CROSSCURRENTS

CONTEMPORARY

POLITICAL ISSUES

CROSSCURRENTS

CONTEMPORARY

POLITICAL ISSUES

FIFTH EDITION

EDITED BY

MARK CHARLTON
TRINITY WESTERN
UNIVERSITY

AND

PAUL BARKER
BRESCIA UNIVERSITY
COLLEGE

THOMSON
NELSON

Australia   Canada   Mexico   Singapore   Spain   United Kingdom   United States

THOMSON
NELSON

Crosscurrents: Contemporary Political Issues
Fifth Edition

Edited by Mark Charlton and Paul Barker

**Associate Vice President,
Editorial Director:**
Evelyn Veitch

Acquisitions Editor:
Mike Thompson

Senior Marketing Manager:
Wayne Morden

Senior Developmental Editor:
Katherine Goodes

Production Editor:
Tannys Williams

Senior Production Coordinator:
Hedy Sellers

Copy Editor/Proofreader:
Wendy Yano

Design Director:
Ken Phipps

Cover Design:
Angela Cluer

Cover Image:
© Bob Krist/Corbis

Compositor:
Brenda Prangley

Printer:
Transcontinental

**Library and Archives Canada
Cataloguing in Publication**

Crosscurrents : contemporary political issues / Paul Barker, Mark Charlton, eds. —5th ed.

Includes bibliographical references.
ISBN 0-17-641515-7

1. Canada—Politics and government—1993– —Textbooks. 2. Canada—Social policy—Textbooks. I. Barker, Paul, 1953– II. Charlton, Mark, 1948–

FC635.C76 2005   971.07'1
C2005-903548-X

Table of Contents

Contributors

Philip L. Bryden is Dean of the Faculty of Law of the University of British Columbia.

Daniel Cere is director of both the Newman Centre at McGill University and the Institute for the Study of Marriage, Law & Culture.

Daniel Cohn is a professor of political science at Simon Fraser University.

Andrew Coyne is a columnist with the *National Post*.

Faron Ellis teaches politics at Lethbridge Community College, where he also serves as Director of the Citizen Society Research Lab.

Thomas Flanagan is a professor of political science at the University of Calgary.

Colleen M. Flood is a professor of law at the University of Toronto.

H. Patrick Glenn is a professor of law at McGill University.

Andrew Heard is a professor of political science at Simon Fraser Universty.

John L. Hiemstra is a professor of political science at the King's University College, Edmonton.

Robert J. Jackson is a professor of political science at Carleton University.

Harold J. Jansen is a professor of political science at the University of Lethbridge.

Christopher Kam is a professor of political science at the University of British Columbia.

David Kilgour is a member of Parliament for Edmonton–Strathcona.

Michael Krashinsky is a professor of economics at the University of Toronto.

Justice Kenneth Mackenzie is a member of the British Columbia Court of Appeal.

Robert Martin recently retired from teaching law at the University of Western Ontario.

Justice Beverley McLachlin is Chief Justice of the Supreme Court of Canada.

Patrick J. Monahan is a professor of law at Osgoode Hall Law School, York University.

F.L. Morton is a professor of political science at the University of Calgary.

Paul Nesbitt-Larking is a professor of political science at Huron University College.

John A. Olthuis is a lawyer specializing in Aboriginal issues.

Clifford Orwin is a professor of political science at the University of Toronto.

Anthony A. Peacock is a professor of political science at Utah State University.

Jonathan Rauch is a writer in residence at the Brookings Institute and frequent national columnist in the United States.

John H. Redekop teaches political science at Trinity Western University.

Claude Ryan was a premier of Quebec and respected commentator on public issues.

Justice Mary Saunders is a member of the British Columbia Court of Appeal.

Donald J. Savoie holds the Clement–Cormier Chair in Economic Development at the Université de Moncton.

Tim Schouls teaches political science at Capilano College.

Justice Duncan Shaw is a member of the British Columbia Supreme Court.

David P. Shugarman is a professor of political science at York University.

Beverley Smith is a former president of Kids First Parents Association of Canada and a commentator on family issues.

Margaret Somerville is founding director of the McGill Centre for Medicine, Ethics and Law.

Roger Townshend is a lawyer specializing in Aboriginal issues.

Michael Walzer is a member of the School of Social Science at the Institute for Advanced Study in Princeton, New Jersey.

Nelson Wiseman is a professor of political science at the University of Toronto.

Introduction

In the first edition of *Crosscurrents: Contemporary Political Issues*, we stated our desire to develop a collection of readings that would not only challenge students to think through a number of contemporary political issues but also foster in students an understanding of and tolerance for the views of others. To achieve this, we felt that a text structured in the form of a debate or dialogue on leading political issues provided an ideal format. We find it gratifying that a number of our colleagues have shared this goal and have used the previous editions in their introductory political science or Canadian politics courses.

CHANGES TO THIS EDITION

In preparing a new edition of *Crosscurrents*, we have maintained the basic structure and format of previous editions. The fifth edition addresses eighteen issues, somewhat fewer than previous editions, in response to requests to keep the new edition shorter. For each issue, an introduction provides the reader with the necessary background and places the subject in the context of more general principles of concern to the study of politics. Two essays then present conflicting viewpoints. Finally, a postscript offers a short commentary on the debate and suggests readings for students to explore the topic further.

From the comments of the reviewers, it is clear that *Crosscurrents: Contemporary Political Issues* is used in general introductory courses and in Canadian politics courses to about the same degree. Therefore, we have tried to select topics appropriate to both and have retained the public policy section that covers a variety of issues. People who use the text in an introductory course may find the public policy section more helpful in the early part of such a course, which often deals with ideologies and concepts relating to rights and the role of the state in society.

A NOTE FOR FIRST-TIME USERS

In introducing the first edition of *Crosscurrents* we set out our rationale for developing a reader using the debate format. We still believe that the rationale for using this format for teaching introductory courses is as strong as ever and bears repeating for those who may be picking up this text for the first time.

There are three good reasons, we believe, for using the debate format. First, studies have shown that students learn and retain more information when they are engaged in an active learning process. Yet the reality in most Canadian universities is that students in introductory courses face ever larger class sizes, which militate against discussion and active student involvement. While students generally come to political science courses with a great deal of interest and enthusiasm, they frequently find themselves slipping into a pattern of simple note taking and passive learning.

Second, most introductory political science courses must of necessity address abstract principles and concepts and cover a great deal of descriptive material concerning processes and institutions. At the same time, students come to these courses expecting that they will discuss and debate what is going on in the chaotic world of politics. Unfortunately, it is often difficult for them to relate the debates of everyday political issues to the broader and more abstract principles encountered in their introductory courses. Without a reference point, discussions of contemporary issues may seem more like interesting "current events" digressions, with little direct relationship to the overall propositions being dealt with in the lectures.

Third, students frequently bring to their readings an uncritical awe of the authority of the published word. When confronted with a series of readings by the leading authorities on each subject, there is a strong temptation for students to think that the text presents the "final" word on the subject. They assume that further discussion and debate can add little new to the issue.

With these thoughts in mind, we have endeavoured to develop a collection of readings that will serve as a resource for a more interactive style of teaching, whether it be in classroom or tutorial discussion situations or in a more formal debate setting. Because of the flexibility of the format, *Crosscurrents* can be employed in the classroom in several ways.

(i) Some may wish to assign the chapters simply as supplementary readings reinforcing material covered in lectures, and to use them as points of illustration in classroom lectures or discussions.

(ii) The readings may be used as a departure point for essay assignments in the course. To encourage students to develop their critical skills, they could be asked to write an assessment of the arguments and evidence presented in one of the debates. Alternatively, students could select one side of the debate and write an essay developing their own arguments in favour of that view.

(iii) Others may wish to use the readings as a means of organizing weekly discussion sessions into a debate format. On each topic, two students may be asked to argue the case for opposing sides, and these arguments could be followed by group discussion. This format requires students to adopt a particular point of view and defend that position. Because the necessary background material is provided in the readings, this format is very easily adapted to large courses where teaching assistants are responsible for weekly tutorial sessions.

ACKNOWLEDGMENTS

We would like to express our appreciation to the many reviewers who offered very helpful comments and suggestions: Gerry Boychuk, University of Waterloo; Andrew Heard, Simon Fraser University; Susan Franceschet, Acadia University; Darin Nesbitt, Douglas College; Alexandra Dobrowolsky, St. Mary's University; and John von Heyking, University of Lethbridge. We are particularly indebted to those authors who graciously agreed to write original essays or revise earlier ones specifically for this volume, as well as to the authors and publishers who have granted us permission to use their published work. In addition, we want to acknowledge the excellent support of Katherine Goodes of Nelson in helping us to bring this project to completion. The careful and detailed work of Tannys Williams as production editor and Wendy Yano as copy editor was also much appreciated. Finally, we would be remiss not to mention the patient support of our families who, in their indirect ways, have contributed to this volume.

Mark Charlton, Langley, B.C.
Paul Barker, London, Ontario

About the Editors

Mark Charlton teaches political studies and is Dean of Research and Faculty Development at Trinity Western University, Langley, British Columbia. Professor Charlton received his Ph.D. in political science from Laval University, where he studied as an Ontario–Quebec Fellow. He is author of *The Making of Canadian Food Aid Policy* (1992), editor of *Crosscurrents: International Relations* (2004), and co-author of the *Thomson Nelson Guide to Research and Writing in Political Science* (2005). He has also published a number of articles in *International Journal, Études Internationales, Journal of Conflict Studies,* and the *Canadian Journal of Development Studies.*

Paul Barker teaches political science at Brescia University College, London, Ontario. Professor Barker received his Ph.D. from the University of Toronto. He has written articles on public policy that have appeared in *Canadian Public Administration, Canadian Public Policy,* and the *Canadian Journal of Law and Society.*

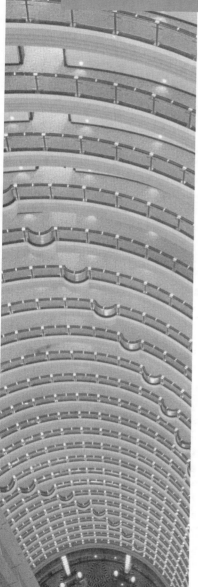

PART ONE

CANADIAN SOCIETY AND POLITICAL CULTURE

Is the Canadian political culture becoming Americanized?

Can Native sovereignty coexist with Canadian sovereignty?

Will conservatism and the Conservative Party fail?

Is the Canadian Political Culture Becoming Americanized?

✔ **YES**
PAUL NESBITT-LARKING, "Canadian Political Culture: The Problem of Americanization"

✘ **NO**
ANTHONY A. PEACOCK, "Socialism as Nationalism: Why the Alleged Americanization of Canadian Political Culture Is a Fraud"

In the eyes of the world, Canada and the United States are very much alike. The two countries share a language, occupy the same geographic space, and support the operation of free markets. The similarity between the two countries also extends to beliefs and attitudes about government—in other words, the political cultures of the two nations are comparable. Canadians and Americans both believe in a modestly sized public sector and exhibit an unwillingness to offer elected officials much leeway. Other countries may give government a large role, but not Canada and the United States.

But at the same time some believe that the two countries are separated by differences in how they approach political life. Americans have been more suspicious of government than Canadians, a view revealed in their determination to ensure that the political power is always shared. On the other hand, Canadians have been more positively disposed toward government. Since Confederation, when government was crucial to the birth of the nation, Canadians have seen purpose in government. For many Canadians, these differences in political culture are fundamental to the uniqueness of Canada. Inherent in the Canadian political culture are a sense of community and an appreciation of the value of collective efforts and public institutions. Such an attitude curtails the often rapacious individualism found in purely liberal political cultures, the best example of which is that of the United States.

For those who see and cherish these differences, there are disturbing changes now taking place in the attitudes of Canadians toward government and public life. There is a declining trust in elected officials, and voters have become less attached to traditional parties and more enamoured of new vehicles of representation. Once valued public policies are now under attack, and the downsizing of government has become an important goal. A belief in individual entitlement, fuelled in part by the newly entrenched Charter of Rights and Freedoms, has emerged as well, pushing aside more communitarian sentiments. For many, these and other

2

developments mean only one thing: the Americanization of the Canadian political culture. The toleration, the sense of collective purpose, the respect for authority—all this and more is being lost. The way Canadians think about politics is changing, and it is a change to be regretted because it threatens to engulf Canada in what has been called the *possessive individualism* of the American political culture.

Not all accept that Canada's political culture is inherently different from that of the United States. From this view, the world's appreciation of the two nations is the correct one: the two are basically the same. Efforts to argue otherwise, to contend that Canada is more community oriented, more caring, distort the basic reality and lead to ill-advised ventures in government policymaking. Moreover, the changes that are taking place in the Canadian political culture hardly amount to an Americanization, for Canada has always been like the United States; rather, the changes reflect the globalizing forces that are transforming all countries. One decidedly beneficial effect of this change is that Canada rids itself of attempts to make it different from its southern neighbour.

A third view of the state of Canada's political culture is possible. Perhaps Canada is different from the United States, though not by much, and this difference still prevails. In politics, it has always been possible to separate Canada and the United States. This was true at Confederation and it remains true today.

In the readings, Paul Nesbitt-Larking argues that indeed the political culture of Canada is being Americanized. He also argues that this offers little cause for celebration, for it spells the end of what it means to be Canadian. Anthony A. Peacock rejects the notion that the political cultures of the two countries are different, and contends that both are now undergoing a transformation wrought by the forces of technology and globalization.

✔ **YES**

Canadian Political Culture: The Problem of Americanization

PAUL NESBITT-LARKING

Living next to you is in some ways like sleeping with an elephant; no matter how friendly and even-tempered the beast, if I may call it that, one is affected by every twitch and grunt. Even a friendly nuzzling can sometimes lead to frightening consequences.

–Pierre Trudeau, speech to the National Press Club,
Washington, D.C., March 25, 1969

For a very long time, and certainly since the American Declaration of Independence in 1776, the destiny of Canada has been shaped through its complex interconnections with the political words and deeds of those other European descendants who live to the south of us. Canada is, and always has been, an American nation. Carved and crafted from a process of "defensive expansionism,"[1] in which the harsh wilderness of this northern part of the American continent was stitched together in east-to-west chains of settlement, often "in defiance of geography,"[2] Canada, in its very existence and longevity, is a major North American achievement. Less obviously, political and governmental life in Canada reflects two centuries of an ambivalent relationship with Americans and their way of life, in which Canadians have alternately incorporated and rejected American influences. Americans are a self-confident people who share a common heritage grounded in an evolving covenant to sustain the most perfect political system of freedom and opportunity. Through their enterprise and determination, Americans have translated the ideals of their founders into enormous economic, cultural, military, and political achievements. It is no idle boast to claim that the United States of America is the greatest nation on Earth.

When Americans are asked to name their "best friends" in the international community, most name the British; when they are asked with whom they conduct the most international trade, Japan is mentioned most often. These responses strike many Canadians as curious. Canada is in fact America's largest single trading partner, and, when probed, a majority of Americans expresses a strong and genuine affinity toward Canadians. What these findings reveal is best expressed by former prime minister Pierre Trudeau in the above quotation: a combination of benign ignorance and careless presumption. Americans do not think much about Canada or Canadians at all, and when they do, they think of Canadians as Americans, with some curious characteristics, who happen to live in another place. Over the past two hundred years, Americans have made gracious and consistent overtures to Canadians to join them in their great republic, and they have never been able to understand the apparent stubbornness with which a succession of Canadian leaders has resisted. American leaders have frequently regarded Canada as an odd little anomaly with its monarchical traditions and its chronic French-English tensions. Such Americans approximate Trudeau's elephants: they do not know their own strength and therefore are often unable to appreciate the damage or the offence they cause. Trudeau's tone is mild in its mockery, and it is possible to argue that his choice of animal attributes too much benevolence to the Americans. The American approach to Canada, as it has crafted its independent foreign policy throughout the past eighty years, might better be described as "bear-like" in its angry malevolence rather than elephantine in its passive tolerance. Whenever it is hungry, hurt, or under a perceived threat, the bear is prone to attack, lashing out against all who offend it or merely get in its way. While the Americans have uttered no serious threats to invade Canada since the late nineteenth century, they have interfered aggressively in our domestic and foreign affairs and, in so doing, have acted in ways that are at best insulting and undiplomatic and, at worse, in contravention of established international law and precedent. An egregious instance of undiplomatic interference is the recent ambassadorship of Paul Cellucci. Appointed by President George W. Bush, Cellucci was ambassador to Canada from 2001 to 2005. Using his ambassadorial role as a partisan bully pulpit, Cellucci lambasted Canadian governments over their domestic and foreign policy positions, far exceeding the bounds of normal diplomacy.

While it is possible to argue about the extent to which the American impact on Canada has been elephantine, bear-like, or both, it is indisputable that it has been of great magnitude. Our economy is dominated by American capital. American direct investment in Canada is currently about $225 billion (USD) and U.S.-based corporations own many of Canada's most profitable industries. Since the 1950s, Canada's military strategy and structure have been shaped in deliberate synchronization with those of the United States through a series of bilateral and multilateral agreements. Whether we refer to it as "culture" or the "entertainment industry," Canada is dominated by American material. The vast majority of the movies or TV shows we watch or the magazines we browse through originate in the United States. In political terms, the American influence has also been profound. Many of our major political institutions have been deliberately shaped to reflect, if not entirely replicate, their American counterparts, including federalism, the Senate, the Supreme Court, and the Charter of Rights and Freedoms. Our political practices and processes have also come to approximate the American pattern in certain ways. In the early twentieth century, Canada adopted the American practice of selecting political leaders through holding large-scale party conventions; in recent decades, commentators have referred to the "presidentialization" of the role of Canada's prime minister. At the deepest level, many Canadians have been enthusiastic followers of the American way of political life and have come to admire American political values and beliefs. These Canadians have attempted to convince other Canadians of the superiority of the American way and to encourage them to incorporate American values into Canadian political parties, institutions, and practices. The struggle between those who value American political ideals and those who wish to preserve a distinctive Canadian set of ideals has been raging since the Declaration of Independence in 1776. In presenting the principal features of this ideological conflict throughout this paper, I shall explain why I believe Americanization is potentially so damaging to Canada and Canadians, and how eternal—or at least periodic—vigilance is the price of remaining Canadian.

POLITICAL CULTURE AND IDEOLOGY

Unlike most concepts in political science, "political culture" has a clear and definite beginning. The term was invented by Gabriel Almond and first used in an article in 1956.[3] Like other American political scientists of his era, Almond was determined to develop political analysis into a more rigorous and scientific discipline than it had been in the early decades of the century. The United States had emerged from the Second World War as the leading military, moral, and economic power in the world, with associated opportunities and dangers. In order to exert a meaningful influence on an unstable and rapidly changing environment, the American state required detailed and accurate analyses of political character in other parts of the world. Aware of the imprecision of existing accounts of political life in other countries, Almond adapted the "structural-functionalist" sociological framework of Talcott Parsons as a basis for developing a systematic understanding of political characteristics. Introducing political culture, he said: "Every political system is embedded in a particular pattern of orientations to political action. I have found it useful to refer to this as the political culture."[4] By this, he meant that it is possible to identify coherent and distinctive patterns of beliefs, values, and attitudes toward political institutions and practices among each of the world's political communities. Almond and his colleague Sidney Verba attempted to identify such political orientations among the citizens of England, Mexico, Germany, the United States of America, and Italy in *The Civic Culture*.[5] On the basis of their analyses of responses to survey data, Almond and Verba produced portrayals of the distinctive political cultures of each country based upon rigorous methodological techniques and consistent quantified measures.

Almond and Verba's study generated great interest and admiration and gave rise to over a decade of research based upon their model. The systematic study of political culture was undertaken in many countries, including Canada.[6] Despite its widespread success and acceptability, the approach also attracted its critics. Prominent among the criticisms were the following: that in its assumption of the civic perfection of the United States of America, the political culture approach provided an arrogant, partial, and distorted image of political values, beliefs, and attitudes in other countries; that there were serious methodological flaws inherent in attempting to capture something as deep, nebulous, and "holistic" as culture merely through adding up a series of quick responses to questions by individuals; and, perhaps most damning of all, that in the increasingly turbulent and conflictual years of the 1960s and early 1970s, the approach could offer little to explain mass discontent, institutional paralysis, sudden change, or socioeconomic breakdown. By the mid-1970s, the huge research industry generated by Almond had dwindled to almost nothing and political scholars turned their attention to other matters. In the Canadian case, the decline of interest in political culture was marked by a series of influential anti-American articles, reflecting a more general pro-Canadian assertiveness that was prominent at the time.[7]

Regrettably, in turning away from the "Americanized" version of political culture, the Canadian political science community abandoned a very important subfield of enquiry. With all its faults, the path-breaking work of Almond had alerted us to the importance of how people feel about political issues and how they make sense of their political experiences. In criticizing Almond and others for their failure to achieve the exacting standards of full scientific rigour, it is easy to overlook the obscurity of the concept of culture and the difficulties inherent in working with it. Raymond Williams referred to culture as one of the two or three most difficult words in the English language.[8] Ongoing disputes at the core of political science over the very meaning of "politics" itself attest to the continued controversies surrounding this concept. When politics and culture are put together in a composite concept, definitional difficulties are multiplied.

Despite these challenges, it is possible to adapt the core of meaning inherent in Almond's approach, adding to it insights derived from other scholars in the field. The central criticisms of Almond pertain to the manner in which the concept was (ab)used—both methodologically and ethically—rather than to the concept itself. In building on Almond, my own definition of political culture incorporates the following additional insights. First, political cultures should be seen as "events" as well as states of affairs; political cultures are generated, produced, reproduced, modified, and even transformed by people in their daily activities; people are strongly conditioned through their socialization to the symbolic worlds into which they are born and in which they grow up, but they also, in their turn, contribute to the reproduction of those symbolic orders. Second, political cultures are literally "mundane" or everyday; many of the political values, beliefs, attitudes, and symbols that we hold most dearly are so taken for granted and unquestioned that we are often not aware of them. Third, I define politics more broadly than Almond, as the manner in which people come to decide on the appropriate distribution of valued resources, as well as on the making of those rules that govern us. The processes of politics are both cooperative and conflictual; politics happens everywhere there are things to be distributed and rules to be made. To summarize: Political cultures happen as people, operating in an already constituted symbolic field of political cultural concepts and practices, convey to each other conceptions of the distribution and uses of valued resources and of the making of decisions and rules.

As I conceptualize them, political cultures are vague, nebulous, and shifting phenomena, and they are difficult to measure in any precise way. One of the most promising ways in which to explore political cultures is through the employment of the related concept of ideology. Political cultures consist of loose and semi-formed ideas, beliefs, and feelings about political institutions and practices. Ideologies are partial appropriations from political cultures, arising from the conscious and deliberate attempts of the intellectual leadership of particular social groups (known as "ideologues") to achieve a definitional monopoly of the political world, which will be accepted by as many people as possible, and which accords with the particular interests of their group. Ignoring the complexities and subtleties of political cultures and focusing on a narrow and self-interested band of values and beliefs, ideologues seek to convince others of the way things are, the way they ought to be, and, less obviously, the way it is possible for them to be. In so doing, ideologues hope that their "construction of reality" will convince others sufficiently to effect political change in their favour. Ideologues employ a range of political movements and associations to achieve their ends, including political parties, political institutions, interest groups, the media, the bureaucracy, and the educational system.

Canadian political culture has provided fertile "clay" for a broad range of ideologues, who have attempted to mould and shape it according to their particular interests. Arguably the most important ideological struggle over the past two hundred years has been that between "individualism" and "communitarianism." Canadian political culture, in contradistinction to the American political culture, has managed to sustain a balance between these two principal ideological tendencies. As will become clear in the next section, another way of saying that communitarianism continues to be part of the Canadian equation is to say that Canadians have been consistently seduced by the promise of the American dream, but have periodically drawn back in order to develop and sustain distinctive institutions and practices that counter those American values.[9]

INDIVIDUALISM AND COMMUNITARIANISM

The quantitative approach to political culture, developed by Almond and his followers, did not recognize the importance of the ideological opposition between individualism and communitarianism. The reason for this is readily apparent: the model of political reality devised by Almond came from an ideological individualism so profoundly entrenched and successful that it had completely overwhelmed the American political culture. It rarely occurred to American students of political culture to think beyond the limits of their individualistic premises. The entire apparatus of methodology, questions, and comparisons among nations was premised upon this unquestioned individualism. It seems hardly surprising that when Almond and his colleagues applied their benchmarks, the United States routinely emerged as the most "perfect" political culture.

Students of political culture in Canada, however, have enjoyed full access to three other approaches to the study of political culture that have enabled them to reflect upon the Canadian experience of individualism versus communitarianism. These are the "fragments" approach, associated with Louis Hartz, Kenneth McRae, and Gad Horowitz[10]; the "historical-developmental" approach, best expressed in the synthesis offered by Seymour Martin Lipset[11]; and the more recent empirical attitudinal surveys of Michael Adams, Matthew Mendelsohn, and Edward Grabb and James Curtis, among others.[12] There are large-scale differences between the three approaches with respect to their theoretical presuppositions and methodological approaches. What unites them, however, is their propensity to portray the evolution of Canadian political culture as an ongoing struggle between the American forces of possessive individualism on the one hand and the European forces of conservative order and socialist collectivism on the other hand. "Possessive individualism" is a phrase originating in the work of C.B. Macpherson, which distils the essence of the pure ideology of individual property rights and freedom from interference, first developed in the work of John Locke.[13] The term "communitarianism" best combines the anti-individualistic impulses of traditional conservatism and socialism. As its name implies, communitarianism is a belief system that stresses both the logical and the moral necessity of thinking about political life in terms of the requirements of the community or the collectivity, rather than in terms of the isolated and abstracted individual. In considering those distinctively Canadian forces that have opposed possessive individualism throughout the past two centuries, communitarianism is best able to convey the alternating right-wing and left-wing critiques of American liberalism.[14]

The fragments approach to political culture argues that the principal "white settler" societies were established by ideologically homogeneous and cohesive colonies of Europeans, whose founding characteristics established the ideological parameters of those societies throughout the succeeding generations. Louis Hartz describes the powerful and pervasive force of liberal individualism in the United States, arguing that even in the twentieth century, its domination of the political culture can explain the early death of American socialism, the reluctant collectivism and populist character of the New Deal era, and the anticommunist vehemence of McCarthyism.[15] Kenneth McRae illuminates the importance of feudalism in the French-Canadian fragment, as well as loyalty to the British Crown among the English-Canadian fragment, in the establishment of a society in Canada that, while fundamentally sharing in the liberal individualistic ethos of the American political culture, exhibited elements of a political culture of cautiousness, moderation, gradualism, compromise, and order.[16] McRae also makes reference to the incursion of modest doses of left-wing culture with the settlement of parts of the

Canadian west by later European fragments, ideologically committed to socialism.[17] These themes are further amplified by Gad Horowitz in his seminal account of the development of ideologies in Canada. Horowitz goes much further than Hartz and McRae in pointing out the critical importance of the communitarian elements in Canada's historical development.[18] Horowitz also moves his analysis away from the Hartzian notion that the founding ideologies of the fragments "congealed" early and remained unchanged.

The manner in which historical developments, notably major events, shape the emergence of a political culture is explored in detail in the work of Seymour Martin Lipset. Since the early 1960s, Lipset has been developing a comparative analysis of the political cultures of Canada and the United States. On the basis of his understanding of comparative patterns of settlement, formative historical events, such as the American Revolution and the Canadian "counterrevolution," and a broad array of sociological data on such matters as crime rates, divorce rates, and church attendance, Lipset comes to concur with Horowitz that differences between the Canadian and American political cultures are profound indeed[19]:

> My central argument is that the two countries differ in their basic organizing principles. Canada has been and is a more class-aware, elitist, law-abiding, statist, collectivity-oriented, and particularistic (group-oriented) society than the United States.... The United States remained throughout the 19th and early 20th centuries the extreme example of a classically liberal or Lockean society, one that rejected the assumptions of the alliance of throne and altar, of ascriptive elitism, of mercantilism, of noblesse oblige, of communitarianism.[20]

While Lipset stresses the fundamentally liberal individualist character of both Canada and the United States and argues that, in the global context, "the two resemble each other more than either resembles any other nation,"[21] his framework of comparison, like mine, is between the two countries, and the distinctions are substantial enough to be noteworthy.

Recent empirical surveys of Canadian and American attitudes sustain the view that Canada is a more communitarian polity. Michael Adams's data reveal that over the past decade both Canadians and Americans have been shifting in their attitudes away from support for traditional authorities toward greater individualism. However, Americans have moved strongly in the direction of possessive individualism, competitiveness, patriarchy, and exclusionary defensiveness. For their part, Canadians have diverged from the American path and shifted strongly toward socially oriented individualism, self-expression, and fulfillment through altruism and inclusiveness.[22] Both Adams and Edward Grabb and James Curtis highlight the important point that while the American South skews the United States toward its characteristic values of possessive individualism and exclusionary defensiveness, Quebec skews Canada toward socially inclusive individualism and a comfort with statism, secularism, and communitarianism. In a key table summarizing measures of individualism, Grabb and Curtis's data show that for three out of the four variables that achieve significant national differences, the United States is more individualistic. Moreover, the pattern of American individualism is as strong in the north as it is in the south.[23] Matthew Mendelsohn, in a summary of his findings, remarks that at the beginning of the twenty-first century, Canada remains: "more collectivistic, more open to diversity, more supportive of state intervention, more deferential, and more prepared to find solidarity with people in other countries than its southern neighbour."[24] This is despite a decade of globalization, continental economic integration, federal and provincial neoliberal fiscal policies, and the consequent erosion of the Canadian welfare state.

Despite the historical pervasiveness of communitarian elements in Canada's political culture, and the eloquent passion of many of its supporters, possessive individualistic ideology is currently in global ascendancy.[25] If there is a communitarian response to these trends, it is to be found in the reactionary and defensively hostile impulses of religious and nationalistic fundamentalisms. Such social forces have grown in panic response to the rapid onset of a global economy and culture seemingly bereft of morality and meaning. Canadians have worked hard to sustain a more balanced and inclusive communitarian polity that celebrates diversity, openness, and polyethnic traditions. Given the current political landscape in the United States and beyond, such a balance seems increasingly challenging to sustain. In the next section, I turn my attention to the dangers for Canada associated with incorporating too much possessive individualism and narrow defensiveness: the problem of Americanization.

THE PROBLEM OF AMERICANIZATION

To speak of Americanization as a problem is not to adopt a narrowly ethnocentric, anti-American point of view. A large majority of Canadians was horrified at the attacks of September 11, 2001, in which thousands of innocent lives were lost, and chose to express their solidarity in empathetic support and acts of kindness. Canadians continue to express strong bonds of affection for Americans and an admiration for many aspects of the American way of life, notably the exuberant spirit of entrepreneurship. There is even a small minority of Canadians who would welcome a union of the two countries. Equally, not all Americans are defensive possessive individualists. American scholars, notably Robert Bellah and Robert Putnam, have expressed deep reservations about the consequences of the early and monopolistic domination of individualist liberalism as the American creed and its continuing effects on the American polity. The equation of individualism and libertarian freedom with "Americanism" itself has permitted the ideological intolerances of authoritarian populism and "witch hunts" and has discouraged forms of state-led and communitarian solutions to America's problems that have been made possible elsewhere. Globalization, in its economic, cultural, and militaristic forms, represents the universalization of Americanism in the form of global capitalism, global media, and the American military presence overseas.

Americanism is rapidly becoming so dominant that communitarian ideological perspectives are in jeopardy. Ideologies in themselves do not die, but given the will and the opportunity, ideologues can so determine and shape political culture that a given people come to believe that only one ideological position is desirable or possible. A political culture can be so imbued with a particular ideological orientation that all others dwindle and fade. Once this is in process, political support for previously existing institutions and practices, which run counter to the interests of the prevailing ideology, falls away. The institutions and practices of the Canadian nation-state have been built on the basis of a political culture characterized by some degree of communitarianism. Once these diminish beyond a certain point, Canada itself is in question. This point was grasped, in a work of brilliant insight, by conservative scholar George Grant, in 1965. In his *Lament for a Nation*, Grant understood that the uncritical adoption of American technocratic politics and economics, as well as the culture of populist consumerism, would undermine Canada to the point where its continued existence ceased to be relevant. He noted, "The impossibility of conservatism in our era is the impossibility of Canada."[26] Put simply, Grant was arguing that if nobody loves the country or regards the relationship between the generations as a communitarian trust, then the nation-state itself will become little more than a practical container. The subtitle of Grant's book is "The Defeat of Canadian Nationalism." There has never been a massive Canadian nationalism—at least not in English Canada—but there have been assertive moments of resistance to Americanization. The continued viability of Canada depends upon the capacity and willingness of Canadians to recognize those economic, cultural, and political signs of the eroding Canadian balance, and to work tirelessly in order to redress the imbalances.

For nearly two decades, Canada's principal political parties and political leaders have been actively promoting economic policies of Americanized possessive individualism. At the federal level, with the marginal exception of the early 1980s, when the Liberal Party attempted to forge a limited new "national policy," both Liberal and Progressive Conservative governments have driven the ideological agenda toward free-market solutions. As in the construction of any ideological perspectives, the politicians have argued that their proposals are not merely sound, but that "we have no choice." In the 1970s, the Liberals argued that too many demands had been made on the federal system and that it was impossible to continue to provide the kind of extensive and responsive public service that had developed throughout the 1950s and 1960s. They promoted monetary and fiscal policies that increased unemployment, facilitated a decrease in the public sector, and squeezed middle-class incomes through higher interest rates and taxes. In the 1980s, the Progressive Conservative Party pointed out that Canadians had been victims of fiscal irresponsibility, and they began to talk of the need to cut the national deficit. They continued the trend against communitarianism in Canada through their modest attempts at public sector cutbacks, their privatizations and deregulations, but mostly through their two free trade agreements and the introduction of the regressive Goods and Services Tax. The Progressive Conservative government hoped that these policies would stimulate noninflationary growth in the economy. In the 1990s, the emphasis on the national deficit intensified, and the Liberal Party perpetuated the trend toward Americanization, with their massive cuts to the federal public sector as well as cuts in transfer payments to the provinces. The radical downsizing of the federal government inevitably had an impact on the provinces. In some of them, notably Alberta and Ontario, right-wing governments went even further than the federal Liberal Party in radical reductions to the size and scope of the public sector on the basis of American-style populist individualism, promoting a generalized distrust of government and large-scale tax cuts designed to curtail redistributional policies.

In the 1990s, two new major parties came onto the federal scene. One of them, the Reform Party, which became the Canadian Alliance, was a strong proponent of possessive individualism and committed to further radical cuts in public spending. It advocated reductions in transfers to individuals and regions, large-scale tax cuts, and the diminution of the power of the federal state to enforce national standards. The Canadian Alliance and the Progressive Conservative Party united in 2003 to form the Conservative Party of Canada. Its new platform continued the general thrust of Canadian Alliance policies, calling for tax cuts, deregulation, and greater powers to the provinces. Of all the political parties and politicians in contemporary Canada, very few have been active promoters of policies to enhance the communitarian essence of Canada, or even to slow its decline. The Liberal Party under Prime Minister Paul Martin has redressed the balance to some extent, restoring funds to public services, such as health, education, social assistance, Canadian culture, aid to Aboriginal peoples, and foreign aid. The minority party status of the Martin Liberals has enhanced the power of Liberal Party backbenchers and the more communitarian political parties, the Bloc Québécois and the New Democratic Party. Despite this trend, however, the fiscal strategy of the Martin government has simultaneously transferred massive resources and fiscal authority to the provinces while increasing military expenditure and cutting personal and corporate taxes. The combined impact of these measures has been to jeopardize the longer-term revenue potential of the federal state, rendering it decreasingly able to act on behalf of Canadians and to devise renewed programs of national scope.

Behind the political parties have been the most important special interest groups. Many prominent corporate organizations, such as the Canadian Council of Chief Executives, the Canadian Federation of Independent Business, and the Canadian Taxpayers Federation, have actively promoted greater economic integration into the United States as well as policies designed to cut the public sector and reduce taxes on the corporate elite. The corporate elite has been strongly supported by most of Canada's leading journalists, intellectuals, and academics. Some of them have, while attacking collectivism, continued to promote the rhetoric of a united Canada, which cherishes its distinctiveness. In this respect, they have offered some resistance to Americanization insofar as they have advocated the old-style orderly and conservative forms of "elite accommodation" through which Canada's distinctive communities are able to achieve a modus vivendi. In other words, they have advocated the kind of political arrangements that the Progressive Conservatives attempted to promote in the 1980s with the Meech Lake and Charlottetown Accords. The ideals of such accords, based upon bilingualism and multiculturalism in a finely balanced Canada consisting of "a community of communities," continue to be supported at the highest levels. In modified form, such is the agenda of the current Liberal and Conservative parties.

The problem for Canada is that the refined and noble politics of cultural pluralism and mutual respect has been promoted through anachronistic and elitist political practices from which most citizens have felt excluded. This is why Michael Adams and others have detected a growing wariness on the part of Canadians regarding traditional authorities. The politics of elite accommodation also runs directly counter to the anticollectivist impulses of economic possessive individualism. The cultural message of economic liberalism stresses narrowly defined rights, absolute freedom from restraint, and a rejection of those virtues associated with family, community, and society, such as love, tolerance, charity, duty, loyalty, and patriotism. There are signs that the hold of such qualities in the Canadian political culture is diminishing. An angry Canadian public rejected the Charlottetown Accord in 1992. The accord had been designed to provide a new compromise among Canadians in terms of their constitutional rights, as well as to restate the commitment of Canadians to a unified nationhood and distinctive national identity. Canadian voters punished the architects of the plan, the Progressive Conservative Party, by almost completely rejecting them in the federal election of 1993. In their place, English Canadians supported the Reform Party, while many Quebecers turned to the Bloc Québécois; both political organizations did not accept bilingualism and multiculturalism.

The decline in support for the traditional parties, the growing disrespect for politicians, the growth of support for narrowly defined single-issue political movements, and a generalized sense of the atomization of political society all point to a growing individuation of Canada's political culture.[27] The rapidly declining trust in Canada's political institutions, political parties, and politicians is reported in Neil Nevitte's *The Decline of Deference*.[28] Nevitte's data demonstrate that "confidence in governmental institutions is declining while non-traditional ... forms of political participation are increasing. In political matters, people are becoming less deferential, less compliant, more inclined to speak out...."[29] Similar findings are reported by Harold D. Clarke and his colleagues in *Absent Mandate*, which also tracks Canadian public opinion in the 1980s and 1990s.[30] Clarke et al. report strong declines in partisan loyalty and attachment over these decades, in conjunction with growing disaffection, detachment, and negativity concerning politicians and parties.[31] Their final chapter is entitled "The Politics of Discontent," and a key feature of that chapter is their characterization of an "angry and cynical" electorate.[32] Concluding their work, Clarke et al. refer to the Canadian political situation as one of "permanent dealignment," by which they mean a consistently fragmented and volatile relationship between citizens and parties.[33] In the context of such permanent dealignment, communitarian attachments to persons and places become strained. Despite the fact that dealignment and disaffection can be dangerous to a political community, blind deference is no better. Deference is always a thin and brittle basis for a political community and is, in the final analysis, as damaging as possessive individualism. Disaffection and the decline of deference are, therefore, in some respects positive forces and represent the kind of assertive enhancement of political efficacy and political participation that Adams refers to as "the balance of individual autonomy with a sense of collective responsibility."[34] However, in contemporary Canada, the principal ideological forces that have picked up on the mood of popular anger and cynicism offer individuated solutions, which serve to amplify people's negativity, deepening and broadening their defensive possessiveness rather than encouraging their communitarian imaginations to seek new ways in which to invigorate the body politic.

The Canadian public have demonstrated that they are not bound to the traditional political parties and that they are prepared to vote for new "anti-party" parties in numbers large enough to elect entire "Official Oppositions" to the House of Commons. The Canadian Alliance represented an American-style populism that it made hegemonic in the west of Canada. The Bloc Québécois offers the only true communitarian option in Canada, one that is, of course, grounded in demands for a distinctive and independent Quebec state to reflect the aspirations of the people of Quebec. To some extent, the success of Quebec nationalism is a reflection of the poverty of any true pan-Canadian national vision either inside French Quebec or in the rest of Canada. Current political discourse in Canada is punctuated by the claims and counterclaims of single interest groups, to which citizens are encouraged to adhere on the basis of their narrowly defined personal and individual desires. Among the most recent crop of such groups are gun owners angry about gun control, victims of crime angry about the lack of compensation in the criminal justice system, and religious traditionalists angry at the prospect of the right of civil marriage being extended to gays and lesbians. At present there is little to unite the various single-issue groups other than a shared belief in entitlement based on a conception of the state as a repository of goods and legal precedents that are "up for grabs."

The impact of the changing composition of Canada's political culture, as well as of the work of the ideologues of possessive individualism, has been acutely felt. Despite the efforts of small Canadian nationalist groups, such as the Council of Canadians, and an assortment of individuals, including some prominent politicians and journalists, the federal state has been radically Americanized in the past decade: NAFTA and the GST are accomplished fact; Air Canada, Canadian National Railways, and Petro-Canada, corporations designed with explicit public and nation-building purposes, have been partially or totally privatized; major regulatory agencies, such as the Canadian Radio-television and Telecommunications Commission, have lost many of their regulatory powers; federal Crown corporations, notably the CBC, have suffered enormous budget cuts; and there have been radical reductions in the size and scope of the state. The effects of these cuts have reverberated in the quality of life at the provincial level: The "social safety net" has been lowered; universal provision of social services, which nurtures a communitarian ethos, has been rapidly replaced with "means-tested" and limited provision of social services, which targets and stigmatizes the poor; public systems of health care and education are being eroded to the point where partial privatization of so-called core or essential services seems highly probable; the gap between the rich and the poor is increasing as the middle class, which carried much of the burden of redistribution in the 1980s, becomes increasingly reluctant to share.

In furtherance of these trends, the liberal-individualistic message of radical decentralization is currently being hotly promoted by Canada's richest and most influential special interest group, the Canadian Council of Chief Executives. The Canadian Council of Chief Executives and the Conservative Party are both promoting a new Canada in which principal socioeconomic and political control is devolved to the provinces and in which there is little more than some vague sentiment to hold the country together. If there is radical decentralization in the future, those ties of common citizenship that bind us will fall away, and the already weak voices for Canada will become even weaker. There is growing evidence of parochial assertiveness and a "beggar-thy-neighbour" attitude among opinion leaders in Canada's more affluent provinces, Ontario and Alberta. As the voices for a pan-Canadian vision diminish, so the logic of an independent Quebec state will increase. Once Quebec has gone, the remaining nine provinces and the territories will have very little left to hold them together. As they enter further into the liberal-individualistic ethos of free trade in the North American continent, an ethos buttressed by new World Trade Organization agreements that severely restrict the scope of sovereign states in controlling capital flows, so the patent absurdity of continued independence for a culturally fractured, socioeconomically divided, and geographically split Canada will become increasingly clear. We will have rationalized Canada out of existence.

CONCLUSION

Given the ideological assault of Americanizing possessive individualism on Canada's political culture, and the efficacy of that assault in terms of major changes in public policy, what is the prognosis for Canada? The spirit of self-centred individualism and defensive exclusionism does not bode well for the continued existence of Canada. Traditional conservatives would argue that any nation that has lost its sense of organic connectedness is in poor health. When the phrase "The West wants in" became the rallying cry for the foundation of the Reform Party, it was taken to mean that the western provinces wished to partake of the benefits and burdens of full and equitable citizenship. Regrettably, the phrase has come to be associated instead with a narrowly focused acquisitiveness, opportunistic rent-seeking, and an unwillingness to share natural advantages with those persons and regions less fortunate in the country. Under such circumstances, it seems improbable that the wealthier provinces, such as British Columbia, Alberta, and Ontario, will be able to see much sense in sustaining Canada as a unified nation-state. The deficit cutting and public-sector gutting economic policies of the Liberal Party and the Conservative Party are actively promoting this kind of fragmentation. And yet there do continue to be some modest signs of Canadian distinctiveness. As mentioned earlier, public opinion research reveals Canadians in the late 1990s to be more communitarian, statist, committed to social order, and supportive of public health care than Americans.[35] Moreover, it is always possible that the decline of public provision, the growing inequality, and the increasing immiseration of the poor will so offend the communitarian impulses of our political culture that Canadians will reject further trends toward possessive individualism.[36]

On the cultural front, there seems to be little patriotism or spontaneous love of country. There are occasional glimpses, such as when Canada won two hockey gold medals in the 2002 Winter Olympics. But other than these infrequent moments, it simply appears that few people care very much. Over a century ago, the French intellectual Ernst de Renan referred to a nation as an act of will, as "a daily plebiscite." There seems to be very little active will to nurture Canada. While it is possible to be reserved in one's patriotism, our continued silence in the context of accelerated Americanization is deafening. Not only is there an atmosphere of listless apathy about the nation, but also increasing numbers of English Canadians have exhibited an unwillingness to accept even the modest and unexceptional claim of Quebec to be a "distinct society." Such an uncompromising stance would be welcomed in the radically individualistic melting-pot homogeneity of the United States, but it makes little sense in Canada. It is possible that there are sufficient numbers of French Quebecers who could be persuaded to remain in a Canada of "two solitudes" united through mutual and distanced respect. The ultimate consequence of the logic of hard-line opposition to distinct society status is to drive those moderate Quebecers into the welcoming arms of the separatists.

Canada is in jeopardy. Our neighbours to the south have consistently stated that they would welcome Canada as a part of their great country. Such a solution might make sense. Here we might recall the sarcastic and self-pitying vitriol of George Grant, who said: "Perhaps we should rejoice in the disappearance of Canada. We leave the narrow provincialism and our backwoods culture; we enter the excitement of the United States where all the great things are done."[37] Such an eventuality would be a tragic loss to a world that desperately needs the model of polyethnic and multicultural tolerance provided by Canada. Perhaps, given the newfound assertive and anti-elite rebelliousness of Canadians, we will simply reinvent the country and craft something new, authentic, and beautiful. Maybe, in this globalized, postmodern age in which Canada's greatest claim to international distinctiveness is to be a country that is so tolerant of pluralities of differences among its own citizens that it really has no substantive core, Canada will actually become the first "post-nation": an address with no fixed identity, whose very openness will be an exemplar to the remainder of the world, whose new soft tribalisms will gradually infiltrate the remainder of the planet, including America, imbuing them with Canadianism and creating the ultimate global village.

NOTES

1. The phrase comes from H.G.J. Aitken, "Defensive Expansionism: The State and Economic Growth in Canada," in W.T. Easterbrook and M.H. Watkins, eds., *Approaches to Canadian Economic History* (Toronto: McClelland and Stewart, 1967), pp. 183–221.

2. W.A. Mackintosh, "Economic Factors in Canadian History," in Easterbrook and Watkins, eds., *Approaches*, p. 15.

3. Gabriel Almond, "Comparative Political Systems," *World Politics* 18 (1956): 391–409.

4. Ibid., p. 396.

5. Gabriel Almond and Sidney Verba, *The Civic Culture* (Boston: Little Brown, 1963).

6. See Jon Pammett and Michael Whittington, eds., *Foundations of Political Culture: Political Socialization in Canada* (Toronto: Macmillan, 1976); Richard Simeon and David Elkins, "Regional Political Cultures in Canada," *Canadian Journal of Political Science* 7 (1974): 397–437; John Wilson, "The Canadian Political Cultures: Towards a Redefinition of the Nature of the Canadian Political System," *Canadian Journal of Political Science* 7 (1974): 438–483; Elia Zureik and Robert Pike, eds., *Socialization and Values in Canadian Society: Political Socialization* (Toronto: Macmillan, 1975).

7. Donald Smiley, "Must Canadian Political Science Be a Miniature Replica?" *Journal of Canadian Studies* 9 (1974): 31–42; C.B. Macpherson, "After Strange Gods: Canadian Political Science 1973," in T.N. Guinsberg and G.L. Reuber, eds., *Perspectives on the Social Sciences in Canada* (Toronto: University of Toronto Press, 1974), pp. 52–76; Alan Cairns, "Political Science in Canada and the Americanization Issue," *Canadian Journal of Political Science* 8 (1975): 191–234.

8. Raymond Williams, *Keywords: A Vocabulary of Culture and Society* (London: Fontana, 1976), p. 76.

9. This point is elaborated by Stephen Brooks, *Canadian Democracy: An Introduction*, 3rd ed. (Toronto: Oxford University Press, 2000), p. 34, who attributes a range of economic and cultural policies to a series of deliberate "refusals in the face of Americanizing pressures."

10. Louis Hartz, *The Founding of New Societies* (New York: Harcourt, Brace and World, 1964); Kenneth McRae, "The Structure of Canadian History," in Louis Hartz, *The Founding of New Societies*, pp. 219–274; Gad Horowitz, "Conservatism, Liberalism, and Socialism in Canada: An Interpretation," *Canadian Journal of Economics and Political Science* 32 (1966): 143–171.

11. Seymour Martin Lipset, *Continental Divide: The Values and Institutions of the United States and Canada* (New York: Routledge, 1990).

12. Michael Adams, *Fire and Ice: The United States and Canada and the Myth of Converging Values* (Toronto: Penguin, 2003); Matthew Mendelsohn, *Canada's Social Contract: Evidence From Public Opinion*. Discussion Paper P101. Public Involvement Network, Canadian Policy Research Networks (November 2002); Edward Grabb and James Curtis, *Regions Apart: The Four Societies of Canada and the United States* (Toronto: Oxford University Press, 2005).

13. C.B. Macpherson, *The Political Theory of Possessive Individualism* (London: Oxford University Press, 1962). The dominance of possessive individualism in the American tradition has been well established in the key political cultural contributions to American society, notably: Alexis de Tocqueville, *Democracy in America* (New York: Doubleday, Anchor, 1969); Louis Hartz, *The Liberal Tradition in America* (New York: Harvest, 1955); David Riesman, *The Lonely Crowd: A Study of the Changing American Character* (New Haven: Yale University Press, 1962); Robert N. Bellah, Richard Madsen, William M. Sullivan, Ann Swidler, and Steven M. Tipton, *Habits of the Heart: Individualism and Commitment in American Life* (New York: Harper and Row, 1986); and Robert Putnam, *Bowling Alone: The Collapse and Revival of American Community* (New York: Simon and Schuster, 2000).

14. Sylvia Bashevkin, "The Politics of Canadian Nationalism," in Paul Fox and Graham White, eds., *Politics: Canada* (Toronto: McGraw-Hill, 1995), pp. 40–47.

15. Hartz, *The Founding of New Societies*, pp. 107, 111–112, 119.

16. McRae, "The Structure of Canadian History," p. 239.

17. Ibid., p. 270.

18. Horowitz, "Conservatism, Liberalism and Socialism in Canada," p. 148.

19. General interpretations of the comparatively communitarian character of Canada, proffered by McRae, Horowitz, and Lipset, are rejected by Janet Ajzenstat and Peter J. Smith, "Liberal-Republicanism: The Revisionist Picture of Canada's Founding," in idem., eds, *Canada's Origins: Liberal, Tory, or Republican?* (Ottawa: Carleton University Press, 1995), pp. 1–18. Not only do they claim that there is little Tory conservatism in the Canadian political tradition, but they go further in regarding the Upper and Lower Canadian establishments of the nineteenth century as fundamentally "liberal," and their principal rebel opponents, such as Mackenzie and Papineau, as "civic republican." While this is not the place to engage in detailed debate with Ajzenstat and Smith, I am in fundamental disagreement with their characterizations. Not only do they ignore the abundant evidence of elitist, ascriptive, affective, and particularistic practices on the part of the governing classes, but they also promote the idea that "civic republicanism" is "antiliberal." The ideology is better interpreted,

by Louis Hartz among others, as "left" or radical liberalism. While it is true that Mackenzie and Papineau "scorn ... the nineteenth-century liberal constitution" (p. 8), the basis of their opposition is not antiliberalism, but antiauthoritarianism. There is little evidence to support the claim that the nineteenth-century rebels were against the basic principles of possessive individualism. Their rallying cry was not for the abolition of capitalism, but for responsible government and genuine democratic rights.

20. Lipset, *Continental Divide*, p. 8.

21. Ibid., pp. 214, 219, 225. Neil Nevitte has recently produced comparative survey data to illustrate the fact that, in the context of the advanced industrial nations, Canada and the United States are often closer to each other than to any other nations. He goes further and argues that Lipset's claims that Canadians are more deferential, law-abiding, and passive than Americans is not supported in his data. See Neil Nevitte, *The Decline of Deference* (Peterborough: Broadview Press, 1996), pp. 105–106.

22. Adams, *Fire and Ice*, pp. 39, 97, 123.

23. Grabb and Curtis, *Regions Apart*, p.181.

24. Mendelsohn, Canada's Social Contract, p.1.

25. The historical tradition of communitarianism and collectivism is mentioned in numerous sources, including Rand Dyck, *Canadian Politics: Critical Approaches* (Toronto: Nelson, 1996), p. 286; Michael Whittington and Richard Van Loon, *Canadian Government and Politics: Institutions and Processes* (Toronto: McGraw-Hill Ryerson, 1996), p. 99; and Brooks, *Canadian Democracy*, pp. 52–55.

26. George Grant, *Lament for a Nation* (Toronto: McClelland and Stewart, 1965), p. 68.

27. Peter Dobell and Byron Berry, "Anger at the System: Political Discontent in Canada," in Fox and White, *Politics: Canada*, pp. 4–9; Maclean's/Decima polling data, *Maclean's*, 2 January 1995.

28. Nevitte, *The Decline of Deference*, pp. 56, 79, 267, 291. Nevitte uses his data to interpret recent changes in the Canadian political culture as evidence of a general move toward postindustrial, postmaterialist, and postmodern values, pervasive throughout the West, and he specifically downplays the "Americanization" thesis. Nevitte's method of calculating the degree of "Americanization," outlined in footnote 2 on page 314 of his book, is designed to assess the "cultural lag" thesis that Canadian value changes lag behind those of the United States. Nevitte takes a series of dimensions in which he measures the change in both Canadian and American values from 1981 to 1990. One of these dimensions is "confidence in government institutions." According to Nevitte's data, "confidence in government institutions" declined from 49.6 percent in 1981 to 31.8 percent in 1990 in the United States, a decline of nearly 18 percentage points. In Canada, the comparable change was from 36.9 percent in 1981 to 29.4 percent in 1990, a decline of 7.5 percentage points. Using his calculus of "cultural lag," Nevitte declares Canada to be the leader of the trend in 1990 (Table 9-2, p. 292). The fact that the U.S. figure in 1990 more closely approximates the Canadian figure in 1981 than the Canadian 1990 figure approximates the American 1981 figure— Nevitte's criterion for Canada as the cultural leader—is, in my opinion, inadequate as a measure of the degree of Americanization. It is, of course, possible to argue that the Americans are becoming more like Canadians. However, it seems equally plausible to postulate that the profound loss of confidence, tracked in the American data, has a more moderate, yet still substantial, echo effect in Canada.

29. Ibid., p. 267.

30. Harold D. Clarke, Jane Jenson, Lawrence LeDuc, and Jon H. Pammett, *Absent Mandate: Canadian Politics in an Era of Restructuring*, 3rd ed. (Vancouver: Gage, 1996).

31. Ibid., pp. 22, 61, 65, 67.

32. Ibid., pp. 176–180.

33. Ibid., p. 185.

34. Adams, *Fire and Ice*, p.123.

35. Footnote 12. See also: George Perlin, "The Constraints of Public Opinion: Diverging or Converging Paths," in Keith Banting, George Hoberg, and Richard Simeon, eds., *Degrees of Freedom: Canada and the United States in a Changing World* (Kingston: McGill-Queen's University Press, 1997), pp. 71–149.

36. For data in support of these claims, refer to Statistics Canada, *Canada at a Glance, 2000* (www.statcan.ca), "Persons with Low Income After Tax." The percentage of Canadians with low incomes declined only marginally from 3,744,000 in 1993 (13.1%) to 3,163,000 in 2001 (10.4%). Given the economic boom of this era and the conservatism of the measure (*after* tax income), the failure to deal with poverty is troubling. The failure was particularly pronounced among children. In 2002, 35 percent of female-headed sole parent families had low incomes according to Statistics Canada. A United Nations report on *Child Poverty in Rich Nations* (2000) calculated the Canadian child poverty rate at 15.5 percent. More detailed—and disturbing—data on child poverty are contained on the Campaign 2000 website (www.campaign2000.ca) where, according to their 2004 Report, over a million Canadian children continue to live in poverty, an increase in child poverty between 1989 and 2000. This is despite pledges made by all major Canadian political figures in the late 1980s to eradicate child poverty by 2000.

37. Grant, *Lament*, p. 8.

✗ NO
Socialism as Nationalism:
Why the Alleged Americanization of
Canadian Political Culture Is a Fraud
ANTHONY A. PEACOCK

Writers on America do not simply speak of the United States; they have also constructed the concept of "Americanism" or "Americanization," which refers to such fundamental developments of modernity as cultural homogenization, democratization, and degeneration. America so conceived may exist outside of the United States and involve no actual Americans. Once this point is reached, it becomes clear that real America is no longer at issue: an idea or symbol called "America" has taken over.

–James W. Ceaser, *Reconstructing America:*
The Symbol of America in Modern Thought

INTRODUCTION

As my title suggests, the word "nationalism" in Canada has become synonymous with the word "socialism," with the policy preferences of Canada's socialist or social democratic community, a community that prefers public over private enterprise. The proposition, supported by those I will refer to in this article as Canadian nationalists, that Canada's political culture is distinguishable from its American counterpart by our greater collectivism or our greater use of public enterprise, is, I submit, a fraud. And it is a dangerous fraud at that.

The nationalist characterization of Canadian–American relations amounts to little more than a caricature, disregarding those fundamental features, including American public enterprise, that identify Canadian and American political culture.[1]

More importantly, the nationalists' argument masks the definitively noncollectivist, noncommunitarian nature of Canadian public enterprise. Not only is Canadian public enterprise divisive, tending to pit one region of the country against another, it also undermines the preconditions of any real Canadian community, surrendering to centralized, bureaucratic authorities the task of self-government that should be left to private individuals and to communities themselves. Having lost sight of the very distinction between community and government, the nationalist advocacy has ironically resulted in the emaciation of Canadian identity rather than its cultivation or clarification. In their simplistic characterization of the alleged conflict between the United States and Canada, a conflict that typically takes shape as one between the "insensitive," "materialistic" individualism of the United States and the more "caring," "compassionate" collectivism of Canada, the nationalists have inadequately explained how American political culture has produced not less, but more, of a sense of community, more of a sense of collective identity, and more of a feeling of national pride than anything produced so far in Canada. There seems to be a connection between individualism and community that the nationalists have to date overlooked.

Since the 1960s, when the social democratic agenda of Canadian nationalism, with its demand for greater protection of Canadian political culture, took hold of Canadian public policy, Quebec nationalism has ballooned, English-speaking Canada has lost whatever semblance of identity it may have enjoyed prior to the 1960s, and cultural relativism has become the mantra of law reform and education. Is this mere coincidence?

In this article, I suggest not. What has kept Canadians from realizing or recapturing their identity has little to do with America and much more to do with the destructive policies and disingenuous messages about who they are, perpetuated by Canada's opinion-forming classes: its political elites, its media, its university professors, and other intellectuals.

If we understand political culture in its literal sense as what we have grown in Canada to constitute our politics and our political character, we should see the antisocialistic, free-market movement afoot today as a refreshing attempt to recover a self-reliant, community-oriented individualism, an individualism that provided Canadians a pride and respect before the era of big government and the culture of dependency and entitlements erased what sense of ourselves and self-reliance we had.

NORTH AMERICA: ONE BIG HAPPY FAMILY, BOURGEOIS AND LOVING IT

It is a commonplace among advocates of Canadian nationalism that Canadians are culturally distinct from Americans. This, of course, is not true. The differences between Canadians and Americans are ephemeral, not essential. Canadians and Americans prefer the same television, the same music, the same sports, and the same magazines, enjoy the same cuisine, and vacation at the same destinations. They seek the same things out of life. As George Grant pointed out a generation ago, the identity shared by Canadians and Americans runs deeper than economics or politics, extending to the very faith that gives purpose and meaning to all who live in the Western world.[2] The tough questions that face Canadians respecting politics and culture are the same tough questions that face Americans. The central issue in both cases is whether anything distinctive about Canada or the United States can survive the universalizing and homogenizing effects of modern technology, which makes people, and the objects they desire in life, more and more the same despite whatever differences in appearance persist. "Lying behind the immediate decisions arising from our status within the [American] empire is the deeper question of the fate of any particularity in the technological age. What happens to nationalist strivings when the societies in question are given over, at the very level of faith, to the realisation of the technological dream?"[3]

The technological dream is what Canadians pursue, just as Americans do. We seek economic growth; take pride in our jobs, our industriousness, and our ingenuity; and measure the success of our politicians by how effectively they manage the debt and the deficit.

Listen to Canadian nationalists and our cultural spokesmen, however, and one gets a different impression. As David Frum has remarked:

> Canada is a big, rich, North American nation, where people live in suburbs, drive to work, shop in malls, invest their money in mutual funds, listen to country music, and resent paying taxes. But watch a Canadian movie, read a Canadian novel, flip through most Canadian magazines, or turn on the news, and you'll see a different country; a poor, struggling hinterland of the American empire, where people live in outposts, work for the government if they work at all, collect groceries from food banks, listen to folk singers, and enjoy paying taxes.[4]

The gap between official Canada and actual Canada[5] has to be maintained by the nationalist community because to do otherwise would undermine the moral and political legitimacy of the protectionist enterprise.

The free trade debate of the late 1980s exemplified nationalist rhetoric, a rhetoric that at the time had little to do either with the stakes at issue or with the nationalists' real concern. The real concern of the nationalists was not the transitory issues of depleted social programs, a tarnished environment, or the loss of water to American farmers that free trade might precipitate, although the nationalists protested these issues vociferously. The real concern of the nationalists was that the higher standard of living brought about by more open trade with the United States would cause Canadians to rethink the value of those "nation-building" (read big government) projects that had become the darling objects of cultural protectionism. The wealth and increased freedom free trade would bring might lead Canadians to consign to the dustbin, permanently, those projects that had brought nationalists, and their constituencies, wealth and augmenting, centralized power.[6]

On the other hand, the strong argument for free trade, more than the promise of material prosperity, was precisely the destruction of that official dogma that had become the sine qua non of nationalist indoctrination. Free trade presented Canadians with the opportunity to inaugurate a nationwide self-recognition.[7]

If we were to look for a common thread linking Grant's and Frum's observations, it would be that politics, conceived in any serious sense as a choice between different ends, is over. Modern nations pursue the same ends. This includes Canada and the United States. In the most fundamental respect, Canadian and American politics are aligned. The only serious question is one of means, of how best to achieve the ends Canadians and Americans tend to agree upon. This means that the respective states in Canada and the United States should not be distinguished by ideological differences, as the cultural protectionists suggest. Rather, if we are to think—and legislate—precisely, we should distinguish the Canadian and American states by their greater or lesser efficacy at resolving the same given problems. This, I believe, is what Canadians are coming to recognize.

The nationalists suggest that the political cultures of Canada and the United States can be distinguished on the basis of the different ends they pursue. If they are honest enough to concede that the objects of Canadian and American politics are little different, the nationalists will claim that each country pursues these ends by different means. This too, we will see, is a canard.

MULTICULTURALISM, GROUPISM, AND THE POLITICS OF IDENTITY: AMERICAN, NOT CANADIAN, ORTHODOXY

Political commentators in Canada have gone to great lengths trying to establish that Canadians and Americans differ from one another on ideological or cultural grounds, asserting recently, for instance, that our distinctiveness lies in our bilingualism, our multiculturalism, or our greater pluralism. It has also been suggested, as I indicated in the introduction, that Canada's uniqueness lies in its greater collectivist inclinations or its public enterprises, that Canada is more community oriented, less individualistic than the United States, even if we pursue the same political and economic goals.

Again, these ruminations are not only false but in the case of multiculturalism and our alleged greater pluralism reflect the influences of an American phenomenon, the politics of identity, which eventually made significant inroads into Canadian public policy.

Canada is not bicultural or bilingual. French speakers live, for the most part, in Quebec, English speakers in the rest of Canada. There are bilingual Canadians, but they tend to live in bureaucratized Ottawa and slowly unilingualizing Montreal (more and more English speakers are leaving the city every year).[8] As for Canadians whose bilingualism does not involve French and English, they are irrelevant, no different from what we find in the United States.

Canada is, similarly, no more multicultural or pluralist than the United States, nor is it less assimilationist. If statistics count for anything, Canada's population is more uniform than that of the United States, not less. And this has been so for a number of decades. As Peter Brimelow reported in 1986, responses to the 1981 census indicated that Canada was ethnically much more homogeneous than the United States, as well as much more British. This was particularly the case when English-speaking Canada was considered apart from French-speaking Canada. Of all Canadians surveyed in 1981, over 40 percent told census-takers that they were British in origin. By contrast, in the United States only 14 percent reported being British and another 8 percent claimed to be Irish. (Canadian census-takers classified the Irish as British.) The percentage of Asians were roughly the same in Canada and the United States, but in the United States there were significantly more blacks and Hispanics as a percentage of the population.[9]

These trends have not changed very much in the intervening decades. Recent scholarship has predicted that whites will make up less than 50 percent of the American population sometime during the twenty-first century.[10] There is little evidence suggesting such a rapid transformation would take place in Canada. In short, Canada is no more multicultural or diverse than the United States.

If Canadians believe that their political culture is more tolerant of group politics than that of the United States, that racial and ethnic diversity is better facilitated here through policies of bilingualism and multiculturalism and a constitution that promotes and protects multicultural diversity, again, we might rethink our position. It is true that federal and provincial governments invite racial and ethnic groups to differentiate themselves from other Canadians, frequently paying these groups to do so. Section 27 of the Charter of Rights and Freedoms also provides that the "Charter shall be interpreted in a manner consistent with the preservation and enhancement of the multicultural heritage of Canadians."

But recent trends in American institutional politics, increasingly tutoring racial and ethnic groups, such as Mexican Americans, to define themselves as racial minority claimants,[11] have encouraged greater differentiation between cultural groups in the United States as well, even if, as in Canada, the differences between these groups are more artificial, more exaggerated, than real. "What is undeniably clear," Peter Skerry has written, "is that contemporary political institutions and culture encourage many Mexican Americans to 'assimilate' precisely by defining themselves as an oppressed racial minority."[12] Mexican Americans, like other ethnic and racial groups in the United States, have been invited by politicians, civil rights legislation, public interest law firms, the academic community, and other powerful groups to distinguish themselves from mainstream America, asserting their ostensible victim status. In doing so, however, Mexican Americans join a host of other groups who have asserted a similar status, if on the basis of other characteristics, such as gender or sexual preference, rather than race or ethnicity.

In short, the politics of identity, at work in Canada since the 1970s, has been at work in the United States even longer, since roughly the late 1960s when the civil rights lobby, supported by the United States Supreme Court and others, transformed civil rights initiatives and related public policy into affirmative action for designated classes of citizens.[13] Group identity, group politics, and recognition of group rights have been as prevalent in the United States as in Canada, Canadian policy, in fact, following the American lead. The persistence of opinions north of the border asserting otherwise, even among the most astute observers of Canadian and American politics, is hard to comprehend in light of the significant and mounting evidence to the contrary.[14]

The attempt on the part of the Canadian government, and its intellectual acolytes in the universities and the media, to differentiate Canada from the United States on the basis of our nationwide bilingualism, our greater tolerance for group differentiation, our multiculturalism, or our diversity is, then, misleading. Official bilingualism does not reflect a greater tolerance for group differentiation in Canada. If anything, it reveals a transparent attempt on the part of the federal government to appease the demands of isolated elements of Quebec nationalism in the face of widespread, vocal opposition to the policy both inside and outside Quebec. Canada's experiment with bilingualism has been an unmitigated exercise in social engineering.[15] And its nationalist ideology has transposed the ethnic reality of Canada and the United States, obscuring the strikingly similar nature of their English-speaking populations.[16]

If we consider, on the one hand, the legacy of American public enterprise[17] and the volume of public interest laws that have been passed in the United States,[18] and, on the other hand, the distinctive nature both of American community and of Canadian and American political and institutional structures, it is also apparent that Canada is no more collectivist than the United States. Like its American counterpart, Canadian collectivism—communitarianism as it is some-times referred to (I identify the two here)—is both antediluvian and dangerous: antediluvian because it fails to recognize the dynamism and transient quality of modern technological life; dangerous because in failing to recognize reality for what it is, its diagnoses and proposals for reform, when not entirely irrelevant, promote a soft, and more frequently than not, hard, despotism. As David Bercuson and Barry Cooper have pointed out, real communitarians believe in real communities. But real communities have all but disappeared from Canada, as well as from the rest of the modern world. This theme, the subject of volumes of sociological and political commentary, is apparently lost on communitarians who, in their evocations for a more "helping" or "caring" society, work with a romantic vision of a Canadian community that has never existed and likely never will exist.[19]

Canadians are not polis-dwelling pagans. Nor are they the commiserating vil-lage people of Rousseau's social contract. They are sophisticated, technological individuals who have come to reject the welfare state and public enterprise in Canada for the same reason Americans have rejected these things in the United States: not because they do not understand their machinations or because they have been duped by a conservative attack on them, but because they see them for what they are—a tax consuming, bureaucratic vortex that costs more and more to provide less and less. Public enterprise, and we might add collectivism in general, in Canada and the United States is on the wane, not because Canadians and Americans have been overtaken by a vulgar, malevolent individualism, but because the welfare state that residents of both countries have generously sup-ported for so long has proven to be enormously inefficient.

Even if we assume that real communities could exist in Canada, nationalist and collectivist prescriptions for such communities would undermine them, as the legacy of such policies since the 1960s demonstrates.

The problem of Quebec nationalism provides a case in point. Charles Taylor has attributed the rise of Quebec nationalism during the Quiet Revolution and after to the emergence in Quebec of a French-speaking business class and political intelligentsia.[20] Another cause, perhaps no less significant, has been the increasing dependency on the federal welfare state that has taken place in Quebec since the 1960s. The growth of federal control in Quebec, as in all provinces, has caused many Quebecers, like other Canadians, to move to regain their lost autonomy, even if this means resorting to regional or ethnic nationalism. Should we not expect such nationalism to augment as the federal government expands its mandate?

Whatever the relationship between the federal welfare state and Quebec nationalism, it is clear that the collectivist prescriptions of the nationalists have not improved Canadian community. Public enterprise in Canada rarely serves the public because Canada's political and institutional structures, to a much greater extent than similar structures in the United States, seldom work to serve the interests of the whole country. It is difficult, for instance, to explain to an Albertan that Petro-Canada was in her best interests[21]; that the CBC has not been preoccupied from its inception with the welfare of Central Canada, treating political issues, not unlike the National Film Board of Canada, from a perspective that is neither right-wing nor middle-of-the-road but definitively left-wing[22]; or that the National Policy has not benefited Ontario and Quebec to a greater extent than Canada's "regions." In just what sense are these policies or enterprises "public"? "National"?

Inaugurated in earnest in the 1960s and institutionalized after 1980, when Pierre Trudeau and the Liberal Party unveiled a series of interventionist policies, including the National Energy Program, Canadian nationalism, as I indicated in the introduction, has served as little more than a rhetorical subterfuge for Canada's Left.[23] Under the pretext of "nationalism," Canadian social democrats and their ideological hangers-on have demanded from government, and received, regulation of the economy, education, social programs, medicine, and the media. Champions of communications monoliths, such as the CBC and the NFB, or of regulatory bodies, such as the Canadian Radio-television and Telecommunications Commission, have claimed that these tributaries of government are necessary to preserve the national interest. Canadians, however, have increasingly come to recognize that these entities of state have served as little more than instruments of social democratic indoctrination, more concerned with controlling the future than with preserving the past, with acquiring power than with promoting patriotism.[24]

The left-leaning orthodoxy of the CRTC was once again evident in 2004 when the Commission approved broadcasts of Al-Jazeera, the Qatar-based Arab-language news service that has provided a platform for Islamic terrorism, while only months earlier having denied an application from the Fox News Channel to broadcast in Canada. Fox News threatens liberal media bias in Canada the same way it has threatened liberal media bias in the United States. As has typified the Left's response to Fox News south of the border, Fox's application for a broadcast licence in Canada generated hostility, denunciation of its news personalities, and other attacks from those in Canada's media and political establishment irked by the possibility that their monopoly on what Canadians view as news might be threatened. After protests from many in Canada who wanted to watch America's most successful and widely viewed news channel, the CRTC relented and granted Fox a broadcast licence in November 2004. The licence, however, only allowed Fox to broadcast to digital cable subscribers and only came after vocal protests from the Canadian Association of Broadcasters that Fox's renewed application should be denied.

The Fox News incident again illustrated how Canada's political, media, and opinion-forming elites have monopolized Canadian political culture, maintaining a left-wing anti-American orthodoxy in news presentation through such national censors as the CRTC. The assumption underlying government regulation of Canada's culture is that Canadians cannot think on their own. They must be told what to read, what to watch, what to listen to by their nationalist guardians. The same patronizing assumptions have been used by economic nationalists who, in their attacks on foreign investment and free trade during the last forty years, have claimed to know better than Canadians themselves how they should run their economic and social lives.

INDIVIDUALISM AND COMMUNITY: THE INEXTRICABLE LINK

One reason nationalism has failed to achieve its objectives is the incommensurability of its social democratic policies with the development and maintenance of communities. Communities require individualism—individual autonomy and responsibility—for their generation and maintenance. Cultural protectionists and nationalists tend to assume the opposite: that individualism is incompatible with community, that broad personal autonomy will not result in a strong sense of national or local identity, or a sense of civic pride.

In his contribution to this debate, Professor Nesbitt-Larking remarks that "the cultural message of economic liberalism [meaning America] stresses narrowly defined rights, absolute freedom from restraint and a rejection of those virtues associated with family, community, and society, such as love, tolerance, charity, duty, loyalty, and patriotism." Leaving aside the dubious suggestion that Americans are less loving, tolerant, or charitable than Canadians—the implication here, I believe—one would have to read far and wide among the works of Alexander Hamilton, James Madison, or John Adams, or the icons of economic liberalism—Adam Smith, Friedrich Hayek, or Milton Friedman, for instance—to find any assertion of a connection between economic liberalism and a rejection of those virtues associated with family, community, or society. On the contrary: A central theme running throughout the texts of economic liberals is the impossibility of achieving such virtues without the self-restraint, discipline, and responsibility demanded, and cultivated, by free markets, qualities without which families and communities disintegrate. The mere existence of the United States should be proof enough that duty, loyalty, and patriotism are not incommensurate with economic liberalism or individualism (or their "cultural message"). In fact, individualism would seem to be the necessary precondition for such things.

Presuming individualism and community to be incompatible is an oversight that has led nationalists and collectivists to timeworn interpretations both of Canadian–American relations and of conservatism. William Mitchell and Randy Simmons have observed that welfare economists typically view "the unseemly, raucous, and self-interested competition of the market" as debasing individuals. By contrast, they assume that political actors are better informed and less selfish than market actors, and can readily and accurately divine the public interest. "[S]ince the political process is considered costless, the public interest is easily achieved. And political conflict debases no one." As Mitchell and Simmons suggest, however, the welfare economists get things perfectly backwards: It is the political process that is costly and political conflict that tends to be debasing, not the market. The political responses of the welfare economists to perceived market failures generally make things worse, not better. Mitchell and Simmons conclude: "we think [the United States'] chief problems stem not from market difficulties but from political intervention in otherwise robust markets."[25]

So too in Canada. Welfare economists have interfered in the Canadian economy for over a generation, at significant and unnecessary cost to Canadians. Canadians have responded to these problems, attempting to regain control of their lives and communities, with a newfound conservatism. Yet it is a conservatism the meaning of which has been lost on collectivists and nationalists alike. Conservatives have rarely sought the simplistic objectives attributed to them by their welfare economist critics. As David Frum notes, "Conservatives want to roll back the state not because they envision human beings as selfish individualists who must be left alone to make as much money as they can, but because they see the functions of real communities being usurped by overweening governments."[26] In Canada, our national character and civic community have been undermined as government has expanded. Our understanding of community has been degraded and we take little interest in our surrounding environment. Municipal politics, for example, is a low priority for most Canadians and is rarely reported. Similarly, relative to the United States and Britain, there are few philanthropists in Canada who have been moved by a spirit of civic pride to establish great museums, libraries, or universities. "We are *not*, in fact, a highly community-spirited people; we are merely a highly taxed people."[27]

To listen to our political and intellectual elites, however, a different impression of Canada is conveyed, one based, I suggest, not on the real-world, everyday lives of Canadians, but on idealistic, self-flattering visions, on stereotypes and doctrinaire interpretations.

If we are to overcome our misgivings and recapture an identity that for almost a century was a source of significant northern pride, we will have to turn away from the nationalist prescriptions and commonplaces that have comprised the standard version of Canadian political culture presented to us over the last generation.

SOCIALISM, NATIONALISM, AND THE REVOLT OF THE ELITES

Peter Brimelow remarked that "popular journalism has accustomed Canadians to regard a selective cross-section of their business world as 'the Canadian establishment,' imbued with exciting if intangible power and privilege."[28] As Brimelow highlighted, however, the real Canadian establishment was something quite different, an alliance of politicians, bureaucrats, educators, and members of the media that emerged contemporaneously with the development of the welfare state.[29] The real Canadian establishment more closely approximates what Christopher Lasch described in *The Revolt of the Elites and the Betrayal of Democracy* as the emergent thinking classes: well-educated, well-connected individuals who live in a sanitized world of ideas and abstractions, divorced from physical reality and reflecting the experiences of life in an artificial world where everything that resists human manipulation has been excluded. The credo of these new classes is control. "In their drive to insulate themselves against risk and contingency—against the unpredictable hazards that afflict human life—the thinking classes have seceded not just from the common world around them but from reality itself."[30]

Lasch's description comports with Canada's new knowledge class of university professors, journalists, lawyers, and others seeking greater government control over the economy and culture in the name of the national interest. What the advocates of Canadian nationalism and those proclaiming the increasing Americanization of Canadian political culture really lament is not the loss of Canadian identity per se but the loss of a *socialist* vision of Canada that demands, as the price of Canadian citizenship, state control over how we should lead our lives, what literature we should read, what programming we should watch, what songs we should listen to, where we should send our children to be nursed and educated, how we should ship our goods, and even what airlines we should fly and where we should buy our gas.

The bankruptcy of this vision, the idea that somehow our collective soul depends on things such as Petro-Canada or the CNR, or that our national identity can only be held together by bureaucrats, to say nothing of the expense nationalism has cost, has recently become apparent to Canadians. In the late 1980s and early 1990s, Canadians adopted increasingly expansive free trade, despite the nationalists' misleading, frequently hysterical, protestations. Canadians rejected the pro-Quebec, pro-welfare state Meech Lake and Charlottetown Accords. They displaced—apparently permanently—the federal Progressive Conservative Party with the genuinely conservative Reform Party of Canada (now the Conservative Party of Canada). In two of the three most productive provinces in the country, they elected Conservative governments that did more to wean Canadians from bureaucratic largesse and paternalism than any other governments in Canadian history.

These developments have not augured well for the nationalists, who have witnessed their authority over the lives of Canadians dissipate. The response has been predictable enough: intransigence and a denial that Canadians know what they are doing, even that their newfound conservatism is "un-Canadian."

Two things deserve emphasis here. First, although the products of culture—political or otherwise—are by no means matters of indifference, they are seldom matters of national distinction, even if they are at times subjects of national pride. What is unique, for instance, about Mordecai Richler, Margaret Atwood, or Bryan Adams is not that they are Canadian but that they are excellent at what they do. The cross-cultural, transpolitical nature of their work is reflected in how well they sell outside of Canada. That our pride in these artists originates in their recognition outside our borders is proof that Canadians are quite capable of recognizing excellence, even if their government seems intent on blinding them to it.

Related to this observation is a second, more important one: Nationalism and the preoccupations of cultural protectionism divert us from the real issues that confront Canadians. As the foregoing analysis suggests, the political movement that purports to protect Canadian culture from Americanization is both misleading and dangerous: misleading because it misrepresents the facts of reality, and dangerous because Canadian culture is not threatened by the United States but, as George Grant suggested, by something much more pervasive and elusive, the same thing that threatens American culture. The war of cultures is not between Canada and the United States. It is rather, in Neil Postman's words, "between technology and everybody else."[31]

The dynamism of commercial republics, which both Canada and the United States are, presents problems that governments in both countries must confront: soaring governmental spending, excessive taxation, rising crime, dilapidated educational standards, urban decay, family disintegration, and threats to national security. To the extent that we consume ourselves with affectations over whether the privatization of Petro-Canada or the existence of split-run American magazines will lead to a loss of control over Canada's culture—allegations that themselves, ironically, presume that culture to be hopelessly shallow—we divert our attention from the real issues of the day: how we should better manage our economy, preserve individual freedom, deal with our violent criminals and juvenile offenders, reform our schools and universities, redesign our cities, reunite our families, and fight terrorism. But diversion, I suggest, is part of the political agenda of cultural protectionism.

The word "culture" fits the moral and political relativism fostered by the politics of identity. An amorphous concept that means many things to many people, "culture" frequently refers to popular culture (music, art, and film) but at a deeper level refers to moral and intellectual phenomena, phenomena that are distinct from, sometimes in tension with, or even antithetical to, one another.[32]

The indiscriminate use of "culture" to refer to such distinct concepts as justice, truth, morality, freedom, and the like hides from analysis the real issues we should be talking about in Canadian politics. It also serves the political purpose of fortifying the relativism promoted by those on the cultural left who wish to smooth over distinctions in rank and order between individuals and groups, and the moral and political activities they represent. When we describe as irresolvable differences of culture or preference the distinctions between Quebec nationalism and English-speaking liberal constitutionalism, the relative merits of Aboriginal self-government and other forms of self-government, feminist versus more traditional views of the family, heterosexual marriage versus same-sex marriage, or heterosexual parenting versus homosexual parenting, we dodge admittedly delicate and difficult issues, but we do so at the price of intellectual rigour.

Similarly, when we refuse to discuss issues of privatization, open markets, or government deregulation because they are considered to be antithetical to Canadian political culture, we insulate ourselves from understanding the real issues at stake in the debate over Canada's future; in particular, whether the complex network of rules, content regulations, trade barriers, subsidies, expropriations, and the like, all intended to protect our so-called cultural industries, are really worth supporting or are not just mechanisms for providing pork to a nationalist clientele.

Cultural protectionism serves to immunize the nationalists' projects from the scrutiny they deserve, allowing designated public enterprises to hide behind the mantle of what is alleged to be necessary to protect Canadian identity, an identity that can only take one shape—social democratic—and that will necessarily create a system of inequality in which certain favoured constituencies will enjoy the spoils of government while other groups, generally self-sustaining, will remain outside the fold of government largesse.

Some of the dangers presented by Canadian nationalism and the campaign to advance a distinct Canadian culture—political or otherwise—are, then, an unequal distribution of political power, an undermining of the rule of law and equal treatment that the social engineering and redistributive platform of nationalism promotes,[33] an augmenting of bureaucratic waste and coercion, an empty and self-righteous anti-Americanism, and, ultimately, dishonesty.

To date, the movement in Canada that has sought to free Canadians from the yoke of nationalism has been conservatism. Conservatism has protected Canadians from the indiscriminateness and social and economic levelling of that collectivist ideology that lies at the heart of the nationalist enterprise. If it does not have the answers to all of our political problems, Canadian conservatism has at least diagnosed more accurately, and perhaps less sanctimoniously than its ideological counterparts, the problems that we need to address. If we must choose, we should choose more of it, not less.

NOTES

1. I am following, roughly, Peter Brimelow's characterization. See Peter Brimelow, *The Patriot Game: National Dreams and Political Realities* (Toronto: Key Porter Books, 1986), pp. 136–137:

   [A] common Nationalist misinterpretation of Canada's economic culture ... a caricature, ignor[es,] among other things, the American "public enterprise" tradition that produced the Tennessee Valley Authority, the notoriously powerful New York State Parks Commissioner Robert Moses, and—predating the Bank of Canada—the Federal Reserve system.

2. See George Grant, *Technology and Empire: Perspectives on North America* (Toronto: Anansi, 1969), p. 64.

3. George Grant, *Lament for a Nation* (Toronto: Macmillan, 1965), p. ix.

4. David Frum, *What's Right: The New Conservatism and What It Means for Canada* (Toronto: Random House, 1996), pp. 3–4.

5. Ibid., p. 4.

6. Ibid., pp. 200–201.

7. Ibid., pp. 202–204.

8. For an excellent account of how the city of Montreal has been changed for the worse by Quebec nationalism, see Mordecai Richler, *Oh Canada! Oh Quebec! Requiem for a Divided Country* (Toronto: Viking, 1992).

9. Brimelow, *The Patriot Game*, pp. 138–139.

10. For commentary on the significance of this development and how to respond to it, see Michael Barone, *The New Americans: How the Melting Pot Can Work Again* (Washington, DC: Regnery Publishing, Inc., 2001).

11. Peter Skerry, *Mexican Americans: The Ambivalent Minority* (Cambridge, MA: Harvard University Press, 1993), p. 7.

12. Ibid., p. 365.

13. See Nathan Glazer, *Affirmative Discrimination: Ethnic Inequality and Public Policy* (New York: Basic Books, 1975); and Herman Belz, *Equality Transformed: A Quarter-Century of Affirmative Action* (New Brunswick, NJ: Transaction Publishers, 1991).

14. See, for instance, Thomas Sowell, *Civil Rights: Rhetoric or Reality?* (New York: William Morrow, 1984); Abigail M. Thernstrom, *Whose Votes Count? Affirmative Action and Minority Voting Rights* (Cambridge, MA: Harvard University Press, 1987); and Terry Eastland, *Ending Affirmative Action: The Case for Colorblind Justice* (New York: Basic Books, 1997).

15. Brimelow, *The Patriot Game*, p. 96.

16. Ibid., p. 139.

17. See note 1.

18. Richard A. Epstein provides a good account of this in *Simple Rules for a Complex World* (Cambridge, MA: Harvard University Press, 1995).

19. See David J. Bercuson and Barry Cooper, *Derailed: The Betrayal of the National Dream* (Toronto: Key Porter Books, 1994), pp. 14–16.

20. See Charles Taylor, *Reconciling the Solitudes: Essays on Canadian Federalism and Nationalism* (Montreal and Kingston: McGill-Queen's University Press, 1993), esp. pp. 3–22, 166–167.

21. For a discussion of the meaning and purpose of Petro-Canada, the National Energy Program, and other federal incursions into the Canadian petroleum business, see Peter Foster, *The Sorcerer's Apprentices: Canada's Super-Bureaucrats and the Energy Mess* (Don Mills, ON: Collins, 1982); and *Other People's Money: The Banks, the Government and Dome* (Don Mills, ON: Collins, 1983).

22. See Barry Cooper, *Sins of Omission: Shaping the News at the CBC* (Toronto: University of Toronto Press, 1994).

23. Brimelow, *The Patriot Game*, pp. 18, 132.

24. Ibid., pp. 144, 146.

25. William C. Mitchell and Randy T. Simmons, *Beyond Politics: Markets, Welfare, and the Failure of Bureaucracy* (Boulder, CO: Westview Press, 1994), pp. 3–4.

26. Frum, *What's Right*, p. 5.

27. Ibid., pp. 5–6; emphasis in original.

28. Brimelow, *The Patriot Game*, p. 19.

29. Ibid., p. 18.

30. Christopher Lasch, *The Revolt of the Elites and the Betrayal of Democracy* (New York: W.W. Norton & Company, 1995), p. 20.

31. Neil Postman, *Technopoly: The Surrender of Culture to Technology* (New York: Vintage Books, 1993), p. xii.

32. Mark Blitz, "How to Think about Politics and Culture," *The Political Science Reviewer* 25, no. 5 (1996): 9–11. As Blitz points out (p. 11),

    ... what we need for a good moral education is not identical to what we need for a good intellectual education. Indeed, they may both conflict. The areas of similarity (the need for "discipline" in both, for example) should not blind us to the areas of difference—the need, for example in one but not the other, to be unconventional and, even, irreverent.

33. See Friedrich A. Hayek, *The Constitution of Liberty* (Chicago: University of Chicago Press, 1960), p. 232:

    Those who pursue distributive justice will in practice find themselves obstructed at every move by the rule of law. They must, from the very nature of their aim, favor discriminatory and discretionary action. But, as they are usually not aware that their aim and the rule of law are in principle incompatible, they begin by circumventing or disregarding in individual cases a principle which they often would wish to see preserved in general.... [T]he ultimate result of their efforts will necessarily be, not a modification of the existing order, but its complete abandonment and its replacement by an altogether different system—the command economy.

POSTSCRIPT

In his essay, Paul Nesbitt-Larking paints a picture that must be familiar to many. Government restraint, strident interest groups, growing public intolerance and anger—these are signs of the times. And Nesbitt-Larking argues, convincingly, that these are all manifestations of the growing Americanization of Canadian political life. Canada has always battled the threat of Americanization, and now it faces the prospect of finally losing this protracted war. Yet, it may be possible that Nesbitt-Larking exaggerates his case. Canada still has a national health care program, the United States does not; Canada still has a disciplined political process, the United States does not; and Canada still has a sense of community, the United States does not. Moreover, recent surveys—uncovered by Nesbitt-Larking—reveal that Canadians remain different from Americans in their basic attitudes.

Nesbitt-Larking might be challenged in another way. Perhaps the changes taking place are what Canadians want, and they may be considered to be beneficial. One of these changes is a weakening of the deferential attitude Canadians hold toward leaders and political elites. As Nesbitt-Larking himself admits, this development can be seen in a positive light. Perhaps the costs of Americanization are acceptable in view of the development of a more vibrant and democratic polity in Canada. What is happening is not really the Americanization of Canada, but rather the democratization of a nation held back by vestiges of traditional conservatism.

Anthony A. Peacock has written a very provocative essay. He characterizes any differences in the Canadian and American political cultures as ephemeral, and accuses Canadian nationalists of attempting to graft onto Canada a foreign belief system, namely socialism. Perhaps most arresting is his claim that the United States is at least as caring and community-oriented as Canada, and that individualism and communitarianism go hand in hand. Also interesting is Peacock's argument that the changes now being experienced in Canada represent an attempt to recover a former self distorted by works of Canadian nationalists.

Peacock is convincing—and refreshing. As he says, Canadians and Americans do tend to enjoy the same things. Furthermore, it does seem that governments in Canada have introduced policies and programs that seem to be some distance from the wishes of ordinary Canadians. But his assertions nevertheless raise some queries. Surely, Peacock misses some important differences between Canadians and Americans; the two are similar, but not the same. Moreover, can the CBC, economic regulations, energy boards, and assorted other government initiatives really be the work of only a handful of socialist-minded nationalists? May they not be true reflections of the political culture of Canada and its inherent collectivism? There may also be some who believe that Peacock's effort is merely a conservative's dream of an Americanized Canada.

For students wishing to pursue the debate, it is first necessary to gain a general overview of Canadian political culture. For this, one would do well to read David Bell's *The Roots of Disunity: A Study of Canadian Political Culture*, 2nd ed. (Toronto:

Oxford University Press, 1992). Shorter treatments of Canada's beliefs about politics include David V.J. Bell, "Political Culture in Canada," in Michael S. Whittington and Glen Williams, eds., *Canadian Politics in the 21st Century*, 6th ed. (Scarborough: Thomson Nelson, 2004); Stephen Brooks, "Political Culture in Canada: Issues and Directions," in James P. Bickerton and Alain-G. Gagnon, eds., *Canadian Politics*, 4th ed. (Peterborough: Broadview Press, 2004); and Neil Nevitte and Mebs Kanji, "New Cleavages, Value Diversity, and Democratic Government," in James P. Bickerton and Alain-G. Gagnon, eds., *Canadian Politics*, 4th ed. (Peterborough: Broadview Press, 2004). An examination of the American political culture might also be appropriate, for which Herbert McCloskey and John Zaller's *The American Ethos: Public Attitudes Towards Capitalism and Democracy* (Cambridge: Harvard University Press, 1984) would be suitable. A text that gives a more nuanced view of the possessive or competitive individualism of Americans is Richard J. Ellis, *American Political Cultures* (New York: Oxford University Press, 1993).

Students might then want to access comparative studies of American and Canadian political cultures. Such studies include Gad Horowitz, *Canadian Labour in Politics* (Toronto: University of Toronto, 1968), ch. 1; Seymour Martin Lipset, *Continental Divide: The Values and Institutions of the United States and Canada* (New York: Routledge, 1990); Richard M. Merelman, *Partial Visions: Culture and Politics in Britain, Canada, and the United States* (Madison: University of Wisconsin Press, 1991); and George Perlin, "The Constraints of Public Opinion: Diverging or Converging Paths?" in Keith Banting, George Hoberg, and Richard Simeon, eds., *Degrees of Freedom: Canada and the United States in a Changing World* (Montreal and Kingston: McGill-Queen's University Press, 1997). More recent works include Michael Adams, *Fire and Ice: The United States and Canada and the Myth of Converging Values* (Toronto: Penguin, 2003) and Edward Grabb and James Curtis, *Regions Apart: The Four Societies of Canada and the United States* (Toronto: Oxford University Press, 2005).

A large part of the debate revolves around changes in the political culture of Canada. For an important work on this subject, students should consult Neil Nevitte, *The Decline of Deference* (Peterborough: Broadview Press, 1996) as well as Neil Nevitte, ed., *Value Change and Governance in Canada* (Toronto: University of Toronto Press, 2002). As for manifestations of these changes in the operation of the Canadian political system, the following texts and readings are of some relevance: Harold Clarke et al., *Absent Mandate: Canadian Politics in the Era of Restructuring*, 3rd ed. (Toronto: Gage, 1996); Alan Cairns, *Charter Versus Federalism: The Dilemmas of Constitutional Reform* (Montreal and Kingston: McGill-Queen's University Press, 1992); and Reg Whitaker, "Canadian Politics at the End of the Millennium: Old Dreams, New Nightmares," in David Taras and Beverly Rasporich, eds., *A Passion for Identity*, 3rd ed. (Scarborough: Nelson Canada, 1997).

Finally, central to Peacock's essay is Canadian nationalism. For a start on this subject, students might examine Sylvia B. Bashevkin, *True Patriot Love: The Politics of Canadian Nationalism* (Toronto: Oxford University Press, 1991).

Can Native Sovereignty Coexist with Canadian Sovereignty?

✔ **YES**
JOHN A. OLTHUIS AND ROGER TOWNSHEND, "The Case for Native Sovereignty"

✘ **NO**
THOMAS FLANAGAN, "Native Sovereignty: Does Anyone Really Want an Aboriginal Archipelago?"

In Canada, the subject of Aboriginal rights has never been high on the political agenda. Most Canadians have a vague awareness of the deplorable living conditions on many Indian reserves, but that is about all. The demands of Native people for land, greater autonomy, and even self-government have received little notice. More "immediate" issues such as constitutional reform, Quebec separatism, western alienation, or free trade with the United States have usually pushed Native issues off the list of urgent public issues.

However, the dramatic events surrounding the Oka crisis of 1990 did more to change public perceptions of Native issues than any other single event. Reacting to municipal plans to expand a local golf course onto traditional Native lands, armed Mohawk Warriors began erecting barricades in an effort to stop the work. The protest soon escalated into a full-scale confrontation between the Quebec provincial police and Mohawk Warriors, in which one police officer was killed. Soon a second set of barriers was erected on the Kahnawake reserve near Montreal as a demonstration of support. As the situation appeared to become more violent, Quebec Premier Robert Bourassa called in the Canadian armed forces to restore order to Oka. For the first time in twenty years, Canadian troops were deployed against fellow citizens.

For federal and Quebec officials, the issue was straightforward. The Mohawks, in using arms and barricades to press their case, had broken the law and needed to be brought to justice like any other citizens who had committed illegal acts. Land claims and other grievances would be settled only when arms were surrendered and the lawbreakers brought to justice. But the Mohawks rejected this view. It was not just a matter of land claims that was at stake. It was, the Warriors claimed, a question of sovereignty. The Mohawks occupied sovereign territory that had never been surrendered to any British or Canadian government. Thus the Mohawks had every right, as any other sovereign nation, to take up arms to defend themselves. It was the police and army who were acting illegally.

At the heart of Native grievances is the Indian Act, 1867, which set the tone for successive federal government dealings with Native people. Under this act, elected Indian band councils, not traditional political institutions, deal with the Department of Indian Affairs and Northern Development. Band councils are granted limited powers, but all financial decisions are ultimately subject to the approval of the minister responsible for Indian Affairs. Thus sovereignty remains undivided and concentrated in the hands of Ottawa. Band councils are like fledgling municipal governments, able to exercise only those powers specifically delegated to them.

Native leaders have long argued that this relationship is humiliating and paternalistic. The real aim of the Indian Act, they argue, has been to use the band councils as an instrument for destroying traditional Native institutions and for assimilating and integrating Native people into the larger Canadian society. For moderate Native leaders, the solution has been to negotiate some greater delegation of powers to the band councils. But for a growing number of Native leaders this is not enough. Only when the full sovereignty of Indian nations is recognized will Native people be able to overcome their degrading colonial status.

In the wake of the Oka crisis, Native issues were suddenly given a more prominent place on the Canadian political agenda. The government of Brian Mulroney appointed a royal commission on Aboriginal questions, and gave Native leaders an increasingly prominent role in discussions leading up to the constitutional proposals of 1992. The Charlottetown Accord appeared to address many Native concerns. The accord included a recognition of the inherent right of Aboriginal people to self-government and the commitment to make these Aboriginal governments one of three orders of government along with Ottawa and the provinces. Federal and provincial governments would have committed themselves to negotiating self-government agreements with those Native bands that wished to do so, while a series of future First Ministers' Conferences were promised to give ongoing consideration to Aboriginal constitutional issues.

However, many remained sceptical of the accord. Non-Native critics wondered what a third order of government meant. What form would Native self-government take? How would it mesh with the notion of a sovereign Canada? At the same time, many Native people felt that the accord had not gone far enough. After all, the accord stated that Aboriginal laws could not be inconsistent with those Canadian laws that are deemed essential to the preservation of peace, order, and good government. This was hardly a recognition of Native sovereignty.

With the defeat of the referendum, many of the questions surrounding the issue of Native sovereignty were left unresolved. In October 1996, the Royal Commission on Aboriginal Peoples published its five-volume report. Although the commission made over four hundred specific proposals, the report has quietly passed from public attention. This complacency was due in part to the lukewarm response of the Liberal government, which stated that the estimated $30-billion cost of implementing the report's recommendations was too great to accommo-date in the present economic circumstances. Instead, the Liberal government introduced the First Nations Governance Act, which the government stated was designed to ensure financial and political accountability and to "modernize" the Old Indian Act. Many Native groups opposed the pending legislation, arguing that, rather than a step forward, the legislation would in fact turn Aboriginal communities into the equivalent of municipalities and open the door to the expansion of provincial powers in Native affairs. When Parliament was prorogued in December 2003, the First Nations Governance Act was allowed to die on the order paper and has not been re-introduced.

In the following essays, three specialists in Native issues debate the meaning of Native sovereignty and its relationship to the concepts of a sovereign Canada. John Olthuis and Roger Townshend, lawyers who have done extensive work on Native land claims and Aboriginal constitutional issues, set out the case for Native sovereignty. Thomas Flanagan of the University of Calgary argues that the demand for Native sovereignty as it is posed by Native leaders is incompatible with the continued existence of Canada.

✔ **YES**
The Case for Native Sovereignty
JOHN A. OLTHUIS AND ROGER TOWNSHEND

There is a great divide in perceptions between aboriginal people in Canada and non-aboriginal people. The non-aboriginal Canadian takes as self-evident the legitimacy of the Canadian state and its jurisdiction over Canadian territory. The average aboriginal person, on the other hand, views much of the power exercised by the Canadian state as illegitimate, oppressive, and as infringing on the powers of First Nations. To the extent that non-aboriginal Canadians are aware of this perception among aboriginal people, they are likely bewildered by it and have trouble seeing either a reasonable basis for it or any practical ways in which such a view could be acted on. Yet it is precisely this divergence of views that has caused and will continue to cause confrontations in the political area (such as regarding constitutional amendments) and confrontations on the ground such as at Kanesatake (Oka).

Although non-aboriginal Canadians rarely question the legitimacy of the Canadian state, most thoughtful people would likely be distressed at how flimsy the logical justification for Canadian sovereignty indeed is. There is no question that prior to European contact native nations in North America had stable cultures, economies, and political systems. They unmistakably exercised full sovereignty over their lands, although in somewhat different ways than did European nations. It would be arrogant and ethnocentric to recognize only a European model political organization as a sovereign state. The initial contact of Europeans with native nations generally treated them as allies or as enemies, but in any event, as nations to be treated as equals with European states. How then did this change? International law then and now recognized changes in sovereignty based on conquest, discovery and settlement, or treaty.

There is nothing in Canadian history that could qualify as a conquest in the international law sense. Treaties with First Nations fall into two rough categories. There are "peace and friendship" treaties, which, if anything, reinforce the concept of the equal nationhood of First Nations. There are also treaties that read as land transactions, which by their silence concerning matters of jurisdiction would seem to provide little help in rooting a claim that they are a source of Canadian sovereignty. Furthermore, there are vast areas of Canada where there are no treaties whatsoever. Thus the invocation of treaties is wholly unsatisfactory as a foundation of Canadian sovereignty. What is left is the doctrine of discovery and settlement. The difficulty with this is that it was intended to apply only to lands that were vacant. Its initial application to a claim of European jurisdiction required the step of considering the aboriginal people as legal nonpersons. In fact, the "discovery" of the Americas sparked lengthy theological and judicial debates in Europe about whether indigenous people indeed were or should be treated as humans. Thus the only justification for Canadian sovereignty (of course, inherited from British sovereignty) that has an air of reality to it requires, as a precondition, a judgment that aboriginal people are not human. This is surely repugnant to thinking Canadians.[1]

Despite the logical flimsiness of its assertion of sovereignty, the British (and later the Canadian state), after an initial period of nation-to-nation dealings, has treated aboriginal people as subjects and indeed as less-than-equal subjects. After the onset of European settlement, Canadian Indian policy has been aimed at assimilating aboriginal people into Canadian society. This integration was to be achieved on an individual level and preferably to be achieved by entry into the working-class level of society. Efforts of aboriginal people to interact as a group with Canadian society or to integrate at a higher level of Canadian society met with suppression. For example, for many years an aboriginal person who graduated from university automatically ceased to be an "Indian" in the eyes of the federal government. The policy of assimilation came to a head in 1969 with the notorious White Paper that called for the termination of Indian status. This document was resoundingly rejected by aboriginal people and in fact became the catalyst for the Canada-wide political organization of First Nations. This policy of assimilation has been a complete and utter failure. The political resistance of First Nations to assimilation into Canadian society has never been stronger. Most aboriginal people, in a fundamental way, view the Canadian government as a foreign government and not one that is "theirs." This should hardly be shocking, since it was only in 1960 that aboriginal people were able to vote in federal elections. Neither have aboriginal communities lost their social, cultural, and economic distinctiveness. The Canadian government has tried long and hard to change this, but it has failed. Its attempts have only created much human misery. The residential school system, where Indian children were separated from their families and forbidden to speak their language and often even sexually abused, was one of those attempts. Another attempt was the criminalization of traditional native religious ceremonies. Also, the native traditional economy has in many parts of the country been seriously impaired both by the environmental effects of development activities and directly by legislation restricting hunting rights. Yet the attachment of aboriginal people to the land remains unbroken.[2]

So what options are open? The dismal social conditions in which many aboriginal people in Canada live are the results of failed assimilationist policies of the Canadian government. Aboriginal people firmly believe that the political key to a better future is the recognition of jurisdiction of First Nations. This must be a jurisdiction that goes well beyond a municipal government–type of jurisdiction, and that would allow and encourage the development of new types of structures that would reflect the distinct cultural, political, economic, and spiritual aspects of aboriginal society. This must be a jurisdiction that is provided with sufficient resources to be viable. It would indeed mean a fundamental restructuring of the institutions of the Canadian state or, perhaps more accurately, a rolling back of the jurisdiction of the Canadian state to allow aboriginal institutions to flourish. It is this approach that could allow for a just and peaceful coexistence of First Nations in the Canadian state.

The defeat of the proposed constitutional amendments in 1992 was a missed opportunity to begin to pursue this path. These amendments were rejected by both non-aboriginal and aboriginal people. However, it must be realized that they were rejected for very different reasons. The rejection of the Charlottetown Accord by non-aboriginal people seems to have little to do with the aboriginal proposals in the accord. To the extent that these were a factor, non-aboriginal Canadians were probably disposed to view them as giving too much to First Nations. First Nations, on the other hand, rejected the accord because it was too small a step in the direction they wanted to go.

It is puzzling that the idea of native sovereignty should be so threatening to non-aboriginal people. The very nature of the Canadian political system involves a division of powers between federal and provincial governments. It is but an easy step in theory to implement another order of government and provide for an appropriate division of powers. This would not be a challenge to the very essence of Canada since the sharing of jurisdictional powers between different government institutions is already part of the essence of the Canadian state. Canadian sovereignty is also leaking at the other end with increasing globalization and trade agreements. It becomes confusing, then, why Canada should be unwilling to share jurisdiction with First Nations if it is indeed willing to modify its sovereignty with relation to the provinces and also at the international level. Nor would the idea of native sovereignty within a federal state be an uncharted course. In the United States, a country hardly known for being progressive, it is an established legal doctrine that Indian tribes are "domestic dependent nations." The implementation of this concept extends to separate tribal justice and court systems.

Many non-aboriginal Canadians may be troubled by the idea of native sovereignty since they feel that aboriginal people should be able to achieve their social and economic goals by participation as individuals within Canadian society. This misses the entire point of native difference. Most aboriginal cultures have a distinctive and tangible collective nature that goes well beyond the sum of the individuals that constitute them and that would be destroyed by assimilation on an individual basis. The failure of many non-aboriginal Canadians to appreciate this reflects only that liberal individualism is such a pervasive ideology in Canadian society that it is barely recognizable as an ideology at all and often viewed as ultimate truth. (This appears to be the position taken by Thomas Flanagan in the opposing article.) By definition, a group with a culture that differs at significant points from liberal individualism cannot be accommodated within a purely individualistic framework, particularly when any integration with a larger society can only take place on an individual basis. It is true that a society that permits or encourages interaction on a collective basis is not a "liberal democracy" in the sense of the term used by Flanagan. This is the very point. A "liberal democracy" is not an acceptable political structure for most aboriginal people. Fortunately, Canada has never been a "liberal democracy" in a strong sense, as Flanagan seems to admit. For that matter, whether or not "liberal democracy" is a meaningful term is questionable, since the concepts of liberalism and democracy can come into sharp conflict (for example, when a majority wishes to suppress rights of a minority).

Others may view the kind of structural diversity advocated in this article to be extremely impractical. As Flanagan admits, it is not unprecedented—he cites the Ottoman Empire as an example. There are also analogies less unfamiliar to Canadians—the position of Indian tribes in the U.S. system is one. Another example, in a context without an aboriginal element, is that the social and political structure of the Netherlands permits and encourages structural diversity based on philosophical or confessional communities. But apart from whether operating models exist or not, the alternatives to recognizing aboriginal jurisdiction must be looked at realistically. Flanagan's alternative is to do more consistently what the Canadian government has been trying to do for a century. This has failed utterly, and has created much suffering and resentment in the process. What is there to lose in trying something different? Demands for the recognition of aboriginal jurisdiction are not going to go away. If "legitimate" avenues for advancing these demands are shut down, other means may be sought. The continued peace and security of Canada may well depend on accommodating aboriginal jurisdiction.

Respect for the cultural distinctiveness of aboriginal people requires the recognition of institutional forms of First Nations governments with sufficient resources to exercise jurisdiction meaningfully. The sad history of the treatment of aboriginal people by the Canadian state also cries out for redress in the form of recognition of native sovereignty. Nor should this recognition be viewed as completely impractical or as entailing the very destruction of the Canadian state.

NOTES

1. For more detail on the international law aspects of this, see, for example, O. Dickason, "Concepts of Sovereignty at the Time of First Contact," in Dickason and Green, eds., *The Law of Nations and the New World* (Edmonton: University of Alberta Press, 1989).

2. For more examples of the failure of the policy of assimilation and native resistance to it, see, for example, Diane Engelstad and John Bird, eds., *Nation to Nation: Aboriginal Sovereignty and the Future of Canada* (Concord: House of Anansi Press, 1992).

✗ NO

Native Sovereignty: Does Anyone Really Want an Aboriginal Archipelago?

THOMAS FLANAGAN

"... words are wise men's counters, they do but reckon by them: but they are the money of fools...."

—Thomas Hobbes, *Leviathan* (1651), I, 4

In the spirit of Hobbes, before we can debate native sovereignty, we should be clear on what we are talking about. I have elsewhere defined sovereignty as "the authority to override all other authorities." More specifically, it is

> a bundle of powers associated with the highest authority of government. One is the power to enforce rules of conduct.... Another is the power to make law, [also the power of] raising revenue, maintaining armed forces, minting currency, and providing other services to society. Moreover, in the British tradition sovereignty implies an underlying ownership of all land. Finally, sovereignty always means the power to deal with the sovereigns of other communities as well as the right to exercise domestic rule free from interference by other sovereigns.[1]

That is the abstract meaning of sovereignty in the vocabulary of political science. In this sense, it is a conceptual property of the approximately 190 states that make up the international state system. Most of the entities that possess sovereignty belong to the United Nations or, like Switzerland, could belong if they should decide to apply for membership.

Sovereignty can only pertain to states. It makes no sense to speak of sovereignty unless there is, as in the classical definition of the state, an organized structure of government ruling over a population within defined territorial boundaries. Native societies in what is now Canada did not possess sovereignty before the coming of the Europeans; neither the concept nor the underlying institutions were part of the culture of their hunting-gathering societies. Of course, hunting-gathering societies have political processes that assign rank and dominance within communities and involve conflict between communities, but the political processes of stateless societies are not the same thing as statehood and sovereignty.

As a way of increasing their political leverage in contemporary Canada, native political leaders have adopted the classical language of statehood to describe their communities. What used to be called bands or tribes are now called "nations," and these nations are said to have possessed sovereignty from the beginning and to possess it still.[2] This strategic use of language has served native leaders well in their struggle for greater power within the Canadian polity, but politically effective assertions should not be confused with intellectually persuasive analysis.

When native leaders in Canada now claim to possess sovereignty, they typically mean one of three things, each of which is related to a particular political situation. In what follows, I will argue that all three of these meanings are incompatible with the continued existence of Canada and the maintenance of essential Canadian political traditions. It is not that words alone can destroy Canada; words in themselves do not accomplish anything. But words such as "native sovereignty" are the verbal symbols of political projects that cannot be reconciled with Canadian institutions.

1. Some native leaders, for example those from the Mohawk communities of Kahnawake and Kanesatake in Quebec, speak of sovereignty in the robust sense described above, that is, the international sense. They hold that the Mohawks on their territory constitute a sovereign, independent state not part of Canada or the United States. This sovereign state should be admitted to the United Nations and in other respects become part of the international community. A Mohawk elder told the Royal Commission on Aboriginal Peoples in March 1993: "You have no right to legislate any laws over our people whatsoever. Our lands are not yours to be assumed. You are my tenant, whether you like it or not."[3]

While I respect the honesty of this position, I do not take it seriously as a political proposition. In the ten provinces, Canada has over 600 Indian bands living on more than 2200 reserves, plus hundreds of thousands of Métis and nonstatus Indians who do not possess reserves. These scattered pieces of land and disparate peoples are not going to be recognized as independent sovereign states, now or ever. They are simply not viable as sovereign states paying their own way and defending their interests in the international community. Nor is there any practical way to weld them into a single sovereign state. Native peoples are deeply divided by language, religion, customs, and history and in no way constitute a single people. They are not seeking emancipation from the tutelage of Indian Affairs in order to lose their identity in some supratribal bureaucracy.

2. The concept of sovereignty, as originally formulated by the philosophers Jean Bodin and Thomas Hobbes, was thought to be a set of powers located in a single seat of authority—perhaps the monarch, perhaps the parliament, but in any case one sovereign. However, sovereignty can also be divided. Indeed, the classical definition of federalism implies a system of divided sovereignty, in which two levels of government each have shares of sovereign power guaranteed in a constitution that cannot be changed unilaterally by either level of government acting alone. In such a context, it is at least verbally meaningful to speak of giving native peoples a constitutionally entrenched share of sovereign authority.

This is more or less the political theory contained in the Charlottetown Accord. According to that document, "The Constitution should be amended to recognize that the aboriginal peoples of Canada have the inherent right of self-government within Canada," and aboriginal self-governments should be recognized as "one of the three orders of government in Canada."[4] Although the terms federalism and sovereignty were not used, the most straightforward way to interpret the scheme proposed by the Charlottetown Accord is as an extension of divided sovereignty in a federal system from two to three levels. Although none of the details were worked out, the accord would have endowed aboriginal self-governments with many of the attributes of provinces: an entrenched constitutional basis of authority, participation in constitutional amendment procedures, representation in the Senate, a role in fiscal federalism, broad legislative jurisdiction, and so on.

This proposal cannot be dismissed on a priori grounds. There is no self-evident reason why federalism must be based on only two levels of government. Why not a "third order"? There are in fact many reasons why not, but they are more practical than conceptual.

First, as mentioned above, there are in Canada over half a million status Indians belonging to more than 600 bands on more than 2200 reserves scattered across all 10 provinces. No one has proposed a workable mechanism by which this far-flung archipelago could be knit together into a single political entity, or even a small number of such entities. On the contrary, it was widely assumed in the debate on the Charlottetown Accord that the focus of self-government would be the band, or perhaps small clusters of closely related bands organized into tribal councils. Indeed, one of the widely touted advantages of the third order of government is its alleged flexibility, which would allow different bands or groups of bands to have their own institutions of government, criminal justice systems, schools, and so on.

But surely realism must intervene at some point. We are talking about six hundred bands with an average population of less than a thousand, mostly living on small, remote pieces of land without significant job opportunities, natural resources, or economic prospects. There would be virtually no revenue base, let alone the pool of human skills necessary to operate modern public services. How are such small, isolated, and impoverished groups of people supposed to support and operate an untried system of government incorporating a degree of complexity not seen since the medieval Holy Roman Empire?

However, this is only the initial objection. Hard as it would be to harmonize 2200 reserves into a workable third order of government in a multitiered federal system, the problem is actually much more difficult than that. At any given time, more than half of Canada's status Indians live off reserve. They reside almost everywhere in the rest of Canada, from remote wilderness areas to the city centres of Vancouver, Toronto, and Montreal. Moreover, in addition to status Indians, there are perhaps another half million (the true number is impossible to ascertain) Métis and nonstatus Indians, that is, people of partly Indian ancestry who are not registered under the Indian Act but have some degree of identity as native people. A small number of Métis live in territorial enclaves (the Métis settlements of northern Alberta), but most are mixed in with the general population of Canada. Again, there is every conceivable kind of social situation. There are Métis hunters, trappers, and fishermen in the northern forests; Métis farmers on the Prairies; and Métis business owners, professionals, and workers in Winnipeg and other major cities.

How could one create a third order of government embracing all aboriginal people, as the Charlottetown Accord purported to do, when most of these people do not live in defined territories? Since no one, thank God, was talking of forcibly relocating populations to create separate territories, the only other approach would be to create a racially defined system of government for aboriginal people no matter where they live.

Now there is a historical model for such a system, namely the Ottoman Empire that ruled the Middle East and southeastern Europe from the fifteenth century until it was dismembered after the First World War. Throughout this immense territory, members of numerous Christian churches (Maronite, Coptic, Chaldean, Greek Orthodox, Armenian Orthodox, etc.) lived alongside the adherents of several Islamic sects (Sunni, Shi'ite, Druze, etc.). There were also important Jewish populations in most parts of the empire. All these ethno-religious communities were allowed a substantial degree of autonomy, including not only religious freedom but also their own systems of private law, so that matters such as marriage, family, and inheritance were regulated within their separate communities.

It was an admirable system in its way, ruling a colourful, polyglot population for five centuries—no mean achievement in itself. But I doubt it is a model Canadians want to imitate, for it was in no sense a democracy. There were no elections or other institutions of representative government. The sultan was theoretically an autocrat, but in fact rule was carried out by the imperial bureaucracy. The empire existed to collect taxes, keep internal order, and wage war against the neighbouring Persian, Russian, and Austro-Hungarian empires.

Like all liberal democracies, Canada is based on an entirely different set of political principles, most notably the twin concepts of the rule of law and equality under the law. The legal equality of all citizens is what makes democracy possible. As John Stuart Mill argued cogently in his *Considerations on Representative Government,* people cannot participate peacefully and cooperatively in one political system unless they feel themselves part of a single community: "Free institutions are next to impossible in a country made up of different nationalities."[5] A territorial definition of the polity is essential to this system of liberal democracy. Political and civil rights must be contingent on residence within a specific territory, not membership in a specific race or ethnic group.

Admittedly, Canada as a liberal democracy is challenged by the linguistic cleavage between English and French as well as the ethnic diversity of our aboriginal and immigrant population. But, at least prior to the Charlottetown Accord, the solutions toward which we groped were always liberal democratic ones based on legal equality within defined territorial jurisdictions. The French fact in Canada was recognized by creating the province of Quebec, which, although it happens to have a French majority, is a province similar in principle to all the others. Similarly, the contemporary Northwest Territories, although it has a native majority, is a territorial, not an ethnic polity. The same will be true of Nunavut when it comes into being. It will be a territory within which an Inuit majority will control a liberal democratic system of government; it will not be an Inuit ethnic polity.

The aboriginal self-government provisions of the Charlottetown Accord would have changed this by authorizing an ethnically defined third order of government to sprawl across existing territorial jurisdictions. It was a departure from, not an extension of, our federal system of liberal democracy. It is so incompatible with our system that it probably would not have worked at all. But to the extent that it had any effect, it would have encouraged the segmentation of native people. Wherever there were appreciable numbers of Indians and Métis in our cities, they would have been encouraged to develop their own schools, welfare agencies, justice systems, elective assemblies, and other paraphernalia of government. Instead of being encouraged to take advantage of the opportunities of Canada's urban society and economy, as so many immigrants from the Third World are now doing, native people would have been led to withdraw further into a world of imaginary political power and all too real dependence on transfer payments.

Finally, even if they could have been made to work in their own terms, the aboriginal self-government provisions of the Charlottetown Accord would have set up unacceptable pressures to create segmentary arrangements for other groups. In addition to setting up the third order of government across the country, the accord provided for unique aboriginal participation in national political institutions: aboriginal senators, possibly with a "double majority" veto over legislation on aboriginal matters[6]; aboriginal members of the House of Commons[7]; and aboriginal nominations to the Supreme Court, as well as a special advisory role for an aboriginal Council of Elders.[8] It would not have been long before other groups demanded similar treatment: women's organizations, visible minorities, the disabled, gays and lesbians, and so on. Indeed, demands of this type were heard during the referendum on the accord. Reservation of Senate seats for women was a major issue in certain provinces, notably British Columbia; and Joe Clark promised to revisit the situation of the disabled once the accord was passed. Even if Canada's liberal democracy could have survived the distinct society for Quebec and the third order of government for aboriginals, it could not survive if every identifiable group set out to entrench its political power in the Constitution. It would be the end of equality before the law, and ultimately of liberal democracy itself.

3. A third possible meaning of native sovereignty is the assertion that selected aspects of Canadian law, whether federal or provincial, simply do not apply to Indian bands or other native communities. There have now been many incidents

of this type, for example, the assertion by Manitoba and Saskatchewan bands that, regardless of provincial legislation, they can run gambling casinos on their reserves. Now the application of provincial legislation to Indian reserves is a complex and contentious area of the law. The general principle formulated by Douglas Sanders, one of the preeminent experts in the field of native law, is this: "Provincial laws apply to Indian reserve lands if they do not directly affect the use of land, do not discriminate against them and are not in conflict with federal Indian legislation."[9] It may well be that the capricious way in which provinces exploit gambling for their own purposes while forbidding private entrepreneurs to enter the field conflicts with the Indian Act, with Section 91(24) of the Constitution Act, 1867, or some other constitutional protection of Indian rights. But this involves interpretation of the Canadian Constitution; it has nothing to do with assertions of native sovereignty. The appropriate remedy is to seek an interpretation of the Constitution by bringing an action before the courts. Wrapping the issue in declarations of sovereignty only obscures the real question.

It is hardly consistent for Indian bands to continue to receive their full range of governmental benefits, including social assistance from provincial authorities, while maintaining that their "sovereignty" allows them to ignore provincial legislation whenever they choose. This self-contradictory position is an obvious nonstarter.

For the sake of clarity, let me repeat that I am not opposing the desire of Indian bands to open casinos on their reserves. Any form of legal entrepreneurship by anyone in Canada should be applauded (though there are serious concerns that in practice the gambling industry may tend to sprout criminal connections that will be as destructive for natives as for anyone else). My point is simply that, whatever the merits of Indians opening casinos on their reserves, it is not a matter of sovereignty.

Up to this point, the tone of my essay has been unavoidably negative, because I was asked to argue the negative side in a debate about native sovereignty. Let me take the opportunity in closing to state my views in a more positive way.

Status Indians in Canada have suffered terribly under the regime of the Indian Act and the Department of Indian Affairs. Bureaucratic socialism has been a failure wherever it has been tried, whether in Eastern Europe or North America. As quickly as possible, Indian bands should receive full ownership of their reserves, with the right to subdivide, mortgage, sell, and otherwise dispose of their assets, including buildings, lands, and all natural resources. As much as possible, they should assume the self-government responsibilities of small towns or rural municipalities. What happens afterward should be up to them. This kind of devolution of power is already possible under federal legislation; it has taken place in a few cases, such as the Sechelt band of British Columbia, and is being negotiated by other bands across the country. It does not require an elaborate metaphysics of sovereignty.

However, a large and ever-increasing majority of native people do not live on reserves and never will, except for occasional visits. For this majority, neither self-government nor sovereignty can have any meaning except to the extent that they, as Canadian citizens, participate in the government of Canada. For them, the political illusion of self-government is a cruel deception, leading them out of, rather than into, the mainstream of Canadian life. Their future depends on fuller participation in the Canadian society, economy, and polity. They are, to all intents and purposes, internal immigrants, and for purposes of public policy their problems are fundamentally the same as those of other recent immigrants.

It is now twenty-five years since Pierre Trudeau became prime minister of Canada. One of his government's early projects was the famous White Paper on Indian affairs, which articulated an approach similar to the one stated here, namely to encourage the social, economic, and political integration of natives into Canadian society. Sadly (as I see it), native leaders totally rejected the White Paper and set off along the opposite path of emphasizing separate institutions and political power, pursuing the elusive goals of land claims, aboriginal rights, self-government, and sovereignty. As far as I can see, a quarter-century of this political approach has produced hardly any beneficial results. There are more native politicians and lawyers than there used to be, but economic and social conditions seem not to have improved at all. We still read every day about unemployment rates of 90 percent on reserves, of Third World standards of housing and health, of endemic alcoholism, drug addiction, violence, and family breakdown.

What the black economist Thomas Sowell has written of the United States is equally true of Canada:

> Political success is not only relatively unrelated to economic advance, those minorities that have pinned their hopes on political action—the Irish and the Negroes, for example—have made some of the slower economic advances. This is in sharp contrast to the Japanese-Americans, whose political powerlessness may have been a blessing in disguise, by preventing the expenditure of much energy in that direction. Perhaps the minority that has depended most on trying to secure justice through political or legal processes has been the American Indian, whose claims for justice are among the most obvious and most readily documented.... In the American context, at least, emphasis on promoting economic advancement has produced far more progress than attempts to redress past wrongs, even when those historic wrongs have been obvious, massive, and indisputable.[10]

In the last analysis, the most harmful thing about the quest for sovereignty is the opportunity cost. The "brightest and best"—the leaders of native communities—are led to devote their talents to a cause that produces nothing except ever-growing levels of discontent and disappointment.

NOTES

1. Mark O. Dickerson and Thomas Flanagan, *An Introduction to Government and Politics: A Conceptual Approach*, 3rd ed. (Scarborough: Nelson, 1990), pp. 35–36.

2. See Menno Boldt and J. Anthony Long, "Tribal Traditions and European-Western Political Ideologies: The Dilemma of Canada's Native Indians," *Canadian Journal of Political Science* 17 (1984): 537–553; Thomas Flanagan, "Indian Sovereignty and Nationhood: A Comment on Boldt and Long," ibid., 18 (1985): 367–374; Boldt and Long, "A Reply to Flanagan's Comments," ibid., 19 (1986): 153.

3. Debbie Hum, "Ottawa Has No Right to Impose Its Law on Natives: Mohawk," *The Gazette* (Montreal), March 18, 1993.

4. Charlottetown Accord, Section 41.

5. John Stuart Mill, *Considerations on Representative Government* (Chicago: Henry Regnery, 1962; first published 1861), p. 309.

6. Charlottetown Accord, Section 9.

7. Ibid., Section 22.

8. Ibid., Section 20.

9. Douglas Sanders, "The Application of Provincial Laws," in Bradford W. Morse, ed., *Aboriginal Peoples and Law: Indian, Metis and Inuit Rights in Canada* (Ottawa: Carleton University Press, 1985), p. 453.

10. Thomas Sowell, *Race and Economics* (New York: David McKay, 1983), p. 128.

POSTSCRIPT

The main purpose of the article by John A. Olthuis and Roger Townshend is to demonstrate that Native claims to sovereignty have a strong historical and moral basis. Moreover, the authors argue that there is plenty of room to accommodate broader notions of Native sovereignty that would not lead to the destruction of the Canadian state as Thomas Flanagan suggests. Nevertheless, even if we accept their argument, there still are a number of nagging practical questions that remain. Would all of the more than 600 tribal bands in Canada be given equal sovereign status? Or would sovereignty be granted to some kind of pan-Indian confederation? Would such a body constitute a third level of government as envisaged in the Charlottetown Accord? If sovereignty is recognized, and outstanding land claims resolved, would federal and provincial governments, preoccupied with deficit reduction measures, simply withdraw access to all services currently provided? Would small and dispersed Indian bands be able to fund and staff the social, economic, and governmental programs that self-government would necessitate?

One intriguing response to some of these questions has been put forward by Thomas Courchene and Lisa Powell in a volume entitled *A First Nations Province* (Kingston: Institute of Intergovernmental Affairs, 1992). They suggest that instead of creating a third order of government, a First Nations province could be created that would represent Native aspirations, providing the powers, institutions, and ability to carry out intergovernmental relations in largely the same manner as provinces presently do.

The notion of a third level of government was taken up by the Royal Commission on Aboriginal Peoples. In its final report, the commission recommended that an Aboriginal order of government be recognized, which would coexist with the federal and provincial orders of government. According to the commissioners, "The governments making up these three orders are sovereign within their own several spheres and hold their powers by virtue of their inherent or constitutional status rather than delegation. They share the sovereign powers of Canada as a whole, powers that represent a pooling of existing sovereignties" (p. 244). Although the commission found that Aboriginal communities may choose from one of three different models of Aboriginal government, they recommended that a House of First Peoples be created as a third chamber of Parliament. The House of First Peoples would have power to veto certain legislation that "directly affect[s] areas of exclusive Aboriginal jurisdiction ... or where there is a substantial impact of a particular law of Aboriginal peoples" (p. 418). Although Aboriginal responses to the report were positive, government complacency and the ongoing preoccupation with unity issues relating to Quebec have ensured that these recommendations have largely been ignored. Some fear that it will take further Oka crises to put the issue of Native sovereignty back at the top of the public policy agenda.

Not everyone sympathetic to Native concerns feels that these demands should be pressed in terms of claims to sovereign statehood. For example, Menno Boldt and J. Anthony Long point out that sovereignty is really a Western European concept based on notions of territoriality and hierarchical authority that are foreign to traditional Native culture. In their article "Tribal Traditions and European-Western Political Ideologies: The Dilemma of Canada's Native Indians," *Canadian Journal of Political Science* 17, no. 3 (September 1984): 537–555, Boldt and Long argue that reliance on the concept of sovereignty has led many Native leaders to reinterpret their own history in a selective way that actually legitimizes European-Western philosophies and conceptions of authority: "The legal-political struggle for sovereignty could prove to be a Trojan Horse for traditional Indian culture by playing into the hands of the Canadian government's long-standing policy of assimilation" (p. 548).

Although Native issues have been ignored for so long, a number of excellent books on the subject have appeared in recent years. *Pathways to Self-Determination: Canadian Indians and the Canadian State,* edited by Leroy Little Bear, Menno Boldt, and J. Anthony Long (Toronto: University of Toronto Press, 1984) is a useful set of essays (many written by Native leaders) for beginning to explore these issues. *Nation to Nation: Aboriginal Sovereignty and the Future of Canada,* edited by John Bird, Lorraine Laud, and Murray MacAdam (Concord: House of Anansi Press, 2001), contains a series of thirty essays that deal with the issues surrounding sovereignty, land claims policy, and Native/non-Native relations. Also useful are the following volumes: J. Frideres, *Native People in Canada: Contemporary Conflicts,* 3rd ed. (Scarborough: Prentice-Hall, 1988) and B. Morse, *Aboriginal Peoples and the Law: Indian, Metis and the Inuit Rights in Canada* (Don Mills: Oxford, 1984).

Perhaps the most detailed resource on this issue is the five-volume Report of the Royal Commission on Aboriginal Peoples. Especially useful on the issues of sovereignty and self-government is the volume titled *Restructuring the Relationships* (Ottawa: Report of the Royal Commission on Aboriginal Peoples, Volume 2, 1996). For a critical perspective on the issue of Native sovereignty, see Melvin Smith, *Our Home and Native Land?* (Victoria: Crown Western, 1995).

Two of Canada's noted political scientists have recently published books on Aboriginal policy from quite diametrically opposed perspectives. Tom Flanagan published *First Nations? Second Thoughts* (Montreal: McGill-Queen's University Press, 2000), which sets up to refute what he sees as the primary "myths" surrounding the debate over Aboriginal rights. Alain Cairns, in *Citizens Plus: Aboriginal Peoples and the Canadian State* (Vancouver: University of British Columbia Press, 2000), looks at ways in which the gap between Aboriginal people and non-Aboriginal people can be bridged in a way that respects the distinctive needs of First Nations peoples.

Will Conservatism and the Conservative Party Fail?

✔ **YES**

NELSON WISEMAN, "Going Nowhere: Conservatism and the Conservative Party"

✘ **NO**

FARON ELLIS, "Twenty-First Century Conservatives Can Succeed"

In 2003, members of the Progressive Conservative Party and the Canadian Alliance party agreed to combine their forces to create a new national political party. The two representatives of conservatism in Canada would be replaced by one single entity called the Conservative Party of Canada. Not surprisingly, the new party subscribed to beliefs and principles associated with modern conservative thinking. Government would be small, elected officials would be accountable, and individual rights and freedoms would be emphasized. Progressive social policies, such as health care and the environment, would be respected, but the well-being of the country would rest on the efforts of individual Canadians and not on government.

The genesis of the Conservative Party lay in developments that took place in the preceding decade. The Progressive Conservatives historically had been the standard-bearer of conservatism in Canada. But in the late 1980s, the Reform Party rose in an attempt to more accurately represent those with conservative views (and to better serve interests in the West). The two parties tangled in federal elections, each frustrated in the belief that the other had divided the conservative vote. The result was easy victories for the Liberal Party of Canada. Faced with this situation, efforts were made to unite the two parties of conservatism. Initial efforts managed only to alter the makeup of the Reform Party and to give it a new name (somewhat awkwardly, the Canadian Reform Conservative Alliance, shortened to Canadian Alliance). Eventually, the endeavour to unite the Right led to serious discussions between the leaders of the two conservative parties and creation of the Conservative Party of Canada. Canada would now have a single, united party dedicated to conservative principles and ready to govern.

The question is whether Canadians are ready to accept conservatism and its representative. Early indications suggest an answer in the negative. In the 2004 federal election, the new Conservative Party won 99 seats and helped force the ruling Liberals into a minority situation. But the objective had been victory, and the popular vote for the new party fell short of the combined vote of the two former conservative parties in the previous election. Following the election, the party seemed indecisive about major matters and its positions on crucial issues—same-sex marriage and child care—failed to resonate with Canadians. For some supporters, the problem lay with the failure of the party to properly reflect conservative beliefs. But there was also a suspicion of another answer to the difficulties of the party: Canada was not ready for conservatism.

In the minds of some, Canada has never been and for the foreseeable future will never be suited to conservatism and conservative parties. In the past, conservatism had been less hostile to government than its modern counterpart and more willing to respect traditions. But it largely lost out to the emerging liberalism and its focus on individualism and progressive policies that challenged past practices. In this environment, the Progressive Conservative Party experienced mostly failure and had to watch the triumphant Liberal Party of Canada become the nation's governing party. Modern conservatism differs from the old conservatism and indeed reflects some of the attributes of the old liberalism (which causes some to call it "neoliberalism," or a new variety of liberalism). However, it seems that the country has moved on and embraces a liberalism that provides a role for active government, one that has little time for ideas and parties that have qualms about same-sex marriages, easy access to abortion services, and state support for regulated child care. In other words, modern conservatism fits uneasily, if at all, into the Canadian reality. Accordingly, the Conservative Party faces only disappointment.

There are others, however, who feel differently and believe that Canada is ready for a party that advocates limits on government and that reminds people of the importance of traditional institutions such as the family and church. The challenge is to ensure that the party plays to its strengths and resists the temptation of the Liberals' way—which is to be all things to all people. It must also ensure that extremists in the party—those who wish to use the state to impose moral choices on the citizenry—are unable to wield much power or gain much notice.

In the readings, Nelson Wiseman, a professor of political science at the University of Toronto, argues that modern conservatism and the Conservative Party have little future in Canadian politics. Faron Ellis, a political scientist at Lethbridge Community College, makes the case that Canada is fertile ground for modern conservatism and that the Conservative Party can position itself to take advantage of this situation.

✔ **YES**

Going Nowhere: Conservatism and the Conservative Party
NELSON WISEMAN

This is a tale of two quite different conservative philosophies and two quite dissimilar Conservative parties that share the same labels but differ in thought and development. According to our story, one variant of conservatism has failed and the other soon will. The fortunes of both Conservative parties are related to the shortcomings of the conservative ideologies that have infused them. The denouement to this account is—alas for conservatives and Conservatives—the continuing hegemony of liberalism and the Liberal Party in Canadian politics.

To be sure, the Conservative Party has had its moments in the sun and may again. The flickering periods of success have been relatively brief, best seen as temporary interregnums between long periods of Liberal rule. Conservatives, serving as a default option for the electorate, have prevailed when Liberals have faltered. The conservative impulse, in both its older manifestation and its newer incarnation, is a minoritarian one in Canada. The overarching mainstream ideology—liberalism—has been the principal guide in Canadian political thought. The periodic, transitory victories of the Conservative Party have come as reactive jerks to an otherwise popular Liberal Party when it appears arrogant and tired. Chastened by the electorate from time to time, the Liberals have consistently bounced back in a way that they did not in Britain, where the social democratic Labour Party displaced them. Canada's Liberals have also been more effective in capitalizing on Canada's changing social composition than have the Conservatives.

The older Canadian conservative tradition and Conservative Party are those of the nineteenth century. Genetically rooted in British conservatism or Toryism, early Canadian conservatism was a reaction to American revolutionary liberalism. The conservative creed—carried to Canada by decamped and expelled American Loyalists—was expressed earlier, in a Gallic manifestation, by French Canada's quasi-feudal structures and ideological disposition. Conservatism was reinforced by the War of 1812 and by Britain's imperial control of British North America's political and economic systems: thus, the early influence of a high Tory right in the form of Upper Canada's Family Compact and Lower Canada's Chateau Clique. In French Canada—which appeared more like pre-liberal, pre-revolutionary Old France than Europe's liberal, revolutionary New France—the ultramontane Roman Catholic establishment came to hold sway a few decades after the Conquest. It deferred to British leadership in matters of state (the Church opposed Papineau's 1837 rebellion against the English) and economy (it preached the virtues of subsistence farming for the *habitants* and denigrated worldly materialism). In exchange for its fealty to the British Crown, the conservative clerical class was left at the commanding heights of French Canada's separate, segregated culture and society. It was a mutually reinforcing division of labour: The economically dominant British—driven by a possessive individualist outlook—tended to industry, trade, and commerce protected by a strong, centralized state, while the economically subordinate French Canadians looked inward with pride for spiritual, religious inspiration to preserve their traditional conservative ways. Canada's founders were America's anti-revolutionary liberals—those with a Tory streak buttressed by their British connection—working with French conservatives.

The new conservatism—and the new Conservative Party—are that of the early twenty-first century. Unlike the old conservatism, it is not at all repelled by America. Proximity and attraction to America's evolving neoliberalism (known as "neoconservatism" there) pollinate the new conservatism. Both Canadian liberalism and the new Canadian conservatism have drawn heavily on American thought and models, while the older conservatism and Conservative Party had greater British impetus. Post-Loyalist American farmers carried American liberal ideas of freedom, equality, and individualism when they pioneered the western reaches of Upper Canada in the early nineteenth century. Later, early twentieth-century American farmers transplanted then-current American notions when they homesteaded the western reaches of the prairies. Canadian liberalism was buttressed by a massive influx of many radical nineteenth-century Britons who had experienced the rise and success of the anti-Tory, liberal British Reform Party. Upper Canada's population exploded from 77 000 in 1811 to 952 000 by 1851. British liberalism, streaked by conservatism, was sustained by the opportunities afforded by Canada's expanding frontier economy where land was free or cheap. Liberalism grew and further eclipsed conservatism because while Old World social structures, such as rigid class divisions and a state-sanctioned church, could be wistfully imitated, they could not maintain their early hold. They were not native to, nor an organic part of, the North American reality and came to be rejected. Other Canadian realities, however, favoured some Old World notions such as a strong state. That was indispensable to the settlement of the Canadian West and the building of a national economy and culture using Crown corporations.

Modern conservatism rejects the liberal Keynesian paradigm that took hold after the Second World War. In the Keynesian schema, the state endeavoured to guide macroeconomic supply and demand, society's gross production and consumption. It did so by manipulating the levers of fiscal policy, public-sector spending, and taxation. Modern conservatism, in contrast, seeks to completely unfetter free-market practices by shrinking the state, accommodating *laissez-faire*, privatizing state enterprises, deregulating, liberalizing trade regimes, outsourcing state functions to profit-motivated contractors, and cutting back social entitlements.[1] The agenda of the new conservatism is offloading and downsizing government activities. The focus is not on what the state can do to manage the economy but on what private enterprise, acting freely, can do to boost it. The state's potential role as social engineer in the form of affirmative action programs for disadvantaged groups is ridiculed and rejected. On some social issues, such as abortion and gay marriage, however, the new conservatism's partisans are divided.

Times change, ideas evolve, political parties reinvent themselves, and new groups of Canadians appear as older ones fade and die off. Although the polity is always in flux, successful institutions, ideologies, and political parties outlive their competitors and shift with the changing temper of the times. The weakness of the federal Conservatives is, in part, a product of political geography: the key to winning federal power is to capture the larger cities. There, the Liberals have consistently dominated since the 1960s. In most provinces, in contrast, the road to provincial power is to win the rural and outlying districts, where Conservatives have been more successful.[2] The key to winning the votes of the ever-changing electorate has been to change with it. An example is the success of Ontario's provincial Progressive Conservatives during their unmatched dynasty of 42 consecutive years of power between the 1940s and 1980s. They had the ability to change as Ontarians changed. That party's formula was to bridge the Old Ontario and the New Ontario, maintaining its Anglo-Saxon rural/small town supporters while augmenting them with those in the growing, more ethnically and ideologically diverse metropolitan centres. The party was by turns—sometimes simultaneously as need be—"progressive" and "conservative,"[3] a contradictory formula that worked. In contrast, the federal Conservatives and their Conservatism, for the most part, have played the role of handmaidens or followers in the political and policy arenas rather than trailblazers. The opponents of conservatism successfully characterized the party and its ideas as reactionary, as perpetrators of an inegalitarian status quo that serves established interests.

THE OLD CONSERVATISM

Classical conservatism, as articulated by Edmund Burke, had a tiny leftist tinge to it in that it was receptive to change so long as society's fundamental institutions were preserved. In this view, organic change—where the polity's components worked together harmoniously for the beneficial maintenance of the whole system—was natural and welcome. Fundamentals were to prevail over innovations when they clashed. This older strand of conservatism harked back to the wisdom of the ages. There is a quaint, archaic flavour to it. It warns of the dangers of experimentation and cautions people to do and think as their forebears did. It sees man as born flawed, he and his world as imperfect. Classical conservatism (known in its British manifestation as Toryism and expressed as a form of quasi-feudalism in early French Canada) knitted together a number of interconnected and reinforcing principles. They included, in addition to an adherence to tradition, the importance of maintaining social order through a strong authority, an authority that demanded and deserved deference. Order required protecting the weak as well as the strong. It meant a strong, centralized, and authoritative—but not necessarily big–government. Classical conservatism was less optimistic about human nature than liberalism and placed less faith in government's wisdom and planning abilities than socialism urged.

Classical conservatism embraced hierarchical institutions as guarantors of stability. These institutions–such as the Crown, the church, the military, and the patriarchal family (and other hierarchies like corporations and universities)–were organized and understood to provide reinforcement and direction to the community's common interests. Such institutions worked as partners, in collaboration; they neither competed with each other nor were internally driven. In this cosmology, political society is a hierarchically structured organic-corporatist-communitarian entity comprised of unequal classes–some more privileged than others–all sanctioned by heredity and tradition and relating to each other cooperatively. It was a compassionate conservatism in that, out of a sense of *noblesse oblige*, society's privileged were duty-bound to protect and aid the poor and less fortunate. Classical conservatism's collectivist and elitist elements were considered natural as well as necessary bulwarks against revolutionary chaos, class conflict, and fearful anarchy. The old conservatism thus viewed democracy's stirrings and unshackled individual freedoms with suspicions of "mobocracy."

The creation of the modern Canadian state was a conservative triumph over liberalism in that market logic–absorption by the American economic behemoth–was resisted on nationalist grounds. Politics trumped the economic allure of continental integration. Nevertheless, the old conservatism was always a minoritarian impulse in the political culture; it infused Canadian liberalism but did not displace it as the dominant outlook. The state's Tory institutions were deployed in the interests of liberal acquisitiveness and economic expansion. The old conservatism, for example, underwrote private enterprise at public expense for national economic development and "national purpose"[4] in projects like the Canadian Pacific Railway.

Joe Clark made much of the old conservatism's notion of community, describing Canada as a "community of communities." Even Brian Mulroney, who preached an aggressive market liberalism and reversed the Conservatives' protectionist posture vis-à-vis the United States, came to describe Canada's universal social programs as a "sacred trust" not to be violated, for they were "a cornerstone of our party's philosophy."[5] Socialists, however, had first championed such programs while old conservatives opposed their implementation by welfare liberals. Perhaps one of the last gasps of old conservatism came on the eve of the 2003 merger of the old Conservative Party and the Canadian Alliance. Lowell Murray, a Conservative senator and former Mulroney cabinet minister, wrote that as a Conservative,

> We believe that government's job is to provide stability and security against the excesses of the market. Democratic politics must define the public interest and ensure it always prevails over more private ambitions. To that extent the

forces of technology and globalization need to be tamed.... Reform [the new] conservatism which is what the Alliance [party] practises [sic] relies on people's fear of moral and economic decline.... It spoils all the good arguments for the market economy by making a religion of it, pretending there are market criteria and market solutions to all of our social and political problems.[6]

THE OLD CONSERVATIVE PARTY

John A. Macdonald's old Conservative Party was undeniably successful; it won five of Canada's first six elections. The party, however, floated on the shaky foundations of a shifting coalition of forces rather than being constructed on solid pillars. Indeed, the very first Conservative government was actually a Liberal-Conservative one, bringing together anti-American Tories and Montreal-based English Canadian financiers and business liberals seeking to build an economic empire via railway construction. This alliance drew on the support of Quebec's conservative *Bleus* and some of Canada West's Reformers who were also tied to railway interests. The old Conservatives' triumphs lay in Macdonald's skills in organizing and dispensing bureaucratized patronage: some Conservative constituency associations operated like employment agencies where individual party activists formally applied for government positions, trading on their financial or campaigning contributions. Such procedures were considered normal and legitimate, based on the idea that "to the victor belongs the spoils."[7] Wilfrid Laurier's Liberal machine proved no less adept at using the glue of patronage. Notwithstanding its brokerage orientation, the old Conservative Party differed from the Liberal Party in that it was the carrier of what there was of the old conservatism.

The old Conservative Party's undoing was its failure to continue to broker successfully between British and French on issues of language and religion. French Catholic Quebec was upset with Métis leader Louis Riel's execution and the suppression of French language schooling in New Brunswick, Ontario, and especially Manitoba. The party became identified as fiercely Protestant and British. Quebec was lost to the party as it further distanced itself from the Québécois on issues of international empire, war, and conscription. The Conservatives could thus not muster enough support in Quebec to win more than four seats in any of the four elections between 1917 and 1926; they won none in 1921. Six decades later, the story had not changed much. Only two seats in Clark's governing caucus in 1979 were from Quebec and, in 1980, only one. The party did not select a French Canadian leader until it was in its death throes in the 1990s (when they selected Jean Charest). The John Diefenbaker Conservative victory in Quebec in 1958 and Mulroney's landslides there in the 1980s were false indicators of Conservative viability in Quebec, for the party benefited from the fleeting tactical acquiescence of Quebec's old and new nationalists, the Union National and the Parti Québécois, as well as, in Mulroney's case, the provincial Liberals.

Another source of the Conservatives' undoing was, paradoxically, their most notable policy accomplishment: the National Policy of 1879. The construction of a Trans-Canada railway, the settlement of the West, and the imposition of tariffs facilitated the development of central Canada's nascent industrial economy. The tariff, a regionally discriminatory transportation policy, as well as the power of financial institutions associated with the Conservatives of Montreal's St. James Street and Toronto's Bay Street, turned the West against the party. It became a Liberal stronghold and a wellspring for third-party protest (in the form of the Progressives, Social Credit, and the CCF). R.B. Bennett's Conservatives held power during the Depression and came to be blamed for it. Diefenbaker swept the West in 1958 in part because his populism and background were so different from those, like Ontario's Colonel George Drew, who preceded him. The party had anointed a progressive, populist Westerner, John Bracken, as its leader during the Second World War, but the country was not prepared to switch leaders then or in the war's aftermath. The challenge to the ruling Liberals then was from the left (the CCF) rather than the right. Bracken's singular contribution to the party was to change the "Conservative" brand to "Progressive Conservative," but the party did not live up to its new billing.

The chronic electoral weakness of the old Conservative Party was evidenced in the thirty elections between 1896 and the party's last outing in 2000: it won nine of them, but in only six did it win a majority of seats. In all three elections that returned Conservative minorities, the party attracted fewer voters than the Liberals. The "government party," the Liberals, have held office in parts of all but 26 of the past 110 years. The old Conservatives served as the natural "opposition party." A telling sign of their vulnerability came in Canada's first multiparty election in 1921: they ran third behind the upstart, loosely organized Progressives, who themselves became a dilapidated annex of the Liberals. Between 1993 and 2000, the old Conservatives, claiming that they were the only "national" alternative to the Liberals, ran last in a five-party system in all three elections. The relatively few Conservative victories in the twentieth century were more rebuffs for the perceived shortcomings of Liberal regimes rather than Conservative mandates. In only four of the twenty-five elections since 1921 have the Conservatives won with wide national support.

Unlike parties of principle like the Progressives, CCF-NDP, Social Credit, Reform Party, and Canadian Alliance, the old Conservative Party styled itself, like the Liberal Party, as a brokerage party. Its strategy was to build a tent large enough to hold Canadians from all strata of society. It operated as a cadre party—deferring to its leader and his coterie on major issues of policy. No Conservative convention or policy gathering debated or endorsed free trade or the GST before their institution by the leader. Gaining a few seats and a higher vote share is deemed a victory by a small party like the NDP, but Conservatives measured their leader by a higher standard: outright victory. The more they found themselves relegated to the opposition benches, the more a mindset of defeat and self-destructive tendencies set in. A "Tory Syndrome"[8] took hold, where a weak election performance led Conservative partisans to attribute failures to their leader, which weakened him and his ability to take the party forward.

As a near perpetual opposition party, the old Conservatives projected the image of nay-sayers with little or no experience in fashioning public policy or responsibility for public administration. More often than not, the party's MPs appeared uncoordinated in their opposition roles, many tending to work at cross-purposes with their leader. When they occasionally did hold office, as in the Meighen, Bennett, Diefenbaker, and Clark years, they offered incoherent and unsynchronized policy direction or struggled with crises beyond their control (the Depression and skyrocketing oil prices in the 1970s).

The Mulroney Conservative victories in the 1980s were the fruit of a tenuous alliance of Western Canadian rural, fiscal, and social conservatives on the one hand and Quebec nationalists on the other. There had always been substantial Conservative support in Ontario and the Maritimes—the very creatures of Loyalism—but it had not been sufficient to propel the party to power. Quebec's francophone Conservatives were an *ersatz* phenomenon, first and foremost nationalists whose nationalism transcended any liberal-conservative-socialist cleavage such as that of English Canada. Once Quebecer Mulroney left the stage, the party plummeted in the province from sixty-three seats in 1988 to one in 1993 and reverted to its longstanding marginal position.

Sociodemographic change eroded the historic bases of support for the old Conservative Party in English Canada. The Maritimes' constantly shrinking share of the population in the twentieth century made the region count for less and less. Loyalist and early post-Loyalist rural Ontario was transformed into an increasingly urban, multicultural, kaleidoscopic society. The Liberals benefited. The outcome of the four minority elections between 1957 and 1965 reflected that change: southern, metropolitan Ontario's swing seats determined whether Conservatives or Liberals would come out on top as the rest of the country was in a state of electoral stasis with few seats changing hands. Immigrants, soon naturalized as citizens, were more favourably disposed to the Liberals, as was a rising class of young, upwardly mobile, urban professionals. These groups saw Liberal immigration and urban policies more positive than those of the Conservatives. Old Tory Toronto, once a Conservative stronghold, became a Liberal bastion. The Conservatives' battles against bilingualism and the maple leaf flag (they fought to retain the Red Ensign with its Union Jack) did not resonate with either Quebecers or Ontario's newer ethnic minorities. The Liberals reinforced their standing with these groups, and the Conservatives weakened theirs, on issues such as multiculturalism, affirmative action programs, and social policy. The old Conservatives represented the Old Canada, disproportionately those of British ethnic descent, Protestant, and rural/small town. They could not shake that image.

THE NEW CONSERVATISM

The new conservatism is a modern variant of the old liberalism. The new conservatism or neoliberalism gives priority to the individual over the community in the economic sphere. Immense business corporations are seen as individuals. Community is defined atomistically as the sum of its self-governing, equally free-willed individuals. Margaret Thatcher captured this sentiment with her observation, "There is no such thing as society." The new conservatism, unlike the old conservatism, is loath to use the state to protect the public good or broad community interest at the expense of the private freedoms—the negative liberties—of its autonomous individuals. An exception is made for the state's war-making and police functions. The new conservatism depicts society as a one-class citizenry rather than as a society of unequal classes, as both Tories and socialists do. Thus, the new conservatism favours the mechanics of an individual-based participatory form of democracy; it embraces the use of referenda and the potential recall of elected representatives, seeing representatives as delegates charged with communicating, unmediated, their electors' views. It does not see politicians, as Burke and the old conservatism did, as trustees elected to exercise their personal judgment of what is best, and held to account in elections on the basis of stewardship.

The new conservatism views the state as a constantly renewed and voluntary arrangement among contemporaries. This jettisons the old conservatism's conceptualization of state and society as an inherited ancient bond that links past, present, and future generations. The new conservatism claims to move on popular impulse, operating on the principle that society is a compact among equal citizens. Hierarchical and monarchical institutions—like an appointed upper house and the Crown's residual prerogatives exercised by the prime minister—are condemned as outdated remnants of the old conservatism. The new conservatism lambastes the old conservatism for offering an unreal, inferior understanding of the existing socioeconomic order and how it should work. The old conservatism is indicted as a reactionary vision of the future.

The new conservatives, however, are divided on the moral, as opposed to economic, sphere of human behaviour. The same-sex marriage issue demonstrates their division. Libertarian conservatives tolerate traditionally proscribed acts—homosexuality, abortion, suicide, drug use, etc.—so long as such behaviour is freely chosen. Social conservatives have kept the faith with old conservatives in the moral sphere. Unlike libertarian, they believe government must not remain neutral on moral issues. Social conservatives look to government to preserve and promote traditional values and institutions such as the traditional family and to do so in the schools, the law, and the media. They condone teaching religion in schools as part of education's bedrock function. In contrast, libertarians would leave the teaching of religious doctrines to the educational marketplace. Social conservatives are also distinguished by their positions on issues such as fetal rights, capital punishment, and criminal sentencing. It is a comment on its evolution that the old Conservative Party, by the 1990s, had come to look at abortion and gay rights more favourably than the new conservatives in the Reform/Alliance party which upheld the moral cudgels of the Old Canada.

Where the libertarian and social conservative tendencies of the new conservatism merge is on rejection of state intervention in economic matters except for state intervention in support of private enterprise. Their common objective goes beyond "shrinking the state" to reducing its very capacity to act. They would place much of the traditional public policy agenda beyond the reach of government and, consequently, beyond the reach of citizens who may wish to have their government steer a more collectivist course. The new conservatives would limit the instrumentality of government in pursuit of social justice objectives because they are wedded to free-market solutions. This dampens the prospect for public embrace of the new conservatism because Canadians have become inured to and expect government action in the liberal reform tradition. Preoccupation with individual and corporate rights towers over considerations of social and economic justice for the new conservatives. But, "Like nature itself, the market order knows neither justice nor injustice," writes Cy Gonick. "Social obligation, the idea of solidarity between self and community, has no place ..." in this logic.[9]

Nationalism is a litmus test differentiating the old and new conservatism. Tory conservatism expressed itself in a certain anti-Americanism. David Orchard, the anti–free trade crusader, carried its banner in his bid for the old Conservative Party leadership in 1998 and 2003. Red Tories and old-style Burkean Tories had been nationalist communitarians who opposed class struggle but promoted a national identity to counter American influence. Liberalism and the Liberals, in contrast, had not been philosophically or historically linked to statism or collectivism until Pierre Trudeau led them. The closer the new Conservative Party moves toward contemporary American conservatism, the farther it moves away from the Tory nationalism that had informed the old Conservative Party. The last Conservative leader who underlined the links between his party and its British Conservative Party roots was Robert Stanfield; he cited both Burke and the pioneering British Tory factory legislation of the nineteenth century as part of Canadian conservatism's legacy.[10]

THE NEW CONSERVATIVE PARTY

There is no single genesis for the new Conservative Party: origins include some elements of the populist agrarian revolt of the 1920s, the Social Credit phenomenon of the 1930s, the appearance of the Reform Party in the 1980s, and the demolition of the old Conservative Party in the 1990s. Initially, prairie populism was diametrically opposed to the old conservatism and old Conservative Party. Social Credit, preaching the virtues of monetary reform, wedded it with messianic evangelicalism. Its logo was a green Christian cross on a white background. Preston Manning, the founding Reform Party leader, is the godson of Social Credit's founder, "Bible" Bill Aberhart. Manning's father, Ernest, took over Aberhart's immensely popular *Back to the Bible Hour* radio broadcasts and served as Alberta's premier for a quarter-century. Reflecting and leading the transmutation of Social Credit, he went from serving as Alberta's anti-bank treasurer in the 1930s to director of the Canadian Imperial Bank of Commerce in the 1960s. In that decade, he called for a merger of Conservative and Social Credit partisans into a new Conservative party that stressed "Social Conservative ideals and principles." He wrote of "the responsibility of governments to give first consideration to human beings as individuals (as persons) rather than to human beings in the aggregate." He defined the family as the "most fundamental unit of human association," and pointed to the public's "spiritual resources" and "the Sovereignty of God." The "Social Conservative," wrote Manning, "will speak of a 'society of great individuals,' before he will speak of a 'great society,'"[11] a term used by welfare liberals in the American Democratic administration at that time.

Social Credit did fade and disappear as the elder Manning recommended, but the younger Manning resurrected the division on the Right in the 1980s with the Reform Party. The spark for its ignition was the blatant favouritism shown by Mulroney's old Conservatives for Quebec's aerospace industry at the expense of Manitoba's. Reform smashed the old Conservatives' base in English Canada beyond the Atlantic region. The policy inclinations of Reform's activists, however, limited the party's appeal. A survey of the party's 1992 Assembly—attended by the elder Manning who termed it a "crusade"—showed that 96 percent of delegates agreed that courts were too lenient with criminals, 99 percent agreed that government ought to reduce its deficit as much as possible, 96 percent thought the welfare state made people less willing to look after themselves, 98 percent opposed a constitutional veto for Quebec, and 97 percent opposed increased government efforts to further multiculturalism.[12] Reform (and its successor, the Canadian Alliance) competed with the old Conservatives for the same minoritarian right-wing vote with failing results for both of them, especially the Conservatives. Some policy convergence facilitated their merger. Electoral arithmetic compelled it. In 1997, the economic and fiscal planks in the old Conservative and Reform platforms were near carbon copies. Where they differed was on Quebec, bilingualism, immigration, institutional reform, and "morality" issues. In the 2000 election, Joe Clark's old Conservatives somewhat tempered their market liberalism. They spoke of social safety nets and equalization payments because Atlantic Canada was their only remaining base.

The base of the new Conservative Party, like its predecessor party and Reform/Alliance, continues to be the West and in English Canada's rural/small town districts. In its first outing, the new party proved to be less than the sum of its parts: the combined vote for the two older parties had been nearly 38 percent in 2000, but the new merged party garnered less than 30 percent in 2004. Chronic weakness in large cities and irrelevance in Quebec are fatal shortcomings as cities account for increasing numbers of Canadians. The 2004 results speak for them-selves: of fourteen major urban centres for which Elections Canada broke out the vote,[13] the new Conservatives led the popular vote in only three (Calgary, Edmonton, and St. John's). In four centres (Halifax, Montreal, Vancouver, and Victoria), they were beaten by the NDP as well as the Liberals. In the largest city, Toronto, they won no seats and drew no more votes than the NDP. The combined vote for the Bloc Québécois and the NDP nearly equalled the vote for the Conservatives.

Data (excluding Quebec) drawn from the 2004 Canadian Election Study reveal the new Conservative Party's limited growth potential. In the 2000 election, the old Conservatives led as voters' second-choice party, but the new Conservatives badly trailed both the Liberals and the NDP on this score in 2004. Nearly half of respon-dents agreed that "Stephen Harper is just too extreme." Public opinion overwhelm-ingly supported increased government funding for health care and education. There was less public support for cutting personal taxes (the Conservatives' signature policy) than for increased social housing. The ratio of Liberal-to-Conservative sup-porters was more than three-to-one among the steadily growing numbers of mem-bers of visible minorities. The Conservatives trailed the NDP among this group as well. The Conservatives did have the lead among self-described religious funda-mentalists (over half) and (nearly half of) Protestants. Nevertheless, the party did gain about the same vote level (outside Quebec) as the Liberals.[14] The billion-dollar gun registry boondoggle and the "sponsorship" scandal in the run-up to the elec-tion discredited the Liberals in the eyes of many voters.

THE FUTURE: GOING NOWHERE

Even after the scandals and internecine disputes that rocked the Liberals, the Conservatives fell short in 2004. Their prospects are bleak. Without substantial gains in metropolitan Canada and Quebec, they remain perpetual also-rans. Their best prospect is to eke out a plurality of seats. In that scenario, however, they would still be overwhelmed by the other parties and Canada's overriding liberal-social democratic ethos. A majority election victory for the new Conservative Party would be but a necessary, not sufficient, condition for the new conservative philosophy to prevail. As new Canadians settle in the New Canada of cos-mopolitan, polyethnic big cities, the Conservatives' Old Canada base—rural/small town, Protestant English Canada—continues to shrivel. The Conservatives do have strength and substantial potential in English Canadian suburbs and exurbia, areas encircling the cities' cores, as demonstrated during the Mulroney years. The party may yet capitalize on that potential if Harper fails and the party selects a leader in the older mould of a more centrist conservatism—one in the line of Clark, Mulroney, or Ontario's Bill Davis or John Tory. If and when the Conservatives pre-vail however, it will likely be for a relatively brief period—the Conservative stretch in office from 1984 to 1993 was atypical.

Harper inadvertently acknowledged his reconciliation to permanent minoritarian status on the eve of the opening of the Thirty-Eighth Parliament in 2004. He, along with the Bloc Québécois and NDP leaders, wrote a joint letter to the Governor General, effectively signifying, in a way that the old Conservatives had never done, that they no longer consider themselves a competitive national alternative to the dominant Liberals. It was *de facto* recognition by the Conservatives that they are but one player in an increasingly institutionalized multiparty system and not a viable shadow government. As Canada inches its way toward a more proportional voting system, the Conservatives and their conservative outlook will probably suffer as new parties chip away at their base and further marginalize it.

Conservatism and the Conservative Party have had an embedded place in Canada's political culture, but their influence is more likely to wane than wax. The new conservatism of the late twentieth century may prove to have been a passing phenomenon. So long as Canadians invest in defining themselves by who they are not—Americans—and so long as the new conservatism is driven by similar ideas and demographic forces to those in the U.S., the appeal of the new conservatism is limited. The new Conservative Party's prospects brighten greatly if Quebec secedes from Canada, for the party would then be competitive with the Liberals. Paradoxically, the party that forged Canada may only regain power if the country breaks apart.

NOTES

1. Stephen McBride and John Shields, *Dismantling a Nation: The Transition to Corporate Rule in Canada,* 2nd ed. (Halifax: Fernwood, 1997), p.18, and John Shields and B. Mitchell Evans, *Shrinking the State: Globalization and Public Administration "Reform"* (Halifax: Fernwood, 1998).

2. Timothy L. Thomas, "An Emerging Party Cleavage: Metropolis vs. the Rest," in Hugh G. Thorburn and Alan Whitehorn, eds., *Party Politics in Canada,* 8th ed. (Toronto: Prentice-Hall, 2001), chapter 30.

3. John Wilson, "The Red Tory Province: Reflections on the Character of the Ontario Political Culture," in Donald C. MacDonald, ed., *The Government and Politics of Ontario,* 2nd ed. (Toronto: Van Nostrand Reinhold, 1980).

4. Reg Whitaker, *A Sovereign Idea: Essays on Canada as a Democratic Community* (Montreal: McGill-Queen's University Press, 1992), p. 20.

5. Quoted in Colin Campbell and William Christian, *Parties, Leaders, and Ideologies in Canada* (Toronto: McGraw-Hill Ryerson, 1996), p. 52.

6. Lowell Murray, "Don't Do It, Peter," *The Globe and Mail,* June 23, 2003.

7. Gordon T. Stewart, "Political Patronage under Macdonald and Laurier, 1878–1911," *American Review of Canadian Studies* 10, no. 1, (1980).

8. George C. Perlin, *The Tory Syndrome: Leadership Politics in the Progressive Conservative Party* (Montreal: McGill-Queen's University Press, 1980).

9. Cy Gonick, *The Great Economic Debate* (Toronto: James Lorimer, 1987), p. 130.

10. Robert L. Stanfield, "Conservative Principles and Philosophy," in Paul Fox and Graham White, eds., *Politics: Canada*, 8th ed. (Toronto: McGraw-Hill Ryerson, 1995), pp. 307–311.

11. E.A. Manning, *Political Realignment* (Toronto: McClelland and Stewart, 1967), pp. 65–70.

12. Keith Archer and Faron Ellis, "Opinion Structure of Party Activists: The Reform Party of Canada," *Canadian Journal of Political Science* 27, no. 2 (June 1994): Table 5, pp. 295–297.

13. http://enr.elections.ca/Major Centres_e.aspx, consulted on November 3, 2004.

14. Elisabeth Gidengil and Neil Nevitte, "Something Old, Something New: Preliminary Findings of the 2004 Canadian Election Study," Seminar presentation, University of Toronto, October 22, 2004.

✗ **NO**

Twenty-First Century Conservatives Can Succeed
FARON ELLIS

> In order that our free will may not be extinguished, I judge that it could be true that fortune is the arbiter of half our actions, but that she lets the other half, or nearly that, be governed by us.
>
> —Niccolo Machiavelli, *The Prince* (1513) XXV

Included in Machiavelli's message to sixteenth-century princes is advice that modern political parties should also consider. Although they cannot control their entire fate, they can control some. By making provisions to help withstand the ravages of fortune that may beset them, by way of their opponents or by other uncontrollable circumstances, they are better armed to accomplish their goals: to guide public policy, voters, and public discourse toward their objectives and away from their opponents'. For conservatives, this includes finding a set of core principles that, after considerable compromise by all the disparate and divergent interest that make up the loosely knit Canadian conservative movement, they can agree to champion as the best way to achieving at least some of their objectives. For the new Conservative Party of Canada, the overall task is similar, but complicated by the structural requirement of building those common objectives into an organization capable of fulfilling its purpose: to successfully compete for votes in a manner that affords it the opportunity to form a national government and implement conservative principles.

Ideologically, Canadian conservatism has been comprised of an often fractious, complex mix of several, seemingly contradictory ideological streams. Elements of Toryism, business liberalism, nationalism, and populism, among others, have all enjoyed periods of support,[1] making Canadian conservatism, like most ideologies, a very amorphous entity. The new Conservative Party, on the other hand, is a political party, and parties are first and foremost organizations. As organizations operating within a larger institutional context, parties have different demands placed on them than do movements or ideologies. Parties are subject to different pressures for accommodating the wide variety of perspectives that underpin their overall ideological constituency, as well as subject to standards of compromise and cooperation that are unique to them as organizations. Parties must inevitably make decisions about what constitutes their core ideology, values, or principles. They must also determine how much of each competing sub-ideology will be represented and how far the party will go in accommodating the more peripheral elements of the ideological coalition. Attempting to accommodate too many peripheral elements often comes at the expense of fulfilling the party's ultimate purpose: successfully competing for votes.

In an era of brokerage parties and electronic politics, competing for votes within a moderate, liberal-pluralist political culture means that Canadian parties cannot afford to become too ideologically doctrinaire in either their policies or their leadership selection. But neither can they become so amorphous, or as organizations so unfocused, as to be void of any tangible identity onto which voters can grasp and thereby attach their often transient partisan and voting loyalties. All parties must attempt to define their identities, their core principles or ideologies, positively, on their own terms, or risk surrendering that opportunity to their opponents who are likely to do so negatively and on much less favourable terms. New parties face great challenges along this dimension. It is therefore more important for them to establish an identity that is their own creation, prior to attempting to broker a coalition large enough to form a government. It is my contention that a libertarian-conservative core identity—based on a limited-state that promotes not only economic liberty, but also moral and social liberty—offers the best prospects for success for conservatives and the new Conservative Party.

I must begin, however, by conceding half, or nearly that much, of Professor Wiseman's argument. For he is correct in his assertion that the new Conservatives will fail if they continue to pursue an Old Canada vision with values rooted in the nineteenth century and that survive primarily in rural Canada. He is also correct in his assertion that conservatism will continue to be at best a default option for voters who tire of corrupt or arrogant Liberal governments if Conservatives continue to be united by no greater principles than their mutual distaste for Liberal regimes.

As long as conservatives refuse to embrace the overriding, mainstream, libertarian political culture of contemporary Canada, including the ascendancy of pluralism and individual rights as the primary virtues in a developing liberal-pluralist-democracy, Conservatives will continue to suffer from a schizophrenia that will betray their unreadiness to govern to an increasingly cynical electorate. To deny that liberalism is the foundation of Canadian political culture, and is here to stay, is a prescription for failure. Simply attempting to rebuild previously failed coalitions would be as irrational as it has been unproductive.

But the continuing hegemony of liberalism in Canada need not necessitate continued Liberal Party of Canada hegemony. As Wiseman correctly concedes, the Canadian Liberal Party has become at best a liberal-social-democratic pretender. To that we can add overly statist. In their quest to provide continuing rationale for a strong national government and federal powers more generally, Liberals provide Canadian voters with a statist response to virtually every social, economic, and political issue, real or imagined. In the process, the federal Liberals have become so illiberal that they can no longer legitimately claim the mantle of liberty's defenders. These conditions all but necessitate a libertarian-conservative response to Liberal Party electoral hegemony.

It is here where the new Conservatives can succeed. By consistently following a few simple principles, albeit most involving tough choices, considerable courage, and tremendous resolve, Conservatives can build a new, mainstream party around a core set of libertarian-conservative principles that will make the new party capable of consistently competing for power. This will require a leap of faith for some. But as the evidence and rationale that follows will demonstrate, accommodating Canadian liberalism's new manifestations in a complex, urban, pluralistic polity is not as radical a transformation for the new Conservatives as it may first appear. The libertarian core of both the former Reform and Alliance parties, as well as the disparate remaining non-Tory elements of the Progressive Conservative Party, have several common foundational elements upon which a more grand party can be built—and to which many mainstream voters can be recruited. What remains to be seen is whether or not Conservatives have the vision and discipline to build an enduring political institution upon those foundations.

VARIOUS KINDS OF CONSERVATISM

All the forms of conservatism that have emerged in all the federal and provincial party systems over the years can be distilled down to three:

1. Toryism of the nineteenth century—combining a reverence for tradition with support for state maintenance of an ordered and structured society—that in various incarnations sputtered through the twentieth century.

2. Libertarian conservatism in the form of nineteenth-century liberalism—with its emphasis on economic liberty, free markets, capitalism, and a limited state—that reappeared in the late twentieth century as neoconservatism or neoliberalism.

3. Social conservatism of the nineteenth century—with its emphasis on traditional, primarily religious moral values and opposition to advancing liberal-pluralism—that manifested itself in the late twentieth century as the religious right.

Innumerable hybrids of one or more elements of each have appeared in the various parties, movements, and factions that have called themselves conservative over the past two hundred years.

The most important dimensions of conservatism at the beginning of the twenty-first century revolve around the relative unity of conservatives in support of fiscal conservatism and the need for dismantling much of late twentieth-century left-wing social engineering. There exists, however, a wide gulf between libertarian and social conservatives on moral issues, and each has recently taken up common cause with populists in an effort at improving their fortunes. Each errs in doing so, but for different reasons, which shall be elaborated upon later.

Conservatives should relegate Toryism, with its accompanying statism, to the dustbin of history or to the Liberals and their socialist allies. Social conservatism should be tolerated, in the same manner in which all competing ideas should be tolerated, but not adopted as part of the defining identity of the new Conservative Party. Hybrids should also be rejected because of their tendency to be amorphous to the point of providing conservatism's enemies with frequent and ample opportunities to distort and mischaracterize the Conservative Party to voters. Only by defining a core libertarian-conservative identity will the new Conservatives find the ideological consistency necessary to become an electorally successful, enduring national coalition capable of being more than a temporary default option for voters who tire of corrupt or arrogant Liberal regimes.

REFLECTIONS ON THE WISEMAN "DOOMED TO FAILURE" THESIS

Many grains of truth are contained in Nelson Wiseman's review of Canadian conservative history. Like most undergraduate students of Canadian politics, I was introduced early to the Hartz-Horowitz "Tory touch" fragment thesis, and to Wiseman's application of the thesis to the study of Canadian prairie political culture.[2] Both continue to serve as exemplary readings for conceptualizing and teaching Canadian political culture, as much for their utility in engendering critical thinking as for their other virtues. The thesis posits that the political cultures of new societies are primarily fragments cast off from the European ideological dialectic. Separated from the dialectic, political cultures of new societies lose the impetus for change and remain frozen fragments of the prevailing ideology at the time of their founding. Having been founded at a time when liberalism dominated, North American political cultures are primarily liberal. But because Canada contained a quasi-feudal French element and an English Tory element at its founding, the Canadian political culture, although primarily liberal, is touched with Toryism, thereby making a synthesis out of liberalism and into socialism a possibility. Because a full critique of the thesis is outside of the parameters of this debate, I will direct readers to previous rebuttals and restrict my comments to the following.[3]

Initially, pining for the virtues of a mythical Toryism while at the same time portraying all libertarian (neoconservative or neoliberal) elements of conservatism as inherently vicious is in keeping with the standard statist attack on the new Right. It is typically the purview of hostile academics and media pundits, but not necessarily that of Canadian voters. It is no coincidence that the death of the Progressive Conservative Party, and by default the "Tory touch" mythology, was bemoaned more by the former than the latter. After all, without a party vehicle to which the myth can remain attached, the Tory element of the dialectic appears more difficult to substantiate and the Marxist tautological house of cards begins to collapse. Without Toryism, the desired end state of socialism becomes unattainable. Liberalism triumphs as the final political culture, leaving Toryism a relic of the past and socialism a never to be achieved nightmare. But the next generation of Marxist academics need not despair. They will likely find enough Toryism within the Liberal Party of Canada, at least in its statist and anti-American manifestations, to keep the myth alive.

The fact that a wide variety of left-wing pundits see so much to mourn in the death of the Progressive Conservative Party should give Conservatives cause for celebration. For it was the Tory element of the coalition that failed Conservatism in the 1980s and has been at least partially responsible for keeping Conservatives from succeeding since. Conservatives should bid a fond farewell to the vanguard of former Progressive Conservative "red Tories" and rejoice in the extinguishing of fellow travellers from their ranks.

Secondly, it is correct to assert that if the new Conservatives remain geographically anchored in the West and rural ridings, they are likely destined to perpetual opposition. But history need not dictate a predetermined future. Canadian voters are characterized by a number of traits, and among these is their well-deserved reputation for vote switching.[4] The persistent shattering, rebuilding, or creating anew of electoral coalitions and partisan alignments is one of the most enduring features of Canadian party systems.[5] Not only do Canadian voters regularly realign their partisan attachments in tectonic shifts that shatter the old order, they also exhibit a high degree of vote switching between non-monumental elections. Wiseman implies this when he states that Toronto used to be a Conservative bastion but is now a Liberal fortress. While downtown Toronto ridings may represent tough territory for the new Conservatives for some time to come, opportunity awaits them in the suburbs of central Canadian cities, with voters who are tired of bearing an increasingly disproportionate burden for a multiplicity of statist schemes designed to address issues that affect them only marginally, or not at all. Many are current Liberal party voters who, as a group, have demonstrated the highest rates of vote switching over the past several federal elections. Evidence abounds to suggest that the Liberal coalition, although consistently the largest, is also the most susceptible to erosion.[6] This alone should give pause to those who believe the Conservative coalition would be most susceptible to fracturing under a proportional representation electoral system.

However, if the new Conservatives do not immediately begin to define a libertarian vision for these voters, and continue to let their opponents define conservatism as inhospitable to central suburban voters' personal and collective ambitions, Conservatives will not succeed. Wiseman demonstrates this adequately when he borrows a tactic from Reform's early critics[7] by placing particular emphasis on former Alberta Premier Ernest Manning's influence on the party. By assuming that what the elder Manning or his mentor Alberta Premier William Aberhart stood for in the 1930s to be equivalent to what Preston Manning or the millions of Reform voters stood for in the 1990s, it is possible to build a caricature of Reform as reactionary agents of their own privilege. However, it stretches credibility to assume that what rural, Depression era voters appreciated about their parties is similar enough to what contemporary voters saw in Reform, its successor the Canadian Alliance, or the new Conservatives, to account for the millions of votes conservative parties have mustered in the last four federal elections. But the political problem remains: conservatism's opponents have been more successful at defining conservative parties' identities than have Conservatives. Politically, the reactionary case has been repeatedly made, and it has repeatedly stuck. When supported by frequent, often outlandish public comments by senior party officials—primarily undisciplined members of Parliament—an image of Reform,[8] the Alliance,[9] and to a certain extent the new Conservatives,[10] emerged that didn't mesh with members' and voters' core values. In all cases, the parties have tended to be mischaracterized as much more socially conservative, more pro-American, and more anti-French than were either their memberships or their voting bases.[11]

Reform's image problem continued in spite of the fact that even a cursory review of the academic literature analyzing membership opinion defeats many of the charges. It is here where Professor Wiseman's critique is particularly instructive. The fact that he has reviewed the attitudinal data that Archer and I collected at the 1992 Reform Assembly is laudable. But when he chooses to make such selective use of it in support of his mischaracterizing of Reform, ignoring altogether data that refutes the mischaracterization, his analysis becomes polemical.

For example, he cites the data that suggest virtually all Reform delegates agreed that the federal government should seek to reduce its federal deficit as much as possible—neither a surprising nor unreasonable finding given the soft question and the fact that the federal government of the time was continuing to borrow between $30 and $40 billion annually on its way to building a half-trillion dollar national debt. Be that as it may, he is correct to cite evidence that fairly characterize Reformers as fiscally conservative. Yet he also characterizes the party as anti-abortion and anti-gay, upholding the "moral cudgels of the Old Canada." This in spite of the fact that at the same convention, delegates clearly held more solidly libertarian than socially conservative positions on a number of issues. They demonstrated this in their policy debates and in their opinion structure.[12] By a two-to-one margin 1992 Reform delegates stated they were pro-choice on the abortion issue (61.5 percent agreed abortion is a private matter to be decided by a woman, 30.9 percent disagreed and 7.5 percent were uncertain).[13] Less than half of all delegates took a socially conservative position on the only homosexuality question that was asked. The mischaracterization aptly demonstrates the challenges that Reform–Alliance encountered and that the new Conservatives have yet to resolve: the ability to positively define a vision for conservatism before the many entrenched interests—who correctly view Conservatives as a threat to their state-sponsored privilege—fill in the many unknowns with negatives. To put an end to this pattern, Conservatives must be much more active in defining and defending a coherent vision of the place for conservatism within the mainstream of Canadian liberalism. The fact that their opponents' tactics are as predictable as they are transparent should make that task much easier for the new Conservatives than it was for Reform.

Finally, despite his general characterization of libertarian conservatives as atomistic hedonists with no collective consciousness, and the corresponding implication that socialists have a monopoly on what constitutes social justice, Wiseman is correct to state that conservatives tend to be relatively united on economics but divided on moral matters. More problematic is his inclusion of "the role of the state" on his list of "conservatives' common objectives." Rather than united on this matter, what constitutes the appropriate role for the state is often one of the most contentious issues dividing the various factions within conservatism. While it is true that there exists general agreement among conservatives about reducing the state's capacity to excessively engage in socialist economic engineering, there is much less unity with respect to the state's role in dealing with moral issues—a point Wiseman concedes about the moral divisions but not about the state's role in defining or regulating moral decision making.[14]

The problem for libertarian conservatives, and many voters who shied away from Reform, is their suspicion that social conservatives want to simply replace left-wing economic social engineering with right-wing moral engineering. Libertarian conservatives are as opposed to the latter as they are to the former. They share these sentiments with growing legions of Canadian voters who have become either suspicious of or hostile to forty years of statist public policy and the corresponding price tag. But these same voters, when faced with a choice, have repeatedly demonstrated that they are likely to reject the suspicion of right-wing moral engineering before they get a chance to reject left-wing social engineering. Which brings us to the choice Conservatives now face: which type of party and which vision of conservatism are they prepared to champion to the Canadian voter.

While I will not presume to prescribe to the members, leaders, and voters of the new Conservative Party what specific policy measures that they may want to adopt, I will offer a few suggestions as to the direction their policy positioning should take as the party seeks to define its identity and its new electoral constituency. Initially, Conservatives need to fill the policy void with clear, articulate, and consistent fiscally conservative, non-statist economic policy. Secondly, they need to define a libertarian core vision that includes drawing a line in the sand across which social conservatives will not be allowed to drag the party. And most importantly, they must avoid the populist trap by setting clear limits on the party's planned use of populist decision-making mechanisms.

FILLING THE CONSERVATIVE POLICY VOID

For Conservatives, winning the battle over the evils of government deficits should not be considered a victory in the overall war on socialist fiscal policy. The past three Liberal budgets and the explosion in planned expenditures for the next five years should demonstrate clearly enough that much work is still needed. Conservatives must make the case for deep middle-class tax cuts, an end to corporate welfare, spending reprioritization, and reduced business taxes. They must present Canadians with a comprehensive, bold, and clear fiscally conservative economic platform. The comprehensiveness of the platform, and the conviction with which it is delivered, will attract voters and at least partially inoculate the party against open-ended charges of recklessness or of harbouring hidden agendas.

Central to the economic platform must be a clear vision for a limited state that most Conservatives agree should underpin most other planks of a comprehensive conservative agenda. The vision should be bold, but not reckless. When told by pollsters and pundits that Canadian voters are not as interested in tax cuts as they are in health care spending, Conservatives should rise to the challenge of convincing more voters of the wisdom contained in their vision rather than shirk from it and yield the economic agenda to their competitors. Conservatives should emulate past successes where they have led rather than followed public opinion. The fight against deficit financing and the battle in support of free trade should serve as reminders to Conservatives of how voters have handsomely rewarded them when they demonstrated leadership.

Conservatives must also be cautious about being distracted in their economic policy development by national unity or regionalism issues. Most importantly, they must resist the temptation to adopt a series of "special case" exemptions from the limited-state agenda for the sake of vote buying in Quebec or Atlantic Canada. The mobilization strategy for Quebec and the East should be based on the conviction of principle and the consistency and comprehensiveness of the vision rather than opportunistic piecemeal regional graft. Dedication to the rule of constitutional law, including respect for the division of federal powers, is consistent with a libertarian, non-statist approach to economic issues. It is consistent with an overall agenda of reducing centralized social engineering and in support of provincial equality and autonomy. Corporate welfare in the form of subsidies to regionally based aerospace companies, hugely disproportionate equalization asymmetry, and employment insurance rules should be as anathematic to Conservatives as are billion-dollar gun registry bureaucracies and affirmative action agendas.

DEFINE THE CORE LIBERTARIAN IDENTITY

Conservatives should heed the advice that Alberta Premier Ralph Klein provided the first United Alternative Convention by adopting social and moral policies that are consistent with their economic positions. That is, if Conservatives can justify the legitimacy of limiting the state from excessively interfering in Canadians' economic lives, they should be able to justify, with equal conviction and consistency, the legitimacy of limiting the state from excessively interfering in Canadians' personal lives. By boldly articulating the moral legitimacy of individual liberty, the rule of law, political freedom, responsive and accountable governing institutions, and free political expression, Conservatives can succeed in defining an identity for themselves that is consistent, principled, and enduring.

Social conservatives need to be assured that they are welcome in the coalition, but that a dismantling of left-wing social engineering will not be accompanied by a corresponding increase in right-wing moral engineering. Ensuring that the libertarian core is established early in the formative years of the new party, and communicating this clearly, is both honourable in that it will allow social conservatives to make informed decisions about their participation, and necessary in order to attract moderate voters who are still repelled by the possibility of a social conservative hidden agenda. Social conservatives need to understand that by remaining within the mainstream of the Conservative coalition they are likely to achieve about half of what they want, or nearly that much. But social conservative zealots who refuse to defer to party policy, or who plan to continue championing their moral causes at the expense of the greater good of the party, should be thoroughly, swiftly, and efficiently extinguished from the ranks of the new Conservatives.

Libertarian conservatives must also make an articulate case for the moral legitimacy of pluralism. Although Canadian conservatives have succeeded in making their opposition to state-sponsored programs well known, because their opposition extends to programs that are targeted at identifiable groups, they have been much less successful at defending themselves against charges that their opposition to state funding for specific groups equates to hostility toward the groups themselves. It is here where libertarians have failed Canadian conservatism most: by not countering the charges of intolerance with a staunch defence of the diversity that is by definition a necessary component of pluralism.

Liberal-pluralism entails a diversification of power and the existence of a plurality of organizations that are both independent and non-inclusive. Central to this is a limited state that leaves individuals free to voluntarily enter into multiple associations with others. But it is more. Pluralism entails not only the recognition and articulation of diversity or differentiation. It is a normative as well as a descriptive concept. It assumes a particular belief content that contains its own morally authoritative claim on legitimacy. Pluralism asserts that not only do differences exist, but also that difference itself is a moral good. Difference above likeness, dissent above unanimity, choice above conformity, and change rather than the status quo are all fundamental to pluralism. Advocating for the liberty to voluntarily enter into non-inclusive associations without state interference requires the recognition of the presence of other competing associations with which one chooses not to associate. Libertarians further argue that these choices and associations are private and that the state should not be making decisions about which groups are to be publicly sponsored and which are not. But in advocating for private choice, diversity and competing perspectives are assumed. Libertarians owe it to conservatism to firmly establish that it is as philosophically supportive of diversity and choice in private moral matters such as marriage and abortion as it is for private religious or economic associations. Libertarians must also begin to vigorously counter all charges to the contrary from both within and outside of the conservative movement.

AVOID THE POPULIST TRAP

Both social conservatives and libertarians have periodically attached themselves to populism. Recently, the various elements of conservatism have created a populist trap that has had the effect of limiting electoral success. Social conservatives often embrace populism in the naïve hope that through populist mechanisms they can somehow stem the tide of an increasingly secular, liberal political culture. Libertarians, although philosophically opposed to social conservative moralizing, don't fear the consequences of putting their differences to the test of a populist dispute resolution mechanism. The combination of the two doesn't usually represent a threat to libertarians on the policy front. Libertarians know that under most direct democracy scenarios they will come out winners when the mainstream liberal-pluralist political culture expresses its collective will in favour of rights, autonomy, choice, and liberty. Even a referendum on same-sex marriages today would likely face even odds. A vote on abortion would be a slam dunk in favour of choice. But in not fearing the outcome of populist decisions, libertarians too often and too easily surrender their philosophical objections to the potential for majority tyranny. By legitimizing the populist dispute resolution mechanism, libertarians legitimize the majoritarian principles contained in them, and thereby legitimize the potential for the suppression of individual rights, autonomy, choice, and liberty, so long as it is done democratically. Libertarians should stop surrendering to populist expediency and begin a concerted defence of libertarian-pluralism.

Populism has also been thought to offer Conservatives an escape from having to take firm stances on moral issues so as to not alienate one or the other key elements of the contemporary coalition. And herein lies the populist trap. It is a function of both excessive cleverness and an unwillingness to adopt firm positions on divisive policy domains. By substituting populist direct democracy decision-making mechanisms for firm policy stances, Conservatives institutionalize unknowns into their parties' platforms and their identities. By definition, direct democracy contains a quality of the unknown. For if a party's policy platform dictates the eventual public policy outcome, the direct democracy decision-making exercise is meaningless. Likewise, institutionalizing direct democracy decision-making severely restricts the party from taking firm positions on controversial issues when needed, most importantly during election campaigns. Both create uncertainty in the minds of voters. No one can say for sure what the party stands for because, prior to consulting the people, it does not know where it stands. More importantly, the institutionalized uncertainty affords the party's opponents with ample opportunity to fill in the unknowns with negatives, especially when supported by the often-extreme utterances of undisciplined party members. It also serves to deny other conservatives the ammunition needed to defend their positions with any certainty, clarity, or conviction. No party can afford to turn over definition of its own identity to its opponents. New parties with high levels of unknown quantities can afford it the least.

The populist trap plagued Reform in its attempt to expand its base outside of Western Canada. It helped turn much of the Alliance's 2000 election campaign into a fountain of comedic material and political ridicule of its leader. Although new Conservative leader Stephen Harper has so far successfully avoided building a populist trap of his own making—witness the noticeable lack of advocacy for a referendum to resolve the same-sex marriage issue—he has suffered from a residual populist trap hangover from the Reform–Alliance era. It stalled the new Conservatives momentum in the 2004 election and quite possibly was the single biggest issue to forestall their ascension to government.

As such, it is necessary for the new Conservative Party to carefully define its proposed use of referenda: limiting its use to only constitutional or other grand institutional change. Free parliamentary votes should remain, but for a more comprehensive list of categories well beyond simply divisive social or moral issues. Its position on the use of the notwithstanding clause must be clarified. Its members of Parliament and other party officials must exercise the discipline necessary to act as a cohesive organization, something they have been much more adapt at under Harper's leadership than at any time over the past ten years. Ideological populists, and those willing to use populism as an excuse for lack of discipline, should be told, respectfully, that their opinions would be better expressed through an advocacy group than from within a party organization, and their presence should be extinguished.

As part of this process, Conservatives must judiciously avoid the temptation to enlist help from mercenary interest groups: social conservative, populist, or otherwise. They tend to be the most undisciplined of all associates, will tarnish the party's image with moderate voters, and will abandon the party when their most zealous pursuits are not realized. Their potential for short-term electoral help is dwarfed by the detriment they will cause to the long-term objectives of establishing a broadly based coalition built upon a libertarian core. And once associated with their causes, it will be difficult for the party to overcome the founding identity that will have been implanted in the minds of many voters. Trying to extricate the negativity by purging itself of these associations at a later date will likely also prove futile. Few elections have been won on the slogan, "trust us now that we have turned on our former friends."

CONCLUSION

By defining its own identity centred on a comprehensive, consistent libertarian core identity, conservatives and the new Conservative Party can build the foundations for an enduring and competitive national political party. Instead of denying the continued progression of liberalism in Canada, Conservatives can succeed by championing individual liberty, pluralism, choice, and a limited state. By eschewing both left-wing social engineering and right-wing moral engineering, by standing in defence of liberty in moral as well as economic affairs, Conservatives can define a place for conservatism in the mainstream of Canada's liberal-pluralist political culture. If carefully organized and executed with discipline, the new Conservatives have the opportunity to end Liberal Party hegemony and establish themselves as a legitimate governing party for the twenty-first century.

NOTES

1. See William Christian and Colin Campbell, *Political Parties and Ideologies in Canada*, 3rd ed. (Toronto: McGraw-Hill Ryerson Ltd, 1990).

2. For concise versions of each, see Gad Horowitz, "Conservatism, Liberalism and Socialism in Canada: An Interpretation," pp. 90–106; and Nelson Wiseman, "The Pattern of Prairie Politics," pp. 351–368; both in Hugh G. Thorburn and Alan Whitehorn, eds., *Party Politics in Canada*, 8th ed. (Toronto: Prentice Hall Canada, 2001).

3. See Nelson Wiseman, "Canadian Political Culture: Liberalism with a Tory Streak," pp. 56–67; and Janet Ajzenstat and Peter J. Smith, "The 'Tory Touch' Thesis: Bad History, Poor Political Science," pp. 68–75; both in Mark Charlton and Paul Barker, eds., *Crosscurrents: Contemporary Political Issues*, 4th ed. (Scarborough: Thomson Nelson, 2002).

4. See Harold D. Clarke, Jane Jenson, Lawrence Le Duc, and Jon H. Pammett, *Absent Mandate: Interpreting Change in Canadian Elections*, 2nd ed. (Toronto: Gage Educational Publishing Company, 1991).

5. See R.K. Carty, "Three Canadian Party Systems: An Interpretation of the Development of National Politics," in Hugh G. Thorburn and Alan Whitehorn, eds., *Party Politics in Canada*, 8th ed. (Toronto: Prentice Hall Canada, 2001), pp. 16–32; and R.K. Carty, William Cross, and Lisa Young, *Rebuilding Canadian Party Politics* (Vancouver: UBC Press, 2000).

6. For evidence, see Jon H. Pammett, "The People's Verdict," in Jon H. Pammett and Christopher Dornan, eds., *The Canadian General Election of 2000* (Toronto: Dundurn Press, 2001), pp. 293–317; and Andre Turcotte, "Canadians Speak Out," in Jon H. Pammett and Christopher Dornan, eds., *The Canadian General Election of 2004* (Toronto: Dundurn Press, 2004), pp. 314–337.

7. See Sydney Sharp and Don Braid, *Storming Babylon: Preston Manning and the Rise of the Reform Party* (Toronto: Key Porter, 1992). For a critique of these early analysts, see Tom Flanagan, *Waiting for the Wave: The Reform Party and Preston Manning* (Toronto: Stoddart Publishing Co., 1995).

8. Faron Ellis and Keith Archer, "Reform at the Crossroads," in Alan Frizzell and Jon H. Pammett, eds., *The Canadian General Election of 1997* (Toronto: Dundurn Press, 1997), pp. 111–133.

9. Faron Ellis, "The More Things Change... The Alliance Campaign," in Jon H. Pammett and Christopher Dornan, *The Canadian General Election of 2000* (Toronto: Dundurn Press, 2001), pp. 59–89.

10. Faron Ellis and Peter Woolstencroft, "New Conservatives, Old Realities: The 2004 Election Campaign," in Jon H. Pammett and Christopher Dornan, eds., *The Canadian General Election of 2004* (Toronto: Dundurn Press, 2004), pp. 66–105.

11. For an analysis of Reform opinion structure as it is impacted upon by ideology, see Faron Ellis and Keith Archer, "Ideology and Opinion Within the Reform Party," in Hugh G. Thorburn and Alan Whitehorn, eds., *Party Politics in Canada*, 8th ed. (Toronto: Prentice Hall Canada, 2001), pp.122–134. For a comparison of attitudes of party members in Canada with specific analysis of ideological divisions, see William Cross and Lisa Young, "Policy Attitudes of Party Members in Canada: Evidence of Ideological Politics," *Canadian Journal of Political Science* 35, no. 4 (December 2002): 859–880.

12. See Faron Ellis, *The Limits of Participation: Members and Leaders in Canada's Reform Party* (Calgary: University of Calgary Press, 2005).

13. See Keith Archer and Faron Ellis, "Opinion Structure of Party Activists: The Reform Party of Canada," *Canadian Journal of Political Science* 27, no. 2 (June 1994): 277–308. More recently, delegates attending the new Conservative Party's convention adopted as policy by a margin of 55 percent to 45 percent the most libertarian position available by committing the party to passing no legislation that would restrict abortion choice. See Conservative Party of Canada, "Results of the March 17–19 2005 Founding Policy Convention."

14. See Cross and Young, "Policy Attitudes of Party Members," for a comparison of Alliance and PC members' attitudes.

POSTSCRIPT

In his article, Nelson Wiseman sees only dim prospects for modern conservatism and the Conservative Party in Canadian politics. Though there are many reasons for this fate, the main one appears to be that modern conservatism is out of step with the beliefs of most Canadians. Yet, one has to wonder about this claim. For Wiseman, most Canadians supposedly believe in government that takes a leading role in shaping society and providing services, but the past decade or so has witnessed government cut both spending and taxes—an action consistent with conservatism and the platform of the Conservative Party. Wiseman also points to what many think to be the Achilles heel of the Conservative Party—namely its potential to support reactionary or extreme stances on moral issues. But polling suggests that those who make up the party steer well clear of positions that would limit access to abortion services or attempt to marginalize gays and lesbians. And as for Wiseman's belief that certain elements of the electoral map—large cities, certain regions of the country—are beyond the grasp of the Conservative Party, it can be argued that Canadians are more than capable of switching their allegiances. Nothing in Canadian politics is set in stone.

For his part, Faron Ellis is much more positive about the chances of conservatism and the Conservative Party. Indeed, it seems that Conservatives need only be themselves and electoral success will come their way. But as with Wiseman, there are questions. Ellis says that Conservatives and their party should stick to an economic platform that finds little favour with "special case" funding for the likes of Quebec and Atlantic Canada. However, the electoral success of the Conservative Party rests in part on breakthroughs in these regions, so to say no to their requests appears self-defeating. Ellis is also tough on social conservatives and the populists who wish for more direct democracy—both must be clearly secondary to the libertarian element of the Conservative Party. Ellis' stance here would certainly make things easy for the party, but some might argue that in effectively simplifying the essence of the Conservative Party he also ignores important aspects of its makeup. In other words, to win the Conservative Party must almost deny itself, or at least parts of it. Finally, Ellis believes that the future of Canada lies in the "continued development of liberalism," which means a greater emphasis on "individual liberty, pluralism, choice, and a limited state." Yet, as Wiseman suggests, such a characterization seems to leave Canada little different from the United States, a development that many Canadians seem unwilling to embrace right now.

For an understanding of the new Conservative Party of Canada, one might start with Faron Ellis and Peter Wollstencroft's contribution in Jon H. Pammett and Christopher Dornan, eds., *The Canadian General Election of 2004* (Toronto: Dundurn Group, 2004). The article discusses the origins of the party and contains references to documents necessary for appreciating the position of the Conservative

Party. The publication *Policy Options* in various editions (March 2004, June/July 2004, and September 2004) also has some good pieces on the party and its prospects. With this understanding of the party, students might wish to back up and acquire a better picture of the overall party system in Canada as well as predecessors to the Conservative Party. For these insights, Hugh Thorburn and Alan Whitehorn's *Party Politics in Canada,* 8th ed. (Toronto: Prentice-Hall Canada, 2001) is the place to go. R. Kenneth Carty, William Cross, and Lisa Young's *Rebuilding Canadian Party Politics* (Vancouver & Toronto: UBC Press, 2000) helps to sort out the past, present, and possible future of party politics in Canada. Also useful is James Bickerton and Alain-G. Gagnon, "Political Parties and Electoral Politics," in James Bickerton and Alain-G. Gagnon, eds., *Canadian Politics,* 4th ed. (Peterborough: Broadview Press, 2004). For some deep history on conservative parties in Canadian politics, a good source is Dan Azoulay, *Canadian Political Parties: Historical Readings* (Toronto: Irwin Publishing, 1999).

The debate addresses not only the Conservative Party but also the ideology of conservatism. For information on conservatism and the competing ideologies in Canadian politics, a good place to start is Colin Campbell and William Christian, *Parties, Leaders, and Ideologies in Canada* (Toronto: McGraw-Hill Ryerson, 1996). There are also some useful chapters on this topic: David Bell, "Political Culture in Canada," in Michael Whittington and Glen Williams, eds., *Canadian Politics in the 21st Century,* 6th ed. (Scarborough: Thomson Nelson, 2004); Raymond Bazowski, "Contrasting Ideologies in Canada: What's Left? What's Right?" in James Bickerton and Alain-G. Gagnon, eds., *Canadian Politics,* 3rd ed. (Peterborough: Broadview Press, 1999); and Neil Nevitte and Mebs Kanji, "New Cleavages, Value Diversity and Democratic Governance," in James Bickerton and Alain-G. Gagnon, eds., *Canadian Politics,* 4th ed. (Peterborough: Broadview Press, 2004).

A number of books have been written about conservative parties in Canadian politics that preceded the formation of the Conservative Party of Canada. These include Jeffrey Simpson, *The Discipline of Power: The Conservative Interlude and the Liberal Restoration* (Toronto: MacMillan, 1980); George Perlin, *The Tory Syndrome: Leadership Politics in the Progressive Conservative Party* (Montreal and Kingston: McGill-Queen's University Press, 1980); Tom Flanagan, *Waiting for the Wave: The Reform Party and Preston Manning* (Toronto: Stoddart, 1995); Trevor Harrison, *Of Passionate Intensity: Right Wing Populism and the Reform Party of Canada* (Toronto: University of Toronto Press, 1995); and Faron Ellis, *The Limits of Participation: Members and Leaders in Canada's Reform Party* (Calgary: University of Calgary Press, 2005).

PART TWO

THE CONSTITUTION AND FEDERALISM

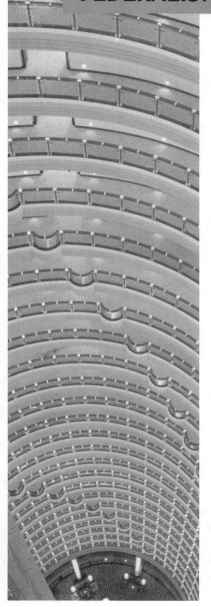

Is the Canadian Charter of Rights and Freedoms antidemocratic?

Should the federal government play a leading role in health care?

Are Canada's child pornography laws unconstitutional?

Is the Clarity Act good for Canada?

Is the Canadian Charter of Rights and Freedoms Antidemocratic?

✔ **YES**
ROBERT MARTIN, "The Canadian Charter of Rights and Freedoms Is Antidemocratic and Un-Canadian"

✘ **NO**
PHILIP L. BRYDEN, "The Canadian Charter of Rights and Freedoms Is Antidemocratic and Un-Canadian: An Opposing Point of View"

Do terminally ill patients have the right to a doctor-assisted suicide? Should women have unrestricted access to abortion without fear of criminal penalty? Does freedom of expression include the right to produce and distribute pornography? Are Sunday shopping regulations a violation of freedom of religion? Should people be able to marry same-sex partners? All of these questions raise difficult issues regarding the relationship between individual citizens and their government. In essence they each pose the same questions: What civil rights does an individual have and how are they to be protected from the intrusive arm of the state?

In choosing to establish a system of parliamentary government on the "Westminster model," the founders of Canada adopted a British solution to this problem. Parliament would be supreme and would act as the ultimate guarantor of individual rights and freedoms. This solution reflects an implicit trust in both Parliament and the basic democratic values of civil society. It assumes that civil liberties are so deeply engrained in the national political culture that parliamentarians and citizens alike would never seriously consider using the power of government to infringe upon them. Public opinion and tradition would act as a powerful constraint against any violation of the fundamental civil and political liberties that are considered to be an inherent part of a democratic system. With the establishment of a federal system in Canada, courts were given the task of deciding whether federal and provincial legislatures were acting within their respective jurisdictions, not whether their actions violated civil and political liberties. There was no perceived need to give such rights special judicial protection that put them outside the reach of legislators.

Not everyone was happy with this solution. They pointed to a long history of both provincial and federal governments' trampling of the rights of citizens. In the early part of this century, British Columbia passed laws denying Asians the right to vote in provincial elections. During the Second World War, the federal government arbitrarily seized the property of Japanese Canadians and placed them in internment camps without due process of law.

These experiences, and others, convinced many Canadians that greater protection of civil rights was needed. The Americans provided an alternative solution: define the rights of citizens in a written constitutional document that is beyond the reach of the legislature. The courts, through the power of judicial review, can then pass judgment on whether the legislation passed by a government infringes on civil liberties. John Diefenbaker began to move Canada in this direction in 1960, when his government passed the Canadian Bill of Rights. But this bill was simply an act of Parliament and applied only to the federal government. As a result, Canadian courts made only limited use of the Bill of Rights.

With the adoption of the Canadian Charter of Rights and Freedoms as part of a larger constitutional package, the government of Pierre Trudeau brought in a new era in 1982. With the entrenchment of the Charter in the Canadian Constitution, not only were Canadians given an explicit definition of their rights, but also the courts were empowered to rule on the constitutionality of government legislation.

There is little doubt that the adoption of the Charter has significantly transformed the operation of the Canadian political system. Since the adoption of the Charter, the Supreme Court of Canada has been involved in virtually every issue of any great political significance in Canada. As a result, there has been a growing public awareness about the potential "political" role that the Supreme Court now plays in the lives of ordinary Canadians. Increasingly, Canadians define their needs and complaints in the language of rights. More and more, interest groups and minorities are turning to the courts, rather than the usual political processes, to make their grievances heard. Peter Russell has described the dramatic impact of the Charter on Canadian politics as having "judicialized politics and politicized the judiciary."

Has the impact of the Charter been a positive one? Has the Charter lived up to its promise to enhance Canadian democracy through the protection of civil liberties? Robert Martin, a former law professor at the University of Western Ontario, feels that the impact of the Charter has been largely a negative one. In particular, he argues that the Charter has had an antidemocratic effect on the country and has accelerated the Americanization of Canada. In contrast, Philip Bryden, Associate Dean of the Faculty of Law at the University of British Columbia, argues that the Charter plays an essential role in protecting and enhancing the quality of Canadian democracy.

✔ YES
The Canadian Charter of Rights and Freedoms Is Antidemocratic and Un-Canadian
ROBERT MARTIN

INTRODUCTION

On April 17, 1982, the Canadian Charter of Rights and Freedoms became part of our Constitution. Everyone who has written about the Charter agrees its effect has been to change profoundly both our politics and the way we think. Most of the commentators have applauded these changes. I do not.

I believe the Charter has had decidedly negative effects on Canada. It has contributed to an erosion of our democracy and of our own sense of ourselves. It is time for a serious and critical stocktaking.

Let me be clear that I am not suggesting the Charter itself has actually *done* any of this. A central problem with the Charter has been its contribution to our growing inability to distinguish between the concrete and the abstract. The Charter is simply words on a piece of paper. What I will be addressing are the uses to which the Charter has been put by human beings. I will look at the antidemocratic effects of the Charter and then turn to an analysis of its un-Canadian character.

THE CHARTER IS ANTIDEMOCRATIC

By their nature, constitutions express a fear of democracy, a horror that the people, if given their head, will quickly become a mindless mob. As a result, constitutions, all constitutions, place enforceable limitations on the powers of the state and, more particularly, on the lawmaking authority of the people's representatives.

Prior to 1982, the Canadian Constitution did contain such limitations. Our central constitutional document, the British North America Act of 1867, divided lawmaking authority between Parliament and the provincial legislatures and, thereby, limited that authority. But these limitations were purely functional. The authority to make laws about education, for example, rested with the provinces. Ottawa could not make laws about education, and if it attempted to do so, the attempt could be struck down by the courts. The courts had no authority to tell the provinces how to exercise their authority over education, to tell them what kind of laws they should make about education.

This is what changed in 1982. The federal division of powers remained, but for the first time substantive limitations were placed on lawmaking authority. The judges were given the power to strike down laws that, in their opinion, were inconsistent with the Charter.

It is crucial to understand basic distinctions between legislators and judges. Any Canadian citizen over the age of eighteen is eligible to be elected to Parliament or a provincial legislature. Elected members are directly accountable to their constituents. They must face reelection at least once every five years. By way of contrast, to become a senior judge in Canada you must be a lawyer and you must have been one for ten years. You are appointed until age seventy-five through a closed process that a former chief justice of Canada described as "mysterious," and you are made constitutionally independent, directly account-able to no one.

The defining feature of representative democracy in Canada has been that it is up to the elected members of our legislatures to resolve issues of social, economic, and political policy, subject, of course, to the approval or disapproval of the people, which is expressed at periodic elections. This has changed since the adop-tion of the Charter. Judges can now overturn deliberate policy decisions made by the elected representatives of the people where those decisions do not accord with the way the judges interpret the Charter. This is undemocratic. Some of our com-mentators call this "counter-majoritarian," but the phrase is pure obfuscation.

We seem to be experiencing great difficulty today in grasping this simple truth about the antidemocratic nature of judicial review of legislation. One explanation for our difficulty is that we have forgotten that liberalism and democracy are not the same thing. Liberalism is about individual rights, about the ability of individ-uals to do as they please without interference from the state. Liberalism makes protection of the autonomy of the individual more important than the promotion of the welfare of the collectivity. Democracy is, and always has been, about the interests of the collectivity, about majority rule, about power to the people.

There is an inherent and irreconcilable tension between liberalism and democ-racy. This tension has always been built into our political system, a system that is ordinarily described as liberal democracy.

The Charter is a liberal document. It sets out fundamental notions about the rights of the individual that have always been at the core of liberalism. More to the point, the Charter has led to a shift in emphasis in Canadian liberal democracy. The balance has been tilted in favour of liberalism and away from democracy.

Members of the judiciary, led by the Supreme Court of Canada, have shown little restraint in arrogating to themselves a central policymaking role. In 1984, they conferred upon themselves the distinction "guardian of the Constitution." They haven't looked back.

Our judges have not hesitated to substitute their views of acceptable or desir-able social policy for those of our legislators. When the judges have not agreed with the policy decisions of our elected representatives, they have invalidated the legislation that expresses those decisions. But the judges have been prepared to go further. They have shown themselves willing to write legislation, to even go to the point of imposing financial obligations on the state.

The willingness to interfere with the traditional policymaking functions of legislatures has not been restricted to the courts. Administrative tribunals now sit in judgment on the validity of legislation, and boards of inquiry set up under human rights acts rewrite legislation and create new legal responsibilities for individuals.

We have become more and more inclined to seek to resolve the central questions agitating our society in the courtroom, rather than through the political process. The result of this is to surrender to lawyers control of the social agenda and of public discourse.

In a similar vein, the Charter has given a great boost to interest group politics. Indeed, an active judicial role and interest group politics seem made for each other.

Interest group politics is antidemocratic in two respects. It erodes citizenship, the essential precondition to democratic politics. People are induced to define themselves according to their race or sex or sexual preference or some other ascriptive criterion, rather than as citizens. And, in practice, interest group politics has meant seeking to use the courts as a means of short-circuiting or bypassing democratic processes.

The Charter has thus, in an institutional sense, had an antidemocratic effect. But it has also reinforced ideological currents that are antidemocratic. The most important of these stem from our growing obsession with "rights."

Our fascination with rights has been central to a process through which we seem to have come to prefer the abstract over the concrete. "Rights" appear to be more attractive than real things such as jobs or pensions or physical security or health care. We have been persuaded that if we have "rights" and these "rights" are enshrined in a constitution, then we need not concern ourselves with anything else. It is difficult to describe as "democratic" a public discourse that avoids addressing actual social and economic conditions.

Rights discourse itself encourages antidemocratic tendencies. The inclination of persons to characterize their desires or preferences as "rights" has two unfortunate results. First, there is an inevitable polarization of opposing positions in any debate. And, second, the possibility of further discussion is precluded. If you assert that something is your "right," my only possible response is, "No, it isn't."

Finally, the interest in rights has done much to promote individualistic and, therefore, antisocial ways of thinking. My impression is that many people view their rights as a quiver of jurisprudential arrows, weapons to be used in waging the ceaseless war of each against all.

THE CHARTER IS UN-CANADIAN

It is difficult to imagine any single event or instrument that has played a more substantial role in Americanizing the way Canadians think than has the Charter. The Charter clearly did not begin this process, but it has, since 1982, been central in it.

The basis for my assertion about the Americanizing effects of the Charter is a recognition that, historically and culturally, the Charter is an American document. This truth is seldom adverted to. As a technical drafting matter, the Charter, it is true, was the creation of Canadian lawyers. But the document's roots lie elsewhere. The idea of enshrining the rights of the individual in a constitution and then protecting those rights through judicial intervention is uniquely American. It may well be a good idea, but no one who had the slightest acquaintance with our history could call it a Canadian idea.

"Life, liberty, and the pursuit of happiness" are not simply words in the Declaration of Independence; they are essential notions defining the American experience. Up until 1982, the central Canadian notions were profoundly different. Our social and constitutional watchwords were "peace, order, and good government."

That has changed. I now teach students who are convinced that we did not have a Constitution, that we were not a proper country until we adopted the Charter. We have worked diligently to abolish our own history and to forget what was once our uniqueness. We are now told that the Charter is a basic element in defining what it means to be Canadian. And many Canadians do appear to believe that we can understand ourselves through our approach to the constitutional protection of rights.

The Charter has promoted our Americanization in other ways besides helping persuade us that we don't have a history. We have, as has already been noted, become more individualistic in our thinking and in our politics over the last decade. Again, it would be foolish to see the Charter as the only cause of this, but it is noteworthy that the decade of the Charter has seen an increase in the concrete indications of social alienation—crime, marital breakdown—as well as in more subtle forms—incivility, hostility, and so on. There was a time when one had a palpable sense, on crossing the border, of entering a different society. This is no longer true.

The Charter has led us to forget our uniqueness as Canadians and to disregard our history. It has had an incalculable effect in Americanizing both the way we think and the way we see ourselves. We have become incomparably more individualistic. Our collective sense of ourselves, and our idea of responsibility for each other and the society we share, has been seriously weakened.

Like Americans, we now believe there must be a legal remedy for every social ill. Like Americans, we put "me" first.

CONCLUSION

Many Canadians have contrived to forget that most of the things that once made Canada a fine country—physical security, health care for all, reasonably honest and competent government, sound education—came about through the political process, not as gifts from beneficent judges.

The fact is that during the period the Charter has been part of our Constitution, ordinary Canadians have seen a steady erosion of their standard of living. Unemployment is high and rising. Social services, health care, and pensions are threatened. Not only has the Charter not been of any help in preventing this erosion, it has served to distract our attention from what has been going on.

The great beneficiaries of the Charter have been the lawyers. They are consulted on issues of public policy, they pronounce on the morality or desirability of political and social beliefs and institutions, their advice is sought in a vast array of situations. The number of lawyers grows exponentially as does the cost of retaining their services.

The Charter has, to judge by media commentators, become the basis of our secular religion. And the lawyers are the priests. At some time Canadians will decide to take control of their agenda back from the lawyers. That is when we will begin to give serious thought to repealing the Charter.

✘ NO

The Canadian Charter of Rights and Freedoms Is Antidemocratic and Un-Canadian: An Opposing Point of View
PHILIP L. BRYDEN

Robert Martin's essay launches a two-pronged attack on the Canadian Charter of Rights and Freedoms. The Charter is, according to Professor Martin, both antidemocratic and un-Canadian, and the sooner we Canadians come to our senses and realize that our lawyers have hoodwinked us into believing that the Charter is a good thing, the better off all of us (except maybe the lawyers) will be. My own view is that Professor Martin's essay presents a caricature of both the Charter and modern Canadian democracy, and that when we put the Charter in a more realistic light we will see that the Charter can, and does, make a valuable contribution to Canada's democratic system of government.

The more powerful of Professor Martin's criticisms is his argument that we should get rid of the Charter because it is antidemocratic. Its attraction is that it contains a germ of truth. Like most half-truths, however, it hides more than it reveals.

In its simplest terms, the argument that the Charter is antidemocratic rests on the superficially plausible idea that if nonelected judges are empowered to overturn the decisions of elected politicians, the document that gives them this power must be antidemocratic. The usefulness of the argument lies in its reminder to us that the greatest challenge for a court that has the kind of authority granted by our Charter is to interpret the vague but meaningful generalities on which this authority rests—ideas such as freedom of expression, fundamental justice, and equality—in a way that is consistent with our commitment to democratic government. Where the argument begins to mislead is when its proponents assume that because some judges have had difficulty meeting this challenge in the past, the whole enterprise is doomed to failure.

More specifically, two myths that underpin the notion that the kind of judicial review created by our Charter is inherently antidemocratic need to be exposed. The first myth is that the decisions of our elected legislators and the will of the majority of the electorate are one and the same. Democratic government as it is practised in late-twentieth-century Canada bears little resemblance to the workings of the Athenian polis or a New England town meeting. That observation is neither a disavowal of our current system of representative democracy nor an assertion that the way we presently govern ourselves stands in no need of improvement. It is, however, a reminder that when skeptics examine the record of judicial review using our Charter and point out some court decisions that deserve criticism, we should be evaluating that judicial performance against the reality of parliamentary government in Canada today and not against some romanticized portrait of government of the people, by the people, and for the people.

The second (and ultimately more damaging) myth is that majority rule is, or ought to be, all that modern democratic government is about, and it is in perpetuating the myth that "there is an inherent and irreconcilable tension between liberalism and democracy" that Professor Martin makes his most serious error. My point is not simply that we need a Charter to protect us from the tyranny of the majority, though I think it is dangerously naive to believe that our fellow citizens are somehow incapable of tyranny. Rather, I want to suggest that democratic government as we should (and to a significant extent have) come to understand it in Canada consists of a complicated web of commitments to each other, only one of which is the commitment to government that in some meaningful way reflects the will of the people.

A belief that important decisions can only be taken after a free and public discussion of the issues, a willingness to abide by a set of rules that govern the way we make authoritative decisions, an acceptance of significant constraints on the use of force—these and many other commitments, some contained in the Charter and others not, are not mere side effects of modern Canadian democracy. They lie at the very heart of democratic government in Canada. And they are part of the reason why the Canadian system of government—notwithstanding all its shortcomings—is respected by people around the world.

This is, I freely acknowledge, a liberal conception of democratic government. Moreover, I recognize that there are other visions of democracy—the kind of Marxist democracy practised by Chairman Mao's Red Guards during the Cultural Revolution, for example—that leave no room for special protection of those who are not able to identify themselves with the will of the majority. For very good reasons, however, Canadians have accepted a liberal notion of democracy, and our commitment to this version of the democratic ideal was firmly in place long before we adopted the Charter.

The real issue is not whether placing some constraints on our legislators is inherently antidemocratic—it isn't. Instead, we ought to ask whether Canadian judges using the Charter can play a useful role in enhancing the quality of our democracy. The answer to this question is not obvious, but I believe that our judges can play such a role, and that by and large our experience during the first few years of the Charter bears this out.

Robert Martin leaves the impression that the Charter has fundamentally undermined the power of our elected representatives to shape the laws that govern our society. If we take a closer look at both the structure of the Charter and the judicial record in interpreting the Charter, however, I find it very difficult to see how that impression can be substantiated.

Because of the types of rights it does (and does not) guarantee, the Charter has little relevance to large and important areas of our political life, notably economic and foreign policy. The judiciary did not bring us free trade with the United States—our political leaders did. And our elected representatives, not our judges, will decide the shape of any new trade pact we may enter into with the United States and Mexico. Our elected representatives decided to commit our troops in the Persian Gulf War, and they, not our courts, will decide what role we play in other trouble spots around the world.

Where the Charter has had some potential to conflict with social policy, our judges have tended to be rather reluctant to accept claims that individual rights should override important governmental interests. Thus our Supreme Court has decided that provincial Sunday closing laws reasonably limit freedom of religion, that Criminal Code prohibitions on hate speech and obscenity are acceptable constraints on freedom of expression, and that mandatory retirement at age sixty-five reasonably limits our right to equality. We may or may not agree with the wisdom of these and other decisions upholding the right of our politicians to pass laws that place reasonable limits on our constitutionally protected rights and freedoms, but this is certainly not the record of a judiciary that is attempting to undermine democratic government in Canada.

This is not to say that Charter litigation is meaningless because the government always wins. Our courts have made important decisions upholding the rights of refugee claimants, of people accused of crimes, of women, gays and lesbians, and many others. Once again, many of these decisions have been controversial, but I believe they have raised our sensitivity to the concerns of people whose interests are not always well represented through our political process. And in so doing, I would argue, they have enhanced the quality of Canadian democracy.

Professor Martin seems to believe that the Charter has undermined our sense of ourselves as a collectivity and contributed to the rise of a political life that is alternatively characterized by narrow interest group politics or pure selfishness. To the extent that this description of contemporary Canadian politics has an aura of authenticity about it, however, I think it confuses cause and effect. The popularity of the Charter (indeed much of the need for a Charter) arises from the fact that Canadians understand the diversity of their interests and want to incorporate into their democratic system of government a recognition of the vulnerability of some of those interests.

This diversity of interests was not created by the Charter, and getting rid of the Charter is not likely to usher in a return to a mythical golden age of harmony and communitarian spirit. Throughout our history Canadians have recognized and sought to give legal protection to our diversity on regional, linguistic, religious, and other grounds, and I suspect that only someone from Ontario could imagine characterizing this as an erosion of citizenship.

Again, the problem of the fracturing of our sense of ourselves as a political community that Professor Martin identifies is a real one, and it is a challenge for supporters of the kind of political ideals that the Charter represents to realize their goals in a way that does not irreparably undermine other political values that are important to us. What Professor Martin fails to do, in my view, is make a convincing case that it is not possible for us to meet this challenge or that it is not worthwhile for us to try to do so.

Professor Martin's second criticism of the Charter is that it is un-Canadian, by which he seems to mean that the Charter contributes to the "Americanization" of Canadian political life. It would be foolish to deny the influence of the United States Bill of Rights on both the content of the Charter and the political will that animated its adoption. In my view, however, Professor Martin is wrong in his attempt to characterize the Charter as a species of cuckoo in the Canadian political nest that seeks to supplant domestic institutions and traditions with unsavoury ideas from south of the forty-ninth parallel.

In response to Professor Martin I would begin with the rather obvious point that even if some of the important ideas embedded in the Charter were imported into Canada from abroad, so is much of the rest of the apparatus of Canadian government. Canada's parliamentary and common law traditions were imported from England; our federalism was imported (albeit in a substantially altered form) from the United States in 1867; and our civil law traditions were imported from France. In each instance we have made these traditions our own, in some instances by performing major surgery on them in the process.

The Charter itself follows in this tradition of domesticating foreign political ideas and structures. For example, a central element of the American Bill of Rights is the protection of the right to private property. The drafters of the Canadian Charter (wisely in my view) decided that our normal political processes were adequate for the protection of the rights of property owners and that judges should not be given this responsibility under the Charter. In addition, the Charter recognizes certain rights of French and English linguistic minorities, expresses a commitment to our multicultural heritage, and contains approaches to equality and other rights that set it off as a document that is quite distinctive from the American Bill of Rights. The Charter's roots may lie in American soil, but the tree that springs up from those roots is distinctively Canadian.

The more subtle but significant point on which Professor Martin and I disagree is that he seems to use the term "Americanization" as a sort of shorthand for most of what he doesn't like in contemporary Canadian political life. No doubt there are plenty of Canadians who prefer the kind of life we had in the 1970s (or the 1950s for that matter) to the kind of life we have today. What is unclear to me, however, is how unemployment, family breakdown, the consequences of massive public sector debt for our social welfare programs, and the other things that trouble Professor Martin about life in Canada in the twenty-first century can be laid at the door of the Charter.

In fairness, Professor Martin doesn't ascribe these social ills to the Charter itself, but he says that the Charter has "served to distract our attention from what has been going on." If the Charter has served to distract Canadians from thinking about the problems of high unemployment and threats to the continued viability of our present schemes for delivering social services, universal health care, and pensions, this is certainly news to me. And I dare say it would come as news to those who took part in the 1993 federal election campaign that revolved around these very issues. Professor Martin is probably correct when he states that the Charter is not going to be of much help in addressing these problems, but nobody ever claimed that it would. More important, we shouldn't assume that because the Charter doesn't address these important problems, the issues the Charter does address are somehow insignificant.

The Charter does not represent the sum of Canadian political life, any more than the American Bill of Rights represents the sum of political life in the United States. From a political science standpoint, what the Charter represents is a special way of addressing a limited range of issues that we feel are unlikely to get the kind of attention they deserve in the ordinary process of electoral politics, and a formal commitment to ourselves that the ideals such as freedom, justice, and equality that the Charter enshrines deserve a special place in our democratic political life. I think this was a commitment that it was wise for us to make in 1982, and that Canadians are right to be proud of this new and distinctive feature of our democracy.

POSTSCRIPT

Robert Martin has more recently expanded his critique of both the Charter and the role of the Canadian Supreme Court in a strongly written book entitled, *Most Dangerous Branch: How the Supreme Court Has Undermined Our Law and Democracy,* (Montreal: McGill-Queen's University Press, 2004). In this book, Martin writes: "As someone who is committed to the maintenance of constitutional democracy, I cannot avoid seeing the Court as a collection of arrogant and unprincipled poseurs, largely out of control."

But Martin is not the only one to express serious reservations about the impact of the Charter on Canadian political life. One of the most caustic critiques of the Charter has been written by Michael Mandel. In his book *The Charter of Rights and the Legalization of Politics in Canada* (Toronto: Wall and Thompson, rev. ed. 1994), Mandel argues that the Charter has led to the "legalization of politics in Canada." Because the scope of interpretation of the Charter is very broad, judges make highly political decisions. They are not just interpreting the law according to some technical, objective criteria, but are actually making the law, usurping the role traditionally reserved only for elected legislators. Because of the high cost of litigation, the legalization of politics, according to Mandel, leads to a conservative, class-based politics that works against socially disadvantaged groups.

Like Martin, Seymour Lipset, a noted American sociologist, argues that the Charter threatens to erase the cultural differences between Americans and Canadians by transforming Canada into a "rights-centred" political culture. See his *Continental Divide* (New York: Routledge, 1990). Christopher Manfredi argues that part of this Americanizing influence is reflected in the frequency with which Canadian judges cite American precedents when making their decisions.

Because of the growing importance of the Charter to Canadian politics, there has been a steady flow of books on this subject in recent years. In addition to the works cited above, students will find the following helpful: Rainer Knopff and F.L. Morton, *Charter Politics* (Scarborough: Nelson, 1992); Patrick Monahan, *Politics and the Constitution: The Charter, Federalism and the Supreme Court* (Toronto: Carswell, 1987); and David Beatty, *Putting the Charter to Work* (Montreal and Kingston: McGill-Queen's University Press, 1987). A book written by a civil rights activist who supports Philip Bryden's arguments is Alan Borovoy's *When Freedoms Collide: The Case for Our Civil Liberties* (Toronto: Lester & Orpen Dennys, 1988). See also Janet Hiebert, *Charter Conflicts: What Is Parliament's Role?* (Montreal: McGill-Queen's University Press, 2002); Christopher Manfredi, *Judicial Power and the Charter, Canada and the Paradox of Liberal Constitutionalism,* 2nd ed. (Toronto: Oxford University Press, 2001); and Peter McCormick, *Supreme at Last: The Evolution of the Supreme Court of Canada* (Toronto: Lorimer, 2000).

If we accept Martin's argument that we should be concerned about the impact of the Charter, what can be done? Is Martin's closing suggestion that many Canadians may begin thinking about repealing the Charter a likely outcome? Perhaps a more likely development is that Canadians will begin to take a more careful look at the record of individual judges and to demand more say in their appointment. The question of whether Parliament should review the appointment of Supreme Court judges is taken up in Issue Nine.

Should the Federal Government Play a Leading Role in Health Care?

✔ **YES**
ANDREW HEARD AND DANIEL COHN, "The Federal Government Should Stay Involved: The Case for a Strong Federal Role in Health Care"

✘ **NO**
PAUL BARKER, "The Case Against a Strong Federal Role in Health Care"

Federalism is a form of government that divides powers and responsibilities between national and regional governments. The intent behind selecting this type of governing arrangement is to increase the chances that local differences are respected while simultaneously allowing for the achievement of country-wide goals. At first glance, it may seem that the two levels of government would operate independently, each looking after their respective duties. But in reality, they often interact in the making of public policies. The lack of clarity in a nation's constitution, the refusal of policies to fit easily into legislative categories, and the sheer competitiveness of governments are some of the factors that lead to a high degree of *interdependence* in federal states. In light of this quality, there is a continuous struggle to sort out the roles of federal and provincial governments. Some areas of policy will, eventually, fall mostly to national governments (e.g., national security) and others to provincial ones (e.g., education). But with some policies there will be disagreement and confusion over who should assume prominence. In Canada, this last situation prevails in relation to health care.

The Canadian health care system (or medicare) offers comprehensive physician and hospital care to all citizens at no direct cost. It is an impressive policy accomplishment and often ranks as the most important public issue in the minds of Canadians. For this reason alone, it is felt that the federal government should take a leading role in the area of health care—medicare is truly a national program and appreciated as such by all Canadians. Supporters of a strong federal role also point to the need for a single authority to offer direction on reforms to the health care system. Medicare needs to continually change to ensure that Canadians continue to receive effective health care, and some believe that the federal government is best positioned to orchestrate the introduction of necessary reforms. The Canadian health care system has also become an important symbol of Canadian values, a situation that also seems to argue for a strong federal presence.

There is, however, a view that suggests that it is unwise for the federal government to assume a lead role in health care. One reason for this is legal: health care is largely a provincial responsibility. The rule of law, an important element in any constitutional democracy, would be allegedly weakened without the provinces directing medicare. A further argument against a strong federal role is that the health system would perform better with the provinces largely in charge. Medicare is in reality ten provincial plans (plus three territorial ones) knitted together by a commitment to principles contained in a piece of federal legislation called the *Canada Health Act*. Accordingly, the provinces have much more experience with health care and much more expertise as well. More generally, it is felt that the national government ought to be spending its time on matters that are more clearly national in scope.

There are also some who feel that the two orders of government should share duties when it comes to health care. It might be said that this is the way it has been done in the past. The federal government sets out the broad principles of health care and provides much needed financial assistance while the provinces administer the health care plans. A closer look, however, at the history of medicare shows that there has always been a lead player in health care, whether it was the federal government in the initial stages of medicare or the provinces in the more recent years. At the moment, the federal government appears to be attempting to re-assert itself. Through various health care accords and a national commission, it has sought to play a guiding role in the reform of the Canadian health care system. The question for this debate is, in a way, whether this recent development bodes well for health care in Canada.

In the readings, Andrew Heard and Daniel Cohn, two political scientists at Simon Fraser University, claim that the Canadian health care system requires a strong hand from the federal government. Paul Barker, one of the editors of *Crosscurrents*, makes the case against a strong presence for Ottawa in health care.

✔ YES
The Federal Government Should Stay Involved: The Case for a Strong Federal Role in Health Care
ANDREW HEARD AND DANIEL COHN

Health care is one of the most important areas of public policy. Canada's system of provincial-run single-payer, universal health insurance plans (popularly known as medicare) enjoys widespread and stable long-term public support.[1] Included in this public judgment is the belief that the maintenance of medicare is a joint responsibility of the federal and provincial governments.[2] Our medicare system has become an important symbol of Canadian identity. The universal and comprehensive medical care that all Canadians are entitled to is one of the most visible differences between Canadian and American cultures.[3] From its public proposal in 1945 through to today, the federal government has played a lead role in creating and guiding medicare. While provincial premiers have taken turns protesting the federal government's invasion of "exclusive" provincial jurisdiction, a brief analysis shows that the federal government is completely justified in taking a lead role. Far from being an invader, it is simply continuing to protect a system it helped develop decades ago. At its heart, medicare in Canada draws its strength from providing basic medical care for all Canadians, regardless of which province they happen to live in. The federal government has an important role to continue to shape and protect this national treasure.

Some historical context is vital to understanding the reasons why the federal government plays a substantial role in health care and also why that role is on solid constitutional ground. When the Fathers of Confederation settled on a division of powers between the national and provincial governments, the guiding principle was that the federal government would be responsible for most important issues, and the provinces would deal with matters of more "local and private concern." Health care then was still very primitive, with only the most rudimentary care available; indeed, it was well into the twentieth century before contact with a doctor was actually likely to improve one's chances of survival. At the time of Confederation, most hospitals were run by religious orders, with a few others set up by other charitable groups or municipalities. The *Constitution Act, 1867* gave the provinces jurisdiction over charities, hospitals, and insane asylums while the new federal government gained control over marine hospitals and quarantine. These are the only direct references to health care in the formal Constitutional documents. All that the provinces were explicitly granted in 1867 was the right to keep an eye on the churches and municipalities that ran the few small hospitals existing at the time. In addition, the provinces were responsible for licensing physicians, as a consequence of their jurisdiction over "property and civil rights"; civil rights in this context meant one's rights in property and not the idea of civil liberties we think of today.

Canadian society responded to such profound disruptions in the twentieth century as the Great Depression and World War II with new ideas about the role of the state to foster the social welfare of its citizens. The original division of powers between the federal and provincial governments in the *Constitution Act, 1867* proved unable to adapt to the new social and economic realities of the twentieth century. First, the Great Depression showed the necessity of providing people with some insurance against unemployment. The courts ruled that this was a provincial responsibility because of their control of most employment contracts, but the provinces simply did not have the financial resources to implement employment insurance. As a result, the *Constitution Act, 1940* was passed to enable the federal government to take responsibility for this area of public policy. Similarly, the post–World War II era saw the acceptance of a universal pension scheme and supplemental benefits as a way to care for senior citizens. Again, the provinces had constitutional responsibility without the practical ability to provide these benefits. A constitutional amendment was passed in 1951 to allow the federal government to create the Canada Pension Plan, and another in 1964 authorized it to provide Old Age Benefits; these amendments preserved provincial jurisdiction as well, because Quebec preferred to launch its own version of these schemes. Thus, the context of the period in which medicare was first created was an era of increasing federal government responsibility for social welfare programs—with the full agreement of the provincial governments at the time. Far from being a constitutional invader, the federal government was welcomed by many as a white knight.

Without federal policy leadership it is doubtful that most Canadians would have public health insurance today, as the provinces proved very reluctant as a group to be policy innovators. While Saskatchewan's CCF-NDP governments are popularly given credit for "inventing" medicare, it must be pointed out that Canadians would have had a complete public health insurance plan at the end of World War II if the provinces had accepted the proposals that Ottawa put forward in 1945. Instead they walked out of the post-war reconstruction conference. Rebuffed when it first raised the topic of public health insurance, the federal government offered to subsidize the creation of universal, single-payer, provincially run hospital and diagnostic services insurance in 1957, as well as insurance for physician bills in 1966, only after support for each measure had reached critical mass in provincial capitals and with voters.[4]

In order to evaluate the merits of the federal government's role in health care policymaking, we must first identify medicare's actual character and scope. Canada's system of provincially run, single-payer, universal health insurance plans is not a coherent country-wide program, nor does it represent the full extent of public involvement in the financing of health care. Rather it should be seen as the backbone of a framework within which each province has designed its own system for financing and delivering health care. This framework provides provincial governments with unparalleled autonomy in designing their own health care systems. In a recent study of health care policymaking in federations, K.G. Banting and S. Corbett found that all of the federal governments that they studied played some role in structuring health care and that Canada had the most decentralized health care policymaking process among the countries studied.[5]

In order to qualify for the full value of the transfers that provinces are entitled to under the Canada Health Transfer,[6] they must abide by the five conditions of the *Canada Health Act*. These govern the way that they manage and finance physician, hospital, and diagnostic services:

- Universality: All permanent residents of the province must be eligible to join the plan.

- Comprehensive: All medically necessary services must be insured. In practice, there is no agreed list of services. Rather, it has been left up to each province to determine what is and is not medically necessary (subject to objections from the federal health minister).[7]

- Accessibility: Services must be reasonably available and there can be no out-of-pocket charges to patients for those services covered by a provincial plan. Initially, only hospital and diagnostic services were covered by this ban on user fees. However, *The Canada Health Act* extended this ban to physician services. This act also specifically gave the federal minister the power to reduce a province's subsidy by one dollar for each dollar of user fees that it allowed.

- Portability: The plan must provide coverage for members travelling outside of their province.

- Public Administration: The plan must be run by an agency responsible to the provincial legislature on a not-for-profit basis.

As noted above, in comparative terms, Canadian provinces have a great deal of autonomy. However, even the five terms noted above are less stringent than they would first appear. The federal government has only rarely found provinces to be so far out of compliance as to warrant penalties, in the form of deductions from their transfer payments.[8] The power exercised by successive federal governments to ensure compliance with these terms has been so light it has raised questions from the Auditor General of Canada.[9] In fact, since 1977, provinces are not even required to spend the money sent to them by Ottawa, or the supporting tax powers that Ottawa has given them (through programs such as the Canada Health Transfer and its predecessors), on the provision of health care. For the financing and delivery of health care goods and services other than physician, hospital, and diagnostic services—important items provided outside of hospitals such as dentistry, optometry, physiotherapy, nursing homes, and elder and home care—even the loose rules of the *Canada Health Act* do not apply.

It has been suggested that Ottawa is trying to play a greater leadership role now that it is flush with budget surpluses. A good example is the 2000 First Ministers' health accord. This deal provided some money "string-free" but also set aside some money that provinces could only use for the purchase of new "health technology." While many thought this meant the provinces were compelled to use the money to buy more state-of-the-art diagnostic equipment so as to cut queues, in fact any equipment used in the health care system was eligible, including lawn mowers.[10] Therefore, it is a bit difficult to argue that the federal role should be reduced further, as Canadian provinces already have more autonomy than sub-national jurisdictions in other major federations, and the rules that constitute the existing, minimal federal framework tend to be enforced very moderately and with great discretion.

A federal role is also required because the provinces have proven reluctant to manage health care. When Saskatchewan created its physician insurance plan in the early 1960s, doctors went on strike to protest the loss of professional autonomy that they felt would result. The strike ended with an agreement that set the terms for the subsequent spread of provincial physician insurance plans. Provincial governments would be responsible for overall funding, but would leave professional management of care in the hands of physicians who would work (for the most part) as private entrepreneurs, billing the province on a fee-for-service basis. Those who wanted could "opt-out" and bill their patients directly either for the same fee set by the province or an additional amount. In these cases, the patient would apply to the province for reimbursement at the provincially set rate. As concern moved from building provincial health systems in the 1950s and 1960s to placing them on a more financially sustainable footing in the 1970s and 1980s, the provinces proved unwilling to make the tough choices needed to control health costs because it would involve confronting the medical profession and other powerful interest groups.

What started as a concession to ease the concern of a few doctors became a means for provinces to avoid managing their health care systems and a potential threat to health care accessibility. This was exacerbated in 1977 when Ottawa agreed to grant the provinces more leeway in how they managed their health care systems. Instead of being reimbursed 50 cents on the dollar for providing services Ottawa approved of, provinces received a block grant to spend as they wished. Therefore, if the provinces could not keep costs under control they, not Ottawa, would be responsible for the extra costs. User fees provided a loophole that would allow provinces to avoid managing their problems or paying the price for their inability to manage: if the physicians' fee chart was kept artificially low, the patient—not the province—was on the hook for the extra costs. In some provinces, there were substantial problems accessing care without user fees. Most notable in this regard was Ontario, where more than half of all anesthesiologists and more than one third of obstetricians were extra-billing. It was at this point that Ottawa stepped in and banned extra-billing with the introduction of the *Canada Health Act*. It is worth pointing out that the decision to ban user fees for physician, hospital, and diagnostic services was seen as so essential that the *Canada Health Act* received unanimous support in the House of Commons on final reading.[11]

This pattern has been repeated on other occasions as well, with the majority of provinces refusing to make the tough decisions necessary to manage their health care systems until Ottawa takes some determined action that compels the provinces to face their problems. The most recent example of this is the wave of hospital rationalizations that swept the provinces during the 1990s and the early years of the new millennium. Although some provinces, such as Alberta, acted on their own, most did less than they could have done until confronted with the cuts to transfers implemented by the federal budgets in 1994–95 and 1995–96. Given that the majority of provinces are reluctant to either innovate or manage their health care systems, a minimal federal health policy framework is necessary to ensure provinces maintain the key features of the program, let alone modify it so as to take better account of the reality of modern health care by providing universal access to home care and pharmaceutical coverage.

Finally, health care is both an expensive and extensive activity, representing a relatively consistent 10 percent annual share of Canada's gross domestic product. In today's dollars, health spending is about $100 billion when including both public and private expenses. If health care's share of the gross domestic product were to rise, Canada's international economic competitiveness could be undermined. Because the maintenance of this competitiveness is a major concern and responsibility of the federal government, Ottawa has no choice but to take a hand in health policy and not simply restrict its role to financier of provincial policy. This is especially the case in that medicare provides Canada with a competitive advantage over the United States in many vital industries, including automobile manufacturing. Without even counting associated industries and services, automobile manufacturing is Canada's number one source of export earnings.[12]

With an appreciation of the actual nature and extent of the federal government's role in health care, one can examine the constitutional grounds for this role. Some provincial leaders trumpet health care as the "exclusive jurisdiction" of the provinces and feel that any federal involvement violates the Constitution. Like many good myths, this view has some real basis in fact. Indeed, the opening words of section 92 of the *Constitution Act, 1867* declare: "In each Province the Legislature may exclusively make Laws in relation to Matters coming within the Classes of Subject next hereinafter enumerated..." This statement is followed by a list of areas of public policy, including charities, asylums, and hospitals. Some believe that this is conclusive evidence that the federal government is treading on provincial toes by daring to legislate on insured medical treatments. However, there are two crucial pieces of the puzzle that must also be fitted into the picture before one can draw proper conclusions on the subject.

First, the whole constitution is much more than just the literal words found in the documents comprising the formal Constitution of Canada. If those documents were to be taken literally, then the federal government would be fully entitled to exercise its powers of reservation and disallowance to veto any provincial legislation to which it objected. While the constitutional documents list certain areas of public policy as the "exclusive" jurisdiction of one level of government or the other, the modern reality is that just about every area of public policy is affected by the activities of both levels of government. For example, the federal government has "exclusive" jurisdiction to legislate on criminal law, but major changes are almost always discussed first with the provincial governments in an effort to get a consensus of support before amending the Criminal Code. A complex pattern of interaction among all governments is sustained right across the policy spectrum.

Secondly, modern Canadian federalism depends to an enormous extent upon "fiscal federalism," which has origins in the formal Constitution but has developed into a much broader and more substantive framework through intergovernmental agreements. These arrangements have allowed the provincial governments to implement important policies that would otherwise have remained only possibilities within the provinces' theoretical jurisdiction. The profound differences in economic activity across this country mean that Canadians would have vastly different provincial public services if the provincial governments relied exclusively on the income generated within their provinces. A belief in the basic equality and worth of Canadians fostered the development of a succession of financial schemes to transfer money from the federal government to the provinces so that Canadians across the country would receive roughly similar benefits. At various times, those federal funds have accounted for up to half of some provincial budgets. Without funding from Ottawa, Canadians living in several provinces would almost certainly still not have comprehensive medical coverage. There is simply no way that the poorer provinces could have afforded to implement the medicare programs that are so appreciated by all Canadians today.

The main federal involvement in medicare is the transfer of money to the provinces, with some conditions attached, rather than legislation aimed purely at regulating insured medical services. The conditions, as we discussed above, are aimed at maintaining some common benefits for Canadians across the country. The crux of the debate then really revolves around the constitutionality of these conditional grants.

There are two basic grounds for justifying the federal government's ability to set some conditions on the grants given to the provinces. The first is the notion of the "federal spending power." In its essence, this idea suggests that the federal government is free to make gifts to the provinces and to attach some conditions upon the receipt of those gifts. While some debate over the extent of the federal spending power, there can be little doubt about its basic constitutionality. In *Reference re Canada Assistance Plan* (1991), the Supreme Court of Canada upheld the basic ability of the national Parliament to create conditional block grants and to alter their terms unilaterally.[13] A key point for the court was that the federal legislation principally sets the terms under which federal money can be transferred and does not attempt a broader regulation of a provincial matter. The *Canada*

Health Act would appear to satisfy this approach to the federal spending power. The only real "enforcement" under the act is the withholding of federal funding, and actual enforcement is sporadic and limited.[14] If a provincial government were to violate any one of the five main conditions of the *Canada Health Act*, the federal government *may* withhold funds after consulting with the provincial government; the withholding is discretionary. The only mandatory withholding of funds is provided in the case of a province that permits extra-billing; the federal government's contribution for health care is reduced on a dollar-for-dollar basis. The *Canada Health Act* might be constitutionally vulnerable if the provinces could establish that the impact of the federal legislation negated their ability to exercise their policy powers on the matter.[15] However, the provincial governments are ultimately free to pursue their own policies if they are prepared to substitute their own revenue for the money that the federal government would otherwise donate. As a result, the act seems to be consistent with the Supreme Court's view that federal legislation under the spending power must concern conditions of dispensing its own funds and not attempt a broader, independent regulation of provincial matters.

The other possible constitutional justification relies on the POGG power, which the courts have interpreted to flow from the opening words of section 91 of the *Constitution Act, 1867* that empower the federal government to "make laws for the Peace, Order, and Good Government of Canada." In an enduring contradiction, the courts have declared this statement to mean that the federal government may pass laws that would normally be in provincial jurisdiction, when the plain English reading of this whole clause seems to explicitly preclude federal legislation on matters listed in section 92 as belonging to the provincial legislatures. As bizarre as this may seem, it is nonetheless an important doctrine of the Constitution and has been developed by the courts for well over a century now.

The federal Parliament may, in two general sets of exceptional circumstances, pass laws that would normally be matters for the provinces. The first is in times of emergency, but this does not apply to health care. The other set of circumstances is when there is a matter of "national concern" or with "national dimensions" involved. Both of these could possibly apply to the *Canada Health Act*. Health care is so vital to Canadian society that the most basic tenets of public health insurance need to be set nationally. If some provinces strayed from the agreed programs, the viability of the coast-to-coast coverage of all Canadians could be seriously threatened. Minor provincial variations could be tolerated, but any significant deviation would undermine medicare. In the case of extra-billing, some doctors charging small amounts would not threaten public health care, but many doctors charging substantial fees would be a very different stress. Events in the early 1980s showed how quickly extra-billing could spread to defeat the basic premise of public health care. By 1983, 62 percent of anesthetists and 39 percent of obstetricians in Ontario were charging their patients significant amounts for any operations they performed.[16] In particular regions of Ontario, every single member of a medical specialty was extra-billing, charging fees that could reach as high as $400 for the delivery of a baby. While many doctors waived fees for their poorest patients, such a situation presented other people with an expensive outlay for health care. What was supposed to be a universal program of health care funded from insurance premiums and tax dollars soon threatened to degenerate into a patchwork across the country; in most provinces all insured services remained free, but in others the extra-billing meant that Canadians living in those provinces faced significant charges for basic health care and hospital treatment. Had the federal government not intervened in 1984 and the trend of extra-billing continued, the medicare system may not have survived into the twentieth-first century in a form we would recognize.

These circumstances might possibly meet the test laid down by the Supreme Court of Canada in the *Crown Zellerbach* case.[17] In that decision, the court held that federal legislation could be enacted under the POGG power on matters of provincial jurisdiction, if provincial inaction or inability would lead to the collapse of a particular regulatory scheme. The corollary of this position could occur if one or more provinces wilfully pursued contrary policies that seriously undermined a public policy in which there was a real national interest. The real-world experience of provincial innovation with extra-billing indicates that the medicare system might require federal legislation if it is to survive.

In conclusion, it is both desirable and constitutional for the federal government to play a substantial role in health care. Canadians deeply value the comprehensive medicare programs that insure everyone across the country for a comprehensive range of treatments, as well as ensuring that their coverage moves with them across the country. Federal grants have permitted all Canadians to enjoy relatively comparable levels of health care that simply could not have been achieved without the federal government. A 2003 Ekos poll found that, in the public's eyes, the single most important aspect of the Canadian health care system was equal access to health care for all Canadians.[18] While there are still differences in treatment and waiting times from province to province, those differences pale in comparison to what might exist without the lead role taken by the federal government. Provincial autonomy in health care still exists; any province could pursue their own objectives if they are prepared to fund medicare themselves. So far, at least, provincial governments have decided to abide by the collective vision of health care that successive federal governments have defended. Even the richest provinces have concluded it is better to abide by the national policy preferences. It is important to note, too, that provincial autonomy does not necessarily mean advancements in health care. The track records of some provincial governments in experimenting with extra-billing in the 1980s and hospital closures in the 1990s and early 2000s demonstrate that provincial innovations can have a very negative impact on health care. Ultimately, the federal–provincial dynamic provides a system of healthy checks and balances that depends upon a national consensus to survive. Medicare is a unique policy area that accommodates differences in provincial political cultures while transcending them at the same time. Medicare was created thanks to the leadership shown by the federal government and that role is needed just as much today.

NOTES

1. Matthew Mendelsohn, *Canadians' Thoughts on their Health Care System: Preserving the Canadian Model through Innovation* (Ottawa: Commission on the Future of Health Care in Canada, 2002).

2. Antonia Maioni, "Federalism and Health Care in Canada," in Keith G. Banting and Stan Corbett, eds., *Health Policy and Federalism: A Comparative Perspective on Multi-Level Governance* (Montreal: McGill-Queen's University Press, 2002), p. 177.

3. Peter C. Newman, "Remembering Pierre Berton," *MacLean's Magazine* (13 December, 2004): 36–38.

4. D. Cohn, "The Canada Health and Social Transfer: Transferring Resources or Moral Authority?" in P.C. Fafard and D.M. Brown, eds., *Canada: The State of the Federation, 1996* (Kingston: Queen's University Institute of Intergovernmental Affairs, 1996), pp. 169–171.

5. K.G. Banting and S. Corbett, "Health Policy and Federalism: An Introduction," in K.G. Banting and S. Corbett, eds., *Health Policy and Federalism: A Comparative Perspective on Multi-Level Governance* (Montreal: McGill-Queen's University Press, 2002).

6. From 1977 to 2005, there were three different federal transfers to the provinces for the nominal support of medicare and to which the terms of the *Canada Health Act* applied after it passed in 1984. From fiscal 1977/78 to 1996/97, there was the Established Program Financing (EPF) transfer, which funded medicare and post-secondary education. In the 1995/96 budget (effective 1996/97), this was merged with the Canada Assistance Plan (CAP), which funded social programs, including the cost of medical and health services for low-income families not covered by medicare (called "extended health" services), to create the Canada Health and Social Transfer (CHST). In the 2004/05 budget, the CHST was split into the Canada Health Transfer and the Canadian Social Transfer.

7. This has led to federal–provincial disputes as to what should be covered. The most persistent case surrounds the unwillingness of some provinces to fund abortion services. See Laura Eggerson, "Abortion Services in Canada: A Patchwork Quilt with Many Holes," *Canadian Medical Association Journal* 164 (20 March, 2001): 847–849.

8. K.G. Banting and R. Boadway, "Defining the Sharing Community: The Federal Role in Health Care," in H. Lazar and F. St-Hilaire, eds., *Money, Politics and Health Care: Reconstructing the Federal-Provincial Partnership* (Montreal: Institute for Research on Public Policy, 2004), pp. 15–16.

9. Auditor General of Canada, *Status Report of the Auditor General of Canada to the House of Commons* (Ottawa: Office of the Auditor General of Canada, September 2002), chapter 3.

10. L. Priest, "Fund for Medical Machines Buys Lawn Tractors," *The Globe and Mail* (2 April, 2002): A1.

11. S. Heiber, and R. Deber, "Banning Extra-Billing in Canada: Just What the Doctor Didn't Order," *Canadian Public Policy* 13, no. 1, (1987): 62–74; M. Begin, "Revisiting the Canada Health Act: What Are the Impediments to Change, A Speech to the Institute for Research on Public Policy," (Montreal: Institute for Research on Public Policy, 20 February, 2002); Joseph Magnet and Sandra Rodgers-Magnet, "Medicare Under Siege," *The Globe and Mail* (29 December, 1983): A7.

12. Industry Canada, "Trade Data Online Database," (Ottawa: Industry Canada, accessed on 25 February, 2005): http://strategis.gc.ca/sc_mrkti/tdst/engdoc/tr_homep.html; D. Hakim, "This year Ontario May Pass Michigan in Making Vehicles," *New York Times* (27 November, 2004): C1.

13. *Reference re Canada Assistance Plan*, [1991] 2 *Supreme Court Reports*, 525.

14. Sujit Choudhry, "The Canada Health Act and the Social Union: The Need for Institutions," *Osgoode Hall Law Journal* 38 (2000): 39.

15. Dale Gibson, "The Canada Health Act and the Constitution," *Health Law Journal* 4 (1996): 1.

16. Magnet and Rodgers-Magnet, "Medicare Under Siege."

17. *R. v. Crown Zellerbach*, [1988] 1 *Supreme Court Reports*, 401.

18. Ekos Research Associates, "Romanow Tracking Poll (November 2004)" (accessed on 17 March 2005): http://www.ekos.com/admin/articles/Romanow24Nov2003.pdf.

✗ **NO**
The Case Against a Strong Federal Role in Health Care
PAUL BARKER

A major issue in Canada is whether the federal government should take the lead in the area of health care. There is great concern about the Canadian health care system itself, but a related concern is which level of government should assume the dominant position in ensuring that Canadians receive effective health care services. In the past, the federal government has been central to the introduction of hospital and physician programs, the core elements of the publicly funded health care system in Canada known as medicare. More recently, it has reached agreements with the provinces that require the latter to introduce health care reforms that are consistent with the wishes of the federal government. Some are comfortable with the federal government in this role and believe that a service as important to all Canadians as health care requires a great deal of direction from the centre. Not only will this increase the chances of ensuring that all parts of the country have access to medically required care, but it will also confirm health care as an important symbol of Canadian citizenship and values.

There are others, however, who are uneasy with a strong federal presence in the area of health care. They believe that such a presence may violate the country's Constitution, which authorizes the provinces to handle most aspects of health care. The federal government has authority to act on public health matters and to provide health services to specific groups. But legal responsibility for the major elements of the Canadian health care system—hospital care, physician services, community-based care, and prescription drugs—rests with the provinces. Those who find little favour in a major federal role in health care also believe that the goal of providing high quality care will be best achieved by the allowing the provinces to head the effort at reforming health care services. The sheer experience and expertise of the provinces, garnered through three decades of directly administering their health plans, almost alone make the case for this argument. A final contention is that a strong federal role in health care draws the national government away from a concern more pressing than health: the security of the country. Canada needs a national government able to guide it in a world that is increasingly volatile and decidedly unsympathetic to nations unprepared and poorly equipped. Implicit in this last argument is the notion that medicare should become more of a health care program and less of a symbol of Canadian beliefs and values.

LEGAL ARGUMENT

The legal argument against the primacy of the federal government in health care relies on two considerations. One is that such a role may violate the terms of the Constitution. The written Constitution places the great bulk of responsibility for health care with the provinces, yet federal actions in this area take little notice of the division of powers. The other consideration is that a strong federal presence offends the spirit of the Constitution and its treatment of health care. Even if a constitutional challenge to aggressive federal actions in health care were to fail, it could still be argued that a strong federal role takes insufficient heed of the intent of the Constitution to have the provinces carry the brunt of the load in the field of health care.

Both provisions in the Canadian Constitution and accompanying judicial review suggest that responsibility for the Canadian health care system lies mostly with the provinces. Section 92(7) of the *Constitution Act, 1867* states the provinces have legislative responsibility for hospitals, and case law has interpreted other heads of provincial powers as giving the provinces authority over such matters as the regulation of doctors, the training of health professionals, and the operation of social insurance plans. It thus seems fair to conclude that "[w]hen it comes to health, the provinces hold the front lines."[1] However, it would be wrong to argue from this that a federal presence is obviously unconstitutional, for there are powers in the Constitution that give authority to the federal government to act in the area of health. The most important of these is the federal spending power, which allows the federal government to transfer funds to the provinces and place conditions on the use of these funds as long as these conditions fall short of an attempt to regulate provincial behaviour. Many believe that federal conditional grants for health—which have formed the basis for Ottawa's involvement in medicare—respect the limits of the federal spending power.[2] They allow the federal government to shape provincial activities in health care without crossing the line by attempting to effectively legislate elements of provincial health plans. The question of the constitutionality of the federal actions hinges in part on the veracity of this claim.

It seems clear that traditional federal conditional grants for health care are safe from any constitutional challenge. These grants simply stipulate that the provinces follow some quite general requirements in return for receiving financial assistance from the federal government. For instance, the provinces should endeavour to ensure that their plans offer a "comprehensive" set of services and are "universal" in the sense that all residents are covered. Similarly, residents must have "reasonable" access to health care services, and efforts ought to be made to make health benefits "portable" and administered on a non-profit basis. All of these conditions or requirements give the provinces some flexibility in the management of their plans (or stipulate requirements that no government would do otherwise even in the absence of the stipulations). But other aspects of the federal role paint a different picture. The *Canada Health Act*, a piece of federal legislation, outlines the aforementioned general conditions, but it also includes a further condition: namely, that provincial plans prohibit hospital user fees and physician charges at point of service. This prohibition is achieved by reducing federal grants to the provinces equal to the amount of user fees and physician charges levied in the province; a province that levies, for example, two million dollars in hospital user fees loses the same amount in federal funding. This condition, unlike the other conditions in the federal legislation, appears to be more precise in its aim and more determined to shape a particular aspect of provincial plans—in other words, there is no room for flexibility, and hence this condition takes on the character of a regulatory activity. Recent federal–provincial accords also suggest that the federal government has become more specific in its requests. In the accords, the provisions state that new monies must be spent on particular areas (e.g., primary health care, home care), and some even go so far as to require the purchase of particular items relating to health care (diagnostic imagining machines).[3] As with the prohibition on charges and fees, these too appear to be an attempt to regulate provincial behaviour and hence constitute an unconstitutional use of the federal spending power.

A defence against this last claim can be made based on a distinction between compulsory regulation and voluntary regulation.[4] Clearly, a federal law that forces the provinces to do something within the latter's jurisdiction would be in violation of the Constitution. This is compulsory regulation. But it is argued that the use of the federal spending power in health care does not engage in this type of regulation. Rather, it engages in a voluntary form of regulation—here, the provinces can either accept or reject the health care conditions. Admittedly, a rejection of federal conditions means less or even no federal money, but still the absence of compulsion is apparent. The problem with this line of defence is that there is an element of compulsion. In light of the high cost of health care, the provinces really have no choice: they must gain access to the federal funds and hence must observe the accompanying conditions. It is an offer the provinces are unable to refuse.

The second consideration in the legal argument against a strong federal role is that such a role is inconsistent with the spirit or overall intent of the Constitution. An impressive number of heads of power in section 92 of the *Constitution Act, 1867* place most of the responsibility for health care services with the provinces. These heads include property and civil rights, matters of a local or private nature, and management of hospitals. Accordingly, surveys of constitutional responsibility of health care inevitably conclude that the overall aim of the Constitution is to allow the provinces to take the lead in health care. Some might argue that this is an artefact of circumstance, that the Fathers of Confederation would have allocated powers differently if they had been able to foresee the import of health care to the nation. But the centrality of the provinces is also a product of judicial review, which is of much more recent vintage. And for some legal scholars, it makes sense to place responsibility with the provinces—the drafters of the British North America Act were more prescient than we give them credit for.[5] A primary federal role thus seems out of place, for the relevant law and the accompanying spirit appear determined to give the provinces pride of place in the area of health care. Of course, it is possible that a strong federal role might be ruled consistent with the letter of the law. The federal spending power, for instance, might be invoked to support aggressive federal actions in the area of health care, and there is case law to back up such an interpretation. In this guise, the spending power means that Ottawa "may attach to any grant or loan any conditions it chooses, including conditions it could not directly legislate."[6] But surely this is equivalent to engaging in an end-run on the Constitution, an activity that hardly respects its spirit.

Recent developments supply some evidence for revealing how the spirit of the law goes unrecognized. In 2001, the federal government set up a commission to study the future of health care without any provincial participation in its activities. As Richard Simeon says, it seems strange to examine medicare without the inclusion of government entities most identified with health care.[7] Not surprisingly, the report of the commission talks insistently about the need for federal leadership and a strong presence at the centre.[8] In 2003, the federal and provincial governments agreed to an accord stipulating that new federal monies had to be spent on particular areas, and a year later another accord followed the same line of development.[9] As mentioned already, the accords can be seen in violation of the letter of the law. But perhaps the greater injury is to the spirit because the accords reverse the process that is to be expected: the federal government submits its plans and the provinces inevitably accept them. The provinces have attempted to introduce their own plans for reform into the proceedings, but these have been summarily rejected. The accords also made provision for a national body—the Health Council of Canada—whose main task is to monitor the implementation of the provisions contained in the accord of 2003. This, too, represents a failure to appreciate the intent of the Constitution, for the council endeavours to track the behaviour of the provinces and report on any shortfalls. More ambitiously, it also seeks to provide some leadership on issues it deems important to the health of Canadians (for example, waiting lists). The council, while well intentioned, fails to respect the fact that it is the provinces that are largely responsible for the maintenance and development of the Canadian health system. Supporters of the council are quick to point out that the council includes members from provincial governments, but the fact is that the federal government initiated the proposal without effusive support from the provinces (and, indeed, Quebec and Alberta refused to accept the body). As with many developments in health care, the council was a price that the provinces had to pay in order to get federal funding.

POLICY ARGUMENT

Any federal state seeks to establish arrangements between the two levels of government in order to produce the best policies and programs possible. The legal division of powers is one such arrangement. But sometimes a state's constitution fails to allocate responsibilities in a way that provides for good public policy, and a disjunction between the legal and desired division of roles emerges. In this situation, a need to supplement or amend the legal structure becomes evident. However, with respect to health care in Canada, no such disjunction exits. As shown, the Canadian Constitution places responsibility squarely with the provinces, and, as will be shown now, this is an allocation that contributes to an effective and equitable health care system in Canada. A strong federal leadership role in health care is thus not only inconsistent with the Constitution, but also detracts from the effort to produce good health care programs in Canada.

The policy argument against a strong federal role in health care begins with a consideration of claims made in favour of giving the provinces primacy in formulating and implementing health care programs. In a federal state, the policy role of the national government can be derived from an attempt on the part of central authorities to address the failings of the provinces; such an exercise thus requires first an understanding of the benefits of leaving policy to the provinces.[10] There are at least three reasons for believing that the aim of producing good health care policy will be best met by strong provincial leadership. One reason is that the provinces are better positioned than the federal government to determine the differing health care preferences of individual Canadians across the country. Although all Canadians wish for an effective health care system, they may differ in how this is best achieved. Some may feel that a strong hospital sector is necessary to achieve this end, while others may believe that a more community-based approach is preferable. Similarly, the provinces may differ on the appropriate decision-making structures in relation to health care—nearly all provinces have set up regional health authorities, but the membership, structure, and duties of these bodies are not the same across the country.[11] The fear associated with a strong federal role is that the national government will be insensitive to these differing preferences in its attempt to offer a national health care system; a major attraction of federalism is its capacity to reflect the diversity of a nation, yet a too-strong national government can nullify this quality.

A second and related reason is that the provinces are better informed on what it takes to build a workable health care system. The greater expertise stems from the past thirty years of making and carrying out health care programs. During these years, the federal government has participated in making the Canada health care system a success, but its role has largely been related to providing for conditional grants—not running health care programs. It has been the banker of health care, not the maker. A case might be made that the federal government is not at an informational disadvantage in the early stages of developing a country's health care system; but medicare in Canada has long left this stage of development and now finds itself in a period of renewal, which requires a level of expertise derived from close experience working with health care programs. Such challenges as reorganizing the delivery of primary health care (including the redefining of responsibilities of health care workers), rationalizing the supply of hospital services, and determining the efficacy of medical procedures are hardly suited for an order of government with little familiarity with the intricacies of health care services. Moreover, the informational requirements also extend to an appreciation of the political dynamics associated with health care reform. It is not enough to know what has to be done: success in health care also depends on knowing how it is to be done. And, again, the provincial governments are better positioned to understand the local politics of health care.

A third and final reason for provincial primacy in health policy is that it increases the chances of policy experimentation. A strong federal role does not necessarily rule out experimentation, but a strong provincial role guarantees a country with ten laboratories in which to test new ideas. The attraction here is that one or two provinces may experiment with a proposed change in the health care and not put the entire health care system in harm's way. If the innovation tests well, the other provinces can elect to incorporate it into their health systems; if it fails, then little damage is done. A famous U.S. Supreme Court justice nicely captures the essence of this third benefit of provincial primacy:

> It is one of the happy incidents of the Federal system that a single coura-geous state [or province] may, if its citizens choose, serve as a laboratory, and try moral, social, and economic experiments without risk to the rest of the country.[12]

At present, there is evidence of the desire of some provinces to experiment. Among these provinces, Alberta is arguably the most ambitious. It believes that medicare would benefit if the private sector were more greatly involved in health care through the provision of necessary health care services. The province has also believed at times that various types of direct patient charges might ease the pres-sure on provincial health care plans. Most experts find little research to support such initiatives, but the latter have not been thoroughly tested in Canada. Experimentation can help eliminate the uncertainty about privatization and do so without incurring the possibility of injury to the entire Canadian health care system.

The preceding suggests that substantial policy benefits arise from giving the provinces primacy policy over health care. It is also true, however, that this same arrangement can lead to some costs. Any significant differences in provincial health care programs may dissuade some Canadians from moving from one province to another, for example, to take a new job. This would be an undesirable development because a smooth-functioning market needs people to use their skills in the most productive way. A province may also make decisions that have unwanted effects on other provinces; for instance, it may refuse to provide full heath care coverage to residents visiting from other parts of the country. The aforementioned costs are associated with losses in efficiency in that provincial decisions on health care may have negative effects on the allocation of scarce resources in the country. But the more important cost might be in relation to equity and the aim of any nation to instil an element of fairness in its provision of public services throughout the country. Provinces acting on their own without central direction may produce a health system that fails to provide all Canadians with a set of roughly comparable health care services. Considerations of fairness suggest that it is appropriate that health care programs—in either their structure or effect—be fairly similar across Canada. Unity considerations also come into play at this point: a country with widely disparate levels of services may produce tensions and animosities between regions that threaten the viability of the country.

All of these possible costs point toward the need for a federal role that reduces the prevalence of the difficulties created by the provinces. But this need not be a strong role. What is required here is what the federal government has done in the past, which is to set out some general conditions that remind the provinces of their commitment to making medically necessary health care accessible to all Canadians. And the emphasis here is on a *gentle* reminder, for the provinces mostly act as one in relation to the broad strokes of health policy (though as mentioned differences in details may appear). A perusal of provincial health plans reveals a great deal of similarity in terms of their basic contours, and a review of provincial planning for the future again reveals similar thinking (reform of physician and hospital care, more community-based services, greater emphasis in promotion and prevention). In the past couple of years, the federal government has felt it necessary to become more aggressive in monitoring the provinces and to make available monies only for certain services and programs. But many of these services and programs have been under consideration by the provinces for several years. There is, in other words, no need for a federal role in health care policy that goes beyond the general conditions contained in the *Canada Health Act*. And even if provincial plans were to diversify more in the future, an argument could still be made for limiting Ottawa's role. Canadians may decide that the benefits of differentiation more than compensate for the loss in comparability. Alberta may begin to charge patients directly, Quebec may pursue more aggressively its use of for-profit imagining clinics, and Ontario may lean heavily on nurse practitioners to solve its perceived shortage of doctors—and Canadians may accept these developments with little notice. The balance between achieving similar health plans and allowing the provinces to go their own way has historically been in favour of the former, but this balance is not set in stone. Indeed, opinion surveys show that Canadians are willing to try new ways of delivering and financing health care.[13]

PHILOSOPHICAL ARGUMENT

The philosophical argument against a strong federal role in health care is that such a role draws the national government away from its primary role of providing security for the nation. Accordingly, "philosophical" in this context refers to the well-known belief in liberal philosophy that the core duty of any national government is to provide for stability. Under certain circumstances, when peace and stability reign, a national government can afford to concern itself with matters unrelated to security. But most of the time, discussions of national leadership typically relate to the development of foreign and defence policies that protect a nation against aggressors. At present, Canada is in need of this kind of leadership, but it is not clear that its national government is meeting this need. Ultimately, the philosophical argument against Ottawa taking the lead in the reform of the Canadian health care system is that it is needed more elsewhere.

In allocating powers in a federal state, there is little disagreement about assigning responsibility for national security to the central government. If there is any issue that has country-wide dimensions and surmounts regional differences, it is security and the literal survival of the nation. The *Constitution Act, 1867* reflects this belief by giving Ottawa authority over such matters as the military, navy, militia, and overall defence of the country. There is also little argument that this issue must be a primary concern—if not *the* primary concern—of any national government. Without security and the provision of some kind of order, there can be no basis for a workable society. As Thomas Axworthy writes, "... we should never forget that the first principle of the state is to promote the human security of our own citizens...."[14] Despite this understanding, there are signs that the federal government is falling short of carrying out its most important duty.

One sign is the questionable capacity of Canada to defend itself against potential threats to its security. Once, Canada had one of the largest armed forces in the world, but now they are a pale shadow of their former selves. Andrew Cohen writes that Canada's armed forces "are among the weakest in the industrialized world," and notes that our expenditures on defence measured in terms of their share of GDP rank seventeenth among the nineteen members of the North Atlantic Treaty Organization.[15] Not surprisingly, Canada finds itself hard-pressed to deal with terrorism both in and outside its borders, and its contributions to addressing other international threats are disappointing. In the eyes of our allies, our intentions are good, but our capabilities are woeful—Canada is "a kind of well-meaning Boy Scout."[16] Another sign is the decline in its ability to conduct relations with other countries. As with its armed forces, the Canadian foreign service was once a presence in world affairs, but now that time is gone. Maintaining the security of the nation relies not only on armaments, but also on men and women skilled in the arts of diplomacy. Unfortunately, Canada appears largely without the necessary diplomatic and conceptual skills for navigating the world of international politics.

Arguably the most dispiriting sign is the inability of the national government to define a role for Canada in the post–Cold War era. At times, this inability seems to stem from a desire to withdraw from world affairs, to have no real role, and to rely on others to sort out the complexity of international relations. But other times, it appears as a failure to apply the necessary attention to an important issue. The national government understands the need to undertake such a role, for only it can provide the necessary framework for addressing the security of Canada. However, its priorities appear to lie elsewhere, in health care and other domestic issues. In the 2004 federal election, the prime minister declared that the number one priority of a Liberal government would be health care and that reducing waiting times represented the "litmus test" of his government's most important commitment.[17] In other words, the federal government would direct it energies toward ensuring that Canadians do not have to wait as long for health care services. With this kind of sentiment, there should be little wonder about the absence of an articulated position for Canada to take in world affairs. Ensuring that Canadians have timely access to health care is important, but it should not be the primary preoccupation of a national government.

For some, there is much exaggeration about the failings of the national government in the area of defence and foreign policy. There are indications that the federal government is aware of the threat of terrorism—for example, it has directed additional funds to this area and passed new anti-terrorist legislation—and the state of the armed forces is not as bad as some claim. Even so, the actions of the federal government may still seem wanting. For a national government to carry out its duty to defend the country, it is not enough to provide a defence of the citizenry. This role, if fully exercised, can also be used to give definition to a nation. Cohen, for one, believes a decision on part of the federal government to re-engage itself in world affairs would have a uniting effect:

> What we do abroad will enrich us at home. For a country forever wondering if it has a future, indeed doubting that if it has one, the new Canadian internationalism could become an instrument of pan-Canadian unity, taking us beyond the boundaries of language and race and region, drawing on all elements of a truly diverse society.[18]

Of course, it is contended that this is exactly what the federal government is doing with health care, using it to give definition and unity to Canada. Moreover, it is also believed that a withdrawal of the federal government from a leadership position in health care would put at risk the nation-building capability of this public program. But as suggested, greater involvement in foreign affairs can accomplish the same purpose while at the same time ensuring the security of the nation. For those who believe that the commitment to health care is too deep-rooted to be so easily replaced, it has to be remembered that universal health system has only been a part of Canada for the past thirty or so years.[19] What also has to be remembered is that it is the underlying values of government programs that are important and not the programs themselves. Medicare has served admirably in reminding Canadians of what is means to be a Canadian, but other programs can also perform this function just as well.

There is also the possibility that lessening the importance of health care to Canadians may actually be beneficial in a sense other than allowing the federal government to better attend to the security of the country. The reform of health care at times requires actions that appear threatening to medicare (for example, closing hospitals or de-insuring certain services), and elected officials may be reluctant to take such actions in the glare of public attention on health care. The fact that major adjustments to health care involve the participation of first ministers also points to the highly charged atmosphere in which health care reform takes place. A less emotive setting might lead to better health care policy. The de-emphasis of health care could also provide a related benefit, which is to give provincial governments more room in which to allocate their revenues. The national importance of medicare, especially in recent years, has led to provincial budgets that pay a lot of attention to health care and look less favourably on other significant responsibilities. It is often claimed that medicare underpins the notion of Canada as a sharing community. But sometimes it appears as if the emphasis on health care only forces governments and the electorate to concentrate on health and to neglect other activities that make a contribution to Canadian life.[20] The fear is that the underlying sentiment here is not one of sharing, but almost a desperate determination to ensure that one's own health care needs are met.

CONCLUSION

For the most part, the federal role in health care in Canada has been to provide the provinces with financial assistance with the stipulation that provincial health plans observe some general conditions. This is a role that recognizes the primacy of the provinces in health care. The provinces are allowed to shape their plans with little interference from federal authorities, a situation consistent with the constitutional framework and with the requirements of sound public policy. It also increases the chances that the national government will concern itself with truly national matters and not be distracted by issues that can be handled by the other order of government. Accordingly, a strong federal role in health care upsets traditional arrangements for health care and puts at risk the benefits of these arrangements. At present, some feel that the challenges facing the health care system require federal leadership; Ottawa needs to use its spending power (and financial resources) to force the provinces to make the necessary reforms in their health care plans. But the policy benefits of such action will be negligible—the provinces are better positioned to reform the medicare—and it will be contrary to the spirit of the Constitution. Moreover, a strong federal role in health care reform will draw away the national government from its true purposes.

NOTES

1. Andre Braen, "Health and the Distribution of Powers in Canada," in Tom McIntosh, Pierre-Gerlier Forest, and Gregory P. Marchildon, eds., *The Governance of Health Care in Canada* (Romanow Papers, Volume III) (Toronto: University of Toronto Press, 2003), p. 30.

2. See, for example, Peter Hogg, *Constitutional Law of Canada,* Loose-leaf Edition (Toronto: Thomson Carswell, 1997), p. 6.8 (a) or 6.15–6.19.

3. First Ministers' Meeting—Communique on Health (September 11, 2000); 2003 First Ministers' Accord on Health Care (February 5, 2003).

4. Hogg, *Constitutional Law of Canada,* p. 6.8 (a) or 6.17–6.18.

5. Braen, "Health and the Distribution of Powers in Canada," p. 42.

6. Peter Hogg, quoted in Keith Banting and Robin Boadway, "Defining the Sharing Community: The Federal Role in Health Care," in Harvey Lazar and France St-Hilaire, eds., *Money, Politics and Health Care: Reconstructing the Federal-Provincial Partnership* (Montreal & Kingston: The Institute for Research on Public Policy and the Institute of Intergovernmental Relations, 2004), p. 6.

7. Richard Simeon, "We've Tied the Commission's Hands," *The Globe and Mail* (13 April, 2001): A13.

8. Commission on the Future of Health Care in Canada, *Building on Values: the Future of Health Care in Canada,* (November 2002), chapter 2.

9. First Ministers' Meeting, *A 10 Year Plan to Strengthen Health Care* (September 2004).

10. Robin Boadway, "The Folly of Decentralizing the Canadian Federation," *Dalhousie Review* 75, no. 3 (Winter 1996): 333–334.

11. Carolyn Tuohy, *Accidental Logics: the Dynamics of Change in the Health Care Arena in the United States, Great Britain, and Canada* (New York: Oxford University Press, 1999), p. 98.

12. Harvey Rosen et al., *Public Finance in Canada,* 2nd ed. (Toronto: McGraw-Hill Ryerson, 2003), p. 166.

13. Matthew Mendelsohn, *Canadians' Thoughts on Their Health Care System: Preserving the Canadian Model Through Innovation* (Saskatoon: Commission on the Future of Health Care in Canada, June 2002), pp. 9–13.

14. Thomas Axworthy, "Choosing Canada's Role in the World," *National Post* (16 October, 2004), RB1.

15. Andrew Cohen, *While Canada Slept: How We Lost Our Place in the World* (Toronto: McClelland & Stewart, 2003), p. 27.

16. Michael Ignatieff, quoted in J.L. Granatstein, *Who Killed the Canadian Military?* (Toronto: Harper Flamingo Canada, 2004), p. 179.

17. Liberal Party of Canada, *A Fix for a Generation: The Paul Martin Plan for Better Health Care* (2004).

18. Cohen, *While Canada Slept,* p. 203.

19. Michael Bliss, "The Great Myths of Medicare," *National Post* (7 September, 2004), A1, A9.

20. In Ontario, for example, the expenditures of the provincial government are coming to close to representing nearly half of all *program* expenditures.

POSTSCRIPT

In a calm and measured way, Andrew Heard and Daniel Cohn show why many believe the federal government ought to play an important role in health care in Canada. Ottawa was integral to the introduction of medicare, and it has been essential to pushing reluctant provinces into adopting necessary health care changes. It has also been there when the very survival of medicare seemed at risk. For those who fear that the federal government may be trodding all over the Constitution, Heard and Cohn argue convincingly that such fears are unfounded. There are, however, a few spots where the two authors are not totally convincing. They say that the provinces are not up to the task of making necessary reforms, yet one wonders whether the provinces are truly incapacitated. The two also state that the provinces are free to reject federal transfers if they dislike the attached conditions, but acknowledge that these transfers are essential to the well-being of many provinces. Heard and Cohn are also impressed with the fact that the provinces possess a great deal of autonomy in comparison with sub-national states in other federations. But it fails to follow that this opens the door for a stronger federal presence in Canada. Perhaps the Canadian provinces are just better able to handle health care than their counterparts in other locales.

In his effort, Paul Barker is concerned that a strong national role will run roughshod over the spirit of the Constitution if not the actual provisions and judicial interpretations. He also seems impressed with the ability of the provinces to make sound health policy and thinks that a strong federal role leads to the neglect of more proper duties of the federal government. All of this is perhaps worthy of consideration, but the arguments are vulnerable. As Barker admits, the legal case against a strong federal role seems to rest largely on the rather shaky grounds that somehow the spirit of the Constitution—which is not really defined—is somehow violated. He also thinks a strong provincial role is necessary to preserve different approaches to the delivery and financing of health care, but later on says that provincial health plans are largely similar. Do we really need to preserve the possibility of differences when few differences actually appear in provincial plans? As for his belief that a strong federal role leads to the neglect of the security of the nation, it omits the possibility that a federal government might be able to do both. Finally, his belief that medicare should assume less importance seems misguided: Canadians believe strongly in this program and seem less than willing to give it up as symbol of this country's beliefs and values.

Students interested in this debate might begin with articles that provide an overview of federalism and health care in Canada: Antonia Maioni and Miriam Smith, "Health Care and Federalism" in Francois Rocher and Miriam Smith, eds., *New Trends in Canadian Federalism*, 2nd ed. (Peterborough: Broadview Press, 2003); Antonia Maioni, "Health Care in the New Millennium," in Herman Bakvis and Grace Skogstad, eds., *Canadian Federalism: Performance, Effectiveness and*

Legitimacy (Toronto: Oxford University Press, 2002); and Alan Davidson, "Dynamics Without Change: Continuity of Canadian Health Policy," *Canadian Public Administration* 47, no. 3 (Fall 2004). Two additional pieces might also be consulted for a close-up view of the most developments relating to the federal role in health care: Gerard Boismenu and Peter Graefe, "The New Federal Tool Belt: Attempts to Rebuild Social Policy Leadership," in *Canadian Public Policy* XXX, no. 1 (2004) and Tom McIntosh, "Intergovernmental Relations, Social Policy and Federal Transfers After Romanow," *Canadian Public Administration* 47, no. 1 (Spring 2004). The next step might be to examine how the Constitution treats health care, and for this one should refer to Peter Hogg, *Constitutional Law of Canada* (Toronto: Carswell, 2001), chapter 6; Andre Braen, "Health and the Distribution of Powers in Canada," in Tom McIntosh, Pierre-Gerlier Forest, and Gregory P. Marchildon, eds., *The Governance of Health Care in Canada* (Toronto: University of Toronto Press, 2004); and Dale Gibson, "The Canada Health Act and the Constitution," *Health Law Journal* 4 (1996).

To participate in this debate, students need to understand the policy implications of assigning health to one level of government or another. Robin Boadway and his colleagues have provided a useful framework for addressing this most important issue: Robin Boadway, "Recent Developments in the Economics of Federalism," in Harvey Lazar, ed., *Canada: The State of the Federation 1999/2000* (Montreal & Kingston: McGill-Queen's University Press, 2000) and Keith Banting and Robin Boadway, "Defining the Sharing Community: The Federal Role in Health Care," in Harvey Lazar and France St-Hilaire, eds., *Money, Politics and Health Care: Reconstructing the Federal-Provincial Partnership* (Montreal and Kingston: Institute for Research on Public Policy & the Institute of Intergovernmental Relations, 2003). Allan Maslove also provides some direction on this issue as well: Allan Maslove, "National Goals and the Federal Role in Health Care," in National Forum on Health, *Canada Health Action: Building on the Legacy: Striking a Balance Between Health Care Systems in Canada and Elsewhere*, vol. 4 (Ottawa: Her Majesty the Queen in Right of Canada, 1998). For differing views on the actual impact of allocating major responsibility for health care to one level of government or the other, students should consult the following publications: Gregory P. Marchildon, *Three Choices for the Future of Medicare* (Ottawa: Caledon Institute of Social Policy, April 2004); Michael Rachlis, *The Federal Government Can and Should Lead the Renewal of Canada's Health Policy* (Ottawa: Caledon Institute of Social Policy, February 2003); Commission on the Future of Health Care in Canada, *Building on Values: The Future of Health Care in Canada Final Report* (Saskatoon: Commission on the Future of Health Care in Canada, November 2002), chapter 2; various chapters in Tom McIntosh, Pierre-Gerlier Forest, and Gregory P. Marchildon, eds., *The Governance of Health Care in Canada* (Toronto: University of Toronto Press, 2004); Antonia Maioni, "Decentralization in Health Policy: Comments on the ACCESS Proposals (and comments by John Richards)," in Robert Young, ed., *Stretching the Federation: The Art of the State in Canada* (Kingston: Institute of Intergovernmental Relations, 1999); and Thomas J. Courchene, *Redistributing Money and Power: A Guide to the Canada Health and Social Transfer* (Toronto: C.D. Howe Institute, 1995), chapter 5.

In his article, Barker argues for a federal government that spends more time on security policy and less on health care. For sources on the state of Canada's foreign and defence policies, students might look at the following: Andrew Cohen, *While Canada Slept: How We Lost Our Place in the World* (Toronto: McClelland & Stewart, 2003); J.L. Granastein, *Who Killed the Canadian Military?* (Toronto: HarperFlamingo Canada, 2004); and the February 2005 issue of *Policy Options*. These sources are largely critical of Canada's attempts to provide sound arrangements for the security of the country. Different interpretations of Canada's relations with the rest of the world include Jennifer Welsh, *At Home in the World: Canada's Global Vision for the 21st Century* (Toronto: HarperCollins, 2004); Laura Macdonald, "In the Shadow the Superpower: Beyond Canada's Middle Power Image," in Michael Whittington and Glen Williams, eds., *Canadian Politics in the 21st Century* (Toronto: Thomson Nelson, 2004); Andrew Cooper, "Canadian Foreign Policy after September 11: Patterns of Change and Continuity," in James Bickerton and Alain-G. Gagnon, eds., *Canadian Politics,* 4th ed. (Peterborough: Broadview Press, 2004); and the set of articles in Janine Brodie and Linda Trimble, eds., *Reinventing Canada: Politics of the 21st Century* (Toronto: Prentice-Hall, 2003). Finally, the federal government has recently released a policy statement that seeks to give greater definition to Canada's foreign policies. The statement entitled *A Role of Pride and Influence in the World* is available on the website of Foreign Affairs Canada.

Finally, an appreciation of the history of medicare in Canada is required. For this, one might read Malcolm G. Taylor, *Health Insurance and Canadian Public Policy: The Seven Decisions that Created the Canadian Health Insurance System* (Montreal & Kingston: Institute of Public Administration of Canada, 1978). There are more recent histories available, but Taylor's work is almost magisterial in its telling of the story of medicare.

Are Canada's Child Pornography Laws Unconstitutional?

✔ **YES**

JUSTICE DUNCAN SHAW, "Opinion in *R. v. Sharpe*," (1999), 169 D.L.R. (4th) 536

✘ **NO**

CHIEF JUSTICE BEVERLEY MCLACHLIN, "Opinion in *R. v. Sharpe*," (2001), 194 D.L.R. (4th) 1

In early 1999, the British Columbia Supreme Court ruled unconstitutional a provision of the Criminal Code that makes possession of child pornography a criminal offence. John Robin Sharpe, a private citizen, had been charged under this provision and had sought to overturn the charge by having the law declared unconstitutional. Justice Duncan Shaw, who presided over the case, noted in his decision that all parties to the legal proceedings agreed that the provision violated the section of the Canadian Charter of Rights and Freedoms protecting freedom of expression. Where the parties disagreed was on whether the prohibition amounted to a reasonable limit. The Charter contains a section that allows for limits on rights and freedoms if the limit can be considered reasonable in a free and democratic society. Justice Shaw decided that the provision could not be considered a reasonable limit.

The government of Canada appealed the decision to the British Columbia Court of Appeal, but lost on a split decision. On further appeal to the Supreme Court of Canada, however, the government fared much better. In a unanimous decision, the highest court in the land found that the prohibition on possession of child pornography could be considered a reasonable limit. Mr. Sharpe had therefore lost his legal battle on the issue of the constitutionality of the Criminal Code provision, and would now have to face charges of possession of child pornography. In its decision, the Supreme Court specified a few exceptions to the reach of the child pornography law, but none of these applied to the respondent.

Central to the case *R. v. Sharpe* was the definition of a reasonable limit and its application to the Criminal Code. In an earlier case, the Supreme Court had set down a test for determining the reasonableness of a limit on a right or freedom protected in the Charter of Rights and Freedoms. To constitute a reasonable limit, the law under review has to have a pressing and substantial goal. In other words, the legislation must pursue an important societal objective. This part of the test is relatively easy to pass, for courts are reluctant to suggest that any piece of government legislation is not important in one way or another. More difficult is the second part of the test, which deals with proportionality. Under this part, it must be shown that the means in the legislation are rationally connected to the overall end or purpose. For instance, in R. v. Sharpe the federal government had to prove that prohibitions on the possession of child pornography would help in the battle against child pornography and against the commission of sexually related offences. A second aspect of the proportionality test requires that the legislation limit the restricted freedom as little as reasonably possible; and a third and final element of proportionality demands that government lawyers show that the benefits of the restriction outweigh the costs. In R. v. Sharpe, the B.C. Supreme Court (and subsequently the B.C. Court of Appeal) found that the legislation and its sponsor, the federal government, failed to meet the test of reasonableness. The Supreme Court of Canada, however, decided that the prohibition on possession of child pornography (with some exceptions) could be seen as a reasonable limit on Mr. Sharpe's freedom of expression.

The decisions in R. v. Sharpe led to a great deal of controversy. Justice Shaw was the recipient of death threats, as was Mr. Sharpe. In the House of Commons, a member of Parliament proposed the use of the notwithstanding clause in the Charter of Rights and Freedoms after the release of Justice Shaw's decision. This clause, which is rarely employed, authorizes the overriding of Charter court decisions and the consequent re-enactment of the laws declared unconstitutional by the judiciary. The proposal fell just short of acceptance. The Supreme Court's decision assuaged many concerns, but it worried civil liberties associations. They felt that the decision was unclear in its applications to various situations involving child pornography. Also, some legal commentators felt that the Supreme Court had bowed to public pressure. The court, they sensed, had made a political decision, not a legal one.

The story of John Robin Sharpe and child pornography did not end with the decision of the Supreme Court of Canada. On being tried, Sharpe was found guilty of possessing pornographic *pictures* of children (sentence of four months' house arrest) but was acquitted on charges of possessing and distributing *written* child pornographic material. The acquittal, based on the ground that his written materials had some artistic merit, led to an attempt on the part of the federal government to amend the Criminal Code to make it more difficult to gain such acquittals. The proposed legislation, after three years, is still being considered by Parliament. During the federal election of 2004, the Conservative Party accused the prime minister of supporting child pornography because of his government's failure to agree to an opposition motion to criminalize all forms of child pornography. This action, which many believed to be an unfair accusation, gravely hurt the chances of the Conservative Party in the election. Finally, Robin Sharpe, in 2004, was found guilty of indecent assault of a young boy that took place a quarter of a century ago. Sharpe was sentenced to two years in jail.

The two readings for this debate are abridged versions of the decisions rendered by the British Columbia Supreme Court—written by Justice Shaw—and by the Supreme Court of Canada—written by Chief Justice McLachlin.

✔ **YES**
Opinion in *R. v. Sharpe*
JUSTICE DUNCAN SHAW

[1] Shaw J.:— The accused John Robin Sharpe challenges the constitutionality of child pornography provisions set out in Section 163.1 of the *Criminal Code*, R.S.C. 1985, c. C-46. Mr. Sharpe contends that the impugned provisions violate the *Canadian Charter of Rights and Freedoms,* and in particular Sections 2(*a*), 2(*b*), 2(*d*) and 15.

[2] A *voir dire* has been held to hear the constitutional challenge. This is my ruling.

[3] There are four charges against Mr. Sharpe.

Count 1
He, on or about the 10th day of April, 1995, at or near Surrey, in the Province of British Columbia did have in his possession for the purpose of distribution or sale, child pornography: computer discs containing a text entitled "Sam Paloc's Flogging, Fun and Fortitude—A Collection of Kiddiekink Classics," contrary to Section 163.1(3) of the *Criminal Code.*

Count 2
He, on or about the 10th day of April, 1995, at or near Surrey, in the Province of British Columbia did have in his possession child pornography: computer discs containing a text entitled "Sam Paloc's Flogging, Fun and Fortitude—A Collection of Kiddiekink Classics," other writings and photographs, contrary to Section 163.1(4) of the *Criminal Code.*

Count 3
He, on or about the 13th day of May, 1996, at or near the City of Vancouver, in the Province of British Columbia did have in his possession, for the purpose of distribution or sale, child pornography: books, manuscripts and stories, contrary to Section 163.1(3) of the *Criminal Code.*

Count 4
He, on or about the 13th day of May, 1996, at or near the City of Vancouver, in the Province of British Columbia did have in his possession child pornography: books, manuscripts, stories and photographs, contrary to Section 163.1(4) of the *Criminal Code.*

[4] The evidence indicates that there were two seizures of materials from Mr. Sharpe. The first was by Canada Customs. That seizure was of computer discs containing a text entitled "Sam Paloc's Flogging, Fun and Fortitude—A Collection of Kiddiekink Classics." As a result of that seizure Mr. Sharpe was charged with Counts 1 and 2.

The second seizure was at Mr. Sharpe's home pursuant to a search warrant (the validity of which will be contested at a later point in this trial). That seizure was of a collection of books, manuscripts, stories and photographs said by the Crown to constitute child pornography. Many of the seized photographs are of nude boys displaying their genitals or anal regions.

[5] The challenges by Mr. Sharpe are on s-s. (4) and s-s. (1)(*b*) of s. 163.1 of the *Criminal Code*. Subsection (4) prohibits simple possession of child pornography. Subsection (1)(*b*) sets out part of the definition of child pornography, that part including material which counsels or advocates the commission of sexual offences against children. [...]

[7] Mr. Sharpe invokes the following provisions of the *Canadian Charter of Rights and Freedoms:*

2. Everyone has the following fundamental freedoms:
   (*a*) freedom of conscience and religion;
   (*b*) freedom of thought, belief, opinion and expression, including freedom of the press and other media of communication;
   . . . . .
   (*d*) freedom of association.
   . . . . .

15 (1) Every individual is equal before and under the law and has the right to the equal protection and equal benefit of the law without discrimination and, in particular, without discrimination based on race, national or ethnic origin, colour, religion, sex, age or mental or physical disability.

[8] The Crown relies upon s. 1 of the *Charter:*

1. The *Canadian Charter of Rights and Freedoms* guarantees the rights and freedoms set out in it subject only to such reasonable limits prescribed by law as can be demonstrably justified in a free and democratic society.

SIMPLE POSSESSION: SUBSECTION (4)

[9] I will deal first with Mr. Sharpe's contention that s-s. (4) of s. 163.1 is unconstitutional.

[10] It will be observed on reading s-s. (4) that the word "possesses" is not limited; any purpose will suffice to make possession of child pornography a crime. Subsection (4) is to be contrasted with s-s. (2) and s-s. (3) which prohibit possession for purposes of publication, sale or distribution.

Evidence

[11] The Crown led evidence from two expert witnesses. The first was Detective Noreen Waters of the Vancouver Police Department. She is an expert in the investigation of child pornography. She testified that with the advent of the Internet

there has been a veritable explosion of the availability of child pornography. She observed that as a result of simple possession charges laid under s-s. (4), the police have been able to obtain search warrants and carry out searches which have assisted them in finding child molesters. Detective Waters also pointed out that children are abused when they are exploited in the production of filmed or video-taped pornography.

[12]The second expert witness was Dr. P.I. Collins, a specialist in Forensic Psychiatry, particularly with respect to sexual deviancy and pedophilia. Dr. Collins is a clinician (as distinct from a researcher) who specializes in treating persons with sexual deviancy problems. His patients include homosexual pedophiles, men whose sexual preference is boys.

[13]Dr. Collins offered several reasons why, in his view, child pornography is harmful to children. The first is that some pedophiles show children sexually explicit depictions of children with adults, or adults with other adults, in order to lower inhibitions and to make the depicted conduct appear to be normal. The second is that pornography excites some child molesters to commit offences. The third is that child pornography augments or reinforces the "cognitive distortions" of pedophiles. Dr. Collins explained that cognitive distortions are erroneous beliefs by which pedophiles justify their aberrant behaviour. Examples of cognitive distortions are that child-adult sex is natural and that it does no harm to children. The fourth reason offered by Dr. Collins is that children are abused in the making of pornography and that pornographic films or photographs are a record of their abuse.

[14]To support his views Dr. Collins relied upon certain studies, two of which were put in evidence. The first was by W.L. Marshall, Ph.D., entitled "The Use of Sexually Explicit Stimuli by Rapists, Child Molesters, and Non-offenders," published in the May 1988 *Journal of Sex Research,* Vol. 25, No. 2. This article addresses the "inciting" element of pornography. Dr. Marshall states, at p. 284:

> One very important set of observations of the present study concerns the use of sexually explicit materials by sex offenders as an inciter to commit their illegal behaviors. Slightly more than one third of the child molesters and rapists claim to have at least occasionally been incited to commit an offense by exposure to one or the other type of the sexual materials specified in this study.

[15]It should be noted that the materials used in the study were sexually explicit "hard-core" pornography. Dr. Marshall points this out, at pp. 283–84:

> It is important to recall that the sexually explicit materials of interest in this study refer to what is often called "hard-core" pornography; that is, depictions that are very explicit, showing genital contact, etc. and which leave nothing to the imagination. Also the content of these explicit materials was restricted to either depictions of sex with children or sex between adult men

and women that was either mutually consenting or forced by the man upon the woman. Therefore, the present findings cannot be construed as relevant to any broader issues concerning pornography in general.

[16]The second article referred to by Dr. Collins is entitled "Use of Pornography in the Criminal and Developmental Histories of Sexual Offenders" by D.L. Carter, R.A. Prentky, R.A. Knight, P.L. Vanderveer and R.J. Boucher of the Massachusetts Treatment Centre. The study was published in the *Journal of Interpersonal Violence*, Vol. 2, No. 2, June 1987, p. 196. The purpose of the study was to examine possible differences between rapists and child molesters in exposure to and experience with pornography. The subjects of the study were convicted rapists and child molesters.

[17]The study found that child molesters have a greater exposure to pornography than rapists and use it more often than rapists in association with criminal offences. The study also showed that child molesters use pornography more often than rapists to relieve impulses to commit offences. Under the "Discussion" part of the study, the authors state, at p. 205:

Child molesters, however, indicated significantly more exposure than rapists in adulthood and were more likely both to use such materials prior to and during their offences and to employ pornography to relieve an impulse to commit offenses.

[18]The phenomenon of pornography relieving impulses to commit offences was further addressed, at p. 207:

The "use of sexual materials to relieve an impulse to commit an offense" (item I) was our test of the "catharsis hypothesis," the notion that the use of pornography relieves pent-up sexual tension that might otherwise be directed at an individual. We found support for this hypothesis among child molesters. That is, child molesters report that they were more likely than rapists to employ pornography as a means of relieving an impulse to act out. This finding should not be construed to suggest that pornography functions to inhibit sexual acting out. The use of pornography to relieve an impulse does not preclude its role in intensifying an already active, and in many cases rich, fantasy life. Such intensification is supported by the greater use of pornography prior to offenses by child molesters. *Thus if an individual is prone to act on his fantasies, it is likely that he will do so irrespective of the availability of or exposure to pornography.* [Emphasis added.]

[19]The study used a broad selection of sex materials, from depictions of nude individuals on the one hand, to depictions of persons engaged in explicit sexual acts on the other. The materials included photographs, films, cartoons, magazines and books. Despite the wide range of materials used, the study did not address the

differences in effect of the kinds of pornography (explicit sex or simply nudes) on the persons being studied. However, the article reported on earlier studies which found that "mildly erotic stimuli" inhibited aggression while "highly erotic stimuli" increased aggression. The authors state, at p. 197:

> Earlier studies reported that exposure to pornography inhibited aggression (Baron, 1974: Frodi, 1977). Subsequent studies, however, have found that although mild erotic stimuli inhibited aggression, highly erotic stimuli in fact increased reported aggression in a laboratory setting.

[20] Dr. Collins testified that pedophiles often used pornography as an aid to masturbation. He was asked about the relieving effect versus the inciting effect of pornography. He was unable to say whether the relieving effect or the inciting effect was greater, but noted that a study on the subject is underway at the present time by a Dr. Ronald Langevin.

[21] There was no evidence led of any study demonstrating that "cognitive distortions" cause any significant increase in the danger that pedophiles pose to children. However, as was pointed out in the *Carter et al.* study, a person who is prone to act out his fantasies will likely do so irrespective of the availability of or exposure to pornography. In my view, without reasonable supporting evidence, I should give only minimal weight to the "cognitive distortions" point.

[22] As for written material which counsels or advocates illegal sexual relations with children, there was no evidence to show its harmful effect. However, in my view, it is reasonable to assume that the dissemination of such material does pose some risk of harm to children.

[23] I make the following findings of fact based upon the evidence:

1. Sexually explicit pornography involving children poses a danger to children because of its use by pedophiles in the seduction process.

2. Children are abused in the production of filmed or videotaped pornography.

3. "Highly erotic" pornography incites some pedophiles to commit offences.

4. "Highly erotic" pornography helps some pedophiles relieve pent-up sexual tension.

5. It is not possible to say which of the two foregoing effects is the greater.

6. "Mildly erotic" pornography appears to inhibit aggression.

7. Pornography involving children can be a factor in augmenting or reinforcing a pedophile's cognitive distortions.

8. There is no evidence which demonstrates an increase in harm to children as a result of pornography augmenting or reinforcing a pedophile's cognitive distortions.

9. The dissemination of written material which counsels or advocates sexual offences against children poses some risk of harm to children.

Legal Analysis

[24] Crown counsel concedes that s-s. (4) violates the guarantee of freedom of expression set out in s. 2(*b*) of the *Charter*. I agree with this concession. Crown counsel contends however that s-s. (4) is saved by s. 1 of the *Charter* as being a reasonable limit prescribed by law which is demonstrably justified in a free and democratic society.

[25] Crown counsel does not concede that there has been any violation of s. 2(*a*), s. 2(*d*) or s. 15 of the *Charter*.

[26] Because of the Crown's concession that s-s. (4) violates s. 2(*b*) of the *Charter*, the dispute becomes whether s-s. (4) may be justified under s. 1 of the *Charter*.

[27] Insofar as counsel and I are aware, the constitutionality of s. 163.1 has thus far been addressed in only one other court decision, *Ontario (Attorney General) v. Langer* (1995), 97 C.C.C. (3d) 290, 123 D.L.R. (4th) 289 (Ont. Ct. Gen. Div.)); leave to appeal to S.C.C. refused (1995), 42 C.R. (4th) 410n, 126 D.L.R. (4th) vii. In *Langer*, the court dealt with an application by the Crown to forfeit paintings and sketches seized from an art gallery. The paintings and sketches depicted explicit sexual relations between adults and children. The court held that the depictions had artistic merit and did not pose a realistic risk of harm to children, and ordered that the paintings and sketches be returned to the person from whom they had been seized.

[28] The learned trial judge, McCombs J., dealt with the constitutionality of s. 163.1. In a researched and detailed decision, he held that s. 163.1 violated s. 2(*b*) of the *Charter* but was justified under s. 1.

[29] In dealing with s. 1, McCombs J. addressed the proportionality tests set out in *R. v. Oakes* (1986), 24 C.C.C. (3d) 321, 26 D.L.R. (4th) 200 (S.C.C.). In respect of the "minimal impairment" test, he said, at pp. 325–26:

> This objection ignores the reality that, on the basis of the opinion evidence which I have accepted, private possession of child pornography poses a realistic risk of harm to children, by reinforcing cognitive distortions, fuelling fantasies, and its potential use in "grooming" possible child victims. It is entirely reasonable and within the legitimate objectives of Parliament to criminalize private possession of child pornography.

[30] The final proportionality test addressed by McCombs J. was the weighing of the legislative objectives of s. 163.1 against the effects of the prohibitions. He said, at pp. 327–28:

> The final branch of the proportionality test includes a weighing of the legislative objectives against the effects of the legislation. Even if legislation

otherwise meets s. 1 criteria, a provision will not constitute a reasonable limitation if its effects are so deleterious that they outweigh the importance of its objectives.

The child pornography provisions, designed to protect children, do indeed limit the fundamental freedom of expression. However, in the contextual approach that is required, it is appropriate to bear in mind the type of expression that has been limited. As Dickson C.J.C. observed (*Keegstra*, *supra*, at p. 47):

> "...it is equally destructive of freedom of expression values, as well as the other values which underlie a free and democratic society to treat all expression as equally crucial to those principles at the core of s. 2(*b*)."

The expression inherent in the production of child pornography is not crucial to the principles which lie at the core of freedom of expression. There is no evidence to support the contention that the effects of the legislation are so deleterious that they outweigh the pressing and substantial objective of the legislation.

[31] On my reading of *Langer*, it is evident that the court did not deal with the "weighing of effects" test formulated in *Dagenais v. Canadian Broadcasting Corp.* (1994), 94 C.C.C. (3d) 289, 120 D.L.R. (4th) 12 (S.C.C.). As noted above, the s. 1 analysis in *Langer* ended with the weighing of the legislative objectives against the effects of the legislation. *Dagenais* was not cited, likely because it had only recently been decided and may not have been drawn to the court's attention.

[32] The "weighing of effects" test in *Dagenais* was articulated by Lamer C.J.C., who said, at pp. 324–25:

> While the third step of the *Oakes* proportionality test has often been expressed in terms of the proportionality of the objective to the deleterious effects, this court has recognized that in appropriate cases it is necessary to measure the actual salutary effects of impugned legislation against its deleterious effects, rather than merely considering proportionality of the objective itself. For example, in *Reference re: ss. 193 and 195.1(1)(c) of the Criminal Code (Man.)* (1990), 56 C.C.C. (3d) 65, [1990] 1 S.C.R. 1123, 77 C.R. (3d) 1, Dickson C.J.C. (who characterized the objective of the impugned *Criminal Code* solicitation provisions as the curtailment of the social nuisance caused by the public display of the sale of sex) applied the third step of the proportionality analysis by considering (at p. 76) whether "the obtrusiveness linked to the enforcement of the provision, when weighed against *the resulting decrease in the social nuisance associated with street solicitation,* can be justified in accordance with s. 1." (emphasis added)

and further, at p. 325:

In my view, characterizing the third part of the second branch of the *Oakes* test as being concerned solely with the balance between the objective and the deleterious effects of a measure rests on too narrow a conception of proportionality. I believe that even if an objective is of sufficient importance, the first two elements of the proportionality test are satisfied, and the deleterious effects are proportional to the objectives, it is still possible that, because of a lack of proportionality between the deleterious effects and the salutary effects, a measure will not be reasonable and demonstrably justified in a free and democratic society. I would, therefore, rephrase the third part of the Oakes test as follows: there must be a proportionality between the deleterious effects of the measures which are responsible for limiting the rights or freedoms in question and the objective, *and there must be a proportionality between the deleterious and the salutary effects of the measures.*

[33] In my view, it is appropriate in the present case to consider the proportionality between the deleterious effects and the salutary effects of the prohibition of simple possession of child pornography.

[34] I will now enter upon the weighing process. First, the salutary effects. The prohibition combats practices and phenomena which, at least arguably, put children at risk. These include: the use by some pedophiles of sexually explicit images in the grooming process leading to sexual relations with children; the abuse of children in the making of pornography and the preservation of that abuse in photographs or films; the confirmation or augmentation of cognitive distortions of some pedophiles; the incitement of some pedophiles to commit offences against children; and the advocacy or counselling of the commission of sexual offences against children.

[35] There are factors which go to the weight to be attached to the effectiveness of the prohibitions in combatting the foregoing practices and phenomena. There is no evidence which demonstrates any significant increase of danger to children related to the confirmation or augmentation of cognitive distortions caused by pornography. There is no evidence that "mildly erotic" images are used in the "grooming process." Only assumption supports the proposition that materials that advocate or counsel sexual crimes with children have the effect of increasing the occurrence of such crimes. Sexually explicit pornography is used by some pedophiles to relieve pent-up sexual tension. A person who is prone to act on his fantasies will likely do so irrespective of the availability of pornography. There is no evidence that the production of child pornography will be significantly reduced if simple possession is a made a crime.

[36] I turn now to consider the detrimental effects. I start by repeating s. 2(*b*) of the *Charter*:

2. Everyone has the following fundamental freedoms:

. . . . .

(b) freedom of thought, belief, opinion and expression, including freedom of the press and other media of communication.

[37] Freedom of expression plays an important role in this case. The personal belongings of an individual are an expression of that person's essential self. His or her books, diaries, pictures, clothes and other personal things are intertwined with that person's beliefs, opinions, thoughts and conscience. In *Ford v. Quebec (Attorney General)*, [1988] 2 S.C.R. 712, 54 D.L.R. (4th) 577, dealing with the right of people to use the language of their choice, it was held that "freedom of expression" should be broadly interpreted. The court said, at p. 749:

> It is also the means by which the individual expresses his or her personal identity and sense of individuality. That the concept of "expression" in s. 2(b) of the Canadian *Charter* and s. 3 of the Quebec *Charter* goes beyond mere content is indicated by the specific protection accorded to "freedom of thought, belief [and] opinion" in s. 2 and to "freedom of conscience" and "freedom of opinion" in s. 3. That suggests that "freedom of expression" is intended to extend to more than the content of expression in its narrow sense.

[38] The court included "individual self-fulfilment and personal autonomy" within freedom of expression: (*supra*, at p. 767). The same notion was articulated in *R. v. Keegstra* (1990), 61 C.C.C. (3d) 1 (S.C.C.), by Dickson C.J.C. at p. 49:

> Another component central to the rationale underlying s. 2(b) concerns the vital role of free expression as a means of ensuring individuals the ability to gain self-fulfillment by developing and articulating thoughts and ideas as they see fit.

[39] The proportionality tests under s. 1 of the *Charter* include a consideration of the fundamental values that underlie the *Charter*. In *Keegstra, supra,* Dickson C.J.C. said, at p. 29:

> ... the balancing exercise in s. 1 is not restricted to values expressly set out in the Charter ...

[40] Dickson C.J.C. at p. 29 cited the following passage from *R. v. Oakes, supra,* at p. 346:

> The court must be guided by the values and principles essential to a free and democratic society which I believe embody, to name but a few, respect for the inherent dignity of the human person, commitment to social justice and equality, accommodation of a wide variety of beliefs, respect for cultural and group identity, and faith in social and political institutions which enhance the participation of individuals and groups in society. The underlying values and principles of a free and democratic society are the genesis

of the rights and freedoms guaranteed by the Charter and the ultimate standard against which a limit on a right or freedom must be shown, despite its effect, to be reasonable and demonstrably justified.

[41] What weight will be given to these values will depend upon the particular circumstances. As Dickson C.J.C. said in *Keegstra* at p. 29:

Undoubtedly these values and principles are numerous, covering the guarantees enumerated in the Charter and more. Equally, they may well deserve different emphases, and certainly will assume varying degrees of importance depending upon the circumstances of a particular case.

[42] One significant value underlying the *Charter* is the individual's reasonable expectation of privacy. It is well described in *R. v. Dyment* (1988), 45 C.C.C. (3d) 244, 55 D.L.R. (4th) 503 (S.C.C.), *per* La Forest J., at p. 254:

The foregoing approach is altogether fitting for a constitutional document enshrined at the time when, Westin tells us, society has come to realize that privacy is at the heart of liberty in a modern state: see Alan F. Westin, *Privacy and Freedom* (1970), pp. 349–50. Grounded in man's physical and moral autonomy, privacy is essential for the well-being of the individual. For this reason alone, it is worthy of constitutional protection, but it also has profound significance for the public order. The restraints imposed on government to pry into the lives of the citizen go to the essence of a democratic state.

[43] An important aspect of privacy is an individual's right of privacy in his or her own home. In the present case, the police entered Mr. Sharpe's home pursuant to a search warrant and seized his collection of materials alleged to be pornographic.

[44] The case law on freedom of expression reflects the *Charter*'s concern for the right of privacy. *R. v. Keegstra, supra,* deals with the constitutionality of the *Criminal Code* ban on the wilful promotion of hatred against identifiable groups (s. 319(2)). The prohibition expressly excluded "private conversations" and this exclusion was an important factor in the court (by a 4–3 majority) upholding the legislation. Dickson C.J.C. for the majority said, at p. 56:

In assessing the constitutionality of s. 319(2), especially as concerns arguments of overbreadth and vagueness, an immediate observation is that statements made "in private conversation" are not included in the criminalized expression. The provision thus does not prohibit views expressed with an intention to promote hatred if made privately, indicating Parliament's concern not to intrude upon the privacy of the individual.

[45]*Canada (Human Rights Commission) v. Taylor,* [1990] 3 S.C.R. 892, 75 D.L.R. (4th) 577, deals with a provision of the *Canadian Human Rights Act* which prohibits repeated communication by telephone of any matters likely to expose others to hatred or contempt. The constitutionality of the legislation was upheld by a 4–3 decision. Dickson C.J.C. for the majority dealt with the privacy point, at pp. 936–37:

> I do not disagree with the view that telephone conversations are usually intended to be private; it is surely reasonable for people to expect that these communications will not be intercepted by third persons. Moreover, in determining in *Keegstra* that the criminal prohibition of hate propaganda in s. 319(2) of the *Criminal Code* is not constitutionally overbroad, I relied to an extent upon the fact that private communications were not affected. The connection between s. 2(*b*) and privacy is thus not to be rashly dismissed, and I am open to the view that justifications for abrogating the freedom of expression are less easily envisioned where expressive activity is not intended to be public, in large part because the harms which might arise from the dissemination of meaning are usually minimized when communication takes place in private, but perhaps also *because the freedoms of conscience, thought and belief are particularly engaged in a private setting.* [Emphasis added.]

[46]McLachlin J. for the minority also addressed the question of privacy. She said, at p. 967:

> The benefit obtained from prohibiting private conversations between consenting individuals is arguably small, since only those who are already receptive to such messages are likely to be interested in receiving them. On the other hand, the invasion of privacy may be significant. Without suggesting that prohibition of offensive telephone calls could never be justified, the fact that private communications are banned cannot but enhance the significance of the infringement of the rights of the individual effected by s. 13(1) of the Act.

[47]*R. v. Butler* (1992), 70 C.C.C. (3d) 129, 89 D.L.R. (4th) 449 (S.C.C.), addresses the constitutionality of the obscenity provisions of the *Criminal Code*. The court by a 7–2 majority upheld the obscenity provisions. Writing for the majority, Sopinka J. took account of the fact that the prohibitions did not touch the private use or viewing of obscene materials. He said, at p. 166:

> Fourthly, while the discussion in this appeal has been limited to the definition portion of s. 163, I would note that the impugned section, with the possible exception of s-s. (1) which is not in issue here, has been held by this court not to extend its reach to the private use or viewing of obscene materials.

[48] I will now specify what I consider to be detrimental effects arising from the prohibition of simple possession of child pornography.

[49] First and foremost, the invasion of freedom of expression and personal privacy is profound. Further, the prohibition extends to all persons including those who make no harmful use of pornography. They may be collectors of pornography, whether out of prurient interest or simply out of curiosity, but with no harmful intent. The prohibition also includes pedophiles who, instead of preying on children, use pornography for very private purposes, such as relief from their affliction by masturbation. As noted earlier, sexually explicit pornography is used to relieve pent-up sexual tension of otherwise potential aggressors. Whether or not this cathartic effect outweighs the harm caused by the possession of pornography is not known, but it is nonetheless a significant factor to take into account. The ban includes "mildly erotic" pornography, such as is included in s-s. (1)(a)(ii), although the evidence indicates that "mildly erotic" pornography has the effect of reducing sexual aggression against children. As for materials that counsel or advocate sexual offences against children, there are no doubt collectors who are not affected by such literature, but who are nonetheless subject to criminal sanctions arising from mere possession. A magazine or a newspaper may contain some material said to be pornographic. Although the balance of the publication may be quite within the law, the offending material will make possession of the magazine or newspaper illegal: *R. v. Popert* (1981), 58 C.C.C. (2d) 505 (Ont. C.A.). Purchasers of such publications will have to become their own censors.

[50] I turn then to weigh the salutary effects against the detrimental effects. In my opinion, the detrimental effects substantially outweigh the salutary effects; the intrusion into freedom of expression and the right of privacy is so profound that it is not outweighed by the limited beneficial effects of the prohibition.

[51] As pointed out earlier, an individual's personal belongings are an expression of that person's essential self. Books, diaries, pictures, clothes and other belongings are personal and private expressions of their owner's beliefs, opinions, thoughts and conscience. The simple possession prohibition deals with a very intimate and private aspect of a person's life and, in my view, that fact should be given considerable weight. I find that the limited effectiveness of the prohibition is insufficient to warrant its highly invasive effects.

[52] In arriving at this conclusion, I have taken into account that the *Criminal Code* contains what I consider to be powerful measures to tackle the problem of harm to children arising from pornography. Under s-s. (2) and (3) of s. 163.1, the making, printing, publishing, importing, distribution, selling or possessing of child pornography for the purpose of publication, distribution or sale, are made criminal. These measures aim not only at the sources but also at the means of dissemination of child pornography. In addition, the obscenity provisions under s. 163 provide an element of protection of children. See *R. v. Butler, supra,* p. 151.

[53] In conclusion, I find that s-s. (4) fails the "weighing of effects" proportionality test formulated in *Dagenais* and is therefore not saved under s. 1 of the

Charter. As s-s. (4) is in violation of s. 2(*b*) of the *Charter* and is not justified under s. 1, s-s. (4) must be and is declared void.

[54] Mr. Sharpe also raised s. 2(*a*), s. 2(*d*) and s. 15 of the *Charter.* In light of the conclusion I have reached in respect of s. 2(*b*) and s. 1, I need not address s. 2(*a*), s. 2(*d*) and s. 15.

[55] It follows from the declaration that s-s. (4) is void that Counts 2 and 4, being based upon s-s. (4), must be and are dismissed.

[...]

✗ NO

Opinion in *R. v. Sharpe*
CHIEF JUSTICE BEVERLEY MCLACHLIN

MCLACHLIN C.J.C. (IACOBUCCI, MAJOR, BINNIE, ARBOUR AND LEBEL JJ. CONCURRING):—

I. INTRODUCTION

[1] Is Canada's law banning the possession of child pornography constitutional or, conversely, does it unjustifiably intrude on the constitutional right of Canadians to free expression? That is the central question posed by this appeal.

[2] I conclude that the law is constitutional, except for two peripheral applications relating to expressive material privately created and kept by the accused, for which two exceptions can be read into the legislation. The law otherwise strikes a constitutional balance between freedom of expression and prevention of harm to children. As a consequence, I would uphold the law and remit Mr. Sharpe for trial on all charges.

[3] The respondent, Mr. Sharpe, was charged on a four-count indictment after two seizures of material. The first seizure was made by Canada Customs. It consisted of computer discs containing a text entitled "Sam Paloc's Boyabuse–Flogging, Fun and Fortitude: A Collection of Kiddiekink Classics." Two charges were laid with respect to this material–one for illegal possession under s. 163.1(4) of the *Criminal Code*, R.S.C. 1985, c. C-46, and one for possession for the purposes of distribution or sale under s. 163.1(3) of the *Code*. The second seizure was at Mr. Sharpe's home pursuant to a search warrant the validity of which will be contested at trial. Police officers seized a collection of books, manuscripts, stories and photographs the Crown says constitute child pornography. Again, two charges were laid–one of simple possession and one of possession for the purposes of distribution or sale.

[4] Mr. Sharpe brought a preliminary motion challenging the constitutionality of s. 163.1(4) of the *Criminal Code*. He does not challenge the constitutionality of the offence of possession for the purposes of distribution and sale, which will go to trial regardless of how this appeal is resolved. Mr. Sharpe contends that the prohibition of possession, without more, violates the guarantee of freedom of expression in s. 2(*b*) of the *Canadian Charter of Rights and Freedoms*. The trial judge ruled that the prohibition was unconstitutional, as did the majority of the British Columbia Court of Appeal. The Crown appeals that order to this Court.

[5] The Crown concedes that s. 163.1(4)'s prohibition on the possession of child pornography infringes the guarantee of freedom of expression in s. 2(*b*) of the *Charter*. The issue is whether this limitation of freedom of expression is justifiable

under s. 1 of the *Charter,* given the harm possession of child pornography can cause to children. Mr. Sharpe accepts that harm to children justifies criminalizing possession of some forms of child pornography. The fundamental question therefore is whether s. 163.1(4) of the *Criminal Code* goes too far and criminalizes possession of an unjustifiable range of material.

[...]

V. ANALYSIS

A. The Values at Stake

[21] Among the most fundamental rights possessed by Canadians is freedom of expression. It makes possible our liberty, our creativity and our democracy. It does this by protecting not only "good" and popular expression, but also unpopular or even offensive expression. The right to freedom of expression rests on the conviction that the best route to truth, individual flourishing and peaceful coexistence in a heterogeneous society in which people hold divergent and conflicting beliefs lies in the free flow of ideas and images. If we do not like an idea or an image, we are free to argue against it or simply turn away. But, absent some constitutionally adequate justification, we cannot forbid a person from expressing it.

[22] Nevertheless, freedom of expression is not absolute. Our Constitution recognizes that Parliament or a provincial legislature can sometimes limit some forms of expression. Overarching considerations, like the prevention of hate that divides society as in *Keegstra, supra,* or the prevention of harm that threatens vulnerable members of our society as in *Butler, supra,* may justify prohibitions on some kinds of expression in some circumstances. Because of the importance of the guarantee of free expression, however, any attempt to restrict the right must be subjected to the most careful scrutiny.

[23] The values underlying the right to free expression include individual self-fulfilment, finding the truth through the open exchange of ideas and the political discourse fundamental to democracy: *Irwin Toy Ltd. v. Quebec (Attorney General),* [1989] 1 S.C.R. 927 at p. 976, 58 D.L.R. (4th) 577; *Ford v. Quebec (Attorney General),* [1988] 2 S.C.R. 712 at p. 765, 54 D.L.R. (4th) 577. While some types of expression, like political expression, lie closer to the core of the guarantee than others, all are vital to a free and democratic society. As stated in *Irwin Toy, supra,* at p. 968, the guarantee "ensure[s] that everyone can manifest their thoughts, opinions, beliefs, indeed all expressions of the heart and mind, however unpopular, distasteful or contrary to the mainstream. Such protection," the Court continued, "is ... 'fundamental' because in a free, pluralistic and democratic society we prize a diversity of ideas and opinions for their inherent value both to the community and to the individual." As stated by Cardozo J. in *Palko v. Connecticut,* 302 U.S. 319 (1937), free expression is "the matrix, the indispensable condition, of nearly every other form of freedom" (p. 327).

[24]The law challenged in this appeal engages mainly the justification of self-fulfilment. Child pornography does not generally contribute to the search for truth or to Canadian social and political discourse. Some question whether it engages even the value of self-fulfilment, beyond the base aspect of sexual exploitation. The concern in this appeal, however, is that the law may incidentally catch forms of expression that more seriously implicate self-fulfilment and that do not pose a risk of harm to children.

[25]As to the contention that prohibiting *possession* of expressive material does not raise free expression concerns, I cannot agree. The right conferred by s. 2(*b*) of the *Charter* embraces a continuum of intellectual and expressive freedom— "freedom of thought, belief, opinion and expression." The right to possess expressive material is integrally related to the development of thought, belief, opinion and expression. The possession of such material allows us to understand the thought of others or consolidate our own thought. Without the right to possess expressive material, freedom of thought, belief, opinion and expression would be compromised. Thus the possession of expressive materials falls within the continuum of rights protected by s. 2(*b*) of the *Charter*.

[26]The private nature of the proscribed material may heighten the seriousness of a limit on free expression. Privacy, while not expressly protected by the *Charter*, is an important value underlying the s. 8 guarantees against unreasonable search and seizure and the s. 7 liberty guarantee: see *Hunter v. Southam Inc.*, [1984] 2 S.C.R. 145, 11 D.L.R. (4th) 641, 14 C.C.C. (3d) 97; *R. v. Mills*, [1999] 3 S.C.R. 668, 180 D.L.R. (4th) 1, 139 C.C.C. (3d) 321. Indeed, as freedom from state intrusion and conformist social pressures is integral to individual flourishing and diversity, this Court has observed that "privacy is at the heart of liberty in a modern state": *R. v. Dyment*, [1988] 2 S.C.R. 417 at p. 427, 55 D.L.R. (4th) 503, 45 C.C.C. (3d) 244; see also *R. v. Edwards*, [1996] 1 S.C.R. 128, 132 D.L.R. (4th) 31, 104 C.C.C. (3d) 136, at para. 50. Privacy may also enhance freedom of expression claims under s. 2(*b*) of the *Charter*, for example in the case of hate literature: *Keegstra, supra*, at pp. 772–73; *Taylor, supra*, at pp. 936–37. The enhancement in the case of hate literature occurs in part because private material may do less harm than public, and in part because the freedoms of conscience, thought and belief are particularly engaged in the private setting: *Taylor, supra*. However, the private nature of much child pornography cuts two ways. It engages the fundamental right to freedom of thought. But at the same time, the clandestine nature of incitement, attitudinal change, grooming and seduction associated with child pornography contributes to the harm it may cause children, rather than reduces it.

[27]In summary, prohibiting the possession of child pornography restricts the rights protected by s. 2(*b*) and the s. 7 liberty guarantee. While the prurient nature of most of the materials defined as "child pornography" may attenuate its constitutional worth, it does not negate it, since the guarantee of free expression extends even to offensive speech.

[28] This brings us to the countervailing interest at stake in this appeal: society's interest in protecting children from the evils associated with the possession of child pornography. Just as no one denies the importance of free expression, so no one denies that child pornography involves the exploitation of children. The links between *possession* of child pornography and harm to children are arguably more attenuated than are the links between the manufacture and distribution of child pornography and harm to children. However, possession of child pornography contributes to the market for child pornography, a market which in turn drives production involving the exploitation of children. Possession of child pornography may facilitate the seduction and grooming of victims and may break down inhibitions or incite potential offences. Some of these links are disputed and must be considered in greater detail in the course of the s. 1 justification analysis. The point at this stage is simply to describe the concerns that, according to the government, justify limiting free expression by banning the possession of child pornography.

[29] These then are the values at stake in this appeal. On the one hand stands the right of free expression—a right fundamental to the liberty of each Canadian and our democratic society. On the other stands the conviction that the possession of child pornography must be forbidden to prevent harm to children.

[...]

C. Is the Limitation on Free Expression Imposed by Section 163.1(4) Justified Under Section 1 of the Charter?

[78] Crown counsel has conceded that criminalizing possession of child pornography limits the right of free expression. The question we must answer is whether that limitation is reasonable and demonstrably justified in a free and democratic society. To justify the intrusion on free expression, the government must demonstrate, through evidence supplemented by common sense and inferential reasoning, that the law meets the test set out in *R. v. Oakes,* [1986] 1 S.C.R. 103, 26 D.L.R. (4th) 200, 24 C.C.C. (3d) 321; and refined in *Dagenais v. Canadian Broadcasting Corp.,* [1994] 3 S.C.R. 835, 120 D.L.R. (4th) 12, 94 C.C.C. (3d) 289; and *Thomson Newspapers Co. v. Canada (Attorney General),* [1998] 1 S.C.R. 877, 159 D.L.R. (4th) 385. The goal must be pressing and substantial, and the law enacted to achieve that goal must be proportionate in the sense of furthering the goal, being carefully tailored to avoid excessive impairment of the right, and productive of benefits that outweigh the detriment to freedom of expression.

[79] Before we turn to these issues, we must consider the argument that prohibitions on private possession of child pornography can never be justified. Such laws, Southin J.A. asserted, constitute "the hallmark of tyranny" (para. 95). They represent such a fundamental intrusion on basic liberties that they can never be justified in a free and democratic society.

[80] Section 1 of the *Charter* belies the suggestion that any *Charter* right is so absolute that limits on it can never be justified. The argument posits that some rights are so basic that they can never be limited as a matter of principle, precluding

any evaluation under s. 1. This is both undesirable and unnecessary. It is undesirable because it raises the risk that laws that can be justified may be struck down on the basis of how they are characterized. It is unnecessary because s. 1 provides a basis for fair evaluation that upholds only those laws that do not unjustifiably erode basic liberties.

[81]I conclude that the argument that limitations on possession of child pornography can never be justified as a matter of principle must be dismissed. We must conduct a detailed analysis of whether the law's intrusion on freedom of speech can be justified under s. 1 of the *Charter*.

1. Is the Legislative Objective Pressing and Substantial?

[82]I earlier concluded that Parliament's objective in passing s. 163.1(4) was to criminalize possession of child pornography that poses a reasoned risk of harm to children. This objective is pressing and substantial. Over and above the specific objectives of the law in reducing the direct exploitation of children, the law in a larger attitudinal sense asserts the value of children as a defence against the erosion of societal attitudes toward them. While the government in this case did not present attitudinal harm to society at large as a justification for the law's intrusion on the right of free expression, this may be seen as a good incidental to the law's main purpose—the prevention of harm to children.

2. Is There Proportionality Between the Limitation on the Right and the Benefits of the Law?

[83]Parliament can prohibit possession of child pornography. The issue in this case is whether it has done so in a reasonable and proportionate manner having regard to the right of free expression.

(a) Rational Connection

[84]As the first step in showing proportionality, the Crown must demonstrate that the law is likely to confer a benefit or is "rationally connected" to Parliament's goal. This means that it must show that possession of child pornography, as opposed to its manufacture, distribution or use, causes harm to children.

[85]This raises a question pivotal to this appeal: what standard of proof must the Crown achieve in demonstrating harm—scientific proof based on concrete evidence or a reasoned apprehension of harm? The trial judge insisted on scientific proof based on concrete evidence. With respect, this sets the bar too high. In *Butler, supra*, considering the obscenity prohibition of the *Criminal Code*, this Court rejected the need for concrete evidence and held that a "reasoned apprehension of harm" sufficed (at p. 504). A similar standard must be employed in this case.

[86]The Crown argues that prohibiting possession of child pornography is linked to reducing the sexual abuse of children in five ways: (1) child pornography promotes cognitive distortions; (2) it fuels fantasies that incite offenders; (3) prohibiting its possession assists law enforcement efforts to reduce the production,

distribution and use that result in direct harm to children; (4) it is used for grooming and seducing victims; and (5) some child pornography is produced using real children.

[87] The first alleged harm concerns cognitive distortions. The Crown argues that child pornography may change possessors' attitudes in ways that make them more likely to sexually abuse children. People may come to see sexual relations with children as normal and even beneficial. Moral inhibitions may be weakened. People who would not otherwise abuse children may consequently do so. Banning the possession of child pornography, asserts the Crown, will reduce these cognitive distortions.

[88] The trial judge discounted this harm due to the limited scientific evidence linking cognitive distortions to increased rates of offending. Applying the reasoned apprehension of harm test yields a different conclusion. While the scientific evidence is not strong, I am satisfied that the evidence in this case supports the existence of a connection here: exposure to child pornography may reduce paedophiles' defences and inhibitions against sexual abuse of children. Banalizing the awful and numbing the conscience, exposure to child pornography may make the abnormal seem normal and the immoral seem acceptable.

[89] The second alleged harm is that possession of child pornography fuels fantasies, making pedophiles more likely to offend. The trial judge found that studies showed a link between highly erotic child pornography and offences. However, other studies suggested that both erotic and milder pornography might provide substitute satisfaction and reduce offences. Putting the studies together, the trial judge concluded that he could not say that the net effect was to increase harm to children (at para. 23). Absent evidence as to whether the benefit from sublimation equals the harm of incitement or otherwise, this conclusion seems tenuous. More fundamentally, the trial judge proceeded on the basis that scientific proof was required. The lack of unanimity in scientific opinion is not fatal. Complex human behaviour may not lend itself to precise scientific demonstration, and the courts cannot hold Parliament to a higher standard of proof than the subject matter admits of. Some studies suggest that child pornography, like other forms of pornography, will fuel fantasies and may incite offences in the case of certain individuals. This reasoned apprehension of harm demonstrates a rational connection between the law and the reduction of harm to children through child pornography.

[90] The third alleged harm—that criminalizing the possession of child pornography aids in prosecuting the distribution and use of child pornography—was not expressly considered by the trial judge. Detective Waters testified that as a result of possession charges, the police have been able to uncover persons involved in producing and distributing child pornography. The Criminal Lawyers' Association argues that it is dangerous to justify violations of rights on the sole basis that they will assist in the detection and prosecution of other criminal offences. Such reasoning, it argues, could be used to justify many other violations of fundamental

rights. Given the evidence linking possession with harm to children on other grounds, it is not necessary to resolve the question of whether an offence abridging a *Charter* right can ever be justified *solely* on the basis that it assists in prosecuting other offences. It is sufficient to note that the fact the offence of possession aids prosecution of those who produce and distribute child pornography is a positive side-effect of the law.

[91] The trial judge was satisfied that the evidence relating to the fourth alleged harm, the use of child pornography to "groom" or seduce victims, showed a rational connection. The evidence is clear and uncontradicted. "Sexually explicit pornography involving children poses a danger to children because of its use by pedophiles in the seduction process" (para. 23). The ability to possess child pornography makes it available for the grooming and seduction of children by the possessor and others. Mr. Sharpe does not deny that some child pornography can play an important role in the seduction of children. Criminalizing the possession of child pornography is likely to help reduce the grooming and seduction of children.

[92] The fifth and final harm—the abuse of children in the production of pornography—is equally conclusive. Children are used and abused in the making of much of the child pornography caught by the law. Production of child pornography is fueled by the market for it, and the market in turn is fueled by those who seek to possess it. Criminalizing possession may reduce the market for child pornography and the abuse of children it often involves. The link between the production of child pornography and harm to children is very strong. The abuse is broad in extent and devastating in impact. The child is traumatized by being used as a sexual object in the course of making the pornography. The child may be sexually abused and degraded. The trauma and violation of dignity may stay with the child as long as he or she lives. Not infrequently, it initiates a downward spiral into the sex trade. Even when it does not, the child must live in the years that follow with the knowledge that the degrading photo or film may still exist, and may at any moment be being watched and enjoyed by someone.

[93] It is argued that even if possession of child pornography is linked to harm to children, that harm is fully addressed by laws against the production and distribution of child pornography. Criminalizing mere possession, according to this argument, adds greatly to the limitation on free expression but adds little benefit in terms of harm prevention. The key consideration is what the impugned section seeks to achieve beyond what is already accomplished by other legislation: *R. v. Martineau*, [1990] 2 S.C.R. 633, 58 C.C.C. (3d) 353. If other laws already achieve the goals, new laws limiting constitutional rights are unjustifiable. However, an effective measure should not be discounted simply because Parliament already has other measures in place. It may provide additional protection or reinforce existing protections. Parliament may combat an evil by enacting a number of different and complementary measures directed to different aspects of the targeted problem: see, e.g., *R. v. Whyte*, [1988] 2 S.C.R. 3, 51 D.L.R. (4th) 481, 42 C.C.C. (3d) 97. Here the

evidence amply establishes that criminalizing the possession of child pornography not only provides additional protection against child exploitation—exploitation associated with the production of child pornography for the market generated by possession and the availability of material for arousal, attitudinal change and grooming—but also reinforces the laws criminalizing the production and distribution of child pornography.

[94]I conclude that the social science evidence adduced in this case, buttressed by experience and common sense, amply meets the *Oakes* requirement of a rational connection between the purpose of the law and the means adopted to effect this purpose. Possession of child pornography increases the risk of child abuse. It introduces risk, moreover, that cannot be entirely targeted by laws prohibiting the manufacture, publication and distribution of child pornography. Laws against publication and distribution of child pornography cannot catch the private viewing of child pornography, yet private viewing may induce attitudes and arousals that increase the risk of offence. Nor do such laws catch the use of pornography to groom and seduce children. Only by extending the law to private possession can these harms be squarely attacked.

(b) Minimal Impairment

[95]This brings us to a critical question in this case: does the law impair the right of free expression only minimally? If the law is drafted in a way that unnecessarily catches material that has little or nothing to do with the prevention of harm to children, then the justification for overriding freedom of expression is absent. Section 163.1(4), as a criminal offence, carries the heavy consequences of prosecution, conviction and loss of liberty, and must therefore be carefully tailored as a "measured and appropriate response" to the harms it addresses: *Keegstra, supra,* at p. 771. At the same time, legislative drafting is a difficult art and Parliament cannot be held to a standard of perfection: *R. v. Edwards Books and Art Ltd.,* [1986] 2 S.C.R. 713, 35 D.L.R. (4th) 1, 30 C.C.C. (3d) 385; *Irwin Toy Ltd., supra; R. v. Chaulk,* [1990] 3 S.C.R. 1303, 62 C.C.C. (3d) 193. It may be difficult to draft a law capable of catching the bulk of pornographic material that puts children at risk, without also catching some types of material that are unrelated to harm to children. This is what McEachern C.J.B.C. had in mind when he suggested that it is difficult to see how Parliament could have drafted the law in a way that eliminated the possibility of "unintended consequences" (para. 292).

[96]This Court has held that to establish justification it is not necessary to show that Parliament has adopted the least restrictive means of achieving its end. It suffices if the means adopted fall within a range of reasonable solutions to the problem confronted. The law must be *reasonably* tailored to its objectives; it must impair the right no more than *reasonably* necessary, having regard to the practical difficulties and conflicting tensions that must be taken into account: see *Edwards Books and Art Ltd., supra; Chaulk, supra; Committee for the Commonwealth of Canada*

v. Canada, [1991] 1 S.C.R. 139, 77 D.L.R. (4th) 385; *Butler, supra; RJR-MacDonald Inc. v. Canada (Attorney General),* [1995] 3 S.C.R. 199, 127 D.L.R. (4th) 1, 100 C.C.C. (3d) 449; *M. v. H.,* [1999] 2 S.C.R. 3, 171 D.L.R. (4th) 577.

[97]This approach to minimal impairment is confirmed by the existence of the third branch of the proportionality test, requiring that the impairment of the right be proportionate to the benefit in terms of achieving Parliament's goal. If the only question were whether the impugned law limits the right as little as possible, there would be little need for the third stage of weighing the costs resulting from the infringement of the right against the benefits gained in terms of achieving Parliament's goal. It was argued after *Oakes, supra,* that anything short of absolutely minimal impairment was fatal. This Court has rejected that notion. The language of the third branch of the *Oakes* test is consistent with a more nuanced approach to the minimal impairment inquiry—one that takes into account the difficulty of drafting laws that accomplish Parliament's goals, achieve certainty and only minimally intrude on rights. At its heart, s. 1 is a matter of balancing: see *Dagenais, supra; RJR-MacDonald, supra; Ross v. New Brunswick School District No. 15,* [1996] 1 S.C.R. 825, 133 D.L.R. (4th) 1; *Thomson Newspapers, supra.*

[98]Against this background, I turn to the legislation here at issue. Mr. Sharpe argues that s. 163.1(4) fails the minimal impairment test because the legal definition of "child pornography" includes material posing no reasoned risk of harm to children. However, as discussed earlier, properly interpreted, the law catches much less material unrelated to harm to children than Mr. Sharpe suggests. Depictions of kissing, hugging and other activity short of "explicit" sexual activity, works of art even of limited technical value, and family photos of naked children absent proof of a dominant sexual purpose, all fall outside the scope of the law. Many of the other hypothetical examples relied on in the courts below as suggesting overbreadth either disappear entirely on a proper construction of the statutory definition of "child pornography," or are narrowed to the extent that material is caught only where it is related to harm to children. If these were the only grounds for concern arising from s. 163.1(4), I would have little difficulty concluding the provision is carefully tailored to its objective. It should also be remembered that to effect a conviction under s. 163.1(4), as under any other criminal provision, the Crown must establish that the accused possessed the requisite *mens rea;* this requirement, too, limits the reach of the statute.

[99]The fact remains, however, that the law may also capture the possession of material that one would not normally think of as "child pornography" and that raises little or no risk of harm to children: (1) written materials or visual representations created and held by the accused alone, exclusively for personal use; and (2) visual recordings, created by or depicting the accused, that do not depict unlawful sexual activity and are held by the accused exclusively for private use.

[100] Possession of material in these categories is less closely tied to harm to children than the vast majority of material caught by the law. Children are not

exploited in its production. The self-created nature of the material comprising the first category undermines the possibility that it could produce negative attitudinal changes. In the second category, those depicted may well not even look like children. This said, some material in these categories could conceivably cause harm to children. Self-created private expressive materials could conceivably abet negative attitudinal changes in the creator, although since the creation came from him or her in the first place one would not expect the effect to be significant. A self-created private depiction or writing in the possession of the maker could fall into the hands of someone who might use it in a way that harms children. Again, a person's video or photo of him- or herself engaged in a lawful sexual act could present an image that looks like a child, which could possibly come into the hands of someone who would use it to harm children. So it cannot be denied that permitting the author of such materials to keep them in his or her custody poses some risk. However, the risk is small, incidental and more tenuous than that associated with the vast majority of material targeted by s. 163.1(4). Indeed, the above-cited examples lie at the edge of the problematic classes of material. The bulk of the material in these two problematic classes, while engaging important values underlying the s. 2(b) guarantee, poses no reasoned risk of harm to children.

[101] The government's argument on this point is, in effect, that it is necessary to prohibit possession of a large amount of harmless expressive material in order to combat the small risk that some material in this class may cause harm to children. This suggests that the law may be overbroad. However, final determination of this issue requires us to proceed to the third prong of the proportionality test—the weighing of the costs of the law to freedom of expression against the benefits it confers.

(c) Proportionality: the Final Balance

[102] This brings us to the third and final branch of the proportionality inquiry: whether the benefits the law may achieve in preventing harm to children outweigh the detrimental effects of the law on the right of free expression. The final proportionality assessment takes all the elements identified and measured under the heads of Parliament's objective, rational connection and minimal impairment, and balances them to determine whether the state has proven on a balance of probabilities that its restriction on a fundamental *Charter* right is demonstrably justifiable in a free and democratic society.

[103] In the vast majority of the law's applications, the costs it imposes on freedom of expression are outweighed by the risk of harm to children. The Crown has met the burden of demonstrating that the possession of child pornography poses a reasoned apprehension of harm to children and that the goal of preventing such harm is pressing and substantial. Explicit sexual photographs and videotapes of children may promote cognitive distortions, fuel fantasies that incite offenders, enable grooming of victims, and may be produced using real children. Written material that advocates or counsels sexual offences with children

can pose many of the same risks. Although we recently held in *Little Sisters Book and Art Emporium v. Canada (Minister of Justice),* 2000 SCC 69, 193 D.L.R. (4th) 193, 150 C.C.C. (3d) 1, that it may be difficult to make the case of obscenity against written texts, materials that advocate or counsel sexual offences with children may qualify. The Crown has also met the burden of showing that the law will benefit society by reducing the possibility of cognitive distortions, the use of pornography in grooming victims and the abuse of children in the manufacture and continuing existence of this material. Explicit sexual photographs of children, videotapes of pre-pubescent children and written works advocating sexual offences with children—all these and more pose a reasoned risk of harm to children. Thus we may conclude that in its main impact, s. 163.1(4) is proportionate and constitutional.

[...]

POSTSCRIPT

For Justice Duncan Shaw, the key to deciding this case was the weighing of the salutary and deleterious effects of the prohibition on the possession of child pornography. The justice recognized the possible benefits of the prohibition. It could, as he writes, "combat practices and phenomena which, at least arguably, put children at risk." But he was unconvinced that the prohibition did much to affect the risk—the supporting evidence for such a belief was not strong. Alternatively, the prohibition had a clear—and unwanted—effect on one's privacy; and Shaw believed privacy to be an element of freedom of expression. For Chief Justice Beverley McLachlin, the standard of proof that Shaw used for the effect of pornography on children was too rigorous. The courts, she said, require only "reasoned apprehension of harm," not hard scientific evidence, and with this different standard one could see more clearly the deleterious effects of the possession of child pornography.

In some respects, Shaw's decision—as McLachlin herself admitted—was a "courageous" one. Shaw felt that the right of privacy was imperilled by such provisions as the ones dealing with possession of child pornography. But children are precious to any society and, more important, are often defenceless. Typically, the standard of proof in any situation, legal or otherwise, should be high because the stakes are usually high. But it might be necessary to adjust this position when it comes to children and the delicate question of child pornography. Also, legal precedent, which judges are obliged to consider, does seem to require a less rigorous standard. As for McLachlin's decision, it seems at first a paragon of common sense. But unlike Shaw, she appears to struggle little with the issues in this case. It is not as open and shut as she thinks. The fact that she found exceptions to the law also reveals that she, too, may have had doubts about the law.

The *R. v. Sharpe* case requires an appreciation of the history and provisions of the Canadian Charter of Rights and Freedoms. Any course text in Canadian political science will provide you with this (for example, Rand Dyck, *Canadian Politics: Critical Approaches,* 4th ed. [Scarborough: Thomson Nelson, 2004]). The next step is to consult Peter W. Hogg's *Constitutional Law of Canada: 2004 Student Edition* (Toronto: Carswell, 2004) or the loose-leaf version. This text provides an overview of the Charter and discusses rules of interpretation in relation to how judges make sense of Charter sections (chapter 33). Hogg also supplies a readable discussion of much of the relevant case law dealing with freedom of expression, pornography, and the *R. v. Sharpe* decision. For other legal commentaries on the case and child pornography, students might read Robert Martin, "Case Comment: *R. v. Sharpe,*" *Alberta Law Review* 39 (September 2001); Robert Ivan Martin, *The Most Dangerous Branch: How the Supreme Court of Canada Has Undermined Our Law and Our Democracy* (Montreal & Kingston: McGill-Queen's University Press, 2003); and Bruce Ryder, "The Harms of Child Pornography Law," *University of British*

Columbia Law Review 36, no. 1 (2003). Articles on the decisions by the lower courts in *R. v. Sharpe* are also available (recall that two B.C. courts offered decisions in the case): A. Wayne McKay, "*R. v. Sharpe:* Pornography, Privacy, Proportionality, and the Protection of Children," *National Journal of Constitutional Law* 12; Hamish Stewart, "A Judicious Response to Overbreadth: *R. v. Sharpe,*" *Criminal Law Quarterly* 43, no. 2 (March 2000); June Ross, "*R. v. Sharpe* and Private Possession of Child Pornography," *Constitutional Forum* 11 (Winter 2000); and Jack Watson, "*R. v. Sharpe,*" *National Journal of Constitutional Law* 10 (June 1999).

Like all major Supreme Court decisions, the *R. v. Sharpe* finding caused many to wonder about how judges actually make decisions and about the wisdom of allowing appointed officials to decide on what appear to be political and moral issues. For a discussion of how judicial interpretation attempts to fit into the workings of democracies, students might consult the following: Christopher P. Manfredi, *Judicial Power and the Charter: Canada and the Paradox of Liberal Constitutionalism,* 2nd ed. (Toronto: Oxford University Press, 2001); F.L. Morton and Rainer Knopff, *The Charter Revolution and the Court Party* (Peterborough: Broadview Press, 2000); Paul Howe and Peter H. Russell, eds., *Judicial Power and Canadian Democracy* (Montreal and Kingston: McGill-Queen's University Press, 2001); Janet Hiebert, *Charter Conflicts: What Is Parliament's Role?* (Montreal and Kingston: McGill-Queen's University Press, 2002); Patrick James, Donald E. Abelson, and Michael Lusztig, eds., *The Myth of the Sacred: The Charter, the Courts, and the Politics of the Constitution in Canada* (Montreal and Kingston: McGill-Queen's University Press, 2002); Kent Roach, *The Supreme on Trial: Judicial Activism or Democratic Dialogue* (Toronto: Irwin Law, 2001); and Robert Ivan Martin, *The Most Dangerous Branch: How the Supreme Court of Canada Has Undermined Our Law and Our Democracy* (Montreal and Kingston: McGill-Queen's University Press, 2003).

Finally, the federal government, as mentioned in the introduction, is now attempting to amend the Criminal Code in light of the decision and other concerns about child pornography. The Library of Parliament has published a discussion document outlining the government's legislative efforts in this area up to this point. The document, which is available on the website of the Parliament of Canada, is entitled *Bill C-2: An Act to Amend the Criminal Code (Protection of Children and Other Vulnerable Persons) and the Canada Evidence Act.*

Is the Clarity Act Good for Canada?

✔ **YES**
PATRICK J. MONAHAN, "Doing the Rules: An Assessment of the Federal *Clarity Act* in Light of the *Quebec Secession Reference*," in *C.D. Howe Institute Commentary* 135 (February 2000)

✗ **NO**
CLAUDE RYAN, "Consequences of the Quebec *Secession Reference*: The Clarity Bill and Beyond," in *C.D. Howe Institute Commentary* 139 (April 2000)

CLARITY ACT 2000, C. 26

The possibility of the secession of Quebec raises a number of difficult questions. Some of these questions relate to the fate of Canada without Quebec, and others to efforts that might serve to douse secessionist fires in Quebec. Both sets of questions appear to assume that Quebec does indeed have the legal right to secede from Canada, but until recently this assumption had not been tested. In August 1998, the Supreme Court of Canada addressed this issue. It ruled that Quebec could not *unilaterally* secede from Canada. But it also ruled that the rest of Canada was obligated to negotiate terms of secession with Quebec if a *clear* majority of Quebecers indicated their wish to leave Canada on a *clear* referendum question.

The decision of the Supreme Court resolved the basic legal issue—secession only under certain conditions—but in so doing it introduced some new uncertainties. The court, for instance, failed to specify the meaning of a "clear majority." Did this mean that support for secession had to be greater than a mere 50 percent plus one? It did seem to suggest this, but the actual percentage required was unclear. There was also uncertainty about the meaning of a "clear question" and about the nature of secession negotiations. The federal government, for one, felt that the Supreme Court decision demanded legislation that might help resolve some of these new uncertainties. In December 1999, the federal government introduced the Clarity Act. On the matter of a clear question, the legislation stipulated that it would be up to the House of Commons to determine if the question allowed for "a clear expression of the will of the population." If the question failed to accomplish this aim, then no negotiations could commence. On the matter of a clear majority, again the House of Commons would play a major part, for it would have to determine whether the vote amounted to "a clear expression of a will by a clear majority." In so doing, it would have to consider among other things the percentage of eligible voters who took part in the referendum and the size of the actual majority in the vote. Lastly, the bill noted that a constitutional amendment would have to accompany the secession of any province. It also said that negotiations leading to the amendment and secession would involve "at least the governments of all of the provinces and the Government of Canada" and that a number of matters would have to be considered in the negotiations.

The introduction of the federal Clarity Act generated a great deal of debate and discussion—much of it acrimonious. Quebec's minister of Intergovernmental Affairs claimed that the act gave the federal government the authority to decide Quebec's fate. He said that the House of Commons—and not residents of Quebec—now determined the referendum question and how much support was required. The act also gave the federal government or any province a veto over secession. The minister's counterpart at the federal level disagreed with this assessment, saying that the act represented a "reasonable" attempt to deal with the intricacies of secession in Canada. As for the participation of the House of Commons in the secession process, he said that the federal legislature could not possibly walk away from its responsibility to represent all Canadians in such an important process. Others also saw the reasonableness of the act, but thought the act might have been more specific on the key terms. Still others thought the act unnecessary (it did not really go beyond the Supreme Court decision) and served only to provoke Quebec and further divide the country.

The federal government introduced the bill in December 1999, and witnessed its passage in the House of Commons only a few months later. Clearly, the federal government and supporters of the government on this issue were confident of their position. Immediately after the referendum of 1995, Ottawa had promised a new federalism that would strive to meet the demands of Quebec. This was the "Plan A" approach, one that adopted a conciliatory tone toward Quebec. But a new plan, "Plan B," had evolved in the meantime—a much tougher stance—and a major element of this new plan was the Clarity Act. The question was whether this new course was the right course or one that would bring Quebec ever closer to secession from the rest of Canada.

In the years following the passage of the Clarity Act, the push for a sovereign Quebec has weakened. The Liberal Party of Quebec, and not the Parti Québécois, now governs Quebec, and most polls show that Quebecers seem to have lost their taste for a separate Quebec. Some see this as evidence that the Clarity Act has had the right effect, that it has helped slay the separatist dragon and made Canada more united. Others are not so sure and point to the almost cyclical nature of separatist support. Recently, there has also been talk of another constitutional crisis because of the inability of the country to elect a national government that has a strong presence in Quebec. Moreover, the most up-to-date polls suggest a resurgence in support for separatism in Quebec—largely a result of revelations concerning corruption in the operation of a federal program designed to weaken the separatist threat in Quebec. And just to make things really interesting, some now worry that the Clarity Act provides the kind of certainty that facilitates a vote *in favour* of separation. The Clarity Act, it seems, is still relevant.

In the readings, Patrick J. Monahan, a professor of constitutional law at Osgoode Hall Law School, argues that the Clarity Act represents a sound piece of legislation. The late Claude Ryan, former premier of Quebec and respected commentator on Quebec, contends that the legislation was unwise. Both readings address the act before it became law, although the final version differs very little from the one that Monahan and Ryan consider. A copy of the Clarity Act is also provided.

✔ **YES**

Doing the Rules: An Assessment of the Federal *Clarity Act* in Light of the *Quebec Secession Reference*
PATRICK J. MONAHAN

THE CONTENT OF THE ACT

The *Clarity Act* consists of a mere three sections. Section 1 deals with the Supreme Court's requirement of a clear question, section 2 with the requirement of a clear majority, and section 3 with certain aspects of the secession negotiations. The preamble to the bill states that its purpose is merely to clarify the circumstances under which the government of Canada would enter into secession negotiations and that it does not restrict the right of a provincial government to consult its population through a referendum on a question of the province's own choosing.

With respect to a clear question, the bill states that, within 30 days of a provincial government's officially releasing a referendum question on secession, the House of Commons would be asked to express its opinion, through a resolution, as to whether the question is clear. Section 1(3) sets out the standard that must be met in this regard:

> In considering the clarity of a referendum question, the House of Commons shall consider whether the question would result in a clear expression of the will of the population of a province on whether the province should cease to be a part of Canada and become an independent state.

This formulation seems almost a direct quotation from the relevant Supreme Court passages on this issue.

Section 1(5) requires that the House of Commons, in judging the wording of the question, take into account the views of other political actors, including the opposition parties in the legislative assembly of the province whose government is proposing secession. The mandatory nature of this requirement suggests that, if the opposition in the Quebec National Assembly refused to endorse a question as clear, the House of Commons would have difficulty coming to a different opinion. This innovation is important and constructive for the reasons discussed earlier in this *Commentary*. The federal government is prohibited from entering into negotiations on secession if the House of Commons determines that a referendum question is not clear.

In my view, the only controversial aspect of the legislation's treatment of the clear question issue relates to section 1(4), which seeks to deem certain questions unclear. It provides:

For the purpose of subsection (3), a clear expression of the will of the population of a province that the province cease to be part of Canada could not result from

    (a) a referendum question that merely focuses on a mandate to negotiate without soliciting a direct expression of the will of the population of that province on whether the province should cease to be part of Canada; or

    (b) a referendum question that envisages other possibilities in addition to the secession of the province from Canada, such as economic or political arrangements with Canada, that obscure a direct expression of the will of the population of that province on whether the province should cease to be part of Canada.

Arguably, the requirements of section 1(4) go beyond the principles mandated by the Supreme Court of Canada. No doubt the 1995 referendum question, with its convoluted reference to an offer of partnership "within the scope of the Bill respecting the future of Quebec and of the agreement signed on June 12, 1995" was confusing. It is not self-evident, however, that a referendum question that "envisages other possibilities in addition to the secession of the province from Canada, such as economic or political arrangements with Canada" would necessarily obscure the expression of the will of the population of the province on whether it should cease to be part of Canada. As Pellet argues in his recent analysis of the federal legislation (1999, 3), one can imagine Quebecers being asked a question that envisaged some form of continuing association with Canada (a free trade area, for example) without thereby rendering the question unclear.

One way to deal with this concern would be to amend the opening phrase in section 1(4) to require that such matters only be taken into account by the House in reaching its assessment (similar to the formulation in section 1(5)), rather than deeming such questions necessarily unclear.[1]

With respect to the requirement of a clear majority, section 2 of the bill requires that the House of Commons express its view, by resolution, on whether there had been a "clear expression of a will by a clear majority of the population of that province that the province cease to be part of Canada." In forming that assessment, the House is instructed to take into account a number of factors, including the size of the majority of valid votes cast in favor of the secessionist option and the percentage of eligible voters voting in the referendum. The House is also required to take into account the views of other political actors, including the opposition party in the legislature of the province seeking to secede. The federal government is prohibited from entering into secession negotiations unless the House of Commons determines that there has been a "clear expression of a will by a clear majority of the population of that province that the province cease to be part of Canada" (section 2(4)).[2]

Section 2 seems a faithful rendering of the statements of the Supreme Court. Unfortunately, however, it fails to go beyond the analysis offered by the Court itself. In particular, it does not provide any meaningful guidance as to what level of support would be required to constitute a clear majority. Certainly, risks would be associated with the federal government's committing itself to any particular standard in advance of a referendum. However, the alternative, reflected in section 2, is to leave the matter entirely to the discretion of the prime minister until after the ballots have been counted.

Arguably, a preferable approach would be for the government to state clearly in advance the threshold that would have to be achieved in order to trigger secession negotiations. This approach would promote accountability and transparency since it would allow all parties to know in advance the basis on which the federal government would exercise its discretion. It would also reduce the possible confusion and disorder that could result in the aftermath of a very close vote on secession.

Media reports suggest that the federal government refrained from committing itself to a particular threshold because it feared that doing so could give rise to a legal challenge against the bill. It is true that the Supreme Court's opinion stated: "[I]t will be for the political actors to determine what constitutes a 'clear majority on a clear question' *in the circumstances under which a future referendum vote may be taken*" (para. 153; emphasis added). Yet it seems difficult to extrapolate from such a vague statement a prohibition on the advance establishment of any threshold for a clear majority. Otherwise Canadians would be forced to conduct a referendum campaign without any meaningful understanding of the basis on which the judgment as to the existence of a clear majority would be formed.

I remain of the view that it would have been preferable for the legislation to have indicated that a minimum threshold of a majority of eligible voters would be required before secession negotiations could commence, in the manner described earlier. However, even in the absence of such a specification, the legislation does make a contribution to the legal framework by setting out a process to be followed for determining whether a clear majority had been obtained. In the immediate aftermath of a majority "yes" vote, there would be widespread confusion over the consequences of the vote. In setting forth the process that would have to be followed by the political actors at the federal level, the *Clarity Act* at least provides some structure for what would be a very difficult political debate.

Finally, section 3 of the bill specifies that secession would require a constitutional amendment and that the negotiations for such an amendment would involve "at least the governments of all the provinces and the Government of Canada." The reference to the involvement of the provinces can be traced back directly to the Supreme Court's opinion. Moreover, the use of the term *at least* indicates that other political actors may well have a right to play a direct role in the negotiations, a mandate that again is consistent with the Court's reasoning.

Note also the requirement that the negotiations involve "all" the provinces. Legal scholars have an ongoing debate over whether the secession of a province would require the unanimous consent of the provinces or merely that of seven provinces representing 50 percent of the total Canadian population. My own view has been that unanimous provincial consent would be required since the secession of a province would directly affect matters identified in section 41 of the *Constitution Act, 1982* (Monahan 1995, 6–9).[3] In its submissions to the Supreme Court in the *Secession Reference,* however, the federal government refused to take a position on the applicable amending formula and urged the Court to refrain from commenting on this issue, advice that the Court accepted.[4] The requirement that all the provinces participate in the constitutional negotiations does not necessarily lead to the conclusion that they must all consent to an amendment.[5] However, it certainly tends to support such a rule as a practical matter.

Section 3 also indicates certain matters that would have to be "addressed in negotiations," including "the division of assets and liabilities, any changes to the borders of the province, the rights, interests and territorial claims of the Aboriginal peoples of Canada, and the protection of minority rights." Significantly, while such matters would have to be "addressed in negotiations," they need not be addressed in the constitutional amendment itself. This approach is also in keeping with the Court's opinion, which states that there are no predetermined outcomes on any of the matters that would be the subject of negotiations. Thus, while the issue of borders or the territorial claims of aboriginal peoples would have to be considered, they need not result in actual border changes. All that would be required is that both parties be prepared to negotiate such matters in good faith.[6]

AN ASSESSMENT

What overall assessment can be offered of the *Clarity Act*? In general terms, it is a reasonable attempt to give expression to the principles identified by the Supreme Court of Canada. In particular, it focuses on the circumstances that would trigger the duty to negotiate identified by the Court.

The bill is not, as some critics maintain, an attempt to undermine the right of the Quebec government to draft a referendum question of its own choosing, much less to dictate the substantive outcome of the sovereignty negotiations. Rather, it is a reflection of the Supreme Court's own instruction that the political actors give "concrete form to the discharge of their constitutional obligations." With the Court's having imposed on the government of Canada an obligation to negotiate secession if certain conditions are met, it is clearly appropriate and necessary for Ottawa to set out the criteria on which that judgment is to be based. Assuming that the government's criteria are a good faith attempt to give concrete form to the principles identified by the Court, which is the case with the *Clarity Act,* no objection to the legislation can be convincing.

To see clearly why this is so, consider the alternative scenario under which the federal government would be required to enter into secession negotiations whenever requested by Quebec. Under this approach, such negotiations would be obligatory whenever Quebec declared that there was a clear majority on a clear question in favor of secession. In other words, one of the parties to the negotiations could unilaterally dictate to the other the circumstances under which they must be commenced. Such a situation would be directly contrary to the entire framework set out by the Supreme Court, which clearly stated that no single majority or perspective is entitled to trump any other.

Given that Quebec has no right to dictate to the federal government on the issue of commencing negotiations, it follows inexorably that the federal government must be able to state the circumstances under which its independent discretion would be exercised. This is what the *Clarity Act* seeks to achieve.[7]

In fact, it is the Quebec government's own recently introduced legislation on this issue that fails to respect constitutional rights of other governments. Bill 99 states, among other things, that "the Quebec people alone has the right to decide the political regime and legal status of Quebec" (section 2). The bill also states that the Quebec National Assembly is bound only by Quebec law in regard to the exercise of the right to self-determination (section 10). These provisions are a direct contradiction of the Supreme Court of Canada's declaration that Canadian law provides no unilateral right to secession. In short, Bill 99 seems to reflect the very constitutional unilateralism that the Quebec government claims to oppose.

What of the argument made recently by federal Progressive Conservative leader Joe Clark to the effect that the *Clarity Act* is deficient because it "offers no process for those in Quebec, or in the other provinces, who want to renew Confederation" (Clark 2000, A13)? Mr. Clark has proposed amending the legislation to provide a process for enacting constitutional changes dealing with matters such as Senate reform or changes to the division of powers.

With respect, Mr. Clark's criticisms are unpersuasive. First, the *Clarity Act* does not bar or limit the ability of provinces to hold referendums or to pass constitutional resolutions on subjects other than secession. The legislation deals exclusively with the circumstances under which negotiations on secession could be commenced. Any province that wished to initiate constitutional reform on other issues could continue to do so in whatever manner it believed appropriate, without regard to the terms of the legislation.

But what of the argument that the *Clarity Act* should be amended to require the House of Commons to consider such constitutional reform initiatives, or to regulate the manner in which the government can enter into constitutional negotiations on these matters? In my view, such a specification would be not only unnecessary but unwise.

Currently, governments have a general discretion as to the circumstances and the manner in which constitutional reform should be undertaken. Far from posing a problem, this flexibility has proven to be essential for securing provincial consensus for difficult constitutional change. If constitutional amendments in general were made subject to requirements similar to those set out in the *Clarity Act,* achieving constitutional reform would be more difficult rather than less. This is because the legislation, through its insistence on a clear referendum question and a clear majority, *limits* the ability of the federal government to enter into constitutional negotiations or to introduce constitutional amendments. What possible basis could there be for imposing such limitations on the right of the government to enter into constitutional discussions or to enact amendments on matters other than secession?

Consider, for example, the impact such restrictions would have had on the negotiations that led to the Meech Lake Accord. In early 1986, the federal government and the provinces entered into "informal discussions" on proposals that the Quebec government had put forward to secure Quebec's political assent to the constitutional changes that had been enacted in 1982. These discussions eventually led to unanimous provincial agreement to the terms of the Meech Lake Accord in 1987. Prior to that agreement, the House of Commons did not need to take a formal position on whether Quebec had put forward "clear" proposals or on whether there was a "clear majority" supporting them. Ottawa's evaluation of the wisdom and timing of any constitutional negotiations was a purely political rather than a legal matter. This flexibility permitted Ottawa to gauge the level of support for various potential amendments and to ensure that negotiations would not be commenced until there was reasonable assurance that they would prove successful.[8]

There is little doubt that similar flexibility will be essential whenever negotiations are initiated in the future on amendments designed to secure the Quebec government's political assent to the 1982 constitutional amendments. It would therefore be self-defeating for proponents of "Plan A" to seek to bring such negotiations within the scope of the *Clarity Act.* Such legal regulation would only make negotiations more complicated to start and more difficult to bring to a successful conclusion. It would be far better, in my view, to leave consideration of such matters to the political arena, with governments retaining needed flexibility to determine the manner and mode of constitutional negotiations designed to renew the federation.

CONCLUSION: THE TIME TO ACT

The final matter to be considered is whether now is an appropriate time to move ahead with this initiative. Many thoughtful commentators argue that, with the pro-sovereignty forces currently on the defensive, the federal government should have adopted a wait-and-see approach to this file. The Quebec government may decide not to hold a third sovereignty referendum, in which case the *Clarity Act* will be rendered superfluous. Moreover, proceeding with the bill risks reviving the flagging fortunes of the Parti Québécois and helping to create the winning conditions that Premier Bouchard seeks to call and win a referendum.

These arguments have some force, but, on balance, I believe that the federal government was right to introduce the *Clarity Act* and that it should move forward as quickly as possible to enact it into law. The legislation is, on the whole, a reasoned and appropriate elaboration of the constitutional principles identified by the Supreme Court of Canada. It is designed to promote democratic accountability and protection against arbitrary action by government, both in framing the referendum question and in ensuring that there is an appropriate political mandate for fundamental political change. These safeguards are reasonable and appropriate for any society committed to the rule of law.

[...]

NOTES

1. Alternatively, section 1(4)(b) could be amended by replacing the words "that obscure" with the words "to the extent that such a reference would obscure." This amendment would clarify that a sovereignty referendum question could refer to political and economic arrangements with Canada as long as the reference did not obscure the expression of the will of the Quebec population to cease to be a part of Canada.

2. The reference in section 2(4) to a "clear expression of a will by a clear majority of the *population of that province*" could be interpreted as requiring, at a minimum, the consent of a majority of eligible voters. This potential interpretation is reinforced by the requirement in section 2(2) that the government consider the percentage of eligible voters voting in the referendum.

3. The matters identified in section 41, such as the office of the Lieutenant Governor, the use of the English and French languages, and the composition of the Supreme Court of Canada, can be amended only with the consent of the Senate and House of Commons and the legislative assemblies of all ten provinces.

4. In the *Secession Reference*, the Court says it "refrain[s] from pronouncing on the applicability of any particular constitutional procedure to effect secession unless and until sufficiently clear facts exist to squarely raise an issue for judicial determination" (para. 105).

5. It is logically possible that, although all provinces would participate in the negotiations, only seven of them would be required to adopt a resolution authorizing the constitutional amendment.

6. As the Court states in para. 93, a party that failed to act in accordance with the underlying constitutional principles would "put at risk the legitimacy of the exercise of its rights."

7. One hears an alternative argument that the federal government has a right to form a judgment as to when secession negotiations should begin but only after a referendum has occurred, not before. This argument is no more plausible than the one outlined above in the text. If Ottawa is entitled to form an independent opinion on a matter, it is surely also entitled to decide for itself how and when to come to that opinion.

8. Of course, while the negotiations were successful in the sense that they resulted in the unanimous agreement of the federal and provincial governments, the accord ultimately failed to achieve the necessary legislative ratification, in part due to the "closed door" nature of the negotiations that produced it.

REFERENCES

Angus Reid Group. 1999. "Quebecers on a Clear Question and a Clear Majority." December 14. Poll available at Internet website: www.angusreid.com.

Aubry, Jack. 1999. "Referendum rules from PM unwelcome, Charest says." *National Post,* October 30.

Brassard, Jacques. 1997. *Quebec and Its Territory.* Québec: Secrétariat aux affaires inter-gouvernementales canadiennes.

Brun, Henri. 1999. "Avis juridique concernant la notion de majorité dans le *Renvoi relatif à la sécession du Québec.*" Québec. Mimeographed.

Bryden, Joan. 1999. "Liberal MPs' support for secession legislation dwindling: Ontario MPs disapprove: Jean Chrétien risks defeat within his ranks." *National Post,* October 25.

Cameron, David R., ed. 1999. *The Referendum Papers: Essays on Secession and National Unity.* Toronto: University of Toronto Press in association with the C.D. Howe Institute.

Centre de recherche sur l'opinion publique (CROP). 1999. "Research in Public Opinion." Poll available at Internet website: www.pco-bcp.gc.ca/aia.

Clark, Campbell, and Robert Fife. 1999. "Bouchard gives PM 'a flat no' to peace offer on referendum rules." *National Post,* December 1, p. A1.

Clark, Joe. 2000. "Let's get back to plan A." *Globe and Mail* (Toronto), January 3, p. A13.

Crawford, James. 1997. "State Practice and International Law in Relation to Unilateral Secession." Expert report filed by the Attorney General of Canada, supplement to the case on appeal in the *Quebec Secession Reference.*

Dion, Stéphane. 1999. "Referendums on Secession and Requirements for Clarity: Examples from Northern Europe." Note for an address at the Conference of the Nordic Association for Canadian Studies. Reykjavik, August 5.

Ekos Research Associates. 1999. "Fin de siècle: fin de la souveraineté?" December 14. Poll available at Internet website: www.ekos.com.

Franck, T., et al. 1992. "L'intégrité territoriale du Québec dans l'hypothèse de l'accession à la souveraineté." In Commission d'étude des questions afférentes à l'accession du Québec à la souveraineté, *Projet de Rapport,* Annexe. Québec, September.

Grand Council of the Crees. 1995. *Sovereign Injustice: Forcible Inclusion of the James Bay Crees and Cree Territory into a Sovereign Quebec.* Nemaska, Que.: Grand Council of the Crees.

Hogg, P.W. 1999. "The Duty to Negotiate." *Canada Watch* 7 (January–February): 34–35.

Lajoie, Andrée. 1999. "Avis juridique: le sens de l'expression 'question claire' dans le *Renvoi relatif à la sécession du Québec.*" Montréal, Université de Montréal, Faculté de droit. Mimeographed.

Mackie, Richard. 1999. "PM's strategy costs Liberals in Quebec." *Globe and Mail* (Toronto), December 23, p. A1.

Monahan, Patrick J. 1995. "The Law and Politics of Quebec Secession." *Osgoode Hall Law Journal* 33: 1–33.

———. 1997. *Constitutional Law.* Concord, Ont.: Irwin Law.

——. 1999. "The Public Policy Role of the Supreme Court of Canada in the Secession Reference." *National Journal of Constitutional Law* 11 (November): 65–105.

——. and Michael C. Bryant, with Nancy C. Coté. 1996. "Coming to Terms with Plan B: Ten Principles Governing Secession." *C.D. Howe Institute Commentary* 83. June.

Newman, Warren J. 1999. *The Quebec Secession Reference: The Rule of Law and the Position of the Attorney General of Canada.* Toronto: York University, Centre for Public Law and Public Policy.

Pellet, Alain. 1999. "Avis juridique sommaire sur *Le Project de loi donnant effet à l'exigence de clarté formulée par la Cour Suprême du Canada dans son avis sur le Renvoi sur la sécession du Québec.*" Université de Paris X-Nanterre, December 13. Mimeographed.

Quebec Liberal Party. 1991. Constitutional Committee. *A Quebec Free to Choose.* Report of the committee chaired by Jean Allaire. Quebec.

Robertson, Gordon. 1996. "Contingency Legislation for a Quebec Referendum." Paper distributed at the Confederation 2000 Conference, March 8.

Wells, Paul. 1999. "Other provinces would have no say in separation talks, Quebec says." *National Post,* November 19, p. A1.

✗ NO
Consequences of the Quebec *Secession Reference:* The Clarity Bill and Beyond
CLAUDE RYAN

AFTER THE *SECESSION REFERENCE:* MORE RECENT DEVELOPMENTS

On the legal front, the federal government obtained from the Supreme Court almost all the answers it wished concerning the democratic and constitutional validity of a secession referendum process. It was also told something it did not seem to expect: that, if a referendum were held on a clear question and resulted in a clear majority in favor of secession, the federal government and other participants in the Canadian federation would have an obligation to engage the Quebec government in good-faith negotiations to put into effect the clearly expressed will of Quebecers.

The Clarity Bill

In the short term, the federal government has emerged from its Supreme Court initiative with its position reinforced. The legal prospects are now clear enough, and the *Secession Reference* gives it an important tool that it can use at any time if an unforeseen situation emerges. Since it seems that no referendum will be held in the foreseeable future, the federal government should behave with reserve and moderation. Unless it has truly useful, relevant, and timely points to add to the debate, Ottawa should use the current period of respite not to provoke new quarrels with Quebec but to devote time and energy to improving the political aspects of the relationship between Quebec and the Canadian federation.

Although Bill C-20, the federal clarity bill, pursues defensible goals, the means by which the federal government expects to realize them are highly questionable in light of the principles of both federalism and democracy. Had the bill been limited to giving assurances that, in the event of a "yes" vote, Parliament would be convened to examine and assess the situation thus created and to provide guidance as to the appropriate line of conduct, there would have been nothing to say against such an initiative. Such a bill would simply have assured the Canadian population that its representatives in the federal Parliament would be immediately involved in any "yes"-vote situation.

But the clarity bill goes much further. It contains elements that are plainly unacceptable, not only to sovereigntists but also to many federalist Quebecers.

The main problem stems from section 1 of the bill, which states that the federal Parliament would be required to pronounce itself on the clarity of the referendum question as soon as it was made public and that, if the verdict was that the question was unclear, the federal government would be released from its obligation to negotiate in the event of a sovereigntist referendum victory. The bill also stipulates that a question would be considered unacceptable if the Quebec government sought a mandate to negotiate without "soliciting a direct expression of the will of the population of that province on whether that province should cease to be part of Canada," as would any question offering "other possibilities in addition to the secession of the province from Canada, such as economic and political arrangements with Canada."

Federal Intrusion into a Provincial Matter

These provisions of the clarity bill constitute an undesirable intrusion of the federal Parliament into a process that must unfold within Quebec. Indeed, under Canada's federal system, each level of government is deemed sovereign within its jurisdiction. This means that neither one, when acting within that jurisdiction, should have to be subjected to the other's interference. In conformity with this principle, the federal government recognizes in Bill C-20 that "the government of any province of Canada is entitled to consult its population by referendum on any issue and is entitled to formulate the wording of its referendum question." But it contradicts this recognition by a provision in the clarity bill that confers on the federal Parliament direct power of intervention in the referendum process at a stage when, by its own admission, this process lies within the jurisdiction of the Quebec National Assembly.

If the National Assembly has the right to consult Quebecers on secession, it also has the right to do so without being subjected to constraints or meddling from another legislature. According Parliament the power to judge the clarity of the question at the early stage indicated in the bill represents an obvious intrusion in a referendum campaign. Such an intervention would be all the more intrusive if, even before the vote was held, Parliament enjoined the federal government not to negotiate, regardless of the referendum result.

Furthermore, the clarity bill indicates certain criteria that should guide Parliament in formulating its judgment on the clarity of the question. By including these criteria in a law, Parliament would interfere, at least indirectly, in the very process of drafting the question. Such practices, while acceptable in a unitary state wherein regional governments are subject to central tutelage, have no place in a federal system.

From the point of view of democratic principles, article 1 of the clarity bill presents another major difficulty. It is possible that a majority of federal MPs from outside Quebec would adopt a resolution declaring a referendum question unacceptable as a trigger for negotiations, while a majority of Quebec MPs took a different view. In such a situation, even before Quebecers had a chance to speak, the federal government would be forbidden by a majority of MPs outside Quebec to begin any negotiation whatsoever with the Quebec government following a referendum in favor of sovereignty. Such a situation would be not just indefensible in terms of the democratic principle but politically untenable; it could even steer Quebec public opinion in the opposite direction to that intended.

Still at the political level, it would be unrealistic and dangerous for the federal government to be bound in advance by a parliamentary resolution as to what its conduct should be following a referendum in favor of sovereignty. Nobody can predict the kind of events that would then emerge. Instead of being bound by constraints established in a prior context, the federal government should have plenty of room to maneuver when deciding its conduct under the circumstances of a "yes" vote.

Article 2 of the clarity bill also opens the door to a denial of democracy, since it gives Parliament the power to pronounce on the validity of a vote in favor of sovereignty.

There would be nothing illegitimate about that if the bill did not also make it possible for Parliament to make this judgment by using, *a posteriori*, norms other than those generally accepted. The legislation specifies that the majority obtained could be assessed using three criteria: the majority of votes cast, the percentage of eligible voters voting in the referendum, and "any other matter or circumstances it considers to be relevant." This last, open-ended criterion could lead to a damaging denial of democracy.

Without saying so explicitly in Bill C-20, the federal government implies that a majority of 50 percent plus one of votes cast would not in its view be sufficient for the results of a referendum on sovereignty to be acceptable. This position is not inherently unreasonable: the rule of equality of voters already suffers from important exceptions. It is these exceptions that allow Canadians to be governed, as much in Ottawa as in Quebec City, by parties that have obtained less than 50 percent of the popular vote. Premier Bouchard himself heads a government that has a comfortable majority of seats in the National Assembly even though it obtained fewer votes in the last election than Jean Charest's Liberal Party. If these distortions, produced by the divisions of the electoral map and the first-past-the-post voting system, are not considered scandalous in the eyes of the majority of the population, it is because there is at least a tacit consensus that the current system of representation possesses advantages that exceed the contradictions that can result from it. It is not unreasonable, therefore, to question the notion that a simple majority is the best decision rule.

The current case, however, concerns a referendum, not an election. To my knowledge, the simple majority rule has always been in effect when interpreting the results of a referendum held across an entire territory. One could plausibly argue that this rule be modified in the case of a referendum on the irreversible breakup of the country. But Parliament would be ill-advised to impose its views unilaterally on this topic even before a referendum is called and, what is more, to impose them on a referendum that would be held under the authority of the Quebec government. As long as it acted within its jurisdiction, the determination of the decision rule should be up to the National Assembly.

If the decision rule is to be changed, therefore, it is the National Assembly that must change it. The federal government can seek to modify the decision rule, either by negotiating with the Quebec government or by influencing public opinion. Clearly, what is inadmissible prior to the holding of a referendum would be even more inadmissible after the event. Yet that is what Bill C-20 contemplates. The federal government is using highly contestable means to promote ends that are not altogether unreasonable, and the manner in which things are done is fundamental in constitutional affairs.

The Reaction in Quebec

These contentious elements of the clarity bill have prompted numerous criticisms not only among sovereigntists but among federalists as well. If the principles advanced by Quebec federalist opponents of the bill are right—and I am convinced they are—Quebec federalists should not find themselves isolated. They should be able to count on effective support from federalists living elsewhere in the country who also accept these principles. But the national unity debate has been so poisoned by propaganda against "evil separatists" that to raise questions about the wisdom of Ottawa's referendum legislation is to risk suspicion of complicity with separatists at best, or of mental aberration at worst.

Premier Bouchard legitimately wants to unite all those with serious objections to the federal bill and to defend the powers of the National Assembly. However, for Quebec federalists—who are as committed to Quebec's interests as are the sovereigntists—Bill 99,[1] the Quebec government's proposed counterlegislation, leaves much to be desired. First, the response is disproportionate to the issue at hand. Bill 99 takes the form of a constitutional proclamation of the kind that simply cannot be concocted in a matter of a few weeks. Had he wanted to create a broad consensus, Premier Bouchard would have been wise to restrict himself to a rebuttal of the federal law and an affirmation of the National Assembly's freedom of initiative with respect to the matters fettered by the federal clarity bill.

Furthermore, Bill 99 makes no mention of Quebec's being part of the Canadian federal system, apart from a brief mention (in section 6) that the province "is sovereign in the areas assigned to its jurisdiction," by virtue of the "laws and constitutional conventions" of Canada. On the other hand, the bill contains articles that are of dubious constitutional validity in the eyes of many observers. The remaining text would be more applicable to a Quebec that had voted "yes" in the 1995 referendum or one that had given a plurality of its votes in the 1998 provincial election to the Parti Québécois. However slight the margins, a majority voted "no" in 1995 and a plurality preferred Jean Charest's Liberals in 1998. Several clauses of Bill 99 would require significant modification to be acceptable to Quebecers of a federalist persuasion.

A FUNDAMENTALLY POLITICAL PROBLEM

Since the publication of the Supreme Court's *Secession Reference,* public debate has turned primarily on two matters: the clarity of the question to be submitted to Quebecers in any future referendum and the threshold that a "yes" majority must achieve to trigger the obligation on the part of other senior Canadian governments to negotiate. Given that the Court discussed these matters extensively, it was inevitable that commentary be fixed on them. But Byzantine discussions over what constitutes a clear question and a clear majority are far removed from the true heart of the debate.

In effect, the Supreme Court gave its opinion on the question of how a sovereignty project could be conducted in a manner consistent with the Canadian Constitution. There are, however, more important questions to pose—questions of a fundamentally political, rather than legal, nature: Why does a sovereigntist movement exist in Quebec? Why has this movement been so significant over the past quarter-century? What is the best strategy to counter the idea of Quebec sovereignty?

[...]

NOTE

1. The full title is *An Act respecting the exercise of the fundamental rights and prerogatives of the Quebec people and the Quebec state.*

REFERENCES

Bouchard, Lucien. 1998. "La démarche souverainiste est légitime." *Le Devoir* (Montreal), August 22.

Greschner, Donna. 1999. "Goodbye to the Amending Formulas?" In David Schneiderman, ed., *The Quebec Decision: Perspectives on the Supreme Court Ruling on Secession.* Toronto: James Lorimer.

Lisée, Jean-François. 2000. *Sortie de secours: comment échapper au déclin du Québec.* Montréal: Boréal.

Mackie, Richard. 2000. "Referendum won't settle debate regardless of outcome, Quebeckers say." *Globe and Mail* (Toronto), March 6, p. 1.

Monahan, Patrick J. 2000. "Doing the Rules: An Assessment of the Federal *Clarity Act* in Light of the *Quebec Secession Reference.*" *C.D. Howe Institute Commentary* 135. February.

Nadeau, Richard, et al. 1998. "How the wording affects support for sovereignty." *Globe and Mail* (Toronto), March 16.

Pinard, Maurice. 1998. "Un troisième referendum?" Speech delivered to the Council on Canadian Unity. Reprinted in *Bulletin du Conseil pour l'unité canadienne.*

Thomas, David. 1997. *Whistling Past the Graveyard: Constitutional Abeyances, Quebec, and the Future of Canada.* Toronto: Oxford University Press.

Tully, James. 1999. "Liberté et dévoilement dans les sociétés multinationales." *Globe: Revue internationale d'études québécoises* 2 (2).

Woehrling, José. 1999. "The Quebec Secession Reference: Some Unexpected Consequences of Constitutional First Principles." In David Schneiderman, ed., *The Quebec Decision: Perspectives on the Supreme Court Ruling on Secession.* Toronto: James Lorimer.

Clarity Act 2000, c. 26

An Act to give effect to the requirement for clarity as set out in the opinion of the Supreme Court of Canada in the Quebec Secession Reference

[Assented to 29th June, 2000]

WHEREAS the Supreme Court of Canada has confirmed that there is no right, under international law or under the Constitution of Canada, for the National Assembly, legislature or government of Quebec to effect the secession of Quebec from Canada unilaterally;

WHEREAS any proposal relating to the break-up of a democratic state is a matter of the utmost gravity and is of fundamental importance to all of its citizens;

WHEREAS the government of any province of Canada is entitled to consult its population by referendum on any issue and is entitled to formulate the wording of its referendum question;

WHEREAS the Supreme Court of Canada has determined that the result of a referendum on the secession of a province from Canada must be free of ambiguity both in terms of the question asked and in terms of the support it achieves if that result is to be taken as an expression of the democratic will that would give rise to an obligation to enter into negotiations that might lead to secession;

WHEREAS the Supreme Court of Canada has stated that democracy means more than simple majority rule, that a clear majority in favour of secession would be required to create an obligation to negotiate secession, and that a qualitative evaluation is required to determine whether a clear majority in favour of secession exists in the circumstances;

WHEREAS the Supreme Court of Canada has confirmed that, in Canada, the secession of a province, to be lawful, would require an amendment to the Constitution of Canada, that such an amendment would perforce require negotiations in relation to secession involving at least the governments of all of the provinces and the Government of Canada, and that those negotiations would be governed by the principles of federalism, democracy, constitutionalism and the rule of law, and the protection of minorities;

WHEREAS, in light of the finding by the Supreme Court of Canada that it would be for elected representatives to determine what constitutes a clear question and what constitutes a clear majority in a referendum held in a province on secession, the House of Commons, as the only political institution elected to represent all Canadians, has an important role in identifying what constitutes a clear question and a clear majority sufficient for the Government of Canada to enter into negotiations in relation to the secession of a province from Canada;

AND WHEREAS it is incumbent on the Government of Canada not to enter into negotiations that might lead to the secession of a province from Canada, and that could consequently entail the termination of citizenship and other rights that Canadian citizens resident in the province enjoy as full participants in Canada, unless the population of that province has clearly expressed its democratic will that the province secede from Canada;

NOW, THEREFORE, Her Majesty, by and with the advice and consent of the Senate and House of Commons of Canada, enacts as follows:

1. (1) The House of Commons shall, within thirty days after the government of a province tables in its legislative assembly or otherwise officially releases the question that it intends to submit to its voters in a referendum relating to the proposed secession of the province from Canada, consider the question and, by resolution, set out its determination on whether the question is clear.

   (2) Where the thirty days referred to in subsection (1) occur, in whole or in part, during a general election of members to serve in the House of Commons, the thirty days shall be extended by an additional forty days.

   (3) In considering the clarity of a referendum question, the House of Commons shall consider whether the question would result in a clear expression of the will of the population of a province on whether the province should cease to be part of Canada and become an independent state.

   (4) For the purpose of subsection (3), a clear expression of the will of the population of a province that the province cease to be part of Canada could not result from

   (a) a referendum question that merely focuses on a mandate to negotiate without soliciting a direct expression of the will of the population of that province on whether the province should cease to be part of Canada; or

   (b) a referendum question that envisages other possibilities in addition to the secession of the province from Canada, such as economic or political arrangements with Canada, that obscure a direct expression of the will of the population of that province on whether the province should cease to be part of Canada.

(5) In considering the clarity of a referendum question, the House of Commons shall take into account the views of all political parties represented in the legislative assembly of the province whose government is proposing the referendum on secession, any formal statements or resolutions by the government or legislative assembly of any province or territory of Canada, any formal statements or resolutions by the Senate, any formal statements or resolutions by the representatives of the Aboriginal peoples of Canada, especially those in the province whose government is proposing the referendum on secession, and any other views it considers to be relevant.

(6) The Government of Canada shall not enter into negotiations on the terms on which a province might cease to be part of Canada if the House of Commons determines, pursuant to this section, that a referendum question is not clear and, for that reason, would not result in a clear expression of the will of the population of that province on whether the province should cease to be part of Canada.

2. (1) Where the government of a province, following a referendum relating to the secession of the province from Canada, seeks to enter into negotiations on the terms on which that province might cease to be part of Canada, the House of Commons shall, except where it has determined pursuant to section 1 that a referendum question is not clear, consider and, by resolution, set out its determination on whether, in the circumstances, there has been a clear expression of a will by a clear majority of the population of that province that the province cease to be part of Canada.

(2) In considering whether there has been a clear expression of a will by a clear majority of the population of a province that the province cease to be part of Canada, the House of Commons shall take into account

(a) the size of the majority of valid votes cast in favour of the secessionist option;

(b) the percentage of eligible voters voting in the referendum; and

(c) any other matters or circumstances it considers to be relevant.

(3) In considering whether there has been a clear expression of a will by a clear majority of the population of a province that the province cease to be part of Canada, the House of Commons shall take into account the views of all political parties represented in the legislative assembly of the province whose government proposed the referendum on secession, any formal statements or resolutions by the government or legislative assembly of any province or territory of Canada, any formal statements or resolutions by the Senate, any formal statements or resolutions by the representatives of the Aboriginal peoples of Canada,

especially those in the province whose government proposed the referendum on secession, and any other views it considers to be relevant.

(4) The Government of Canada shall not enter into negotiations on the terms on which a province might cease to be part of Canada unless the House of Commons determines, pursuant to this section, that there has been a clear expression of a will by a clear majority of the population of that province that the province cease to be part of Canada.

3. (1) It is recognized that there is no right under the Constitution of Canada to effect the secession of a province from Canada unilaterally and that, therefore, an amendment to the Constitution of Canada would be required for any province to secede from Canada, which in turn would require negotiations involving at least the governments of all of the provinces and the Government of Canada.

(2) No Minister of the Crown shall propose a constitutional amendment to effect the secession of a province from Canada unless the Government of Canada has addressed, in its negotiations, the terms of secession that are relevant in the circumstances, including the division of assets and liabilities, any changes to the borders of the province, the rights, interests and territorial claims of the Aboriginal peoples of Canada, and the protection of minority rights.

POSTSCRIPT

Patrick Monahan's support for the Clarity Act rests on his belief that the federal government was almost obligated to move forward with the legislation. The Supreme Court decision required such action, as did the need to ensure against the possibility that any secession process would be dominated by the government of Quebec. Any breakup of Canada, Monahan believes, should involve all interested parties and not just one. The logic of Monahan's position is hard to contest, but it might be argued that the Clarity Act is simply too brusque, or even clumsy. A more nuanced approach to the secession process might have been preferable. For example, the legislation might have simply said that any secession process should attempt to reflect the decision of the Supreme Court. As well, the legislation might have included some mention of proposals to structure the process of future constitutional reform. For some Quebecers, the basic message of the Clarity Act is negative: we can stop your referendum process. Reference to constitutional reform might have given a more positive connotation to the legislation.

In his article, Claude Ryan makes some good arguments. The Clarity Act does appear to allow the federal government to intervene at a very early stage in any referendum on secession. The legislation also gives the federal government a great deal of flexibility in determining whether a clear majority has been secured. More generally, Ryan argues persuasively that the Clarity Act misses the larger picture: the most important questions relating to Quebec revolve around the origins of separatism and what can be done to counter separatist thinking. As with Monahan, however, Ryan has not established a foolproof position. Without early intervention in any referendum, the federal government may find it too late to act effectively. And Ryan himself may be missing the fundamental point: the separation of Quebec is not just a Quebec issue, but rather one that must involve all of Canada.

Before tackling the Clarity Act in detail, students are urged to secure the necessary historical background. This requires an appreciation of the attempts at constitutional reform over the past forty years, and such can be gained through Peter H. Russell's *Constitutional Odyssey: Can Canadians Become a Sovereign People?* 3rd ed. (Toronto: University of Toronto Press, 2004) and Kenneth McRoberts, "Quebec: Province, Nation or Distinct Society," in Michael Whittington and Glen Williams, eds., *Canadian Politics in the 21st Century,* 6th ed. (Toronto: Thomson Nelson, 2004). Also required is an understanding of both the 1995 referendum in Quebec (and reactions to the results) and the 1998 Supreme Court secession decision. The relevant texts here are David Cameron, ed., *The Referendum Papers: Essays on Secession and National Unity* (Toronto: University of Toronto Press, 1999) and David Schneiderman, ed., *The Quebec Decision: Perspectives on the Supreme Court Ruling on Secession* (Toronto: James Lorimer, 1999). For an updating of the act and its place in the story of constitutional reform, the interested reader might again look at Peter Russell's last chapter in his *Constitutional Odyssey.*

Now, we are ready to tackle a detailed assessment of the act itself. Interested students might begin with the extended treatments of the Clarity Act given by Monahan and Ryan (from which the debate readings are extracted): Patrick J. Monahan, "Doing the Rules: An Assessment of the Federal *Clarity Act* in Light of the *Quebec Secession Reference*," *C.D. Howe Institute Commentary* 135 (February 2000) and Claude Ryan, "Consequences of the Quebec *Secession Reference:* The Clarity Bill and Beyond," *C.D. Howe Institute Commentary* 139 (April 2000). Submissions to the parliamentary committee examining the Clarity Act are also relevant, and the more prominent of these submissions can be found in *Canadian Parliamentary Review* 23, no. 2 (Summer 2000); the entire set of submissions can be found at the parliamentary Internet website. Also of interest is a speech given by Michael Ignatieff entitled "The Coming Constitutional Crisis," an edited version of which can be found in the April 16, 2005 issue of the *National Post* (the speech was given at Osgoode Hall Law School). Ignatieff is the one partly responsible for people thinking again of Quebec separatism and the impact of the Clarity Act on the future of Canada.

PART THREE

INSTITUTIONS

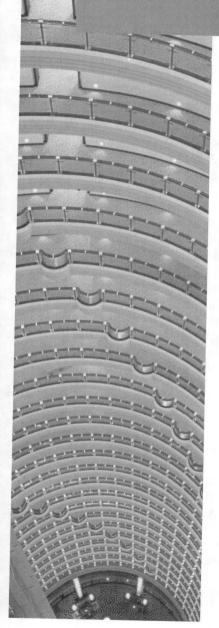

Is the prime minister too powerful?

Should Parliament review Supreme Court appointments?

Should party discipline be relaxed?

Is the Prime Minister Too Powerful?

✔ **YES**

DONALD J. SAVOIE, "*Primus:* There Is No Longer Any *Inter* or *Pares*," in Donald J. Savoie, *Governing from the Centre: The Concentration of Power in Canadian Politics* (Toronto: University of Toronto Press, 1999)

✘ **NO**

PAUL BARKER, "Limits on the Power of the Prime Minister"

Students of Canadian politics appreciate that the prime minister is at the centre of political life in Canada. As leader of the national government, the prime minister determines the priorities that set the public agenda. The prime minister is also able to make appointments to important positions, and acts to represent Canada on the world stage. Perhaps the greatest indicator of power and influence of the first minister is his or her sheer prominence. Canadians might be hard pressed to name the provincial premiers or the chief justice of the Supreme Court of Canada, but few, if any, would experience the same problem with the prime minister.

There is thus little debate about the significance of the prime minister in Canadian politics. What might be debatable, however, is whether the prime minister dominates to the point that he threatens the healthy functioning of democracy in Canada. There are some who believe, strongly, that such is the case. Canada does not really have parliamentary government, they say, but in fact has what might be called "prime-ministerial" government. According to this perspective, the prime minister encounters few constraints on the exercise of his powers. All the typical powers associated with the prime minister—determining appointments, setting the overall direction of the country, representing Canada's interests in foreign dealings— are exercised with very little opposition. The Latin phrase *primus inter pares* ("first among equals") was once used to describe the prime minister's status: the prime minister was powerful (*primus*), but he faced individuals or challengers who were not merely his subordinates but his equals (*pares*) in some respects. Now, it is argued, the prime minister has no equals—he is *primus*, without any qualification.

Any proposition is only as strong as the supporting evidence. A look at Canadian political life does suggest some backing for the thesis of prime-ministerial government. The prime minister appears able to pass bills into law with little difficulty. He also decides who shall sit in cabinet with him and who shall hold the senior positions in the judiciary and the public service. The prime minister is front-and-centre in the media's coverage of Canadian politics; indeed, he might be considered a celebrity or a superstar. The fact that Canadians look instantly to the prime minister in times of trouble also speaks to the primacy of the prime minister. When the terrorist attacks of September 11, 2001, struck the United States, most Canadians turned to the prime minister for guidance on how this country should respond.

The question, however, is whether all this is enough to confirm the prime-ministerial government thesis. The corroborating evidence, to be sure, is impressive, but is it sufficiently impressive to allow us to conclude that Canada is a country with a leader who faces few limits to his power? Some answer in the negative. How, for example, can one ignore the influence of provincial premiers? Canadians may find it difficult to name political leaders in the provinces, but there is little doubt that premiers can frustrate prime-ministerial ambitions. Similarly, members of the prime minister's own government, his cabinet ministers, can make matters difficult for the prime minister—just look at the tussle between former prime minister Jean Chrétien and his finance minister Paul Martin. And, of course, the media present a challenge for the leader of the national government. One day the prime minister may appear invincible, the next day quite vulnerable. Such is the life of any celebrity.

In the readings, Donald J. Savoie, a professor at the Université de Moncton, contends that the prime minister has an undue degree of power. Paul Barker, one of the editors of *Crosscurrents,* argues that Savoie and other supporters of the thesis of prime-ministerial government exaggerate the power open to the prime minister.

✔ YES
Primus: There Is No Longer Any *Inter* or *Pares*
DONALD J. SAVOIE

The prime minister occupies the highest peaks of both the political and adminis-trative mountains, from which he can survey all developments in his govern-ment.[1] This is not to suggest that he can always shape at will all initiatives and move the machinery of government in the direction and at the speed he wishes. There are some constraints to prime-ministerial power, ranging from incessant demands on his time, public opinion, the media—even to inertia, a characteristic found in all large organizations and to which the federal government is certainly not immune. But, no matter the circumstances, the prime minister remains "the boss." Prime Minister Chrétien [was] called the boss, while he, in turn, invariably referred to Pierre Trudeau as "le boss" when he served in Trudeau's Cabinet.

There is no question that a great deal of power is concentrated in the hands of the prime minister, especially when his party enjoys a majority in Parliament. Abraham Lincoln is reported to have provided an account of Cabinet delibera-tions by saying "the Ayes one, the nays seven. The ayes have it."[2] A Canadian prime minister holding a clear majority in Parliament could easily make a sim-ilar claim. Indeed, there have been many instances during the past twenty-five years or so when various prime ministers have chosen to pursue initiatives both large and small without even consulting their Cabinets. Governments are often identified not only in the media, but also in scholarly works by the names of the prime minister, as in the Trudeau, Chrétien, or Mulroney governments, and for very legitimate reasons. Prime ministers have become much more than spokespersons for their Cabinets. They are the focal point of the government and the administration and they clearly dominate inside government. They provide the leadership, the style, and the coherence of the government and the ebb and flow of the fortunes of the government are directly linked to their performance. No single Cabinet minister, regardless of her political base in the party or in the country, can possibly have the same impact as the prime minister. If a minister ever should, it will signal a short-lived government—and no one knows this better than the prime minister.

This [article] looks at the role of the prime minister in government. It examines the levers of power that belong to him or her and the forces that strengthen his hand at almost every turn. [...]

PRIMUS RULES

Canadian prime ministers, again, particularly when they have a majority govern-ment in Parliament, have in their hands all the important levers of power. Indeed, all major national public policy roads lead one way or another to their doorstep. They are elected leader of their party by party members, they chair Cabinet meetings, establish Cabinet processes and procedures, set the Cabinet agenda, establish the consensus for Cabinet decisions; they appoint and fire ministers and deputy ministers, establish Cabinet committees, and decide on their membership; they exercise virtually all the powers of patronage and act as personnel manager for thousands of government and patronage jobs; they articulate the government's strategic direction as outlined in the Speech from the Throne; they dictate the pace of change, and are the main salespersons promoting the achievements of their government; they have a hand in establishing the government's fiscal framework; they represent Canada abroad; they establish the proper mandate of individual ministers and decide all machinery of government issues, and they are the final arbiter in interdepartmental conflicts. The prime minister is the only politician with a national constituency, and unlike members of Parliament and even Cabinet ministers, he does not need to search out publicity or national media attention, since attention is invariably focused on his office and his residence, 24 Sussex. In short, the prime minister is head of government, with limited checks on his power inside government or in Parliament. He is not, however, head of state, a role still played by the governor general as representative of the monarch. This is just as well, since that role is now largely ceremonial.

Each of the above levers of power taken separately is a powerful instrument of public policy and public administration in its own right, but when you add them all up and place them in the hands of one individual, they constitute a veritable juggernaut of power. Other than going down to defeat in a general election, it can only be stopped, or slowed, by the force of public opinion and by a Cabinet or caucus revolt. Even then, public opinion may not be much of a force if the prime minister has already decided not to run again in the next general election. One only has to think back to Trudeau or Mulroney's final years in office to appreciate this. History also tells us that caucus or Cabinet revolts, or even threats of revolts, are extremely rare in Ottawa.

Yet notwithstanding the fact that all these key instruments and so much political power are concentrated in the hands of one individual, one of the main preoccupations of the most senior officials in government is to protect the prime minister. I was reminded of an old political saying on more than one occasion in my interviews with politicians and their advisers: "If the head goes, the rest of the government is sure to follow." Partisan political advisers and Cabinet ministers know that, once exposed, any prime ministerial weaknesses, real or imagined, will serve to stimulate the opposition and the media and make it that more difficult to govern. Accordingly, it is important that the prime minister be protected, but also that his or her hand on the Cabinet and the government machinery not be weakened. Some of the officials on the lookout to protect the prime minister are politically partisan, and one can easily appreciate why they would want to protect him. But others are not partisan and they also regard it as their duty to protect the head of government.

This is true no matter which political party is in power. Permanent officials in central agencies explain this by pointing out that, though they are not politically partisan, they need to be politically sensitive.

There are plenty of subtle and not so subtle hints suggesting that the prime minister towers above his Cabinet colleagues. At the Cabinet table, the prime minister sits at the middle and decides which ministers sit where. The back of his chair is higher than all the others. Whatever may be the case in theory, everyone knows that in practice the secretary of the Cabinet reports directly to him and not to Cabinet and indeed that it is the prime minister alone and not Cabinet who appoints or dismisses the secretary to the Cabinet. His own personal or political office is well staffed and is headed by a deputy-minister-level official. Some of his senior staff members are allowed to attend Cabinet and committee meetings. Ministers, meanwhile, have, relatively speaking, a modest budget for their own offices. These are headed by junior-level officials who are never invited to attend Cabinet meetings.

The prime minister also enjoys a number of special perks not available to his Cabinet colleagues. He is the only government member to occupy an official residence, which is not the case either in Britain or in the United States. If the prime minister wants to contact anyone in Canada, or for that matter in the world, he has at his disposal a highly efficient switchboard capable of tracking down virtually anyone. When Prime Minister Chrétien decided towards the end of a Formula 1 car race that he wanted to talk with Jacques Villeneuve, the PM's switchboard was able to track Villeneuve down in Japan within minutes. No other minister could command this kind of response.

Canadian prime ministers have, since Trudeau, made themselves into television personalities. But the same is not true for Cabinet ministers. A Gallup poll in 1988 revealed that only 31 per cent of respondents could name a *single* Cabinet minister four years after the Mulroney government had come to power. In addition, only 5 per cent of the respondents could identify Don Mazankowski, deputy prime minister and one of the most, if not the most, powerful member of Mulroney's Cabinet.[3]

In Canada, at least since Trudeau, prime ministers rule through good times and bad, with never a hint of serious Cabinet or caucus revolt. British prime ministers can be dumped by their parties even when in office—as Margaret Thatcher can attest—but not, it seems, Canadian prime ministers. Former prime ministers Pierre Trudeau and Brian Mulroney both became extremely unpopular in their latter years in power, all the while without a revolt from either Cabinet or caucus. In both instances, they stayed to the end of their traditional four-year mandate (both Trudeau and Mulroney stayed even beyond their four-year mandates) and their parties went on to suffer humiliating defeats in the next election. [...]

The Canadian prime minister's power extends beyond the federal government. He deals regularly with provincial premiers and territorial leaders. Premiers are first ministers too, a status they jealously guard, and for good reason. The status enables them to deal directly with the prime minister. Indeed, all first ministers, including those from the smaller provinces, believe that they should have full access to the prime minister without having to go through a federal government minister. They know from first-hand experience that the head of government has the power to make things happen and to give a green light to requests and proposals without consulting anyone, if necessary, while a simple Cabinet minister cannot, no matter how solid his standing in government.

In the summer of 1997, Frank McKenna, former premier of New Brunswick, organized a one-on-one meeting with the prime minister. He put two proposals to Chrétien during a golf game: that the federal government support a conference on the economic future of Atlantic Canada and that it cost share a new highways agreement to continue with the construction of a four-lane Trans–Canada highway. The prime minister agreed and instructed his officials to make it happen. One government agency provided some funding to support the conference, and several federal ministers, including Prime Minister Chrétien, attended it. Officials, meanwhile, were instructed to prepare a Treasury Board submission to secure the necessary funding for the highways construction agreement. Within a few weeks, everything had been sorted out and an announcement was made on both an Atlantic Vision conference and a new Canada/Highways agreement. The prime minister did not ask Privy Council and Treasury Board Secretariat officials to prepare a proposal and then to submit it for consideration in the government's decision-making process. His instructions were clear—make these two initiatives happen. This is not to suggest that these two examples represent daily occurrences in Ottawa or that all federal-provincial projects enjoy the same status. But they are revealing in that they are the norm when the prime minister decides to get involved. [...]

PRIMUS IN CABINET

Prime ministers bring their own style to managing their Cabinets and ministers. Trudeau, for example, was much more tolerant of meanderings and long-winded interventions from his ministers at Cabinet meetings than Chrétien, but unlike Chrétien, he was not particularly adroit at handling one-on-one meetings with his ministers. A student of comparative politics writing in the mid-1980s reported that "Canadian Prime Ministers, and particularly Trudeau, were usually powerful but patient."[4] Chrétien, by all accounts, [was] less patient in Cabinet than Trudeau was, but he [was] certainly no less powerful. Mulroney made much more use of humour in Cabinet meetings to make his points than Trudeau did, but both Trudeau and Mulroney relied on extensive Cabinet committee systems to manage the flow of Cabinet papers. Mulroney had a particularly large Cabinet, but he had it operate in an asymmetrical manner by concentrating more power in the priorities and planning and the operations committees.[5] Mulroney also spent more time than Chrétien or Trudeau either cajoling or, if necessary, browbeating his ministers to come to his point of view to establish Cabinet consensus. Clark, meanwhile, relied on a formal inner Cabinet and other ministers in managing his Cabinet and ministers.

To be sure, style and personalities are important in understanding how Cabinet government works, and one is constantly reminded of this by politicians, partisan political advisers, and permanent officials in the interviews. But there are things that transcend both style and personalities when it comes to understanding the workings of cabinet government in a parliamentary system. Put differently, style and personalities do differ, but there are things that remain constant. First, the prime minister has access to virtually all the necessary levers in Cabinet to ensure that he or she is the "boss" in Cabinet, and that if he so wishes—and prime ministers usually do—he can dominate Cabinet deliberations and its decision making. Second, prime ministers are convinced that they need to manage their Cabinet, to have a firm hand in shaping its discussions and decisions for their government to function properly.

The first sign that the prime minister has the upper hand is now evident even before he and his party assume power. Transition planning, a relatively new phenomenon in Canada, has become a very important event designed to prepare a new government to assume power. A former associate clerk of the Privy Council writes that "the first modern effort at transition planning in the public service ... occurred for the June 1968 general election."[6] He adds that transition planning has grown to become an elaborate planning process and now includes "the entire deputy minister community."[7] It is the Privy Council Office (PCO), however, that leads the process and it is clear that the "transition services [is for] the incoming prime minister."[8] Indeed, the focal point throughout the PCO transition planning process is on party leaders or would-be prime ministers. In any event, it would be difficult for it to be otherwise, since in the crucial days between the election victory and formally taking power, the only known member of the incoming Cabinet is the prime minister. For other potential Cabinet ministers, it is a "moment of high anxiety," waiting to see if they will actually be invited to sit in Cabinet, and if so, in what portfolio.[9]

The central purpose of transition planning is to equip the incoming prime minister to have his hand on the levers of power in the government's first few weeks in office. It is now widely recognized that these early weeks can be critical because they set the tone for how the new government will govern.[10] It is also the period when the prime minister, as recent history shows, will make important decisions on the machinery of government and decide which major policy issues his government will want to tackle during its mandate.

Once the prime minister is in office, it quickly becomes clear that his position in Cabinet gives him far more resources than other ministers, including an ability to shape most of its activities and many of its decisions, at least the ones that matter directly to him or in which he has a strong interest. The prime minister hires and fires Cabinet ministers, sets the agenda, and sums up its deliberations and decisions. In any event, ministers do not usually consider themselves to be guardians of any political theory, including the *primus inter pares* theory. Above all, they are politicians, they are deal makers, and they know full well that they stand a much better chance of striking deals if they are in Cabinet, and if they can count on the support of the prime minister at crucial moments. Ministers are also concerned about their own status in Cabinet, in caucus, and in their own ridings. They know that loyalty to the leader, particularly if he has been able to secure a majority mandate, is much valued in the party. In any event, whatever else may be said about Cabinet deliberations, one thing is clear—most ministers would much rather be on the prime minister's side than against him in Cabinet.

The prime minister appoints Cabinet ministers and parliamentary secretaries, and tradition and, more importantly, political realities require that they are loyal to him and in particular to government policy. Should a minister or a parliamentary secretary disagree with a government policy, he or she has two choices—keep quiet and bear it or resign from the post. History suggests that the overwhelming majority much prefer the first option.

It is true that Canada's prime ministers are not completely free to pick and choose ministers. For one thing, ministers are drawn from the legislative branch and so must come from the talent pool on the government side of the House of Commons, or as a last resort the Senate. In addition, no Canadian prime minister would appoint a Cabinet that lacked a proper regional, linguistic, and gender balance. Some have even turned to the Senate to ensure regional balance if the party failed to win a Commons seat in a province or region.[11]

But prime ministers also never lose sight of the need for strong support in Cabinet. Competence and regional balance are, of course, important, but no less important is the need for the prime minister to make Cabinet and the government his. And to do this, he needs a cadre of loyal soldiers in Cabinet. All Canadian prime ministers are certain to appoint well-known loyal supporters to their Cabinet (Trudeau appointed Roméo LeBlanc, Marc Lalonde, Allan MacEachen, and Lloyd Axworthy; Mulroney had Elmer McKay, Bob Coates, and George Hees; and Chrétien brought in David Dingwall, Ron Irwin, Sergio Marchi, and so on). In Canada at least, who supported whom in the party's leadership race will have an important bearing on who ultimately makes it to Cabinet. The strongest rivals to the prime minister will traditionally make it, but their key caucus supporters are not likely to be as fortunate.[12] They will be bypassed for those who supported the prime minister.

How does one become a Cabinet minister? The first step is to become a member of Parliament with the political party asked by the governor general to form the government. The process begins with a run at the party nomination and culminates with several weeks of intense political campaigning, knocking on doors, speaking to local service clubs, and attending all party meetings. Chances are that an individual who successfully navigates his party's nomination process and then goes on to win the riding for his party will be highly motivated and ambitious. Chances are also that he or she will want a seat at the Cabinet table. There are some members of Parliament who are quite happy not to be in the Cabinet. But they are very much in the minority. One minister suggested that "at least 90 per cent of the government caucus, if not more, would welcome an opportunity to sit in Cabinet. For the great majority of us, that is why we run for Parliament."[13]

For those 90 per cent or more, it helps to be from a province with limited representation on the government side (it is unlikely, for example, that Fred Mifflin would have been in the 1997 Chrétien Cabinet if he had been a member of Parliament from Ontario, where the Liberals won all but one seat in the election. He was from Newfoundland and Labrador). It also helps to be noticed. Those with a strong media profile stand a better chance of making it to Cabinet than an unknown backbencher. But one has to be careful in seeking media attention. No prime minister likes to have his Cabinet appointments appear in the press before he makes his choice public. Moreover, as Gerald Kaufman, former British minister, writes, "Voting against the Government on a confidence motion or personally insulting the Prime Minister is not recommended."[14] Unless one represents a riding from a province where few government MPs are elected, the best chance for an MP to make it to Cabinet is to establish a track record of loyalty to the prime minister and to have gained the confidence not only of the prime minister but also of his close advisers.

The prime minister's power of appointment also extends to the chairs and membership of Cabinet committees. These appointments, especially to the chairs, are significant signals as to who is in the prime minister's favour and who is not.

The prime minister is completely free to decide on the kind of committee structure he needs to support the work of his Cabinet. He can [...] overhaul the Cabinet committee structure at any moment without consulting any of his ministers and add new committees or abolish existing ones at the stroke of a pen. The prime minister also decides not only which issues will come forward to Cabinet but when. In addition, the Cabinet does not take votes, which provides the prime minister considerable latitude in defining the consensus.

To have in your own hands the ability to define the Cabinet agenda and to decide if the time is right to discuss a given issue or a proposal in Cabinet is to have an extremely powerful instrument of public policy. The prime minister, as we will see later, is able to draw on senior staff at the centre of government to keep him informed of developments in departments, to let him know what ministers and their departments are thinking, and to help him decide when a given issue should come before Cabinet.

Pierre Trudeau, as is well known, sought to introduce a much more rational approach to Cabinet deliberations and to see to it that all sides of an issue be fully aired before Cabinet made a decision. He established an elaborate Cabinet committee structure to ensure that this would occur. He wanted, he said, to wrestle policy influence away from departments and to give Cabinet the ability to make policy based on competing advice. Indeed, Trudeau decided to overhaul the Cabinet process precisely to break the stranglehold ministers and long-serving deputy ministers had on departments. He felt that major policy decisions and all administrative issues had become the preserve of line departments and that the centre was left ill-equipped to challenge them. The solution—strengthen the centre considerably. Richard French explains, "The Prime Minister's often expressed conviction [is] that Cabinet is less easily captured by the bureaucracy than are ministers operating independently."[15] Peter Aucoin writes that Trudeau launched a major assault on the centre of government to correct "the abuses and excesses of individual ministerial autonomy [which] had to be replaced by a rigorous system of checks and balances within the Cabinet as a collective executive." He adds, "The influence of the bureaucracy had to be countered to ensure that the organizational interests of departments and agencies did not take precedence over required policy innovation and policy coherence."[16] To sum up, Trudeau wanted policy making to be placed firmly in the hands of Cabinet and removed from those of a few powerful ministers and mandarins running government departments. This, in turn, explains why he decided to strengthen the centre of government by enlarging his own office, expanding the Privy Council Office, and establishing new Cabinet committees, effectively giving them the authority to make decisions.

But he saw limits to this approach, notably when he felt there was a chance the discussions would go in the wrong direction. He explained, "If I know that I am going to have a confrontation in Cabinet, if a minister is recommending something and I think it's dead wrong, I won't let him put the thing to Cabinet. I'll see him in my office, I'll set up an interdepartmental committee, I'll meet him privately, I'll say, 'Look, we're on a collision course, this can't possibly be right.' The whole role of the PCO, and the PMO to a certain degree, is to inform me of the genesis of the discussion, how it's going. And if I think it's going in a way that I approve, fine, I'm happy to let the consensus develop. If I think it's not going in the right direction, I ask them to arm me with the arguments and facts and figures."[17] Ministers, meanwhile, are expected to remain loyal to the Cabinet and accept decisions that go against their wishes after Cabinet has reconciled conflicting positions and the prime minister has defined a consensus. The same, however, is not true for the prime minister, who can easily manipulate the Cabinet agenda to get his way.

Some of the respondents revealed that Chrétien [was] on occasion even more direct than Trudeau when seeing proposals that he does not like. One career public servant who worked in the PCO under both prime ministers reports that Chrétien could, before the discussions went too far, simply say to a minister in private or even in front of colleagues, "I know what you are going to recommend. The answer is no. Forget it." Mulroney, in contrast, would, from time to time and depending on the minister, take the time to talk a minister out of a proposal or an idea that he did not like. But the consultations also reveal that Mulroney could be very direct in telling a minister to abandon an idea. In addition, Mulroney would rely on his deputy prime minister, much more than Chrétien, to manage "a stupid idea out of the system."[18]

The prime minister has yet another advantage in securing the upper hand in managing his Cabinet. In chairing Cabinet or a Cabinet committee, the prime minister has full access to unshared knowledge. For each item coming before Cabinet, the PCO will hand a memorandum to the prime minister outlining the major issues, the positions of some of his ministers, and almost always a recommended position. No other minister can come to the Cabinet table with this knowledge, a view of the total picture, knowing what key ministers are going to argue. Such knowledge, if nothing else, enables the prime minister, if he so wishes, to play one Cabinet minister against another, enabling him to establish the Cabinet consensus according to his own thinking. But here again the prime minister has to be careful in choosing the issues he means to influence. The prime minister's summary and decision or his definition of the Cabinet consensus cannot always go blatantly against the sense of the meeting if he is to retain the confidence of his ministers.

Still, interviews reveal that, at least since Trudeau, prime ministers do not hesitate to make use of their power to define Cabinet consensus to tilt decisions in their favour. One senior PCO official explained, "When the prime minister sees that 75 per cent of his colleagues are leaning in his direction, there is no problem, and when he sees that 50 per cent are leaning in his direction, there is still no problem. On very rare occasions, when he sees that he is clearly in the minority with, say, only 25 per cent of ministers leaning in his direction, he will often say to Cabinet, 'I have to reflect on this and I will get back to you shortly on it.' A few days later, he may well direct PCO, through the clerk, to issue a record of decision in his favour or simply hold the matter and have it put on the Cabinet agenda a few months down the road when he thinks that more ministers will speak out in support. My experience with prime ministers is that when they don't have their way the issue is not all that important to them."[19] Another senior PCO official who attended many Cabinet meetings as a notetaker reports that "on more than one occasion, I would take the head count, jotting down the names of the ministers I felt were on the yes side and those on the no side. The consensus was clearly on one side, but I would hear the prime minister draw the consensus on the other."[20]

A minister in the 1993–7 Chrétien government confirms that it is very rare that the prime minister is openly challenged in Cabinet. He reports that "I can only think of three occasions between 1993 and 1997 when the prime minister was openly challenged in Cabinet, and this is not to suggest for a moment that in the end he did not get his way. If my memory is correct, I believe that the prime minister got his way on two of the three occasions. On the third one, I think that the issue simply died, but I am not sure."[21] A senior PMO staff member who attends Cabinet meetings remembers things differently. He reports that he does not recall the prime minister being seriously challenged even once in Cabinet in Chrétien's first mandate. He adds, "That is the problem. Nobody wants to challenge him. In fact, a few of us in PMO do challenge his ideas from time to time, but not so in Cabinet." He went on to report that "on a few occasions ministers have come to me to say that the prime minister has it wrong on this or that issue. I say to them, you are a minister, tell him. A few days later, I will raise the matter with the minister to see if he has challenged the prime minister. Invariably, he will say no and that in the end the matter was not all that important."[22] [...]

THE PRIME MINISTER'S ASSISTANTS

The prime minister does not stand alone at the apex of government dealing with an incessant demand on his time, a hostile opposition in Parliament, a media always at the ready with daily doses of criticism, and a large bureaucracy to direct. He has political assistants and others to help him, to protect him from both internal and external threats, and to assist him in "squeezing forty-eight hours out of the Prime Minister's average day."[23]

Prime ministers, since Pierre Trudeau, have employed anywhere between 80 and 120 staff members in their own offices. Trudeau, as is well known, is the architect of the modern Prime Minister's Office. He felt that the Pearson years lacked a proper planning capacity at the centre, and as a result were marked by confusion and chaos. He resolved that things would be different in his government. He explained, "One of the reasons why I wanted this job, when I was told that it might be there, is because I felt it very important to have a strong central government, build up the executive, build up the Prime Minister's Office."[24] Trudeau, as noted earlier, considerably expanded the size of PMO and identified specific functions and tasks for it to perform. Tom Kent, principal secretary to Prime Minister Pearson, describes the Prime Minister's Office before Trudeau. He writes, "The PMO was then utterly different from what it became in the Trudeau era and has since remained. There was no bevy of deputies and assistants and principal this-and-that, with crowds of support staff."[25]

No prime minister since Trudeau has sought to turn back the clock and cut the size of the office back or to limit its functions to what they were before Trudeau. Mulroney, in fact, did the opposite. He increased the staff at PMO by one-third, increased the office's budget by 50 per cent, and added eight professional staff concerned with policy.[26] When Chrétien came to office, one of the first decisions he made was to abolish the chief of staff position in ministerial offices, a position which Mulroney had established. However, Chrétien decided to retain a chief of staff for his own office, who, as already noted, is ranked at the deputy minister level.

Marc Lalonde, former principal secretary to the prime minister, described the functions of PMO in the following fashion: "The sum total of the role of PMO today—it is a service organization and, as a by-product, it has an advisory capability."[27] There is no question that a great deal of what the PMO does is to provide administrative services and support for the prime minister. Another former PMO staff member made this clear when he wrote that the office "regularly helps [the prime minister] answer thousands of letters; makes travel to a number of public meetings in a single day manageable; enables him to deliver a variety of speeches or addresses within hours of one another, or appear on television programs and hotlines across the country. It regularly brings order to a complex schedule of meetings and consultations; reviews thousands of pages of documents and briefs; mobilizes to help him handle problems or crises."[28]

PMO service functions have been well described elsewhere, and there is no need to go over them in any detail here.[29] Suffice it to note that the office has a director of communications with a staff of about ten people. They handle all relations with the media, including requests for interviews, and they issue press releases, arrange press conferences, prepare speeches, and monitor press reaction and commentaries for the prime minister. They also promote the prime minister's image by, in the parlance of journalism, spinning stories to his political advantage. A correspondence unit handles the prime minister's mail, and an appointment secretariat reviews names for government or patronage appointments. A legislative assistant, as already noted, is exclusively concerned with the activities of the prime minister as a parliamentarian. Another assistant is concerned with caucus relations. Though they have been given various job titles over the years, there have always been regional assistants in the PMO since Trudeau overhauled the office. Their task is to give the prime minister "an additional view of social and political developments in each region."[30] Regional assistants are also responsible for planning and managing the prime minister's visits to their region. However, Chrétien upgraded the position early in his second mandate. In his first mandate, he and his advisers had "not anticipated how much international travel would have to be done by staffers working regional desks and regional travel advance." Chrétien's chief of staff, Jean Pelletier, announced in November 1997 that the office would not separate PMO staffers' roles of "regional assistant and travel advance to free regional assistants to concentrate on regional issues."[31]

To be sure, prime ministers bring their own style and approach to establishing their own offices and they are completely free to shape it as they see fit. Prime ministers can, at any time, restructure, reorganize, or restaff at will. Still, there is a strong bond of loyalty between the staff and the prime minister. The staff is partisan, of course, and enjoys tenure in office as long as that of their leader. Also most senior staff members were comrades-in-arms with the prime minister in previous political battles. But the office, with an annual budget of over $5 million and a person-year complement of about ninety under Chrétien, represents—at the risk of sounding repetitive—the largest concentration of highly paid partisan political advice found in any one place in Ottawa. [...]

REVISITING *PRIMUS*

Current and former ministers report that something happens to a colleague when he becomes prime minister. Things change, they reveal, and one can never be as relaxed with him as was the case before he became prime minister, no matter how close the relationship was. One Cabinet minister explains, "When your colleague becomes prime minister, overnight he assumes a different persona, or perhaps it is us who see him differently. We respect the fact that he has an impossible agenda, that now he has to deal with world leaders, and that we can no longer walk in his office for a relaxed chat. We quickly come to terms with the fact that he can no longer be one of us."[32] A former British Cabinet minister writes that "only those who have served in government fully realize the gulf between a Prime Minister and even the most senior and eminent of his colleagues. Even in casual conversation with them, he ceases to be addressed as 'Anthony' or 'Harold' and, except perhaps when there is no one else present, becomes Prime Minister."[33] Canadian prime ministers are not much different from British prime ministers on this front.

As already noted, students of parliamentary government are writing more and more about a shift towards a presidential form of government. They claim that it is increasingly difficult to write about collective ministerial responsibility or prime ministers as leaders of teams because prime ministers are fast becoming—like presidents—individuals at the top of the pile. Patrick Weller, for one, argues: " ... their [i.e., prime ministers'] control over government activities is regarded as excessive, and their accountability as far too limited. Observers complain that the system has changed from Cabinet government to prime-ministerial government, or that the office of prime minister has been presidentialised."[34] John Mackintosh was the first to express concern over the growing influence of the prime minister in his study of the British Cabinet in 1962.[35] He was later joined by a number of others expressing the same viewpoint, including a highly regarded Cabinet minister, Richard Crossman.[36] Mackintosh answered his critics in the early and mid-1970s, but by the late 1970s he felt it was no longer necessary.[37] He simply made the point that "events since [1962] have done so much to confirm the general case argued in this book" that he felt it unnecessary to make the case.[38] The debate is not limited to Britain. A keen student of Canadian politics suggests that Canada "seems to have created a presidential system without its congressional advantages."[39]

Few observers in Canada believe that the prime minister is still *primus inter pares.* The only time when the Canadian prime minister is still *primus inter pares* is when he chairs a First Ministers' Conference. Premiers are not his political equals, but they shape the discussions at the conference and advance whatever position they wish, even when it is in sharp opposition to the prime minister's position, as Clyde Wells did during the First Ministers' meetings that led to the renegotiation of the Meech Lake Accord.

First ministers now meet on a regular basis and their meetings cover a wide array of topics. The prime minister will consult with the chair of the Annual Premiers' Conference in preparing the agenda. At one meeting, the first ministers agreed to establish a Federal-Provincial-Territorial Ministerial Council on Social Policy Renewal and subsequently agreed to launch a series of joint initiatives.

At the December 1997 meeting, the prime minister reported on the "Team Canada" trade initiative and led a discussion on health care, youth employment, persons with disabilities, and on the development of a national children's agenda.[40] All first ministers have a say in shaping the agenda and all can voice opinions without fearing a demotion at the hand of the prime minister. The prime minister is also not free to define the consensus of the meeting according to his own preferences. It is in this sense that the Canadian prime minister is *primus inter pares* when he chairs a first ministers' meeting. The same cannot be said about Cabinet ministers. They have become much more the prime minister's subordinates than his *pares*. John Crosbie summed up the situation well when he explained why Brian Tobin left the federal Cabinet to become leader of the Liberal Party in Newfoundland and Labrador. He wrote, "In politics, never underestimate the importance of being number one. It is inevitably frustrating to work as a member of a government led by someone else. No matter how much power and authority leaders delegate to you or how well they treat you, they are still number one, and, when they choose to exercise their authority, they naturally have their way. If my leader became trapped by some political circumstance and blurted out a policy pronouncement in my area of responsibility—even if he didn't know much about the subject—I had to live with it. Even if he was completely wrong, I couldn't correct what he had done. But if a person is the leader, he can make the final decision."[41]

This [article] suggests that prime ministers leading a majority government can drive virtually whatever initiative or measure they might favour. Cabinet and Parliament are there, but with a majority of seats a prime minister can manipulate them when it comes to issues that matter a great deal to him. This is more how a United States president operates (without Congress) than what a textbook on British or Canadian politics would suggest is the proper role of the prime minister.

To be sure, prime ministers do not always bypass their Cabinets or only consult them after the fact on the great majority of issues. They will pick and choose issues they will want to direct. Indeed, in some circumstances and on certain issues a prime minister may well decide not to exert his or her authority and let the Cabinet's collective decision-making process run its course. He may also even let government caucus have its day from time to time and accept that a government proposal or legislation should be pulled back and reworked to accommodate the views of caucus members. There are issues on which a prime minister may hold no firm view, and a detached assessment of the costs and benefits of getting involved could suggest that it is best to keep one's political capital in reserve for another day and for another issue.

Prime ministers and their staff, sitting as they do at the apex of power, from where they can survey all developments in the government, come to believe that their political judgment is superior to that of ministers and to value their own opinion over others. After all, they made it to the top of the "greasy pole" while the senior ministers and their advisers, who also tried, did not.

Public opinion surveys also serve to strengthen the hand of the prime minister and his advisers. They no longer need to rely on the views of even powerful regional ministers to gain an appreciation of political developments. Indeed, the most recent public opinion surveys can enable them to challenge the views of ministers. If, say, the minister responsible for Nova Scotia claims that government spending cuts are hurting the party in that province, PMO staffers can point to a public opinion survey suggesting that the majority of Nova Scotians support the government's efforts to deal with the deficit and debt problem. There are now public opinion surveys documenting the views of Canadians on virtually every public policy issue. It is worth noting that a key speech at the 1998 Liberal Party policy conference was by the party's pollster, Michael Marzolini. Marzolini provided the "national-mood numbers," and his speech was as widely reported in the media as the prime minister's own speech.[42]

But there are other forces that serve to strengthen the hand of the prime minister in the machinery of government. We know that globalization has become more than a catchphrase. The emergence of global corporations, and new trade, financial, and communication links are dramatically changing the policy context for national governments in a shrinking world. The nation state, it has been suggested, is being challenged from diametrically opposed directions—from above by international and regional trade agreements and global firms, and from below by the emergence of regionally based nationalism and by linguistic or religious groups challenging the legitimacy of the nation state.

Yet national governments are still the ones being asked to solve many old and new problems. The global economy can set the stage for national and local economies to compete and lay down the rules under which economies and firms must operate. It is hardly possible, however, to imagine a global economy taking shape without conflicts between firms, sectors, regions, and nations or without far-reaching adjustments in some sectors and regions. The designers of the new order in many ways will have to be national politicians and national public services. They alone have the legitimacy.[43] When leaders of national governments come calling in Ottawa, and many do in the course of a year, they always call on the prime minister, and they invariably seek to deal directly with him.[44]

National governments, precisely because of global economic forces, will need to work increasingly with each other and with regional and international trade agreements. They will also need to develop a capacity to move quickly to strike new deals when the time is right, or to change course because of new or emerging political and economic circumstances and opportunities. The focus will be on the heads of national governments because of their ability to unblock files, cut through the decision-making process, and to sign and monitor trade deals.[45] It is the heads of governments that meet at G7, at Commonwealth meetings, at la francophonie, and at the APEC conference. As the national government is being challenged from above and from below, it appears that power is getting even more concentrated at the centre of government.

The Canadian prime minister, unlike the American president, who has to deal with Congress, or the Australian prime minister, who has to deal with a powerful elected and independently minded Senate, has a free hand to negotiate for his government and to make any deal with foreign heads of government adhere. The final hours of negotiations on NAFTA between Prime Minister-elect Chrétien and the United States president, through his Canadian ambassador, are telling. At one point, the American ambassador wondered about Chrétien's political authority to agree to a final deal, given that he had yet to appoint his Cabinet. The ambassador put the question to Chrétien, "What happens if we work all this out and then your new trade minister doesn't agree?" Chrétien replied, "Then I will have a new trade minister the following morning."[46]

It is hardly possible to overemphasize the fact that the Canadian prime minister has no outer limits defining his political authority within the government. To be sure, the media, opposition parties, question period, and public opinion can all serve to inhibit prime ministerial power. Similarly, what may appear at first to be a seemingly innocent incident can take on a life of its own and gain a high profile in the media and force the prime minister to reconsider a government strategy or a proposed initiative. But inside government, the prime minister is free to roam wherever he wishes and to deal with any file he chooses. There is ample evidence to suggest that Prime Ministers Trudeau, Mulroney, and Chrétien have all sought to push back the frontiers of their political authority. Events, the requirements of modern government, the role of the media, the role of first ministers in Canada, and the rise of the global economy have all served to strengthen considerably the hand of the prime minister. [...]

NOTES

1. G.W. Jones, "The Prime Minister's Secretaries: Politicians or Administrators?" in J. Griffith, ed., *From Policy to Administration: Essays in Honour of William A. Robson* (London: George Allen & Unwin, 1976), 36.

2. Quoted in Arthur M. Schlesinger Jr., *The Coming of the New Deal: The Age of Roosevelt* (Boston: Houghton, Mifflin Co., 1959), 518.

3. See John C. Crosbie, *No Holds Barred: My Life in Politics* (Toronto, McClelland and Stewart, 1997), 301.

4. Patrick Weller, *First Among Equals: Prime Ministers in Westminster Systems* (London: George Allen & Unwin, 1985), 8.

5. Evert Lindquist and Graham White, "Analysing Canadian Cabinets: Past, Present and Future," in Mohamed Charih et al., eds., *New Public Management and Public Administration in Canada* (Toronto: IPAC, 1997), 120.

6. John L. Manion and Cynthia Williams, "Transition Planning at the Federal Level in Canada," in Donald J. Savoie, ed., *Taking Power: Managing Government Transitions* (Toronto: IPAC, 1993), 100.

7. Ibid., 108.

8. Ibid., 99.

9. Donald J. Savoie, "Introduction," in *Taking Power,* 8.

10. Ibid., 1.

11. See, among others, James R. Mallory, *The Structure of Canadian Government* (Toronto: Macmillan, 1971), 90–109.

12. For example, John Crosbie, a leadership candidate at the time Brian Mulroney was elected leader of the Progressive Conservative Party, was named minister of Justice when Mulroney came to power in 1984, rather than Allan Lawrence, former attorney general of Ontario, solicitor general in Joe Clark's government in 1979, and opposition Justice critic between 1980 and 1984. Lawrence, however, had supported Crosbie rather than Mulroney in the leadership race. There are many other examples. Doug Young supported Jean Chrétien in his party leadership race, and Chrétien appointed him to Cabinet in 1993 over George Rideout, a highly respected former mayor of Moncton, who had supported Paul Martin.

13. Consultation with a former Cabinet minister in the Mulroney government, Ottawa, March 1993.

14. Gerald Kaufman, *How To Be a Minister* (London: Sidgwide & Jackson, 1980), 19.

15. Richard D. French, "The Privy Council Office: Support for Cabinet Decision-Making," in R. Schultz et al., eds., *The Canadian Political Process* (Toronto: Holt, Rinehart and Winston, 1979), 2d ed., 365.

16. Peter Aucoin, "Organizational Change in the Machinery of Canadian Government: From Rational Management to Brokerage Politics," *Canadian Journal of Political Science* XIX, no. 1 (March 1986): 8.

17. Quoted in George Radwanski, *Trudeau* (Toronto: Macmillan, 1978), 172.

18. Ibid., 173.

19. Consultation with a senior official in the Privy Council Office, Ottawa, November 1997.

20. Consultation with a former senior PCO official, Ottawa, January 1998.

21. Consultation with a former federal Cabinet minister, Ottawa, December 1997.

22. Ibid.

23. A PMO official quoted in Colin Campbell and George J. Szablowski, *The Super-bureaucrats: Structure and Behaviour in Central Agencies* (Toronto: Gage, 1979), 60.

24. Trudeau quoted in Radwanski, *Trudeau,* 146.

25. Tom Kent, *A Public Purpose: An Experience of Liberal Opposition and Canadian Government* (Montreal: McGill-Queen's University Press, 1988), 225.

26. Peter Aucoin, "Organizational Change in the Machinery of Canadian Government: From Rational Management to Brokerage Politics," 22.

27. Marc Lalonde, "The Changing Role of the Prime Minister's Office," *Canadian Public Administration* 14, no. 4 (Winter 1971): 519.

28. Thomas D'Aquino, "The Prime Minister's Office: Catalyst or Cabal? Aspects of the Development of the Office in Canada and Some Thoughts about Its Future," *Canadian Public Administration* 17, no. 1 (Spring 1974): 76-7.

29. See, among others, Richard French, *How Ottawa Decides: Planning and Industrial Policy-making 1968-1980* (Ottawa: Canadian Institute for Economic Policy, 1980), 77-84.

30. See Lalonde, "The Changing Role of the Prime Minister's Office," 526.

31. See "Pelletier reorganizes PMO staffers," *The Hill Times* (Ottawa), 24 November 1997, A1.

32. Consultation with a Cabinet minister, Ottawa, October 1997.

33. Quoted in Simon James, *British Cabinet Government* (London: Routledge, 1992), 94.

34. Weller, *First Among Equals*, 1.

35. John Mackintosh, *The British Cabinet* (London: Methuen, 1962). Professor Mackintosh was also a Labour member of Parliament from 1966 to 1974.

36. See Richard Crossman, *The Diaries of a Cabinet Minister*, vols. 1-3 (London: Hamish Hamilton and Jonathan Cape, 1975, 1976, and 1977).

37. Weller, *First Among Equals*, 4.

38. John Mackintosh, *The British Cabinet*, 3d ed., 1977, 631.

39. Denis Smith, "President and Parliament: The Transformation of Parliamentary Government in Canada," in Thomas A. Hockin, ed., *Apex of Power: The Prime Minister and Political Leadership in Canada*, 2d ed. (Scarborough, Ont.: Prentice-Hall, 1977).

40. Based on material including correspondence made available by the Prime Minister's Office, Ottawa, December 1997.

41. Crosbie, *No Holds Barred*, 476.

42. See, among others, "PM Not Sounding Valedictory Note," *Globe and Mail* (Toronto), 23 March 1998, A3.

43. See, among others, Donald J. Savoie, "Globalization and Governance" (Ottawa: Canadian Centre for Management Development, 1993), 8 and Daniel Bell, "The World and the United States in 2013," *Daedalus*, 116, no. 3 (1984): 19-26.

44. Over a three-day period at the end of November 1997, Prime Minister Chrétien met with the Japanese prime minister, the Chinese president, and the president of the Philippines. See, for example, "Chrétien Plays Host to Leaders," *Telegraph Journal* (Saint John), 27 November 1997, B3.

45. Harlan Cleveland, "The Twilight of Hierarchy: Speculations on the Global Information Society," *Public Administration Review* 45, no. 1 (January/February 1985): 195.

46. Quoted in Edward Greenspon and Anthony Wilson-Smith, *Double Vision: The Inside Story of the Liberals in Power* (Toronto: Doubleday, 1996), 48.

✘ NO
Limits on the Power of the Prime Minister
PAUL BARKER

Many close observers of Canadian politics believe that political power in Canada resides largely with the prime minister and his small group of close advisers. Those who make this argument are careful to admit that the prime minister comes up against some limits, but at the same time they describe Canada as "a kind of monarchy" that is "mandated by democracy."[1] The source of the prime minister's great influence, they say, lies in his access to so many "levers of power."[2] He leads the governing party, controls cabinet and its members, commands the attention of the media, sets the overall direction of the country, and much more. Also important, highly qualified officials located in the central agencies—the "superbureaucrats"—help the prime minister control all relevant matters.[3] There are some who urge caution in adopting the notion that government in Canada amounts to "prime-ministerial government." Keith Archer and his colleagues, for instance, say that the national government is "too large and too complex to be directed by a single individual."[4] But such sentiments appear to receive little attention. According to a popular text in Canadian politics, "[m]ost observers agree that Cabinet government has been transformed into a system of prime-ministerial government."[5] And other reputable sources also diligently outline the case that the prime minister's powers of influence dwarf those of others in the political process.[6]

The belief that the prime minister wields a great deal of power has some merit. The nature of parliamentary government is to situate power in the hands of the political executive, so we expect the prime minister to be influential. But to suggest that this forms the basis of a kind of monarchical democracy goes too far. Though many specific criticisms of the thesis of prime-ministerial government may be made, there are basically two problems with it. One is that it fails to note sufficiently that the prime minister faces some formidable players in the political process. The prime minister is simply not that powerful. There are forces both inside and outside government that can challenge the leader of the governing party. The other problem relates to the conception of competition. The theory of prime-ministerial government assumes that competition for power is viable only when it is patently obvious or present. But prime ministers can be challenged simply by the *threat* of a new competitive force. The prime minister operates in a world of "virtual competition," in which the challenges sometimes appear as only potentialities. The lack of a corporeal presence matters little because the prime minister acts as if the challenges are real. The key implication here is that there is indeed competition in Canadian politics—more so than suggested by a counting of the observable competitors—and that Canada is not nearly as vulnerable to the effects of concentrated power as suggested by those who see the influence of only the prime minister.

INSIDE GOVERNMENT

The idea of an almost domineering prime minister certainly exaggerates the power the prime minister commands outside the formal structures of government; and it can be argued that it is an exaggeration also of the power commanded inside government. Let us begin with the latter. Donald J. Savoie writes that "[it] is hardly possible to overemphasize the fact that the Canadian prime minister has no outer limits defining his political authority within the government."[7] In fact, one *can* overemphasize the influence of the prime minister. Outer limits exist, and one has to look only at the relations between prime ministers and their ministers to see this point. Take, for instance, former prime minister Jean Chrétien and his then-finance minister, Paul Martin. According to Mr. Chrétien himself, the finance minister had a great deal of leeway in the making of fiscal policy. "I am not going to tell my finance minister what to do," said Mr. Chrétien.[8] And this has been the tradition at the federal level: the finance minister runs the budgetary process. Of course, this is not say that the prime minister is shut out of this important process—the national leader can never ignore the economic health of the nation. The fact remains, however, that the finance minister is a powerful player in Canadian politics.

A well-known incident involving Mr. Martin and Mr. Chrétien is telling. In the mid-1990s, the finance minister wanted to announce major pension reforms in his budget. The reforms were risky politically, for they proposed to take away some pension benefits from well-off seniors. The prime minister balked at the changes and asked the finance minister to desist from making his announcement. Mr. Martin challenged the prime minister's counsel not once, but three times. He intimated that he might resign, which the prime minister realized would hurt his government— it could destabilize markets and would make the government look divided. In the end, the two men fashioned a compromise: the announcement would be held back until the next year, but the finance minister could mention the principles of pension reform now. The prime minister had been confronted and he had been forced to accept a compromise. This seems some distance from a prime minister without limits.[9]

There are instances of other ministers taking actions that reveal the limits of prime-ministerial power. Allan Rock, a federal minister of health in the Chrétien government, wanted to raise the profile of the federal government in the Canadian health care system. In early 2000, the health minister outlined a "new plan for health care."[10] Under the plan, Ottawa would be instrumental in effecting changes to the primary health care system and in setting up a national home care program. Both primary health care and home care fall within the jurisdiction of the provinces; accordingly, the new plan held out the possibility of major disruptions in relations between the federal government and the provinces. Many assumed, though, that this would be acceptable because it was thought that the prime minister had given his consent to the initiative. But the prime minister had done no such thing. A minister had announced a major policy initiative with serious implications for federal–provincial relations—without the prime minister's agreement.[11] Eventually, Mr. Chrétien put a stop to Mr. Rock's proposal, but it was clear that cabinet included members who had their own agendas.

The combination of ministerial ambition and backbencher support can also fatally weaken the prime minister. After the election of 2000, many expected Mr. Chrétien to leave office soon and open the way for a leadership race; he had already governed for two full terms and he was getting older. But the prime minister surprised all by saying that he might stay to fight another election in 2004, largely because he believed, correctly, that Mr. Martin and his supporters in the Liberal backbenchers wanted him to resign. The prime minister's speculations on his future infuriated both party members and Liberal MPs who wished to see Mr. Martin become the prime minister, and they began to call for Mr. Chrétien to step down. For a time, the prime minister resisted—he even fired Mr. Martin as finance minister in an attempt to solidify his position. But it was all to no avail; Mr. Martin had made great efforts to gain support of Liberal MPs who failed either to make it into cabinet or who were ignored by the prime minister and his advisors in the Prime Minister's Office. The finance minister also had in place an impressive organization dedicated to making him the prime minister. In August 2002, a humiliated Jean Chrétien announced he would leave office in early 2004, and, by late 2003, he was gone.[12]

For some, the demise of Mr. Chrétien was a product of special circumstances and hardly a sign of inherent prime-ministerial weakness. The former prime minister had been confronted by a minister determined to succeed him and a large group of returning MPs who received nothing from a prime minister unable to give them much. Mr. Chrétien also had no real organization in place to confront his competition—he was too busy running the government. All this may be true. But it is also true that a prime minister had been pushed aside, an unexpected event in the life of an individual who has many levers of power at his behest. [13] A former senior official in the PMO and respected observer of government gives his read of the demise of Mr. Chrétien:

> ... Savoie's 1999 metaphor of an all powerful love-like prime minister casting bolts of electricity into the system would have to be recast in 2003 as Jean Chrétien has been sent into retirement after losing control first of his party, then of his caucus. The events of the past year prove that Canada does not have a dictatorship, friendly or otherwise.[14]

In the government of Paul Martin, there are also signs of conflict between the first minister and elected members of his party. Initially, Prime Minister Martin appeared to look favourably on a decision that would see Canada work with the United States to develop a ballistic missile defence system for North America. But dissent in the party helped produce a contrary decision. The prime minister has also faced resistance from Liberal MPs who disagree with his government's support of legislation favouring same-sex marriage. These two instances of conflict are in part made possible because backbenchers realize that the prime minister is in a minority situation and needs their support. A majority situation might, of course, easily quash these differences. But the fact is that minority governments are part of parliamentary government, and they serve to lessen the power of the first minister.

There is another component of the prime-ministerial thesis that weakens under examination. As part of his attempt to ensure his powerful position, the prime minister (with his advisers) aims to keep his ministers out of trouble so that he "can get things done in areas that matter a great deal."[15] But the prime minister fails in this regard; he is not sufficiently powerful to accomplish this purpose. In these situations, ministers are not acting against the prime minister's wishes. Rather, they are merely being ministers, carrying out their mandates, and in so doing they run into difficulties. One has only to look at the Chrétien government in its later years for confirmation of this point. In early 2000, the minister of Human Resources Development Canada (HRDC) announced that an internal audit revealed that her department had effectively lost track of funds designated for job creation (some accounts put the lost amount at nearly $1 billion). The announcement set off a set of accusations and investigations that greatly hindered the operations of government. The prime minister tried to downplay the problem, saying that "[a]dministrative problems of this nature always exist."[16] But the opposition, the media, and some in the interested public remained unconvinced. The low point of the crisis occurred when the prime minister literally pushed aside, in full view of a television audience, his HRDC minister who was collapsing under the weight of media questioning.

Other members of the Chrétien government also found themselves in trouble. One of the former prime minister's cabinet members jostled over the issue of divorce with a Senator and a Liberal backbencher in the letters section of a national newspaper.[17] Ministers are expected to prevail over lesser members of government, but not in full view of Canadians and not to do so in an imperious fashion. Similarly, the actions of his minister of Indian Affairs and Northern Developed led the leader of a prominent First Nations organization to accuse the federal government of trying to extinguish the Aboriginal population and their culture.[18] More serious was the so-called "sponsorship scandal," in which the minister of Public Works (and his officials) allegedly transferred large amounts of money to Liberal advertising agencies for little or no work. The scandal has attracted a great deal of attention and most likely played some role in producing a minority government for the Liberal Party. It may eventually lead to the end of Prime Minister Martin's government, even though the events under consideration took place while Mr. Chrétien was prime minister.

On balance, it seems that the prime minister cannot really control his individual ministers. At times, they will pursue agendas that are inconsistent with the prime minister's actions. As Herman Bakvis says, "one can ... find examples of ministers carving out their own sphere of influence and taking initiatives."[19] The odd minister may also try to unseat the prime minister—and succeed. At other times, ministers will try to please the prime minister, but the nature of the job—the power and responsibilities—will land ministers in trouble no matter what the prime minister and his central-agency officials try to do. Moreover, it is not just the individual ministers who can constrain the prime minister. The collective ministerial or cabinet decision-making system operates to disperse power. For proponents of the prime-ministerial government thesis, the cabinet system works largely to the advantage of the prime minister. In cabinet, he purportedly sets the agenda, controls the dissemination of information, and makes the final decision (and sometimes he fails to bring his decision to cabinet's attention). But this, too, overstates the case. Most prime ministers realize, sooner or later, that this is a recipe for prime-ministerial overload, and that government functions well only when ministers run their own departments. Consequently, the cabinet system reflects the power of ministers. According to one study of the Chrétien years, the prime minister's "preference [was] to keep out of the hair of his ministers except in the most unusual circumstances."[20] The Privy Council Office (PCO), one of the most important advisory bodies to the prime minister, comes to a similar conclusion. "The tone of government may be set by the Prime Minister and the cabinet," reads a PCO document, "but most of the policies of the government flow from the exercise of the individual responsibilities of ministers."[21]

Government consists of more than just the executive branch. There are the legislature and the judiciary. The functioning of these two branches also contests the notion of an imperial prime minister. Admittedly, the legislature provides less of a challenge for the prime minister than the other two branches. Nevertheless, it can provide a test for the prime minister, and indeed the first minister under pressure can take actions to strengthen this part of government. Prime Minister Martin, for instance, has made a commitment to a number of changes that would strengthen the legislature.[22] Under this plan, party discipline in the House of Commons would be loosened and parliamentary standing committees would be granted more influence. Private members' bills would receive closer consideration and the ethics commissioner would now report to Parliament (and not to the prime minister). A proposal that has already had some effect allows parliamentary committees some say in the appointment of Supreme Court justices.

As for the judiciary, the advent of the Charter of Rights and Freedoms has made the courts a much more important player in Canadian politics. Some downplay the impact of the courts' interpretation of the Charter on other political actors, including the prime minister. But others suggest that the courts, with their interpretation of the Charter, have altered the distribution of power in Canada.[23] Even when decisions that may favour the prime minister are rendered, the transfer of power is taking place because it is the courts that are exercising authority, not the government leader. The prime minister also sometimes fails in an attempt to use the courts to the government's advantage. The Martin government referred its same-sex marriage legislation to the Supreme Court of Canada partly in the hope that the court would find the traditional definition of marriage inconsistent with the Charter of Rights and Freedoms. With this ruling, the prime minister could avoid the politically damaging task of acting against those who still believed in the traditional definition. But the highest court refused to address this issue and simply said that the new legislation outlining a new definition of same-sex marriage was acceptable without saying whether the old definition was unacceptable. The prime minister himself would thus have to apply the death-blow to a definition of marriage still supported by a large part of the electorate. The adjudication of non-Charter issues can also reveal the power of the courts. In 1998, the Supreme Court of Canada laid out the rules that would govern the secession of Quebec from Canada. Though the opinion of the court is non-binding, it has effectively determined how this country might come to an end. Arguably the most important decision affecting Canada was not made by the most important individual in Canadian politics; it was made by others.

OUTSIDE GOVERNMENT

Proponents of prime-ministerial government claim that their theory applies only to developments *within* government. The fact that the provinces or the media may limit the power of the first minister is irrelevant because the theory of prime-ministerial government does not extend outside the halls of government. Yet, these outside forces are sometimes used to demonstrate the power of the prime minister. The media, for instance, allegedly turns the first minister almost into a celebrity, which adds to the influence of the office of the prime minister. Similarly, globalization—another external force—also seemingly plays into the hands of the prime minister because it increasingly requires national leaders to make important decisions. Accordingly, it appears that these outside forces ought to be considered when attempting to assess the power of the prime minister. When this is done, it can be seen that they represent a double-edged sword for the prime minister. The media can place the prime minister in the spotlight and make the leader of the government appear well beyond others in the political process; but the media can hurt the prime minister in at least two related ways. The media practise what some call "gotcha journalism," which is an attempt to highlight the gaffes and mistakes of political leaders.[24] Mr. Chrétien was often the target of this kind of journalism, and Mr. Martin has also experienced at times a rough ride from the media. The media can also use their investigative resources to force an issue onto the political agenda that can hurt the prime minister. The media made much of the former prime minister's attempt to convince a government agency to provide financial assistance to a business concern in Mr. Chrétien's riding. As for the present prime minister, he has so far escaped any media investigations, but during his leadership run the media looked into arrangements relating to his personal affairs.

Globalization, too, may limit the power of the prime minister. Globalization has many meanings and definitions, but basically it focuses on how worldwide forces, especially economic ones, are eroding national boundaries. At present, the nation-state is the primary organizing principle of world politics; however, globalization works to supplant this principle and insert a new one that emphasizes the clout of *supra*national institutions (political and otherwise). In these circumstances, leaders of nation-states, including the prime minister of Canada, should see their power reduced. And in fact there is evidence of weakened leaders, as they accept the dictates of international trade agreements and new tax regimes that demand a common playing field upon which the world's multinational corporations can play.

Proponents of the prime-ministerial government thesis are, however, unconvinced by this kind of analysis. Savoie, for one, says that leaders still maintain great power in a global world because "[t]he designers of the new order in many ways will have to be national politicians and national public services."[25] But this participation of national leaders may be short-lived; they might turn out to be their own gravediggers. Also, those believing in leaders' continued pre-eminence may be guilty of confusing globalization with "internationalization."[26] The latter refers to the heightened interaction between nation-states, a development that strengthens nation-states and their leaders. But globalization is different; its functioning does not really depend on national leaders getting together and making decisions. Globalization seeks to bypass nation-states because it sees them as an obstacle. It is of interest to note that the original proponent of the prime-ministerial government thesis in the Canadian context now admits that the "power that any Canadian prime minister is able to exercise has been leeching away."[27] According to Denis Smith, the prime minister can hardly stand up to the relentless effects of multinational corporations, free trade agreements, and the worldwide financial markets. In plain terms, globalization greatly curbs the influence of the prime minister.

The provinces represent another force outside the national government that reduces the power of the prime minister. In fact, it may be argued that the provinces are more deserving of attention than other forces outside government because they effectively are *within* government at the national level. As many students of Canadian federalism have argued, there are few policy matters that fail to involve both orders of government.[28] One order thus constitutes an extension of the other and vice versa. Another way to see the possible uniqueness of the provinces in the theory of prime-ministerial government is to compare the parliamentary system with the presidential one. Those who see the prime minister as being too powerful point to the separation of powers in the American political system and how this arrangement limits the president. They then note that the absence of such arrangement in Canada strengthens the prime minister. But the supporters of theory of prime-ministerial government fail to finish the story. Government in Canada may not be divided *within* government, but it is divided *between* governments. The operation of the federal principle in Canada (unlike that in the U.S.) gives Canada its own version of the separation of powers. To exclude the provinces in a consideration of the power of the prime minister is to fail to appreciate the full operation of government in Canada. As Richard Simeon and Elaine Willis seem to say, the nature of federalism in Canada almost appears as the natural attempt of any democracy to find ways to ensure that power is never too concentrated:

> In Canada, the closest parallel to divided government is found not in relations between executive and legislative but in federalism itself. Much of the imagery surrounding divided government in the United States is replicated in analyses of federal-provincial relations in Canada. Just as an assertive Congress challenges the president, so do assertive provinces challenge Ottawa.[29]

When one does consider the provinces and their impact on the prime minister, the restraining effect of the provinces can be seen quite clearly. The provinces have constitutional authority over important matters and they represent strong regional interests that can clash with the overall national interest. The sheer size and wealth of some provinces also play a part in relations between the provinces and the prime minister. Recent developments reveal the difficulties the provinces pose for the first minister. Over the past half decade, both Mr. Chrétien and Mr. Martin have attempted to establish a strong role for Ottawa in health care. In these efforts, they have admittedly succeeded in attaching some stipulations to the use of additional financial assistance from the federal government. But the fact remains that the provinces still largely control the shaping and formulating of health policy. More recently, the prime minister has committed his government to the establishment of a national child care program, an area of public policy within the constitutional ambit of the provinces. Not surprisingly, the provinces have resisted the attempt of the prime minister to give structure to the proposed program, and some have demanded that Mr. Martin just provide the necessary cash with few, if any, stipulations. At the moment, it appears as if the prime minister and his responsible minister will be flexible and allow the provinces to spend federal monies on child care arrangements that the provinces find most fitting and appropriate.[30]

Recent events are not the only relevant pieces of evidence when considering federal-provincial relations and the power of the prime minister. The history of federalism, at least since the end of World War II, is the history of declining federal power. "The prominent characterizing feature of the evolution of the Canadian federation in the postwar period," write Robin Boadway and Frank Flatters, "is the gradual but persistent decentralization of fiscal responsibilities from the federal government to the provinces (and their municipalities)."[31] Recently, as reflected in its efforts to affect health care, the federal government and its leader have sought to reverse this trend, to give the national interest—and the prime minister—greater prominence in important areas of public policy.[32] But the trend seems too strong. The money and power have shifted from the federal government to the provinces. The prime minister leads a government that must contend with the reality that it exists in one of the world's most decentralized federal states. The implication of this for the thesis of prime-ministerial government should be clear: The prime minister may not have a United States Congress to deal with, but he does have the provinces.

VIRTUAL COMPETITION

In his article, Donald J. Savoie writes that prime ministers "have in their hands all the important levers of power." But a few paragraphs later, he also writes that "one of the main preoccupations of the most senior officials in government is to protect the prime minister."[33] The power of the prime minister is evidently combined with a rather precarious hold on office, a state of affairs that seems distinctly odd. Surely, a powerful prime minister is free of constant concern for his very survival, yet the reality appears otherwise. Even Mr. Chrétien himself admitted his vulnerability: "It's a survival game played under the glare of light. If you don't learn that, you're quickly finished."[34] The prime minister supposedly governs with few checks; nevertheless, he participates in a game of survival in which all participants—including himself—risk fatal blows.

Part of the explanation for this puzzling state of affairs has already been provided. There are constraints on the prime minister's power. He needs to worry about his situation because he faces challengers. But the near desperate situation of the prime minister depicted in Savoie's writings suggests that something more is at work. The prime minister does countenance challengers whom all can see— cabinet ministers, the provinces, the media. However, he also contends with threats to his position, which amount to competitive forces that are not so evident— a kind of "virtual competition." Normally, we associate competition with entities that are clearly present; but competition can also come in the form of possibilities and potentialities. The result is an individual or organization that possesses a near-monopoly situation but that feels itself to be under siege. In the world of business, this phenomenon is recognized. Powerful companies dominate sectors of the private market, but their chief executive officers admit themselves to be almost terrified by competition. For example, the head of Intel, the fabulously successful maker of computer chips, practises "management by paranoia," and warns other similarly situated business leaders to do the same. Officers of Microsoft, another company in a position of almost complete dominance, utter similar sentiments.[35] The traditional conception of competition demands the existence of clear competitors who force the more powerful actors to adjust their behaviour accordingly; but another conception sees competition in ghostly threats with very imaginable and lethal outcomes.

With this latter notion of competition, the anxiety experienced by the prime minister and his advisers becomes more understandable. The prime minister feels himself to be in a game of survival because he *is* in a game of survival: "The press want to get you. The opposition want to get you. Even some of the bureaucrats want to get you."[36] On the surface, these sentiments of Mr. Chrétien seem mere hyperbole—there are challenges to a prime minister's power, but not to this extent. But perhaps the former prime minister knows better, for he appreciates the possibilities of disaster in his environment. Take, for instance, the opposition. Normally the House of Commons attracts little attention in discussions of the prime minister's power; party discipline reduces the legislature to a bit player in Canadian politics. But a misstep in Parliament, perhaps during Question Period, can damage the prime minister. That is why his senior advisers spend so much time preparing him and cabinet members for their session in the House of Commons. Of course, this is not to say that Parliament rivals the prime minister; but it is to say that members of Parliament have the capacity to ruin a prime minister. Much like a company that can be undermined overnight by a new invention, the prime minister can find himself in serious trouble with a careless response to a question or an insensitive appreciation of a parliamentary matter.

Perhaps even more unsettling in politics (and business) are the threats from the truly unforeseen entities. A prime minister can try to defend himself from the dangers posed by the House of Commons and other well-known elements in the political process. More difficult is a defence against something that essentially emerges from nowhere—a new charismatic leader, a past indiscretion coming to light, a debilitating court decision. In such a world, anything does become possible and prime-ministerial vigilance turns into a practical obsession with challenges to the government.

The important consequence of virtual competition is that the Canadian political process is much less susceptible to the evils of concentrated power than commonly thought. Again, experience in the private sector is instructive. There are well-known companies with positions of incredible influence and wealth who do not act like entities with a near monopoly of the market. Under monopoly conditions, the expectation is that prices will rise, quality will decline, and innovation will disappear. However, this fails to transpire with these companies. Instead, prices fall, quality rises, and innovation takes place.[37] With the appropriate adjustments, the same phenomenon can be seen in political life. Under prime-ministerial government, we should experience high costs, bad public policy, insensitive politicians, and few fresh approaches to societal problems. Some may claim that Canada has all of these, but this would be an exaggeration of the true situation. There are a number of indicators of good government in Canada, a reality that clashes with the predictions of prime-ministerial government. Canada has social policies that are admired around the world, it sometimes serves a useful purpose in foreign affairs (for example, peacekeeping), and the United Nations annually places Canada either at the top of or near the top of the list of the world's best nations in which to live. These outcomes hardly seem consistent with the evils of concentrated power.

CONCLUSION

There is no argument with the claim that Canada's prime minister has substantial influence and that he is the most powerful player in Canadian politics. The objections arise when the claim extends to the notion that the first minister has no real challengers. The thesis of prime-ministerial government suggests that the distance between the prime minister and the other players in the Canadian political process in terms of power is great. The reality, however, is that the gap is not substantial and that it can be bridged. Both inside and outside government there are entities that can remind the prime minister that politics is a game of survival for *all* players. Inside government can be found ambitious cabinet ministers, disgruntled backbenchers, and newly empowered judges; outside government are the media, premiers, provinces, and a world that pays less and less attention to national leaders. To be fair to those who subscribe to the theory of prime-ministerial government, the challenges that emanate from within and from without government are not equally forbidding. The proponents of prime-ministerial government focus on power relations inside government, and one is certainly on more solid ground when trying to argue for the presence of a prime minister without equals *inside* government than when endeavouring to do the same in relation to matters *outside* government. But even inside government the prime minister must be on guard. Moreover, there are always the threats inherent in the world of virtual competition. Many survey the Canadian political process and see very little for the prime minister to worry about; but they do not see what the prime minister sees.

Ultimately, the belief in the all-powerful prime minister founders because it is at odds with the reality of Canada. This country has its problems; nevertheless, it is recognized as a functioning democracy with public policies that stand up well against those of other nations. Unless one believes in benevolent dictatorships, good public policy cannot generally be said to coexist with a political system in which much of the political power lies with one person and his advisers.[38] Canada's national leader is powerful, but not to the point where power turns into a corrupting force. Fortunately, the competitive pressures in Canadian politics are simply too great for us to have reached this point.

NOTES

1. Donald J. Savoie, "The King of the Commons," *Time*, May 3, 1999, p. 64.

2. Donald J. Savoie, *Governing from the Centre: The Concentration of Power in Canadian Politics* (Toronto: University of Toronto Press, 1999), p. 72.

3. Colin Campbell and George Szablowski, *The Superbureaucrats* (Toronto: Macmillan, 1979).

4. Keith Archer et al., *Parameters of Power: Canada's Political Institutions,* 3rd ed. (Toronto: ITP Nelson, 2002), p. 241.

5. Rand Dyck, *Canadian Politics: Critical Approaches,* 4th ed. (Scarborough: Thomson Nelson, 2004), p. 504.

6. See, for example, Savoie, *Governing from the Centre.*

7. Savoie, *Governing from the Centre,* p. 108.

8. Edward Greenspon and Anthony Wilson-Smith, *Double Vision: The Inside Story of the Liberals in Power* (Toronto: Doubleday Canada, 1996), p. 163.

9. Ibid., ch. 16.

10. Robert Fife and Giles Gherson, "Rock Proposes New National Health Plan," *National Post,* January 27, 2000, pp. A1, A11.

11. Anne McIlroy, "Rock's Grand Plan Was News to the PM," *Globe and Mail,* March 4, 2000, p. A3.

12. For more on this, see Susan Delacourt, *Juggernaut: Paul Martin's Campaign for Chrétien's Crown* (Toronto: McClelland and Stewart, 2003).

13. British Prime Minister Tony Blair has also been forced to compete with his finance minister, suggesting that direct ministerial challenges to the prime minister are not so rare. See Elizabeth Renzetti, "Buddies in Bad Times," *Globe and Mail,* April 23, 2005, p. F3.

14. Thomas Axworthy, "Our Public Service Malady: A Diagnosis," *Globe and Mail,* September 27, 2003, p. D4. (In this article, Axworthy is reviewing a new book by Savoie: Donald J. Savoie, *Breaking the Bargain: Public Servants, Ministers, and Parliament* [Toronto: University of Toronto Press, 2003]).

15. Savoie, *Governing from the Centre,* p. 336.

16. Daniel LeBlanc, "Multibillion-dollar Mess Routine, Chrétien Says," *Globe and Mail,* February 1, 2000, p. A5.

17. For the exchange of letters, see the letters section of following editions of the *National Post:* July 10, 2000; July 16, 2000; July 20, 2000; and July 26, 2000.

18. Justine Hunter, "Native Leader Alleges Racist Federal Plot," *National Post,* July 18, 2000, p. A1.

19. Herman Bakvis, "Prime Minister and Cabinet in Canada: An Autocracy in Need of Reform?" *Journal of Canadian Studies* 35, no. 4 (Winter 2001): 65.

20. Greenspon and Wilson-Smith, *Double Vision,* p. 35.

21. Privy Council Office, *Responsibility in the Constitution* (Ottawa: Minister of Supply and Services, 1993), p. 62.

22. For a discussion of these changes, see Peter Aucoin and Lori Turnbull, "The Democratic Deficit: Paul Martin and Parliamentary Government," *Canadian Public Administration* 46, no. 4 (2003).

23. See the debate between Peter H. Russell and F.L. Morton in Mark Charlton and Paul Barker, eds., *Crosscurrents: Contemporary Political Issues,* 3rd ed. (Scarborough: ITP Nelson, 1998), Issue Fourteen.

24. George Bain, *Gotcha! How the Media Distort the News* (Toronto: Key Porter Books, 1994).

25. Savoie, *Governing from the Centre*, p. 107.

26. See Jan Aart Scholte, "The Globalization of World Politics," in John Baylis and Steve Smith, eds., *The Globalization of World Politics: An Introduction to International Relations* (New York: Oxford University Press, 1997).

27. Denis Smith, "Is the Prime Minister Too Powerful?—Yes" in Mark Charlton and Paul Barker, eds., *Crosscurrents: Contemporary Political Issues*, 2nd ed. (Scarborough: Nelson Canada, 1994), p. 159.

28. See, for example, Richard Simeon, "The Federal-Provincial Decision Making Process," in *Ontario Economic Council, Issues and Alternatives—1977: Intergovernmental Relations* (Toronto: Ontario Economic Council, 1977), p. 26.

29. Richard Simeon and Elaine Willis, "Democracy and Performance: Governance in Canada and the United States," in Keith Banting, George Hoberg, and Richard Simeon, eds., *Degrees of Freedom: Canada and the United States in a Changing World* (Montreal: McGill-Queen's University Press, 1997), p. 171.

30. John Ibbitson, "Frazzled in the Forum: A Besieged PM Hangs on," *The Globe and Mail*, April 23, 2005, p. A8.

31. Robin Boadway and Frank Flatters, "Fiscal Federalism: Is the System in Crisis?" in Keith G. Banting, Douglas M. Brown, and Thomas J. Courchene, eds., *The Future of Fiscal Federalism* (Kingston: School of Policy Studies et al., 1994), p. 137.

32. Gerard Boismenu and Peter Graefe, "The New Federal Tool Belt: Attempts to Rebuild Social Policy Leadership," in *Canadian Public Policy* XXX, no. 1 (2004).

33. Savoie, *Governing from the Centre*, pp. 72–73.

34. Savoie, *Governing from the Centre*, p. 313.

35. Robert J. Samuelson, "The Gates of Power," *The New Republic*, April 23, 2001, p. 31.

36. Savoie, *Governing from the Centre*, p. 313.

37. Samuelson, "The Gates of Power."

38. One might also believe in a "friendly dictatorship." See Jeffrey Simpson, *The Friendly Dictatorship* (Toronto: McClelland & Stewart, 2001).

POSTSCRIPT

At first blush, it is difficult to argue with Donald Savoie. He has interviewed many people at the centre of government and they tell him that the prime minister comes up against no real limits to his power. If a minister crosses the prime minister on an important issue, the minister is gone tomorrow. If cabinet challenges the prime minister, then the prime minister either ignores cabinet or waits for his ministers to see the wisdom of his position. If a provincial premier wants something, then the prime minister can make it happen—simple as that. But is it all really that simple? A prime minister who almost casually fires ministers, for example, is unlikely to generate the level of trust necessary for government to succeed. Savoie seems to think the prime minister and his assistants in the Prime Minister's Office can run government almost by themselves (and therefore, losing ministers represents no real cost). But government is much too large and sprawling for this to be possible. The prime minister needs ministers because he needs help. Government is not a one-person show.

In his article, Paul Barker points out additional problems with Savoie's thesis. Ministers can challenge the prime minister—without necessarily facing dismissal—and forces outside government proper can reduce the influence of the prime minister. Savoie may claim that his views pertain only to the internal dynamics of government, but to say that the prime minister prevails within government may not be saying very much. One needs to examine the likes of the media and the provinces to acquire a full appreciation of the operation of parliamentary government. Then there is the case of Jean Chrétien. It is not clear how his demise fits with the notion of a near all-powerful prime minister. But Barker, too, may be guilty of exaggeration—he may, in other words, underestimate the true power of the prime minister. He is impressed with how ministers are able to challenge the prime minister, but it looks as if he has ignored the fact that most of these challenges end with the prime minister getting his way. As for the prime minister failing to keep his ministers out of trouble, this may be seen as amounting to very little. More generally, Barker seems to take little notice of Savoie's interviews with individuals who should know how government works. These individuals make it clear that the prime minister is without any equals and they suggest that no one is even close to the prime minister in terms of pure power.

To begin an analysis of the power of the prime minister, the interested student first needs to understand the system of parliamentary government and the prime minister's formal role in it. For this, one might consult Peter Aucoin, "Prime Minister and Cabinet," in James Bickerton and Alain-G. Gagnon, eds., *Canadian Politics,* 3rd ed. (Peterborough: Broadview Press, 1999) or Michael Whittington, "The Prime Minister, Cabinet, and the Executive," in Michael Whittington and Glen Williams, eds., *Canadian Politics in the 21st Century,* 6th ed. (Scarborough: Thomson Nelson, 2004). Jeffrey Simpson's book *The Friendly Dictatorship* (Toronto:

McClelland & Stewart, 2001) might then be read for an engaging discussion of the thesis of prime-ministerial government. With these readings completed, the student is now ready to tackle Savoie's detailed analysis of prime-ministerial power: Donald J. Savoie, "The Rise of Court Government in Canada," *Canadian Journal of Political Science* 32, no. 4 (December 1999) and Donald J. Savoie, *Governing from the Centre: The Concentration of Power in Canadian Politics* (Toronto: University of Toronto Press, 1999). For a shorter and more recent presentation of Savoie's position, one might read Donald J. Savoie, "Power at the Apex: Executive Dominance," in James Bickerton and Alain-G. Gagnon, eds., *Canadian Politics*, 4th ed. (Peterborough: Broadview Press, 2004) or Donald J. Savoie, "The Federal Government: Revisiting Court Government in Canada," in Luc Bernier, Keith Brownsey, and Michael Howlett, eds., *Executive Styles in Canada: Cabinet Structures and Leadership Practices in Canadian Government* (Toronto: University of Toronto Press, 2005).

To appreciate the genesis of this discussion in Canada (and elsewhere), one should read Thomas A. Hockin, ed., *Apex of Power: The Prime Minister and Political Leadership in Canada,* 2nd ed. (Scarborough: Prentice-Hall, 1977). The belief that the position of prime minister has become almost too powerful is not limited to those who examine Canadian politics. Other parliamentary democracies may also be operating under prime-ministerial government. For more on this, see Patrick Weller, *First Among Equals: Prime Ministers in Westminster Systems* (London: George Allen & Irwin, 1985). Weller has also produced a more recent consideration of cabinet government and the prime minister in Patrick Weller, "Cabinet Government: An Elusive Ideal?" *Public Administration* 81, no. 4 (2003).

Savoie and other liked-minded scholars are not without their critics. A critical examination of the theory of prime-ministerial government can be found in Herman Bakvis, "Prime Minister and Cabinet in Canada: An Autocracy in Need of Reform?" *Journal of Canadian Studies* 35, no. 4 (Winter 2001). The article addresses directly the analysis of Savoie and others who subscribe to the theory of prime-ministerial government, and he provides as well a useful bibliography on the topic of prime-ministerial power. For an account of the fall of former prime minister Jean Chrétien, one might read Susan Delacourt, *Juggernaut: Paul Martin's Campaign for Chrétien's Crown* (Toronto: McClelland and Stewart, 2003). Prime ministers in other countries are also experiencing difficult times, including Prime Minister Tony Blair of Great Britain. See, Geoffrey Wheatcroft, "The Tragedy of Tony Blair," *Atlantic Monthly* (June 2004).

Should Parliament Review Supreme Court Appointments?

✔ **YES**
F.L. MORTON, "Why the Judicial Appointment Process Must Be Reformed"

✘ **NO**
H. PATRICK GLENN, "Parliamentary Hearings for Supreme Court Appointments?"

A good bet for inclusion in a politics exam is a question on how Supreme Court justices in Canada are appointed and whether this appointment process is suitable. A decent answer to the first part of the question is within reach of the diligent student. The federal minister of justice draws up a short list of candidates based on consultations with interested parties, who may include the Chief Justice of the Supreme Court, relevant provincial officials, members of law societies, and the Canadian Bar Association. The justice minister then evaluates the candidates in light of their professional capacity, personal characteristics, and diversity. With this done, the minister and the prime minister discuss the candidates and recommend one of them to cabinet for appointment to the Supreme Court of Canada. This part of the exam question can be nicely answered, thanks in part to the greater willingness lately of the federal government to give us a better view of the selection process.

The second part of the exam question—the suitability of the process—is more challenging. One possible answer is to contend that the process is fine. The process seeks to include interested and expert parties and applies relevant criteria to the assessment of candidates. The centrality of the prime minister and cabinet also confirms the importance of the task. The real test of suitability lies in the results: Do the selected candidates perform well? The consensus is that Canada has been well served by justices of the Supreme Court of Canada. So it seems a good answer is that the present process is more than suitable.

But another answer is possible. Such an answer would start with the observation that the Charter of the Rights and Freedoms has made the Supreme Court of Canada a more central part of Canadian politics. Its decisions on the Charter amount to important statements of public policy, often touching the lives of everyday Canadians (e.g., Sunday shopping, abortion, and same-sex marriage). Accordingly, it seems that the selection of the justices should provide for public input. Following the American practice, we should institute a system in which nominated justices have to appear before a parliamentary committee. Our elected representatives would have a chance to question the nominee on issues of interest to Canadians. This would also open up the process and make the justices better known.

There are, however, some possible problems with such an answer. Potential nominees to the Supreme Court might refuse to stand for nomination if they thought the process provided the possibility of an embarrassing session before a parliamentary committee. There is also the fear that parliamentary hearings would unnecessarily politicize the selection process—for example, opposition members on the committee might see this as an opportunity to criticize the government. As a result, it might be argued that a process that lies somewhere between the status quo and parliamentary hearings would be preferable. Recently, the justice minister consented to appear before a parliamentary committee to explain two appointments to the Supreme Court. Such an adjustment to the present process might be suitable because it gives elected members—and Canadians—greater insights into the selection process without actually placing the nominees before the committee. Another possible answer, recommended by the Canadian Bar Association, is to set up a formal advisory committee that would put forward a short list of candidates to the justice minister. The fact that the committee would include representatives from Parliament would supposedly meet the demand for more public input. The federal government has indicated that it could accept such a proposal.

Clearly, it is difficult to provide a solid answer to questions about the suitability of the process for selecting Supreme Court justices. Perhaps the wisest course of action is to lay out all the options and list their pluses and minuses—and then try to centre on the one that best suits Canada.

In the readings, F.L. Morton, a political scientist specializing in judicial politics (and a newly elected MLA in Alberta), argues for parliamentary hearings. For Professor Morton, there is no doubt about the best answer to the query about the suitability of the present selection process. H. Patrick Glenn, a professor of law at McGill University, contends that Canada should stay with the current selection process. For Professor Glenn, parliamentary hearings and other attempts to include parliamentary representatives into the selection process fail to appreciate the workings of parliamentary government and the crucial difference between law and politics.

✔ **YES**

Why the Judicial Appointment Process Must Be Reformed

F.L. MORTON

It is time to reform the appointment process for Supreme Court judges. Since the adoption of the Charter of Rights and Freedoms in 1982, the Supreme Court has become a powerful actor in Canadian politics. Yet the appointment of our new constitutional masters remains largely unchanged, shielded from any public review or comment. Like the selection of a new Pope, Canadians learn who has been chosen as one of their new constitutional priests only after the decision has been made. This closed system was appropriate to the important but secondary role played by judges under Canada's old regime of parliamentary supremacy. It is completely inconsistent with the powerful new role of judges under the Charter. In a properly organized democracy, the exercise of political power must be ultimately accountable. Under the new regime ushered in by the Charter, this is no longer the case. If we are to prevent constitutional supremacy from degenerating into judicial supremacy, we must amend the appointment process to include some form of public review of the candidates.

There can be no questioning the fact that the Charter has fundamentally altered the role of the Supreme Court in Canadian politics. Prior to 1982, the court rarely obstructed the policy choices of Parliament or provincial legislatures. During this era, most of the Supreme Court's decisions dealt with civil (private) law disputes. Legislatures made these laws and courts applied and interpreted them. If a government believed the court had misinterpreted a statute, this mistake could be quickly reversed by legislative amendment. During the 1950s and 1960s, the court averaged less than three constitutional decisions per year, almost all in the field of federalism. Impact studies found that even a negative division of powers decision rarely prevented a determined government from achieving the same policy objective through alternative legislative means.

The adoption of the Canadian Bill of Rights in 1960 did not change the court's low political profile. In keeping with the then strong British influence in Canadian legal culture, the court interpreted the Bill of Rights in a traditional and deferential manner. In thirty-five decisions over twenty years, the individual rights claimant won only five cases. In only one case did the Supreme Court declare a federal statute invalid. Writing in the late 1960s, one expert accurately described the Supreme Court as "the quiet court in an unquiet country."[1]

The "Charter Revolution" of the 1980s brought this era to an abrupt end.[2] In the first decade following its adoption, the Supreme Court made over 200 Charter decisions. In these first decisions, the court ruled in favour of the rights claimant sixty-seven times, striking down portions of twenty-seven federal and fourteen provincial statutes in the process. These statistics, as impressive as they are, still fail to capture the extent of the court's new influence over public policy—of who gets what, when, and how.

The court has virtually rewritten the law of Canadian criminal process, reversing many of its earlier precedents along the way. It has adopted an exclusionary rule that is at least as rigorous as the American practice.[3] The right to counsel has been interpreted to discourage almost any police questioning of suspects in the absence of counsel[4] and to preclude judicial use of almost any form of self-incrimination at any stage in the investigative process.[5] A comparative study concluded that the accused in Canadian criminal cases now enjoy more rights than in the United States.[6] As a consequence of these decisions, the cost of publicly funded legal aid has skyrocketed. In Ontario, legal aid costs rose from $56 million in 1982 to $213 million in 1992. In Alberta, legal aid costs grew 42 percent in 1992 alone. As predicted by constitutional expert Eugene Forsey in 1982, the Charter has indeed proven to be a gold mine for lawyers.

The judiciary has also made decisions on the basis of the "spirit" of the Charter in a number of controversial social issues. In 1988, the Supreme Court struck down Canada's abortion law in its Morgentaler ruling, notwithstanding the fact that any reference to abortion—pro or con—had been intentionally excluded from the Charter. In a similar vein, lower courts have added homosexuality to the list of forms of discrimination prohibited by the Charter, again despite clear evidence that this option was explicitly rejected when the Charter was being drafted.[7] The court also struck down the federal Sunday-closing law (which it had upheld under the 1960 Bill of Rights), paving the way for wide-open Sunday shopping in most provinces. In the politically sensitive area of language rights, the court has also been active. It struck down several sections of Quebec's Bill 101, the Charter of the French Language, contributing to Quebec's sense of alienation from English Canada and the failed attempts at constitutional reconciliation in the Meech Lake and Charlottetown Accords. The court has aggressively interpreted the official minority language education rights provisions, requiring provinces not just to provide minority language education services, but in some cases separate facilities and even specially designated "minority-only" seats on school boards. The court's decision in the 1985 Singh case forced Ottawa to revamp its refugee determination process, at a cost of over $200 million. In addition to such indirect costs of compliance with Charter decisions, the court ruled that judges have the authority to order "affirmative remedies," such as the expansion of social benefit programs that unfairly exclude (i.e., discriminate against) a disadvantaged group.[8] While the court stressed such remedies could only be used in rare circumstances, within a month lower courts had ordered a costly extension of spousal benefit plans in the homosexual rights cases mentioned above.

Despite the broad sweep of the Charter's impact on Canadian public policy, no one could reasonably object to these decisions if they were simply dictated by the text of the Charter. In other words, if the Supreme Court has simply been giving effect to the clear or intended meaning of the Charter, critics would have to direct their ire at the Charter itself and not the judges. But as anyone familiar with Charter decisions knows, the opposite is much more often the case. There have been only one or two cases involving clear-cut violations of the central meaning of Charter rights. An overwhelming number of Charter claims involve activities that fall on the periphery of the meaning of rights, issues over which reasonable citizens can and do disagree. The court's free speech cases, for example, have dealt not with core issues of political speech, but with questions such as whether types of commercial speech—television advertising or on-street soliciting for purposes of prostitution—are constitutionally protected forms of expression. Judicial answers to questions such as these are purely discretionary, and vary from one judge to another, depending on their judicial philosophy and personal judgments.

Well-intentioned traditionalists have argued that even if all of the above is true, requiring public parliamentary hearings would still do more harm than good: the cure would be worse than the disease. This analysis is usually premised on U.S. experience, most notably the Robert Bork and Clarence Thomas hearings before the Senate Judiciary Committee in 1987 and 1991, respectively. These media-circus events featured aggressive interest group lobbying, strong ideological overtones, and character assassination. Most Canadians were repulsed by these transparent "court packing" attempts and thus sympathetic to the argument that this is one American institution that we definitely do not want to import into Canada. If we tease out the different strands of this argument, however, we find that none are conclusive.

The most obvious criticism of confirmation hearings is that they politicize the process. Special interest groups would leap at the opportunity to influence the choice of the next Supreme Court judge, promoting candidates sympathetic to their objectives and opposing those who are not. This criticism assumes that the current practice is not politicized. In fact, there is growing evidence to the contrary. When Justice Estey retired shortly after the 1988 Morgentaler decision, *The Globe and Mail* reported that "activists in the abortion debate and representatives of ethnic communities are lobbying hard.... Many members of the ruling PC Party's right-wing ... are putting pressure on PM Mulroney to appoint a conservative judge." Member of Parliament James Jepson, one of the most outspoken pro-life Tory backbenchers, explained the importance of the new Supreme Court appointment:

Unfortunately, with the Charter that Trudeau left us, we legislators do not have final power. It rests with the courts.... You have seen the battling in the United States for the [most recent] Supreme Court nominee. Well, it doesn't take a rocket scientist to see we have the same situation here now.[10]

The same kind of pressure is coming from the political left. At a 1991 conference on the Charter and Public Policy, Marilou McPhedran, a leading feminist legal activist in Ontario, challenged several speakers who spoke as if there were no politics in the appointment process. "We're not being completely honest about the present appointment process," she declared. "We've all been involved in judicial appointments."[11] Other sources confirm that feminist organizations such as LEAF and NAC have privately lobbied the government on judicial appointments.[12]

It is hardly surprising that the new role of the court under the Charter has stimulated behind-the-scenes manoeuvring to influence the appointment of ideologically friendly judges. Indeed, it would be more surprising if it had not. It is an axiom of political science that "where power rests, there influence will be brought to bear."[13] The new Supreme Court is no exception. The appointment process has already been politicized. A confirmation hearing would simply bring these politics out into the open.

A related criticism is that the political lobbying that would inevitably accompany confirmation hearings would undermine the rule of law by making the personal preferences of judges more decisive than the content of the law they are supposed to interpret. Once again, this criticism comes too late. As noted above, the approach to interpreting the Charter chosen by the majority of judges has maximized judicial discretion by minimizing the value of the actual text and its intended meaning. This previously heretical view was actually voiced by Justice Estey, after he retired from the court, in an interview with *The Globe and Mail*:

> Justice Estey said it worries him that Canadians still do not realize how decisions vary according to the personality of each judge. As the misconception is gradually corrected, he said, people may lose respect and faith in the institution.... People think a court is a court is a court. But it is elastic. It is always sliding.[14]

Another variation on this criticism is that public hearings for judicial nominees will inevitably lead to American-style judicial activism. This view is wrong. American-style activism is already here. The argument that the Section 1 "reasonable limits" provision makes judicial review under the Charter qualitatively distinct from U.S. judicial review—an opinion very much in vogue in judicial circles—is just legalistic myopia. Section 1 simply gives Canadian judges even more discretion than they already had. True, judges can use Section 1 as a vehicle of self-restraint. But they can just as easily use it in an activist fashion, and that is what they have done. Section 1 has become just another path to the same end.

Another argument against public hearings is that they are inconsistent with the Canadian convention of "ministerial responsibility"—that the justice minister and the prime minister must be "responsible" to the House of Commons for their judicial appointments. Again, this criticism is wrong on two counts. First, the simple fact of holding public parliamentary committee hearings for judicial candidates does not mean that the committee (or the House of Commons) will have a "veto" power, analogous to the U.S. Senate. Presumably this committee, like all parliamentary committees, would be struck in a fashion that reflects the government's majority in the House of Commons. In the final analysis, a government would always have the votes to push through a positive committee recommendation, no matter how badly its nominee had performed.

In this sense, committee hearings would actually strengthen ministerial responsibility, because a government would have something to be responsible for! That is, the opposition and the Canadian people would have the opportunity to learn what kind of judge the government was appointing: an activist or an apostle of judicial self-restraint, a conservative or a liberal. What it means is that prior to final appointment, a government's candidate for the Supreme Court will be expected to field responsible questions about his or her judicial philosophy from a multiparty committee. The purpose of the hearings is not to prevent a government from making appointments to the Supreme Court, but to make it clear—and public—what kind of criteria the government is using.

As U.S. experience indicates, a government's judicial appointments can become an issue at election time. With the adoption of parliamentary committee hearings, an incumbent government could be challenged to defend its appointment record. Whatever else might be said of this, it certainly does not offend any of the tenets of responsible government.

The last criticism is perhaps the most serious and difficult to meet: public hearings will deter qualified men and women from seeking or accepting appointments to the Supreme Court. There is no denying that many qualified candidates would refuse to submit themselves and their families to the kind of dissection and inspection of their private and professional lives—not to mention slander and innuendo—that both Robert Bork and Clarence Thomas had to endure.

My response is twofold. First, the same thing could be said of democratic politics in general. For generations, many of our most qualified citizens have refused to enter electoral politics because they do not have the stomach or the patience for the public scrutiny that comes with the job. Yet even as we acknowledge the seriousness of this problem, we would not for a minute consider abandoning the free elections, freedom of speech, and independent press that can make political life so uncomfortable. To speak bluntly, having decided to share some of the privileges of elected lawmakers, Canadian judges must also be prepared to share some of the disadvantages that come with the exercise of power.[15]

The second reason is more cheerful: adopting the practice of judicial nomination hearings need not mean adopting the way Americans conduct theirs. Canadians have always prided themselves on conducting politics in a more civil and professional manner than their American neighbours. There is no reason this tradition cannot be extended to judicial nomination hearings. If professional norms and courtesy are observed, there is no reason that Canada cannot reap the advantages of this system while minimizing its potential negatives.

To conclude, those who defend the status quo would have us believe that in preserving a British-style judicial selection process with the new U.S.-style judicial review of constitutional rights, Canadians can have the best of both worlds. In fact, this combination can just as easily produce the worst of both worlds—judicial lawmaking with no accountability. The solution to this problem is public hearings for Supreme Court nominees before a parliamentary committee.

NOTES

1. R.I. Cheffins, "The Supreme Court of Canada: The Quiet Court in an Unquiet Country," *Osgoode Hall Law Journal* 4 (1966): 259–360.

2. F.L. Morton, "The Charter Revolution and the Court Party," *Osgoode Hall Law Journal* 30, no. 3 (1992): 627–653.

3. *R. v. Collins*, [1987] 1 S.C.R. 265.

4. *R. v. Manninen*, [1987] 1 S.C.R. 1233.

5. *R. v. Hebert*, [1990] 2 S.C.R. 151.

6. R. Harvie and H. Foster, "Different Drummers, Different Drums: The Supreme Court, American Jurisprudence and the Revision of Canadian Criminal Law under the Charter," *Ottawa Law Review* 24 (1990): 39.

7. *Haig (and Birch) v. Canada* (1992), 5 O.R. (3d) 245; and *Leshner v. Ministry of the Attorney-General* (1992), 10 O.R. (3d) 732 (Ont. C.A.).

8. *Schachter v. Canada,* [1992] 2 S.C.R. 679.

9. F.L. Morton, Peter H. Russell, and M.J. Withey, "The Supreme Court's First One Hundred Charter Decisions: A Statistical Analysis," *Osgoode Hall Law Journal* 30, no. 1 (1992).

10. "Reduced Role for Politicians Urged in Naming of Judges," *The Globe and Mail,* (16 May, 1988): A1.

11. Morton, "The Charter Revolution and the Court Party," p. 638.

12. Ibid. Also see Sherene Razack, *Canadian Feminism and the Law: The Women's Legal Education and Action Fund and the Pursuit of Equality* (Toronto: Second Story Press, 1991), pp. 36–63.

13. V.O. Key, *Politics, Parties, and Pressure Groups* (New York: Thomas Y. Crowell, 1958), p. 154.

14. *The Globe and Mail,* (27 April, 1988): A5.

15. Interestingly, Supreme Court Justice Jack Major believes that the prospect of public hearings would deter few from seeking a place on the Canada's highest court. See "MPs' Scrutiny Won't Scare Off Judges, Major Says," *National Post* (13 June, 2005): A1, A6.

✗ **NO**
Parliamentary Hearings for Supreme Court Appointments?
H. PATRICK GLENN

Should there be parliamentary confirmation hearings for Supreme Court of Canada appointments? There has been only limited discussion of the question in Canada, though a number of themes have emerged. Proponents of hearings have said that the Supreme Court, particularly since the enactment of the Canadian Charter of Rights and Freedoms, exercises important political responsibilities, and that a more openly political appointment process is therefore appropriate. The larger role of the Supreme Court is also said to require increased public knowledge of judges and of judicial aspirants. Confirmation hearings are therefore urged as a means of facilitating public awareness and debate. A further argument, more rooted in a particular philosophy of judicial activity, is to the effect that judges are free to decide cases as they wish and that such unlimited discretion requires political surveillance, at least at the stage of appointment.

Since there have never been confirmation hearings of judicial appointments in Canada, few people have tried to explain or justify their absence. Recently, however, in response to arguments in favour of confirmation hearings, it has been said that the existing process has served Canada well, and better than the confirmation process has served the U.S. ("if it ain't broke, don't fix it"); that changes to the existing process would be difficult to implement and not likely to yield better results; that confirmation hearings would give rise to unseemly and inappropriate attacks on appointees while provoking no meaningful response from them; and that the public ordeal of hearings would deter good candidates from seeking judicial office.

A contemporary observer of this debate would probably come to the conclusion that confirmation hearings should be held. They accord with democratic theory; it is true that the judges of the Supreme Court of Canada, who are accountable to no one for their decisions, render judgments that have major political importance; the arguments against hearings seem both undemocratic and elitist, in seeking to protect important people from public scrutiny. Shouldn't we just get on with it?

There may be more to be said. In particular, it seems worthwhile to ask some further questions as to the compatibility of confirmation hearings with existing Canadian institutions, and as to the relations between law and politics.

I. CONFIRMATION HEARINGS AND CANADIAN INSTITUTIONS

The creation of confirmation hearings for Supreme Court of Canada appointments is related to the existing political institutions of the House of Commons and the Senate, where the hearings would take place; to the Supreme Court itself, whose composition might be affected; and more generally to the Canadian judiciary, for the model of judicial appointment procedure that would be created. In each case, it will be suggested, confirmation hearings are incompatible with existing Canadian institutions and the (justifiable) philosophy that underlies them.

What is the significance of confirmation hearings for the House of Commons and the Senate? In the U.S. model, hearings of Supreme Court nominees are conducted by a committee of the Senate. The hearings are part of the system of checks and balances written into the U.S. Constitution. The executive, in the person of the president, cannot abuse the appointment process (notably to the unelected cabinet), and the Senate holds in effect a veto power over presidential nominees to the cabinet, to executive positions generally, and to the federal judiciary. Moreover, the Senate majority is frequently of a different political allegiance than that of the president. However, neither the Canadian House of Commons nor the Canadian Senate plays the same role as the U.S. Senate. The Canadian parliamentary system is one of responsible government. The government, or the executive, is responsible to the House of Commons in the sense that it can be defeated by the House and turned out of office. However, the party that obtains the majority of seats (or votes) in the House will form the government and also control the House. Canada does not have a system of checks and balances. One may agree or disagree on types of government, but ours is unlikely to change in the foreseeable future, at least in this respect. There are, moreover, reasons for systems of responsible government. They have to do with entrusting government to those who have democratically won it, and requiring them to act ethically and responsibly for the public good, or be voted out. Checks and balances are not seen as useful or efficient devices to ensure this outcome. They are judged to be ineffective and counter-productive, likely to give rise to partisan bickering and disputes over personalities. Canadian governments, with democratic legitimacy, are entitled to govern.

Submitting judicial nominations to a vote of a House of Commons committee will thus usually not result in partisan control of the nomination, since a majority government will control the votes of the committee. If it does not, as might occur in the case of a minority government, would a contrary vote of the committee bar the government from proceeding with the nomination? No one knows the answer to this question, but a partial answer must be, not consistently with our present system of government, and the reasons for our present system of government are as good as they always have been. A vote of a House of Commons committee will thus result in either no control of the government, or control that is incompatible with our system of government. There are very large constitutional questions lurking behind all of this.

Some proposals have called for confirmation hearings before a Senate or joint House of Commons/Senate committee. These proposals were made in the context of a radically reformed Senate; they appear to be unsustainable in its present state. In any event, they raise the same fundamental questions of the legitimacy of control over a government having the support of the House of Commons.

Should there then be public hearings before a House of Commons committee, with no conclusive vote? This would be in a sense a reversal of the U.S. model, which until the twentieth century consisted of a Senate vote with no hearings. Is it publicity alone that is sought? This may depend ultimately on our concept of the relations between law and politics (more on that to follow).

Parliamentary confirmation hearings therefore do not sit well with our political institutions. What about the Supreme Court itself? Does its mandate require appointments only after hearings and the exercise of some form of political control? Here the importance of the Charter and the intermittent activism of the U.S. Supreme Court have dominated the discussion. What is the nature, however, of the Supreme Court of Canada? In the Western legal tradition it has become a rather unique type of court, unlike the highest courts of the U.K., the United States, or France. In each of those countries the jurisdiction of the highest court is more specialized than that of the Supreme Court of Canada. In the U.S., the Supreme Court is a court essentially for federal and constitutional matters only; its constitutional responsibilities dominate its workload. In the U.K., the House of Lords has historically had no constitutional responsibilities similar to those exercised by the Supreme Court of Canada in application of the Charter, and still has no powers to declare enacted law to be inoperative. In France, there are three separate high courts, one for constitutional law, one for administrative law, and one for private law.

The Supreme Court of Canada is the only generalist court amongst these courts. A large part of its docket is given over to criminal appeals, and it continues to hear appeals in all other areas of private and public law. There has been a decline in the number of Charter cases, and, in 2003, such cases accounted for only 11 percent of all cases heard.[1] The Supreme Court is very much a court of law in the traditional sense, deciding individual cases involving individual litigants. Its decisions have important precedential value, but this is true of the decisions of all high courts. It is therefore incorrect to treat the Supreme Court as a fundamentally political institution simply because it has begun to decide Charter cases. It certainly does decide Charter cases, and they are important cases. It is not, however, a court dominated by a political workload, a political agenda, or politically motivated judges. This too is related ultimately to our views concerning law and politics. Do we wish to give dominance to the overtly political part of the court's workload? Its present structure and jurisdiction does not indicate that this need be done.

Finally, what is the relation of confirmation hearings at the level of the Supreme Court to our entire system of judicial appointments? Would hearings be compatible with the system or constitute a useful model for its reform? Canada originally inherited the British system of appointment of judges, which relies on the professional opinion of a very small number of judges, including the Lord Chancellor, to inform the government's choice of members of the judiciary. As well, judges are chosen from a very small and select group of professionals, those barristers who have become Queen's Counsel. This system of appointment was of course appropriate for the British judiciary, which has historically been very small, with much adjudication being left to lay magistrates (the local notables). The Canadian judiciary, however, has become quite unlike the British judiciary. It is much larger; it is composed almost entirely of professional judges; and its members are generally drawn from a very large, unified legal profession (and not from a very small corps of professional pleaders or barristers). In keeping with these changes to the judiciary, the Canadian system of appointment has changed considerably from the British model. At the provincial level, judicial nominating commissions are becoming the rule. These commissions receive applications and nominations for judicial positions, assess qualifications, and make recommendations for appointment (often in the form of short lists) to provincial authorities. At the federal level, the process of screening and recommending judicial candidates has become a major activity of the Ministry of Justice, involving consultation with a committee of the Canadian Bar Association, which provides formal evaluations of all candidates. The process is neither secretive nor internal to the government. It is simply not conducted in a public forum.

These changes in the process of appointing Canadian judges have been occurring gradually and the process of change is certainly not complete. One result of change has been a decline in the importance of political patronage in the appointment process. It is reasonable to think that the quality of the Bench has also been reinforced, since the procedures allow much more information to be processed about a larger number of judicial candidates than would otherwise be the case. Appointments to the Supreme Court of Canada go through a similar, though less formal, process and, unlike the case of the U.S. Supreme Court, there is no criticism of the quality of appointments to the Supreme Court of Canada. It is evident that successive governments have taken the task very seriously and that the visibility of the court has enhanced the likelihood of high-quality appointments.

The underlying political ethic of this appointment process is that of responsible government, that is, it is the task of the government to act, as government, in the public interest. The underlying judicial ethic of the process is that of obtaining a judiciary of the highest quality. Quite absent from the process have been the ideas of checks and balances on government action and of democratic approval of the judiciary. Discussion of the existing judicial appointment process in Canada thus provides little or no support for judicial confirmation hearings, given the underlying principles of responsible government and a judiciary of the highest quality. This conclusion can be seen as without prejudice to the development of judicial nominating commissions, which have as their task the searching out of the best candidates, as opposed to merely eliminating allegedly bad governmental nominations. The Canadian Bar Association has currently proposed that such a commission be charged with nominating a short list of candidates for the Supreme Court to the prime minister and the government. The commission would be partly composed, however, of politicians. What should one make of such a proposal? This brings us, finally, to the larger question of the relations between law and politics.

II. LAW, POLITICS AND CONFIRMATION HEARINGS

The relations between law and politics have already been mentioned, in discussing whether judicial appointments and activity should receive some form of democratic approval (which could logically extend to election of judges), whether confirmation hearings should be held before a parliamentary committee of some kind, and whether the Supreme Court should be treated as a political institution. Since democracy has been a relatively successful form of government, its extension to the judiciary appears to be a good thing. Democracy is a form of politics, however, and its application to law means politicizing the legal process in an explicit manner. Do we want to do this?

One of the most frequently made criticisms of the legal order is that it is ultimately political. Since it is ultimately political, we should do away with the legal charade and apply to the legal process the same methods and techniques that are used elsewhere in politics. Law should be the object of public and transparent political debate and be subject to democratic institutions. The notion of the "political" is here very large and appears to extend to most forms of human interaction. Such an attitude underlies the adoption of systems of election of judges in both the former U.S.S.R. (implementing socialist legality) and the United States (implementing Jeffersonian democracy). We have now had substantial modern experience with the notion of democratizing the legal process, in such a direct way. The problems are both theoretical and practical.

Ultimately our view of judicial activity may be driven by our view of law itself. Is there such a thing, for example, as a natural legal order? The aboriginal population of this country tells us there is. It teaches respect for the natural environment. We should continue to act in traditional ways since these ways do the least violence to the world. If there is such a natural legal order, it does not require elected judges or a democratic legal process. It requires a legal process that will ensure respect for the natural legal order; in the aboriginal legal order, this meant adherence to the wisdom of people recognized as elders. Nor do religiously inspired legal traditions insist on democratic legitimation; legal authority is derived from religious learning and some form of official recognition of such acquired authority. In the Western secular world, these ancient traditions have had and continue to have great influence. The Western legal tradition is remarkable, however, for its insistence that law is presently *made* by those entrusted with the task. This philosophical attitude emerged with the Renaissance, but the Renaissance did not lead to a radical democratization of the legal process. Something else was also at work.

In contemporary liberal societies, people are entitled to different views and different ways of life. Law is used to regulate and conciliate the conflicts which inevitably arise. Since there is no consistently imposed social fabric, law must do more than it does in a society in which common forms of life are accepted by all concerned. In the inevitable turmoil of social relations, the major teaching of the Renaissance was that law had to be separated out from politics. Politics would of course continue to exist and would give the major forms of direction to society. At the level of daily life, however, where decisions are made which affect the individual, it was felt that the political process was too large, too biased, and too crude to regulate the detail of social existence. The person charged with social deviance could not be judged, for example, by those who had made the rules. From the seventeenth century, the notion of an independent judiciary thus emerged, one that was not subject to the political process but was given remarkable institutional liberty to pursue justice in the individual case. This is why Canada has professionalized its judiciary. No one wishes to be judged by those controlled by someone else, or by those fearing sanctions for their decisions, or by those biased by social position or attitude. In short, most of our present legal institutions have been developed, not because it is felt that law is somehow inevitably different from politics—more scientific, more technical, or more neutral— but because it has been felt that every possible effort should be made to provide institutional protection to individuals—in liberal, democratic states—from the brute forces of politics. The separation of law and politics does not deny the political character of law, but assumes it. It then seeks to control and limit the influence of politics through institutional guarantees of fair process, independent decision-makers, and applications of established rules.

The notion of an independent judiciary, one that is not democratically elected and not subject to democratic recall, is thus parallel to and consistent with the political ethic of responsible government. Those entrusted with authority are expected to exercise it in the public interest. There can be no guardians of the guardians, at least in any immediate and direct way. The independence of the judiciary takes the ethic a step further, however, in awarding tenure for life (or its statutory equivalent, the seventy-fifth birthday) to those judged best qualified to have it. Since our judiciary is now a large one, judicial councils have been established to discipline judges for non-judicial conduct, but no political authority can interfere in the judicial decision-making process, and no judge need fear official or popular sanction for unpopular decisions. Most of our legal institutions today thus represent efforts to separate law from politics, because their confusion has been recognized by most people at most times to be highly undesirable. This is particularly so in Canada, where the Charter of Rights essentially protects the individual from majoritarian politics, and where the multicultural character of the society also implies freedom from majority control.

Efforts to democratize and politicize the legal process are visible today because they have been so consistently rejected in the past, and because our existing institutions translate this rejection. It is not that no one thought of parliamentary confirmation hearings before the Charter. It is rather that institutions were created that would—as much as possible—free the legal process from the political one. Judges *are* free to decide as they wish, and since they are institutionally free, they choose to decide according to their best appreciation of existing law. This freedom is given to them because you would not want *your* case to be decided on majoritarian political grounds. Creating judicial confirmation hearings would not change a great deal in the unfolding of history. It would be a small, further step in the politicization of law, however, and as such there should be a presumption against such hearings, as indeed there is in this country.

The practical difficulties in democratizing the legal process have been more significant than the theoretical ones, however, in the jurisdictions that have attempted the process. In the former U.S.S.R., the process of election of judges was party-controlled, in the name of authoritarian, socialist legitimacy, and the result was the opposite of democratic control. In the United States, a populist, majoritarian, monocultural tradition prevailed at the state level (leading to election of state judges) but not at the federal level, where the Bill of Rights was to be enforced by an independent judiciary. At the state level, the election of judges has been the object of ongoing reforms designed to eliminate party influence and corruption while reinforcing the quality of judges. The democratic control has been largely illusory, and voter influence, never strong, has been declining steadily in favour of various forms of judicial nominating commissions. What should we make of the U.S. experience?

As mentioned above, confirmation hearings are a relatively recent phenomenon in the United States, beginning only in this century, shortly before World War II. Why did they come about? Why was the presumption against politicization (federal U.S. judges are appointed and not elected) here reversed? It does not appear to have been the role of the U.S. Supreme Court in deciding Bill of Rights cases that caused the change, since this had been going on for a long time prior to the introduction of confirmation hearings. An independent high court free of political influence and free of democratic pressures in the appointment process is thus entirely compatible with a constitutional democracy. It is even the ideal balance between the will of the majority and individual rights. What appears to have brought about the change, according to U.S. writers, was the process by which appointments to the court became seen as further means of advancing political goals. Today in the United States, there is talk of "transformative appointments," in the sense of appointments that would change the course of decisions of the court, in a broad, political sense (though there is no way of predicting this at the time of appointment). Judges are expected to decide according to a broad, personal political philosophy. There has thus been surprise at the emergence of a group of "legal conservatives" in the court, those who refuse to overrule prior decisions with which they disagree, because of the need for legal stability. Yet if governments are entitled to use the Supreme Court for political objectives, and its judges are expected to act as majoritarian political appointees, then it is normal that the process of appointment be politicized and even radically so. It is also normal that the process be subject to the full range of political debate and struggle, as unedifying and inefficient as it frequently is. There is no practical means of ensuring only serene and enlightened democratic participation in the nomination process. Most importantly, there appears to be no means of politicizing the appointment process without also politicizing the court itself.

The Supreme Court has not become a political battleground in Canada. If we are to struggle toward a rule of law, for individuals, rather than a rule of political power, it is undesirable that it become a political battleground. Its present role as a court of law should remind us of why it is there. Let's leave it alone. One day it may have to decide my case, or yours.

NOTES

1. Supreme Court of Canada, "Statistics 1994–2004," (accessed January 31, 2005) http://www.scc-csc.gc.ca/information/statistics/download/ecourt.pdf.

POSTSCRIPT

In his article, F.L. Morton makes a forceful case for parliamentary hearings. If the Supreme Court is now much more powerful than before, then it seems only sensible to make it more accountable to the public. His contention that the traditional appointment process is already politicized—but only behind the scenes—is also disturbing. It appears that some Canadians get to influence who sits on the Supreme Court, but not others. Yet, some lingering doubts remain about parliamentary hearings. Morton is confident that the basic civility of Canadians would preclude any of the excesses associated with American hearings. But scholarly studies suggest that Canadians are losing this civility (or deferential attitude), and are becoming more like their neighbours to the south. Also, it is unsettling to think that the country could lose some very capable jurists just because of the wish to ask nominees a few questions. For some, this might be too high a price to pay.

There is also the concern about the impact of hearings on the public perception of judicial decision making. At present, most citizens believe that justices offer disinterested interpretations of the law. As Morton shows, this is not an entirely accurate conception of how judges decide—indeed, for Morton, it is patently false. But one might argue, as H. Patrick Glenn seems to, that adjudication of conflicts over the law does involve the application of judicial expertise and wisdom, and that the spectacle of hearings might undermine public confidence in the judiciary. If the electorate believes that judges are merely imposing their own preferences on society, then the legitimacy of the judicial branch of government may be in jeopardy.

Obviously, Glenn is much happier with the present appointment process. He also finds little good to say about public hearings—and seemingly for good reason. If one looks to the American experience, the presence of hearings seems to be sign of a highly politicized court system, one in which the rule of law takes a back seat to the sway of political power. However, Glenn's arguments, like Morton's, are not entirely convincing. He contends that the appointment process in Canada is open and non-secretive; it is simply not carried out in full view of the public. But surely the absence of a public forum turns the process into what Glenn denies it to be: a closed process. Glenn makes the important point that the present appointment practice helps to shield the judicial process from the intrusiveness of politics and majoritarian thinking. But it might be argued that allowing public hearings would not put a large dent in the shield that protects the independence of the judiciary. Glenn concedes as much, but nevertheless seems to argue that hearings go against basic principles regarding judicial appointments. There also appears here to be a fear of the slippery slope—that the small steps toward a more politicized system encourage the taking of larger steps.

Recently, the federal government suggested a possible compromise between the present process and parliamentary hearings. Under the proposed system, an advisory committee–that would include members of Parliament–would advise the federal justice minister on the selection on new appointments to the Supreme Court. With this arrangement, the people's representatives would have some say in the selection process, but the possible costs of public hearings would be avoided. But some might still say it goes too far, while others may contend that it does not go far enough. Perhaps the advisory committee is not really a workable compromise.

To gain a full appreciation of the debate over the selection of Supreme Court justices, one might begin with a general overview of the court. For this, see the chapter on the Supreme Court in Peter Hogg, *Constitutional Law of Canada* (Toronto: Carswell, 2004) or the relevant chapter in Rand Dyck, *Canadian Politics*, 3rd ed. (Toronto: Thomson Nelson, 2004). Interest in the selection of Supreme Court justices has been precipitated in large part by effect of judicial interpretation of the Charter of Rights and Freedoms. A number of articles and books have been written on this topic: Raymond Bazowski, "The Judicialization of Politics," in James Bickerton and Alain-G. Gagnon, eds., *Canadian Politics*, 4th ed. (Peterborough: Broadview Press, 2004); Radha Jhappen, "Charter Politics and the Judiciary," in Michael Whittington and Glen Williams, eds., *Canadian Politics in the 21st Century*, 6th ed. (Toronto: Thomson Nelson, 2004); Janet L. Hiebert, *Charter Conflicts: What Is Parliament's Role?* (Montreal & Kingston: McGill-Queen's University Press, 2002); Christopher Manfredi, *Judicial Power and the Charter: Canada and the Paradox of Liberal Constitutionalism*, 2nd ed. (Toronto: Oxford University Press, 2001); Robert Martin, *The Most Dangerous Branch: How the Supreme Court of Canada Has Undermined Our Law and Our Democracy* (Montreal & Kingston: McGill-Queen's University Press, 2003); and Kent Roach, *The Supreme Court on Trial: Judicial Activism or Democratic Dialogue* (Toronto: Irwin Law, 2001).

With an understanding of the Supreme Court and its growing importance, it is now possible to approach the writings on the selection process. Morton has collected a series of articles on this issue in his book *Law, Politics and the Judicial Process in Canada*, 3rd ed. (Calgary: University of Calgary Press, 2002). Jacob Ziegel, a respected professor of law at the University of Toronto, has also written on this matter: see Jacob S. Ziegel, "Merit Selection and Democratization of Appointments to the Supreme Court of Canada," in Paul Howe and Peter H. Russell, eds., *Judicial Power and Canadian Democracy* (Montreal & Kingston: McGill-Queen's University Press, 2001) and his review of most recent developments affecting the appointment process: Jacob Ziegel, "Choosing Supreme Court Judges," *Literary Review of Canada*, May 2005. The Chief Justice of the Supreme Court of Canada, Beverly McLachlin, gave an important speech in which she conveyed her sentiments about any reform of the appointment process: Beverley McLachlin, "The Judiciary's Distinctive Role in Our Constitutional Democracy," *Policy Options*, September 2003.

In the last few years, a flurry of actions has taken place in relation to the appointment of Supreme Court justices (and that has been precipitated largely by Prime Minster Martin's promise to make the political process more open). In March 2004, the Canadian Bar Association (CBA) put forward its views on the appropriate reform of the appointment process in a document entitled "Supreme Court of Canada Appointment Process" (available at the CBA website). Around the same time, the House of Commons Committee on Justice, Human Rights, Public Safety and Emergency Preparedness held hearings on the matter and released an important report entitled "Improving the Supreme Court of Canada Appointments Process," May 2004 (available at the Parliament of Canada website). The publication provides some good background on the issue of selection and offers arguably the best description of the current appointment process (provided by minister of justice through testimony before the committee). Following this, the government made changes to the appointment process for the purpose of selecting the latest two justices to the Supreme Court of Canada, and a parliamentary ad hoc committee was struck to participate in this process and to prepare a report on its activities. The report, which is available at the federal Department of Justice website, is entitled "Report of the Interim Ad Hoc Committee on the Appointment of Supreme Court Justices," August 2004.

Finally, the minister of justice, in April 2005, released a paper, "Proposal to Reform the Supreme Court of Canada Appointments Process" that set out the thoughts of the federal government on what should be done to the way in which appointments are made to the country's highest court.

The American appointment process is obviously relevant to this debate, so appreciation of this process is in order. Useful are Henry Abraham's two texts, *The Judicial Process: An Introductory Analysis of the Courts of the United States, England, and France*, 6th ed. (New York: Oxford University Press, 1993) and *Justices and Presidents: A Political History of Appointments to the Supreme Court*, 3rd ed. (Toronto: Oxford University Press, 1992); as well as David M. O'Brien's *Storm Center: The Supreme Court in American Politics*, 3rd ed. (New York: W.W. Norton, 1993). The American appointment process is controversial in large part because of Senate hearings on two Supreme Court nominees, Robert Bork (in 1987) and Clarence Thomas (in 1991). For more on these hearings, see Ethan Bronner, *Battle for Justice: How the Bork Nomination Shook America* (New York: W.W. Norton, 1989); and Timothy M. Phelps and Helen Winternitz, *Capitol Games: Clarence Thomas, Anita Hill, and the Story of a Supreme Court Nomination* (New York: Hyperion, 1992).

Should Party Discipline Be Relaxed?

✔ **YES**

DAVID KILGOUR, JOHN KIRSNER, AND KENNETH MCCONNELL, "Discipline versus Democracy: Party Discipline in Canadian Politics"

✘ **NO**

ROBERT J. JACKSON AND PAUL CONLIN, "The Imperative of Party Discipline in the Canadian Political System"

David Kilgour, a member of Parliament from Alberta, has had a rocky relationship with the Progressive Conservative Party over the years. Elected to Parliament in 1979 as a member of the Conservative Party, Kilgour quit the party caucus in April 1987 in protest over the Conservative government's policies for the West and its failure to develop adequate ethical guidelines for elected representatives. Kilgour rejoined the Tory caucus in February 1988, but soon became critical of his party's proposed Goods and Services Tax (GST). On April 10, 1990, he voted against the government's bill authorizing the GST, and as a consequence was expelled from the caucus of the Progressive Conservative Party. Kilgour subsequently crossed the floor to sit as a member of the Liberal Party. He has since been reelected four times as a Liberal member of Parliament.

In April 2005, David Kilgour's parliamentary career took yet another twist. Following revelations of the Gomery Commission into misuse of government funds under the sponsorship program in Quebec, Kilgour announced that he could no longer sit in the Liberal caucus in good conscience. Instead, he indicated that he would henceforth sit as an independent in Parliament and would retire from federal politics when the next election was called.

David Kilgour's troubles with his former party stem from the well-known tradition of party discipline, which requires members of Parliament to vote according to their party's position. Clearly, the member from Alberta has some difficulty with this tradition, and he is not alone. Polls show that only a small percentage of respondents believe that the first priority should be loyalty to his or her party.

Despite this, political leaders have long felt that the principle of party discipline was vital to the functioning of parliamentary government in Canada. When necessary, as in the case of David Kilgour, party officials have shown that they are willing to take strong measures to enforce party discipline—by withholding support for a candidate at election time, by denying parliamentary appointments, or even by expelling a recalcitrant MP from the party caucus.

The rationale for discipline in political parties is a simple one. Canada has a parliamentary system of government that requires that the party in power maintain the support and confidence of the majority of the members of the legislative branch. Without this support, the government would find it difficult to carry out the mandate on which it is elected and, more important, to remain in power. Party discipline is a means of preventing these occurrences.

For many Canadians, as reflected in the following two readings, the debate over party discipline hinges largely on whether or not Canada should move closer to an American model, where members of Congress are seen as being relatively free to vote according to personal conscience and constituency interest. David Kilgour, John Kirsner, and Kenneth McConnell argue that relaxed party discipline would advance the cause of democracy and provide better representation for individual constituents. Robert Jackson and Paul Conlin counter that the weakening of party discipline would give Canada an American-style system in which special interest groups, not elected officials, would control our legislative representatives.

✔ YES

Discipline versus Democracy: Party Discipline in Canadian Politics
DAVID KILGOUR, JOHN KIRSNER, AND KENNETH MCCONNELL

Representative democracy in Canada is so dominated by political parties that some experts believe the party discipline exerted on most votes in our House of Commons and provincial legislatures is the tightest in the democratic world. Defenders of our model argue that many Canadians prefer it this way because each party's candidates can be assumed at election time to share the party's position on every issue. Others contend our executive democracy, patterned on a system prevailing in Great Britain about three centuries ago, requires iron party discipline if our fused legislative and executive branches of government are to function effectively. Another reason, probably the most important, is that our practice makes life easier for leaders of both government and opposition parties.

Unlike in parliamentary systems of nations such as Great Britain and Germany, virtually every vote in Canadian legislatures is considered potentially one of nonconfidence in the government. Even a frivolous opposition motion to adjourn for the day, if lost, can be deemed by a cabinet to have been one of nonconfidence. The whips of government parties have for decades used the possibility of an early election to push their members into voting the party line. The opposition attitude is so similar that we had a few years ago the spectacle of both opposition parties in our House of Commons arguing that a free vote on an abortion resolution would "rip out the heart" of our parliamentary system of government. The constituents of both provincial and federal legislators would be the real winners if party discipline is loosened. Private members from both government and opposition benches could then take positions on government bills and other matters based on assisting their constituents instead of their respective party hierarchies.

PARTY DISCIPLINE IN CANADA

W.S. Gilbert put the present Canadian political reality succinctly: "I always voted at my party's call and I never thought of thinking for myself at all." Canadian members of Parliament are essentially passive observers in the formulation and administration of most national policy. Indeed, Sean Moore, editor of the Ottawa lobbyist magazine *The Lobby Digest*, told a committee of MPs in early 1993 that they are rarely lobbied by the almost three thousand reported lobbyists in the capital because "elected officials play a very minor role in governing."

MPs from all parties vote in solid blocs on almost every issue. Government members do so from a fear that a lost vote on a measure will be deemed by their prime minister as a loss of confidence. This stems from the early- to mid-nineteenth-century British concept that a government falls if it loses the support of a majority in the Commons on any vote.

Besides the threat of parliamentary dissolution, private members are also subject to rewards and punishments from party leadership, depending on how they vote. A "loyal" MP who votes the party line will be a candidate for promotion (if in the government party, perhaps to cabinet) or other benefits from the party, such as interesting trips or appointment to an interesting House committee. A "disloyal" MP who votes against the party leadership may be prevented from ascending the political ladder and could ultimately be thrown out of the party caucus. In light of this, "caucus solidarity and my constituents be damned" might be the real oath of office for most honourable members in all political parties.

Reg Stackhouse, a former Tory MP for Scarborough West, in a submission to the Task Force on Reform of the House of Commons in 1985, commented on the discipline imposed on private members of the government party:

> Not only is it demanded that [the member] vote with the government on crucial matters such as the Speech from the Throne or the budget, but also that he vote, speak or remain silent according to the dictate of the government. Even though a government may be at no risk of falling, it requires this all but unconditional commitment, and renders the member a seeming robot, at least imaginatively replaceable by a voting machine.

This is the major defect in Canadian parliamentary democracy: most MPs are essentially brute voters who submit to any demand from their respective party whips. In Canada's current political culture, a prime minister or premier could in practice on all confidence votes cast proxy votes on behalf of all government members. The same practice prevails in the opposition parties because they think themselves obliged to vote in uniform party blocs virtually always. If not, some of our media, apparently unaware that parliamentary democracy has evolved elsewhere, including in the matters of the parliamentary system in the United Kingdom, report that the opposition leaders cannot control their caucuses. This status quo has persisted for so long primarily because party leaders and policy mandarins obviously prefer it. Measures going into the House of Commons where one party has a majority usually emerge essentially unscathed. Everything follows a highly predictable script: obedient government members praise it; opposition parties rail against it; and plenty of bad measures become law essentially unamended.

The present regional differences and priorities require much better public expression in Parliament, at least if one central institution of our national government is to reflect adequately all parts of the country. Regional voices are frequently suffocated by rigid party discipline and the entrenched habit of the national caucuses to maintain a close eye on what opinion leaders, particularly columnists in Toronto–Ottawa–Montreal, regard as the national interest on any issue. Therefore, reforming the role of MPs is not only essential for parliamentary legitimacy in post-modern Canada, but is vital to "nationalizing Ottawa."

ELIMINATING EXCESSES

A report by the late Eugene Forsey and Graham Eglington *(The Question of Confidence in Responsible Government)* lists a large number of measures defeated in the Westminster Parliament. On most, the cabinet of the day simply carried on, presumably either dropping the failed proposal or seeking majority support for a different measure. For tax bills, the list of such defeats begins in 1834. During 1975, for example, a financial bill of the Harold Wilson cabinet dealing with their value-added tax rate was defeated, but the ministry carried on in office, treating it not as a confidence vote.

The Forsey-Eglington Report also emphasizes that in earlier years, government MPs in Canada were permitted to vote against cabinet measures. For example, between 1867 and 1872, their study lists fully eighteen pages of cases in which Conservative MPs voted against measures of John A. Macdonald's government. The sky did not fall; Macdonald's government was able to function effectively; government MPs could keep both their self-respect and their membership in the government caucus.

The study also provides interesting data about voting in our House of Commons during other periods: in 1896, fully sixteen Conservative MPs voted with Laurier's Liberals to adjourn a Conservative measure intended to restore Catholic schools in Manitoba; in 1981, sixteen Conservative MPs, including three who later became ministers, voted against the final resolution patriating our Constitution.

The all-party McGrath Report on parliamentary reform came to the conclusion that the role of the individual member must be enhanced. As James McGrath himself said in 1985, "I wanted to put into place a system where being a member of Parliament would be seen to be an end to itself and not a means to an end." On the question of nonconfidence, McGrath recommended the following:

- A government should be careful before it designates a vote as one of confidence. It should confine such declarations to measures central to its administration.

- While a defeat on supply is a serious matter, elimination or reduction of an estimate can be accepted.

- In a Parliament with a government in command of a majority, the matter of confidence has really been settled by the electorate.

- Government should therefore have the wisdom to permit members to decide many matters in their own personal judgments.

Reg Stackhouse agrees that party discipline must have limits: "Tight party lines need be drawn only when the government's confidence is at stake, i.e., when the government decides the fate of a bill is absolutely essential to its objectives."

One way to reduce party discipline in the interest of greater fairness for every province would be to write into our Constitution, as the West Germans did in their Basic Law, that MPs and senators shall "not [be] bound by orders and instructions and shall be subject only to their conscience." Party discipline diluted this principle in West Germany, but when combined with another feature of their Constitution—that no chancellor can be defeated in their equivalent of our House of Commons unless a majority of members simultaneously agree on a new person to become chancellor—there now appears to be a more independent role for members of the Bundestag than for Canadian members of Parliament. For example, in the case of the defeat of the minority Clark government in 1979 on its budget, the West German rule would have kept Clark in office unless the Liberals, New Democrats, and Social Credit MPs had agreed simultaneously on a new prime minister who could hold the confidence of a majority of MPs. A similar rule, if adopted by the House of Commons, would inevitably weaken our party discipline significantly because MPs from all parties could vote on the merits of issues, knowing that defeat would bring down only the measure and not the government.

Another approach would be for each new federal or provincial cabinet to specify at the start of their mandate which matters at the heart of their program will be confidence issues. The Mulroney government, for example, might have spelled out in late 1988 that the Canada–U.S. Free Trade Agreement would be a confidence issue. In those situations, party discipline would be justifiable. Otherwise, its backbenchers would be free to vote for their constituents' interests at all times. This restored independence for legislators would lead to better representation for all regions of Canada and much more occupational credibility for Canadian legislators.

A study of the 32nd Legislative Assembly of Ontario (1981–85) indicated that its members voted in uniform party blocs about 95 percent of the time. The same pattern has applied in at least the past four Parliaments in Ottawa. The Canadian pattern indicates that all of the various party leaders could cast a proxy vote on behalf of all their followers without even bothering to have them physically present. It also overlooks that a majority or even a minority government can function effectively without our present stratospheric levels of party solidarity.

THE AMERICAN WAY

In the United States Congress, where admittedly there is a strict separation of powers between the executive and the legislative branches of government, legislation does get passed with far less party loyalty. The constitutional separation of powers and the weakness of party discipline in congressional voting behaviour greatly facilitate effective regional representation in Washington. Unlike the situation in Canada where a government falls if it loses the support of a majority in the House of Commons on a confidence vote, United States presidents and Congress are elected for fixed terms. Neither resigns if a particular measure is voted down in either the Senate or the House of Representatives.

The practices in our two countries are so different that *The Congressional Quarterly* defines party unity votes there as those in which at least 51 percent of members of one party vote against 51 percent of the other party. Under this definition, itself astonishing to Canadian legislators, the *Quarterly* notes that for the years 1975 to 1982 party unity votes occurred in only 44.2 percent of the 4,417 recorded Senate votes and in only 39.8 percent of those in the House of Representatives. This sample, moreover, includes the years 1977 to 1980, the last period before 1993 to 1996 when Democrats controlled the White House and both branches of Congress.

Another feature of the congressional system that fosters effective regional input in national policymaking is territorial bloc voting—something quite unknown in Canada's House of Commons. Representatives from the two political parties of the Mountain states, Sun Belt states, New England states, and others vote en bloc or work together in committees to advance common interests.

A good example of how effective regional representatives can influence the geographic location of federal government procurement, which affects the geographic distribution of the manufacturing sector, is the Southern congressional influence. It played a major role in the postwar concentration of federal military and space expenditures in the South and in the general economic revival and growth of the Sun Belt. And during 1981–82, the height of the "boll-weevil era," the longtime legislative coalition of Southern Democrats and Republicans was successful more than 85 percent of the time, due to mutual areas of agreement and interest.

The point of this comparison is only to emphasize that, unlike the American Congress, Canadian bloc voting makes bipartisan or tripartisan agreement on anything in our legislatures exceedingly rare. In our current political culture, if a government or opposition MP's loyalty to his or her province clashes with the instruction of the party whip, putting constituents' or regional considerations first in his or her way of voting implies considerable risk to one's prospects for party advancement. Backbench MPs in Canada are thus far less able to represent regional interests effectively than are their counterparts in Washington where the congressional system provides the freedom for effective regional representation when an issue has clear regional implications. This, of course, is not to suggest that Canada should duplicate the American congressional style of government. Rather, it is to point out that the best solution to ongoing problems of representative democracy in Canada might be to adopt attractive features from various systems, including the American one.

PUTTING CONSTITUENTS FIRST

Canada is a federal state and federalism means that on some issues the will of the popular majority will be frustrated. If the biggest battalions of voters are to prevail over smaller ones under any circumstances, we should drop the charade that we have a federal system of government that respects minorities in times of stress. The notion that the largest group of Canadians, that is, southern Ontarians and metropolitan Quebecers, must be accommodated always has resulted in discontent everywhere and accompanying feelings of regional irrelevancy.

In an increasingly interdependent world, many Canadians in our outer eight provinces and the territories at least want new or altered institutions that will represent the interest of both "inner Canadians" (those who live in the Toronto–Ottawa–Montreal corridor) and "outer Canadians" effectively. Unless we move away from the notion that "the national interest" is merely a code phrase for the most populous region dominating all corners of the country, frictions between inner and outer Canada are likely to worsen.

If party discipline in Canada were relaxed, representation for all areas of Canada would be improved. It would be easier for, say, western MPs to defy their party establishments, if need be, in support of western issues. Coalitions composed of members of all parties could exist for the purpose of working together on issues of common regional or other concern. The present adversarial attitudes and structures of Parliament or legislatures in which opposition parties oppose virtually anything a government proposes might well change in the direction of parties working together for the common good.

Members of Parliament today represent an average of about eighty-seven thousand voters. At present, few government and opposition MPs have any real opportunity to put their constituents first in votes in the House of Commons. Real power is concentrated in the hands of the party leaderships. Canadian democracy itself would benefit if we put our present mind-numbing party discipline where it belongs—in the history books.

✘ NO
The Imperative of Party Discipline in the Canadian Political System
ROBERT J. JACKSON AND PAUL CONLIN

The fact that Canada has been successful as a state leaves some observers perplexed. The Canadian border encases the second-largest geographic land mass in the world under the authority of one Constitution. At the same time, the country is sparsely populated by a narrow ribbon of inhabitants stretched along the forty-ninth parallel. This widely dispersed population is subject to the pull of global economics dominated by its American neighbour to the south. From its genesis, Canada has been a linguistically and culturally heterogeneous society, and is becoming more so with each successive year. Despite the existence of all these centrifugal pressures, what we know today as Canada has existed and thrived for over a century and a quarter.

It is not by historical accident that Canada occupies the position it does today. On the contrary, the fact that Canada exists is the result of deliberate measures taken by Canadian leaders to establish policies and institutions that transcend diversity and bind the country together. Examples include national economic and social policies, a responsible cabinet/parliamentary system of government, and in particular, the establishment of broadly based and national political parties. Institutional structures, such as political parties, can transcend Canadian diversity and provide poles of allegiance against centrifugal influences. In order to fulfil this function effectively, the parties themselves must act as cohesive units and strive for party solidarity. Strong parties, based on a broad consensus, are thus vital to the effective functioning of responsible government and the Canadian state. Party solidarity, the apex of which is party discipline, is the guiding principle of the party system in Canada.[1]

Party discipline refers to the ability of the leader in a democratic state to enforce obedience on his or her followers in the legislature and in the party organization. The argument for relaxing party discipline is that MPs should not be "trained seals," but should be free to represent the views of their constituents. Members are, after all, elected by their constituents and should be responsible to them. But the issue is not that simple; the Canadian form of government relies on cohesive political parties. In the responsible government model, the party in power is awarded an electoral mandate to enact a legislative program, and its members must support the cabinet and prime minister in order to accomplish this. An MP is not primarily a delegate of his or her constituents. Rather, an MP is elected to serve as a member of a particular party. Within that party, the MP is called upon to deliberate and participate in formulating policies, and then to accept and support the majority decision. The government will not be made more responsive if its members make it more difficult to pass legislation. The prime minister and government must have the means of achieving their objectives.

The Canadian system is premised on the idea that reason and judgment are to be respected in the field of policymaking. Parties must be entrusted to deliberate, decide, and then be judged by the electorate. Otherwise, MPs would be elected to deliberate, but constituents, who have not participated in the deliberations, would retain the right to decide. Such a procedure would be ludicrous. MPs do not and should not directly represent their individual constituencies, provinces, or even regions, polling on every issue to see how they should vote. Rather, they are members of a particular party that provides broad perspectives on national issues. They run under the banner of that particular party and seek the privileges offered by it because they are in general agreement with its broad base of national policy directions, directions that can be influenced and adjusted in caucus.

As a British politician pointed out more than a century ago, "Combinations there must be—the only question is, whether they shall be broad parties, based on comprehensive ideas, and guided by men who have a name to stake on the wisdom of their course, or obscure cliques, with some narrow crotchet for a policy, and some paltry yelping shibboleth for a cry." After all, if MPs do not accept the decision arrived at by their executives and party, which groups will they represent? The special pleading of a particular pressure group that has a narrower conception of the national interest?

Party discipline is a feature inherent in the Canadian model of Parliament, and is inextricably linked to the concept of responsible government and the confidence convention. The Constitution Act, 1867, established that Canada would have a responsible cabinet/parliamentary system of government. This is the basis of our current system whereby the cabinet, as selected by the prime minister, is composed of members of the legislature and must keep the confidence of the House of Commons. The system also presupposes an opposition party or parties that are ready and willing to attack the government in an attempt to alter or reject its legislation. The government must therefore enforce party discipline not only to enact its legislative program, but also for the sake of its own self-preservation.

The United States congressional system of government differs from the parliamentary system in several key areas. Rather than fusing the executive and legislative branches of government, the American system is based on the separation of powers. The president and all of his or her cabinet members are prohibited by the Constitution from simultaneously sitting in the executive and legislative branches. The absence of responsible government and the corresponding absence of confidence convention allows the congressional system to function without party discipline.[2]

Calls for the relaxation of party discipline in Canada are not a recent phenomenon. Like the perennial cure for the common cold, the topic of parliamentary reform provides exaggerated hopes for optimists, then later gives way to despair when it fails. As early as 1923, for example, the MP from Calgary, William Irving, introduced a motion in the House of Commons that would have allowed for the relaxation of party discipline by reducing the number of votes considered to be votes of confidence. The motion was defeated, but to this day "reformers" still look to the United States and see the relaxation of party discipline as the panacea for perceived parliamentary inadequacies. Simplistic prescriptions such as the relaxation of party discipline, while seductive, fail to take into account the complexity of the parliamentary system. It is fallacious to assume that certain selected features of the congressional system can be appended to the parliamentary system without seriously affecting the functioning of the entire system.

Imagine a scenario where party discipline in Canada was significantly relaxed. Issues formerly resolved along party lines, based on consensual lines and accommodation in caucus, would be decided on much narrower grounds. Regionalism and special interests would dominate decision making in the House of Commons, and political parties would cease to serve their function as institutions that bind the country together. The decision-making model now in place, which requires political parties to produce nationally acceptable compromises, would be replaced by an increase in confrontation. MPs liberated from the yoke of party discipline would be saddled by the demands of lobbyists and others representing narrow special interests and regional interests.

Many of the arguments against party discipline are founded on misconceptions about the practice. The very term "whip," the name given to the party member charged with the task of enforcing party discipline, conjures up images of a menacing disciplinarian imposing the will of the party on recalcitrant MPs. This is not the case, however. While there are instances where MPs have been coerced or even threatened with sanctions if they do not conform, party discipline is largely self-imposed. Because the majority of MPs enjoy relatively little job security, they do not relish the prospect of facing reelection. Consequently, never in Canadian history has a government been toppled by a breach in party discipline. Furthermore, recent studies indicate that since 1940, no MP from the governing party has ever broken party ranks during a minority government. Nor has any MP ever left a government with a majority of fewer than nine seats.[3] This indicates that MPs, at least for the sake of their own self-preservation, are willing to tolerate party discipline.

Another misconception is that constituents do not want their MPs to toe the party line. This is a somewhat complex issue owing to the fact that the vote for the executive and legislative representative is fused into the same ballot in parliamentary systems. While it is impossible to determine the exact weight voters give to the individual candidate and the party label, several studies indicate that the determining factor is the party label. One report found that shortly after an election, fewer than two-thirds of respondents could correctly give the name of their recently elected MP.[4] More specifically, from 1940 to 1988, thirty-one MPs ran for reelection in the general election following the parliamentary session in which they revolted against their parliamentary caucus and crossed the floor. Only twelve of them were successful in the election, and three were forced to run under their former party banner. These figures contrast with the argument that the voters will reward an MP for acting independently.

The most recent substantive recommendations for reforming party discipline are embodied in the so-called McGrath Report, released in June 1985. The report had three basic conclusions:

1. There should be attitudinal changes.

2. The parties should relax their discipline.

3. There should be organizational reform.

The committee reported: "We believe the country would be better served if members had more freedom to play an active role in the debate on public policy, even if it meant disagreeing with their parties from time to time." The report then called for an "attitudinal change" by backbenchers and asked the prime minister to accept more dissension and defeat of government measures without recourse to the threat or use of dissolution of the House.

Unfortunately, this part of the report is romantic nonsense for the following reasons:

1. Calls for an attitudinal change are unlikely to be effective. The only practicable reform is one that changes the organization around members.

2. There never was a Golden Age of Parliament, as the report implies. In the period before parties, when Canadian MPs were "loose fish," MPs were not free of financial and other social ties that constrained their voting behaviour.

3. The question should not be whether MPs are free to vote against their parties, but rather, whose interests or groups are they adopting when they do so? Free voting does not mean that MPs are free of pressures to conform with other groups' positions.[5] Is it better to have MPs' behaviour determined by widely based cohesive political parties or narrower interest groups?

The facts also belie the utopian assumptions of the McGrath Report. Since 1985, there has been no real relaxation of party discipline in the House of Commons. The urging cries of "reformers" have had no effect: the reality is that MPs are already free to vote as they wish. The point is that they do not choose to exercise their liberty by taking stands against their parties. They will always be subject to constituents, interest groups, and financial pressures: the only question is whether they will follow the dictates of a broadly based party or those of another group with a narrower conception of the national interest. Those who choose wisely stand solidly with their parties, helping to protect the system of government and providing a counterpoint to the centrifugal influences of our geography and society.

NOTES

1. Robert J. Jackson and Doreen Jackson, *Politics in Canada,* 2nd ed. (Scarborough: Prentice-Hall, 1990).

2. Robert J. Jackson and Doreen Jackson, *Contemporary Government and Politics: Democracy and Authoritarianism* (Scarborough: Prentice-Hall, 1993).

3. Paul Conlin, "Floor Crossing in the Canadian House of Commons, 1940–1992" (Carleton University: Unpublished B.A. (Hons.) research paper, 1993).

4. William Irvine, "Does the Candidate Make a Difference? The Macro-politics and Micro-politics of Getting Elected," *Canadian Journal of Political Science* 15, no. 4 (December 1982).

5. Robert J. Jackson, "Executive–Legislative Relations in Canada," in Jackson et al., *Contemporary Canadian Politics* (Scarborough: Prentice-Hall, 1987), pp. 111–125.

POSTSCRIPT

One's stance on the issue of party discipline depends in part on how one interprets the experience of other countries, particularly the United States. David Kilgour, John Kirsner, and Kenneth McConnell like the freedom that the relaxed party discipline of the American system gives members of Congress to represent their constituents, especially their regional concerns. But Robert Jackson and Paul Conlin are skeptical—they fear that an American-style system of lax discipline leaves the door open to the excessive influence of special interests on members' voting decisions.

But is there another model that could be followed? As Kilgour, Kirsner, and McConnell note, in Great Britain, members of the House of Commons may vote against their party without fear of recrimination on issues that are understood by all not to constitute a vote of confidence. Accordingly, a government may be defeated on a particular bill and still survive. It is suggested that such a practice allows MPs some independence in the legislature without putting at risk the life of a government.

Those wishing to understand how Britain has dealt with the issue of party discipline should read John Schwarz, "Exploring a New Role in Policymaking: The British House of Commons in the 1970s," *American Political Science Review* 74, no. 1 (March 1980): 23–37. Schwarz examines the changes made to British parliamentary traditions to permit a greater amount of "cross-voting." He argues that these changes have greatly strengthened the role of the House of Commons in the legislative process.

Not everyone is convinced that the British experience can be readily adapted to Canada. C.E.S. Franks, in *The Parliament of Canada* (Toronto: University of Toronto Press, 1987), notes that there are a number of factors that make the British experience unique. Because of the much larger number of members in the British House of Commons, party discipline is much harder to enforce. A large number of safe seats make MPs less dependent on party patronage for their postparliamentary livelihood. The cabinet in Britain is much smaller. Long-serving MPs from safe seats, who are not obsessed with promotion to the cabinet, are much less likely to succumb to the brandishments of their leader, as both Margaret Thatcher and John Major have learned to their chagrin. In contrast, there is a much higher turnover among Canadian MPs, who generally do not feel secure enough to challenge a leader they feel is necessary to their own reelection chances.

The applicability of the British experience to Canada is also explored in Peter Dobell, "Some Comments on Party Reform," in Peter Aucoin, ed., *Institutional Reforms for Representative Government* (Toronto: University of Toronto Press, 1985). Dobell is not optimistic about the prospect of Canadian party leaders relinquishing their strong control over party discipline in the near future. However, he does propose some minor modifications that would give some flexibility to individual MPs.

Before succeeding Jean Chrétien as prime minister, Paul Martin, in a speech in October 2002, outlined the ways in which he would bring about parliamentary reforms to enhance the voice of MPs, strengthen accountability, and relax party discipline. His announced plan would introduce a system of identifying three types of parliamentary votes. Only a limited number of votes on "fundamental issues" would require full party support. A second level of votes would require members of cabinet to support the government but allow other party members to vote freely from party discipline. And, the third category of votes would allow all MPs to vote as they wished, without the pressure of party discipline. Martin noted that this would make up the majority of parliamentary votes in the future. On becoming prime minister, Martin kept his promise and implemented the new way of classifying votes. Only time will tell whether the change will have any major effect on the operation of party discipline. For an analysis of Martin's proposals, see Peter Aucoin and Lori Turnbull, "The Democratic Deficit: Paul Martin and Parliamentary Reform," *Canadian Public Administration* 46, no. 4 (Winter 2003).

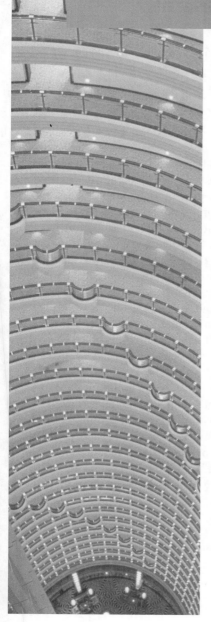

PART FOUR

THE POLITICAL PROCESS

Should representation in Parliament
mirror Canada's social diversity?

Should voting be made mandatory?

Is a Mixed-Member Proportional
electoral system in Canada's interest?

Are "dirty hands" necessary in politics?

Should Representation in Parliament Mirror Canada's Social Diversity?

✔ **YES**
TIM SCHOULS, "Why Group Representation in Parliament Is Important"

✗ **NO**
JOHN H. REDEKOP, "Group Representation in Parliament Would Be Dysfunctional for Canada"

Canada is a representative democracy in which, every four or five years, we choose certain individuals (members of Parliament) to act on our behalf. As our representatives, we empower them to act as our agents and to represent our interests in the national decision-making process. As long as representative democracy has existed there has been debate over the exact nature that representation should take.

Much of this debate has focused on how the representative is expected to carry out his or her duties. Traditionally three different views of representation have been put forward. First, there are those who argue that the representative is to act as a *trustee*. That is, members of Parliament are given a mandate to act as they best see fit on behalf of the interests of the electors. MPs are given considerable leeway to exercise their personal judgment in balancing the interests of their constituents with those of the broader community and in coming up with a policy that best serves the common good. While the representatives can exercise wide latitude in making decisions, the voter will hold them accountable by removing them from office at the end of their term if they are perceived to have failed in adequately representing the voter's interests.

Second, there are those who argue that the representative is to act primarily as a *delegate*. According to this view, members of Parliament should act as they have been instructed to by the voters rather than trusting their own judgment as a guide. Representatives should not stray too far from the explicit wishes of their constituents. A variety of techniques such as constituent surveys, public hall meetings, and telephone referendums have been used in recent years by MPs, especially those from the Canadian Alliance party, before voting on a particular issue in an attempt to ascertain what the "instructions" of the electorate were.

Third, representatives have been seen as first and foremost *party members* who act and vote primarily according to the dictates of the party leadership. This perspective assumes that the representatives in a party act as a team and that the electorate chooses which team they feel best represents their interests. Like the trustee model, the voters must wait until the next election to render a judgment on the success of the representative in representing their interests. The debate that follows in Issue Thirteen addresses weaknesses of the party model of representation and ways that these deficiencies in representative government can be addressed.

In recent years, the debate over representation has shifted toward a more fundamental question—to what extent do the representatives in Parliament reflect the characteristics of ethnicity, language, and gender that are found in the population at large. On one level, this argument suggests that to be truly "representative," Parliament should be composed of the same proportion of social groups as is Canadian society at large. Parliament, in other words, should be a microcosm of Canadian society. If the population is composed of 51 percent women, 6 percent visible minorities, and 4 percent Aboriginal people, then there should be at least the same proportion of representatives elected to Parliament from each of these groups. A basic premise of this argument is that voters, especially those from minority and marginalized groups within society, will not see the decisions of Parliament as being fully legitimate unless the voters see themselves reflected in the social makeup of the legislature. As the social and cultural makeup of Canada changes, our political institutions could increasingly lose credibility if their composition does not adequately reflect the changing face of the country.

However, this argument goes beyond the question simply of increasing the numerical representation of certain social groups, such as women, in Parliament. It argues that representation is important because, once elected, women will act in the interests of women. They will interpret issues and respond to them differently than a male representative would. Thus, the election of women and minority groups to Parliament would result in substantive changes in the content of public policy, as the views of groups once marginalized and unrepresented in the political system are now given voice within the corridors of power. Only those who truly know from experience what it is to be a woman, an Aboriginal person, or a member of a visible minority can truly represent other members of the groups to which they belong in Parliament.

In the following essays, we examine in greater depth this view of representation. Tim Schouls sets out the philosophical case for ensuring that the social diversity of Canada is represented in the Canadian legislature. In response, John Redekop examines the implications of this move away from more traditional definitions of representation and questions both the wisdom and practicality of such an approach.

✔ YES
Why Group Representation in Parliament Is Important
TIM SCHOULS

An increasing number of Canadians are convinced that the system of parliamentary representation in Canada is unfair because it is seen as unrepresentative of Canada's social diversity as a whole. Parliament has long reflected the regional and linguistic composition of Canada by allocating seats in the House of Commons and Senate in a manner that ensures adequate representation of provincial interests at the national level. But this exclusive concern for provincial and regional representation is now being challenged by nonterritorial groups who demand representation on the basis of characteristics that are not tied to geography. These groups argue that if the full diversity of Canada's population is to be reflected in Parliament, its representative character must be expanded beyond that of territory to include guaranteed seats for disadvantaged groups such as women, Aboriginal peoples, ethnic and visible minorities, and people with disabilities. The belief here is that parliamentary representatives must share central experiences and assumptions with those they represent if those representatives are to understand their constituents' needs and interests. Conversely, these groups believe that they cannot be adequately represented if their needs and interests are not advanced by those who share their gender, Aboriginal status, ethnicity, race, or disability.

The conventional Canadian approach to representative democracy, as represented in the article that follows by John Redekop, is generally hostile to claims for guaranteed group-based representation. According to Redekop's view, effective representation does not depend upon representatives and constituents sharing the same personal attributes. Instead, the effectiveness of representatives is measured by the degree to which they are able to present and advance the concerns and claims of their constituents. According to his line of argument, just as lawyers can represent clients who are very different from them, so too can representatives protect the interests of those whose lives have little in common with their own.

While this article will not take direct issue with this more traditional understanding of democratic representation, it will argue that democracy in Canada can be considerably deepened and enhanced when the composition of the House of Commons substantially reflects the social diversity of the Canadian population.[1] No doubt, MPs can represent constituents who are very different from them, but at the same time it is not always obvious that this representation has been effective in cases where the constituents in question have been subject to historical disadvantage and marginalization. Of course, not all groups in Canadian society have been marginalized or have suffered disadvantage, but for those that have, their argument that seats in the House of Commons be guaranteed to them is worthy of serious examination. For democracy implies equality, but, where conditions of marginalization and disadvantage exist, it necessarily follows that some groups possess greater opportunity, and thus privileges and powers that others do not. In the Canadian parliamentary setting, white males from professional and business backgrounds have historically dominated the House of Commons and Senate, and, as a result, it is they who have traditionally held a monopoly upon the political reigns of power. Conversely, many women, Aboriginal peoples, certain ethnic and visible minorities, and people with disabilities claim that they have been marginalized, which means, among other things, that they have been minimally represented in parliamentary discussions and decision-making processes. This article will argue that where political marginalization of groups has historically existed, active reform to secure these groups seats in the House of Commons is a healthy democratic response. Not only will such reform ensure marginalized groups a greater presence and thus a voice in the parliamentary process, but also such reform may encourage the development of legislation and laws that take more fully into account the views of marginalized groups. In short, an active reform process will counteract the current imbalance in political power and so promote greater democratic equality of opportunity and participation in the House of Commons for Canada's socially diverse groups.

GROUP IDENTITY IN CANADA

It could be argued that to focus exclusively upon demands by marginalized groups for political inclusion within the House of Commons is to largely miss the point of group identity politics in Canada. The range of political differences and objectives represented by Canada's diverse population is extensive, pushing far beyond the kinds of solutions that a politics of inclusion within the House of Commons can offer. To be sure, over the last twenty-five years or so Canadians have begun to define themselves in new ways, and the politics of parliamentary inclusion is in large part an initiative that attempts to address those changes. For political purposes, Canadians used to identify themselves largely with their provinces of origin, with their use of French or English as their first language, and with their Catholic or Protestant religion. In response, the House of Commons was set up, both in terms of its allocation of seats and in terms of representation within cabinet, to reflect this geographic, linguistic, and religious diversity. In recent years, however, a new set of identity categories has become increasingly salient for many Canadians, categories associated primarily with changing conceptions of ethnicity and with the newfound political relevance of gender. Immigration and demographic trends of the 1970s to the 1990s have made Canada a far more multiethnic and multicultural country, while strong feminist initiatives during this same time frame have elevated the political status of women. New Canadians with origins in the Caribbean, Africa, Middle East, Central and South America, and Asia identify themselves not simply as provincial residents speaking either English or French, but more importantly as members of ethnic groups with distinctive perspectives and interests to offer to the broader Canadian political agenda. Feminists, meanwhile, point out that the social and political structures of Canada reinforce men's power to the detriment of women. In response, redress of the current structural imbalance of power between men and women constitutes a central component of the feminist political agenda. In short, attachments to geography, language, and religion are receding in their overall political importance. At the same time, attachments to ethnicity and gender are becoming more significant politically. Against these shifting demographic trends, it is therefore not surprising that the conventional geography-based strategy for allocating House of Commons seats is coming under increasing attack.

However, despite the need to address the challenge of representation in the House of Commons for the marginally represented categories of women and ethnic groups, Canadian identity politics is more typically driven by demands for Aboriginal self-government and the recognition of Quebec's "distinct society." Like women and ethnic minorities, Aboriginal peoples and the citizens of Quebec argue that the existing conventions of representation do not grant them standing that is proportional to their numbers in Canada. From the perspectives of their leaders, however, greater representation in Parliament will not guarantee Aboriginal peoples and the citizens of Quebec the kind of legislative power they need to secure their political objectives within Canada. Their numbers are simply too small and their influence too weak to counteract the legislative priorities of the non-Aboriginal, non-Québécois parliamentary majority. Hence, Aboriginal peoples demand an equal partnership with federal and provincial governments based upon the recognition of their inherent right to self-government, while Quebecers demand at minimum an expansion of their powers within the federal system of government so as to increase their provincial autonomy within Canada. Thus, when Aboriginal peoples and Quebecers claim that they do not enjoy equal powers within Canada, they typically seek solutions within the realm of inter-governmental affairs rather than parliamentary representation.

When considering the arguments for greater parliamentary representation for disadvantaged or marginalized groups within Canada, it is important to realize from the outset, then, that the demands for political inclusion by Aboriginal peoples, the citizens of Quebec, women, and ethnic and visible minorities are not naturally all of one piece. Aboriginal peoples and Quebecers demand more autonomy *from* Parliament through self-government and special provincial status (or secession), while women and ethnic and visible minorities demand more autonomy *within* Parliament through elevated levels of representation. In fact, in many respects, the demands of the former two groups are mirror images of those of the latter groups. Be that as it may, the demands for equal representation within Parliament remain an important concern for some groups. The intent of this article is to draw attention to only this very small piece of the larger, often poorly interlocking, Canadian identity puzzle.

REPRESENTATIONAL DEFICITS

On the surface, there is an undeniable, indeed, almost irrefutable, logic attached to the demand that the House of Commons reflect the diversity of the Canadian population. At present, for example, electoral mechanisms organize Canadians into geographically bound constituencies. While Redekop is quite right to point out that dividing voters into constituency groups makes sense from a practical point of view, such a division also carries with it the assumption that voters' primary political identity flows from their attachment to territory. MPs are thus linked to their constituents in geographic terms. The geographical division of the electorate encourages voters to think of their varied interests (whether relating to jobs, social security, the environment, etc.) largely in terms of where they live.

Now, while features associated with geography may well shape citizens' identities in some respects, Canadians also possess diverse identities by virtue of their cultural, gender, ethnic, and religious differences, which have very little to do with geography. It therefore stands to reason that along with geographic affiliation, Canadians may want to be represented by those who share their Aboriginal status, gender, ethnicity, or religious identity. There is an intuitive logic attached to the idea, for example, that when legislative initiatives dealing with abortion, childcare, or pay equity are before the House of Commons, female constituents may want to be represented by women who can identify with these issues because they are women. Similarly, when legislative initiatives dealing with reserve-based economic ventures or housing starts are before the House, it makes sense that Aboriginal constituents may want to have Aboriginal people representing their interests. According to this line of reasoning then, there is clearly something amiss when representation within the House is monopolized by a single group (upper- and middle-class males, for example), a group, moreover, that most likely possesses a relatively limited range of perspectives. Indeed, most well-intentioned Canadians would probably readily admit that where underrepresentation of certain groups exists, reforms ought to be encouraged to stimulate a more proportional balance of representation in the House.

While there have been a few improvements, it is undeniably the case that the composition of the House of Commons is only a very pale reflection of the diverse social characteristics of the Canadian population, as can be seen in the following three examples. In the 1988 federal election, 39, or 13.2 percent, of the MPs elected were women; in the 1993 election, 54, or 18.3 percent, were women; while in the 1997 election, 61, or 20.2 percent, were women. Given that women constitute 51 percent of Canada's population, the severity of their underrepresentation in the House is hard to miss.[2] In the case of Aboriginal peoples and visible minorities, underrepresentation in the House is even more striking.[3] Aboriginal peoples constitute approximately 4 percent of Canada's population, yet they were able to capture only 1 percent of the seats (3 of a total 295) in each of the 1988 and 1993 elections.[4] Visible minorities, meanwhile, while constituting 6.3 percent of Canada's population, captured only 2 percent of the seats (6 out of 295) in 1988, though they improved their fortunes slightly by increasing their share to 3 percent (9 out of 295) in the election of 1993.[5] Compare these lean numbers to the following scenario. If a proportional share of seats were given to each of the three groups mentioned above, women would be entitled to 153 seats, Aboriginal peoples to 12 seats, and visible minorities to 19 seats out of the total 301.[6]

The obvious question here is why do women, Aboriginal peoples, and visible minorities persist in being so severely underrepresented in the House of Commons? There is no short answer to this question, for the barriers that inhibit each group from entering electoral politics are numerous and in many respects different from one another. Women, for example, have traditionally avoided political life at the national level because the heavy demands of family life and a political career often strain significantly against one another. Moreover, the challenge associated with securing financing to contest constituency nominations and run campaigns, coupled with the perception that the fierce competition associated with politics is symptomatic of a male domain, has made the political arena at the national level minimally appealing for many women.[7] Aboriginal candidates share with women the structural barrier of limited financing. In addition, as the Committee for Aboriginal Electoral Reform argues, "Canada's history of assimilationist policies have had an adverse impact on Aboriginal perceptions of Parliament and the value of participating within it."[8] The negative feelings Aboriginal peoples hold against Parliament as a colonial instrument of oppression means that many Aboriginal people are inclined not to vote in federal elections. This in turn discourages parties from fielding Aboriginal candidates as there is little incentive for them to use such Aboriginal candidates, in attempts to win a largely apathetic Aboriginal vote. Barriers inhibiting the participation of visible minorities are also readily identifiable. For example, Daiva Stasiulis argues that for many recent immigrants a significant barrier exists in the form of lack of familiarity with Canada's two official languages and with the customs of the British parliamentary tradition.[9] This barrier is compounded in turn by party politics that tend to identify the issues of Canadian politics along a French–English continuum and to engage in the recruitment of candidates by using old, well-established networks that have little, if any, connections to the immigrant community.

Given these structural barriers, it seems but a small step to justify reforms aimed at securing a proportional number of women, Aboriginal peoples, and ethnic and visible minorities in the House of Commons. Moreover, the case for inclusion only gathers strength when we recognize that the primary reason why women, Aboriginal peoples, and ethnic and visible minorities are absent from the House of Commons is because they have been ignored and marginalized by the male hierarchy that holds power. Given that men dominate the House of Commons, it only stands to reason that they will have greater opportunity and power to advance their perspectives and legislate their preferences. Conversely, it has been well documented that, relative to men, women suffer greater social and economic disadvantage, a condition that in turn means that women have fewer political resources than men. Aboriginal peoples and ethnic and visible minorities, meanwhile, have long struggled against what Iris Marion Young calls cultural imperialism.[10] In the Canadian setting, cultural imperialism has typically manifested itself in the form of English and French cultures establishing society-wide norms. Aboriginal, ethnic, and visible minority cultures, conversely, were traditionally stigmatized as being inferior and in need of transformation to align them more closely with the perspectives and worldviews of the two dominant cultures.

THEORIES OF REPRESENTATION

It is largely in reaction to these structural barriers that numerous calls for reform leading to a more proportional balance of representation in Parliament have been issued over the years. In essence, calls for proportional representation constitute a claim to tip the scales of the currently imbalanced composition of the House of Commons toward a more balanced representation of Canada's social diversity. If the political assumptions associated with white male privilege hamper the capacity of minorities to gain access to the House of Commons, then on democratic grounds surely no effort should be spared to get more minority representatives into the House. Moreover, the urgency that many marginalized groups attach to their claims for inclusion flows directly from the fact that the House of Commons lies at the symbolic heart of representative government in Canada. It is with this state institution more than any other that the primary qualification to become an MP is purely and simply the ability to represent. No doubt, as Redekop points out, many MPs get elected simply because they are better than their opponents in capturing the vote. But in the end, the test of good service is established by the degree to which constituents judge their MP to have been an effective representative on their behalf. This stands in sharp contrast to employment within the judiciary or bureaucracy, for example, where professional expertise and academic qualifications are of first importance. Simply put, legislatures exist to represent the population they serve; this is their central function. It is therefore imperative from the point of view of numerous marginalized groups that, if they are to achieve social and political equality in any meaningful sense, they simply must achieve proportional standing in the parliamentary domain where many of their interests are so regularly considered and debated.

If the case for more proportional inclusion in the House of Commons is so compelling, then why do so many Canadians accept with little trouble the prevailing patterns of white, male-dominated representation? In order to get a handle on this question, it is important that we step back for a moment and examine with some care the conflicting understandings that lie behind the idea of representation itself.

To date, there has been significant agreement in Canada that the practice of parliamentary democracy ought to adhere to a liberal conception of representation. From a liberal point of view, it is the individual who is to be treated as the most important of all political entities. This means that when it comes to representation, each individual is to count equally as one, and no one as more than one. In the context of elections, moreover, this concern for individual equality translates into the well-known slogan One Person, One Vote. What is of principal importance from the liberal point of view, then, is that while group interests can be advanced (given that it is individuals who form groups for the deliberate purpose of promoting common interests), individual interests must not be ignored in the process. Indeed, for liberals, to represent groups exclusively potentially poses two immediate dangers to the individual. First, when MPs represent group interests they tend to regard those interests as held by all members of the group. However, not all group members may hold the same interests. For example, some women may dissent from a particular daycare strategy, yet if women are treated as a group, MPs may be tempted to regard the endorsement of the strategy by some women as an endorsement by all. Focusing upon the interests of each and every individual gets around this problem of universalizing interests. Second, to focus upon the interests of groups brings with it the possibility that MPs will privilege some groups over others. Under this scenario, not only are dissenting individuals within privileged groups left unrepresented, but so too are all members of groups who are not fortunate enough to gain the attention of MPs in the first place.

In the interests of equality of representation, then, representatives are elected to advance the individual interests of their individual constituents. To be sure, the interests of constituents will regularly conflict, and so the MP will be forced to make compromises and secure tradeoffs. The measure of effective representation is determined when, despite being faced by the challenge of conflicting interests, MPs are nevertheless able to take appropriate positions demonstrating that in doing so they have taken the interests of all their constituents into account. The issue, then, is not who is in the House of Commons doing the representing, but rather whether the MP, regardless of personal characteristics, is able to get the job done on behalf of his or her constituents. In short, MPs may well possess different social, ethnic, or sexual characteristics from those they represent, but this should not matter if MPs demonstrate a constant readiness to respond in helpful ways to their constituents' needs.

This liberal argument of representation is certainly a very powerful one. But on its own, this liberal theory simply does not do full justice to the political marginalization and exclusion that many women, Aboriginal peoples, and ethnic and visible minorities experience. As Redekop so powerfully argues, men can represent women (much as a male lawyer can represent a female client) if the issue in question is a legislative initiative to which both men and women agree. But what Redekop fails to take seriously is that with respect to many issues, women,

Aboriginal peoples, and visible and ethnic minorities will want to be represented by those who are like them because they believe that their identities carry with them distinctive experiences that white male MPs will be hard-pressed to understand. Women, for example, may possess experiences and consequently perspectives that are distinct from those of men with respect to the issues of childbearing and childcare, sexual harassment and violence, the division of paid and unpaid labour, and the matter of women's exclusion from significant portions of the economic and political world.[11] Furthermore, with respect to Aboriginal peoples, Ovide Mercredi and Mary Ellen Turpel argue, "As Peoples with distinct cultures, languages, governments, territories and populations in Canada, we must be recognized as full and equal participants in the Canadian political system. We can speak for ourselves and no one else has the political or spiritual authority to speak for us. Canadians cannot speak for us because Canadians are different."[12] What is at issue here is not so much the capacity of MPs to advocate on behalf of their female, Aboriginal, or ethnic and visible minority candidates per se; minorities would certainly endorse any initiative that sees MPs support and advance their political agendas. More directly, what is at issue is the desire of women, Aboriginal peoples, and ethnic and visible minorities to gain a more proportional balance in the House of Commons on the grounds that they have been marginalized and excluded from representing themselves in the past.

At the same time, it is critical to underscore the point that the leaders of marginalized groups do not generally stake their claim for greater inclusion on the grounds that they share common interests, interests, moreover, that they believe only their own representatives are capable of putting before the House of Commons. Such an argument cannot provide the moral foundation for a claim to greater inclusion because the experiences of marginalized groups are normally too varied to be contained within a single common interest. Women have different perspectives on abortion, childcare, and pay equity, for example, while Aboriginal peoples have different perspectives on economic development, land claims, and self-government. Within their respective communities, women and Aboriginal peoples may thus share common policy concerns, but this does not mean that they will also share the same views on how those concerns ought to be handled. Minority groups are not homogeneous, possessing single, distinct policy perspectives. Such images portray far too simplistic a view of the world. Because minority groups do not by definition possess common policy interests, the strength of the argument for greater inclusion in the House of Commons necessarily lies elsewhere.

The argument for greater inclusion in the House of Commons gathers far more strength when considered within the framework of political marginalization or exclusion. The representational claim of marginalized groups is a forceful one because groups want to overcome the barriers of domination that have excluded them from participating in an equitable way in the House in the past. As the argument goes, if the distinct voices and (internally multiple) perspectives of marginalized social groups are not represented in the House, then it is almost certainly the case that the legislative initiatives and policy outcomes of the dominant white male majority will (continue to) prevail. In essence, what marginalized groups are saying is that they have a right to participate in these parliamentary discussions whatever their opinion may be on the matter under consideration. In this sense, the demands for parliamentary inclusion put forward by women, Aboriginal people, and visible and ethnic minorities flow from their common experiences of exclusion as groups, and from their mutual desire to engage more directly in parliamentary debate and decision making. To be sure, as Redekop points out, inclusion in parliamentary debate is not in and of itself enough to guarantee satisfactory legislative outcomes for marginalized groups. Influence can be effective only to the degree that marginalized groups can make their presence felt where power in parliamentary government is exercised—by the majority party and, more particularly, by the prime minister and cabinet drawn from the majority party. At the same time, however, without presence in the House of Commons there is little opportunity for marginalized groups to exercise any influence at all.

The larger point that the leaders of marginalized groups seek to establish, however, is that because white males have traditionally monopolized parliamentary power, they cannot at this juncture in history take the place of the very groups they have marginalized by standing in as their representatives. As social groups, women, Aboriginal peoples, and visible and ethnic minorities need to be represented by other women, Aboriginal peoples, and visible and ethnic minorities because they share identities, which goes along with having been historically excluded. Thus, for example, men may be able to advance women's interests, but what men cannot do is stand in for women when women want to have all their diversity *as women* represented in the House of Commons. This is a task that only women can perform for themselves. Against historical patterns of exclusion, the presence of women in the House of Commons ensures that all the diverse and quite possibly conflicting interests of women will actually be heard and debated in Canada's central representative political arena.[13]

In sum, the proportional presence of women, Aboriginal peoples, and visible and ethnic minorities in the House of Commons matters because this presence would have the effect of counteracting the current hierarchy of white male power. A more sustained and numerically balanced presence would help to raise the profile of marginalized groups and thereby possibly place their multiple issues more regularly before the House. In this vein, Young argues, "The principle of group representation calls for some means by which the needs, interests, knowledge, and social perspective of oppressed or disadvantaged groups receive explicit and formal representation in political discussions and decision-making. The primary argument for such group representation is that where there are social group differences and some groups are privileged and others oppressed, group representation is necessary to produce a legitimate communicative forum."[14] Proportional representation of marginalized groups in the House of Commons would ensure that the full range of views represented by Canada's diverse population would have the opportunity for expression on a consistent and ongoing basis. This may in turn encourage a situation in which "those who had previously monopolized positions of power and influence might be equally encouraged to recognize their partiality and bias."[15]

OBJECTIONS

In the article following, John Redekop raises a number of objections against the arguments put forward thus far. Let me conclude by addressing the three that are most significant.

First, Redekop argues that a politics of parliamentary inclusion based on gender, ethnic, or other minority identities introduces or possibly intensifies divisions between Canadian citizens, divisions, moreover, that arguably may not be of the first importance in the public eye. He points out that Canada has enough trouble as it is building points of commonality between Canadians in Parliament, so why should Canadians further fuel the fire of divisions by paying attention to gender- and ethnicity-based claims to inclusion? Indeed, would it not be far better to encourage citizens to focus on matters of policy instead and try to build alliances across identity differences in support of policy initiatives that all groups can support? To cede to demands for parliamentary inclusion by marginalized groups, argues Redekop, would seem only to add additional stress to an already severely stretched Canadian unity fabric.

There is no easy answer to this objection, for Redekop is undoubtedly right that the demand for inclusion by women, Aboriginal peoples, and visible and ethnic minorities would add a new and potentially divisive dimension to parliamentary politics. However, one way to partly allay these fears of division is to recognize that what marginalized groups are asking for is not to be separated from the structures of Canadian democracy, but rather to be more fully included within them. Contrast, for example, the demands of Quebec separatists with the demands of marginalized groups, and consider which is the more divisive force within Canadian politics. Quebec separatists threaten political unity within Canada because they question the credentials of the Canadian government to exercise any authority over them. Marginalized groups, on the other hand, have drawn attention to their identities only because they want to be more fully included in the political discussions that shape the political identity of Canada as a whole. Thus, although marginalized groups may focus upon the political importance of their social differences, what they are actually doing, as Will Kymlicka puts it, is trying to find avenues for "full membership in the larger society."[16] Seen from this perspective, the demand for greater inclusion by marginalized groups can be seen as an important endorsement of the Canadian parliamentary system.

Redekop's second objection relates to who potentially qualifies for distinct representation within Parliament. If Parliament is to be considered truly representative of Canada's social diversity, Redekop asks, then does this mean that all sectors of the Canadian population should be represented, including, for example, the aged, teachers, students, factory workers, retail sales workers, parents, athletes, and environmentalists? Once we accept the view that the characteristics of people play a role in determining whether they feel adequately represented in Parliament, then we seem to be in the absurd position of having to consider the claims for inclusion by a potentially endless list of groups. Moreover, even if we can establish which groups might qualify for guaranteed representation, Redekop asks further, how do we go about establishing who legitimately belongs to which group? Is the attempt to establish boundaries simply too difficult, given so many people now have what might be called "hybrid" identities (e.g., a person may be both female and Aboriginal)? In other words, on what basis do we distinguish legitimate claims by groups for parliamentary inclusion from those that are not legitimate?

Again, there is no straightforward answer to Redekop's objection, though Anne Phillips points us in a helpful direction. She argues that the case for greater inclusion of women, ethnic groups, and ethnic and visible minorities rests upon "an analysis of the existing structures of exclusion."[17] That is, a system of fair representation does not mean that any or all groups are entitled to specific representation on the basis of some purported principle of equality or fairness. Instead, what we must do is focus upon those particularly urgent instances where the oppression of groups has led to those same groups experiencing a profound degree of marginalization and exclusion from the political process. Proportional representation of groups is thus never simply required, but must be determined on a case-by-case basis in reference to these questions: Has this group been historically oppressed? Will proportional representation in Parliament constitute a significant step in overcoming those conditions of oppression? In other words, what qualifies groups for greater inclusion is the likelihood that without guaranteed access to the arena of policymaking they will be unable to overcome their current experiences of exclusion and marginalization. While this approach does not get around the difficulties associated with defining who is and who is not a member of a disadvantaged group, it at least narrows the field of potential candidates who may be eligible for guaranteed representation. Against these more restrictive criteria, women, Aboriginal peoples, and numerous visible minority and ethnic groups in Canada are able to put forward a very strong case.

Third, Redekop argues that the proposal to move to identity-based representation is condescending toward those groups that would benefit from guaranteed seats because, among other things, such representation would relegate them to the status of second-class MPs. If groups can't make it to the House of Commons on their own, in other words, and are thereby "reduced" to relying upon special governmental facilitation to get them there, they will undoubtedly lack credibility.

No doubt, securing seats through special guarantees does constitute a significant departure from standard electoral practice in Canada. But though a departure, these reform proposals are not in and of themselves condescending to disadvantaged and marginalized groups. Here everything depends on one's perspective. Despite what Redekop says, disadvantaged and marginalized groups are not after guaranteed seats because the dominant male hierarchy has told them that such a course of action would be good for them. To accept the directives of the dominant male hierarchy on these grounds would indeed be condescending. On the contrary, disadvantaged and marginalized groups who make the point are saying that they are after guaranteed seats because this is the only way they will be able to break the stranglehold upon power that the dominant male hierarchy now exercises over them. They would stand for office and get elected through conventional channels, in other words, if they could reasonably expect to be successful in this way. The trouble is that their success is minimized because the dominant male hierarchy (which constitutes a minority in demographic terms) has been very effective at retaining its vast majority of seats in the House since it has at its disposal a disproportional share of the party and electoral machinery needed to win elections. From this perspective, the only way to break this cycle of dominance is to make structural changes that directly challenge the male hierarchy. One way to mount this challenge is through a system of guaranteed seats.

CONCLUSION

Redekop is quite right to point out that the practical complications associated with getting a system of guaranteed seats off the ground are considerable. I have no easy solutions to offer. However, simply because there are practical difficulties associated with reform should not lead us to abandon the project. Advocates of reform tell us that a system of guaranteed seats is an integral component of their larger project to overcome the debilitating cycle of political marginalization and exclusion they now experience. The question is, what is the best route to heeding this call for justice? There is, of course, safety to be had in steering the ship of democratic practice in Canada into the tranquil waters of the status quo rather than into the rocky waters of reform. The latter route may well lead to significant structural damage to the parliamentary ship as we know it. However, avoiding rocky waters also means that those who now hold power will continue to pilot the ship. The message that the marginalized and disadvantaged in Canada draw to our attention is that this inclination toward "safety" may be less than desirable.

NOTES

1. I will leave aside the question of representation in the Senate as this would raise issues that lie beyond the scope of this paper.

2. See Jane Arscott and Linda Trimble, "In the Presence of Women: Representation and Political Power," in Jane Arscott and Linda Trimble, eds., *In the Presence of Women: Representation in Canadian Governments* (Toronto: Harcourt Brace & Company, Canada, 1997), pp. 1–17.

3. At the time that this article was originally written, the official number of Aboriginal and visible minority MPs elected federally in June 1997 was unavailable (see footnote 6).

4. See Committee for Aboriginal Electoral Reform, *The Path to Electoral Equality* (Ottawa: Committee for Aboriginal Electoral Reform, 1991), p. 2.

5. See Daiva Stasiulis, "Deep Diversity: Race and Ethnicity in Canadian Politics," in Michael S. Whittington and Glen Williams, eds., *Canadian Politics in the 1990s* (Toronto: Nelson Canada, 1995), pp. 199–200.

6. In the June 1997 federal election, the number of House of Commons seats contested was raised from 295 to 301. [Editors' note: In the 2004 General Election, six Aboriginal candidates and fifteen visible minority candidates were elected, still short of the proportional representation discussed in the article.]

7. On this point, see Lisa Young, "Fulfilling the Mandate of Difference: Women in the Canadian House of Commons," in Jane Arscott and Linda Trimble, *In the Presence of Women: Representation in Canadian Governments*, pp. 85–86.

8. Committee for Aboriginal Electoral Reform, *The Path to Electoral Equality*, pp. 7–12.

9. Daiva Stasiulis, "Deep Diversity: Race and Ethnicity in Canadian Politics," pp. 200–204.

10. Iris Marion Young, "Justice and Communicative Democracy," in Roger S. Gottlieb, ed., *Radical Philosophy: Tradition, Counter-Tradition Politics* (Philadelphia: Temple University Press, 1993), p. 133.

11. Anne Phillips, *The Politics of Presence* (Oxford: Clarendon Press, 1995), pp. 67–68.

12. Ovide Mercredi and Mary Ellen Turpel, *In the Rapids: Navigating the Future of First Nations* (Toronto: Penguin, 1993), p. 36.

13. For an extensive discussion of this point, see Anne Phillips, *The Politics of Presence*, chapter 2.

14. Iris Marion Young, "Justice and Communicative Democracy," p. 136.

15. Anne Phillips, *The Politics of Presence*, p. 152.

16. Will Kymlicka, *Multicultural Citizenship: A Liberal Theory of Minority Rights* (Oxford: Clarendon Press, 1995), p. 192.

17. Anne Phillips, *The Politics of Presence*, p. 47.

✘ NO

Group Representation in Parliament Would Be Dysfunctional for Canada
JOHN H. REDEKOP

INTRODUCTION

Various critics rightly assert that the Canadian Parliament does not accurately reflect Canada's social diversity. They are also correct when they say that Canada's electoral system plays a major role in producing unrepresentative legislatures. What is at issue in the present discussion is not whether the Canadian Parliament, specifically the House of Commons, should be reformed and the electoral system improved but whether the proposal to adopt group representation, as explained by Tim Schouls, constitutes a desirable and workable change.

As I understand it, the proposal under consideration seeks to remedy the alleged major flaw in Canada's electoral system by guaranteeing parliamentary seats for "disadvantaged groups such as women, Aboriginal peoples, ethnic and visible minorities, and people with disabilities." While additional categories are suggested by the phrasing, we will limit this discussion to these five groups; they encompass about 75 percent of Canada's population. We will also limit this analysis to the House of Commons. Senate reform needs to be discussed in its own right.

It should be noted that the proposal emphasizes the need for "political equality," which apparently means "equal representation" or mathematical proportionality. Thus, since females constitute about 51 percent of the population, they would, in the proposed scheme of "proportional parliamentary inclusion" and "proportional presence," be guaranteed 51 percent of the seats in the elected House of Commons. The other four groups would similarly be guaranteed a percentage of seats in this "identity-based" system of representation.

This essay will demonstrate that identity-based group representation in Parliament, with guaranteed seats, as described by Tim Schouls, is neither desirable nor workable in Canada. On balance, I believe, it would not be an improvement over our present single-member plurality electoral system.

One can think of several reasonable and democratic ways in which our present system could be reformed. One way would be to have half of the House of Commons seats filled by our present form of election—which would enable all Canadians to retain the benefits of having their own MP—with the other half being filled by a proportional representation system as is presently practised in Germany, Japan, and New Zealand. Having half of the MPs elected according to the second system would promote unity and goodwill, for example, by allowing a nationally victorious party to have at least some representation from a province where it got a large number of votes but did not come first in any riding. Such was the situation for the Liberals in the general election of 1980, for example, when they received 24 percent of the popular vote in Saskatchewan and 22 percent in each of Alberta and British Columbia but failed to elect even one member in those three provinces. In those three provinces, thus, the Liberals were unrepresented in the national cabinet.

ARGUMENTS BASED ON IDEOLOGICAL CONSIDERATIONS

In part the case for group representation, as presented in the preceding article, rests on **faulty assumptions**; we will review seven.

1. **The five groups under consideration are all definable entities with basically clear boundaries.** This assumption is important because we would need to be clear about who belongs to a particular group if we want to assign guaranteed seats to that group. While there is no difficulty in identifying the women in Canada, the situation is problematic for the other four groups. Who should be in the Aboriginal group? Would a person who is one-eighth Aboriginal and seven-eighths French-Canadian—and there are many such people—be part of the Aboriginal group or the French-Canadian group or both? What fraction of Aboriginal blood would be required? Would Aboriginal people be allowed to decide on fractions for themselves? Such kinds of problems are legion. The actual membership and boundary problems boggle the mind. Also, should we include in the Aboriginal group those Aboriginal people who don't want to be part of this racially segregated group but would rather participate in the category of general voters? Would we force them to be racially categorized?

Similarly, who would belong to a given ethnic minority? Would we require some racial tests? And what about the millions of Canadians who identify with more than one ethnic group? To ask the question is to think of enough problems to keep a small army of bureaucrats happy for years. Further, would a Chinese-Canadian husband and his Jamaican-Canadian wife vote for different slates of candidates, and would their twenty-year-old daughter living at home vote for a third slate of candidates? Would she have a choice?

Moreover, which ethnic groups and which visible minorities would qualify for separate and guaranteed representation? If we want to accommodate all organized ethnic groups in Canada, we would have to deal with at least 160 of them. If they each got even one seat—and the larger groups would insist on getting more—then more than half of the seats in the House of Commons would be assigned to these ethnic groups. And let us not wiggle out of this dilemma by suggesting that only the larger ethnic groups would be assigned seats. They already tend to win seats on their own. It's the scores of smaller groups that systematically and regularly get no representation. Perhaps one could argue that ethnic groups could be lumped together, for example, East Europeans, people from the Middle East, Blacks from Africa, and so on. But often the greatest animosities exist between neighbouring groups, such as Serbs and Croats, Jews and Arabs, Taiwanese and mainland Chinese, and so on.

Even agreeing on who in Canada should belong to the group termed "disabled" would be very difficult. Are we thinking only of paraplegics or quadriplegics? Do we include the blind? What about the hearing impaired? What about the visually impaired? What about the mentally impaired? What about those with perpetually sore backs? Do we include those who have AIDS? Would people with chronic fatigue syndrome qualify? And what about the thousands who are terminally ill with cancer or some other disease? They are certainly disabled and permanently so. Should these and others who could be listed all be included? They certainly all have disabilities. Furthermore, how much impairment creates disability? Who would decide? And would it be logical to assume that this diverse spectrum of groups would have a common political agenda?

2. Voters can be represented well only by representatives who share their social traits. Schouls states that "parliamentary representatives must share central experiences and assumptions with those they represent if those representatives are to understand their constituents' needs and interests." I find his argument unconvincing.

If we look at the professions of teaching, medicine, and law, for example, we find that effective representation and service do not require social similarity. I am confident that if members of the five identity-based groups were given the choice, the vast majority would rank competence as more important than social similarity. When people are sick, it is more important that they have a competent physician than that they have one from their own ethnic group. Similarly, people generally look for competent teachers, lawyers, mechanics, accountants, photographers, and other professionals and tradespeople. Why should we assume that it would be different when we turn to the profession of politics? Granted, social similarity is a significant asset, but it is not the most important criterion.

3. Parliamentary input will shape parliamentary output. The Canadian political system grants power and authority to a majority party or coalition, not to minority groups whose support is not needed by governments in order to retain office. Clearly, identity-based minorities would influence what is said in legislative debate, but why should we assume that such minority voices would affect legislative output, the policy decisions? (The special situation with the majority composed of women will be discussed later.) In fact, it would likely be the case that the majority rulers, either one party or a coalition, would be inclined to discount and marginalize the input of identity-based MPs with their narrow agenda because the rulers cannot realistically hope to win them over to the perspective of the governing majority. There is nothing to be gained by acceding to the requests of opposition minorities. Majorities can safely ignore such minorities.

Conversely, if these same identity-based MPs were members of the governing party, or even of the official opposition, they would have some hope of influencing policies and platforms, but only if they were prepared to accept substantial compromises.

As I see it, the error in Schouls' apparent assumptions in this regard is that voice equals influence. A second apparent assumption is that representation in itself, even having one or a few MPs advocating a certain perspective, constitutes power.

Both assumptions, in my view, are faulty. All the eloquence one can imagine and a total sharing of social traits with one's constituents carry virtually no weight in legislative debate if there is not a political reason for the decision makers, generally the cabinet, to take such input seriously. A few eloquent MPs may achieve publicity, even popularity, but generally do not have significant influence on legislative output.

4. Political decisions grow out of parliamentary debate. In earlier times, generations ago, public policies may actually have had their genesis in parliamentary debate, but those days have passed. It is now erroneous to assume that important public policies, the type that the five identity-based groups would like to see enacted, are actually shaped in Parliament and are the result of MPs' input and debate. It seems safe to say that at least 98 percent of public policies in Canada are generated by the cabinet—which may get its ideas from many sources including pressure groups—and are not formed or changed to any significant extent by parliamentary debate. Just because an identity-based group has 5 or 10 percent of the MPs does not mean that it has 5 or 10 percent of the influence on public policies.

Schouls states that "marginalized groups," including the five we are considering, "want to be more fully included in the political discussions that shape the political identity of Canada as a whole." I seriously question whether parliamentary debates play a significant role in shaping Canada's political identity. It seems more accurate to say that these five groups would achieve more success in influencing Canada's political identity if they contributed informed input to cabinet members and senior officials before cabinet decisions are made. In this way they could also, with greater credibility, threaten voter retaliation, if need be, a tactic they cannot employ if the constituency they represent votes in its own elections or at least for its own set of candidates and the decision makers have nothing to gain by accommodating them. A group that is electorally hived off by itself should not expect to gain concessions from decision makers who have nothing to gain by making such concessions.

It could be that MPs who represent identity-based groups would become part of a governing coalition. In such a situation they might be able to influence policy decision but in virtually all cases only by making compromises, which is exactly what we have under our present system. In rare instances, such MPs might actually be able to topple a government. Such action would perhaps give the key MPs a sense of power, but it would not bring about the implementation of their political agenda.

5. Women do not participate in politics as much as men do because the women "have been ignored and marginalized by the male hierarchy." In earlier times this assumption was valid, but today it has little validity. My experience and observation lead me to conclude that in most situations, political parties, still dominated by males, bend over backwards to get qualified women to stand as candidates. They do so for the same reason that they often seek out ethnic and other minority people to stand as candidates—they believe that having such candidates increases their chances of victory.

If we want to find out why women remain relatively underrepresented in Parliament (although the situation is gradually improving), we must probe more deeply. Simply blaming men will not do. Electoral results and various studies have shown, as former prime minister Kim Campbell and many others could verify, that women do not necessarily or even disproportionally vote for women. Most female voters, just like most male voters, tend to vote for the candidate or party that they believe to be the best of the options. People are more sophisticated than to vote, blindly, for a candidate on the basis of which bathroom that candidate uses.

It is also the case, of course, that most of society, including many women, still believes that women can make their greatest contribution by providing a strong home setting. As long as that view is dominant there is likely to be a relative shortage of qualified women standing for office and being elected. This point ties in with another important reality, namely, that women have babies and men don't.

Any remaining societal barriers hindering political success by women should, of course, be removed. These barriers may include inadequate childcare in Parliament, inadequate leave policies for pregnancy, or inappropriate financial policies. We should not delude ourselves, however, by assuming that if we guarantee women a certain number of seats in Parliament we are thereby eliminating barriers.

6. "The primary qualification to become an MP is purely and simply the ability to represent." This assumption strikes me as being false. The primary qualification, in our electoral system, to become an MP is to find a way to get more people to vote for you than for any other candidate. Often the person who appears to have the greatest "ability to represent" is not elected. Many explanations come to mind as to why such an outcome is commonplace. For a variety of reasons, a candidate may get a huge sympathy vote. The strongest candidate may not belong to the most popular party or even to a credible party. The incumbent may have done so many favours and created so many IOUs that he can defeat all other candidates even if they are obviously more capable. And a certain party or party leader may sweep a lamentably weak candidate into office by promising major benefits to the candidate's constituency.

Once we acknowledge the fact that "simply the ability to represent" is not the primary qualification to become an MP, then we realize that there are key factors other than sharing social traits that shape political outcomes and that we should not concentrate primarily on social traits.

7. "The presence of women in Parliament ensures that all the diverse and quite possibly conflicting interests of women will actually be heard and debated in Canada's central representative political arena." For better or worse, such an

assumption does not bear up under scrutiny. For one thing, no one can ensure that "all" interests will be presented. The significant subgroups of women, as well as of many other groups, are far too numerous to allow us to accept such an assertion as valid. In our parliamentary system, debate in Parliament will continue to be dominated by differences between government and opposition agendas, not by diverse values and perspectives among men or among women or among Aboriginal people or among ethnic groups. Those differences will, in the main, need to be debated elsewhere.

Moving beyond these ideological assumptions, we need to consider several basic ideological issues.

1. Identity-based representation would increase social fragmentation in Canada. That's exactly the opposite of what Canada needs at present. The biggest question we face is whether we have enough commonality to remain united. The country may not survive the injection of additional cleavages that pit some Canadians against other Canadians. In a free society, having a plethora of organized groups— religious, social, ethnic, economic, athletic, professional, and so on—is a sign of political health. But if these groups are elevated to the point of formal and official electoral competition, then differences tend to overwhelm commonalities.

This country would be dangerously weakened if social differences were incorporated into electoral struggles. We do not need the religious animosities that dominate Irish or Israeli party politics, the ethnic tensions that destroyed Yugoslavia and that perennially threaten Belgium and various other countries, the race-based policies that have bedevilled South Africa and other countries, or a parliamentary division that pits women against men simply because some MPs are women and some MPs are men.

Indeed, I would go so far as to argue that Canada has evolved into a stable, free, and tolerant country largely because our national legislature has not reflected the major cleavages in society and has not let these divisions become dominant in our national political agenda.

2. Identity-based group representation raises insoluble problems of boundary and number. Once we start categorizing people according to their personal traits instead of their possession of citizenship, where do we stop? Groups will quickly realize that to be assigned guaranteed seats is the easiest, indeed, for some the only, way for them to be assured of gaining representation in Parliament. If we guarantee seats for women, we can safely assume that soon homosexual women will want to have the authorities guarantee them a quota of seats because as a small minority group among women, they probably would otherwise not get any.

Quite apart from the long list of groups, especially ethnic groups, that would quickly clamour for guaranteed seats, we would soon see a series of divisions and further divisions within the groups initially assigned seats. This problem raises another key question. Who would decide which groups and subgroups would be guaranteed seats? And would the same authority or authorities decide how many seats each group would get? The whole exercise would undoubtedly generate widespread disappointment, resentment, frustration, and anger.

3. The proposal to move to identity-based representation is condescending toward the five groups under consideration. Today, members of all of these five groups have the right to stand for office and to vote. Increasing numbers do, in fact, stand for office, vote, and win seats. Now, with progress well under way, we are being told that these groups are not good enough to make it on their own.

This proposal is condescending in that it assumes that women, who constitute 51 percent of Canadian society, do not know their own best interests or are too incompetent to vote according to their own best interests. They cannot be trusted to decide which candidates, be they male or female, will be the best representatives for them. They need to be told by the dominant male "hierarchy," to use Tim Schouls' term, that they should vote only for women. That's an insult. Why don't we let them decide for themselves who can best represent their interests? If they want to organize a women's party or if they want to vote for women, let them do so. But surely they do not have to be instructed by men or by our mostly male Parliament what they should do.

The same line of reasoning can be applied to the other groups. It may well be that some categories of voters in some parts of the country will not elect people who are their best advocates. But that's how democracy works. Democracy does not ensure that the wisest and most competent and the most effective representatives will be elected; it can only ensure, generally speaking, that the truly uninformed and the seriously incompetent and the utterly ineffective and those who would seek to destroy freedom do not become representatives in our legislatures.

4. The proposal would create first-class and second-class MPs. Presumably, in an electoral system that incorporates identity-based group representation, some women, some Aboriginal people, some visible minorities, some members of ethnic groups, and some disabled people would still be elected in the open segment of the electoral process in the way that they are elected now. Others would be elected by their own kind to fill guaranteed seats. It seems to me that very quickly a situation would develop in which those who were elected to guaranteed seats would be deemed to be second-class MPs because they were elected with special governmental facilitation. They could not make it on their own the way the others did.

One result of such a development would likely be that those who were elected to guaranteed seats would have less credibility in Parliament. Such a result would, of course, undermine the whole reason for embarking on the exercise in the first place.

5. To a significant extent immigrants should be assimilated into Canadian society; Canada should not serve only as a receptacle for transplanted societies from around the globe and should not tolerate the transplanting of tensions and

animosities that exist in many of those societies. Generally speaking, ethnic groups in Canada should not expect governmental assistance in the perpetuation of their ethnic communities. Analogous to the shifting popularity of religious groups, the survival or disappearance of ethnic groups in Canada is properly the concern of the private sector.

This is, after all, Canada, not the immigrants' former country. Ethnic groups should, as I see it, expect gradual assimilation. In any event, they should not expect the Canadian Parliament to make provision for their segregated survival. Above all, we do not want ethnic cleavages and rivalries built into our Parliament. Guaranteeing ethnic seats would, in my view, seriously increase ethnic antagonisms. Let us assume, for example, that the responsible authorities would guarantee two seats to Indo-Canadians; it could hardly be more, given that half of the total seats would be assigned to women and many other groups would need to be accommodated. Immediately there would be fierce rivalries concerning who should be selected. Should Indo-Canadian Hindus, Buddhists, Sikhs, Muslims, and Christians all be given seats, with the groups taking turns electing their MPs? And what about the growing nonreligious subset?

Would the Canadian government, in trying to be fair, undertake to count the members of the various Indo-Canadian subgroups? It would be a mammoth task to decide which Indo-Canadian groups would get the assigned seats.

Surely it would be much wiser to let Indo-Canadians take their place as Canadians and eventually make their political contributions the way the majority of Canadians do. As a matter of fact, Indo-Canadians have already made important political contributions in various jurisdictions in Canada, even at the cabinet level. The same situation prevails for many other ethnic groups, including Chinese-Canadians and other visible minorities.

What multiethnic Canadian society and its government should promote is the identification and strengthening of areas of commonality. We need all the glue we can find to keep this country united. We do not need an electoral system that emphasizes and reinforces ethnic cleavages and thus also ethnic tensions and rivalries. To put it very candidly, Canadian multicultural policies, in electoral matters and in other areas, should guarantee freedom, tolerance, and respect, but in a truly free society these policies should not underwrite the political costs of ethnic group perpetuation, and they certainly should not undermine democracy in a futile attempt to guarantee ethnic group survival.

6. It would be very unwise to agree with the proposal that "no effort should be spared to get more minority representatives into the House." "No effort spared" means exactly that. These words may be a popular slogan, but the fundamental idea they convey is a great threat to democracy. Do we want the effort made to ban the nomination of nonminority candidates so that the minorities can win? Do we want quotas applied along racial and ethnic lines for the general elections? These and numerous other efforts should not be undertaken.

7. The term "political equality" needs to be clarified and then to be understood and applied appropriately. I have difficulty understanding what Schouls means by this term, one which seems to be central to his thesis. If he means equality of opportunity, then he is on solid philosophical and political footing. If, on the other hand, he means equality of influence or, even worse, equality of political outcome, then we have a serious problem.

Democracy cannot guarantee ideal outcomes. Freedom of choice means choice, including the right to make unwise or less than ideal decisions. It includes the right to make choices—in politics, religion, economics, and so on—that are not the most advantageous to oneself. It includes the right to make illogical choices. In the area of religion, for example, freedom does not ensure even the survival, let alone the good health or expansion, of any one faith. Concerning ethnic group survival in Canada, guarantees of freedom should only provide a climate of opportunity and perhaps some general tax and other minor concessions. They should not attempt to ensure or guarantee anything more.

With reference to the proposal for identity-based group representation, one needs to ask in what way would minority representation create political equality? It would create minority representation and not much more than that. It certainly would not create equality of influence on legislative outcomes.

8. The liberal approach to representation does not insist that MPs ought to represent individuals only. I question the statement that in the liberal perspective "representatives are elected to advance the individual interests of their individual constituents." Liberalism assumes more than that. Certainly Canadian MPs do more than represent individual interests. Even a brief reading of *Hansard* should correct such a misconception. Individual MPs from both sides of the House and from all parties frequently urge policy changes or initiatives to assist companies, towns and cities, ethnic and other groups, categoric groups such as families, women, taxpayers, or the unemployed, and, of course, the country as a whole.

For me, however, the main issue in this regard is not whether individuals or groups should be represented and promoted—clearly the interests of both categories must be upheld—but whether national well-being is being advanced. With Edmund Burke I believe that though individual representatives have specific responsibilities to their own constituencies, they should always balance constituency well-being with national well-being.

9. The election of MPs representing identity-based groups would likely produce chronic governmental instability. Most proportional electoral systems have some means, usually a 1 percent or a 5 percent clause, as in Japan and Germany respectively, to prevent the appearance of numerous one-person, two-person, or three- person parties in the legislature. Under the proposal advocated by Schouls, there could be no threshold exclusion clause. In fact, the whole intent would be to have a series of mostly small, special interest groups in Parliament that would be likely soon to become special interest political parties.

Such a situation would, of course, almost certainly produce a series of Parliaments without a majority party, and, therefore, a sequence of shaky and short-lived governments, unless the 153 or more women decided to govern as a bloc. Thus, in trying to address a problem of underrepresentation we would, in fact, be creating much more serious problems for Canadians.

One of the major reasons for general Canadian political and economic stability, even when separatists threaten to break up the country, is our majority cabinet system with its stability and predictability between elections. If no one party is permitted to field its own slate of candidates in all constituencies in an effort to form a majority government, we might well regularly produce minority governments consisting of numerous groups and parties and, therefore, vulnerable to disintegration in the face of separatist threats or various economic and political crises. We should not toy with such risks.

In passing, we should also note that small ethnic or other groups invited to join coalitions should not expect to make substantial headway with their particular agendas. The larger party or parties leading the coalition would likely have at least several small groups to appease, as best they could, so that each small group would likely get very little of what it wanted.

Such a situation reminds us again that in a democracy compromise is a crucial ingredient. The desire to implement narrow, doctrinaire agendas is not an important component.

10. Political accountability is greater when half or more of the members in a legislature are elected in single-member districts. Single-member districts, as in Canada's present electoral system, tend to create majority governments by disproportionally rewarding that party or those parties that are the most popular. While this system tends thus to distort public preferences, it also tends to produce governmental accountability.

If one believes, as I do, that an effective system of political accountability is a very important factor, then one is prepared to accept the distortion that the system creates. The distortion can, of course, be greatly reduced by the adoption of the dual German electoral system.

Given the broad economic and social scope of governmental activity in our day, it is surely important to know whom to thank and whom to blame. It is much easier to do so if a majority government is in place than if a broad coalition governs. Since most governments tend not to change greatly the general political direction and policies that they inherit when they take office, it seems more important that we should be able to hold governments accountable than that the composition of a legislature accurately reflect the social composition of society.

Furthermore, in the identity-based system of representation being advocated, it is not clear how voters could identify the official loyal opposition, that is, a "government in waiting," the likely alternative to the government of the day. The important distinction between two relatively clear sets of policies and politicians, offering clear alternatives to voters, would become very blurred or even disappear. That would be a serious loss.

11. **Social, religious, or racial fragmentation of society probably constitutes a greater threat to political stability than does the geographical division of the electorate for purposes of electing a legislature.** The proposal makes much of the supposed division of the electorate into geography-based constituencies. Schouls suggests that such a method of dividing voters "rests on the assumption that voters' primary political identity flows from their attachment to geography." As I see it, such an assertion misstates the point. The division of voters into constituency groups is a pragmatic and utilitarian means of getting MPs elected by approximately the same number of potential voters per riding with special provisions made for sparsely inhabited regions. As I see it, this system does not imply primary attachment of voters to territory or to anything else, although in some cases there is considerable racial or religious homogeneity. It is only a convenient way to divide voters, most of whom likely have nongeographic primary attachments, into groups of the desired size.

Above all, these constituency groupings are not based on social, religious, or other social tests, do not reinforce cleavages or animosities, and do not exacerbate tensions.

ARGUMENTS BASED ON PRACTICAL CONSIDERATIONS

1. **The categories and percentages presented in the proposal raise numerous important problems and dilemmas.** In the early sections of the article, Schouls emphasizes the importance of the "New Canadians with origins in the Caribbean, Africa, Middle East, Central and South America, and Asia." If, in his ethnic categories, he includes, as he logically should, all ethnic groups, including those not part of the visible minorities, that come from these regions, then the total becomes considerably greater than the 6.3 percent that he cites. Further, when he introduced his five categories he listed "ethnic and visible minorities" as two groups. What has happened to the ethnic groups that are not visible minorities? Having acknowledged that "numerous visible minority and ethnic groups in Canada are able to put forward a very strong case," Schouls seems to have forgotten about the nonvisible ethnic minorities.

In the scheme before us, 153 seats in the current 301-seat House of Commons would be assigned to women. An additional 12 seats would be assigned to Aboriginal people. Given Schouls' strong commitment to equality, one must conclude that 6 of these 12 would be given to Aboriginal women. Of the 19 seats he would guarantee to visible minorities, we ought to conclude that at least 9 would be given to women. The result would be that 168 seats would be assigned to women, which means that the male voters, with 133 seats, would be seriously underrepresented. Or maybe the 6 aboriginal females would be part of the 153.

The situation becomes additionally complicated if we factor in the people with disabilities, who seem also to have been forgotten somewhere along the way, and, of course, the large groups of ethnic minorities who belong to distinct and cohesive ethnic groups but who, in most cases, are not physically recognizable.

Other complicating factors come to mind. Where would one place an MP, elected to a nonguaranteed seat, who is female, disabled, and Aboriginal? Would she be counted in one or all of those categories, or in none? Even more important, who would decide? And would the number of guaranteed seats be reduced if significant numbers of women and several Aboriginal people and members of visible minorities, or even any of them, managed to get elected to nonguaranteed seats? Surely the authorities could not simply let the number of seats allocated to the "others," the presumably nonvisible minority males, be markedly reduced or the whole scheme would go out of whack in that direction.

The assigning of individuals to the several voting groups would be a national nightmare. How would one categorize spouses in mixed marriages? How would the authorities categorize the children of these marriages? Would every Canadian have to carry a racial or ethnic identity card, a Canadianized version of apartheid? Presumably so, or the overall registering of voters could not be carried out in a way to facilitate the achievement of the stated percentage goals.

Additional major problems would involve the allocation of the twelve Aboriginal seats to the numerous competing groups, the allocation of the nineteen visible minority seats to at least twenty-five visible minority groups, and the allocation of whatever the appropriate number of seats is to people with disabilities. The challenges and problems boggle the mind.

2. We are not told how the electoral system would be altered to ensure that the guaranteed seats would be filled as intended. This is no small matter. Since relatively well-paid, high-status positions as members of Parliament are at issue, we can be assured that there would be a great clamouring for the occupancy and control of these seats. Who would handle the nominations? For example, concerning the women, would various organizations each be assigned certain seats? Would the National Action Committee on the Status of Women be given a bloc? Would Real Women be assigned a large segment, since they seem to represent a high percentage of nonorganized women? Would the women's organizations be allowed to nominate candidates who would compete against one another? Would there be primary elections? If so, who would pay for the costs? What about all of the other women's organizations? Would the guaranteed women's seats be spread across all of the provinces?

And what happens if most of the voters in a given riding don't want to be part of such a guaranteed constituency? Will they simply be told by whoever has the authority to tell them that their MP will be a woman, like it or not? What happens if all of the established parties in one of these ridings refuse to nominate anybody in such an authoritarian situation but a small women's pressure group manages to nominate a woman? Would that female candidate automatically become that riding's "elected" MP?

And what happens if, in a guaranteed woman's riding, a party nominates a male? Would the sex (or gender) police declare the nomination invalid on account of a candidate being of the wrong sex? How would such a ruling be upheld given Canada's commitment to equality? How could such a ruling or policy be justified given all of the official legislative and judicial decisions, not to mention constitutional provisions, spelling out equality of the sexes?

If, perchance, the assumption is that the guaranteed women MPs, more than half of the House of Commons, would not be elected in existing ridings, then how would they be chosen? Would they be selected by women's groups, or one women's group, such as the National Action Committee on the Status of Women, without any connection to a given territory such as a riding? And how could this be seen as fair in that the women get to vote twice, once in the general election and, presumably, once in a women's election? Or are the 153 "guaranteed" female MPs not even going to be elected? If that is the intent, then how could this be done given the stipulations in the Elections Act and the relevant equality provisions of the Charter of Rights and Freedoms?

Furthermore, if it is fair to guarantee a specified number of seats to women, why is it not fair also to specify a number of seats for men? Surely that would be more equitable than giving special guarantees to members of only one sex. Would men be allowed to vote in the women's elections? Would parties still be allowed to nominate women in all of the nonwomen's seats? And what happens if, after all of the ballots are counted, the total number of female MPs comes to 60 or 65 or 70 percent of the House of Commons? That would be a distinct possibility. Would that constitute equality? Would that be more democratic than what we have now?

3. **Who will administer the incredibly complex and probably unworkable scheme advocated in the proposal?** Somebody will have to make many very controversial, often very unpopular, decisions. Some of the dilemmas would involve policy and others would involve implementation and administration. Is it assumed that the last freely elected House of Commons would try to implement this Orwellian manipulation? Is it assumed that the cabinet would issue an order-in-council or that the legislature would enact a statute, perhaps relying on article 33 of the Charter, the notwithstanding clause, to get this whole venture under way without having it aborted by the courts?

CONCLUSION

Tim Schouls is to be commended for urging that the barriers that many women and other groups face in politics should be removed. Unfortunately, guaranteeing seats does not in itself remove barriers. In fact, the proposal being advanced as a remedy creates more barriers than it removes.

Perhaps the major flaw in the proposed scheme is that it fails to accommodate the fundamental principle that democracy cannot, and should not attempt to, guarantee outcomes. Democracy cannot ensure that the ideal will be realized or even that the best option will be chosen. Freedom of political choice, like freedom of religion, includes the right to make wrong choices, wrong as some people or even the majority might define wrong. It includes the right to make choices that are not self-serving, self-advancing, or even well informed.

Throughout history, ideologues have tried to combine idealistic outcomes with democratic means—to do so cannot be ensured and no coercive attempt should be undertaken to try to achieve that goal. Political leaders and common citizens alike must rely on education and persuasion. Either the voters have free choice, within very broad and reasonable limits, or they do not. All else is undemocratic manipulation even if done in the name of democracy and equality. The French Revolution bears solemn witness to that fact. The proposed plan for representation based on group identity ultimately takes away choice, specifically the option to choose that which ideologues and true believers of various sorts deem to be improper and unwise.

The proposed plan, however laudable its genesis and honourable its intent, must be rejected as both undemocratic and unworkable. It risks the achievements that have been made in assisting the politically marginalized groups, and it undermines the prospect for further democratic progress. We must look elsewhere for the agenda for further success.

POSTSCRIPT

In reading this debate, it is interesting to note the absence of discussion of class issues, especially in the article by Tim Schouls. While he is concerned about increasing the representation of those marginalized in society, marginalization is identified primarily with the identity politics of ethnicity and gender. What role does class play in this analysis? Is the issue of class merely subsumed or transcended by issues of ethnicity and gender? What relevance, if any, does class analysis have to this debate?

Will Kymlicka is one theorist who Schouls uses to develop the philosophical basis for his argument. See Kymlicka's *Multicultural Citizenship: A Liberal Theory of Minority Rights* (Oxford: Clarendon Press, 1995) for a defence of granting differentiated rights to ethnic groups based on their vulnerability. For an interesting critique of this position, see Brian Walker, "Plural Cultures, Contested Territories: A Critique of Kymlicka," *Canadian Journal of Political Science* 30, no. 2 (June 1997): 211–234.

A number of good references are useful for pursuing this issue further. For two books that deal with the philosophical dimensions of this debate, see Jane Arscott and Linda Trimble, eds., *In the Presence of Women: Representation in Canadian Governments* (Toronto: Harcourt, Brace & Company, 1997) and Anne Phillips, *The Politics of Presence* (Oxford: Clarendon Press, 1995). For a book that tackles some of the practical difficulties of implementing proportional representation for social groups, see Committee for Aboriginal Electoral Reform, *The Path to Electoral Equality* (Ottawa: Committee for Aboriginal Electoral Reform, 1991).

When the Territory of Nunavut was being created, an interesting experiment in gender representation was contemplated. The Nunavut Implementation Commission proposed the creation of electoral districts that would elect one man and one woman each in order to create the world's first legislature with full gender parity. However, the proposal received only 43 percent of the vote in a referendum and therefore was not implemented. To learn more about this potential experiment in equitable social representation and why it failed to win support, see Jackie Steele and Manon Tremblay, "Paradise Lost? The Gender Parity Plebiscite in Nunavut," *Canadian Parliamentary Review* (Spring 2005): 34–39.

Should Voting Be Made Mandatory?

✔ **YES**
ANDREW COYNE, "The Right to Vote, and the Obligation," in the
National Post, December 20, 2000, p. A19

✘ **NO**
CLIFFORD ORWIN, "You Can Lock Me Up, But You Can't Make Me Vote,"
in the *National Post,* December 20, 2000, p. A18

In recent years a troubling trend has appeared in Canadian political life: the percentage of eligible persons who exercise their right to vote is getting smaller and smaller. Two decades or so ago, the turnout rates for federal elections hovered over 70 percent, but they have now fallen in the last two elections to just over 60 percent. It appears that more and more Canadians are deciding not to participate in a core component of the democratic process. Moreover, these most recent percentages actually overstate the level of participation. Turnout rates in Canada are calculated by dividing the number of people who voted by the number of eligible people *on the electoral list.* If the denominator had been simply the number of people eligible to vote—some fail to get on the electoral list—the turnout rate for two most recent federal elections would have just been above 50 percent. It should not be surprising to learn that this fall in voter participation has given Canada one of the lowest turnout rates among democracies.

A number of reasons have been put forward to explain the decline in turnout. One is that Canadians have become disillusioned with politics and feel that they have little or no ability to influence government action. There is, in other words, a kind of democratic malaise that has infected the political process, and the falling turnout rates are simply a symptom of this problem. Another explanation is the absence of choice: political parties now differ very little. A further factor may be that people increasingly use other mechanisms—interest groups, for example—to influence governments; voting in order to sway the decisions of government is ineffective. For some, the explanation is obvious: Canadians have finally figured out that the costs of voting outweigh the benefits. A single vote will never decisively influence an election, so why bother to incur the costs of voting (which might include taking time from work or arranging for a babysitter).

After the 2000 election, Canada's chief electoral officer, Jean-Pierre Kingsley, expressed his concern about the declining percentage of Canadians turning out to vote. With some trepidation, he also suggested a solution, namely mandatory voting. He sensed that many might feel uneasy about such a solution, but concluded that "sometimes in order to save democracy, you have to do things that might seem to turn a little bit against it." Canada is not the only country faced with declining turnout rates, and the chief electoral officer referred to some countries that have resorted to requiring their citizens to vote; in these places, he noted, more than 90 percent of the eligible population votes. Mandatory voting may seem like an affront to democracy itself, which the chief electoral officer appreciated, but it may be necessary in order to strengthen democracy.

There are in fact some sound justifications for mandatory (or compulsory) voting. One just suggested is that democracy may be seriously weakened without aggressive or even coercive action to maintain voting. Another related argument revolves around how the act of voting is perceived. Typically, it is seen as a right to be exercised or not. But given its import to the functioning of democracy, it might be more properly viewed as an obligation. There are certain things that one must do to ensure the health of society, and voting may be counted among these. A further rationale for compulsory voting is that it increases the chances that all societal interests will be taken into consideration at election time. With voluntary voting, the fear is that those who fail to vote are families and individuals who are relatively less well off. The trend in turnout rates is disturbing not only because of the percentage of people who are not voting, but also because of the composition of this group.

Some, of course, are not persuaded by these and other arguments. A major concern with the proposal is, quite simply, its compulsory nature. In a free and democratic country, it is desirable to keep compulsory acts to a minimum. Yet here is a proposal that places obligation at the very heart of the democratic process. There is also the concern that mandatory voting will, ironically, lead to more apathy. Politicians will no longer have to work hard to get their supporters out to vote, and voters will act in a way expected of people who are forced to do something rather than being able to choose to do it of their own free will.

Andrew Coyne, a columnist for the *National Post,* makes the case for mandatory voting. Clifford Orwin, a professor of political science at the University of Toronto, makes the contrary case.

✔ YES
The Right to Vote, and the Obligation
ANDREW COYNE

For someone who is actively engaged in preventing people from participating in elections—via the election law's limits on so-called "third-party" advertising—Jean-Pierre Kingsley is perhaps ill-placed to be talking up the benefits of making participation compulsory. On the other hand, for a newspaper that recently head-lined an editorial "Disenfranchise Them" (with regard to federal prisoners), *The Post* is perhaps not the ideal voice to argue that the decision to vote or not should be left to the free will of the individual.

Which is to say that the debate on whether voting should be made mandatory, touched off by the chief electoral officer's musings this week, is not so simply resolved. If it were only a matter of individual rights, that would be one thing—though Lord knows there are lots of other things we are either required to do or forbidden from doing, most of which entail a more profound invasion of personal liberty than having to mark a ballot, and with less warrant, in as much as we are so enjoined *for our own good*.

But voting isn't like wearing a seatbelt. It doesn't just engage the interest of the voter, but everyone else's interests as well. By casting his ballot, the voter is not just deciding how he will live his life, but how others will live theirs. For that reason, the right to vote is not like other rights, such as the right not to be impris-oned without trial, or the right to speak freely. The latter are rights that inhere in every person, by virtue of their humanity. The right to vote, by contrast, is a right restricted to citizens. It is a privilege conferred on members of the club, by the other members. We don't let citizens of other countries vote in our elections, and properly so, since they are not subject to our laws.

If the right to vote is conferred by the majority, and if it can be taken away by the majority (as *The Post* urges we should do to prisoners), then we are clearly dealing with something other than an ordinary right. Is it possible that voting might fall under that category of activities that are both a right and an obliga-tion? There are other examples. You are legally obliged, if called, to serve on a jury: That's why it's called jury duty. The system would collapse if it were other-wise. Should we not view an election as a kind of trial, the voters as a kind of jury, bound by the same civic duty?

Well, you may say, the members of a jury are called upon to decide the fate of another. A citizen who does not vote, on the other hand, merely agrees to have his fate decided by others. Shouldn't he have that right? But it is not his own gov-ernment that suffers from his inaction, but everybody's. When barely 60% of the electorate bother to show up at the polls, as in the most recent election, the result has correspondingly less legitimacy, the government has less authority. Which may well encourage others not to vote the next time.

A mandatory voting law would not compel you to vote for a particular party—or any of them. Wherever such laws apply, including Australia, Belgium, Greece, Brazil and Argentina, voters retain the option of formally declining the ballot. Likewise, you could always spoil your ballot, or vote for a fringe candidate, or otherwise register your dissatisfaction. The only right such a law would infringe is the right to sit on your duff, the sacred liberty of layabouts.

Opponents look at it the other way. If people are too lazy or stupid to vote, maybe it's best that they didn't. If a mandatory voting law increased the quantity of votes, the overall quality of the vote might be diminished. In fact, there's good reason to think the contrary is the case: The non-voters are the smart ones. Each individual vote, after all, makes very little difference to the outcome (yes, even in Florida). Rationally, it may not be worth the time it takes to drive to the polling station.

The present system, in other words, depends upon voters acting irrationally—which is to say, only the irrational vote: those too angry, too zealous, too plain addled to think things through. Or else it rewards those with an unusually large interest in controlling the levers of power: the axe-grinders and the favour-seekers and interest groups of all kinds.

A compulsory system, on the other hand, alters the balance of costs and bene-fits in favour of exercising the franchise: If you don't vote, you pay a fine. Or, if that offends your delicate libertarian sensibilities, how about this: If you *do* vote, you get a tax credit. Either way, the incentive is for rational non-voters to become rational voters.

Sure, the decline in voter turnout is more the symptom than the disease, reflecting a belief that nothing much is at stake. But every little bit helps. And the fact that fewer and fewer people are involved itself contributes to the increasing vacuity of our elections. You have to pay your taxes. You have to buy insurance for your car. What's the big deal if you have to vote as well?

✗ NO
You Can Lock Me Up, But You Can't Make Me Vote
CLIFFORD ORWIN

Like every proud citizen of a liberal democracy, I cherish my right to vote. I never fail to exercise it. Sometimes, I do so by making a point of not voting.

The logic of this is elementary, but Jean-Pierre Kingsley, Canada's chief electoral officer, just doesn't get it. As reported in this newspaper yesterday, he has suggested that Parliament consider making voting compulsory. Dismayed by the decline of the voting rate in Canada, he points to countries such as Belgium and Australia, where voting is a legal duty and more than 90% of the citizens perform it.

Let's say Mr. Kingsley gets his way, that Parliament legislates our obligation to participate in electing it, and that, as a consequence, more of us do. Just what would such an increase signify? Only that votes that were formerly free and for that very reason significant have become unfree and thus less so; that votes that once attested to uncoerced decisions on the part of those who cast them now attest to coerced ones. That the motive of exercising a democratic privilege has been corrupted by the attachment of a sanction.

Mr. Kingsley sees it as a loss for democracy if only half of eligible citizens vote. Perhaps. But to command them to do so would clearly be a loss for freedom, which Canada, as a liberal democracy, must respect no less than equality. Indeed, our very equality is above all one of our rights or freedoms, which are not to be abridged without a powerful reason. My right to vote, precisely as a right, implies my right or freedom not to do so. Think of it as a precious right not to have my ballot counted.

If our politicians did act as Mr. Kingsley suggests, they would really be rubbing our faces in it. On top of everything else they make us do, now they would be making us vote *for them*. To vote is not a neutral act of citizenship, like paying your taxes or stopping on red. To vote is to vote for someone. What's more, it's to vote for someone chosen from among those on the ballot. It is thus a highly constrained choice. As a citizen of a liberal democracy, I have every right to decline it. I may do so because I find the choice offered unpalatable. I may do so because I find it indifferent. I may do so because, as in the recent Toronto mayoral election pitting Mel Lastman against the 27 dwarfs (number approximate, apologies if I overlooked anyone), the outcome is a foregone conclusion. I may do so because election day finds me under the weather. (If I missed a vote under the new dispensation, would I have to bring a note from my doctor?) I may do so simply because I'm busy that day with tasks all of which I rank ahead of voting. All are legitimate reasons; to criminalize them just doesn't make any sense. And if I abstain out of apathy or listlessness, well, that may not be pretty, but in a liberal society neither reason is, nor should be, illegal.

Of course I do vote most of the time, and so should you. Precisely because we do so freely, our vote enjoys a significance that it otherwise would not. By bestirring ourselves, we pass a litmus test that ought not to be discarded. In a society otherwise democratic, there is this slight remnant of a principle of natural aristocracy: all have the right to vote but only if they're willing to make the effort required to do so. The apathetic are permitted to disenfranchise themselves. Make voting mandatory and all those citizens who otherwise couldn't be bothered to do so will flock (make that slouch) to the polls. Will the quality of our public life really improve thereby?

I won't make the absurd claim that should voting be made compulsory here, Canada would cease to be a liberal democracy. (Obviously Australia and Belgium remain ones.) But I do think that as far as it goes it would be illiberal. Mr. Kingsley himself describes it as repulsive. Just look at most of the regimes of the past century in which voting has been mandatory—and, since these regimes were fascist or communist, utterly meaningless.

In any case, my own survey suggests that in Canada, at least, voting rates would actually fall as a result of the criminalization of minding one's own business. Since my research budget is low, I just took my own pulse, which began to quicken. My mind, usually frightening in its clarity, clouded with adrenalin. I began to imagine myself as a prisoner of conscience. (Would the Reverend Jesse Jackson visit me in my frostbitten northern Selma?) For make no mistake about it, if voting were compulsory, I'd refuse to do it. And having done the crime, I'd proudly do the time. Just don't sentence me to serve it in the parliamentary visitors' gallery.

POSTSCRIPT

In a short space, Andrew Coyne makes a persuasive argument for mandatory voting. To survive and flourish, democracies *need* people to vote. Voting is thus not really a right, but an obligation. Mandatory voting may involve an element of coercion, but it also recognizes that this very element of coercion is sometimes necessary to ensure people carry out their obligations to society. Moreover, the very fact that a rational calculation of costs and benefits may encourage non-voting also seems to demand drastic action. People want democracy to survive (and by implication want others to vote), but they see little reason for themselves to vote. If we all calculate this way, democracy will fast disappear.

But Coyne might be a little too narrow in his analysis. He may not be taking sufficient heed of the view (possibly wrong-headed though it may be) that voting is the exercise of a right and that all voters should possess the liberty to vote or not. Clifford Orwin is certainly aware of this sentiment and believes that mandatory voting would be an affront to a free society. Moreover, he is convinced that many (including himself) would suffer any penalty in order to protest against a system of compulsory voting. Orwin's objections are, of course, fine in theory, but they pay scant attention to declining turnout rates. Rhetoric about freedom and democracy does little to address the fact that more and more people are failing to participate in the democratic process.

A good place to begin an examination of the debate issue is Jeffrey Simpson's *The Friendly Dictatorship* (Toronto: McClelland and Stewart, 2001). This text includes an informative and readable chapter on declining turnout rates in Canada. For additional background, students might also read A. Brian Tanguay, "Reforming Representative Democracy: Taming Canada's Democratic Deficit," in James Bickerton and Alain-G. Gagnon, eds., *Canadian Politics,* 4th ed. (Peterborough: Broadview Press, 2004). Students should then consult the following articles on the declining turnout in the crucial federal elections of 2000 and 2004: Jon H. Pammett, "The People's Verdict," in Jon H. Pammett and Christopher Dornan, eds., *The Canadian General Election of 2000* (Toronto: Dundurn Group, 2001) and Jon H. Pammett and Lawrence Leduc, "Behind the Turnout Decline," in Jon H. Pammett and Christopher Dornan, eds., *The Canadian General Election of 2004* (Toronto: Dundurn Group, 2004). The diligent student might also peruse the relevant chapters on voter turnout in Neil Nevitte et al., *Unsteady State: The 1997 Canadian Federal Election* (Toronto: Oxford University Press, 2000) and André Blais et al., *Anatomy of a Liberal Victory: Making Sense of the Vote in the 2000 Canadian Election* (Peterborough: Broadview Press, 2002). The website of Elections Canada, an agency of the Canadian government, also contains some pertinent articles on the 2004 election in its online journal *Electoral Insight* (January 2005).

An examination of declining voter turnout naturally leads to a search for the factors responsible for this development. For insights into this matter and the more general question of variation in turnout rates among democracies, students should read the following articles: Centre for Research and Information on Canada, "Voter Participation in Canada: Is Canadian Democracy in Crisis?" and Elisabeth Gidengil et al., "Turned Off or Tuned Out? Youth Participation in Politics," both in George A. MacLean and Brenda O'Neill, eds., *Ideas, Interests, and Issues: Readings in Introductory Politics* (Toronto: Pearson Prentice Hall, 2006); André Blais et al., "Where Does Turnout Decline Come From?" *European Journal of Political Research* 43, no. 2 (2004); André Blais and Agnieszka Dobrzynska, "Turnout in Electoral Democracies," *European Journal of Political Research* 33 (1998); and Mark N. Franklin, "Electoral Participation," in Lawrence LeDuc, Richard G. Niemi, and Pippa Norris, eds., *Comparing Democracies: Elections and Voting in Global Perspective* (London: Sage Publications, 1996). The aforementioned website of Elections Canada also contains an interesting article by André Blais and his colleagues entitled "Why Is Turnout Higher in Some Countries than in Others?" These articles suggest a number of ways to combat falling (and low) turnout rates, one of which is compulsory voting. Another reading that seeks to understand voting behaviour is Michael D. Martinez, "Turning Out or Tuning Out? Electoral Participation in Canada and the United States," in David M. Thomas, ed., *Canada and the United States: Differences that Count*, 2nd ed. (Peterborough: Broadview Press, 2000). The problem of voting turnout is not unique to Canada, of course, and to gain an appreciation of the situation in the United States one might look at Martin P. Wattenberg, *Where Have All the Voters Gone?* (Cambridge: Harvard University Press, 2002).

In the debate, Coyne argues for the adoption of compulsory voting. To learn about the operation and success of such a system of voting in one country (Australia), students might consult M. Mackerras and I. McAllister, "Compulsory Voting, Party Stability, and Electoral Advantage in Australia," *Electoral Studies* 18 (1999) and Lisa Hill, "On the Reasonableness of Compelling Citizens to 'Vote': The Australian Case," *Political Studies* 50, no. 1 (2002). For more on compulsory voting, students might access the website of the International Institute for Democracy and Electoral Assistance. Finally, the issue of turnout rates and compulsory voting brings us face-to-face with one of the more interesting issues in political science, which is why people vote at all. Some political scientists contend that a rational individual should never vote. For an interesting test of this proposition, see André Blais and Robert Young, "Why Do People Vote? An Experiment in Rationality," *Public Choice* 99 (1999). Also see André Blais, *To Vote or Not to Vote: The Merits and Limits of Rational Choice* (Pittsburgh: University of Pittsburgh Press, 2001).

Is a Mixed-Member Proportional Electoral System in Canada's Interest?

✔ **YES**
JOHN L. HIEMSTRA AND HAROLD J. JANSEN,
"Getting What You Vote For"

✘ **NO**
CHRISTOPHER KAM, "The Limits of Electoral Systems and
Electoral Reform—or How I Came to Love SMP"

Canadian elections produce curious results. In the 2000 federal election, the victorious Liberal Party won the majority of seats with less than a majority of the popular vote. In the national election of 2004, the same Liberal Party failed to get the majority of the seats, but the percentage of seats it won was greater than the percentage of voters it attracted. In the 2001 B.C. election, the winning party won nearly all of the seats while securing only 58 percent of vote; in the 1997 New Brunswick election, the provincial Liberals did win *all* the seats—with only 60 percent of the vote. Clearly, in all these elections, the winners got more than they deserved. Just as clearly, it meant that the losers received less than they deserved. In the 2004 federal election, the NDP received almost 16 percent of the vote but managed to win only 6 percent of the seats; in the two aforementioned provincial elections, the losing parties attracted 40 percent of the vote while winning almost no seats.

On viewing these outcomes, one might be tempted to conclude that the Canadian electoral process had simply got the math wrong. Surely, the percentage of seats won should roughly reflect the percentage of votes won. But that is not how elections work in Canada. Instead, the electoral system divides the country into constituencies or ridings and then declares the winner in each constituency to be the one who receives the most votes. With these rules, a party may win many seats by small margins, with the result that the disjunction between the distribution of seats and votes emerges. In the Canadian electoral system, there is no reward for coming second, third, or any place other than first. Only the candidate with the greatest number of votes gets to sit in legislative assemblies. It is this quality that leads to the curious results.

Of course, an explanation is not a defence. For some, the single-member plurality system, the name given to Canada's election system, is unacceptable. The system plainly distorts the preferences of voters; it gives some parties too many seats and others too few. In a democracy, it might be argued that an electoral system should strive to represent the true wishes of the people. But this fails to occur in

Canada. Accordingly, various types of proportional representation (PR) electoral systems have been proposed to establish a greater equality between the percentage of votes and percentage of seats won. One type of PR system has become especially popular: this is the mixed-member proportional (MMP) system. Under MMP, some seats are still selected through the old system, but others are allocated in such a way to ensure that in the end the percentage of seats is proportional to the percentage of votes. One of the attractions of MMP is that it soothes the concerns of those who feel that we are moving too fast with electoral reform. MMP manages to mix the old with the new, a seemingly acceptable arrangement.

But many still remain uncomfortable with MMP and PR in general. Some feel this way because they fear that the reforms inevitably lead to weak coalition governments, while others believe that it produces elected officials without any constituency responsibilities. Arguably, a more important concern is the inability of PR systems to work well with the possibility of the cycling of majorities in government. Research has shown the voting can lead to one majority being easily trumped by another. PR proponents claim that their system will more accurately reflect the will of the people, but the fact is that there is no one majority that registers the wishes of the electorate—there are many. In light of the inherent instability of government actions, it might be preferable to have an electoral system that allows voters to more easily identify elected officials responsible for the offerings of government. If so, MMP and other versions of PR become unattractive because of their tendency to produce multiparty coalitions. Alternatively, the single-member plurality system (SMP) looks ideal because it usually elects single-party majority governments. In coalition governments, the existence of many policy-makers makes it easier to escape responsibility; in majority governments, the presence of only one party enhances efforts directed at ensuring accountability.

At various times, the reform of the electoral system has been an important issue. Now seems to be such a time. The results of recent elections have led to serious questioning of the plurality system (though, admittedly, the general public evinces little concern). Also, some of the provinces have begun careful examinations of the way they elected public officials, and B.C. held a referendum in May 2005 on whether it should adopt a new electoral system called single-transferable vote. The fact that Canada is one of the few nations that still uses the single-member plurality approach has encouraged reform efforts as well. Eventually, Canada may join other countries in adopting one form or another of proportional representation. In the past, political interests—the beneficiaries of the current system—have stymied reform. But they may be insufficiently influential this time.

In this debate, John Hiemstra, Harold Jansen, and Christopher Kam debate the merits of introducing a system of MMP in Canada. John L. Hiemstra is a professor of political science at the King's University College, Edmonton, Alberta. Harold J. Jansen is a professor of political science at the University of Lethbridge. Christopher Kam is also a professor of political science, at the University of British Columbia.

✔ **YES**
Getting What You Vote For
JOHN L. HIEMSTRA AND HAROLD J. JANSEN

In 2002, Paul Martin gave a widely quoted speech in which he lamented what he called Canada's "democratic deficit."[1] Although Martin's commitment to improving the functioning of Canadian democracy is admirable, he as of yet has not demonstrated a clear commitment to the one reform that would substantially improve Canada's democracy: replacing Canada's outdated single-member plurality electoral system with a system of proportional representation. An almost universally accepted principle of democracy is that governments should make decisions by majority rule. The plurality system rarely produces conditions where this can happen and, in doing so, fails to reflect Canadians' political opinions in the House of Commons. In fact, using the plurality electoral system to elect the House deepens divisions within Canada, weakens the accountability of members of Parliament (MPs) to electors, and undermines representative democracy. Many Canadian provinces are addressing their democratic deficits by seriously examining electoral system reform; it is time for the federal government to join them.[2]

This essay argues that the plurality method for electing MPs to the House of Commons should be replaced with a system of proportional representation (PR). There are many variants of PR in use around the world, but the one that we advocate for Canada is a mixed-member proportional (MMP) electoral system. MMP would make every vote count, enhance national unity, give an accurate reflection of the political opinions of Canadians in the House, and strengthen MPs' sense of obligation to the voters. This essay draws on national and provincial examples to make this case since both levels currently use the plurality electoral system.

A MODEST REFORM

In Canadian federal elections, we use the single-member plurality electoral system to decide who will be our representatives in the House of Commons. The country is divided into 308 single-member districts, each of which elects one MP to the House. The winner in each district is decided by the plurality formula. Simply put, the candidate in a riding who wins more votes than the other candidates—even if less than 50 percent—is the winner and takes a seat as MP in the House of Commons.[3]

Adopting MMP would require only modest reforms to our current system, which could be implemented by a simple act of Parliament and without a constitutional amendment. The number of federal MPs per province is determined by several factors, of which population is the most important. Under the plurality system, the provinces are carved into geographical electoral districts with one MP elected in each district. Under MMP, this would continue to happen, but only half of the MPs allocated to each province would represent single-member districts as they do now. The other half would be chosen from party lists provided by the parties and would be awarded to each party in such a way as to ensure that each party's representation in Parliament matches its share of the popular vote in that province.

For example, under the plurality formula in 2004, the Conservative Party won 26 of Alberta's 28 seats and the Liberal Party won the remaining two. If the election had been held under MMP,[4] fourteen MPs would have been elected in single member districts. The Conservatives would likely have won thirteen of those and the Liberals one. The remaining fourteen MPs would not represent specific districts, but would be divided between the parties to make sure that their overall share of Alberta's representation in Parliament reflects their share of the vote. These MPs would be elected off of party lists provided by each party. The Conservatives' 62 percent of the vote would have entitled them to eighteen MPs, so they would have added five list MPs to the thirteen elected in single-member districts to bring their total to eighteen. The Liberals' share of the vote would have entitled them to six seats, so they too would have received five list seats to bring them up to the proper total. The NDP and Green Party—neither of which would likely have won any seats in the single-member seats—would each have received two seats from party lists to make sure that their seat totals in Alberta reflected the support they have there. In this way, MMP would ensure that each party earns the number of seats to which they are entitled.[5]

Although calculating the number of seats each party would receive is more complicated than under the plurality system, voting in a federal election under MMP would be straightforward. Voters would vote twice: once for the candidate they would like to represent their particular district in the House of Commons and a second vote for the party list they prefer. The local candidate they support may even be from a different party. Voters in countries around the world seem to have no trouble using MMP; there is no reason to expect that Canadians would, either.

There are many variations in how MMP systems have been implemented throughout the world. But the increased popularity of MMP reflects an emerging consensus that MMP systems offer the "best of both worlds."[6] Voters continue to have an individual MP who is "theirs" and can deal with problems they are having with government, one of the advantages of the plurality system. At the same time, voters benefit from having their ideas reflected accurately in Parliament, the major advantage of proportional representation. An MMP system would ensure that voters get what they vote for.

MAKING EVERY VOTE COUNT

As a democratic state, all Canadians should have a say in the composition of the House of Commons, since it deliberates on and approves the laws that govern us all. Sadly, Canada's plurality electoral system repeatedly fails to deliver just and equitable representation when it allows the "winner to take all."

The plurality system is often unjust when it fails to give each vote its "due." In the 1997 federal election, for example, more than 60 percent of voters supported parties other than the Liberal Party, yet they were represented in the House of Commons by less than half of the members of Parliament. In 1984, the Progressive Conservatives won half the vote, but won three-quarters of the seats in the House of Commons. Seen another way, the other half of the electorate had their views represented by only a quarter of the MPs. In 2004, 50.2 percent of voters cast votes for candidates who did not get elected. Thus, they were represented by an MP from a party that they did not support. The plurality system effectively disenfranchised a majority of the voters in the 2004 election.

The injustice done by the plurality electoral formula is illustrated even better by the results of two recent provincial elections. In the 2001 British Columbia provincial election, Gordon Campbell's Liberal Party won 97 percent of the seats (77 out of 79) with only 58 percent of the vote. That left the 21 percent of voters who supported the NDP with only two seats, and the 21 percent who supported other parties with none. Even more dramatically, the plurality system can give every seat to one party, as happened in the 1987 New Brunswick election, when Frank McKenna's Liberal Party won 100 percent of the seats with 60 percent of the popular vote. This left the other 40 percent of the voters unrepresented by the party they supported. It is no surprise that British Columbia and New Brunswick are two of the provinces seriously considering whether to abandon their plurality systems for some alternative.[7] British Columbia and New Brunswick are not isolated cases, either. In the words of one of Canada's leading scholars of political parties and elections, lopsided provincial election results are the "dirty little secret" of provincial politics.[8]

The other serious defect in the plurality electoral system is its inequity; that is, it often makes your vote count for less than others. For example, in the 2000 federal election, 1 051 209 voters in Ontario supported the Canadian Alliance party but the plurality system gave them only two seats in that province. In British Columbia, the plurality system rewarded the 797 518 Canadian Alliance voters with twenty-seven seats. In other words, it took fewer than 30 000 B.C. Alliance voters to elect an MP, while in Ontario, it took over half a million to do so. Clearly, a vote for the Alliance in British Columbia was worth a lot more than a vote in Ontario.

Plurality is a "winner takes all" system that almost always overrewards the winning party. In contrast, MMP is widely recognized as a just and equitable system that accurately translates the percentage of the vote each party wins into a proportionate percentage of seats in the House of Commons. MMP would greatly reduce the injustice and inequity that is so common in the plurality system. In short, MMP would give you what you vote for, which is reason enough to adopt it in Canada.

MMP AND GOVERNMENT EFFECTIVENESS

Proportional representation systems such as MMP are almost always acknowledged as the fairest electoral systems.[9] Yet some still reject any kind of PR for Canada because they fear it would make the government ineffective. They argue that the plurality method produces stable and effective majority governments out of minority electoral returns, while MMP would produce unstable and ineffective minority governments. This implies that Canadians must make an unacceptable choice between the value of effectiveness and the values of justice and equity. Fortunately, the facts show that we do not have to make this decision.

The experiences of other countries indicate that the improved representation provided by PR need not come at the expense of effective government. Arend Lijphart, a noted expert on electoral systems, found in a comparative study of established democracies that countries using PR maintain public order and manage the economy as well as countries that use majoritarian electoral systems, such as plurality.[10]

Besides this comparative evidence, we can look at Canada's experience with minority governments. Canada has had effective government since well before Confederation. Yet there does not seem to be any connection between this effectiveness and the plurality electoral system being able to produce majority governments. In the fourteen elections since 1962, Canada's plurality system produced six minority governments, which is not exactly a stellar record.[11] In spite of these minority governments, Canada's governments have generally been effective. In his seminal study of Canada's Parliament, C.E.S. Franks concludes that "there is no evidence that minority parliaments are less efficient than majorities."[12]

It is true that minority governments have tended to fall more quickly than majority governments in Canada. However, this is less due to the inherent instability of minority governments than to the incentive the plurality system gives to some parties to collapse minority governments. The large parties know that a small shift in the vote toward their party will often be magnified into a large increase in seats and into a majority government for them. The Liberal Party lost the 1979 election, for example, but, after bringing down a minority Conservative government, recaptured a majority government in 1980 with only a 4 percent shift in the popular vote!

If Canada adopted MMP, minority and coalition governments would undoubtedly be more common. But we have already seen that the frequent minority governments under the plurality system in the past did not render the government ineffective. Nor is it the case that coalition governments are automatically weak or unstable. In PR systems like MMP, political parties normally win a steady percentage of the vote in each election. This neutralizes the incentive plurality gives to parties to collapse minority or coalition governments. Since forcing an election under MMP would likely not dramatically alter party strengths, parties are encouraged to work for just policy compromises within Parliament. Thus coalition governments will be able to "get things done" for Canada. The improvement is that coalitions get things done while involving a majority of the MPs who truly represent a majority of Canadians. PR gets rid of artificial majority governments that make decisions on important issues such as the reform of health care with the support of less than half of the voters.

Critics also suggest that PR causes unstable governments by promoting too many small parties. Under plurality, however, Canada has already produced many small parties, a contradiction of "Duverger's law," which asserts that a plurality electoral system tends to produce a two-party system. This diversity of smaller parties should not be denied since it reflects the real political views of Canadians. Moreover, except for Ontario and Quebec, the province-wide lists required by MMP would have relatively few MPs. Thus, parties would still require a significant proportion of the vote to earn a seat in the House of Commons from these party lists.

MMP CAN INCREASE NATIONAL UNITY

Some critics also argue that MMP would be detrimental to national unity. They charge that it would magnify divisions between regions and between English and French cultures. While the plurality electoral system has treated this diversity unfairly, some claim that at least this system has kept our country stable and united. The facts show, however, that quirks in plurality actually serve to worsen these divisions in Canada.

One tendency of the plurality system is to "reward" small, regionally concentrated parties. Canadian history is full of examples of small, regional parties that have won substantial representation in Parliament. Parties like the Progressives, Social Credit, the Creditistes, and the Reform Party have flourished under SMP by being able to translate a relatively small number of votes into a relatively large share of the seats. Particularly troublesome is the tendency of SMP to reward regionally concentrated parties that, in some cases, have promoted separatism or a sectional view of Canada. The plurality system has multiplied their negative impact by rewarding them with far more seats than their electoral support warrants. In the 2004 federal election, for example, the separatist Bloc Québécois (BQ) won 72 percent of the seats in Quebec with the support of only 49 percent of Quebec voters. In 1997 and 2000, fewer than 40 percent of Quebec's voters supported the Bloc, but it still won a majority of the province's seats in the House of Commons in both elections. This also occurred in Quebec provincial elections where the plurality system has allowed the separatist Parti Québécois to form four majority governments even though the party has never won a majority of the votes. In 1998, the PQ won a majority government (76 out of 125 seats) with 42.9 percent of the vote, even though the provincial Liberal Party had the support of more Quebec voters, with 43.6 percent of the vote! Because of this, Quebec is also one of the provinces furthest down the road of electoral reform.[13]

Another bias of the plurality electoral system is that it hurts small, nationally oriented parties with supporters dispersed across the country. For example, the NDP is a national party with a social democratic vision that has some support in all regions of the country. Yet, under the plurality system, it always receives fewer seats in the House of Commons than its support would justify. In the 2004 federal election, for example, the NDP earned only nineteen seats (6.2 percent) in the House of Commons, even though the party earned 15.7 percent of the vote, spread across the country. Even more shocking is that the NDP won almost half a million more votes than the BQ, but earned only about a third of the seats. Under MMP, the NDP would have won 47 seats, a fair reflection of its national support. Unfortunately, the plurality system hurts small parties with support dispersed across the regions, even when they try to appeal to all Canadians, wherever they might live.

The plurality system is also predisposed to overreward large parties in regions where they have strong support while underrewarding them where their support is weak. Thus, Canada often lacks truly national parties in the House. When large parties win the majority of the seats in one region but none in another region, divisions in Canada are perpetuated and worsened. For example, in the 1980 federal election, the Liberal Party formed the government but did not win a single seat in British Columbia, Alberta, or Saskatchewan, although it won over 20 percent of the vote in these provinces. Meanwhile, it won 74 of 75 seats, or 99 percent of the seats, in Quebec with 68 percent of the popular vote. In 2004, over one and a half times as many people voted for the Conservative Party in Quebec than in Saskatchewan, but the plurality system's distortions gave the Conservatives thirteen seats in Saskatchewan, and none in Quebec. While the Conservatives are undoubtedly strongest in the West, the electoral system does not reflect the depth of their support in Central and Eastern Canada. Even the Liberal Party, which enjoys relatively widespread national support, is a victim of this distortion. Only 46 percent of the total votes received by the Liberals in 2004 were cast in Ontario, but 56 percent of Liberal MPs came from that province, exacerbating the perception that the Liberals are only an "Ontario party." This flaw leads voters to develop a regionally skewed perception of the parties' support. It also handicaps the governing and opposition parties' ability to include regional viewpoints in their caucus discussions. In fact, plurality gives parties an incentive to favour regions where they might receive large electoral payoffs, while ignoring other regions.

The weaknesses of the plurality system, Alan Cairns concludes, make Canada's electoral system "divisive and detrimental to national unity."[14] MMP is a better way to handle Canada's regional divisions since it gives seats to national parties in direct proportion to the percentage of popular vote they win in the election. Since every vote counts in MMP, parties have a strong incentive to take a national viewpoint on issues and to search for votes in all regions. While MMP allows voters to develop and support regional parties, it does not unfairly reward these parties. It also encourages the growth of parties that will integrate the regions of Canada.[15]

Why does Canada remain stable even though the plurality system produces minority governments and encourages destabilizing regional parties? Much of the answer lies in Canada's strong, democratic, and tolerant political culture. Adopting PR would not suddenly change this. Nor would PR transform Canada into an unstable regime like pre–World War II "Weimar Germany."[16] Canada's strong, democratic political culture has kept and will continue to keep our system stable. Canada with MMP would more likely resemble modern Germany, which has used MMP for over five decades and remains eminently stable and unified.[17]

THE PLURALITY SYSTEM PRODUCES FALSE MAJORITY GOVERNMENTS

Another claim for the plurality electoral system is that it allows voters to select a government at the same time as they elect their representatives. Indeed, forming a cabinet is largely routine in Canada's parliamentary system, where the party winning the most seats usually forms the government. But it is an illusion to suggest that voters purposefully or automatically select a government. In fact, the majority of Canadians have not been involved in selecting most of Canada's governments. Since World War II, only two of our national governments have been formed by a party that won a majority of the popular vote in an election (1958 and 1984).[18] Over time, the plurality system is producing majority governments that rest on the support of an increasingly small proportion of the electorate.[19]

In practice, the plurality system routinely allows a minority of voters to select the majority of the seats, and thus to select the government. This problem with plurality is closely related to Canada's multiparty system. In the 1997 federal election, when five major parties contested the election, the plurality system translated the Liberals' 38.5 percent of the vote into a majority government. These results were not an anomaly; such distortions occur repeatedly in federal and provincial elections. The fact that there are five parties in Parliament reflects the diversity of political visions in Canada, a reality that ought to be reflected in our foremost representative and debating legislative chamber.

The plurality electoral system frequently magnifies a small shift in the vote to determine who will form the next government. In the 1979 election, Joe Clark's Conservatives were supported by 36 percent of Canadians and took 48 percent of the seats to form a minority government. The Liberals gathered 40 percent of the vote and took 40 percent of the seats. In the 1980 election, the Liberals increased their share of the vote by only 4 percent but won a clear majority government with 52 percent of the seats. And in the following election of 1984, a shift of 17 percent of the vote to the Mulroney-led Tories allowed them to increase their seats by 38 percent, from 37 percent to 75 percent of the seats!

Defenders of the plurality electoral system often cite this property of the plurality system as a desirable feature. They argue that the sensitivity of the plurality system to small shifts in the popular vote allow voters to defeat governments.

Besides the question of whether it is appropriate for a tiny minority of voters to determine who will or will not form a government, the problem is that this mechanism works inconsistently under plurality. While a shift in the popular vote may cause a change of government; often it does not. The actual seat totals depend on a number of factors, including the regional distribution of the vote, the number of political parties, and the division of the vote between these parties. The relationship between seats and votes under the plurality system is not a smooth line on a graph; it is far more random than that. This type of chancy outcome in the formation of governments under plurality is illustrated pointedly in two provincial elections in British Columbia. The NDP failed to form the government in 1986 when its 42.6 percent of the vote translated into 31.9 percent of the seats. In the 1991 election, however, NDP popular support dropped to 41 percent of the vote, yet it took 68 percent of the seats and formed the new government. Sometimes, plurality allows a party to win more seats and form the government with fewer votes than the main opposition party. In the 1979 federal election, for example, the Conservatives formed the government when they won 36 percent of the vote and 136 seats while the Liberals won 40 percent of the vote and only 114 seats.

Selecting a government through the plurality electoral system has the further side effect of distorting the public's perception of the parties' strengths. A month after the 1988 federal election, nobody remembered that the Tories won 57 percent of the seats with only 43 percent of the vote. The public is constantly reminded of the percentage of seats a party won, but not the percentage of the vote it won. Yet Mulroney used his minority electoral support to pass the highly unpopular Goods and Service Tax as well as the controversial Free Trade Agreement with the USA. In a democracy, majorities ought to consult minorities in making policy; the plurality system allows minorities to determine policy without necessarily having to consult the majority.

The plurality system is often associated with a party system with only two political parties. The diversity and complexity of Canadian society, however, has meant that Canada has developed many political parties. It is a mistake to think that we can solve the problems created by the plurality system by abolishing Canada's multiparty system rather than reforming the electoral system itself. We must accept that Canadians have deeply held political views and choose different parties to express these views. Political parties ought to play the critical role of providing an integrated set of principles around which they harmonize the many diverse and sometimes conflicting policies into a coherent platform. This would give voters a real choice. The democratic answer to voter differences is to amend our electoral system so that it responds to the diversity of beliefs and actions of Canadians, and not to force the system to produce the result the critics want. The real challenge is to allow the deeply held political views of Canadians to be properly, safely, and fairly expressed in politics. People with different ethnic, religious, or ideological views often arrive at, or endorse, a particular policy for their own distinct reasons. An MMP system will give no viewpoint a hegemonic grip on the system, instead forcing all parties to discuss their real differences as a means of arriving at mutually acceptable policies. The end result is that governments elected by proportional representation tend to reflect the preferred policies of citizens much better than do those elected by the plurality system.[20]

Since MMP would make the House of Commons accurately reflect the opinions and views of Canadians, it would be better to shift the duty of forming governments away from "chance" and to our MPs. This would give the majority of voters a stronger say in the creation of government. It would place the task of forming governments in the hands of our MPs who currently hold the power of dissolving governments. This conforms with and develops Canada's parliamentary theory.

THE PLURALITY SYSTEM WEAKENS REPRESENTATIVE DEMOCRACY

Indeed, voters would have a greater say over all aspects of their MPs' actions if MPs were obliged to represent their supporting voters. What we see in Canada today is that the plurality electoral system is weakening representative democracy. Representative democracy was created in response to the increasing number of citizens entitled to be involved in politics, but who lacked the time or energy to study political issues and devise fitting solutions. Most Canadians expect their representatives to engage actively in policymaking for them. Even so, plurality fails to give representatives a clear mandate from the voters and does not allow voters to hold MPs responsible for their actions.

Instead, the plurality system is increasingly encouraging Canadians to weaken or even bypass representative democracy. The weakening of the relationship between voters and representatives occurs because plurality requires politicians and parties to compromise too early in the process. Before an election, politicians are forced to develop lowest common denominator policies that will appeal to a plurality of voters in each riding. For example, some voters believe the state should strongly intervene to protect the environment while others believe market forces will correct environmental problems. In response to this spectrum of opinions, most political parties develop a compromised platform that homogenizes the environmental views of Canadians. While this is done to attract the wide range of voters necessary to win a plurality of votes in a single district, it undermines wide-ranging debate about environmental policy in the House of Commons.

Early compromises on policy produce pragmatic, look-alike parties. Election campaigns increasingly focus on party leaders and image and downplay principles, policy platforms, and the teams of politicians behind the leaders. Pragmatic parties make principled discussion rare in the House of Commons and foreclose the opportunity for accommodation between principled party platforms. Consequently, voters seldom know what their MPs and parties stand for and find it difficult to hold them accountable. At the same time, MPs do not receive clear mandates from voters. In these and other respects, plurality weakens the relationship between voters and representatives.

Increasingly, voters are turning away from these indistinct parties. Many are abandoning the electoral process altogether, as Canada's decreasing levels of voter turnout indicate.[21] Some are turning to interest groups for better representation. Political parties are responding to this challenge to their representative role by merely becoming brokers for interest groups. Other voters are pushing reforms such as recall, referenda, and initiative, which bypass representative democracy.[22] Thus, the dynamic set in motion by plurality actually encourages voters to bypass their representatives, a process that is undermining the very essence of representative democracy.

IMPROVING THE QUALITY OF REPRESENTATION

In opposition to plurality, an MMP electoral system would strengthen Canada's political system by encouraging a new dynamic. MMP encourages strong political parties, but would also encourage them to define how they are distinct from the others in order to attract votes. In order to compete effectively, parties would need to develop clearer principles and to define their policy platforms. This would allow political parties to become vehicles for voters to give mandates to MPs and to hold them accountable between elections. MPs would clearly be obliged to act in accordance with the principles and policies that they agreed to with supporters. This would include serving the individual voters according to these principles, if the parties want to maintain electoral support. MPs with a sense of obligation to voters would be a clear advance over the plurality system that limits voters to rubber-stamping or jettisoning representatives at election time.

One common criticism of MMP systems is that they create "two classes" of MPs, namely, those elected in single-member districts and party list MPs. The argument is that those MPs who represent single-member districts have different responsibilities than those who are elected from party lists. The evidence from Germany, the country with the longest experience with MMP, suggests that such concerns are misplaced. The German experience has been that party list MPs do get involved in constituency work, often focusing on single-member districts where their party lost. There is also little evidence in the German case to suggest that party list MPs are more likely to be cabinet ministers than MPs elected by SMP.[23]

Evidence from other countries shows that PR has been superior to the plurality electoral system in bringing minority parties into legislatures. It has also increased the parliamentary representation of women, ethnic groups, and cultural minorities.[24] Significantly, PR has done so without extensive affirmative action programs. PR has also allowed parties to improve the overall quality of individual MPs on their lists. PR also allows citizens to be free to join the political party of their choice and to decide whether their party's MPs will be "trustees" who will independently deliberate on issues; "delegates" who mechanically reflect their views; "mirrors" that reflect their gender, age, ethnic, or other characteristics; or defenders of their party's interests and positions.[25] If "party bosses" dominate under MMP, it will be the fault of those who create parties that tolerate them and of the voters who support them.

MMP allows parties and governments to be as good or as flawed as the people they represent. It leaves the public free to decide which groups or principles or approaches it want represented, by creating parties to reflect these concerns. MMP ultimately leaves the voters to decide which parties they want to be represented by in the House of Commons. For example, if 7 percent of Canadians support the Green Party's approach to environmental issues, MMP will give it 7 percent of the seats, no more and no less.

CONCLUSION

Democratic principles are the foundation upon which political life in Canada rests. The plurality and MMP electoral systems are structures through which Canadians can exercise their democratic choices. But structures are not neutral. They reflect values that the people in a society want the system to advance and thus encourage citizens to act in a certain way. The dominant value of the plurality system is stability—which it is supposed to achieve by translating a minority of votes into a majority government. In spite of the plurality electoral system, however, Canada has frequently produced minority governments. The plurality system also produces electoral outcomes that aggravate and intensify Canada's regional divisions. Too many outcomes of the plurality electoral system have been chancy, unfair, and inequitable. Also, plurality has encouraged the growth of pragmatic and brokerage parties that weaken the incentives of MPs to represent their voters. In spite of these problems, Canada remains a stable, democratic political system.

Since Canada is stable in spite of the plurality system, it has ample room to add the values of justice and equity to stability by adopting a MMP electoral system. MMP makes every vote count and produces results that are proportionate to what voters desire. MMP would also best serve Canada's distinctive needs. It would increase Canada's stability by improving regional representation in major parties, while reducing the unjustified strength of small divisive parties that happen to have regionally concentrated support.

The biggest asset of MMP, however, is that it enhances representative democracy by encouraging MPs and parties to develop a clearer profile on principles and policies. Voters will have a better idea of the mandate they are giving to MPs and thus be able to hold MPs accountable for their principles, policies, and political actions. An MMP electoral system should be adopted in Canada, since it is the fairest and most effective way to fix Canada's real democratic deficit.

NOTES

1. The speech is reprinted in *Policy Options* 24 (December 2002–January 2003): 10–12; available online at http://www.irpp.org/po/archive/dec02/martin.pdf.

2. In October 2004, British Columbia's Citizens Assembly on Electoral Reform recommended that B.C. adopt the single transferable vote form of proportional representation. B.C. voters voted on this proposal in a referendum in May 2005. Quebec has introduced a draft bill that would replace their single-member plurality electoral system with a form of MMP. Prince Edward Island has committed to a referendum on electoral reform. New Brunswick's Commission on Legislative Democracy recommended that New Brunswick adopt a mixed-member proportional electoral system. Ontario is in the process of establishing a British Columbia–style Citizens Assembly. See the essays in Henry Milner, ed., *Steps Toward Making Every Vote Count: Electoral System Reform in Canada and Its Provinces* (Peterborough: Broadview, 2004).

3. Only 44 percent of MPs elected in 2004 won their seats with a majority of the vote in their constituencies. In fact, one MP won a seat with the support of fewer than 27 percent of the voters in his constituency!

4. We are assuming that half of the seats would be allocated in single-member districts and the other half would be allocated from party lists for the entire province. We are also assuming that voters would support the same party with their list vote as they supported in single members.

5. See David M. Farrell, *Electoral Systems: A Comparative Introduction* (New York: Palgrave, 2001), pp. 97–111, for more details on how MMP works in Germany. See the Law Commission of Canada, *Voting Counts: Electoral Reform in Canada* (Ottawa: Law Commission of Canada, 2004), pp. 83–125, for a detailed discussion on how MMP might be implemented in Canada.

6. Matthew Soberg Shugart, "'Extreme' Electoral Systems and the Appeal of the Mixed-Member Alternative," in Matthew Soberg Shugart and Martin P. Wattenberg, eds., *Mixed-Member Electoral Systems: The Best of Both Worlds* (Oxford: Oxford University Press, 2001), pp. 25–51.

7. See Henry Milner, "First Past the Post? Progress Report on Electoral Reform Initiatives in the Canadian Provinces," *Policy Matters.* 5, no. 9 (September 2004): 19–23 (available online at http://www.irpp.org/pm/archive/pmvol5no9.pdf).

8. R. Ken Carty, "Doing Democracy Differently: Has Electoral Reform Finally Arrived?" Timlin Lecture, 1 March 2004, University of Saskatchewan.

9. Andrew Reynolds and Ben Reilly, *The International IDEA Handbook of Electoral System Design* (Stockholm: International Institute for Democracy and Electoral Assistance, 1997), p. 62.

10. Arend Lijphart, "Democracies: Forms, Performance, and Constitutional Engineering," *European Journal of Political Research* 25 (1994): 1–17; see also Arend Lijphart, *Patterns of Democracy: Government Forms and Performance in Thirty-Six Countries* (New Haven: Yale University Press, 1999), chapters 15 and 16.

11. The plurality system not only fails to produce regular majority governments but frequently fails to produce the strong oppositions needed to effectively run a parliamentary system. See Alan C. Cairns, "The Electoral System and Party System in Canada, 1921–1965," *Canadian Journal of Political Science* 1 (1968): 55–80.

12. C.E.S. Franks, *The Parliament of Canada* (Toronto: University of Toronto Press, 1987), p. 50.

13. Quebec has introduced a draft bill to replace its electoral system with a form of MMP. See also Milner, "First Past the Post?" 24–29.

14. Cairns, 92.

15. Harold J. Jansen and Alan Siaroff, "Regionalism and Party Systems: Evaluating Proposals to Reform Canada's Electoral System," in Henry Milner, ed., *Steps Toward Making Every Vote Count* (Peterborough: Broadview, 2004), conclude that MMP would be among the best choices to prevent exacerbating regional conflicts.

16. Enid Lakeman reports that if Weimar Germany had used plurality, the Nazis would likely have won all the seats, cited in Michael Lind, "A Radical Plan to Change American Politics," *The Atlantic Monthly* 270, no. 2 (August 1992): 73–83.

17. In a review of the research on this question, Louis Massicotte, "Changing the Canadian Electoral System," *Choices* 7, no. 1 (February 2001): 21, states that claims of PR undermining democracy have been "discredited." Massicotte's study is available online at http://www.irpp.org/choices/archive/vol7no1.htm.

18. Richard Katz, "Electoral Reform Is Not as Simple as It Appears," in Henry Milner, ed., *Making Every Vote Count* (Peterborough: Broadview, 1999), p. 101, points out that if rejected ballots are included in the vote totals for the 1984 election, then even the Mulroney government did not have the support of a majority of voters, leaving only one government that had the support of a majority of the electorate.

19. Richard Johnston, "Canadian Elections at the Millennium," *Choices* 6, no. 6 (September 2000) (available online at http://www.irpp.org/choices/archive/ vol6no6.htm).

20. G. Bingham Powell, Jr., *Elections as Instruments of Democracy: Majoritarian and Proportional Visions* (New Haven: Yale University Press, 2000), chapter 9.

21. Although it is easy to overstate the impact of electoral systems on turnout, most comparative analyses of turnout find that proportional representation systems are associated with higher turnout. See Pippa Norris, *Electoral Engineering: Voting Rules and Political Behaviour* (Cambridge: Cambridge University Press, 2004), chapter 7.

22. See Nick Loenen, *Citizenship and Democracy: A Case for Proportional Representation* (Toronto: Dundurn, 1997), chapter 5, for a comparison of PR with these other reforms.

23. Louis Massicotte, Á *la recherche d'un mode de scrutin mixte compensatoire*. Document de travail, Québec, Secrétariat à la réforme des institutions démocratiques, Décembre 2004, chapter 8. Available online at http://www.institutions-democratiques. gouv.qc.ca/publications/mode_scrutin_rapport.pdf.

24. Norris, chapter 8, demonstrates that PR enhances the representation of women. The effect for ethnic minorities is more complex. The plurality system represents minorities well if they are geographically concentrated, but has a harder time when minorities are dispersed. See Norris, chapter 9.

25. Several conflicting definitions of representation confuse this debate; see Hanna Fenichel Pitkin, *The Concept of Representation* (Los Angeles: University of California Press, 1967).

✗ NO
The Limits of Electoral Systems and Electoral Reform— or How I Came to Love SMP
CHRISTOPHER KAM

Being asked to defend Canada's single-member plurality (SMP) system is akin to a public defence lawyer being asked to defend an irascible *but nonetheless innocent* client from a series of false charges. SMP is not a perfect electoral system (and my defence of SMP does not take that form), but it is far from the worst, and certainly claims that SMP is the principal source of Canada's political ills are overstated, as are predictions on what the adoption of proportional representation (PR) (including mixed-member proportional [MMP]) would accomplish.[1] One of the most visible problems with arguments that critique SMP and laud PR is the casual use of terminology employed to evaluate electoral systems and political outcomes—terms like fairness and representation, for example. Once these standards are themselves evaluated in light of the inherent difficulties involved in aggregating individual preferences into social choices, one begins to appreciate the arbitrary nature of the case against SMP. There is, in addition, a tendency to project onto SMP aspects of parliamentary government that some people find uncomfortable (e.g., a high level of party cohesion). The result is that SMP is blamed for problems that are not of its making and that electoral reform is predicted to generate more change than it can reasonably be expected to deliver.

THE CASE AGAINST SMP

Complaints against SMP originate from the system's disproportionality—the fact that it does not provide a one-to-one match between parties' vote shares and their parliamentary seat shares. This stands in contrast to PR systems (of whatever variety), which are designed to ensure a one-to-one match between vote shares and seat shares. SMP's disproportionality is systematic: large parties generally obtain more seats than votes; small parties—unless they are regionally concentrated—receive fewer seats than votes. The magnitude of these seat bonuses and penalties is not set in stone, varying by country and election, and depending on whether the SMP system's vote-to-seats curve is stretched out and fairly flat or compressed and very steep. Ideally, however, the disproportionality of SMP helps to divide clearly electoral (hence parliamentary) winners from losers (Powell 2000), something that PR does not do.

SMP's disproportionality has knock-on consequences. First, the seat bonus enjoyed by large parties tends to generate manufactured majorities. In other words, SMP turns electoral pluralities into parliamentary majorities, thus clashing with the notion that democracy is rule by the majority. These manufactured majorities then go on to govern in an unrepresentative fashion, interpreting their manufactured parliamentary majority as if it were a broadly based electoral majority. The result is policy at odds with the preferences of the majority of citizens. The Mulroney government's passage of the unpopular Goods and Services Tax and the Canada–U.S. Free Trade Agreement might be seen as an example of this sort of politics.

This (apparently) unrepresentative politics is compounded by the fact that SMP penalizes smaller parties. It does so by mechanically discounting votes of second or lower placed candidates, which are called wasted votes. This mechanical effect then leads voters to transfer strategically their support from smaller parties to a larger party that might successfully defeat the party they like least. There are two reinforcing consequences to this dynamic: first, people who cast what turn out to be wasted votes lose interest in the political process; and second, the political marketplace fails to provide voters with a full menu of policy choices—suppressing again voters' interest in the political process. Indeed, what voters are left with is a bland competition between two large parties that offer such similar middle-of-the-road policy platforms as to make the electoral choice between them all but meaningless. The large parties can get away with this lack of imagination primarily because SMP provides them with an artificial monopoly on parliamentary seats.

The pattern of wasted votes, just like SMP's disproportionality, is systematic not random. The Canadian experience is for parties to receive no parliamentary seats in some region while sweeping virtually all of the seats in another—despite, in some instances, having relatively similar vote shares in both regions. These "electoral deserts" undermine even the major parties' capacity to act as vehicles of the national interest. The counter-strategy politicians find easiest to execute in these circumstances is to develop regional appeals—hence Canada's experience with the Progressives, Social Credit, Reform Party, and Bloc Québécois.

It would appear that PR of some form is the logical corrective to these problems: with a proportional electoral system, voters will be able to choose (perhaps sincerely) from a broader array of parties, producing a far more ideologically and geographically representative parliament and cabinet. Ideally, the cabinet will itself be a majority coalition cabinet formed on the basis of a publicly announced pre-election agreement (so that voters will not have to factor the outcome of unpredictable coalition negotiations into their electoral calculations). In this respect, the cabinet and its policies will be supported by true rather than a manufactured majority, and its policies can therefore be said to be both democratic and representative.

THEORETICAL CONSTRAINTS ON THE AGGREGATION OF PREFERENCES

Unfortunately for PR's proponents, the argument that I have just set out cannot be logically sustained. The assumed connection between voters' preferences and electoral and parliamentary outcomes that underlies the pro-PR position, and which might suggest replacing SMP with a variant of PR is particularly problematic. A good deal of social choice theory warns us against thinking that there is a straightforward connection between the preferences of individual voters and collective outcomes (Arrow 1963; Gibbard 1973; Satterthwaite 1975; McKelvey 1976; Riker 1982), and precisely because of these social choice results we must handle concepts such as fairness, representation, and majority rule with great care.

Consider the following example. The 1997 Canadian Election Study asked survey respondents to comment on the importance they attached to a variety of election issues, including reducing the deficit and protecting social programs. The cross-tabulation of the responses is set out below. One notes, for example, that 35.5 percent of respondents thought it very important to reduce the deficit and to protect social programs. In contrast, just 0.4 percent of respondents felt neither goal was important. Of note is that *majorities* (note the plural) of voters felt deficit reduction (60.1 percent) and protection of social programs (62 percent) to be very important election issues.

How might the voters in Table 1 translate their expressed preferences on these matters into support for or opposition to various deficit reduction and social program protection policy packages? Given a few mundane assumptions about how people choose between alternative goods (e.g., between ice cream flavours, cars, and—yes—even policy packages), it is fairly easy to show that there is no single

TABLE 1

IMPORTANCE OF ELECTION ISSUES IN 1997: DEFICIT REDUCTION AND SOCIAL PROGRAMS

Importance of Reducing the Deficit	Importance of Protecting Social Programs			
	Not Very	Somewhat	Very	Total
Very	3.9	20.7	35.5	60.1
Somewhat	1.1	10.7	21.4	33.2
Not Very	0.4	1.2	5.1	6.7
Total	5.4	32.6	62.0	

N = 3810
139 Cases dropped due to non-response

Source: 1997 Canadian Election Study. Cross-tabulation of items CPSA2F by CPSA2B.

policy that the voters prefer over all others. This is because there is no single or "true" majority in the electorate. To see this, note that 60.1 percent of voters feel that parties' policies should lay great stress on deficit reduction while 62.0 percent feel that parties' policies should greatly stress the protection of social programs. However, if a party were to offer a policy package that heavily emphasized deficit reduction and the protection of social programs, the party would find that just 35.5 percent of voters (in the top right cell)—a clear minority—actually prefer this policy. By definition, there is another majority (comprised of the 100 − 35.5 = 64.5 percent of voters in the other cells of the table) that prefers a different policy.

The case is made more precisely and generally in Appendix 1. The appendix shows that one can always find a majority to endorse and overturn any given policy proposal (i.e., any combination of deficit reduction and social program protection). This is known as a voting cycle or cycling, and it is a common affliction of group choice. What is a voting cycle and what does it imply? I (and you too probably) have well-defined preferences over ice cream flavours. Personally, I prefer pistachio to vanilla to chocolate, and if you place three servings of each flavour in front of me, I have no problem choosing which I prefer and which, therefore, I will eat first. More than that, I know that because I prefer pistachio to vanilla, and vanilla to chocolate, I must prefer pistachio to chocolate. Were it not so, I could not choose which flavour to eat; I would sit staring at the three bowls of ice cream thinking to myself, "which of these do I really prefer?"

This is not necessarily the case with a group such as the electorate. If we voted on which flavour of ice cream we preferred to eat, it is quite possible (indeed, it is almost inevitable) that we would find that we preferred pistachio to vanilla to chocolate to pistachio! Think of the consequences: if we, as a group, were given a straight choice between any two flavours, we could choose sensibly, but if a third choice were offered, we could not—we would cycle endlessly over pistachio, vanilla, chocolate, and pistachio again. Of course, our electoral system would give us a result, but that result would really be a random draw, and we could always put together a majority to overturn that result and get another "majority-preferred" flavour of ice cream. This is a devastating result: it means that group choices are inherently unstable and arbitrary.

One can reasonably define a fair democratic *process* with citizens voting without harassment at regular intervals, political parties competing freely and legally for citizens' votes, and the media commenting without restriction on political actors and events. (On these process grounds, every election in Canada over the past century has been reasonably fair.) What voting cycles reveal is how arbitrary—hence meaningless—terms such as *fair, democratic*, and *representative* are when applied to political *outcomes*.[2] Thus when proponents of PR (of whatever variety) claim that PR will deliver parliaments and policies that more accurately and fairly represent the will of the majority, we are clearly entitled to ask, "Which majority would that be and why would it be fair to represent their interests rather than another majority's?" The Canadian electorate, as I have just shown, is comprised of many majorities at once, and we have on hand no sensible criteria to determine which of these simultaneous majorities is the true one. Indeed, the very concept of a monolithic "true" majority is largely a chimera, as therefore are notions that political outcomes (e.g., election results, parliamentary votes, or policies) are inherently fair or unfair, representative or unrepresentative, or somehow indicative of a democratic mandate or general will.[3] Criticisms that SMP is inherently unfair, undemocratic, or unrepresentative are, for the very same reasons, quite empty and cannot be used to justify its abolition anymore than they can be used to advance the case for the adoption of PR.

A response to all this might be that I have presented an atypical, even fanciful, model of electoral choice that is, in addition, too simplistic to provide general insights about politics. There are a number of convincing defences to such charges. First, the data in Table 1 are not fictional; they are derived from a representative sample of Canadian voters. Consequently, one can safely assume that distribution of preferences shown in Table 1 accurately reflected the distribution of preferences in the Canadian electorate in 1997. Moreover, consideration over these issues has been shown to have influenced how people voted at the 1997 election (Nevitte, Blais, Gidengil, and Nadeau 1999). Second, the voting cycle is not an artefact of my model's simplicity. In fact, only simpler models of electoral politics, predicated on a single-issue dimension, can avoid voting cycles.[4] Such models are of little relevance to the Canadian case, however, because Canadian politics has almost always operated in at least two-issue dimensions, one reflecting a class or economic cleavage, the other reflecting an ethno-linguistic cleavage marking French/Catholic–English/Protestant tensions (Johnston, Blais, Brady, and Crête 1992)–and cycling is endemic to multi-dimensional politics.[5] Indeed, the hard reality of politics is that voting cycles are ubiquitous: *all* electoral systems succumb to them, and to the extent any electoral system avoids them, it does so only by violating some obvious standard of sensibility (Arrow 1963).[6]

THE UNCOMFORTABLE REALITIES OF PARLIAMENTARY GOVERNMENT

The above example can be extended to parliamentary politics. Some passing knowledge of what goes on in Parliament is all that is required to assure one that parliamentary politics is not completely bogged down by cycling: MPs do not shift back and forth in division after division so as to reject motions and bills that they have just passed. Yet parliamentary politics–just like Canadian electoral politics– is multidimensional. So what prevents voting cycles from taking over Parliament? In the main, two factors provide stability to parliamentary politics: party unity and agenda control. Majority governments can count on the support of their MPs, thus providing Cabinet and Parliament with the monolithic majority required to avoid cycling. In other words, the cohesion of the majority party ensures that there is one and only one majority in Parliament.

The absence of a unified parliamentary majority would not necessarily lead to chaotic parliamentary politics. This is because the Canadian Parliament (like most other parliaments) provides Cabinet with significant control over the parliamentary agenda. For example, only ministers can introduce bills that require the expenditure of public monies.[7] This provides the government with a good deal of control over what happens in Parliament. Indeed, as Appendix 1 shows, control over the agenda—that is, what issues will be voted on and in what order—is all that the government requires to achieve its most preferred outcomes.

There are a number of lessons here. First, one should be cautious about casting party cohesion in a purely negative light; party cohesion serves several vital functions (see following), including preventing voting cycles from emerging in Parliament. Second, it cannot be said with certainty that majority governments in Canada retain power and pass policies solely because of their manufactured majorities. A majority government could use agenda control to obtain its preferred policies, and it might well have to if its policies arouse significant opposition among its own MPs.[8] Third, if cabinets can dominate parliaments by way of sophisticated agenda control rather than by the brute application of a cohesive manufactured majority, then absent an overhaul of the rules of the House, electoral reform will not have much effect on parliamentary politics. Single-party majority, coalition, and minority governments will still be able to achieve their desired policies by strategically manipulating the parliamentary agenda. Fourth, concomitant parliamentary reform to loosen the cabinet's agenda control (so that net effect of reform is to limit single-party majority government *and* to weaken the cabinet's control over Parliament) risks generating cyclical parliamentary politics. Cyclical—that is, random and unstable—parliamentary politics is not just undesirable in and of itself; it undercuts reformers' capacity to predict with confidence what electoral reform will deliver. For all these reasons, I tend not to place great weight on either the normative charge that manufactured majorities are bad things or the positive charge that electoral reform will, by itself, change parliamentary outcomes.

ACCOUNTABLE RATHER THAN REPRESENTATIVE GOVERNMENT

So far, I have painted a fairly bleak picture of democratic government. If we cannot sensibly speak of democracy as representative of majority interests, and if political outcomes are due either to voting cycles or strategic manipulation, why do we bother with it at all? The key is to develop a retrospective conception of representative democracy. That is, instead of reasoning forward from citizens' preferences to political outcomes, one must reason backward from policy outcomes to citizens' objectives. In this retrospective conception of democracy, accountability replaces representation as the main evaluative criterion. Accountability exists when citizens have the capacity to *identify* and *sanction* underperforming political agents (e.g., governments or MPs) (Przeworski, Stokes, and Manin 1999, 10; Powell 2000). Identification is high when it is clear who is responsible for the content of parliamentary outputs and outcomes. Underperformance can be defined in a number of ways as a voter wishes. It may be simply that the voter dislikes the state of the world after four or five years of the incumbent's administration. Alternatively, a voter might assess what the incumbent promised against what the incumbent has delivered, and in this way gauge the incumbent's managerial effectiveness. On this view of democracy, elections provide voters with a minimal veto on the identity of the government (Riker 1982). Yet as long as this veto is applied in such a way that more (less) effective agents are re-elected (defeated) more often than not, we can expect politicians to a) try to honour promises and b) work harder (than they might under alternative institutional rules) to please voters.

On the whole, SMP does a better job of providing the conditions required for accountability than PR—and MMP in particular—does. SMP eases the identification problem for voters because it tends to generate single-party majority governments. Our Westminster parliamentary system then provides these governments with the power required to enact their policy programs. Under these conditions, it is easy for voters to identify the political agent responsible for the content of public policy (i.e., the government) and to gauge the government's effectiveness at implementing its policy program. Should the government fail to deliver on its promised policies, or should those policies turn out to be unsatisfactory, the voter has the option of voting against the government at the next election. Furthermore, because a few votes lost under SMP can cost the government many seats, SMP provides voters with the capacity to inflict sharp sanctions on underperforming political agents.[9]

This can be contrasted with MMP. MMP encourages coalition government. Coalition government is not inherently bad, but it does complicate the identification problem for voters because they cannot tell which coalition partner is responsible for the government's successes or failures. The flatter votes-to-seats curve of PR (i.e., the fact that a few votes won or lost does not have a sharp impact on the number of seats a party gets) lessens the severity of electoral punishment, as does the fact that a party's inclusion or exclusion from government depends not only on its seat shares (which voters can alter via their votes), but also the party's ideological location (which voters cannot alter). In addition, mixed electoral systems allow unpopular or ineffective incumbents to escape direct judgment by voters in their districts and obtain a parliamentary seat via the party list.[10] In short, MMP severely limits the capacity of voters to sanction underperforming political agents.

Naturally, there are implicit assumptions and gaps between theory and reality in this retrospective vision of democracy. Party cohesion is an implicit element of this retrospective vision of democracy. If MPs, especially government MPs, vote as they (or their constituents wish) without regard to their party platforms or positions, voters cannot easily know who is responsible for parliamentary outputs and cannot therefore effectively judge the government's performance. Indeed, by *insisting* that their MPs act as constituency rather than party delegates, voters may well be denying the governing party *and* themselves the means to achieve accountable governance.[11] This principle tends not to be well understood, and yet it is at the core of modern parliamentary government, essentially a system of party-based government.[12] If we wish our MPs to represent constituency interests (as problematic as that notion is) without regard to the survival of a cabinet and its ability to execute a policy program, the correct institutional reform is the adoption of presidential government rather than the replacement of SMP with PR.

Minority government represents another challenge to the internal consistency of this retrospective vision of accountable government. Certainly, the historical pattern of Canadian electoral politics suggests that PR is as likely to result in serial minority government (as in Norway, Sweden, and Denmark) as in majority coalitions. The challenge inherent in serial minority government does not spring from the government side of the House but from the opposition side. On my argument, Cabinet's control of the agenda offers sufficient logical ground for voters to hold the government responsible for parliamentary outputs. The danger, it seems to me, is that electoral reform will bring with it a demand that House rules be reformed so as to distribute parliamentary power in a more proportional fashion, much as they were in New Zealand in the run-up to the adoption of MMP. This creates incentives for opposition parties to eschew government (which demands greater parliamentary discipline and political risk than opposition) in favour of shaping policy from the opposition benches, a pattern that is well-established in Scandinavian countries (Strøm 1990). Insofar as this creates a governmental system in which power is divorced from responsibility, the result may be labelled normatively undesirable; regardless, it obscures clarity of responsibility.

Caught up alongside this worry is the Liberal Party's domination of Canadian politics. Over the past 100 years, the Liberals have been the country's natural party of government. This is not because the Liberal Party has been highly popular with voters, but rather because the Liberals occupy a policy position that is, *on average*, closer than any other political party to what most Canadians prefer. With Liberals so positioned, the argument goes, it has become impossible for voters to discipline them effectively using SMP. It may be time to use PR to generate a system of coalition government, in which the Liberals, while almost always being in government, will at least have to bargain with a coalition partner (Johnston 2001).

This is a coherent argument for PR in that it does not rest on tenuous claims of representation or fairness; indeed, it flows from the retrospective vision that I have just articulated. Nevertheless, I think that I can question this position without contradicting myself. First, I would argue that PR will discipline the Liberals far less than one might like. Serial Liberal minority government remains as likely an outcome as coalition government, especially in view of the (federal)

Canadian tradition of eschewing coalitions. Moreover, even if coalitions were to occur regularly, cagey Liberals might form oversized three-party coalitions to ensure that the coalition itself occupies a multidimensional policy space. With the Liberals almost certainly the dominant partner in any coalition, they could then use agenda control *within the cabinet* to achieve their preferred outcomes. (Colloquially, one might think of this as the Liberals playing off both coalition partners against one another.) Second, given the multidimensional character of Canadian politics and the existence a significant uncoalitionable anti-system party (the Bloc Québécois), there is more reason to predict that Canada under PR will resemble Italy more than Germany, with our Liberals playing the part of the Italian Christian Democrats, a fixed part of a set of revolving cabinets.[13] Finally, there is a risk that the Liberal Party itself will fragment. This should not be celebrated; despite its flaws, the Liberal Party is one of the country's few integrative institutions. The only thing worse than a Canada with a dominant Liberal Party may well be a Canada without one. Admittedly, I cannot prove these assertions, but I do think that they deserve attention and debate. At the very least, one should recognize that the confidence bounds on the predictions of what PR is likely to deliver are very wide.

FINAL CONCERNS: DISILLUSIONMENT AND ELECTORAL DESERTS

This leaves two final complaints about SMP, that it exacerbates voter alienation and creates electoral deserts. The first of these is easily dismissed: voter disillusionment and political cynicism are cross-national phenomena, occurring in a variety of countries irrespective of their electoral systems (Pharr, Putnam, and Dalton 2000).[14] While these patterns are worrisome and deserving of study and attention, this simple evidence suggests that larger forces than electoral systems are behind voters' increasing cynicism.

This leaves the complaint that SMP creates electoral deserts, and it is the one that I take most seriously. Canada remains a country with too much geography, and the attendant centre-periphery tensions frequently push the polity to its limits. Quite sensibly, then, most Canadians highly value regional representation in Parliament (Bricker and Redfern 2001, 23). In the Canadian context, the amelioration of regional electoral deserts is the strongest argument in favour of PR. Even so, I have reservations. Regional, even separatist, appeals are not automatically undercut by PR or mixed systems as the Bavarian CSU and the Italian Northern League demonstrate. However, if eliminating or reducing electoral deserts is the objective of electoral reform, let me suggest a more modest and sensible change, namely the adoption of a mixed-member majority (MMM) system with just 20–25 percent of MPs chosen from regional or provincial lists.[15] As this system is not designed to achieve proportionality (the list seats are just added to the district seats), it preserves the majoritarian character of the current system (which on my retrospective conception of democracy is no bad thing and which better conforms to the assumptions of Westminster parliamentary government) while ensuring that parties have solid chances of obtaining seats in every region.[16]

CONCLUSION

I have tried to avoid repeating common arguments against PR—that it will result in unstable and ineffective Italian-style government, for example. It may or it may not. I have, however, demanded that the arguments against SMP and for PR be internally consistent and correctly attributable to the electoral system. Internal consistency and correct causal attributions are not mere academic details; changing an electoral system is a costly and potentially risky business, and it should not be done without a good deal of sound analysis. We are all well aware of this when it comes to our cars: replacing the alternator when the battery that is dead is costly and useless, and if that alternator is installed incorrectly, it can short out the car's electoral system entirely, making a bad situation even worse. The irony is that people appear to be more willing to overhaul their political institutions than tinker with their cars despite knowing much more about the latter than the former.

Almost every argument that PR's proponents make for PR and against SMP fails in these respects. This is especially the case with the argument that SMP should be replaced by PR because the latter is a fairer, more representative and democratic system. I have shown that this argument is internally inconsistent. The many overlapping, frequently contradictory majorities that exist in any electorate generate voting cycles make it impossible to say what is a fair or representative outcome. A retrospective conception of democracy predicated on ensuring accountable governance is more logically defensible, and SMP tends to do a better job than PR at identifying and punishing underperforming political agents. This is particularly the case with MMP systems that allow constituency losers to obtain parliamentary seats via the party list.

Proponents of PR make a stronger case when they argue that PR will ameliorate Canada's electoral deserts. That said, one should not expect (or even desire) PR to alter the character of parliamentary politics. Quite apart from the incentives inherent in the electoral system, the parliamentary nature of Canadian government will continue to favour high levels of party cohesion and cabinet domination of the parliamentary agenda. In view of this, a better reform—if one is really required—might be to adopt a consciously majoritarian mixed system. Such a system does not run against the retrospective—accountable conception of democracy and is more compatible with the Canadian form of parliamentary government. Even so, one is entitled to ask whether, if that is all that electoral reform can (perhaps) accomplish, the costs justify the unpredictable benefits.

APPENDIX 1. CYCLING IN THE CANADIAN ELECTORATE

This appendix uses a spatial model to illustrate the cycling argument that I have set out above. The main assumptions underpinning this spatial model are as follows:

1. Voters prefer policies that are closer to their most preferred (i.e., ideal) positions and are indifferent between policies that are equally distant from their ideal positions Thus, for example, the 35.5 percent of the respondents in the top right cell will support policy packages that reduce the deficit and protect social programs: the more a policy package cuts the deficit and protects social programs, the more the voters in the top right cell like it; the less the package does of these things, the less they like it. This is a trivial assumption. It is equivalent, for example, to assuming that if a person prefers chocolate ice cream to vanilla, they will tend to order chocolate ice cream rather than vanilla when they go to the ice cream parlour.

2. Voters weight deficit reduction and protection of social programs equally (i.e., that voters are indifferent between an extra dollar spent on social programs and added to the deficit and a dollar taken from social programs and subtracted from the deficit).

3. The psychological distances that voters perceive between a) "not very important" and "somewhat important," and b) "somewhat important" and "very important" are equal on each policy dimension.[17]

These last two assumptions overlap a bit, but what they mean is this: Let's say that a voter whose preferred position is "somewhat-somewhat" on social programs and deficit spending is told that they cannot have their most preferred (i.e., ideal) policy package. Instead, they must choose between policy packages that either a) place little importance on deficit reduction and some importance on protecting social programs, or b) place lots of importance on deficit reduction and some importance on protecting social programs. On these assumptions, the hypothetical voter is indifferent between these two alternative policy packages. They are equally far apart from this voter's ideal policy package, and so to that voter it's "six of one, half-dozen of another."

These assumptions allow one to depict the distribution of preferences displayed in Table 1 in terms of a two-dimensional policy space as shown in Figure 1. Now let's say that these voters decide to vote on a set of policies to deal with the deficit and social programs. If democracy is consonant with majority rule, a simple majority is sufficient to pass a new policy. I have marked the status quo (SQ) in the middle of the space, a policy that places some but not a great deal of importance on these two issues—but this starting location is not critical to my argument, and other status quo policies below the semi-circular curve could just as well be chosen. The curve itself is an indifference curve: all voters above and to

FIGURE 1

A SPATIAL MODEL OF DEFICIT REDUCTION AND THE PROTECTION OF SOCIAL PROGRAMS: FROM SQ TO A

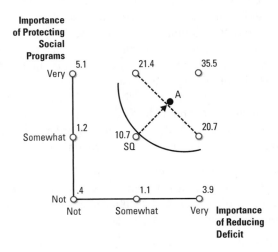

the right of SQ prefer policies inside this curve to policies (including SQ) that lie beyond it. Consequently, we find a massive majority (35.5 + 21.4 + 20. 7 = 77.6 percent) of voters in favour of moving policy to point A.

This initial majority would not agree to move policy beyond A toward the "very-very" position because beyond A the policy's distance from voters at the "somewhat-very" or "very-somewhat" positions would increase—hence, they would not like any such policy package as much as they like A. However, assume that policy B was offered up as an alternative to A. What would happen? As the indifference curves in Figure 2 indicate, B is closer to the ideal points of the 35.5 percent of voters who want a "very-very" policy package and to the ideal points of the (20.7 + 3.9) 24.6 percent of voters who want more deficit reduction. This provides B with a majority of 60.1 percent, so clearly B should replace A as the democratically preferred policy. Finally, consider what might happen if B were voted on against C—the ideal point of the 35.5 percent of voters who want a "very-very" policy package. The situation is depicted in Figure 3 (page 316), and clearly a majority of 62 percent (35.5 + 21.4 + 5.1) supports C over B; C thus replaces B as the effective policy package.

FIGURE 2

A SPATIAL MODEL OF DEFICIT REDUCTION AND THE PROTECTION OF SOCIAL PROGRAMS: FROM A TO B

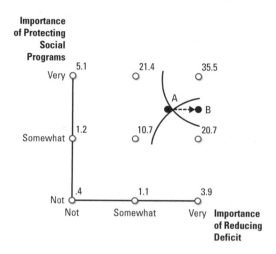

Review what has occurred: via a sequence of overwhelming majority votes the electorate has adopted a policy package (C) that is preferred by little more than a third of all voters. Is this a fair, representative, or democratic outcome? Well, the move from SQ to C has been endorsed by successive majorities of 77.6 percent, 60.1 percent, and 62 percent, and in that respect the outcome seems representative and democratic. Yet barely a third of the electorate actually prefers this policy, and hence it is difficult to label C a fair, representative, or democratic outcome. What if a government were to institute C as its policy? The government could honestly and correctly claim that its policy was supported by a majority of voters. However, the opposition could just as well claim that there is no democratic mandate for C—and indeed, if A were paired against C, 64.5 percent (100 − 35.5) of the electorate would vote for A! In other words, we could well end up in a voting cycle in which the electorate expresses majority preferences for A over C over B over A.

WHY AGENDA CONTROL IS CRUCIAL

In any multidimensional space, agenda control provides a sophisticated agenda setter with the capacity to achieve their most preferred outcome (McKelvey 1976). To illustrate this idea, return to Figures 1–3, and imagine that these figures now

FIGURE 3

A SPATIAL MODEL OF DEFICIT REDUCTION AND THE PROTECTION OF SOCIAL PROGRAMS: FROM B TO C

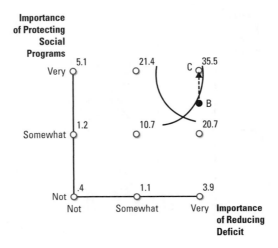

represent the distribution of preferences and seat shares in a parliament, with a minority government intent on a policy of aggressive deficit reduction and social program protection (i.e., a "very-very" policy position). Despite controlling just 35.5 percent of the seats, this government can achieve its ideal policy by structuring a sequence of divisions (i.e., an agenda) that pits SQ against A, A against B, and B against C.

NOTES

1. It is worth emphasizing at the outset that MMP is at root a system of proportional representation. The constituency votes—though they may have the advantage of connecting voters to a single constituency representative—have no real effect of the system's aggregate dynamics, the latter governed by the electorate's party votes. Thus, save for a few details here and there, one does not need to construct an argument against MMP specifically; generic complaints against PR apply just as well.

2. Proponents of PR might seek refuge behind a notion of descriptive representation—that is, the argument that Parliament will better reflect observable characteristics of the voting public. This form of representation is extremely weak theoretically, however (Pitkin 1967). For example, how likely is it that the women and racial minorities who might enter Parliament via party lists will faithfully reflect the class composition

(hence interests) of Canadian society? The honest answer must be "very unlikely": the new MPs will be drawn overwhelmingly from the middle and upper classes. These sorts of problems undermine theories of descriptive representation.

3. The same argument can be used to dismiss the normative claim that a MP's job is to represent his or her riding's interests in Parliament, i.e., that the MP should ignore the party whip and vote as his or her constituents wish. In most cases, it is simply impossible to define sensibly the collective preferences of a constituency.

4. A unidimensional model can (given the same assumptions about voters' preferences that I have made above, to wit, that they prefer outcomes closer to their ideal points) avoid voting cycles—and through this device come to some judgment about the relative outcome-based merits of various electoral systems (e.g., Powell and Vanberg 2000; McDonald, Mendes, and Budge 2004).

5. Lest this all be abstruse, consider how my grandfathers, both blue-collar Catholics voted. My paternal grandfather, an anglophone, consistently voted his class interests—NDP. My maternal grandfather, with the same class interests, but a prairie-based francophone, voted Liberal, clearly an ethno-linguistic expression. In this respect, my grandfathers' voting patterns reflect the multidimensional nature of Canadian politics.

6. The situation is even more complex than I have indicated. All electoral systems also provide incentives for voters to misrepresent their sincere preferences (Gibbard 1973; Satterthwaithe 1975). We are all familiar with this behaviour in SMP systems—voters fleeing from smaller parties to defeat the lesser of two large party evils—*but it occurs in some fashion or other in all electoral systems*. The practical upshot of this is that voters' preferences are endogenous to the electoral system, i.e., we cannot tell if preferences are a cause or an effect. This is precisely why simulations of how Canadian elections would have played out under MMP or some other system are of limited value: if MMP had been used, Canadian voters would have altered their voting behaviour in response to the strategic incentives inherent in MMP.

7. To take another example, legislative committees only get to review bills after second reading, by which time the general tenets of the bills in question have been defined and the committee's scope thereby limited.

8. Canadian MPs do, in fact, break ranks and dissent against their parties more than one might think. The first Chrétien government, for example, saw its MPs rebel on 12 percent of whipped divisions (Kam, forthcoming). Of course, MPs still overwhelmingly vote their party positions. There is, nevertheless, more flexibility in the system than most people realize.

9. One might argue that the steepness of SMP's vote-to-seats curve is a perverse reward system because with just a few additional votes a party can go from opposition to government. This is more fiction than fact, however: because incumbent governments tend on average to lose rather than gain votes SMP's steep votes-to-seats curve generally operates as a sanction not as a reward. Powell (2000, 67–68) reaches a similar conclusion: political responsibility is clearest, and punishment most severe in majoritarian systems such as Canada's.

10. Shugart and Wattenberg (2003) write off this effect as a mere technicality, but they are mistaken. A central task of an electoral system is to allow voters to throw the rascals out, and to the extent that an electoral system prevents this, it is deficient and sows the seeds of voter disillusionment. Japanese voters, for example, were exceedingly

angry to discover that their mixed system allowed the politicians that they had dismissed in single-member districts to return to office via the party list (McKean and Scheiner 2000, 450–451).

11. If voters do not, however, insist upon this, they may logically take a lack of cohesion within a party as evidence of its leaders' political incompetence on the grounds that if leaders cannot convince their own MPs to support their policies, the leaders must not have good policies or must not be terribly persuasive politicians.

12. This misunderstanding appears to be independent of the electoral system because German voters exhibit a similar ambivalence toward the role of their MPs (Paltzelt 2000, 43–48).

13. I am not trotting out the common complaint that PR will result in unstable and ineffective government. Instead, the problem may well be that Canadian politics under PR will be too rigid in that Cabinet will always contain the same Liberal faces and produce the same Liberal policies regardless of electoral outcomes.

14. The Norwegian Storting (elected via list PR), for example, struck a commission to investigate the causes of public cynicism and disillusionment. German political commentators also worry about *verdrossenheit.* (voter disillusionment).

15. To avoid contradiction, I should note that my mixed system would ban candidates from simultaneously running in a constituency seat and on a party list. This is, however, a weak response to the "avoidance of defeat" problem because the top positions on every party list are, for all intents and purposes, invulnerable, a fact that only underscores my reservations about MMP.

16. Here again, I might argue that electoral reform is not quite the right answer to the problem. Regional tension is fuelled by a pattern of executive federalism that does not mesh well with our parliamentary institutions, and which is conducted by disjointed federal and provincial parties (Johnston 1980). In other words, Liberals in Ottawa are entirely different in personnel and philosophy from the Liberals in British Columbia. As a result, party affiliation does not help to bridge federal–provincial tensions as it does in the United States and Germany (Filippov, Ordeshook, and Shvetsova 2004). One might argue that the solution to this problem is to give the provinces a more direct stake in the federal Parliament, perhaps by reforming the Senate along the lines of the German *Bundesrat.* However, I think that electoral reformers make a reasonable argument when they point out the serious constitutional obstacles to Senate reform. To adhere to Senate reform under these conditions allows the perfect to be the enemy of the good.

17. This last assumption is not critical. The critical assumption is rather that voters equally weight the two issues, so that, for example, a voter sees the policy distance involved in moving from "not very" to "somewhat" on deficit reduction as about the same policy distance as moving from "not very" to "somewhat" on social program protection.

REFERENCES

Arrow, Kenneth. 1963. *Social Choice and Individual Values.* Second Edition. New Haven: Yale University Press.

Bricker, D., and M. Redfern. July–August 2001. "Canadian Perspectives on the Voting System." *Policy Options*: 22–24.

Filippov, M., P. Ordeshook, and O. Shvetsova. 2004. *Designing Federalism: A Theory of Self-Sustainable Federal Institutions*. New York: Cambridge University Press.

Gibbard. A. 1973. "Manipulation of Voting Schemes: A General Result." *Econometrica* 41: 587–601.

Johnston, R. 1980. "Federal and Provincial Voting: Contemporary Patterns and Historical Evolution." In D. Elkins and R. Simeon, eds., *Small Worlds: Parties and Provinces in Canadian Political Life*. Toronto: Methuen.

Johnston, R. July–August 2001. "A Conservative Case for Electoral Reform." *Policy Options*: 7–14.

Johnston, R., A. Blais, H. Brady, and J. Crête. 1992. *Letting the People Decide: Dynamics of a Canadian Election*. Montreal and Kingston: McGill-Queen's University Press.

Kam, C. Forthcoming. "Demotion and Dissent in the Canadian Liberal Party." *British Journal of Political Science*.

McDonald, M., S. Mendes, and I. Budge. 2004. "What Are Elections For? Conferring the Median Mandate," *British Journal of Political Science* 34: 1–26.

McKean, M., and E. Scheiner. 2000. "Japan's New Electoral System: la plus ça change..." *Electoral Studies* 19: 447–477.

McKelvey, R.D. 1976. "Intransitivities in Multidimensional Voting Models and Some Implications for Agenda Control." *Journal of Economic Theory* 12: 472–482.

Nevitte, N., A. Blais, E. Gidengil, and R. Nadeau. 1999. *Unsteady State: The 1997 Canadian Federal Election*. Don Mills: Oxford University Press.

Paltzelt. W. 2000. "What Can an Individual MP Do in German Parliamentary Politics." In L. Longley and R. Hazan, eds., *The Uneasy Relationship Between Parliamentary Members and Leaders*. London: Frank Cass.

Pharr, S., R. Putnam, and R. Dalton. 2000. "Trouble in the Advanced Democracies." *Journal of Democracy* 11(2): 5–25.

Pitkin, Hanna. 1967. *The Concept of Representation*. Berkeley: University of California Press.

Powell, G. Bingham. 2000. *Elections as Instruments of Democracy: Majoritarian and Proportional Visions*. New Haven: Yale University Press.

Powell, G. Bingham, and G. Vanberg. 2000. "Election Laws, Disproportionality and Median Correspondence: Implications for Two Visions of Democracy," *British Journal of Political Science* 30: 383–411.

Przerworski, A., S. Stokes, and B. Manin. 1999. *Democracy, Accountability, and Representation*. Cambridge: Cambridge University Press.

Riker, W. 1982. *Liberalism Against Populism*. San Francisco: Freeman.

Satterthwaite, M. 1975. "Strategy Proofness and Arrow's Conditions." *Journal of Economic Theory* 10: 187–217.

Shugart, M., and M. Wattenberg. 2003. *Mixed-Member Electoral Systems: The Best of Both Worlds*. Oxford: Oxford University Press.

Strøm, K. 1990. *Minority Government and Majority Rule*. New York: Cambridge University Press.

POSTSCRIPT

The two articles present some good arguments, but they also leave some questions unanswered. John Hiemstra and Harold Jansen nicely reveal the benefits of mixed-member proportional (MMP) system, but one wonders whether they understate the possible costs of such a system. Coalition governments, an inevitable result of MMP in Canada, may produce policies whose coherence is lacking. The benefit of single-member plurality (SMP) is that a single voice typically determines policy, but the multiple voices in MMP may produce government outputs that endeavour to satisfy the demands of the varied parties in government. Hiemstra and Jansen are little worried with the prospect of two types of MPs under MMP. But it seems possible that those unattached to a constituency may find themselves a little lost, especially in light of the fact that constituency work makes up the bulk of the work of most elected representatives. The two authors also applaud MMP because of its ability to ensure appropriate representation in government. But again one wonders. The presence of coalition governments will produce power arrangements in government that fail to reflect the distribution of the vote in the legislature. A minor party, with little of the popular vote, may team up with a more powerful party to secure its aims in exchange for support. In other words, there is no guarantee that the distribution of the popular vote will be recorded in the actions of government. MMP addresses concerns of representation in the legislative branch, but may have little effect on the distribution of support in the most powerful branch in parliamentary government—namely the executive branch.

In his article, Christopher Kam takes an interesting line of attack against MMP and its kinds. Most critics of proportional representation (PR) rely on the kind of arguments outlined in the preceding paragraph, but not Kam. He thinks the key consideration is the fact that voting is capable of producing multiple majorities. As a result, the claim that PR better represents the will of the people is baseless because there is no one real will of the people. In this kind of environment, the key is not to erect electoral systems that reflect wishes of voters, but rather ones that allow voters to better identity the true powers in government—which SMP nicely does. But do parliamentary systems really produce a cycling of policies, with one majority replacing another? As Kam himself says, cabinet control of the agenda and party discipline—key components of parliamentary government—can nullify this cycling effect. If so, then the argument against MPP on this ground seems to fall away.

Students wishing to pursue the subject of electoral reform might begin with Heather MacIvor's short overview of electoral reform in Heather MacIvor, "A Brief Introduction to Electoral Reform," in Henry Milner, ed., *Making Every Vote Count: Reassessing Canada's Electoral* System (Peterborough: Broadview Press, 1999). Other useful introductions to elections and electoral reforms are Eric Mintz, David Close, and Osvaldo Croci, *Politics, Power and the Common Good: An Introduction to Political Science* (Toronto: Pearson Education Canada, 2006), chapter 10; John Courtney, *Elections* (Vancouver: UBC Press, 2004), chapter 6; and Roger Gibbins and Loleen Youngman, "The Institutional Expression of Multiple Identities: The Electoral Reform Debate," in Thomas M.J. Bateman and Thomas Epp, eds., *Braving the New World: Readings in Contemporary Politics*, 3rd ed. (Toronto: Thomson Nelson, 2004). The next step is to dive into the detailed analyses of the first-past-the-post system and its main competitors. Here, students might start with J. Paul Johnston and Harvey E. Pasis, eds., *Representation and Electoral Systems: Canadian Perspectives* (Scarborough: Prentice-Hall, 1990). This text contains many of the classic articles on electoral reform in Canada, including the seminal article by Alan C. Cairns and the response to his article by J.A.A. Lovink. Most recent examinations of electoral reform (such as MMP) include Henry Milner, ed., *Making Every Vote Count: Reassessing Canada's Electoral System* (Peterborough: Broadview Press, 1999); Henry Milner, "The Case for Proportional Representation," in Hugh Thorburn and Alan Whitehorn, eds., *Party Politics in Canada*, 8th ed. (Scarborough: Prentice-Hall, 2001); Louis Massicotte, *Changing the Canadian Electoral System* (Montreal: Institute for Research on Public Policy, February 2001); and the entire July–August 2001 issue of *Policy Options*. A rigorous analysis of electoral reform and MMP can also be found in Law Commission of Canada, *Voting Counts: Electoral Reform in Canada* (Ottawa: Law Reform Commission, 2004). Students would be well-advised to read this report, which is available at the website of the Law Commission of Canada (some university libraries may also have hard copies).

The issue of electoral reform is not merely a matter of concern for academics. Provincial governments in Canada have been looking long and hard at this issue, and some seen poised to make some changes. For more on developments in the provinces, students should see Henry Milner, ed., *Steps Toward Making Every Step Count: Electoral Reform in Canada and Its Provinces* (Peterborough: Broadview Press, 2004). This text also offers good general articles on electoral reform, which makes it a book that must be read by all interested in this debate topic. A report related to this text is Henry Milner, "First Past the Post? Progress Report on Electoral Reform Initiatives in Canadian Provinces," in *Policy Matters* 5, no. 9 (September 2004).

The experience of other countries with the plurality system and proportional representation is relevant to the discussion of electoral reform in Canada. On this topic, the following might be consulted: Arend Lijphart and Bernard Grofman, eds., *Choosing an Electoral System: Issues and Alternatives* (New York: Praeger, 1984); Vernon Bogdanor and David Butler, eds., *Democracy and Elections: Electoral Systems and Their Political Consequences* (Cambridge: Cambridge University Press, 1983); and Michael Dummett, *Principles of Electoral Reform* (Oxford: Oxford University Press, 1997). Especially relevant are Matthew Soberg Shugart and Martin P. Wattenberg, ed., *Mixed-Member Electoral Systems: The Best of Both Worlds?* (Oxford: Oxford University Press, 2001), and the aforementioned

Steps Toward Making Every Vote Count: Electoral Reform in Canada and Its Provinces.
Both contain pieces on the operation of MMP in other countries. Also, special attention may be given to Arend Lijphart, "Democracies: Forms, Performance, and
Constitutional Engineering," *European Journal of Political Research* 25 (1994): 1–17.
What makes this article so central to the debate is that it denies that one must
concede a decline in the effectiveness of government in order to introduce PR. For
more on Lijphort's work, students might want to consult Arend Lijphort, *Patterns
of Democracy: Government Forms and Performance in Thirty-Six Countries* (New
Haven and London: Yale University Press, 1999), chapters 15–16.

Are "Dirty Hands" Necessary in Politics?

✔ **YES**
MICHAEL WALZER, "Political Action: The Problem of Dirty Hands,"
in *Philosophy and Public Affairs* 2, no. 2 (1973): 160–168, 174

✘ **NO**
DAVID P. SHUGARMAN, "Democratic Dirty Hands?" in Paul Rynard and
David P. Shugarman, eds., *Cruelty and Deception: The Controversy Over
Dirty Hands in Politics* (Peterborough: Broadview Press, 2000)

Political life in Canada includes public officials who act questionably and then protest that no wrong was done. Some of these actions are clearly corrupt while others may be trying to serve some public purpose—either way, the public official will deny that a moral issue is involved. Most of us want little to do with politicians who engage in these kinds of actions, especially those who act solely for private gain. But there are some morally suspect public officials to whom we extend some degree of acceptance. These are politicians who are required to act undesirably—to break a law or utter a falsehood—in order to serve the public interest. They know they are acting wrongly, and we may know it too, but the circumstances demand action that would be ordinarily condemned. What differentiates this kind of politician from the morally bankrupt type is the recognition of some moral wrong being committed. A feeling of guilt and remorse attends the former type of politician while no such feeling is found in the latter.

The expression "the ends justify the means" is often used to describe the phenomenon of people acting badly for the purpose of achieving a greater good. In political life, it is called "dirty-hands politics." Time and time again, elected (and appointed) officials face a difficult dilemma: whether to take an action that might benefit many but would constitute an improper or even immoral act. There is the presidential hopeful who has the capacity to do good things for his or her country, but who must make shadowy deals with unsavoury types to win office. There is also the country's chief law enforcement officer who must break the law in order to provide for public safety. When examined closely, political life appears rife with dirty-hands situations. Recently, it was alleged that funds from a government program aimed at raising the profile of Canada in Quebec were improperly used to support the Liberal Party of Canada. The revelations disturbed many Canadians, but some said that this was a small price to pay for fighting the separatist threat. The party leaders knew they were doing wrong, but the unity of the country was at stake.

In some countries, dirty hands are not really an issue. The precariousness of rule and the weakness of moral and legal codes make this the case. However, in democracies, dirty hands are a concern. Democracies like to think of themselves as based on the rule of law and observant of accepted moral practices. Accordingly, dirty-hands politics fits uneasily into democratic life. Nevertheless, there are some who believe that democracies must accept politicians with dirty hands. Without this acceptance, public life would suffer and even the security of a country could be put at risk. At the extreme, it is thought that the moral politician—one who refuses to practise dirty-hands politics—is dangerous.

But many adherents to democracy have trouble with dirty hands in politics. For them, what seems dangerous is not the threat to morality in politics, but rather the acceptance of a type of politics that so clearly contradicts democratic practice. Dirty-hands politics invites us into a world of calculation in which we count on all-knowing leaders to decide whether to observe laws and moral precepts. It also assumes that the beneficial effects of our acts are well known, that a politician who breaks the law or lies to the electorate knows with certainty that all will turn out well. But life, especially political life, is rarely so certain. To observe understood rules seems safe, and certainly more consistent with democratic practices. There may be short-run costs with such a stance (some advantageous consequence may be lost), but the long-term gain will be appreciable: democracy will be strengthened. In the end, dirty-hands politics amounts to a kind of "moral Machiavellianism," in which any action is fine so long as it results in a beneficial outcome and so long as the individual undertaking the action possesses a guilty conscience.

In the readings, Michael Walzer, a professor in the School of Social Science at the Institute for Advanced Study in Princeton, New Jersey, argues for the acceptance of politicians with dirty hands. David P. Shugarman, a political science professor at York University in Toronto, contends that dirty-hands politics rarely has a place in any democracy.

✔ **YES**
Political Action:
The Problem of Dirty Hands
MICHAEL WALZER

In an earlier issue of *Philosophy & Public Affairs* there appeared a symposium on the rules of war which was actually (or at least more importantly) a symposium on another topic.[1] The actual topic was whether or not a man can ever face, or ever has to face, a moral dilemma, a situation where he must choose between two courses of action both of which it would be wrong for him to undertake. Thomas Nagel worriedly suggested that this could happen and that it did happen whenever someone was forced to choose between upholding an important moral principle and avoiding some looming disaster.[2] R.B. Brandt argued that it could not possibly happen, for there were guidelines we might follow and calculations we might go through which would necessarily yield the conclusion that one or the other course of action was the right one to undertake in the circumstances (or that it did not matter which we undertook). R.M. Hare explained how it was that someone might wrongly suppose that he was faced with a moral dilemma: sometimes, he suggested, the precepts and principles of an ordinary man, the products of his moral education, come into conflict with injunctions developed at a higher level of moral discourse. But this conflict is, or ought to be, resolved at the higher level; there is no real dilemma.

I am not sure that Hare's explanation is at all comforting, but the question is important even if no such explanation is possible, perhaps especially so if this is the case. The argument relates not only to the coherence and harmony of the moral universe, but also to the relative ease or difficulty—or impossibility—of living a moral life. It is not, therefore, merely a philosopher's question. If such a dilemma can arise, whether frequently or very rarely, any of us might one day face it. Indeed, many men have faced it, or think they have, especially men involved in political activity or war. The dilemma, exactly as Nagel describes it, is frequently discussed in the literature of political action—in novels and plays dealing with politics and in the work of theorists too.

In modern times the dilemma appears most often as the problem of "dirty hands," and it is typically stated by the Communist leader Hoerderer in Sartre's play of that name: "I have dirty hands right up to the elbows. I've plunged them in filth and blood. Do you think you can govern innocently?"[3] My own answer is no, I don't think I could govern innocently; nor do most of us believe that those who govern us are innocent—as I shall argue below—even the best of them. But this does not mean that it isn't possible to do the right thing while governing. It means that a particular act of government (in a political party or in the state) may be exactly the right thing to do in utilitarian terms and yet leave the man who does it guilty of a moral wrong. The innocent man, afterwards, is no longer innocent.

If on the other hand he remains innocent, chooses, that is, the "absolutist" side of Nagel's dilemma, he not only fails to do the right thing (in utilitarian terms), he may also fail to measure up to the duties of his office (which imposes on him a considerable responsibility for consequences and outcomes). Most often, of course, political leaders accept the utilitarian calculation; they try to measure up. One might offer a number of sardonic comments on this fact, the most obvious being that by the calculations they usually make they demonstrate the great virtues of the "absolutist" position. Nevertheless, we would not want to be governed by men who consistently adopted that position.

The notion of dirty hands derives from an effort to refuse "absolutism" without denying the reality of the moral dilemma. Though this may appear to utilitarian philosophers to pile confusion upon confusion, I propose to take it very seriously. For the literature I shall examine is the work of serious and often wise men, and it reflects, though it may also have helped to shape, popular thinking about politics. It is important to pay attention to that too. I shall do so without assuming, as Hare suggests one might, that everyday moral and political discourse constitutes a distinct level of argument, where content is largely a matter of pedagogic expediency.[4] If popular views are resistant (as they are) to utilitarianism, there may be something to learn from that and not merely something to explain about it.

I

Let me begin, then, with a piece of conventional wisdom to the effect that politicians are a good deal worse, morally worse, than the rest of us (it is the wisdom of the rest of us). Without either endorsing it or pretending to disbelieve it, I am going to expound this convention. For it suggests that the dilemma of dirty hands is a central feature of political life, that it arises not merely as an occasional crisis in the career of this or that unlucky politician but systematically and frequently.

Why is the politician singled out? Isn't he like the other entrepreneurs in an open society, who hustle, lie, intrigue, wear masks, smile and are villains? He is not, no doubt for many reasons, three of which I need to consider. First of all, the politician claims to play a different part than other entrepreneurs. He doesn't merely cater to our interests; he acts on our behalf, even in our name. He has purposes in mind, causes and projects that require the support and redound to the benefit, not of each of us individually, but of all of us together. He hustles, lies and intrigues *for us*—or so he claims. Perhaps he is right, or at least sincere, but we suspect that he acts for himself also. Indeed, he cannot serve us without serving himself, for success brings him power and glory, the greatest rewards that men can win from their fellows. The competition for these two is fierce; the risks are often great, but the temptations are greater. We imagine ourselves succumbing. Why should our representatives act differently? Even if they would like to act differently, they probably cannot: for other men are all too ready to hustle and lie for power and glory, and it is the others who set the terms of the competition.

Hustling and lying are necessary because power and glory are so desirable—that is, so widely desired. And so the men who act for us and in our name are necessarily hustlers and liars.

Politicians are also thought to be worse than the rest of us because they rule over us, and the pleasures of ruling are much greater than the pleasures of being ruled. The successful politician becomes the visible architect of our restraint. He taxes us, licenses us, forbids and permits us, directs us to this or that distant goal—all for our greater good. Moreover, he takes chances for our greater good that put us, or some of us, in danger. Sometimes he puts himself in danger too, but politics, after all, is his adventure. It is not always ours. There are undoubtedly times when it is good or necessary to direct the affairs of other people and to put them in danger. But we are a little frightened of the man who seeks, ordinarily and every day, the power to do so. And the fear is reasonable enough. The politician has, or pretends to have, a kind of confidence in his own judgment that the rest of us know to be presumptuous in any man.

The presumption is especially great because the victorious politician uses violence and the threat of violence—not only against foreign nations in our defence but also against us, and again ostensibly for our greater good. This is a point emphasized and perhaps overemphasized by Max Weber in his essay "Politics as a Vocation."[5] It has not, so far as I can tell, played an overt or obvious part in the development of the convention I am examining. The stock figure is the lying, not the murderous, politician—though the murderer lurks in the background, appearing most often in the form of the revolutionary or terrorist, very rarely as an ordinary magistrate or official. Nevertheless, the sheer weight of official violence in human history does suggest the kind of power to which politicians aspire, the kind of power they want to wield, and it may point to the roots of our half-conscious dislike and unease. The men who act for us and in our name are often killers, or seem to become killers too quickly and too easily.

Knowing all this or most of it, good and decent people still enter political life, aiming at some specific reform or seeking a general reformation. They are then required to learn the lesson Machiavelli first set out to teach: "how not to be good."[6] Some of them are incapable of learning; many more profess to be incapable. But they will not succeed unless they learn, for they have joined the terrible competition for power and glory; they have chosen to work and struggle as Machiavelli says, among "so many who are not good." They can do no good themselves unless they win the struggle, which they are unlikely to do unless they are willing and able to use the necessary means. So we are suspicious even of the best of winners. It is not a sign of our perversity if we think them only more clever than the rest. They have not won, after all, because they were good, or not only because of that, but also because they were not good. No one succeeds in politics without getting his hands dirty. This is conventional wisdom again, and again I don't mean to insist that it is true without qualification. I repeat it only to disclose the moral dilemma inherent in the convention. For sometimes it is right to try to succeed, and then it must also be right to get one's hands dirty. But one's hands get dirty from doing what it is wrong to do. And how can it be wrong to do what is right? Or, how can we get our hands dirty by doing what we ought to do?

II

It will be best to turn quickly to some examples. I have chosen two, one relating to the struggle for power and one to its exercise. I should stress that in both these cases the men who face the dilemma of dirty hands have in an important sense chosen to do so; the cases tell us nothing about what it would be like, so to speak, to fall into the dilemma; nor shall I say anything about that here. Politicians often argue that they have no right to keep their hands clean, and that may well be true of them, but it is not so clearly true of the rest of us. Probably we do have a right to avoid, if we possibly can, those positions in which we might be forced to do terrible things. This might be regarded as the moral equivalent of our legal right not to incriminate ourselves. Good men will be in no hurry to surrender it, though there are reasons for doing so sometimes, and among these are or might be the reasons good men have for entering politics. But let us imagine a politician who does not agree to that: he wants to do good only by doing good, or at least he is certain that he can stop short of the most corrupting and brutal uses of political power. Very quickly that certainty is tested. What do we think of him then?

He wants to win the election, someone says, but he doesn't want to get his hands dirty. This is meant as a disparagement, even though it also means that the man being criticized is the sort of man who will not lie, cheat, bargain behind the backs of his supporters, shout absurdities at public meetings or manipulate other men and women. Assuming that this particular election ought to be won, it is clear, I think, that the disparagement is justified. If the candidate didn't want to get his hands dirty, he should have stayed at home; if he can't stand the heat, he should get out of the kitchen, and so on. His decision to run was a commitment (to all of us who think the election important) to try to win, that is, to do within rational limits whatever is necessary to win. But the candidate is a moral man. He has principles and a history of adherence to those principles. That is why we are supporting him. Perhaps when he refuses to dirty his hands, he is simply insisting on being the sort of man he is. And isn't that the sort of man we want?

Let us look more closely at this case. In order to win the election the candidate must make a deal with a dishonest ward boss, involving the granting of contracts for school construction over the next four years. Should he make the deal? Well, at least he shouldn't be surprised by the offer, most of us would probably say (a conventional piece of sarcasm). And he should accept it or not, depending on exactly what is at stake in the election. But that is not the candidate's view. He is extremely reluctant even to consider the deal, puts off his aides when they remind him of it, refuses to calculate its possible effects upon the campaign. Now, if he is acting this way because the very thought of bargaining with that particular ward boss makes him feel unclean, his reluctance isn't very interesting. His feelings by themselves are not important. But he may also have reasons for his reluctance. He may know, for example, that some of his supporters support him precisely because they believe he is a good man, and this means to them a man who won't make such deals. Or he may doubt his own motives for considering the deal, wondering whether it is the political campaign or his own candidacy that makes the bargain at all tempting. Or he may believe that if he makes deals of this sort now he may not be able later on to achieve those ends that make the campaign worthwhile, and he may not feel entitled to take such risks with a future that is not only his own future. Or he may simply think that the deal is dishonest and therefore wrong, corrupting not only himself but all those human relations in which he is involved.

Because he has scruples of this sort, we know him to be a good man. But we view the campaign in a certain light, estimate its importance in a certain way, and hope that he will overcome his scruples and make the deal. It is important to stress that we don't want just *anyone* to make the deal; we want *him* to make it, precisely because he has scruples about it. We know he is doing right when he makes the deal because he knows he is doing wrong. I don't mean merely that he will feel badly or even very badly after he makes the deal. If he is the good man I am imagining him to be, he will feel guilty, that is, he will believe himself to be guilty. That is what it means to have dirty hands.

All this may become clearer if we look at a more dramatic example, for we are, perhaps, a little blasé about political deals and disinclined to worry much about the man who makes one. So consider a politician who has seized upon a national crisis—a prolonged colonial war—to reach for power. He and his friends win office pledged to decolonization and peace; they are honestly committed to both, though not without some sense of the advantages of the commitment. In any case, they have no responsibility for the war; they have steadfastly opposed it. Immediately, the politician goes off to the colonial capital to open negotiations with the rebels. But the capital is in the grip of a terrorist campaign, and the first decision the new leader faces is this: he is asked to authorize the torture of a captured rebel leader who knows or probably knows the location of a number of bombs hidden in apartment buildings around the city, set to go off within the next twenty-four hours. He orders the man tortured, convinced that he must do so for the sake of the people who might otherwise die in the explosions—even though he believes that torture is wrong, indeed abominable, not just sometimes, but always.[7] He had expressed this belief often and angrily during his own campaign; the rest of us took it as a sign of his goodness. How should we regard him now? (How should he regard himself?)

Once again, it does not seem enough to say that he should feel very badly. But why not? Why shouldn't he have feelings like those of St. Augustine's melancholy soldier, who understood both that his war was just and that killing, even in a just war, is a terrible thing to do?[8] The difference is that Augustine did not believe that it was wrong to kill in a just war; it was just sad, or the sort of thing a good man would be saddened by. But he might have thought it wrong to torture in a just war, and later Catholic theorists have certainly thought it wrong. Moreover, the politician I am imagining thinks it wrong, as do many of us who supported him. Surely we have a right to expect more than melancholy from him now. When he ordered the prisoner tortured, he committed a moral crime and he accepted a moral burden. Now he is a guilty man. His willingness to acknowledge and bear (and perhaps to repent and do penance for) his guilt is evidence, and it is the only evidence he can offer us, both that he is not too good for politics and that he is good enough. Here is the moral politician: it is by his dirty hands that we know him. If he were a moral man and nothing else, his hands would not be dirty; if he were a politician and nothing else, he would pretend that they were clean.

[...]

That is the dilemma of dirty hands as it has been experienced by political actors and written about in literature of political action. I don't want to argue that it is only a political dilemma. No doubt we can get our hands dirty in private life also, and sometimes, no doubt, we should. But the issue is posed most dramatically in politics for the three reasons that make political life the kind of life it is, because we claim to act for others but also serve ourselves, rule over others, and use violence against them. It is easy to get one's hands dirty in politics and it is often right to do so.

NOTES

An earlier version of this paper was read at the annual meeting of the Conference for the Study of Political Thought in New York, April 1971. I am indebted to Charles Taylor, who served as commentator at that time and encouraged me to think that its arguments might be right.

1. *Philosophy & Public Affairs* 1, no. 2 (Winter 1971/72): Thomas Nagel, "War and Massacre," pp. 123–144; R.B. Brandt, "Utilitarianism and the Rules of War," pp. 145–165; and R.M. Hare, "Rules of War and Moral Reasoning," pp. 168–181.

2. For Nagel's description of a possible "moral blind alley," see "War and Massacre," pp. 142–144. Bernard Williams has made a similar suggestion, though without quite acknowledging it as his own: "many people can recognize the thought that a certain course of action is, indeed, the best thing to do on the whole in the circumstances, but that doing it involves doing something wrong" (*Morality: An Introduction to Ethics* [New York, 1972], p. 93).

3. Jean-Paul Sartre, *Dirty Hands,* in *No Exit and Three Other Plays,* trans. Lionel Abel (New York, n.d.), p. 224.

4. Hare, "Rules of War and Moral Reasoning," pp. 173–178, esp. p. 174: "the simple principles of the deontologist ... have their place at the level of character-formation (moral education and self-education)."

5. In *From Max Weber: Essays in Sociology,* trans. and ed. Hans H. Gerth and C. Wright Mills (New York, 1946), pp. 77–128.

6. See *The Prince,* chap. XV; cf. *The Discourses,* bk. I, chaps. IX and XVIII. I quote from the Modern Library edition of the two works (New York, 1950), p. 57.

7. I leave aside the question of whether the prisoner is himself responsible for the terrorist campaign. Perhaps he opposed it in meetings of the rebel organization. In any case, whether he deserves to be punished or not, he does not deserve to be tortured.

8. Other writers argued that Christians must never kill, even in a just war; and there was also an intermediate position which suggests the origins of the idea of dirty hands. Thus Basil The Great (Bishop of Caesarea in the fourth century A.D.): "Killing in war was differentiated by our fathers from murder ... nevertheless, perhaps it would be well that those whose hands are unclean abstain from communion for three years." Here dirty hands are a kind of impurity or unworthiness, which is not the same as guilt, though closely related to it. For a general survey of these and other Christian views, see Roland H. Bainton, *Christian Attitudes Toward War and Peace* (New York, 1960), esp. chaps. 5–7.

✗ NO
Democratic Dirty Hands?
DAVID P. SHUGARMAN

DIRTY HANDS OR BASIC HUMANITY?

The theoretical defence of dirty hands has to be understood as an ethical argument which, from the perspective of those making the connection, sets out the best way of combining morality with power. Walzer presents two examples to demonstrate what dirty-hands acts are and why they ought to be approved. They are meant to illustrate the nature of the moral problems faced by decent politicians and to persuade us that choosing to be devious and cruel, despite our normal repugnance to so act, is at times the best way to operate. In my view they are, to the contrary, useful examples for showing serious weakness not only in Walzer's updated version of moral Machiavellism but in the dirty-hands position generally, especially when we consider its repercussions and implications for democratic politics.

The first of Walzer's examples I want to review is the one he regards as the more dramatic of the two. In point of fact it is, in Walzer's discussion, his second example. I want to begin with it because it is a cruelty case, clearly much "bloodier" than the other example, but I will argue that, ironically, in important respects it is not a persuasive example of dirty hands. Walzer presents us with a politician who comes to national power while his country is at war with a colony. He wins election on a platform promising decolonization and peace, and his commitments are genuine. However, as soon as the new leader arrives in the colony to negotiate a peace settlement, he finds that terrorists have placed bombs in various apartment buildings in the capital, and they are set for detonation within hours. Luckily, a terrorist leader has been captured who is thought, on good grounds, to know where the bombs are. But the terrorist won't talk. So the national leader, who had made it clear in his campaigning that he regards torture as an absolute evil, orders the man tortured to try to get him to divulge the whereabouts of the bombs before hundreds or thousands of innocent people are blown up. That is the end of the scenario. We don't know whether the torture tactics paid off or not.

Now, there is something terribly contrived, almost to the point of being incredible, about this example: if this is meant as a *realpolitik* illustration, it is difficult to believe that anti-colonialist forces would engage in terrorism the day that a new leader, elected on a platform of effectively giving up the fight against independence, arrives to negotiate a transfer of power. Also, the new leader might well have considered other options: prevailing upon the rebel terrorist to reconsider, given the new government and new policy; ordering the evacuation of everybody in the apartments within twenty-four hours (which might have the effect of weakening the terrorists' standing with their public and, furthermore, might have moved the terrorist leader to co-operate); but no, Walzer treats this as an *in extremis* situation. There is no other option; this is the politician's last chance to save lives. But we can set aside questions about the credibility of the scenario to focus on whether or not this is really an account of dirty hands and to examine what, for Walzer, is the moral of the story.

What is especially important to Walzer's account, and what makes his contribution to the dirty-hands problem so interesting and innovative, is that we are asked to understand that this is a leader who knowingly authorizes commission of a moral crime and is willing to accept a moral burden, which is his guilt. It is the acknowledgement and acceptance of guilt, says Walzer, that "is the only evidence he can offer us, both that he is not too good for politics and that he is good enough." The national leader is then Walzer's archetypal "moral politician" who is so because we see his dirty hands: "If he were a moral man and nothing else, his hands would not be dirty; if he were a politician and nothing else, he would pretend that they were clean."[1] This is a seductive account of an ideal leader landing in a crisis situation and dealing with it. He does so both by accepting a moral paradox that meets the social psychology of decent citizens and by expressing that paradox as a result of his strength of character, his own individual psychology. I think there are important problems with such an account.

Consider some other difficult critical situations we could find ourselves in. Normally, we don't physically push people: but pushing someone out of the way of an oncoming vehicle is hardly a dirty-hands illustration—though he or she may be bruised and shaken by the push; and pushing or pulling a child away from another child whom the first child is about to strike with a dangerous object may be paternalistic, but it's not dirty hands. There is no reason in either of these cases for someone to feel guilty about intervening. Injury or deceit is not involved, but it is easy to imagine cases where either could be necessary. Imagine pretending to be wealthy and promising a million dollars to a gullible kidnapper who is about to beat up your spouse and child unless you pay a ransom; after he releases them, you renege on the promise. Imagine having to kill or torture someone to get a key he or she is carrying that will open the freezer in which this person has locked your spouse or child, when the police and locksmiths are hours away. You are a good person, you don't normally deceive people, you believe keeping your word is a mark of your integrity and humanity, you've never killed anyone, are against capital punishment, and feel strongly about the importance of Article 5 of the United Nations Declaration of Human Rights that forbids torture and inhuman treatment. In the extreme situations I've instanced, you wouldn't be wrong to do what you wouldn't normally do, and while you might regret having to do what you did, there would be no reason for you to feel guilty or to be punished.

I suggest here that in such cases, one has to see the need to move away from absolutist deontology—the one that says, "I have a duty to myself and others never to depart from the moral principles I believe that I and everyone else mu⸢

follow"—and to recognize when an exceptional circumstance, an extreme situation, requires making an exception to generally sound ethical principles. In this view, recourse to dirty hands is an extreme exception to democratic politics rather than a staple of it and resort to such tactics is the result of a failure of politics and a turn to war. We would be mistaken to think of this as a move or "surrender" to consequentialism. Of course, unless we thought about the consequences of our act and those of not doing it, we wouldn't know whether to call this an exceptional circumstance or not. But such a move is also consistent with the notion of duty to humanity, and can be an expression of our humanity—considerations fundamental to Kantian moral philosophy, though departing from Kant's own commitment to an exceptionless categorical imperative and his rejection of considering the consequences of actions. It is a mistake to see such a move as one away from principles, as unprincipled and compromising (using compromise in a derogatory fashion). It is misleading to depict the world as a place where most people can be expected to be, and expect others to be, pure deontologists *except* for "gifted" politicians who are expected to know that they cannot be.

[...]

FAIR ELECTIONS?

The other example of a defensible dirty-handed move that Walzer provides focuses on trickery and illegalities rather than on cruelty, but in some respects it is more disturbing. It has to do with the rigging of an election. An honest leader deliberates on whether to make a deal with a corrupt ward boss. In return for delivering votes, the ward boss demands that the politician, once elected, pay him back with a number of school construction contracts. The politician would be buying votes and committing himself to deliver favours with public funds—patronage. Walzer suggests that when the stakes are high enough, his hypothetical candidate (is he hypothetical? Jack Kennedy apparently did make deals with the Mafia, as well as with shady ward bosses in Illinois to win Chicago, and the state in 1960) will set aside his scruples and make the deal. And, says Walzer, "we want him to make it, precisely because he has scruples about it."[2]

There are several serious problems with this example.[3] First, there is a potentially dangerous contagion effect of supporting and applauding people who contravene rules governing fair elections: if it gets around that this is what it takes to win, it will be difficult to expect others not to do so in the future.[4] A similar point was made by Justice Brandeis of the US Supreme Court seventy years ago: "Decency, security and liberty alike demand that government officials shall be subject to the same rules of conduct that are commands to the citizen. In a government of laws, existence of the government will be imperiled if it fails to ˥aw scrupulously. Crime is contagious. If the government becomes a ⌐ls contempt for law."[5] There is also something obviously con- . supposedly democratic politician flouting fundamental values

333

of democracy. "The cultivation of the capacity for judicious vice in the ruler sits oddly with the values of public accountability and relative openness characteristic of genuine democracy."[6]

Then (as was also problematic in the first example) the claim that citizens can know a politician and his psyche so intimately that they understand how badly he's going to feel is dubious. In the US people running for the kinds of positions where dirty hands might make a difference—governor, senator, president—spend hundreds of thousands, usually millions of dollars on public relations, advertising campaigns, and public opinion polls to project both an image and an attractive platform. During an election campaign, people have enough trouble getting important issues clarified without being expected to know a candidate's inner motives and deeply held moral convictions.

Additionally, Walzer's "we" in this case is outrageously presumptuous. While it no doubt includes members of Nixon's Committee to Reelect the President—who helped organize and finance support for the Watergate burglars and White House plumbers, and who were convinced they were supporting a great American to achieve great goals—it doesn't include me, nor should it include people who value democratic procedures and principles and are prepared to live by them, even when their agenda and candidates may be defeated.

The notion that winning elections justifies rigging them calls for a remarkably schizoid moral sensibility on the part of both leaders and led. It requires a belief in the tragic heroism of a moral expert who can be trusted to be dishonest because he has carefully weighed the ethical costs of dishonesty against the ethical benefits of what that dishonesty will bring and who will experience psychological trauma as a result. In fact, Walzer's example collides with the theory it is supposed to strengthen when we ask how his successful politician is to do penance. Why would a successful politician feel or admit guilt at having done something that paid off in victory and that was done with the assumed consent of his supporters? How would a successful politician be punished? By not electing him again? Why?

What this example recommends is excusing fraud at election time, nullifying the value of elections. People then consent to an empty mandate. But we cannot claim that the dirty hands are democratic, any more than we could use the term *democratic* to refer to bogus elections. The proposition that it is democratic for a democracy to disenfranchise itself is logically and practically incoherent. It is like saying that, as an example of their freedom, free persons will voluntarily submit themselves to slavery. In this regard, "free slaves" and "democratic dirty hands" are not paradoxes, they are oxymorons.[7]

DEFENSIBLE AND INDEFENSIBLE DIRTY HANDS

There are a number of different facets or aspects of dirty-hands deeds; clearly, some are acceptable in extreme circumstances. In this regard there is the humorous example of the British military officer portrayed by Peter Sellers in the anti-war movie *Dr. Strangelove*. The Sellers character is stationed at a US nuclear-bomber air-command base commanded by a renegade madman who, using a secret code, signals American warplanes to drop nuclear weapons on Russian sites. When the British officer finds out what has happened, he first tries to reason with the base commander, then, realising he is dealing with insanity, tries to play along in order to extract the code and halt the bombing mission. When the base comes under attack by loyal American troops, the commander kills himself. The Sellers character attempts to phone the White House to inform the President of what has happened. But the base's military phone lines have been cut, and the only phone that is still working is a pay phone. The long-distance operator refuses to put a call through until Sellers pays for a connection, so he breaks into the coin depository of a nearby soda pop machine—and is berated by another soldier for this violation of private property, despite the fact that the change for the phone call might prevent nuclear war.

So a good man tries deception, then breaks the law to try to avert disaster. This is a dirty-hands case, but in a conventional rather than Walzerian sense. The notion that the Sellers character should feel guilty for shooting up a pop machine or trying to deceive a crazed warmonger, and that he or we should think he has done something seriously wrong in order to do right, is as bizarre, ludicrous, and dangerously confusing as the situation he finds himself in. Of course, he has not had to torture or kill anyone to try to get the secret code, but, if he had, "we" would have thought it justifiable and we would not expect him to be punished for it.

Now let us consider two examples that come without any satirical intent and that are unacceptable. They concern recent unfortunate historical cases. MKULTRA was a program of mind-control experimentation funded and organized by the American Central Intelligence Agency and implemented at the Allen Memorial Institute of McGill University in Montreal by its director, Dr. Ewan Cameron. At least 77 persons who thought they were being given the best treatment possible to cure their psychological problems were instead used as part of a program to investigate mind-control techniques. They were given a hallucinogen (the drug LSD) and assorted other experimental drugs without their permission or knowledge. Stansfield Turner, a director of the CIA during Jimmy Carter's presidency, wrote that the unit conducting these experiments had an enormous grant of autonomy from oversight or review "and a few well-intentioned, but terribly misguided individuals badly abused the CIA's privilege of keeping secret so much of what it does." In a democracy, according to Turner, "we should never turn over the custody of [high ethical] ideals to any group of individuals who divorce themselves from concern for the public attitude. The crimes against humanity perpetrated by zealots ... are too many, [and] without accountability the temptations of acting in secret [are] too great."[8]

One response to MKULTRA offers an example, one of the few,[9] of a dirty-hands public servant who seems to have been troubled at the time and later aware that deceptive treatment and duplicitous use of mental patients was morally problematic and perhaps even wrong: appearing before the US Senate Select Intelligence and Human Resources Committee, one of the principal figures in charge of the MKULTRA program, Dr. Sidney Gottlieb, testified that all the work he did and authorized was "extremely unpleasant, extremely difficult, extremely sensitive." But, sounding like someone who saw himself as a noble warrior fighting the good fight of the Cold War, Gottlieb also testified it was "above all ... extremely urgent and important."[10] The fact that over 70 people had their psyches disturbed for years and, in some cases, had their lives ruined was a price they were unfortunate enough to be required to pay for "desirable ends," such as counteracting the efforts of communist countries to brainwash Western operatives and soldiers. They paid by being subjected to the kind of brainwashing "we" wanted to be able to counter or inflict on the other side.

Our final example refers to the infamous presidency of Richard Nixon. In 1969–70, the Nixon administration secretly approved over 3600 B-52 air attacks against suspected Viet Cong and North Vietnamese installations in Cambodia. These attacks were kept secret from Congressional committees and authorities. Large parts of Cambodia were devastated, thousands of Cambodians were killed; it made no appreciable difference to how the Americans fared in Vietnam, but it contributed to the strengthening of the Khmer Rouge, who then ended up slaughtering their own people in one of the most brutal campaigns of this century. The secret bombing of a nation with which the Americans were not at war owed much to the devious minds and machinations of Henry Kissinger, Nixon, and Alexander Haig.

As Nixon's right-hand man in foreign affairs (first as national security advisor, then as secretary of state), Kissinger enjoyed a reckless, imperialistic, and hubris-filled tenure, apparently failing to appreciate that he was living in a democratic society in the twentieth century. Tony Judt points out that Kissinger was fascinated by, and identified with, the diplomacy and politics of Count Metternich and believed they were applicable to contemporary international relations.[11] However, Metternich operated in an early nineteenth-century hereditary Austrian empire. As Judt notes, this was a context where "all power was vested in the emperor and his ministers. There were no constitutional constraints, no electoral constituencies to placate or inform, no committees to consult. The imperial foreign minister and chancellor answered only to his emperor and to their shared view of the imperial interest."[12] Kissinger—a Nobel Peace Prize winner, respected scholar, and towering figure in public policy—had hands that were continually filthy. He saw himself representing America's best interests and was unwilling and unprepared to let democratic demands get in the way of his Machiavellian maneuvers. Like his president, he was obsessed with, and talented at, concealment and the spreading of disinformation. The historical record shows, says Judt, that Kissinger was "resistant to the constraints of policy-making in a constitutional republic with multiple governing branches." As practical examples of an outstanding dirty-hands leader on dirty-hands programs, Kissinger, the bombing of Cambodia, and the MKULTRA program offer us powerful evidence for rejecting the arguments of moral Machiavellism.

What I think the examples show (and we could have added Lyndon Johnson's lies in 1964 about being the "peace candidate," Watergate, Iran-Contra, RCMP dirty tricks, and many others)[13] is that the dirty-hands position is terribly misleading, insofar as it seeks to convey a great truth about the close relationship between leadership, morality, and democracy. The picture painted of the dirty-hands leader is a composite of wily negotiator, clever manipulator, no-nonsense general, and "father-knows-best" moral actor. It is a highly romanticized view of leadership and a dangerous one. The only place we find such leaders is in hero-producing histories, fiction, and Hollywood movies. It is dangerous for precisely those reasons that Acton and Mill appreciated, and that ethical realists at times so acutely emphasize, but at other times unfortunately neglect: the use of power without checks and balances leads to its abuse.[14]

Dirty-hands defenders accuse their allegedly deontological opponents of being too moral (or of being moral purists), but the moral Machiavellian position is, in fact, buoyed by a moral righteousness of its own, the sense that, because of the high stakes and the nature of one's opponents, a leader needs to act in support of a cause in ways that are beyond normal judgements of good and evil. There may be something to this as an *in extremis* rationale, so long as we are addressing reactions in life and death situations and during war, but this is, I suggest, light years away from justifying electioneering trickery. Yet Walzer's treatment of the logic of dirty hands remains the same for both his dramatic and pedestrian examples.

With respect to *in extremis* issues, it is instructive to refer to the meaning of "hard cases" in law. Moral Machiavellians see politics as an arena of hard cases where leaders must repeatedly overcome adversity and prevent great suffering. When judicial decisions depart from normal principles of law to meet cases of hardship—suffering, privation, adversity—the term used to describe such an outcome is "hard case." It is generally recognized that "hard cases make bad law." In a like manner, we ought not to let hard, exceptional cases determine how we are to operate and understand the workings of ethical politics in a democracy. To deal with special circumstances, we may very well require the admission of exceptions to generally recognized, practical principles of ethical conduct. It is a mistake, however, to make the exception the rule.

Operating on democratic principles means that when an important plan of action is contemplated, a context of relevant information and the reasons for the plan should be widely disseminated, easily accessible, and addressed to the largest possible audience of citizens. As Sissela Bok argues, *where there is a case to be made for departing from accepted norms, reasons should, nonetheless, appeal to generally recognized considerations of justice in social relations.* We need to ask questions like: Does the recommended deviation prevent or reduce harm? Does it contribute to achieving benefit? Is it the thing to do because of considerations of fairness? Does it contribute to trustworthiness and so serve the cause of veracity?[15] If these considerations figured in political deliberations, and if citizens and not their representatives were to decide on the acceptability of probable risks, it would not be easy to get one's hands dirty in politics, and it would seldom be right to do so.

Moral Machiavellians, in contrast, contend that the only ways of dealing with dirty-handed politicians are for citizens to be willing to get their own hands dirty or to be spectacularly discriminating and psychologically prescient when choosing leaders. In other words, we should be electing leaders who we expect will do the nasty things they think need to be done on our behalf and then feel terrible about it, so terrible that they would welcome punishment. Indeed, Walzer tells us that the main failing in Machiavelli's own articulation of dirty hands is that "he does not specify the state of mind appropriate to a man with dirty hands."[16] So here the main checks on a leader's wide discretion and possible abuse of power are not constitutional rules, political institutions, or democratic values, but rather the psychology of the individual mover and shaker. This is a position that has little practical purchase because, as Walzer himself points out, "In most cases of dirty hands moral rules are broken for reasons of state ... [and] moral rules are not usually enforced against [this] sort of actor largely because he acts in an official capacity."[17] In defending dirty hands and trying to find a place for them within democracy, Walzer is reduced to emphasizing the need for a political culture that values moral rules highly and takes their violation seriously, while simultaneously acknowledging that it is the remarkable individual who belongs to such a culture who is the quintessential dirty-hands politician. This is like recommending a recipe that is bound to be botched before it gets to the table.[18]

[...]

NOTES

An earlier version of this essay was first presented to the Dirty Hands Workshop held at York University, December 1993.

1. Michael Walzer, "Political Action: The Problem of Dirty Hands," *Philosophy and Public Affairs* 2 (Winter, 1973): 167–168.

2. Walzer 166.

3. When Kenneth Howard deals with the example, he finds it a trivial one or one that doesn't even bear the designation of a dirty-hands problem because it is too much like normal political activity! W. Kenneth Howard, "Must Public Hands Be Dirty?" *The Journal of Value Inquiry* II (Spring 1977): 32.

4. C.A.J. Coady, "Dirty Hands," *A Companion to Contemporary Political Philosophy*, ed. Robert E. Goodin and Philip Petit (Oxford: Blackwell, 1995) 426.

5. Mr. Justice Louis D. Brandeis, dissenting in *Olmstead v. United States* 277 US 438, 475 (1928).

6. Coady 426.

7. See Ian Greene and David P. Shugarman, *Honest Politics* 173. Arguments that the term democratic ought not to be applied to cases where majoritarian decisions undermine basic democratic values and processes and reduce effective equal participation rights of citizens are presented by Robert Dahl in *Democracy and Its Critics* (New Haven: Yale University Press, 1989) 170–172 and Alan Gewirth, *The Community of Rights* (Chicago: University of Chicago Press, 1996) 324–325.

8. Quoted by Anne Collins, *In The Sleep Room* (Toronto: Key Porter Books, 1997) 32.

9. The case of Cyrus Vance's decision to resign from the Carter inner circle after lying to allies about the US's commitment not to use force to release American Embassy hostages in Iran would seem to be another. See Dennis Thompson, *Political Ethics and Public Office* 18, 19.

10. Collins 34.

11. Tony Judt, "Counsels on Foreign Relations," *New York Review of Books* XLV:13 (August 13, 1998): 54–60.

12. Judt 59.

13. These examples are discussed in *Honest Politics*, Ch. 7.

14. This and the preceding three sentences are, with slight revision, from Shugarman, "The Use and Abuse of Politics," *Moral Expertise: Studies in Practical and Professional Ethics,* ed. Don MacNiven (New York: Routledge, 1990) 215.

15. Sissela Bok, *Lying: Moral Choice in Political and Private Life* (New York: Pantheon Books, 1978) 75–77.

16. Walzer 176.

17. Walzer 149.

18. This and the preceding two sentences are from "The Use and Abuse of Politics" 215.

POSTSCRIPT

At first glance, Michael Walzer's position is unacceptable. A democracy that condones dirty hands will not long survive—it is too much of a contradiction. But a second look causes us to pause. Dirty-hands politics just recognizes that good men and women will be put into positions (usually not of their own making) that may require them to take difficult actions. Sometimes the prisoner may have to be tortured or the electoral rules bent to achieve an important purpose, and sometimes political parties may have to use tainted money to achieve important policy objectives. In a perfect world, politicians would be moral and law abiding. But politics is anything but a perfect world. On occasion, one has to hide the truth or break the law.

Yet David Shugarman reveals the soft underbelly of the dirty-hands argument. If *one* politician—however desirable—buys votes, then why shouldn't another politician, and still another. The downward slope toward widespread electoral corruption is a slippery one. Shugarman recognizes that an absolute position against morally suspect actions is unrealistic—extreme situations may require the betrayal of some beliefs—but we recognize that this is rarely done and can be argued to be in the service of some higher moral requirement. However, Shugarman *does* appear at times to be bordering on an absolutist position. He wants any possible situation of dirty-hands politics to be deliberated and debated. But there may be situations where there is neither the time nor the will to do so. Sometimes quick action is called for, and sometimes the democratic citizenry may want its leaders to get their hands dirty.

The student interested in the subject of dirty-hands politics might begin with Ian Greene and David P. Shugarman's *Honest Politics: Seeking Integrity in Canadian Political Life* (Toronto: James Lorimer, 1997). The text includes chapters on dirty-hands politics and other issues relating to the question of politics and morality. The next book to consider is Paul Rynard and David P. Shugarman, eds., *Cruelty and Deception: The Controversy over Dirty Hands in Politics* (Peterborough: Broadview Press, 1999). The text provides the full version of Shugarman's piece in this debate and many other insightful articles on dirty politics. It also includes excerpts from some of the classic statements on dirty-hands politics (e.g., Machiavelli, Weber). After this, one might refer to a text that conveys the results of a survey addressing Canadians' views on ethics in political life: Maureen Mancuso et al., *A Question of Ethics: Canadians Speak Out* (Toronto: Oxford University Press, 1998).

For additional treatments of dirty-hands politics, the following could be consulted: Dennis Thompson, *Political Ethics and Public Office* (Cambridge: Harvard University Press, 1987); Peter Madsen and Jay M. Shafritz, eds., *Essentials of Government Ethics* (Toronto: Penguin Books, 1992); Stanley Benn, "Private and Public Morality: Clean Living and Dirty Hands," in S.I. Benn and G.F. Gaus, eds.,

Public and Private Morality in Social Life (New York: St. Martin's Press, 1983); and Amy Gutmann and Dennis Thompson, eds., *Ethics and Politics: Cases and Comments,* 3rd ed. (Belmont, Calif.: Wadsworth Publishing, 1997). Also, the afore-mentioned *Cruelty and Deception* text includes a comprehensive listing of the relevant literature on dirty hands in politics.

As well, students should read the unedited version of Walzer's seminal piece on dirty hands. It is difficult, but it will reward those who believe in the importance of the issue of dirty-hands politics. The citation for the article is Michael Walzer, "Political Action: The Problem of Dirty Hands," *Philosophy and Public Affairs* 2, no. 2 (1973). It can also be found in a number of collections on ethics and politics, including Madsen and Shafritz's text listed above.

Finally, students interested in dirty-hands politics and corruption in government will want to read the soon-to-be-released report of the Commission of Inquiry into the Sponsorship Program and Advertising Activities (otherwise known as the Gomery Commission). The report will address claims of political and bureaucratic wrongdoings in the implementation of a federal program directed at making Quebecers more aware of Canada and its national government. Reports of the Office of the Auditor General and the Public Accounts Committee of the Canadian House of Commons also examine these claims (reports are available on the web-sites of the two bodies). Articles on the Gomery Commission and the "sponsorship scandal" can be found in *Policy Options* 26, no. 5 (June 2005).

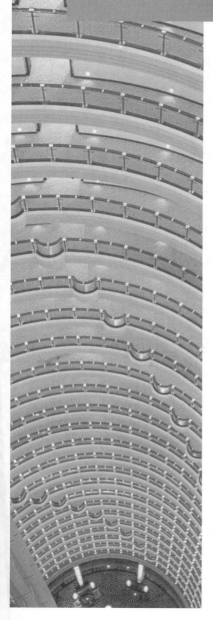

PART FIVE

PUBLIC POLICY

Is a private health care system necessary?

Is same-sex marriage beneficial for society?

Does Canada need a national child care program?

Should religious beliefs be excluded from consideration of public policy?

Is a Private Health Care System Necessary?

✔ **YES**
MARGARET SOMERVILLE, "Getting Past the Myth of Medicare" in the *National Post*, June 21, 2004, p. A10

✘ **NO**
COLLEEN M. FLOOD, "Two-Tier Medicine Isn't the Answer" in the *National Post*, June 21, 2004, p. A10

REBUTTAL
COLLEEN M. FLOOD, "Two-Tier Care Is Not the Answer,"
MARGARET SOMERVILLE, "'Two-Stream,' Not 'Two-Tier,'"
in the *National Post*, August 3, 2004, p. A11

In recent years, the confidence of Canadians in their publicly funded health care system—known as medicare—has declined. The principles of the system promise reasonable access to a set of comprehensive hospital and physician services with no charges at point of service, but users of the system increasingly feel that it is faltering. Long waiting lists make access to care difficult and too many Canadians are without a family doctor. The quality of care at times also leaves something to be desired—partly because of the lack of appropriate medical technology—and stories of patients becoming sick in hospitals appear to be increasing. Perhaps the most disconcerting symptom of decline is the appearance of advertisements in Canada's national newspapers that invite Canadians to come to America to receive their care without the wait. Medicare was once a proud achievement, but it now seems in need of serious repair.

One possible type of repair is to institute a health care system consisting of private and public sectors. Any Canadian can elect to receive care from the private sector, but many provinces prohibit securing private insurance for medically required care provided outside of medicare (no such prohibitions exist for non-medically required care and thus Canada has a private market for dental care, home care, prescription drugs, and other services). Accordingly, the patient would have to pay the bill for a private medical service, an expense that only the wealthiest individual would accept (and other obstacles make it difficult even for this group to secure care). But the end of the prohibition on private insurance would entice more into the private sector. With this development, it would be hoped that pressures on the public system would lessen. Allowing a thriving private system of health care would purportedly benefit all parties. Those who remain in the public system would get faster access to care and more money would be available to address concerns of quality. For those in the private sector, there would be few instances of waiting, and presumably they could purchase as high a quality of care as they wished.

But this solution to the ailments of medicare may have its faults. Doctors and nurses could leave the public system in droves, searching for higher levels of remuneration in the market-based private sector. The result is that medicare would be starved of necessary personnel. It is also possible that the easy procedures would gravitate to the private sector, leaving medicare with the task for providing the more difficult—and more expensive—services. Most unsettling, those who leave the public system may vote in a manner that restricts the flow of funds into medicare. Why support financially a system that offers one no direct benefit? The ultimate result, it is argued, would be a two-tiered system: a private one for the well-off, a public one for the less well-off.

The case for two systems of care thus seems vulnerable. Yet, it is interesting to note that Canada is the only developed country that actively works against the emergence of a private system parallel to the public sector. The countries most similar to Canada—the other Anglo-American democracies—all have two health care systems for the provision of medically necessary care. Critics of the two-system approach are quick to point out the health care systems in these countries are hardly without their own difficulties, and in fact these difficulties may exceed those in Canada. But it remains that Canada is alone in its determination to prevent the emergence of a private system working alongside their public counterpart. All of this, though, may not matter, for the Supreme Court recently ruled that prohibitions on the purchase of private health insurance for medically required care in Quebec violate the Canadian Charter of Rights and Freedoms. The decision of the court may lead to a thriving private market for hospital and physician services.

In the readings, Margaret Somerville, founding director of the McGill Centre for Medicine, Ethics, and Law, presents an argument for considering a two-sector health care system for Canada. Colleen Flood, a professor of law at the University of Toronto and a holder of a Canada Research Chair in health care, follows with criticisms of such a proposal. The two authors then each provide additional commentaries on the wisdom of implementing a health care system with two sectors. All four pieces were drafted before the Supreme Court of Canada released its decision on the constitutionality of Quebec's laws affecting the purchase of private health insurance.

✔ **YES**
Getting Past the Myth of Medicare
MARGARET SOMERVILLE

Recently, a friend dying of cancer was admitted to the emergency room of a Montreal teaching hospital. There was little privacy and, as one expects, lights on and loud noise 24 hours a day. The corridors were full of patients. On one occasion, I saw an old lady—a corridor inmate—eating her evening meal while the man in the bed next to her used a bedpan. After my friend had spent five days in "Emerge," I wanted to try to get him moved and asked him for permission to "make a fuss"—my "informed consent" training kicked in. He refused. He said it might mean worse treatment for him. Eventually, I felt my obligations as a friend trumped those as an ethicist and I intervened, in a way that would not be available to everyone, without telling him. He was moved to a room within an hour.

The room's state of disrepair was classic Third World motif. It reminded me of a "workers' holiday camp" in Hungary I had stayed in after the communist regime collapsed. Paint was peeling from the walls, there were gouges in the plaster, and the floor was in need of repair. A rolled-up towel was stuffed into the slit between the window and sill, to stop an icy winter draft. Last week, I visited another friend in another Montreal teaching hospital, a physician who was recovering from surgery. He pointed out the 1950s-colour paint peeling from the damaged walls and woodwork. Interesting that he only noticed the paint as a patient, although he works in this hospital system.

The state of the paint might seem trivial, but it signals other, much more serious problems. Rundown hospital facilities are deeply depressing and have a negative impact on the morale of health care staff, even if they try to prevent that. Low morale could be one cause of the alarmingly high rate of treatment errors in hospitals documented in recent research. During his three days in hospital, my physician friend identified three—and probably four—clear mistakes in his treatment. Most patients would not recognize these had occurred.

Then just this month, an outbreak was reported of 780 cases of clostridium difficile infection in five Montreal hospitals over the last 18 months, which has killed at least 79 patients. It is being blamed in part on old, difficult-to-clean hospital facilities, inadequate numbers of cleaning staff and possibly inadequate supervision of those there are, and a lack of private rooms and follow-up testing. One hospital asked its housekeeping staff to clean contaminated rooms and then tested; they were still highly contaminated.

Nurses are also in short supply. Patients report that proper care isn't forthcoming unless family members agitate for it. More and more frequently, patients who can afford it are hiring their own nurses to care for them in hospital. That is not a one-tier health care system. And all, or all but one, of the mistakes my physician friend experienced were committed by nurses. Nurse training must be ongoing and junior nurses need careful supervision. That's impossible when there aren't enough senior nurses and those that are on staff are overwhelmed.

And then there's the "waiting list" problem. Last week, yet another friend who is a family practitioner told me he examined a patient and found a mass in her abdomen that he thought was almost certainly a uterine fibroid, a non-emergency condition. He phoned to book a vaginal ultrasound and was given a date nearly five months in advance. His intuitions made him uneasy and he said it was urgent, although he felt guilty for doing so. The patient was given an appointment in four weeks. She was diagnosed with probable ovarian cancer. A hospital physician to whom I told this story was very surprised. He has also seen a woman with a similar presentation last week and said she had an ultrasound the same day. Small wonder people choose to go to hospital emergency rooms, to say nothing of implementing principles of equal access to treatment, justice and fairness.

So if we all know the health care system needs fixing, what is required to do that?

At a practical level: We need people to speak out constantly and provide facts such as those outlined above. Then, we must be open to all possibilities, including a two-stream system—public and private systems operating side by side—as in England and Australia, which are not radically conservative countries. It is ethically unacceptable for Canadian politicians to reject, out-of-hand, potentially better options simply out of adherence to a fixed ideology.

It is also ethically unacceptable for these politicians to publicly trumpet the virtues of the single-payer health care system while traveling to the United States for their own treatment—an option many Canadians cannot afford. As a safeguard on the integrity of their own decision-making, politicians and their families should be required to use the same Canadian system they approve for others.

Canada's medicare system is shrouded in myth. Myths convey important shared values essential to our personal and collective spirit and identity. But in the case of health, our myths are getting in the way of providing people with quality care. We must establish a system that recognizes all Canadians are entitled to all medically necessary health care and allows them timely access to that—but that does not necessarily mean providing health care only through a public system.

So, while politicians should promise and provide more money for the health care system, we need to demand they do more. We should vote for the ones who are courageous enough to state publicly that all ethical options for change should be on the table. At the moment, most of them seem to see doing that as a huge political risk.

✗ NO
Two-Tier Medicine Isn't the Answer
COLLEEN M. FLOOD

Last week, the Supreme Court of Canada heard a case that could overturn medicare. Quebec doctor Jacques Chaoulli and his patient, George Zeliotis, claim their Charter rights have been violated by a Quebec law prohibiting the sale of private insurance for medically necessary hospital and physician services. They want this law, and similar laws in other provinces, overturned. They want a flourishing private market for health care: a two-tier system where doctors can work in the public sector and top up their incomes in the private sector; and a system where people with private insurance or their own private means can jump queues in public hospitals.

By contrast, arguments for one-tier medicare are often advanced on the grounds of equity; that it is wrong for a rich person with cancer to get a higher standard of treatment than a poor person with cancer. Health care is, after all, the one great leveller. Serious disease can tear families apart, but at least with public insurance it will not destroy them financially.

Advocates of two-tier often contend all Canadians would be better off since those with private resources would no longer burden the public sector and waiting lists would fall. The trouble with this argument, appealing as it may intuitively seem, is that there is no evidence to support it. Countries such as the U.K. and New Zealand, which allow people to buy faster, high-quality hospital and physician services in the private sector, have much longer waiting lists than in Canada. In the U.K. and New Zealand, just under 10% and 35% of the populations, respectively, have private insurance. Everybody else has to put up with long waiting lists in the public sector. And the private sector doesn't do the tough stuff; it doesn't provide the cancer care and the cardiac treatments. It does the easy, high-volume procedures.

Why don't waiting lists fall when people are allowed to buy private insurance? First, there are only a limited number of doctors. If specialists shift their efforts and energies to the private sector to do high-volume procedures such as knee operations, then they have less energy and time for public knees (or hearts, or cancer, etc.). And because it takes a goodly number of public dollars to train doctors (as well as many years), this is not a problem that one can assume the market will respond to. Second, of course, the well-to-do and the well-insured will not continue to lobby governments for improvements in health care. With the political incentive diminished, the public system will wither and waiting lists will grow. Third and finally, in order for the private tier to succeed, the pubic tier must be second-rate. Otherwise, why would anyone purchase care privately?

Advocates of private insurance often point out that Canada is alone in not allowing private funding for hospital and physician services. But in fact, the public-private distinction is blurred in many countries with enormous tax and public subsidies shoring up the private insurance system and laws trying to prevent private insurers doing what their natural inclination is to do—avoid risk. Private insurers make money by avoiding risk and thus even being wealthy doesn't assure you of coverage. Ironically, the fact that you need health care, because you have cancer, will mean you can't get private insurance. Even in the United States, they had to bring in medicare for the over 65s—largely because many of the elderly couldn't get private insurance; they were risk-rated out.

Several groups appearing before the Supreme Court are arguing for a middle ground. These groups include the Canadian Medical Association (CMA) and a number of senators, led by Senator Michael Kirby, who was the chairman of the Senate committee that released a report on medicare in October, 2002. They agree with Messrs. Chaoulli and Zeloitis that those laws prohibiting the sale of private insurance breach the Charter unless the Quebec provincial government guarantees timely treatment to its citizens. If the Quebec government does not do this, it must allow its citizens the opportunity to purchase private insurance.

The senators and the CMA appear to be taking the middle ground, but behind their moderate stance is a serious attack on universal access. There is no assurance if they are successful that Quebec or any province will put in place waiting-time guarantees. Alberta and British Columbia may embrace the notion of two-tier and welcome its imposition by the Supreme Court. In pursuit of a policy goal of waiting-time guarantees, both the Senate and the CMA are willing to sacrifice universal health care from coast to coast.

The Chaoulli case (and crumbling political support) has been a wake-up call to the incumbent federal government to do something about waiting times, and that is a good thing. The lesson from examining other jurisdictions is that where there is a political will to do something about timeliness, waiting times can be tackled and lowered. More money is not necessarily needed, but better management is undoubtedly part of the solution. Canadians shouldn't give up on medicare and should rest assured that all health care systems struggle with waiting-time issues. The only country that doesn't is the United States, but it leaves 44 million people uninsured, and these people can only dream of getting on to a waiting list.

People who say private insurance is good say that pubic waiting lists will diminish if Canadians can purchase private insurance. They are wrong. For most Canadians, a two-tier system will mean an era of more, not less, waiting. When thinking about the pros and cons of two-tier medicare, ask yourself this question: How would your grandmother fare? Could she afford private insurance and would she qualify? Like democracy, our one-tier health care system may indeed be the worst kind of system—except for all the others.

REBUTTAL
Two-Tier Care Is Not the Answer
COLLEEN M. FLOOD

In her article, *Getting Past the Myth of Medicare,* Prof. Somerville suggests that a parallel private system might be a solution to medicare's problems. In such a system, people with private insurance would be able to purchase faster treatment than is available in the public system.

More private funding for medicare sounds like a good idea. Many people intuitively think that if we had a two-tier system then fewer patients would use the public system and doctors and nurses would have more time to deal with patients that remain.

But if this were true, then why do the headlines in New Zealand, the UK and Australia (all countries with two-tier systems) sound depressingly familiar? All the problems that plague the Canadian system plague other countries that allow people to jump queues in the public system.

What would happen if we introduce a two-tier system in Canada? Presently, as is the case in many countries around the world, we don't have enough physicians and nurses and most are already working at full capacity. If we had a private sector operating alongside the public sector, then at least some of these doctors and nurses would spend all or part of their time working in the private sector.

That would be fine if the burden on the public system declined proportionally, but it wouldn't: the sickest and the poorest people would be left in the public sector and it would be left to perform the most intensive and expensive kinds of treatment. Waiting lists in medicare would grow.

Remember that waiting lists in the UK and New Zealand are longer than in Canada for most indicators and in Australia are similar to those in Canada. Two-tier has not eliminated waiting for care except for the fortunate few with private insurance.

Prof. Somerville seems to support that Australian two-tier system and suggests we should look to that as an example. But there are enormous cross-subsidies in Australia from taxpayers to the private insurance system to keep it afloat.

Despite paying taxes for the private system, not many taxpayers benefit from this contribution since they cannot afford the insurance premiums. The millions of Australian dollars poured into the private system could have been poured into public hospitals to deal with waiting times but for political reasons these monies were devoted to the private insurance system.

Many of us, physicians and patients alike, are frustrated with medicare; we want it to work better for those we love and for ourselves. It is easy to come up with horror stories of packed emergency wards, peeling paint, and poor care. But it is just as easy to do this in countries that have two-tier medicine.

We should be careful not to let frustration and emotion destroy what is best about medicare. Prof. Somerville is right in saying that we should be open to all sorts of ways of improving our system, including reviewing private options in funding and delivery. But we can't act on anecdote and intuition; we have to act on the best available evidence. And the evidence is clear; a two-tier system will make our system worse rather than better.

REBUTTAL
"Two-Stream," Not "Two-Tier"
MARGARET SOMERVILLE

Not all private/public health care systems are the same. Some are "two-tier" and ethically unacceptable. Others are "two-stream" and acceptable. Moreover, not-for-profit private health care eliminates some business-based problems you identify.

Doctors already "work in the public sector and top up their incomes in the private sector"—to quote your earlier article—in a wide variety of ways, some challengeable under medicare rules.

It's also already true that "people with private insurance or their own private means can jump queues in public hospitals." People privately accessing diagnostic technology are then treated in the public system much sooner than those who must wait for diagnosis. Likewise, people getting organ transplants outside Canada go into the public system on return, while others die waiting for organs.

You state "health care, after all, is the one great leveler." Sadly, many sick Canadians experience their time in the health care system as taking them down to a *lower* level of existence—which is no criticism of the dedicated health professionals who achieve the superhuman in extraordinarily difficult circumstances. Rather illness, not health care, is the great leveler.

You claim that "the private sector doesn't do the tough stuff ... cancer care and cardiac treatment." That isn't true, for example, in Australia's mixed public/private system. My 58-year-old brother died of cancer in Australia last year. He was treated for over four years in the private sector. I saw him often and never saw conditions such as I described in my article. Also, last time I checked, "the fact that you need health care, because you have cancer, will mean you can't get private insurance," was not true in Australia.

Saying a two-stream system means "the well-to-do and the well-insured will not continue to lobby governments for improvements in health care" is like saying that people who have houses don't care about homeless people. Indeed, better care in the private stream is likely to create pressure for the same level of care in the public stream if we have a sense of justice.

It's true that "the public-private distinction is blurred in many countries." But, in practice, those countries already include Canada. Around 30% of our health care is paid for privately.

You speak of "sacrific[ing] universal health care" by changing medicare. Universality in the Canada Health Act means everyone must be covered by medicare. But it doesn't speak to the major current issue: Is the range, quality and timeliness of healthcare provided by medicare adequate?

I wholeheartedly agree with you that "better management is undoubtedly part of the solution." But what constitutes that needs very subtle and nuanced analysis and understanding. Dr. Harry Zeit's letter in the *Post,* responding to our articles, is a powerful signpost.

The system must be designed to nurture the healing encounter between patients, health care professionals and the system. What is needed cannot be captured just in statistics (although they are valuable), but requires a comprehension of what Dr. Zeit calls its current "soul-destroying" nature. In the best of all worlds, we would have a public system that could do all that and more. The reality is we don't. Ethically, therefore, we must search for ethical alternatives that can bring us closer to that goal.

POSTSCRIPT

In her articles, Margaret Somerville paints a picture of health care in Canada that may be depressingly familiar to many people. Dilapidated hospitals, crowded emergency rooms, treatment errors, humiliating invasions of privacy, and fewer and fewer health personnel: these are the qualities that we increasingly associate with medicare. Especially revealing—given the nature of the debate here—is the use of private personnel to look after loved ones in hospital. There is simply not enough care even for those fortunate enough to get into the hospital, so we have to search for help outside the public system to make sure things work well inside the system. For Somerville, it is a myth to believe that Canada has a fully funded health care that is equally available to all. And it is a dangerous one at that, for it lulls us into accepting the present state of medicare when we should be contemplating changes.

All of Somerville's claims may be true. But it does not necessarily follow that the appropriate response is a two-sector health care system for Canada. As Colleen Flood argues in her article, countries with private systems running alongside the public ones still seem to have waiting lists. Flood also provides some good reasons for why this is the case, which helps builds the case against a private system. Perhaps it would wiser to focus on fixing the public system. A couple of years ago, the federal government set out an ambitious agenda for doing just that. Though it is too early to determine the success of the agenda, it does appear to have some potential. Moreover, the provinces over the years have been working hard to introduce reforms.

As shown, Flood pokes some holes in the argument for a parallel private system. But her article also elicits some queries and concerns. Flood thinks the supply of health personnel is fixed in the short term, so the introduction of a private system would only work by taking doctors from the public system with predictable results. However, it is possible that the supply might increase more quickly if the health care system becomes more attractive to doctors and nurses—and to voters. Perhaps more disturbing is her discussion of the court case in which a Quebec doctor and his patient argue against the prohibitions on private insurance on the grounds that they violate the Canadian Charter of Rights and Freedoms. It may be true that the prohibitions help uphold the principles of medicare, but it is unsettling to think that this must come at the cost of violating individual rights and freedoms. This is especially so in light of the fact that access to medicare is difficult, seemingly leaving the patient with nowhere to go: medicare is inaccessible and private care is too expensive. The majority of the Supreme Court justices also found this troubling and declared the prohibitions unconstitutional.

An attempt to tackle the issue of two health care systems should start with the views of Canadians about the current arrangement for health care in Canada. As mentioned, we are beginning to lose confidence in medicare. Two studies that provide details on this development (and other related ones) are Matthew Mendelsohn, *Canadians' Thoughts on Their Health Care System: Preserving the Canadian Model Through Innovation* (Saskatoon: Commission on the Future of Health Care in Canada, June 2002) and Julia Abelson et al., "Canadians Confront Health Care Reform," *Health Affairs* 23, no. 3 (May/June 2004). Terrence Sullivan and Patricia Baranek's *First Do No Harm: Making Sense of Canadian Health Reform* (Toronto: Malcolm Lester, 2002) also addresses Canadians' views of medicare. The next task is to acquire an appreciation of the present state or condition of medicare so that we can better understand the background to the demand for a private sector. On this matter, there is agreement that medicare could operate better, but disagreement on the extent of the problems facing the health care system. The best thing for students to do is to dive into the literature and determine for themselves the actual state of medicare: Commission on the Future of Health Care in Canada, *Building on Values: The Future of Health Care in Canada* (Saskatoon: Commission on the Future of Health Care in Canada, 2002); Fraser Institute, *How Good Is Canadian Health Care? 2004 Report by Nadeem Esmail and Michael Walker with Sabrina Yeudall* (Vancouver: Fraser Institute, 2004); David Gratzer, *Code Blue: Reviving Canada's Health Care System* (Toronto: ECW Press, 1999); David Gratzer, *Better Medicine: Reforming Canadian Health Care* (Toronto: ECW Press, 2002); Michael Rachlis, *Prescription for Excellence: How Innovation Is Saving Canada's Health Care System* (Toronto: HarpersCollins Publishing, 2004); Terrence Sullivan and Patricia M. Baranek, *First Do No Harm: Making Sense of Canadian Health Care Reform* (Toronto: Malcolm Lester, 2002); and Carolyn Hughes Tuohy, "The Costs of Constraint and Prospects for Health Care Reform in Canada," *Health Affairs* 21, no. 3 (May/June 2002).

The heart of the debate deals with the establishment of a two-sector health care system and its possible implications for health care in Canada. Probably the article to start off with is Carolyn Hughes Tuohy, Colleen M. Flood, and Mark Stabile, "How Does Private Finance Affect Public Health Care Systems? Marshaling the Evidence from OECD Nations," *Journal of Health Policy, Politics and Law* 29, no. 3 (June 2004). This article from a prestigious American journal (and which should be available online at any library in a university with a medical school) directly addresses the debate question. Other relevant articles and books include Donna M. Wilson, "Public and Private Health-Care Systems: What the Literature Says," *Canadian Public Administration* 44, no. 2 (Summer 2001); Gillian Currie, Cam Donaldson, and Mingshan Lu, "What Does Canada Profit from the For-Profit Debate on Health Care?" *Canadian Public Policy-Analyse de Politiques* XXIX, no. 2 (2003); Maude Barlow, *Profit Is Not the Cure*: *A Citizen's Guide to Saving Medicare* (Toronto: McClelland and Stewart, 2002); and the relevant articles in Gregory P. Marchildon, Tom McIntosh, and Pierre-Gerlier Forest, eds., *The Fiscal Sustainability of Health Care in Canada* (Toronto: University of Toronto Press, 2004). Most of the publications mentioned in the preceding paragraph are also of some value here. In looking at these and other articles, students should be aware of the complexity of the issue of providing for more private participation in Canadian health care. For some, greater private involvement means a new sector parallel to the existing public sector—the interpretation assumed in this debate—but for others it can mean for-profit firms delivering publicly funded health care, and still for others it can mean charging patients extra for services that are still covered by the public system. For guidance on the multiple meanings of private health care, one is advised to read Raisa Deber et al., "The Public-Private Mix in Health Care," in National Forum on Health Care, ed., *Striking a Balance: Health Care Systems in Canada and Elsewhere* (Saint-Foy Que.: Editions MultiMondes, 1998).

Finally, for an examination of how provinces limit the availability of private insurance for medically required care, one should read Colleen Flood and Tom Archibald, "The Illegality of Private Health Care in Canada," *Canadian Medical Association Journal* 164, no. 6 (2001).

Is Same-Sex Marriage Beneficial for Society?

✔ **YES**

JONATHAN RAUCH, "For Better or Worse?" *The New Republic,*
May 6, 1996

✘ **NO**

DANIEL CERE, "War of the Ring," in Daniel Cere and Douglas Farrow,
eds., *Divorcing Marriage: Unveiling the Dangers in Canada's New Social
Experiment* (Montreal and Kingston: McGill-Queen's University Press,
2004) (revised)

In the United States and Canada, the question of same-sex marriage has become
a highly contested public policy issue. Both countries have defined marriage as a
union of a man and woman, but now this definition is being challenged in order
to allow for marriages between couples of the same sex. In the United States,
movement toward a legal recognition of same-sex marriage has been relatively
slow. In contrast, the shift toward a legal recognition of same-sex marriages in
Canada has been moving forward at a rapid pace.

In the early 1990s, the status of gay rights generally had not been clearly
addressed by the courts. However, in two significant cases in the late 1990s (*Egan
v. Canada* and *Vriend v. Alberta*), the Supreme Court of Canada ruled that the protection of individuals from discrimination in the Charter of Rights and Freedoms
should be extended to include discrimination based on sexual orientation. In subsequent challenges, the courts were asked whether these protections would also
apply in relation to same-sex relationships. In a 1998 decision, the Supreme Court
ruled that it was unconstitutional to differentiate between unmarried same-sex
couples and opposite-sex couples. This led to a number of legislative changes that
basically brought the rights and benefits of same-sex couples into line with those
of opposite-sex couples who lived in "common law" situations.

Despite these changes, same-sex couples could still not marry and have access
to the same legal status and rights that have traditionally accompanied marriage.
The exclusion was based on the fact that marriage, according to the definition
inherited from the English common law tradition, was defined as being between
a man and a woman. In 1993, when two men who had been cohabiting sought a
marriage licence in Ontario they were refused. In the subsequent court case, an
Ontario Divisional Court ruled that the refusal to grant them a marriage licence
was not a violation of the equality provisions of Section 15 of the Charter of

Rights and Freedoms, because nowhere in law were homosexuals prohibited from marrying. They were free to marry like anyone else—as long as they married someone from the opposite sex. Thus, a homosexual who chooses not to engage in a heterosexual marriage is doing so as a matter of choice and therefore is not being discriminated against.

In response to this decision, gay rights activists launched court appeals in three different provinces: Ontario, Quebec, and British Columbia. In each case, the strategy was the same. A same-sex couple would seek to obtain a marriage licence. When refused, they would launch a court case against the government. In these provinces, gay rights activists were successful in getting the courts to recognize the traditional definition of marriage as discriminatory. As a response to these judicial developments, the federal government drafted a new law to redefine marriage. At the same time, it announced that it would forward a reference question to the Supreme Court of Canada, asking for its opinion on whether draft legislation that would entitle same-sex couples to marry under the law was constitutional. Following a statement by the Supreme Court that the proposed legislation was consistent with the Charter of Rights and Freedoms, the federal government introduced a bill in Parliament to change the definition of marriage to a committed relationship between any two consenting adults. After considerable debate, the bill was passed by Parliament on June 28, 2005, with a vote of 158–133. Opponents to the bill stated that their fight against same-sex marriage was only just beginning.

Not surprisingly, the issue of same-sex marriage has generated a great deal of debate. Those in favour of the redefinition of marriage argue that it is the right of gays and lesbians to have access to the institution of marriage. The Canadian Constitution protects individuals against discriminatory action by government, but the traditional definition of marriage purposively denies access to marriage for same-sex couples. The argument for same-sex marriage also stems from a particular understanding of marriage. Marriage is simply an arrangement that allows two people who love each other to come together and to care for one another. Opposite-sex couples clearly are capable of love and caring, but so are same-sex couples. A redefinition of marriage, it is argued, also opens an opportunity for society to demonstrate a greater acceptance of gays and lesbians. Up to this point, it seems that homosexuals have been at best tolerated in both Canada and the United States. Acceptance of same-sex marriage will go a long way toward acceptance of them.

The concerns about redefining marriage to include same-sex couples begin with a reference to tradition. Marriage is a revered institution of Western society, and one does not end it with a few strokes of a legislator's pen. There is also the view that proponents of same-sex marriage misunderstand the purpose of marriage. It is more than uniting a loving couple; it is also about procreation and assuming long-term obligations that are crucial to the functioning of any society. Perhaps the greatest fear stems from the belief that including same-sex couples within the definition of marriage will undermine an institution already weakened by well-intentioned reforms. Many will come to believe that marriage has no real meaning anymore and act in a manner that reflects this sentiment. Already marriage has been rocked in recent years by rising divorce rates, and same-sex marriages may only hasten the collapse of this most important societal structure.

There have been efforts to find an acceptable compromise. It has been suggested that all the rights and benefits of a married couple—except for the marriage licence—be made available to same-sex couples. For all intents and purposes, say some, this would confer marriage status on unions of gay and lesbian couples. Another suggestion is to get government out of the marriage business altogether. Under this arrangement, the role of government would be to record the unions of two people. Whether couples wanted to get married would be a private matter and undertaken by institutions outside of government (such as churches or other social institutions). The point here is that marriage would no longer be recognized in law. Up to this point, proposals such as these have not been enthusiastically received. The offer of marriage without the licence is seen as discriminatory and based on a long-discredited legal approach of creating separate but equal categories of treatment. The idea of making marriage solely a private matter has not been seriously considered by many groups. Sometimes it is difficult to see an important institution in a different light.

In the readings, Jonathan Rauch and Daniel Cere debate the issue of same-sex marriage. Mr. Rauch is a prominent commentator on public issues in the United States. Dr. Ceres is a director at the Newman Centre at McGill University in Montreal.

✔ YES
For Better or Worse?
JONATHAN RAUCH

Whether gay marriage makes sense—and whether straight marriage makes sense—depends on what marriage is actually for. Current secular thinking on this question is shockingly sketchy. Gay activists say: marriage is for love, and we love each other, therefore we should be able to marry. Traditionalists say: marriage is for children, and homosexuals do not (or should not) have children, therefore you should not be able to marry. That, unfortunately, pretty well covers the spectrum. I say "unfortunately" because both views are wrong. They misunderstand and impoverish the social meaning of marriage.

So what is marriage for? Modern marriage is, of course, based upon traditions that religion helped to codify and enforce. But religious doctrine has no special standing in the world of secular law and policy (the "Christian nation" crowd notwithstanding). If we want to know what and whom marriage is for in modern America, we need a sensible secular doctrine.

At one point, marriage in secular society was largely a matter of business: cementing family ties, providing social status for men and economic support for women, conferring dowries, and so on. Marriages were typically arranged, and "love" in the modern sense was no prerequisite. In Japan, remnants of this system remain, and it works surprisingly well. Couples stay together because they view their marriage as a partnership: an investment in social stability for themselves and their children. Because Japanese couples don't expect as much emotional fulfillment as we do, they are less inclined to break up. They also take a somewhat more relaxed attitude toward adultery. What's a little extracurricular love provided that each partner is fulfilling his or her many other marital duties?

In the West, of course, love is a defining element. The notion of lifelong love is charming, if ambitious, and certainly love is a desirable element of marriage. In society's eyes, however, it cannot be the defining element. You may or may not love your husband, but the two of you are just as married either way. You may love your mistress, but that certainly doesn't make her your spouse. Love helps makes sense of marriage emotionally, but it is not terribly important in making sense of marriage from the point of view of social policy.

If love does not define the purpose of secular marriage, what does? Neither the law nor secular thinking provides a clear answer. Today marriage is almost entirely a voluntary arrangement whose contents are up to the people making the deal. There are few if any behaviours that automatically end a marriage. If a man beats his wife, which is about the worst thing he can do to her, he may be convicted of assault, but his marriage is not automatically dissolved. Couples can be adulterous ("open") yet remain married. They can be celibate, too; consummation is not required. All in all, it is an impressive and also rather astonishing victory for modern individualism that so important an institution should be so bereft of formal social instructions as to what should go on inside of it.

Secular society tells us only a few things about marriage. First, marriage depends on the consent of the parties. Second, the parties are not children. Third, the number of parties is two. Fourth, one is a man and the other a woman. Within those rules a marriage is whatever anyone says it is.

Perhaps it is enough simply to say that marriage is as it is and should not be tampered with. This sounds like a crudely reactionary position. In fact, however, of all the arguments against reforming marriage, it is probably the most powerful.

Call it a Hayekian argument, after the great libertarian economist F.A. Hayek, who developed this line of thinking in his book *The Fatal Conceit.* In a market system, the prices generated by impersonal forces may not make sense from any one person's point of view, but they encode far more information than even the cleverest person could ever gather. In a similar fashion, human societies evolve rich and complicated webs of nonlegal rules in the form of customs, traditions and institutions. Like prices, they may seem irrational or arbitrary. But the very fact that they are the customs that have evolved implies that they embody a practical logic that may not be apparent to even a sophisticated analyst. And the web of custom cannot be torn apart and reordered at will because once its internal logic is violated it falls apart. Intellectuals, such as Marxists or feminists, who seek to deconstruct and rationally rebuild social traditions, will produce not better order but chaos.

So the Hayekian view argues strongly against gay marriage. It says that the current rules may not be best and may even be unfair. But they are all we have, and, once you say that marriage need not be male-female, soon marriage will stop being anything at all. You can't mess with the formula without causing unforeseen consequences; possibly including the implosion of the institution of marriage itself.

However, there are problems with the Hayekian position. It is untenable in its extreme form and unhelpful in its milder version. In its extreme form, it implies that no social reforms should ever be undertaken. Indeed, no laws should be passed, because they interfere with the natural evolution of social mores. How could Hayekians abolish slavery? They would probably note that slavery violates fundamental moral principles. But in so doing they would establish a moral platform from which to judge social rules, and thus acknowledge that abstracting social debate from moral concerns is not possible.

If the ban on gay marriage were only mildly unfair, and if the costs of changing it were certain to be enormous, then the ban could stand on Hayekian grounds. But, if there is any social policy today that has a fair claim to scaldingly inhumane, it is the ban on gay marriage. As conservatives tirelessly and rightly point out, marriage is society's most fundamental institution. To bar any class of people from marrying as they choose is an extraordinary deprivation. When not so long ago it was illegal in parts of America for blacks to marry whites, no one could claim that this was a trivial disenfranchisement. Granted, gay marriage raises issues that interracial marriage does not; but no one can argue that the deprivation is a minor one.

To outweigh such as a serious claim it is not enough to say that gay marriage might lead to bad things. Bad things happened as a result of legalizing contraception, but that did not make it the wrong thing to do. Besides, it seems doubtful that extending marriage to, say, another 3 or 5 percent of the population would have anything like the effects that no-fault divorce has had, to say nothing of contraception. By now, the "traditional" understanding of marriage has been sullied in all kinds of ways. It is hard to think of a bigger affront to tradition, for instance, than allowing married women to own property independently of their husbands or allowing them to charge their husbands with rape. Surely it is unfair to say that marriage may be reformed for the sake of anyone and everyone except homosexuals, who must respect the dictates of tradition.

Faced with these problems, the milder version of the Hayekian argument says not that social traditions shouldn't be tampered with at all, but that they shouldn't be tampered with lightly. Fine. In this case, no one is talking about casual messing around; both sides have marshaled their arguments with deadly seriousness. Hayekians surely have to recognize that appeals to blind tradition and to the risks inherent in social change do not, a priori, settle anything in this instance. They merely warn against frivolous change.

So we turn to what has become the standard view of marriage's purpose. Its proponents would probably like to call it a child-centred view, but it is actually an anti-gay view, as will become clear. Whatever you call it, it is the view of marriage that is heard most often, and in the context of the debate over gay marriage it is heard almost exclusively. In its most straightforward form it goes as follows (I quote from James Q. Wilson's fine book, *The Moral Sense*):

> A family is not an association of independent people; it is a human commitment designed to make possible the rearing of moral and healthy children. Governments care—or ought to care—about families for this reason, and scarcely for any other.

Wilson speaks about "family" rather than "marriage" as such, but one may, I think, read him as speaking of marriage without doing any injustice to his meaning. The resulting proposition—government ought to care about marriage almost entirely because of children—seems reasonable. But there are problems. The first, obviously, is that gay couples may have children, whether through adoption, prior marriage or (for lesbians) artificial insemination. Leaving aside the thorny issue of gay adoption, the point is that if the mere presence of children is the test, then homosexual relationships can certainly pass it.

You might note, correctly, that heterosexual marriages are more likely to produce children than homosexual ones. When granting marriage licences to heterosexuals, however, we do not ask how likely the couple is to have children. We assume that they are entitled to get married whether or not they end up with children. Understanding this, conservatives often make an interesting move. In seeking to justify the state's interest in marriage, they shift from the actual presence of children to the anatomical possibility of making them. Hadley Arkes, a political science professor and prominent opponent of homosexual marriage, makes the case this way:

> The traditional understanding of marriage is grounded in the "natural teleology of the body"—in the inescapable fact that only a man and a woman, and only two people, not three, can generate a child. Once marriage is detached from that natural teleology of the body, what ground of principle would thereafter confine marriage to two people rather than some larger grouping? That is, on what ground of principle would the law reject the claim of a gay couple that their love is not confined to a coupling or two, but that they are woven into a larger ensemble with yet another person or two?

What he seems to be saying is that, where the possibility of natural children is nil, the meaning of marriage is nil. If marriage is allowed between members of the same sex, then the concept of marriage has been emptied of content except to ask whether the parties love each other. Then anything goes, including polygamy. This reasoning presumably is what those opposed to gay marriage have in mind when they claim that, once gay marriage is legal, marriage to pets will follow close behind.

But Arkes and his sympathizers make two mistakes. To see them, break down the claim into two components: (1) Two person-marriage derives its special status from the anatomical possibility that the partners can create natural children; and (2) apart from (1), two-person marriage has no purpose sufficiently strong to justify its special status. This is, absent justification (1), anything goes.

The first proposition is wholly at odds with the way society actually views marriage. Leave aside the insistence that natural, as opposed to adopted, children define the importance of marriage. The deeper problem, apparent right away, is the issue of sterile heterosexual couples. Here the "anatomical possibility" crowd has a problem, for a homosexual union is, anatomically speaking, nothing but one variety of sterile union and no different even in principle: a woman without a uterus has no more potential for giving birth that a man without a vagina.

It may sound like carping to stress the case of barren heterosexual marriage: the vast majority of newlywed heterosexual couples, after all, can have children and probably will. But the point here is fundamental. There are far more sterile heterosexual unions in America than homosexual ones. The "anatomical possibility" crowd cannot have it both ways. If the possibility of children is what gives meaning to marriage, then a post-menopausal woman who applies for a marriage licence should be turned away at the courthouse door. What's more, she should be hooted at and condemned for stretching the meaning of marriage beyond its natural basis and so reducing the institution to frivolity. People at the Family Research Council or Concerned Women for America should point at her and say, "If she can marry, why not polygamy?"

Obviously, the "anatomical" conservatives do not say this, because they are sane. They instead flail around, saying that sterile men and women were at least born with the right-shaped parts for making children, and so on. Their position is really a nonposition. It says that the "natural children" rationale defines marriage when homosexuals are involved but not when heterosexuals are involved. When the parties to union are sterile heterosexuals, the justification for marriage must be something else. But what?

Now arises the oddest part of the "anatomical" argument. Look at proposition (2) above. It says that, absent the anatomical justification for marriage, anything goes. In other words, it dismisses the idea that there might be other good reasons for society to sanctify marriage above other kinds of relationships. Why would anybody make this move? I'll hazard a guess: to exclude homosexuals. Any rationale that justifies sterile heterosexual marriages can also apply to homosexual ones. For instance, marriage makes women more financially secure. Very nice, say the conservatives. But that rationale could be applied to lesbians, so it's definitely out.

The end result of this stratagem is perverse to the point of being funny. The attempt to ground marriage in children (or the anatomical possibility thereof) falls flat. But, having lost that reason for marriage, the antigay people can offer no other. In their fixation on excluding homosexuals, they leave themselves no consistent justification for the privileged status of *heterosexual* marriage. They thus tear away any coherent foundation that secular marriage might have, which is precisely the opposite of what they claim they want to do. If they have to undercut marriage to save it from homosexuals, so be it!

For the record, I would be the last to deny that children are one central reason for the privileged status of marriage. When men and women get together, children are a likely outcome; and, as we are learning in ever more unpleasant ways, when children grow up without two parents, trouble ensues. Children are not a trivial reason for marriage; they just cannot be the only reason.

What are the others? It seems to me that the two strongest candidates are these: domesticating men and providing reliable caregivers. Both purposes are critical to the functioning of a humane and stable society, and both are much better served by marriage—that is, by one-to-one lifelong commitment—than by any other institution.

Civilizing young males is one of any society's biggest problems. Whenever unattached males gather in packs, you see no end to trouble; wildings in Central Park, gangs in Los Angeles, soccer hooligans in Britain, skinheads in Germany, fraternity hazings in universities, grope-lines in the military and, in a different but ultimately no less tragic way, the bathhouses and wanton sex of gay San Francisco or New York in the 1970s.

For taming men, marriage is unmatched. "Of all the institutions through which men may pass—schools, factories, the military—marriage has the largest effect," Wilson writes in *The Moral Sense*. (A token of the casualness of current thinking about marriage is that the man who wrote those words could, later in the very same book, say that government should care about fostering families for "scarcely any other" reason than children.) If marriage—that is, the binding of men into couples—did nothing else, its power to settle men, to keep them at home and out of trouble, would be ample justification for its special status.

Of course, women and older men don't generally travel in marauding or orgiastic packs. But in their case the second rationale comes into play. A second enormous problem for society is what to do when someone is beset by some sort of burdensome contingency. It could be cancer, a broken back, unemployment or depression; it could be exhaustion from work or stress under pressure. If marriage has any meaning at all, it is that, when you collapse from a stroke, there will be at least one other person whose "job" is to drop everything and come to your aid; or that when you come home after being fired by the postal service there will be someone to persuade you not to kill the supervisor.

Obviously, both rationales—the need to settle males and the need to have people looked after—apply to sterile people as well as fertile ones, and apply to childless couples as well as to ones with children. The first explains why everybody feels relieved when the town delinquent gets married, and the second explains why everybody feels happy when an aging widow takes a second husband. From a social point of view, it seems to me, both rationales are far more compelling as justifications of marriage's special status than, say, love. And both of them apply to homosexuals as well as to heterosexuals.

Take the matter of settling men. It is probably true that women and children, more than just the fact of marriage, help civilize men. But that hardly means that the settling effect of marriage on homosexual men is negligible. To the contrary, being tied to a committed relationship plainly helps stabilize gay men. Even without marriage, coupled gay men have steady sex partners and relationships that they value and therefore tend to be less wanton. Add marriage, and you bring a further array of stabilizing influences. One of the main benefits of publicly recognized marriage is that it binds couples together not only in their own eyes but also in the eyes of society at large. Around the partners is woven a web of expectations that they will spend nights together, go to parties together, take out mortgages together, buy furniture at Ikea together, and so on—all of which helps tie them together and keep them off the streets and at home. Surely that is a very good thing, especially as compared to the closet-gay culture of furtive sex with innumerable partners in parks and bathhouses.

The other benefit of marriage—caretaking—clearly applies to homosexuals. One of the first things many people worry about when coming to terms with their homosexuality is: Who will take care of me when I'm ailing or old? Society needs to care about this, too, as the AIDS crisis has made horribly clear. If that crisis has shown anything, it is that homosexuals can and will take care of each other, sometimes with breathtaking devotion—and that no institution can begin to match the care of a devoted partner. Legally speaking, marriage creates kin. Surely society's interest in kin-creation is strongest of all for people who are unlikely to be supported by children in old age and who may well be rejected by their own parents in youth.

Gay marriage, then, is far from being a mere exercise in political point-making or rights-mongering. On the contrary, it serves two of the three social purposes that make marriage so indispensable and irreplaceable for heterosexuals. Two out of three may not be the whole ball of wax, but it is more than enough to give society a compelling interest in marrying off homosexuals.

There is no substitute. Marriage is the *only* institution that adequately serves these purposes. The power of marriage is not just legal but social. It seals its promise with the smiles and tears of family, friends and neighbours. It shrewdly exploits ceremony (big, public weddings) and money (expensive gifts, dowries) to deter casual commitment and to make bailing out embarrassing. Stag parties and bridal showers signal that what is beginning is not just a legal arrangement but a whole new stage of life. "Domestic partner" laws do none of these things.

I'll go further: far from being a substitute for the real thing, marriage-lite may undermine it. Marriage is a deal between a couple and society, not just between two people: society recognizes the sanctity and autonomy of the pair-bond, and in exchange each spouse commits to being the other's nurse, social worker and policeman of first resort. Each marriage is its own little society within society. Any step that weakens the deal by granting the legal benefits of marriage without also requiring the public commitment is begging for trouble.

So gay marriage makes sense for several of the same reasons that straight marriage makes sense. That would seem a natural place to stop. But the logic of the argument compels one to go a twist further. If it is good for society to have people attached, then it is not enough just to make marriage available. Marriage should also be *expected*. This, too, is just as true for homosexuals as for heterosexuals. So, if homosexuals are justified in expecting access to marriage, society is equally justified in expecting them to use it. I'm not saying that out-of-wedlock sex should be scandalous or that people should be coerced into marrying. The mechanisms of expectation are more subtle. When grandma cluck-clucks over a still-unmarried young man, or when mom says she wishes her little girl would settle down, she is expressing a strong and well-justified preference: one that is quietly echoed in a thousand ways throughout society and that produces subtle but important pressure to form and sustain unions. This is a good and necessary thing, and it will be as necessary for homosexuals as heterosexuals. If gay marriage is recognized, single gay people over a certain age should not be surprised when they are disapproved of or pitied. That is a vital part of what makes marriage work. It's stigma as social policy.

If marriage is to work it cannot be merely a "lifestyle option." It must be privileged. That is, it must be understood to be better, on average, than other ways of living. Not mandatory, not good where everything else is bad, but better: a general norm, rather than a personal taste. The biggest worry about gay marriage, I think, is that homosexuals might get it but then mostly not use it. Gay neglect of marriage wouldn't greatly erode the bonding power of heterosexual marriage (remember, homosexuals are only a tiny fraction of the population)—but it would certainly not help. And heterosexual society would rightly feel betrayed if, after legalization, homosexuals treated marriage as a minority taste rather than as a core institution of life. It is not enough, I think, for gay people to say we want the right to marry. If we do not use it, shame on us.

✘ NO
War of the Ring
DANIEL CERE

During the 1970s and 80s, most gay and lesbian theorists rejected marriage as an incurably heterosexist institution irrelevant to their concerns. Not surprisingly, the marriage question sparked little interest in a movement that defined itself as being free at last from the constraints of heterosexual conjugality. However, by the late 1990s, marriage was becoming the focus of gay and lesbian advocacy.[1] Within a few short years, a project to impose a new public meaning on the age-old institution was being advanced. Courts and governments began to take up the cause. The gradual deregulation of marriage passed over into an effort to reconstitute marriage on a new model. The war of the ring began, and the situation in the country changed dramatically.

How did the change come about? As recently as 1999, the Parliament of Canada confidently reaffirmed the historic definition of marriage, by a vote of 216 to 55. In 2001, the first same-sex marriage case reached a Canadian provincial court, but the British Columbia Supreme Court rejected the petition, arguing that the common-law definition of marriage could not be changed without an amendment to the country's Constitution. Then, within a year, legal advocates began their full-court press. In July 2002, in *Halpern v. Canada,* the Ontario Superior Court challenged the existing definition of marriage. This controversial judgment was followed by two copycat decisions in the Québec Superior Court and the British Columbia Court of Appeal.[2]

The Ontario decision did not insist that marriage *must* be redefined. However, it did conclude that the existing legal framework was discriminatory since it failed to provide fair public recognition of gay and lesbian unions. *Halpern* suggested three possible remedies:[3] (a) redefine marriage as a union of two persons, or (b) establish a domestic partnership regime that would offer legal recognition for same-sex couples, or (c) abolish marriage as a category in law and set up some kind of neutral registry system. According to *Halpern,* any remedy would have to be implemented "in a manner that accords to same-sex couples a recognition that is full and equal to that enjoyed by opposite-sex couples."

The Ontario court conceded that it was setting in motion a political process that would be "contentious, divisive, troublesome, and potentially at risk of paralysis."[4] Justice Robert Blair warned that the legal redefinition of marriage would not be an incremental change but a profound one. He noted that the consequences

> flowing from such a transformation in the concept of marriage ... are extremely complex. They will touch the core of many people's belief and value systems, and their resolution is laden with social, political, cultural, emotional and legal ramifications. They require a response to a myriad of ...

issues relating to such things as inheritance ... , filiation, biogenetic and artificial birth technologies, adoption, and other marriage[-related] ... matters.[5]

Halpern gave the federal government two years to consider the legislative
options. If the government failed to act, the court would impose the remedy of
redefining marriage.

In response to these developments, the federal government established a parliamentary committee to gauge the views of Canadians. Public hearings began in
January 2003, moving across Canada from Halifax to Vancouver and travelling
to Inuit communities as far north as Iqaluit. Nearly 500 submissions were made
by cultural and aboriginal groups, various civil associations, and faith communities. Then another judicial bombshell. On 10 June 2003, the Ontario Court of
Appeal declared that it would not bother to wait for the government, or for
Canadians, to consider new legislative responses. It struck down the existing law
of marriage as discriminatory, redefining marriage as a "union of two persons."

The federal government immediately hit the brakes on the parliamentary
process. On 12 June, just two days after the decision, it abolished the House of
Commons committee exploring this issue, sweeping aside the contributions of the
numerous individuals and groups that had participated in the hearings. Less than
a week later, on 17 June, the federal cabinet announced that it would draft legislation changing the definition of marriage. Without an electoral mandate, without
the benefit of serious social-scientific research, without adequate democratic
deliberation, without the normal process of judicial appeal, the government repu-
diated the historic definition of marriage and threw its weight behind the project
to redesign that most basic of social institutions.[6]

A few weeks after that, the government went to the Supreme Court of Canada
with a set of reference questions aimed at securing its approval for the new definition. The government initially asked the Court three questions. Was the legislation to redefine marriage within the legislative authority of Parliament? Was it
consistent with the Charter? And were clergy protected from being compelled to
solemnize marriages that violated their religious beliefs? On 28 January 2004, the
new Justice Minister, Irwin Cotler, added a fourth question: Is the traditional
opposite-sex definition of marriage consistent with the Charter?

On 9 December 2004, the Supreme Court delivered its response to the reference
questions. It affirmed Parliament's legislative authority to redefine marriage and
the consistency of the new definition of marriage with the Charter of Human
Rights and Freedoms. It underscored the religious freedom clause but questioned
the jurisdictional authority of the federal government to protect clergy involved in
the solemnization of marriages. Finally, the Court deliberately begged the fourth
question concerning the constitutionality of the traditional definition of marriage.

The supporting arguments may be more significant than the specific conclusions. The justices reject the principle that marriage is a unique social institution
that transcends the power of the state. They argue that marriage is a creature of

the state. They maintain that the state should engage in ongoing social engineering on this institution; that marriage can be "fundamentally modified by law."[7] This view reverses the traditional role of the courts as the protector of the soft-shelled world of marriage against intrusion by the state.

Second, the justices acknowledge that there are "competing" conceptions of the nature of marriage in Canada. However, they firmly side with one particular ideological view of marriage and dismiss the historic definition of marriage as a historically "frozen" tradition inherently bound to religion. They disparagingly compare the historic conjugal understanding of marriage to earlier legal traditions that denied women that status of being "persons."[8] They reject the notion that marriage is a complex multilayered reality involving sex-bridging, generativity, and orientation to children. They conclude that the law must evolve to embrace their close relationship concept of marriage. "The only objective core," they assert, "is that it is the voluntary union of two people to the exclusion of all others."[9] This minimalist ideology of marriage must be legally imposed as the new public norm.

Third, the judges attempt to graft this particular ideology of marriage onto the Charter of Rights and Freedoms. They note that the lower courts have found that "the opposite-sex" conception of marriage "violates the equality guarantee enshrined in section 15 of the Charter."[10] They conclude that the project to redefine marriage "points unequivocally to a purpose which, far from violating the Charter, flows from it."[11] This proposed legislation represents "a promotion of Charter rights and values" and thus "enriches our society as a whole."[12]

The Supreme Court had given the green light and on 1 February 2005 the federal government introduced Bill C-38, the "Civil Marriage Act." Bill C-38 imposes a new norm of marriage as a close committed relationship between consenting adults. The legislation transforms the legal meaning of parenthood by eliminating the concept of "natural parent" from public law and replacing it with the concept of "legal parent." Why? To give any legal weight to natural parenthood would compromise the parental claims of same-sex couples. Therefore, the birthright of children to be connected to their mothers and fathers must be stripped from law in order to tailor parenthood to the interests of adults.

The Civil Marriage Act denounces the historic definition of marriage as discriminatory and unconstitutional. The inner logic of this action necessarily stirs real anxieties about cultural and religious freedom. However, the protection for religious freedom put forward in Bill C-38 is paper thin. The federal government promises that it won't break into the sanctuaries of Canada's churches, mosques and temples to coerce religious officials to solemnize marriages against their conscience. The legislation fails to mention that this "protection" is bogus since the federal government has no jurisdiction over the solemnization of marriage. Furthermore, in those many areas of federal jurisdiction that the government could have offered real and tangible safeguards—charitable status, communications, funding to defend against court challenges, and so on—it is disturbingly silent.

CONJUGAL MARRIAGE OR CLOSE RELATIONSHIPS?

Social institutions are constituted by their shared social meanings. The legal and political imposition of a new authoritative norm of marriage represents a profound shift away from one historic paradigm of marriage to a new and highly controversial conception of marriage. Assessing the social and legal implications of this shift is not an easy task.

Comparative cultural analysis alerts us to the great diversity of forms taken by the marital institution, but it also shows us that marriage invariably displays certain features. Summarizing the historical and cross-cultural evidence, Margo Wilson and Martin Daly, evolutionary psychologists at McMaster University, conclude that marriage is an institution that interacts with a unique social-sexual ecology in human life. It bridges the male-female divide. It negotiates a stable partnership of life and property. It seeks to manage the procreative process and to establish parental obligations to offspring. It supports the birthright of children to be connected to their mothers and fathers.[13]

Canadian law and public policy have long recognized this. In *Egan v. Canada*,[14] Justice La Forest summed up the legal tradition when he stated that marriage is "firmly anchored in the biological and social realities" that men and women "have the unique ability to procreate, that most children are the product of these relationships, and that they are generally cared for and nurtured by those who live in that relationship." However, by the time of *Egan,* a revolt against those realities was already well under way. A new body of academic and legal opinion was busily draining marriage of its core conjugal characteristics: permanence, procreativity, and child-centredness. The move to divest marriage even of its sex-bridging essence was being prepared. Conjugal marriage would be discarded in favour of something else, something built on "pure relationships" or on what scholars sometimes call "close relationship theory."[15]

The British social theorist Anthony Giddens argues that contemporary culture is in the midst of a shift from a culture of marriage to a culture of pure relationships.[16] A pure relationship is one that has been denuded of any goal or end beyond the intrinsic emotional, psychological, or sexual satisfaction that the relationship brings to the adults involved. Pure relationships, unlike marriages, are the ever-changing product of private negotiation. In so far as marriage itself is drawn into this new culture of intimacy, it is placed on a level playing field with all other "long-term" sexual partnerships.[17] Severed from its historic roots in sex difference, permanence, and children, it becomes nothing other or more than a form of intimacy between consenting adults. It is made more pliable, open to constant renegotiation, easily contracted and easily dissolved.[18]

The close-relationship paradigm has not yet been subjected to sustained critical evaluation. Our legal establishment, however, appears very anxious to enthrone it in law. Close-relationship theory provides the framework for the recent recommendations of the Law Commission of Canada in its 2001 report *Beyond Conjugality:*

Recognizing and Supporting Close Personal Adult Relationships. Its influence is also evident in recent court judgments on marriage. Consider, for example, the language of the *Halpern* appeal:

> Marriage is, without dispute, one of the most significant forms of personal relationships . . . Through the institution of marriage, individuals can publicly express their love and commitment to each other. Through this institution, society publicly recognizes expressions of love and commitment between individuals, granting them respect and legitimacy as a couple. This public recognition and sanction of marital relationships reflect society's approbation of the personal hopes, desires and aspirations that underlie loving, committed conjugal relationships. This can only enhance an individual's sense of self-worth and dignity.[19]

What is seldom acknowledged is that this paradigm shift from the conjugal to the close relationship represents a fundamental reinterpretation of the core social purposes of marriage. We are assured that the redefinition it mandates won't make any real difference to society at large; it will simply provide a new measure of dignity to a small and oppressed minority. Evan Wolfson, a prominent same-sex marriage advocate in the United States, dismisses any concern about the big picture with a cheeky rebuke: "Gay people will not use up all the marriage licenses. There's enough marriage to share."[20]

This comforting rhetoric has a familiar ring to it, however. Thirty-five years ago advocates of the liberalization of divorce laws advanced a similar line of argument. At that time, critics of no-fault divorce cautioned that tampering with the meaning of marital permanence could affect the stability of marriage as a social institution. Opinion leaders dismissed those worries, too. No-fault divorce would only make things easier for those hard-pressed couples already headed for breakup, they insisted. Why should it affect stable marriages? There was a lot of talk about all the good things divorce reform would do for the marriage culture. Conjugal culture would be cleansed of bad marriages. Overall marital happiness would be enhanced. With this guarantee, divorce reforms were put into law. The guarantee proved to be fraudulent; divorce rates spiked dramatically, and marital satisfaction declined.[21]

Once again, the experts are confidently telling us that another radical legal change won't make much of a difference. Once again, they are telling us that making marriage more pliable and user-friendly will only enhance Canada's marriage culture. Indeed, Canadians will be able to pride themselves that the change will make their country "rather cool" when compared with other nations.[22] Such facile assurances ought to worry us. So, too, should the apparent inability, or unwillingness, to reckon forthrightly with sex-difference in our social ecology. [23] That difference is something with which close-relationship theory cannot cope. As theories go, it is a blunt instrument. Its very capacity to create "a level playing field" means that it cannot generate any insight into sexual complementarity, male-female bonding, reproduction, or the ties between parents and offspring—which makes it quite unsuitable for dealing with marriage or with marital law.[24]

A CLOSER LOOK AT THE CLOSE-RELATIONSHIP EXPERIMENT

Michel Foucault contends that marriage has fostered a particular type of human identity, namely, the "conjugal self."[25] Be that as it may, marriage has always been the central cultural site of male-female relations. A rich history and a complex heritage of symbols, myths, theologies, traditions, poetry, and art have been generated by the institution of marriage, which encodes a unique set of aspirations into human culture along the axis of permanent opposite-sex bonding and parent-child connectedness.[26]

The proposal to delete sex-difference from the definition of marriage breaks up this code and challenges this heritage, as thoughtful gay and lesbian theorists concede. Ladelle McWhorter, for one, points out that if gay people are

> allowed to participate as gay people in the communities and institutions [heterosexuals] claim as theirs, our presence will change those institutions and practices enough to undermine their preferred version of heterosexuality and, in turn, they themselves will not be the same. [Heterosexuals] are right, for example, that if same-sex couples get legally married, the institution of marriage will change, and since marriage is one of the institutions that support heterosexuality and heterosexual identities, heterosexuality and heterosexuals will change as well.[27]

Heterosexuals are asked to overlook this fact, though it is not in their best interests to do so. Even the Ontario Court of Appeal demands, in effect, that the public meaning of marriage must be revised to take into account "the needs, capacities and circumstances of same-sex couples, not . . . the needs, capacities and circumstances of opposite-sex couples."[28] How reasonable is that, when the reconstitution of marriage to suit same-sex couples is going to have a serious impact on the community most served by the institution?

While most Canadians adhere to the historic conjugal definition of marriage, some are lulled into believing that redefinition will make little difference to their lives and families, and so into compliance with such demands.[29] But that compliance betrays a flawed understanding of the nature of social institutions. Social and economic theorists have rightly underscored the critical importance of institutions as public markers of social meaning.[30] Meaning matters, and the institutions that bear it serve to structure our experiences and to steer them in a particular direction. They define our goals, focus attention on those goals, and direct us toward them. Professor Harry Krause points out that the law "has deeply affected (and helped to affect) family behavior over time," and promises to continue to "shape and channel our future in this most important playground of human existence."[31]

We cannot tinker with the fundamentals of an institution like marriage without expecting significant consequences. Suppose the rules of chess were changed in order to standardize the moves of each of the pieces—what we would be left with would not be chess at all but a curious-looking game of checkers. Marriage, likewise, is not improved by becoming all things to all people. Rather, its capacity to carry its social meaning, and to serve its own distinctive goals, is cast into doubt. Changing the public meaning of an institution changes the social reality.[32] It transforms the understandings, practices, and goods supported by that institution. In this case it alters even the "conjugal self."[33] All of which helps to account for the highly charged nature of the conflict over marriage among those who are paying closer attention.

When we are asked for specifics about the changes that redefinition will bring, we are not altogether reduced to speculation. The couple-centred or close-relationship paradigm has been tried before. It may appear to be the latest fashion, but it has a longer and more checkered history than its advocates care to admit. In fact, today's couple-centred doctrine is a recycled version of the ideologies promulgated over the last century or so by largely discredited social theorists such as Friedrich Engels, Margaret Mead, and Alfred Kinsey. In the 1950s, for example, Harvard's Carle Zimmermann summarized the "new" marriage doctrine being popularized by Soviet Marxists and American sexologists: Marriage must be cut loose from its traditional anchors in permanence, male-female complementarity, and procreation. Marriage must be open to the endless creation of new lifestyles and new family forms. Marriage must be about loving relationships stripped and purified of any connection to the historic commitments and purposes of marriage.[34] Sound familiar?

Already in the 1920s, the Soviet feminist Aleksandra Kollantai was an enthusiastic proponent of this vision of marriage. She believed that marriage must be liberated from the oppressive constraints of permanence and children. A new culture of marriage "would be based only on mutual love." It would rest strictly "on emotional compatibility, common interests, and erotic attraction," and "would be moral only as long as . . . love persisted."[35] Moving words, and more than a little shrewd. Kollantai had embraced Marxism and was anxious to see the "withering of marriage" from a newly emancipated society. She calculated that nudging marriage toward this more pliable notion of pure mutual love would do the trick. As Commissar of Social Welfare, Kollantai was given the opportunity to put theory into practice. The force of the Soviet state was used to implement a set of legal reforms aimed at changing the public meaning of marriage. Policies included the establishment of no-fault divorce, eliminating legal distinctions between cohabitation and marriage, reconstituting marriage as a civil-union regime, universalizing abortion, establishing universal daycare, and other reforms now familiar to Canadians as well.

By the mid-1930s, these state interventions had done some serious damage. Family life in the USSR was destabilized, divorce rates were rising, temporary cohabitation was becoming more and more prevalent, birth rates were declining, and children were falling between the cracks of broken families, often ending up in the streets. The Soviet regime finally saw the writing on the wall and attempted some restorative work; in 1936 it began reversing some of its previous legal reforms. Commissar Kollantai would be amused, however, to learn that Western societies such as Sweden, Holland, and Canada (allowing for political differences) have been treading a similar path, over the last thirty-five years, to that of pre-war Soviet society. [36] And as they slowly but surely implement many of the policies that these earlier reformers experimented with, they are documenting many of the same results: declining marriage rates, declining birth rates, rising divorce rates, more couples in ever more temporary forms of cohabitation, more people struggling as single parents, and the attendant consequences for children.[37]

As was the case in the Soviet Union, not everyone is happy with the experiment. Surveys indicate that the vast majority of young men and women still aspire to committed marriage and family life as the centrepiece of their lives. Indeed, the hunger for a good marriage seems to be more acute among young people today than it was ten years ago.[38] The indications are, however, that these aspirations will often be frustrated and defeated. Social scientists suggest that current trends will have a profound impact on the lives of the millennium generation. "What's going on now is making the sexual revolution of the '60s and '70s pale in comparison," says Dr. Eli Coleman.[39]

Surveying the scene in Canada, sociologist Zheng Wu warns that it would be foolish to underestimate either the magnitude or the tempo of the decline of marriage over the past few decades.[40] Marriage rates fell from 7.1 per thousand in 1987 to 5.1 in 1998. That makes Canada's marriage rate significantly lower than that of the United States (8.4 in 1998) or of England (10.2 in 1998). The divorce rate, which began to spike in the 1960s, now hovers around 40%. The average age for marrying has climbed steeply. In the 1960s, it was 23 for women and 26 for men; now it is 32 for women and 34 for men. (This trend is placing greater stress on women, who must contend with a less merciful biological clock.) The proportion of families headed by married couples has dropped by over 20%. Cohabitation has more than doubled since 1981. Single-parent families have risen 50% since 1981.[41]

This social drift is most pronounced in Québec, which is the trend leader in the movement toward a culture of pure relationships. Currently 30% of Québecers live in cohabitational relationships (the highest in North America). The province's marriage rates have plummeted from 8.5 in the mid-1970s to 3.0 today. Despite the low marriage rates, divorce rates remain spectacularly high, at 47%.

Canadians, in other words, are increasingly having difficulty in forming and maintaining families. They are also bringing fewer children into the world. In 2001, some 40% of married couples were childless. In 1960, the Canadian fertility rate was about 4.0. Today our birth rate has collapsed to 1.5, well below the rate of replacement (2.1); it dropped 25% in the ten years between 1992 and 2002. Québec's fertility rate is even lower at 1.4, and in that province more than half of the children born (58%) are now born outside of marriage.

During the 1970s and 1980s, the baby-boomer generation transformed marriage into a very unstable institution. However, for the vast majority, marriage remained the main hinge of male-female relationships. Things look different now. Male-female relationships no longer revolve around marriage but hang on something so indefinite as to merit only that vaguest of tags, "being in a relationship." Ironically, in the new pure-relationship culture, men and women are drawn together for shorter and shorter periods of time, leaving more and more people flying solo. The recent study by Edward Laumann et al., *The Sexual Organization of the City,* [42] points out that the majority of individuals in urban areas now spend most of their adult lives being single, interspersed with periods of temporary marriage or cohabitation. Only a minority achieve a permanent marriage; fewer and fewer conceive and raise children together.

Katherine Gilday's new National Film Board documentary, *Women and Men Unglued,* poignantly depicts the fragmentation of male-female relationships among Canada's millennium generation. As the pathways to marriage become more difficult to negotiate, many of our young adults are beginning to wonder whether stable marriage is even a possibility. And yet—it is worth repeating—young people still look to a lasting marriage and family as the key to happiness. Canadian survey research indicates that 88% of young Canadians want to marry, 88% want to stay with the same partner for life, and 92% want to have children.[43] If that is really the case, the close-relationship experiment hardly seems designed to meet their needs; nor can it rely on them for support in the long run. So whose needs *does* it serve, and why is it being deployed with such vigour?

ENFORCING THE NEW MARRIAGE REGIME

The deconstruction of conjugal marriage in Canada has not been driven by democratic demand. In fact, the ongoing legal "reform" of marriage has been imposed from the top down. There is a sociological divide on the marriage issue, with support for same-sex marriage coming disproportionately from elite sectors of society—the academy, the legal community, the upper echelons of business and government—and from the media.[44]

That is worth remembering when exposed, as one so often is, to the movement's moralizing rhetoric. Advocates of redefinition, and of the close-relationship ideology that undergirds it, are consistently presented as more caring, more compassionate, more tolerant, and more discerning than their opponents. It is regularly stated, or at least insinuated, that those who reject redefinition are motivated by prejudice, ignorance, hatred, or religious intolerance. What that says about prior generations of Canadians, or about the rest of the world for that matter, may be debated. But what it says about those Canadians—some 67%, according to survey data—who still insist on the traditional definition is only too clear. They are the great unwashed, who lack moral sense and whose voice cannot be trusted.

In the politics of persuasion, rhetoric this hot should not be above suspicion. After all, most of the same Canadians who adhere to the traditional view also applaud the overcoming of unjust discrimination; a significant number of them even want to see formal recognition of gay and lesbian unions,[45] though *not* at the cost of changing the public meaning of marriage. There is no evidence that their position is rooted in prejudice or ill will. Until recently, gays and lesbians themselves regarded marriage as an intrinsically heterosexual institution, and many still do.

Perhaps, then, it is time to stand this charge on its head. Could it be that the language of tolerance and compassion, of diversity and rights—the standard panoply of same-sex marriage rhetoric—is little more than a moralizing veneer concealing other interests? One may choose not to doubt the sincerity of the academic artisans labouring to provide creative justifications for the deconstruction project. However, as Foucault warns, self-righteous moralities often prove to be "supple mechanisms" for advancing special interests in the public market of human relationships. Sexuality and social power—indeed, economic power—are interlaced.[46]

One sign of bad faith on the part of some who wish to entrench close-relationship theory is that they rarely reveal in the political arena just how far they are prepared to go in reconceiving marriage. The opposite-sex stipulation is for them but the first of several restrictions still to be challenged in a much larger deregulation agenda. That agenda—and deregulation, not same-sex marriage per se, *is* the agenda—is already being advanced on several fronts. For example, courts have recently come to the defence of privatized prenuptial agreements that subvert the public "community of life and property" character of marriage. In *Hartshorne v. Hartshorne*,[47] the Supreme Court of Canada concluded that the law must respect the fact that "individuals may choose to structure their affairs *in a number of different ways" and not try* "to second-guess" these freely chosen arrangements. Marriage is here nudged toward a purely private contract or barter system. The door is opened to designer marriages in which the individual partner with the greater resources calls the tune in crafting nuptial deals.

More disturbing is the fact that, off-camera, there is much talk in these circles of cracking open the dyadic restriction on marriage to make room for polygamy. Harry Krause, a respected legal theorist, notes with some satisfaction that polygamy now has "its thoroughly modern advocates."[48] Granted, but this renewed interest in polygamy should tell us something about the social-sexual interests in play here. The tradition of monogamous marriage in Western societies has always been a social practice that constrains the non-egalitarian instincts of aristocratic power. That restraining influence is now facing a serious challenge. Polygamy is the classic public-policy interest of socio-economic male elites with surplus resources to wield in the sexual marketplace.[49]

Room is to be made not only for polygamy, however, but also for polyamory. Academics now hold round-table discussions on the ethics of multiple-partner relationships. Dr. Deborah Anapol, for one, assures us that polyamory is an authentic expression of the multifaceted potential of pure-relationship culture, and so it is.[50] The opening up of marriage to multiple-partnership arrangements, when predicated on an understanding of marriage that is no longer constrained by an interest in permanent male-female bonding, procreation, and the welfare of children, is a rather obvious move. Indeed, it is difficult to see what compelling objection could be brought against it.[51]

Advocates of redefinition do not ordinarily point this out when dealing with the general public. They content themselves with the claim that a gender-neutral definition of marriage, on the close-relationship paradigm, will advance the values of fairness and tolerance. But state establishment of such a paradigm will forge for them a new ring of power, with which still more controversial transformations can be achieved. What they are asking is that law should be recast in a way that effectively denounces the conjugal conception of marriage as irrational, discriminatory, and unconstitutional, and that a new public meaning of marriage should be imposed by the sovereign power of the state. Policy decisions would then have to follow suit in all spheres of public life.[52] This winner-takes-all approach is touted as a "liberal" resolution to the debate.

If this reading of the situation seems exaggerated, consider the language that finds its way even into official court judgments. In *Halpern*, Justice LaForme declared the traditional view "repugnant."[53] *Goodridge v. Department of Public Health* (Massachusetts) includes passages denouncing the special privileges of marriage as a "caste-like system," support for which rests on "invidious distinctions" that are "totally repugnant."[54] Support for such distinctions is said to be "rooted in persistent prejudices against persons who are . . . homosexual." "The Constitution," we are warned, "cannot control such prejudices but neither can it tolerate them."[55]

The threats implicit in such language are not mitigated in the least by a government that promises, as the Canadian government recently did, not to coerce clergy into solemnizing unions against their beliefs. It is cold comfort to know that the state has no plans to do what is seldom even contemplated by totalitarian regimes. And is it not revealing that, in this new legal landscape, such a strange peril should appear on the horizon?

A TIME TO CHOOSE

In the glow of the Liberal government's landmark decision to change the definition of marriage, one of the leading advocates of same-sex marriage, New Democrat MP Svend Robinson, was asked whether he and his partner would soon be wearing wedding rings. The *Globe and Mail* (24 June 2003) recorded his response: "It's been an incredible time for those of us who have struggled for full recognition of gay and lesbian couples' equality rights. Yet I'm still unsure if Max and I will marry anytime soon. After nine years in a committed, loving relationship, how would the state's imprimatur change anything?" Some were confused by Robinson's response. Wasn't gaining that imprimatur the whole point of the struggle to force a redefinition of marriage? Was Robinson somehow dismissing the struggle as unimportant after all? Was he making light of it? On the contrary, if we stop to think about it, we can see that his dilemma was a perfectly natural one.

Marriage, on the historic conjugal view, is a union that includes, but also transcends, the subjective interests of the couple. It shapes the way they act as a couple and the way society acts toward them. It spells out a set of responsibilities and a social protocol. Through its recognition of marriage, the state affirms and promises to support those who accept the challenge of building a permanent and exclusive bond with a person of the opposite sex, a bond that opens outwards toward the future of society through the possibility of conceiving and rearing children. Marriage, to that extent, is a public affair.[56]

On the close-relationship model, however, marriage is reduced to a formalization of one's emotional commitment to a sexual partner. How exactly this kind of marriage serves society is open to debate. Society's support for it has none the less been demanded, in the name of equality, and for this the state's imprimatur is necessary. Once that support has been granted, though—once same-sex marriage has been established as a legal testimony to the full equality of close relationships in general—it is far from obvious why any particular close relationship should be bothered with it. If marriage means little more than having the state involved in one's love relationship, then a studied indifference to it may well be the right approach.

It is sometimes observed that same-sex couples like Svend and Max constitute a minute fraction of the population—well under 1% of all married and cohabiting couples in the country[57]—and that the commitment of these couples to a marriage culture remains uncertain. So perhaps we can all afford to be a little bit indifferent. No matter what happens to the law, same-sex marriages in Canada will surely be few.

That is true enough. But what is at stake in the war of the ring cannot be measured in simple, quantitative terms. Svend's dilemma should remind us of the fact that the battle for marriage is ultimately a battle for public meaning, and that public meaning really does matter. Redefining marriage is a high-risk game for the huge sector of Canadian society sustained by this institution. As a nation guided by the rule of law, we can't have it both ways. Under the rubric of "marriage," we will either have an institution dedicated to male-female bonding, and to procreation and child-rearing, or we will have a quite different institution, dedicated to a close-relationships regime. We, too, must choose, and our choice will make a qualitative, as well as a quantitative, difference to our future.

NOTES

1. Cf. David Chambers, "Couples: Marriage, Civil Union, and Domestic Partnership" in *Creating Change: Sexuality, Public Policy, and Civil Rights,* John D'Emelio, William B. Turner, Urvashi Vaid, eds. (New York: St. Martin's Press, 2002), pp. 281–304.

2. *Halpern v. Canada (A.G.),* [2002] 60 O.R. (3d) 321 (Ont. Div. Ct.) [hereinafter *Halpern* (2002)]; *Hendricks v. Quebec (A.G.),* [2002] J.Q. No. 3816 (Sup. Ct.); *Barbeau v. British Columbia (A.G.),* 2003 BCCA 251.

3. *Halpern* (2002), ibid. at para. 127ff.

4. Ibid. at para. 138.

5. Ibid., at paras. 97–99: "The Courts are not the best equipped to conduct such a balancing exercise, in my opinion. This is not an incremental change in the law. It is a profound change. Although there may be historical examples of the acceptance of same-sex unions, everyone acknowledges that the institution of marriage has been commonly understood and accepted for centuries as the union of a man and a woman. Deep-seated cultural, religious, and socio-political mores have evolved and shaped society's views of family, child-rearing and protection, and 'couple-hood' based upon that heterosexual view of marriage. The apparent simplicity of a linguistic change in the wording of a law does not necessarily equate with an incremental change in that law. To say that altering the common law meaning of marriage to include same-sex unions is an incremental change, in my view, is to strip the word 'incremental' of its meaning." (Justice Robert Blair)

6. The Québec Court of Appeal, in *Ligue catholique pour les droits de l'homme v. Hendricks,* [2004] J.Q. No. 2593 (Qc. C.A.), underlined the legal significance of the federal government's failure to contest recent court decisions declaring the traditional definition constitutionally invalid (para. 24). A federal law cannot be unacceptable in one province yet acceptable in others. If the traditional definition of marriage is unacceptable in Ontario, then it is unacceptable in all of Canada (para. 28). The court thus concluded that recent judicial and political manoeuvres have effectively killed the historic definition of marriage in Canada.

7. Supreme Court of Canada, "Reference re Same-Sex Marriage," Dec. 9, 2004, paras. 24–25.

8. Supreme Court of Canada, "Reference re Same-Sex Marriage," Dec. 9, 2004, para. 22.

9. Supreme Court of Canada, "Reference re Same-Sex Marriage," Dec. 9, 2004, para. 27.

10. Supreme Court of Canada, "Reference re Same-Sex Marriage," Dec. 9, 2004, para. 41.

11. Supreme Court of Canada, "Reference re Same-Sex Marriage," Dec. 9, 2004, para. 43.

12. Supreme Court of Canada, "Reference re Same-Sex Marriage," Dec. 9, 2004, para. 46.

13. "Marriage is a universal social institution, albeit with myriad variations in social and cultural details. A review of the cross-cultural diversity in marital arrangements reveals certain common themes: some degree of mutual obligation between husband and wife, a right of sexual access (often but not necessarily exclusive), an expectation that the relationship will persist (although not necessarily for a lifetime), some cooperative investment in offspring, and some sort of recognition of the status of the couple's children. The marital alliance is fundamentally a reproductive alliance . . . " Margo Wilson and Martin Daly, "Marital Cooperation and Conflict" in *Evolutionary Psychology, Public Policy and Personal Decision,* Charles Crawford and Catherine Salmon, eds. (Mahwah, NJ: Lawrence Erlbaum Associates, 2004), p. 203.

14. [1995] 2 S.C.R. 513 [hereinafter *Egan*].

15. "Close-relationship theory" focuses on the common dynamics—initiation, maintenance, dissolution—present in *all* sexually bonded relationships. The case for same-sex marriage is based on the close-relationship assumption that same-sex relationships are equivalent. In *The Case for Same-Sex Marriage* (New York: Free Press, 1996), p. 109, fn. 6, William Eskridge, Jr., leans on Letitia Anne Peplau and Susan D. Cochrane's "A Relationship Perspective on Homosexuality," in David P. McWhirter et al., *Homosexuality/Heterosexuality: Concepts of Sexual Orientation* (New York: Oxford University Press, 1990).

16. See Anthony Giddens, *The Transformation of Intimacy: Sexuality, Love and Eroticism in Modern Societies* (Cambridge: Polity Press, 1994), and *Modernity and Self-identity. Self and Society in the Late Modern Age* (Cambridge: Polity Press, 1992).

17. Close-relationship theory bleaches out the significance of embodied sexual difference and argues that all committed sexual bonds should be "subsumed under the broader construct of close or primary relationships." John Scanzoni et al., *The Sexual Bond: Rethinking Families and Close Relationships* (Newbury Park, CA: Sage Publications, 1989), p. 9. For a critique of close-relationship theory, see Daniel Cere, "Courtship Today: The View from Academia" in *Public Interest* 143 (Spring 2001): 53–71.

18. David R. Shumway, *Modern Love: Romance, Intimacy and the Marriage Crisis* (New York: New York University Press, 2003), pp. 139–40; Don Edgar, "Globalization and Western Bias in Family Sociology" in Jacqueline Scott, Judith Treas, and Martin Richards, eds., *The Blackwell Companion to the Sociology of Families* (Oxford: Blackwell, 2004), pp. 3–16.

19. *Halpern v. Canada* (2003), O.A.C. 172 at para. 5 [hereinafter *Halpern*].

20. Ben Townley, "U.S. Gay Marriage Debate Rumbles On" (www.uk.gay.com 20 Oct. 2003).

21. See the discussion of Canadian developments by Douglas W. Allen, "Comments on the Justice Minister's Same-Sex Discussion Paper," 1 Apr. 2003 (www.marriageinstitute.ca).

22. "Canada's New Spirit," *The Economist,* 25 Sept. 2003.

23. Advocates of redefinition do occasionally recognize these substantive differences. Cf. William Eskridge, Jr., Gaylaw: *Challenging Apartheid in the Closet* (Cambridge, MA: Harvard University Press, 1999), p. 11.

24. The close-relationship model discovers exactly what it predicts, namely, that same-sex relationships share certain common features with opposite-sex relationships. Thus Justice Blair (*Halpern,* supra note 13 at para. 32) went so far as to say that the former may be "marriage-like in everything but name." But it must be pointed out that close-relationship theory searches for common interpersonal dynamics in all intimate relationships. These patterns hold true for all dyadic relationships—friendship, sibling, same-sex, and opposite-sex relationships. Cf. Susan S. Hendrick, *Understanding Close Relationships* (Boston: Pearson Educational, 2003), pp. 108–9.

25. Michel Foucault, *The History of Sexuality,* vol. 3 (New York: Vintage, 1988), pp. 72–80.

26. Suzanne Frayser, *Varieties of Sexual Experience* (New Haven, CT: HRAF Press, 1985) and George Murdock, *Social Structure* (New York: Free Press, 1965).

27. Ladelle McWhorter, *Bodies and Pleasures: Foucault and the Politics of Sexual Normalization* (Bloomington: Indiana University Press, 1999), p. 125.

28. This on the basis that "the purpose and effects of the impugned law must at all times be viewed from the perspective of the claimant" (*Halpern,* supra note 13 at para. 91).

29. See Dimitra Pantazopoulos, *Ethix: Where Canadians Stand on the Ethical, Moral and Value Issues of the Day*, COMPAS Public Opinion Poll Analysis, Praxis Public Strategies, 28 Nov. 2003.

30. On the "new institutionalism" see, e.g., James M. Acheson, ed., *Anthropology and Institutional Economics* (New York: University of America Press, 1994). For its impact on the study of human sexuality, see Stephen Ellington, Edward O. Laumann, Anthony Paik, and Jenna Mahay, "The Theory of Sex Markets" in *The Sexual Organization of the City*, Edward Laumann et al., eds. (Chicago: University of Chicago Press, 2004), pp. 24–30.

31. Harry Krause, "Marriage for the New Millennium: Heterosexual, Same-Sex—or Not at All?" in *Family Law Quarterly* 34 (2000): 284–85.

32. Wolfgang Kasper and Manfred Streit describe institutions as "the 'software' that channels the interaction of people." In *Institutional Economics: Social Order and Public Policy* (Cheltenham, UK: Edward Elgar, 1998), p. 6. See also Edward Schiappa, *Defining Reality: Definitions and the Politics of Meaning* (Carbondale and Edwardsville: Southern Illinois University Press, 2003) and *On the Nature of Social and Institutional Reality*, E. Lagerspetz, H. Ihaheimo, and J. Kotkavirta, eds. (Sophi: University of Juvaskyla, 2001).

33. Alasdair MacIntyre and others have argued that social institutions are "practices" that embody certain internal goods as well as producing certain external goods. See *After Virtue* (South Bend, IN: University of Notre Dame Press, 1981). The self is shaped by its orientation to these goods. Institutions thus provide unique contexts for pursuing and actualizing particular forms of self-identity, which, as Mary Douglas says, are deeply connected to "defining communities"; see *How Institutions Think* (Syracuse, NY: Syracuse University Press, 1986), chap. 9.

34. See Zimmerman's *Family and Civilization* (New York: Harper and Brothers, 1947), chap. 2.

35. Quoted in Lynn D. Wardle, "The 'Withering Away' of Marriage: Some Lessons from the Bolshevik Family Law Reforms in Russia, 1917–1926" (II, B. 1, 2). For more on the present subject, see H. Kent Geiger, *The Family in Soviet Russia* (Cambridge, MA: Harvard University Press, 1968) and Harold J. Berman, "Soviet Family Law in Light of Russian History and Marxist Theory" in *Yale Law Journal* 26 (1946).

36. See, e.g., Allan Carlson's *The Swedish Experiment in Family Politics* (New Brunswick, NJ: Transaction, 1990) and Brigitte Berger's *The Family in the Modern Age* (New Brunswick, NJ: Transaction, 2002), chap. 2.

37. Research indicates that the reduction of marriage to a pliable close-personal-relationship regime means more unstable and less child-centred marriages. See Maggie Gallagher and Linda Waite, *The Case for Marriage* (New York: Doubleday, 2000), chap. 2; David R. Hall, "Risk Society and the Second Demographic Transition" in *Canadian Studies in Population* 29 (2002): 173–93; Frank Cox, "Qualities of Strong and Resilient Families" in *Human Intimacy: Marriage, the Family and Its Meaning* (Belmont, CA: Wadsworth Publishing, 1999), pp. 4–6.

38. The proportion of Americans between the ages of 18 and 29 who told interviewers that a "happy marriage" is an important part of the "good life" actually increased between 1991 and 1996, from 72% to 86%. See Ira Mark Gellman, "Divorce Rates, Marriage Rates, and the Problematic Persistence of Traditional Marital Roles" in *Family Law Quarterly* 34.1 (Spring 2000): 17.

39. Quoted from Martha Irvine, "Survey Reveals Real-Life Sex and the City," CNN.COM, 9 Jan. 2004, http://www.cnn.com/2004/US/01/09/urban.coupling.ap/; cf. David Hall's talk of a "second demographic transition."

40. "Recent Trends in Marriage Patterns in Canada" in *Policy Options*, Sept. 1998. For summaries of Canadian statistical data see "Updates on Families" in *Canadian Social Trends* 69 (2003); John Conway, *The Canadian Family in Crisis* (Toronto: James Lorimer, 2003); Joanne Paetsch, Nicholas Bala, Lorne Bertrand, and Lisa Glennon, "Trends in the Formation and Dissolution of Couples" in *The Blackwell Companion to the Sociology of Families*, Jacqueline Scott, Judith Treas, and Martin Richards, eds. (Oxford: Blackwell, 2004), pp. 306–31. For American trends, see William Axinn and Arland Thornton, "The Transformation of the Meaning of Marriage" in *The Ties that Bind: Perspectives on Marriage and Cohabitation*, Linda Waite et al., eds. (New York: Aldine de Gruyter, 2000), pp. 147–65; also J. DaVanzo and M.O. Rahman, "American Families: Trends and Correlates" in *Population Index* 59 (1993): 350–86.

41. Data taken from Statistics Canada and Institut de la Statistique Québec.

42. See n. 30 above.

43. Reginald Bibby, *Canada's Teens: Today, Yesterday, and Tomorrow* (Toronto: Stoddart Publishing, 2001), pp. 143–46. In America, 93% rate marriage as one of their most important life goals (Gallagher and Waite, *The Case for Marriage*, p. 23). Brigitte Berger (*The Family in the Modern Age*, p. 59) states that "the vast majority of American men and women have remained loyal to the ideals of the conventional family . . . According to a 1996 census report most American families are still headed up by married couples (78 percent to be precise), marital bonds are still seen as binding (98 percent think marital infidelity to be wrong according to a 1996 University of Chicago sex survey), and . . . most Americans are passionately committed to their children and claim to be guided by conventional principles in the socialization of their children."

44. Canadians unencumbered by marriage, as well as those who have been involved in cohabitational relationships, also indicate more support for this couple-centred view. But it remains the case that proponents of a pure-relationship culture are distinguished by a specific social character (cf. Peter Berger, "General Observations on Normative Conflicts and Mediation" in Peter Berger, ed., *The Limits of Social Cohesion* [Boulder, CO: Westview Press, 1998]). It is also worth noting that lower-income sectors of society are more negatively affected than elite sectors by "decline of marriage" trends. See Theodore Ooms, "Strengthening Couples and Marriage in Low-Income Communities" in *Revitalizing the Institution of Marriage for the Twenty-first Century*, Alan Hawkins, Lynn Wardle, and David Orgon Coolidge, eds. (Westport, CT: Praeger, 2002), chap. 7.

45. Some 37% (i.e., more than half of those who support the traditional definition); see again Pantazopoulos, *Ethix*.

46. Cf. Michel Foucault's analysis of the modern movement toward sexual liberalization in *The History of Sexuality*, vol. 1 (New York: Vintage Books, 1990).

47. 2004 SCC 22.

48. "Marriage for the New Millennium," p. 289. I want to underscore here that what drives all of these developments is a relentless push for the deregulation of marriage by reducing it to a close-relationship regime. Deleting sex-difference as a defining rule does not by itself necessitate these other developments. It is just one move in a larger political game that reaches back to earlier "reforms" and forward to still more controversial transformations.

49. Laura L. Betzig, *Despotism and Differential Reproduction* (Hawthorne, NY: Aldine De Gruyter, 1986).

50. Deborah Anapol, *Polyamory, the New Love Without Limits: Secrets of Sustainable Intimate Relationships* (San Raphael, CA: Intinet Resource Center, 1997). Roger Rubin, former vice-president of the National Council on Family Relationships, argues that the current movement to redefine marriage "has set the stage for a broader discussion over which relationships should be legally recognized." The principles used in support of same-sex marriage are also appealed to in support of polyamorous relationships. See Rubin's "Alternative Lifestyles Today" in M. Coleman and L.H. Ganong, eds., *Handbook of Contemporary Families* (Thousand Oaks, CA: Sage Publications, 2004), pp. 32–33.

51. The Law Commission has already proposed that their new legal category of "close personal relationship" should not be "limited to two people." They argue that "the values and principles of autonomy and state neutrality require that people be free to choose the form and nature of their close personal adult relationships." *Beyond Conjugality*, p. 133, fn. 16.

52. Cf. Jack Knight and Jean Ensminger, "Conflict Over Changing Social Norms: Bargaining, Ideology, and Enforcement" in Mary Brinton and Victor Nee, eds., *The New Institutionalism in Sociology* (New York: Russell Sage Foundation, 1998), pp. 105–26.

53. *Halpern* (2002), supra note 2 at para. 411. His use of the term "repugnant" is a technical one, but cf. para. 212.

54. No. 08860 (Mass. S.J.C. 2003). On 18 Nov. 2003 the court rendered an American version of *Halpern*, with a four-three decision in favour of same-sex marriage. The quoted phrases are drawn from the opinion of Justice Greaney; see also "Opinion to the Senate," 3 Feb. 2004 (section 3 of the opinion of Justices Marshall, Greaney, Ireland, and Cowin).

55. Chief Justice Marshall (section. 3), who in the final sentence above is quoting, in a new context, a statement from *Palmore v. Sidoti,* 466 U.S. 429, 433 (1984).

56. See Gallagher and Waite, *The Case for Marriage,* chap. 2.

57. Recent census data in other Western countries indicate a range of about one-half to one percent.

POSTSCRIPT

In Canada, the argument for same-sex marriage often begins and ends with the claim that it is simply a right afforded gays and lesbians. There is no real attempt to go beyond this point, even though the Charter itself urges all to consider whether rights can be reasonably limited. Accordingly, Jonathan Rauch's piece is welcomed because it seeks to show that same-sex marriage is consistent with some important purposes of marriage—it is, in other words, not just a matter of rights. As Rauch says, society relies on the institution of marriage to provide both stability and care for people when they face serious difficulties, and for Rauch same-sex marriages would help to carry out these functions. Yet, one wonders if Rauch fully appreciates the possible consequences of redefining marriage. As Daniel Cere says in his article, major adjustments have been made to the institution of marriage in the past—making it easier to divorce, for example—and the results have been hardly positive. Then there is the issue of procreation and its place in marriage. Rauch acknowledges the importance of procreation, but his emphasis is clearly on the caring and stabilizing duties of marriage. But it might be argued Rauch's article suffers from a case of misplaced emphasis. What is central to marriage is procreation, not love and caring.

For his part, Cere argues that the move to same-sex marriage represents a fundamental shift in the meaning of marriage. Traditionally, marriage has been about bringing together the two sexes and providing a stable and permanent environment in which to raise children. But same-sex marriage allegedly reduces marriage to just another kind of relationship that allows people to satisfy certain needs. Cere also warns that any redefining of marriage will change the meaning of marriage for heterosexual couples in a way that would most likely weaken the institution of marriage. These are good arguments, but they are not without these weaknesses. Gay and lesbian couples would no doubt claim that they are more than capable of offering a stable family life. Indeed, the point of same-sex marriage is to allow homosexuals to become part of the tradition of marriage and family. As for the effect of same-sex marriage on the meaning of marriage, one might say that the strength of modern societies is their adaptability.

To begin a consideration of same-sex marriage, students might start with a publication of the Law Commission of Canada entitled *Beyond Conjugality: Recognizing and Supporting Close Personal Adult Relationships* (Ottawa: LCC, 2002). The publication—which is available online—has a definite view on same-sex marriage, but it also provides some good background on the history and purpose of the family (and some possible options for reform). Sociological texts on marriage and family might also be consulted at this stage of the investigation. One such text is Agnes Riedmann, Mary Ann Lamanne, and Adie Nelson, *Marriage and Families* (Toronto: Thomson Nelson, 2003). The next step is to acquire some background on developments affecting same-sex marriage in

Canada. One of the best places for this is the website of the federal Department of Justice, which offers a number of reports on the legal decisions and legislative actions in relation to same-sex marriage (an especially good report to read is Department of Justice, *Marriage and Legal Recognition of Same-Sex Unions: A Discussion Paper*, November 2002). The website of the Institute for the Study of Marriage, Law and Culture also provides a rich trove of material on same-sex marriage (and offers a nice way of organizing how one might approach the issue of same-sex marriage). With all the necessary background, the student is now ready to meet head-on the arguments for and against same-sex marriage. Though directed toward an American audience, Jonathan Rauch's *Gay Marriage: Why It Is Good for Gays, Good for Straights, and Good for America* (New York: Henry Holt, 2004) will reward those wishing to better understand the case of same-sex marriage in Canada. The website of EGALE Canada, an organization supporting gays and lesbians, also provides help for those wishing to learn more about the argument for same-sex marriage. For a reading that makes the contrary case, the following publication is essential: Daniel Cere and Douglas Farrow, eds. *Divorcing Marriage: Unveiling the Dangers in Canada's New Social Experiment* (Montreal and Kingston: McGill-Queen's University Press, 2004). The aforementioned website of the Institute for the Study of Marriage, Law and Culture offers additional readings and for a comparison of developments in the United States and Canada, students should see Daniel Cere, "Love and Marriage—and Family Law," *Public Interest* 159 (Spring 2005).

The debate over same-sex marriage is also closely connected with the issue of religious liberty. Opponents of same-sex marriage argue that if the idea becomes enshrined in law, then those who oppose it on religious grounds may not be able to express their views. Thus far, the federal government has argued that the religious freedoms of those who oppose same-sex marriage will be protected. Nevertheless, in British Columbia, a human rights complaint has been launched against the Knights of Columbus, a Catholic lay organization, for refusing to rent its hall, located on church property, for use for a wedding reception for two lesbians. In Alberta, a complaint was made to the provincial human rights commission for statements made by a Catholic bishop opposing same-sex marriages.

Some have attempted to avoid a clash between religious freedoms and gay rights by arguing that the state should get out of the marriage business altogether. Ian Benson, Executive Director of the Centre for Cultural Renewal in Ottawa, for example, argues for a "civil union" approach, which is found in some European countries. Under this model, those who want to benefit from the state's recognition of their relationship would need only to file the necessary documents to have the "civil union" recognized. They would then be entitled to whatever benefits that the government may wish to bestow on such relationships. However, the government itself would not decide whether it would recognize this as a "marriage" in the more traditional sense. This would be done, through some public ceremony held either by a religious body or some other form of social organization. Religious or non-religious groups who wish to recognize same-sex marriages through a public ceremony would be free to do so in the same way that other religious institutions may wish to continue blessing only heterosexual unions. The effect would be to take the decision to recognize and define marriages out of the hands of government and to depoliticize the issue. For a summary of Ian Benson's argument see his article, "The Future of Marriage in Canada: Is It Time to Consider 'Civil Unions,'" available on the website of the Centre for Cultural Renewal.

In the wake of the passage of the same-sex marriage legislation, gay rights advocates heralded June 28, 2005, as a historic day in the development of Canadian human rights. However, opponents call for a continuation of the struggle against the acceptance of same-sex marriage. Just days before the passage of the legislation, Doug Farrow published an article entitled, "Why and How Canadians Should Refuse to Recognize C-38" (it can be accessed at http://www.lifesite.net/ldn/ 2005_docs/Farrow.pdf). Clearly the debate will continue.

Does Canada Need a National Child Care Program?

✔ **YES**
MICHAEL KRASHINSKY, "Canada Needs an Early Childhood Education and Care Program"

✘ **NO**
BEVERLEY SMITH, "Equal Benefit to Children: What It Really Means"

Issues of public policy are like puzzles waiting to be solved. If we look carefully, each policy issue presents us with a number of pieces that have to be put together to make things right. Take, for example, what is at the heart of this particular debate, namely the care of young children. One piece of this specific policy puzzle is the parents, who simultaneously may want to pursue careers while providing loving care for their young ones. There is also the government, which in this case desires action that is both effective and equitable. A third piece, of course, is the children. A final piece to consider might be the requirements of the larger society. Society depends on a productive citizenry, so a population that works is key to its functioning. But society also relies on such core institutions as the family, and it might be thought that the family benefits from anything that keeps it tied together. A successful child care policy takes these pieces and fits them in a manner that pleases all.

A strong contender for solving the child care puzzle is a program that supplies regulated or licensed child care services to all young children at little or no direct cost. For its supporters, who like to call the initiative "Early Childhood Education and Care," the benefits of a national child care program are clear. With the provision of care in a regulated centre, parents are free to enter the labour force knowing that their children are receiving good care. The government likes the program because it is fair—all families may take advantage of it—and because it stands a good chance of success. The children themselves benefit for they are direct beneficiaries of care that must meet certain standards, including the actual provision of care by certified child care providers. And then there is society. It gets an enriched workforce as well as children who form a strong basis for the next generation of productive citizens. A national child care program, it seems, solves the puzzle: the pieces all fit together quite nicely.

But is this really true? Some parents may wish to stay at home and care for their children, but a national program seems to provide these parents with no benefit. The piece of the puzzle that represents the family may thus fit only awkwardly—if at all—with the other pieces. Some also claim that regulated child care really provides little benefit, and that the best it can do is help disadvantaged children. If this is the case, then a universal program covering all young children seems unwise, at least from the perspective of governments wishing to spend their scarce resources wisely. Also disruptive is the concern that a national program weakens the family unit in its efforts to provide an incentive for parents to become working parents and to leave the care of their children to others. In light of all this, a preferred course of action might be either to limit the program to children in need or to provide all families with a cash grant that can be used to provide care for children in any way the family sees fit (including the family using the grant to compensate one parent for staying at home).

However, these solutions, too, are not totally satisfactory. A policy that targets only disadvantaged families risks stigmatizing the recipients of the child care benefits, and one that simply hands cash over to families may fail to provide sufficient guarantees that the benefits will be directed toward the children. And they both seem, administratively speaking, too complicated. Supporters of a national program see their proposal as an extension of the school system, with children starting school a few years earlier than has been the case—hence the name "early childhood education and care." For some, this seems much easier to implement. But administrative simplicity is not necessarily the key to any child care program. So we appear to be back at the start, looking for a solution to the child care puzzle.

In the readings, Michael Krashinsky, a professor of economics at the University of Toronto, outlines the case for a national child care program based on the use of regulated child care centres. Beverley Smith, a child care researcher and former head of the children's group Kids First Parents Association of Canada, contends that the wisest course of action is not to proceed with a national child care program but rather to place money directly in the hands of families with young children.

✔ **YES**
Canada Needs an Early Childhood Education and Care Program
MICHAEL KRASHINSKY

The issue of child care first emerged on the Canadian policy agenda almost 40 years ago. Despite numerous political debates and promises, very little public money has been spent on child care, and that money has been targeted largely to very poor parents whose children are "at risk." The political landscape began to change in the late 1990s when Quebec introduced a universal program of $5-a-day (now $7-a-day) child care for all children under school age. The policy debate was joined in the rest of Canada late in 2004 when the new Martin federal government announced a promise to spend $5 billion over the next five years. While a full child care program will cost significantly more than $1 billion per year (in the end, at least ten times this amount will probably be needed), the Martin commitment represents a major step in that direction and sets us on the road toward a major new social initiative. Of course, child care is a provincial responsibility, so launching a child care program will require the cooperation of the provinces, and negotiations are going on between Ottawa and the provinces as I am writing these words.

It is my view that Canada needs a high quality public program in early childhood education and care (which I will refer to from here on as "ECEC"), and that such a program will ultimately strengthen Canada both economically and socially. The argument for such a program, which I will develop below, can be summarized in a relatively straightforward way:

1. A considerable majority of mothers with young children are working in the labour force.

2. These mothers are not going to stop working for pay, and any policy to induce them to do so is going to be far more expensive than even the best child care program imaginable.

3. While their mothers are working, young children require some kind of care, but many of the current care arrangements are of low or, at best, uncertain quality.

4. High quality ECEC "matters." By this I mean that low quality care hurts children, while high quality care benefits them.

5. The benefits are more than just a quality-of-life issue. Children who receive higher quality care enter school better able to learn, and have greater success in school, and go on to higher productivity and better wages when they eventually enter the labour force. These successful children pay higher taxes, are healthier, and require fewer publicly financed remedial social services.

6. A good ECEC program will help women to combine paid work and family life, and more mothers will enter the labour force as a result. The productive work that they do enriches Canada and provides tax revenues that go a long way toward paying for the ECEC program.

Since each of these points is important in the overall argument for ECEC, it is worth developing each of them a bit more.

1. A considerable majority of mothers with young children are working in the labour force. In 1967, Canada's centenary year, most young children were still cared for full-time in their own homes by their mothers. The labour force participation rate of mothers with preschool children was about 17 percent (that is, one in six young mothers had paid work, and five in six were at home full-time). But things were about to change considerably. The following table shows the percentage of several different groups who were employed (%EMPL), focusing on mothers with partners and with children since 1976 (I focus on mothers with partners, since many single mothers face very heavy work disincentives; the figure for prime-age males is provided because it provides a point of comparison; the percentage employed is somewhat smaller than the labour force participation rate because it omits the unemployed):

Year	%EMPL of Mothers Youngest Child <3	%EMPL of Mothers Youngest Child 3–5	%EMPL for Mothers Youngest Child 6–15	All Males 25–44
1976	27.7%	36.2%	45.7%	90.9%
1981	40.0%	46.2%	55.4%	90.1%
1986	51.2%	55.5%	62.1%	86.2%
1991	57.2%	62.4%	70.3%	83.5%
1996	61.2%	63.4%	71.4%	82.9%
2001	63.6%	68.5%	75.7%	85.9%

(Source: Statistics Canada, Labour Force Survey)

What this table shows is the "sea change" that has occurred in the last thirty years in the attitudes of mothers toward paid work. (It is worth noting that children are of course a shared responsibility of mothers and fathers; I focus on mothers because all our evidence suggest that it is mothers who provide the largest share of child care in most homes, and mothers whose lives and employment are most affected by the presence of young children.) In 1976, most (about two out of three) mothers with young children were not looking for paid work; in 2001, most were looking for paid work. This shift represents perhaps the most important labour force phenomenon of the period, and it simultaneously has major implications for the Canadian economy and for Canadian children.

It is interesting to speculate on why this change has happened. Young women consider a life-long attachment to the labour force to be the norm. High salaries make work attractive; discrimination against working women is less than in the past; families are smaller; men are expected to participate in raising children (and some actually do); women are staying in school longer; and so on. But while this speculation may be interesting, it is somewhat irrelevant. Because whether or not we can explain why mothers are in the labour force, the fact is that they are— which leads us to point 2.

2. These mothers are not going to stop working for pay, and any policy to induce them to do so is going to be far more expensive than even the best child care program imaginable. Anytime a society goes through a major shift in attitudes, there is a tendency to look backward to what may seem with hindsight to be a "simpler" time. In this case, that simpler time would be one in which mothers stayed at home happily caring for their children, and public child care was not on the political radar screen.

There could be an interesting debate on whether in fact women were better off or happier in such a world, or whether this arrangement was in the long-run interest of children. It is my view that women stayed out of the labour market in the past only because of explicit discrimination and social pressure that made it difficult for any but the most determined young women to pursue careers when they had young children, and that modern attitudes make any regression to such a time unlikely. But such a debate is surely moot, since there is no evidence that any reasonable public policy could ever return us to such a world.

In practical terms, the only way to induce mothers with young children to stay out of the labour force would be to provide them with significant cash incentives to do so. These kinds of policies are sometimes mentioned as a way to avoid serious expenditures on child care. But there has been no discussion of what kinds of cash incentives would be needed to have a significant impact on labour force participation. Let's take a look at such a policy.

If we wanted to provide money to induce mothers with young children to leave the labour force, we would probably have to work through the tax system. One way to do that would be to provide a generous tax credit to non-earning parents, and eliminate this credit when the earned income of that parent rises above a certain amount. In economics terms, the net effect of such a program would be to reduce the effective take-home wage of the working mother, while providing an income transfer to families with non-working mothers. How large would the income transfer have to be to have a significant effect?

In an earlier piece Gordon Cleveland and I worked through exactly such a calculation.[1] It turns out that a 2.8 percentage point drop in the labour force participation rate of mothers with young children would have required a $1400 tax credit in 2002. Now in that year, about 65 percent of the women with preschool children were employed. One estimate of the cost of a good child care program would be about $9400 per child in 2002. Suppose that we assume that parents paid 20 percent of this cost, so that a child care program would cost the government about $7500 per child. What would happen if we just gave this money to mothers with young children if those mothers stayed home?

We can answer this by extending what we already know: that a $1400 tax credit would buy us a 2.8 percentage point drop in the labour force participation rate. Making the assumption that all effects are linear, we would conclude that a $7500 tax credit would buy us 2.8 x 7500 ÷ 1400, or a 15 percentage point drop. This would reduce the 65 percent labour force participation rate down to 50 percent. This drop is significant, but it is hardly overwhelming. Multiplying the cost per recipient by the number of mothers who would receive the tax credit, we estimated that the short-run cost of such a program would be at least $7.5 billion per year. In the longer run, the program would be even more expensive, because we know that mothers who stay at home for a significant period of time earn less in the future when they return to work, which would add to the lost taxes in the future. This cost is more than the cost of a comprehensive child care program that would direct good care and early education to all Canadian children.

Let's carry this "thought-experiment" a little further. What would we need to do to return the labour force participation rate to the levels of 1967? Since in 1967, only 17 percent of mothers with young children were in the paid labour force, we would need approximately a 50 percentage point drop in the labour force participation rate. Redoing the math, this means an income transfer program of roughly $25,000 per family (essentially, we would have to replace most of the income earned by the working mothers, who earned an average of about $32,000 in 2002). Since the money would go to about 85 percent of the roughly one-and-a-half million mothers with young children, such a program would cost about $32 billion per year, even ignoring all the lost tax revenue that would not be collected from all the mothers who are no longer working.

The "bottom line" in all this is simple: mothers with young children are working, and they are going to continue to do so. Any attempt to reverse this trend would cost far more than even the best child care program that we could imagine. And this reality leads us to point 3.

3. While their mothers are working, young children require some kind of care, but many of the current care arrangements are of low or, at best, uncertain quality. If mothers with young children are in the labour force and are going to stay there, then the obvious question is what happens to those children. The answer should leave us uneasy. If we leave Quebec out of the mix (in Quebec, the government offers significant subsidies to all children in regulated child care facilities), we find that there are more than twice as many children between the ages of 2 and 5 in unlicensed informal care arrangements as there are in licensed regulated child care facilities. While many of the licensed facilities are quite good, licensing standards are relatively low in many provinces, and recent evaluations

of child care centres found a significant number (especially among centres that were incorporated as "for-profit" operations) providing a less than desirable level of care. Workers in these centres are in general quite poorly paid, because parents cannot afford the cost necessary to provide higher salaries, and this means that centres have trouble attracting and retaining well-trained staff.

But child care centres provide the best care in the child care "industry." What of the children in unregulated unlicensed facilities? In many cases, these children receive no better than custodial babysitting, with little or no early educational experiences. In some cases, the care providers lack the skills to find other jobs, and lack the training to provide proper care to the children they take in and care for.

Why should we care about the care of other people's children? Hillary Clinton's book *It Takes a Village* derives its title from the African proverb that it takes a village to raise a child. Children are more than just the "property" of their parents. The welfare of Canadian children affects all Canadians. In the language of economists, children carry with them a significant "externality." By this, economists mean that the benefits of children extend far beyond their own families. When children receive high quality care, they grow up to become more productive happy and involved citizens, and that makes Canada a better place to live.

The benefits are not just matters of the happiness of children or their civic involvement as adults. When children grow up to be more productive, they pay higher taxes and consume fewer dollars of welfare and other social services. In other words, they contribute to Canadian society in a myriad of ways, and those contributions flow to everyone else in Canada.

Furthermore, when high quality child care is available at relatively low cost, more parents will enter the labour force. These parents will pay higher taxes and themselves consume fewer social services, and again the benefits flow to all the other taxpayers in Canada.

Does this mean that we do not trust parents to care for their own children? Not at all. The problem is that the working parents of young children often lack the financial resources to buy the high quality care that their children need, and that even when they can afford good care, they have a hard time judging exactly what kind of care they should purchase. In this argument, we provide high quality ECEC to children for much the same reasons as we provide public education to them at a later age. We trust parents, but we also think that they need public programs to help them discharge their responsibilities.

For most families, the high cost of child care occurs at exactly the time in the family's financial history when resources are scarcest. Working parents are at the beginning of their working lives and have incomes that are well below what they will be later on. At the same time, they are struggling to purchase houses and cars and the other capital assets that older families often take for granted. Although in theory families could borrow against future earnings to finance child care expenditures, in practice this is hard to do. Thus most young families face difficult choices, in which every dollar spent on child care is a dollar not available for other important essentials.

In addition to the financial strains is the difficulty that most parents face in evaluating the quality of the care they purchase. To the casual observer, this statement may seem strange. After all, this is child care, not rocket science, and all parents are themselves involved in providing care to their own children. Shouldn't parents be able to judge the quality of care provided by babysitters and child care centres? In fact, the dynamics of caring for a large number of children in groups are difficult to evaluate without significant expertise. Parents are not around during the day when care is being provided, and the effect of bad quality care may take years to surface. Children cannot easily report to their parents about the quality of care received. As a result of all this, studies find that parents tend to substantially overrate the quality of the purchased care their children are receiving. And if parents do this, then they are probably not going to be anxious to pay for better care (when they already believe that their children are well cared for).

The bottom line is that many of the children of working parents are not getting care of sufficiently high quality. And this leads us to points 4 and 5.

4. High quality ECEC "matters". Low quality care hurts children, while high quality care benefits them.

5. The benefits are more than just a quality-of-life issue. Children who receive higher quality care enter school better able to learn, and have greater success in school, and go on to higher productivity and better wages when they eventually enter the labour force. These successful children pay higher taxes, are healthier, and require fewer publicly financed remedial social services.

The evidence on the effect of child care is quite clear. When parents work, children are harmed if they are placed in low quality child care arrangements. But in contrast, high quality child care arrangements have a positive impact on children.

The evidence is particularly dramatic for disadvantaged children. For example, the Head Start program in the United States has had a significant impact on children since its inception in the 1960s. The Caroline Abecedarian Project provided high quality child care to a small experimental group of low-income at-risk children and has demonstrated persistent long run positive effects.

The general gains for all children are naturally less dramatic, but they are nonetheless positive and important. The best study to date is an ongoing one supported by the National Institute for Child Health and Human Development (NICHD) in the U.S. It finds that the quality of child care matters. The overall outcomes for children in child care centres were about the same as for children cared for exclusively by their parents. But in general, children in high quality child care centres did significantly better than children in low quality child care arrangements. Furthermore, children in high quality child care centres did better than children cared for exclusively by their parents.

This last result may seem surprising. Does this mean that child care matters more than parental care? Or that parental care harms children? Not at all. The study also found that good quality care at home is very important in determining children's outcomes. What this all means is that high quality early education and care is extremely important in supplementing the care that is provided in the home. Incidentally, this is something that parents have always known. In my 1998 study with Gordon Cleveland, I reported figures which showed that almost half of all non-working parents with 2- to 4-year-old children supplemented parental care with some kind of part-day early educational program.[2] They do this because they know that early education matters, and that it benefits children even when they are cared for full-time by their own parents. When parents can afford supplementary educational programs, the data show that they use them.

But why should we be surprised by this? Recent scientific evidence has been showing how important early stimulation is in building intelligence in children. For years, good parents have invested large amounts of time and resources in providing wide and varied experiences for their children because they believe that effort devoted to young children will pay off throughout the children's lifetimes. The data support what would seem intuitively obvious: high quality early childhood education and care matter.

The following quote from *Neurons to Neighbourhoods: The Science of Early Childhood Development* presents a balanced assessment of the effects of child care quality, and indicates some of its key features:

> In sum, the positive relation between child care quality and virtually every facet of children's development that has been studied is one of the most consistent findings in developmental science. While child care of poor quality is associated with poorer developmental outcomes, high-quality care is associated with outcomes that all parents want to see in their children, ranging from co-operation with adults to the ability to initiate and sustain positive exchanges with peers, to early competence in math and reading.... The stability of child care providers appears to be particularly important for young children's social development, an association that is attributable to the attachments that are established between young children and more stable providers. For cognitive and language outcomes, the verbal environment that child care providers create appears to be a very important feature of care.[3]

Of course, high quality child care not only matters to children, it also matters to their parents. Prior to 1970, child care was provided for young children almost exclusively within families. But this could only take place by essentially moving half of all adult Canadians (generally the female half) out of paid employment and into the household. By the time children were grown, and mothers were free to enter the labour force, their skills had eroded and good jobs were hard to find. Knowing this, few young women prepared for careers that required high levels of training and skill. The economic cost of this was tremendous, which leads us to the final point.

6. A good ECEC program will help women to combine paid work and family life, and more mothers will enter the labour force as a result. The productive work that they do enriches Canada and provides tax revenues that go a long way toward paying for the ECEC program.

Working women have enriched Canada to an enormous extent. That value is what generated the massive costs that I calculated earlier for any program that would remove working mothers from the labour force. Because these mothers are very productive workers and generate large amount of income, any program that would get them to leave the labour force voluntarily would have to be very expensive.

We can get at this value another way. What is the value of the productivity of all working mothers with young children? In our 2003 study (*Fact and Fantasy: Eight Myths About Early Childhood Education and Care*), Gordon Cleveland and I estimated the wages earned by these mothers in 2000, and came up with a figure of just under $27 billion. But this is only the tip of the iceberg.

We know that when people leave the workforce for any length of time, their skills erode and their productivity declines. We estimated that this would double the loss to the Canadian economy if all mothers were to stay home, so the loss would mushroom to about $53 billion, about 5 percent of Canada's GDP. And the story does not end there. The resulting reduction in the workforce would make Canada's economy smaller, and hence attract less investment into the economy. Since working mothers account for roughly 7.5 percent of the workforce, a rough guess would be that when the dust settled, the economy would be 7.5 percent smaller. This pushes the loss up closer to $80 billion. Finally, history shows that when women leave the labour force to care for children, many never return to paid work. And women who stay out of the labour force for long periods do not invest as much into their own education and training, further reducing their productivity. All of this would push the cost up even further.

Lost productivity is real. It means that we have fewer resources to devote to all our needs—less for housing, less for education, less for medical care, and less for retirement. And in the end, lower productivity means lower tax revenues. The taxes paid by working mothers exceed the costs of high quality child care programs. This can be illustrated very simply. Taxes are roughly 40 percent of GDP in Canada. That means that the $80 billion in GDP mentioned earlier would itself generate about $32 billion in taxes. But when Gordon Cleveland and I estimated the cost of a good child care program for Canada in 1998 that would provide good quality care to all children aged 2–5 of working parents, and would also provide enriched early educational programs to all children 2–5 whose parents cared for them at home, we came up with a cost to the government of just over $5 billion, much less than the taxes collected.

Now of course these numbers are a bit misleading. Not all the tax revenue collected from working mothers is available for child care programs. Some of that money supports employment insurance programs for those parents; some supports medical care programs for those families; some supports the roads and transit systems that those parents use to get to work, and so on. But the point of this calculation is to suggest that child care expenditures are not simply a social program. Those expenditures help free up the time of working women, and those working women contribute significant amounts to the Canadian economy and to the government coffers. In a very real sense, expenditures on child care pay for themselves several times over.

It is all of this that leads Cleveland and me to conclude that child care would be a good investment for the Canadian government. Child care expenditures free up parents to enter the labour force and contribute to the Canadian economy. And child care expenditures invest in the future productivity of Canadian children. Making very conservative estimates of these payoffs, we concluded that there would be at least a two-to-one return on dollars invested in the early childhood care and education.

It seems useful to conclude by addressing two of the most common objections raised to significant public expenditures on child care. Critics often suggest that expenditures on child care would discriminate against families that prefer to raise their own children. And critics often ask whether Canada can afford the cost of a significant investment in young children, given the other pressures on public spending. Following the style of the rest of this discussion, let me address these two points in turn:

7. An ECEC program does not discriminate against stay-at-home parents. The discrimination argument is something of a "red herring" which deflects us away from the real issues. Any public program favours those who use it over those who do not. Thus public health care does not favour those who stay well, employment insurance does not favour those who do not lose their jobs, and funds for universities do not favour those who do not pursue higher education. In this sense, the real discrimination in an ECEC program is in favour of families with children and against families without children. This is because funds flow to all families with children, whether or not the parents of those families are in the labour force.

Earlier, I argued that early education worked as an important supplement for parental care, even when parents stayed at home to care for their own children. For this reason, I have always favoured a comprehensive ECEC program that would provide high quality child care in licensed facilities to children whose parents worked, and that would also provide part-day early educational programs to parents who chose to remain at home. Young children benefit from peer play and stimulation by peers and stimulating environments. This needs to be provided to all children, whether or not their parents are in the paid labour force. Just as we provide kindergarten to all children, recent research on early education emphasizes how important it is to provide early learning experiences to children before they enter formal schooling.

In some ways, the discrimination argument is itself a throwback to an earlier time when most children were raised by stay-at-home mothers. If most mothers were staying at home to care for their own children, why should the government provide a special service to the small fraction who were choosing to enter the labour force? Because of the productivity of those mothers and the importance of child care, even that version of the argument fails. But in an era when most mothers with young children are in the labour force, and when the majority of those children are currently receiving inadequate child care, the argument fails completely. It is hardly discrimination to provide services to young children who will clearly benefit from those services. And it is no more discrimination when we provide ECEC to young children than when we provide public education to those children when they are several years older.

Of course ECEC services are not free. Good child care is expensive. And this leads to the final point.

8. Canada can afford a high quality ECEC program. The initial commitment of the Paul Martin government was to $5 billion over five years. Everyone who has studied child care knows that this is only the first step, and that a good program would cost a good deal more. Gordon Cleveland and I set the cost to the government at just over $5 billion in 1998, but our program would have covered only children from 2 years of age and up, and although we allowed for a rise in the currently inadequate wages of child care workers, it is unclear whether more money might not be needed in the long run.

But it is also worth keeping these figures in perspective. As I suggested earlier, the value of working mothers to the Canadian economy today is probably about $80 billion. Looking only at working mothers, ECEC expenditures probably pay for themselves.

Furthermore, ECEC has been shown to have positive payoffs in the future productivity of the children in the program. In that sense, the real issue is whether Canada can afford not to invest in early childhood education. We seldom ask whether Canada can afford to provide children with a primary school or high school education, or whether we can afford the public funding of universities. We all understand that these are silly questions—a modern economy depends above all on a well-educated workforce. Yet current research suggests that educational dollars are at least as well-spent when they are directed at young children.

It takes taxes to support public programs. It is easy for critics to suggest that the weight of the Canadian public sector is dragging down the economy, and that international competitiveness depends on cutting public services to the bone. This is a counter-productive argument. International investors are attracted to stable countries with productive healthy workforces. Investments in public infrastructure that guarantee that kind of environment are what make us internationally competitive. Investment in early childhood education and care is just such an expenditure, one which Canada would be wise to make.

NOTES

1, Gordon Cleveland and Michael Krashinsky, *Fact and Fantasy: Eight Myths about Early Childhood Education and Care* (Toronto: Childcare Resource and Research Unit, 2003).

2. Gordon Cleveland and Michael Krashinsky, *The Benefits and Costs of Good Child Care* (Toronto: Childcare Resource and Research Unit, 1998).

3. Jack P. Shonkoff and Deborah A. Phillips, *From Neurons to Neighbourhoods: The Science of Early Childhood Development* (Washington, DC: National Academy Press, 2000), pp. 313–314.

✗ NO
Equal Benefit to Children: What It Really Means
BEVERLEY SMITH

Over the past twenty years there have been various proposals for a national child care program in Canada based on regulated child care centres. In its February 2005 budget, the federal government has now promised such a system. It will work with provincial governments to make child care spaces available to all families with young children, heavily subsidized by the state. Though the intentions behind a countrywide child care program may be good, there are serious problems with the one-sidedness of the proposal. For one, the plan exaggerates the need for child care facilities and ignores the evidence that other forms of child care are in demand. Some parents prefer to stay at home to look after their children. Others choose grandma care, care by parents in shifts, care by a parent with a home-based office, telecommuting, or part-time paid work during school hours only. The federal plan also assumes that non-parental care in regulated centres is the only way to ensure the highest level of quality of child care. But, again, the evidence suggests otherwise, that families also offer a nurturing environment for young children. And then there is the issue of choice. The current plan provides financial assistance for only one type of child care. A fair program would offer families a choice of care arrangements and then let them decide which arrangement best suits their needs. The absence of choice opens up the possibility that this new program discriminates against some families and is in violation of the Canadian Charter of Rights and Freedoms.

In light of these criticisms of a universal, non-parental child care program, it is preferable to provide assistance to all families regardless of whether they use regulated child care centres. The argument of this paper is not that government is wrong to provide assistance to families with young children. Rather, the argument is that the assistance should be given equally to all children, not only to those in daycare.

NEED FOR CHILD CARE CENTRES

Proponents of a universal child care program say there is a need for more spots in child care centres. They point to the large gulf between the number of children in child care centres and the total number of children in the relevant age groups, and assume that the difference between the two represents the unmet demand for child care. But there are many alternatives to child care centres. Parents embrace a wide variety of child care arrangements when seeking to provide care for their children. Some rely on relatives in the home, while others depend on non-relatives in or outside the home—and these are only a few of the alternative arrangements.[1] What is also often ignored is that a sizeable proportion of parents are actually working for pay at home, a development that undercuts the claim that licensed child care facilities are essential for parents, especially mothers, to enter the paid labour force. It might be argued that alternatives to regulated care are used only because they are relatively inexpensive. But such an idea ignores the huge salary sacrifice made by the caregiver in such situations, often a full income. This is actually for most families the most costly option, but still these families—even those in poverty—use these alternatives because they want to. In 1996, the Canadian Council on Social Development, in its publication "The Progress of Canada's Children," found "[m]any parents go to extraordinary lengths so that one can be at home when the children are young, often living below the poverty line to do so."[2]

There are also other indicators that suggest that the focus on child care centres is simply wrong. One is that many parents prefer part-time employment over full-time work in order to spend more time with their children. Also, the provincial government of Quebec offers a child care plan that greatly reduces the cost of licensed centres, yet many families still choose not to participate in the plan.[3] According to polls and surveys, Canadians want diversity in their child care arrangements. The Vanier Institute, a research body that focuses on the family, recently found that most Canadians feel that their children should be cared for by a parent or relative. Interestingly, the survey also found that care offered in regulated daycare centres ranked fifth among seven choices (and this ranking held in Quebec as well as in other parts of the country).[4] And even though many parents say they cannot afford to be home with the child, this paper makes the case that if we agree what are the "best interests" of the child, then the only appropriate national policy should be to enable those to come to fruition. If daycare is not the preferred option, then to promote it alone is arguing for the second-best interests of the child.

Clearly, instead of ignoring the preferences of parents, public authorities should address them. Given the demand for a wide variety of child care arrangements, it is curious why governments are so determined to focus on only one type of care. The main reason is probably the desire to have women earning and paying tax full-time all their lives. This agenda is barely hidden and even admitted in some documents. Gordon Cleveland and Michael Krashinsky, supporters of a licensed child care program, have written, "... if all child care costs were fully subsidized, the rate of full-time employment (as a percent of all mothers) would increase from 29 percent to 52 percent, suggesting that child care subsidies will have a particularly strong positive effect on full-time work."[5] But this is not the most commonly expressed reason for the government's proposal. The one we hear is that daycare is better for children, and that high quality care can only be provided through regulated child care facilities. The emotional assertion is then made that daycare is as dear to our hearts as is universal public education or free medical care—a sacred right. The use of the term "early childhood education and care" to describe recent government-initiated child care proposals cleverly and emotionally makes the reader think that if you fail to put your child in daycare you are against educating a child at all. How mistaken. As a teacher and parent for 30 years, I am convinced that the most well remembered learning experiences are with someone who loves the child. The parent is the first and main caregiver. Parents may feel reassured that strangers can provide adequate care in their stead, but demoralizing parents into thinking they are themselves incompetent is unfair. We should not forget what is involved in earliest stages of life—learning to roll over, to crawl, to hold a spoon. This learning time that is exhausting for a parent is absolutely vital to the learning of a child and does not require caregiver training as much as a loving presence. And children are so different from each other that a one-size fits all plan is not likely to be very educationally sensitive. The shy child needs cuddle time. The extrovert needs to play. The elephant lover needs a visit to the zoo; the Lego enthusiast needs time alone to be creative; the water enthusiast needs swim lessons. All educators know that smaller class size is optimal for learning. It is ironic that when a mother gives birth to triplets or quadruplets, the community rushes in to help, knowing she cannot handle that workload alone—but that same adult–baby ratio is the norm in many daycares. How child care centres can claim to be better than the parent is troubling.

QUALITY OF CARE

There are studies that find children can benefit from placement in child care centres that offer a high quality of care. However, what is often not mentioned is that those studies such as Head Start are based on children from very troubled homes whose home-care option was problematic at best. Of course, any structured care is better than mayhem. What these studies also found was that going into the home and helping parents—and not taking the child out of the home—provided great benefit. In other words, the final verdict on daycare being even as good as parental care is still out. We who argue for choice are not saying daycare is bad. But we are daring to say that home-based care is also good, and not to be insulted as lesser. The problem with the national daycare proposal in Canada is its contention that *all* children would do better in child care centres. The best strategy for the state is to enable good care wherever the child is.

Some have suggested daycare should be favoured because at least then society can inspect, regulate, and enforce standards. The claim is then made that there is no guarantee parents will offer good care, so do not fund them. But parents also have high standards to abide by—all child welfare legislation puts a heavy onus on parents and the consequences of any abuse and neglect for a parent are much larger than for a daycare, namely loss of custody of one's own child. Parents hold themselves to a very high standard already not only because the arm of the law imposes one but because of their very strong emotional bond with the child. There are, however, some truly troubling aspects of using child care centres. One is cost. Funding staff well enough to make them not want to quit, funding administrators, and then funding inspectors of staff and administrators will cost billions. How much of our budget do we want to direct just to finding substitutes for parents? Is it not less expensive to fund parenting directly? Further, it will be very difficult to carry out the inspections, and the possibility of centres failing to meet standards looms great large.

The last point to make about quality of care is the wide variation of parenting preferences. Parents do not agree on what is good for their babies and any child care provider will be at his or her wit's end trying to respond to those conflicting opinions. It is not that third parties cannot do as parents suggest—it is that caregivers cannot simultaneously use and not use a soother, or vary ways to toilet train, or vary whether to pick up a crying child. The danger is not only that parents would be displeased but also that the unresponsiveness would be excused as if a one-size standardized approach was best. Such standardizing of our children is not necessarily in the best interests of a democratic nation that fosters creativity.

CHOICE

Child care proponents say having free daycare nearby gives women choices. That is actually true in that it lets them choose daycare. But funding only daycare makes any choice but daycare unaffordable, so it actually restricts choices by penalizing all other options. What it does is to channel women not just into full-time employment instead of part-time but also into only certain styles of employment—away from home, days only. Many polls show that women, if given real funded choice, want a much wider array of lifestyles—even at home full-time for a while. The daycare argument claims many benefits from the one lifestyle it endorses. It says that the child benefits from the high quality of care, the mother benefits from a more productive use of her time, the family benefits from the infusion of additional income, and society and government benefit from the fact that more people are now contributing to the economy and paying taxes. In fact, all those assumptions are flawed. The child benefits as much if not more from loving one-on-one care; the mother who is nurturing the development of another human mind is doing highly productive work; the family benefits in stability and emotional strength from the caregiving work; and the state gets a new generation of taxpayers at nearly no cost. A free democratic society lets its citizens make choices and limits occasions when government makes choices for them. And this is most critically true in relation to one of the most important societal institutions—the family.

Daycare proponents say that only with their style of care can women attain full equality with men and financial independence. They are wrong. The feminist movement has had two waves—one that gave women the vote and let them sit in the Senate, and one that welcomed women into corporate offices and university faculties. If we say women must leave home to have value, we have not come a long way but only half way. Yes, women can have value in any paid work outside the home, but they already have value in their unpaid and vital roles in the home. It is not an either-or situation but rather a both-and one. A third wave of feminism would insist that women can earn income or be caregivers—whatever they prefer—and be respected for both roles and be financially empowered. Anything less insults women. And to say that those who are at home with children are not "working" and not productive is an affront to feminism. Women have always worked, just sometimes without pay or recognition—and it is actually very consistent with women's final push to equality to value the caregiving role, whoever does it. This role itself, historically female, is the last challenge for us to value—the final liberation.

In the end, nobody can decide what is best for your child but you. And in a democracy the role of government is to protect that very right you have to make choices. We have signed charters defending this right and we need a child care plan that enshrines it. Daycare yes, but not only daycare. Fund all care, fund children.

The most disturbing implication of the absence of choice is its possible violation of the Charter of Rights and Freedoms. Section 15 of the Charter provides Canadians with equal benefit under the law, yet child care programs such as the one being proposed by the federal government deny some Canadians this basic right. Only those who use non-parental child care programs will benefit, but not others. The Charter of Rights and Freedoms provides Canadians with basic protections against the actions of government, and one of these protections is to be free of discriminatory actions and to be treated equally. But this is exactly what a child care program based on regulated centres fails to do. International declarations of rights support this view. Principle 6 of the United Nations Declaration of the Rights of the Child states that "the child ... shall, wherever possible grow up in the care and under the responsibility of his parents and in any case in an atmosphere of affection and or moral and material security." Similarly, article 29 (1) of the United Nations Convention on the Rights of the Child states that all parties to the convention "agree that the education of the child shall be directed to the development of the respect for the child's parents, his or her own cultural identity, language and values."

AN ALTERNATIVE

The preceding arguments question the fairness of a child care program that focuses only on one type of care—regulated child care centres. It is a social program and as such is not even constitutionally something the federal government is allowed to do. It is a provincial area of jurisdiction. And already some of the provinces are balking at the federal proposal. Alberta wants to fund all types of care not just daycare. Quebec does not want to be accountable to the federal government because it likes to establish its own legislation. In fact, the only way constitutionally for the federal government to try to reduce the high rates of child poverty in Canada and empower women is through the tax system. Federally, the nation can create tax breaks for dependents and for costs of living, and having and taking care of children would easily fit into those categories. But the tax benefit should be universal, for every child. The current Child Care Expense Deduction is flawed because it is only for daycare use and only for the care of a child in a dual-income home. It favours those with higher incomes and takes no heed of families who elect to stay at home and look after their children. The Canada Child Tax Benefit, another federal program, sends monthly payments to some families with children with the understanding that the benefit will decline as family income increases. But it claws back benefits even for very low-income households, it is not adjusted for the increasing costs of older children, and the very poorest homes—those on welfare—do not even get it since their welfare cheques are cut back because it is seen as income. The current federal tax programs for children are flawed, and the daycare plan does not improve upon them.

Many organizations have suggested we increase the spousal deduction (for caregivers), that we increase the child tax credit and make it universal, that we allow pension credits for caregiving years, or that we do not require receipts for the child care expense deduction. These are all interesting proposals, but the one that makes the most sense is a tax credit initiative for all families with young children. Valued at around $4,000 per child, the benefit would go a long ways toward funding a day care space, but some families would put it towards offsetting salary sacrifice or incidental costs of other types of care.

The aim of this paper is to establish equal funding for all ways to raise children. Some have said that supporting care in the home does not accept the reality of the dual-income household, but let me just say that a crying child needing a mother is also a reality. When daycare advocates say they know it would be nice to be home with the baby but it is not possible nowadays, we should back up and just look at that. They are saying that the "best" care is the care in the home, but are trying to establish a national preference of "second best" care. I beg to ask for better.

CONCLUSION

Ken Dryden, a former hockey star, is the cabinet minister responsible for developing the federal government's child care program. He is a strong proponent of his government's child care initiative. Yet before becoming minister in charge of social development, he gave a speech that reportedly brought tears to the eyes of listeners and was requested so much that it was posted on the Internet. Here is what he said:

> Maybe instead of focusing on work and its effect on families, we should focus on work's effect on kids. The more time I spent at being a parent, the more fun, interesting, fascinating, satisfying it was, the more I wanted to spend on it. Quality time is a crock. It is our own purposeful delusion. In fact essential to quality is quantity. As policy makers we need to understand the real why of time, then to create opportunities for time. More time offers the chance for a richer parent-child experience.[6]

Hearing such statements, I believe that Mr. Dryden has temporarily lost sight of a basic fact. There has always been child care in Canada. There is no shortage of it. It happens wherever there is a child. And there are two kinds of child care in Canada—the paid and the unpaid. There is care done for money and care done for love. We need to ensure that the paid version provides more love, and that the unpaid version has more money.

NOTES

1. Statistics Canada, *The Daily*, February 7, 2005. Cat. 11-01-XIE.

2. Canadian Council on Social Development, *The Progress of Canada's Children 1996* (Ottawa: 1996), p.15–16.

3. See, for example, Jocelyn Tougas, *Reforming Quebec's Early Childhood Care and Education: The First Five Years* (Toronto: Childcare Resource and Research Unit, 2002), p. 74.

4. Reginald Bibby, *A Survey of Canadian Hopes and Dreams* (Ottawa: Vanier Institute of the Family, 2004), pp. 53–55.

5. Gordon Cleveland and Michael Krashinsky, *The Benefits and Costs of Good Child Care* (Toronto: Childcare Resource and Research Unit, 1998), p. 43.

6. "Toward a Different Future: How Can We Help Our Kids Do Better?" (Regina: Work & Family Conference, March 2003).

POSTSCRIPT

In his piece, Michael Krashinsky develops a solid argument for a national child care program that relies on the provision of non-parental child care in licensed facilities. As he says, the greater participation of women in the labour force means that families need help in looking after their children. The fact that current child care arrangements leave something to be desired also points to the need for a more regulated and professional approach to child care, and the same can be deduced from the finding that children appear to benefit from the provision of high quality care. Throw in the additional point that working women contribute greatly to the economy and one seemingly has a fool-proof argument in favour of a national program for young children. As for claims about discrimination, Krashinsky says that stay-at-home mothers are really no different from those who are healthy and take no advantage of a health care program or those who are working and have no need of employment insurance. In other words, there is no discrimination—stay-at-home mothers are free to use a national program, but elect not to do so for one reason or another.

Notwithstanding the logical rigour of Krashinsky's thinking, there are still some aspects of his effort that produce questions. A key element of his argument is the belief that all children benefit from high quality non-parental child care, but there are some experts on child care who believe otherwise. For example, Douglas Willms, a respected social science researcher, concludes that such benefits are limited to children of struggling families. Moreover, one has to wonder what makes up high quality care for very young children. Krashinsky refers to the necessity of "early educational experiences" for children, but this conjures up visions of parents desperately trying to get their two-year-olds to speak or do simple math. Perhaps the only thing that really matters at this stage—which Beverley Smith argues in her piece—is a stable and loving environment, something that can be provided in a number of arrangements. Krashinsky also says that the economy benefits immediately from child care because it allows women to be more productive in their working lives. Yet, the country with the least developed child care system among highly industrialized nations—namely the United States—has arguably the most vibrant economy.

In her piece, Smith is able to convey some concerns about any kind of large-scale non-parental program for young children. She shows that non-parental care is not the type of care preferred by most parents, and that there exists a rich variety of care arrangements available to families. Smith is also not convinced of the benefits of non-parental care, and suggests that the key is simply to provide parents with the means to look for arrangements that they believe to be best for their children. The absence of choice in a national program is also a concern for Smith. Yet, all of these worries may still not fatally weaken the argument for a national program. Parents may indeed prefer, for instance, to look after their children themselves, but the reality is that two income-earners are often necessary. Of course, this does not necessarily require a non-parental program—neighbours or relatives might provide the care—but many might feel more comfortable with a regulated child care setting. Also, at this moment the federal government is signing separate child care deals with many of the provinces, arranging for regulated, non-parental child care. With this action, it appears that the majority of Canadians applaud the movement toward what amounts to a national daycare program.

To understand this debate, students first need to grasp the nature of the child care system in Canada. For this, one might read a publication of the Organization for Economic Cooperation and Development (OECD) entitled *Early Childhood Education and Care Policy: A Country Note, Canada* (which is available at the OECD website). Also useful are Rianne Mahon and Susan Phillips's "Dual-Earner Families Caught in a Liberal Welfare Regime? The Politics of Child Care Policy in Canada," and Jane Jenson's, "Against the Current: Child Care and Family Policy in Quebec," both in Sonya Michel and Rianne Mahon, eds., *Child Care Policy at the Crossroads* (New York: Routledge, 2002). These two articles provide a good history of child care arrangements in Canada and in the province of Quebec (which is singled out because of its universal child care program). For some additional background material (and some interesting analysis), one might also read Rod Beaujot, *Earning and Caring in Canadian Families* (Peterborough: Broadview Press, 2000), chapter 8.

The next step is to look at readings that directly address the wisdom of moving forward with a national program that relies on non-parental care in licensed facilities. There are many readings that support such an initiative: Gordon Cleveland, "Family Policy and Preschool Child Care," and Martha Friendly, "Strengthening Canada's Social and Economic Foundations: Next Steps for Early Childhood Education and Child Care," in *Policy Options* (March 2004); Gordon Cleveland and Michael Krashinsky, eds., *Our Children's Future: Child Care Policy in Canada* (Toronto: University of Toronto Press, 2001); Gordon Cleveland and Michael Krashinsky, *Fact and Fantasy: Eight Myths about Early Childhood Education and Care* (Toronto: Childcare Resource and Research Unit, University of Toronto, 2003); and Susan Prentice, ed., *Changing Child Care: Five Decades of Child Care Advocacy and Policy in Canada* (Halifax: Fernwood Publishing, 2001). One might also access the website of the Childcare Resource and Research Unit, located at the University of Toronto. It contains a rich set of articles on child care. The literature on the other side of the debate is less well-developed. However, there are a series of surveys and statistical studies that throw some doubt on the plan for a national child care program. In his survey of Canadian families entitled *A Survey of Canadian Hopes and Dreams* (Ottawa: Vanier Institute of the Family, 2004), Reginald Bibby found that the great majority of families believe that a parent should be at home to look after preschoolers and that parents rank daycare quite low in terms of preferred types of child care. As well, a Statistics Canada study (*The Daily,* February 7, 2005) found that parents still use a wide variety of child care arrangements. It determined that more and more families are using non-parental facilities—a finding that supports a national program—but it also found the same for care provided in the home by relatives. The latter finding suggests that a national program may go against the wishes of many families. Douglas Willms and his colleagues have provided evidence that suggests a more targeted approach—focusing on disadvantaged families—might make the greatest sense: Dafna Kohen, Clyde Hertzman, and J. Douglas Willms, "The Importance of Quality Child Care," in J. Douglas Willms, ed., *Vulnerable Children* (Edmonton: University of Alberta Press, 2002). There are also some American publications that use some of the literature on child care to reveal the failings of relying on regulated centres. See, for example, Mary Eberstadt, *Home-Alone America: the Hidden Toll of Day Care, Behavioral Drugs, and Other Parent Substitutes* (New York: Sentinel, 2004), chapter 1. Finally, the website of Kids First Parents Association of Canada, an advocacy group, is worthy of consideration because it is critical of attempts to limit government support for children to regulated daycare centres.

As mentioned, the federal government is already trying to provide the basis for a national child care program by signing separate child care agreements with willing provinces. The hope of the federal government had been to devise an agreement that would apply to all provinces, but a few of the provinces at this time are not ready to accept the federal vision for child care in Canada. The website of the prime minister of Canada contains the agreements that have been signed up to this point. One will see that they are very similar in content.

Should Religious Beliefs Be Excluded from Consideration of Public Policy?

✔ **YES**

JUSTICE MARY SAUNDERS, Opinion in *Chamberlain v. Surrey School District #36*

✗ **NO**

JUSTICE KENNETH MACKENZIE, Opinion in *Chamberlain v. Surrey School District #36*

What role, if any, should religious beliefs play in the making of public policy? While this issue has often been contested in the United States, it has generated less debate in Canada. However, this has begun to change in recent years. During the 2000 federal election, the political opponents of Stockwell Day tried to focus attention on his religious beliefs, suggesting not too subtly to voters that such beliefs could make him dangerous if his party won the election.

The relationship between religious beliefs and public policy has probably received the most intense scrutiny in the courtrooms of the province of British Columbia. The issue that triggered this debate was the selection of approved books for primary school children. In British Columbia, the provincial School Act grants school boards responsibility for approving the educational resource materials that teachers use in classrooms. In 1995, the Ministry of Education implemented a new Personal Planning curriculum for kindergarten to grade 7, which included a family life component.

In 1996, the Surrey school board passed a resolution that apparently prohibited the use of educational materials that were not on a prescribed list. The Gay and Lesbian Educators of B.C. (GALE)—an organization that advocates for change in the school system to create a positive environment for homosexual and bisexual persons—had developed a list of books that portray homosexual relationships positively. A teacher in the Surrey school district requested that three books from the GALE list be approved for use in teaching kindergarten and grade 1 students in the Surrey school district. The books were reviewed three times by various levels of the school district administrative staff. All agreed that the books dealt with sensitive material and were likely to cause parental concern over the presentation of same-sex parenting to kindergarten and grade 1 children. The superintendent of schools for the school district declared that the three books were unnecessary for achieving the objectives of the school curriculum. Since use of the books would be controversial among the parents in the community, it was decided that the final verdict should come from the school board, which was elected by that community.

On April 24, 1997, the Surrey school board formally considered the request for approval of the three books. The meeting was widely attended and garnered considerable media coverage. Several submissions were received, including from GALE and from the B.C. Civil Liberties Association. At the end of the presentation, the school board, by a vote of 4–2, passed a resolution declining to approve the books. Following this result, the teacher involved applied to the B.C. Supreme Court for a ruling that the school board resolution be declared invalid, and that an order be issued requiring the school board to pass a resolution approving the books in question.

In the subsequent court case, Justice Mary Saunders of the B.C. Supreme Court determined that indeed the school board's resolution should be quashed. In explaining her decision, Justice Saunders pointed out that the British Columbia School Act required that all schools be run on "strictly secular and non-sectarian principles." This she took to mean that not only should schools not show denominational bias, they should also be "independent of religious considerations." In other words, all religious motivations and reasons should be excluded from policy decisions. Interestingly, in a dispute between the parties over evidence, the justice allowed the petitioner's lawyers to introduce information regarding speeches given by the chair of the school board prior to taking that office, because they gave some insight into the "state of mind" of the board chair in making her decision. The justice seemed to be saying that even if no explicitly religiously based arguments were used, any evidence that decisions taken might be rooted in religious principles could disqualify them from the public arena. Further, while the B.C. School Act states that schools should inculcate the "highest morality" in children, the school board is precluded from making any decisions "based in a significant way on religious considerations." Saunders argued that the principles on which this "highest morality" should be based are to be found in the Charter of Rights and Freedoms.

Saunders's finding was appealed by the Surrey school board to the B.C. Court of Appeal. The ruling of the Court of Appeal reversed the previous decision. The justice noted that the school board's decision to refuse approval of the three books did not violate the School Act and was fully consistent with the Charter. In making this decision, the Court of Appeal noted that "a religiously informed conscience should not be accorded any privilege, but neither should it be placed under a disability." The Court of Appeal particularly rejected the suggestion by Justice Saunders that moral decisions influenced by religion are excluded under the School Act. To accept such a position, the court ruled, "would negate the right of all citizens to participate democratically in the education of their children in a truly free society" and would make "religious unbelief a condition of participation in the setting of the moral agenda" in schools.

This case goes to the heart of some critical questions. Is it permissible for public officials to make decisions that are motivated in part by religious belief? Does the Charter of Rights and Freedoms require that moral beliefs that originate from religious belief be excluded from public debate? Does "secular" essentially mean "non-religious"? What role, if any, should religious convictions play in the public square?

✔ **YES**

Opinion in *Chamberlain v. Surrey School District #36*
JUSTICE MARY SAUNDERS

I. INTRODUCTION

[1] On April 24, 1997 the Surrey School Board passed a resolution not approving three books for use as learning resources for kindergarten and grade one students. The three books depicted children with same-sex parents. This resolution followed a School Board resolution of April 10, 1997 stating that resources from gay and lesbian groups are not approved for use in the Surrey School District.

[2] The petitioners apply under the *Judicial Review Procedure Act,* R.S.B.C. 1996, c. 241, for an order quashing the two resolutions and approving the books for use on the basis that the resolutions infringe the *School Act,* R.S.B.C. 1996, c. 412, and the *Canadian Charter of Rights and Freedoms.*

[3] The issues in this case emerged in an atmosphere of strong public debate in Surrey, in which ideas on civil liberties and human rights are advanced on one side and ideas on parental rights, early education and the role of an elected school board are advanced on the other. Both sides to the debate cite the inherent value of our public school system and attempt to deal with the best interests of children during their early education.

[...]

III. THE CIRCUMSTANCES

[...]

Events Prior to the Two Resolutions

[42] Commencing in at least the fall of 1996, the issue of use in Surrey classrooms of materials depicting or concerning same-sex parents began to focus.

[43] GALE was founded in 1991. Since then members of GALE have developed a list of resources dealing with issues of homosexuality. The GALE list included three books at issue here: *Asha's Mums* by the petitioner Rosamund Elwin Michele Paules; *Belinda's Bouquet* by Leslea Newman; and *One Dad, Two Dads, Brown Dad, Blue Dads* by Johnny Valentine. The GALE list, which has not received Ministerial approval, has been widely circulated to teachers and librarians throughout British Columbia, including Surrey.

[44] In December 1996 and January 1997 Mr. Chamberlain submitted the three books from the GALE list for approval as educational resource material at the kindergarten and grade one levels in the Surrey School District.

[45] Mr. Chamberlain's request for approval of the three books was referred to District administrative staff. The books were reviewed three times, by a Helping Teacher and District Principal, by another District Principal and by an Educational Services Committee comprising four District Principals and four District Assistant Superintendents. Upon each review the books were seen as sensitive and likely to cause parental concern over their presentation of same-sex parents to kindergarten and grade one students.

[46] The Deputy Superintendent and Superintendent of Schools for the School District also reviewed the books. The Deputy Superintendent considered that for kindergarten and grade one levels, the subject of same-sex parents identified in the three books should be left for parents to deal with at home. The Superintendent thought that the three books were not necessary to achieve the learning objectives of the Personal Planning curriculum and, anticipating that a decision approving the books for use in kindergarten and grade one would be controversial among parents, considered that the decision should come from the School Board elected by the community. The three books were then referred to the School Board without a recommendation for approval. The item was set on the agenda for the Board's April 24, 1997 meeting.

[47] On March 17, 1997, while the request for approval was awaiting decision, the BCTF [British Columbia Teachers Federation] passed a resolution which gained broad publicity, authorizing appointment of a Committee to "develop recommendations on strategies for achieving the elimination of homophobia and heterosexism in the public school system." This resolution was the subject of forceful comment within the Surrey School District. For example, one trustee is reported in newspaper accounts to have taken strong objection to the BCTF resolution and to education concerning issues of homosexuality in Surrey schools. Many parents contacted school trustees expressing concern that materials on a GALE list of resources were being used in the Surrey School District.

The Two Resolutions

[48] On April 10, 1997 the School Board passed the following resolution, now known as the GALE resolution:

THAT WHEREAS the parents delegate their authority to us as trustees of public education; and

WHEREAS parents have voiced their concern over the use of Gay and Lesbian Educators of British Columbia (GALE BC) resources in the classroom; and

WHEREAS the Gay and Lesbian Educators of British Columbia (GALE BC) resources or resource lists have not been approved for use in School District #36 (Surrey).

THEREFORE BE IT RESOLVED THAT all administration, teaching and counselling staff be informed that resources from gay and lesbian groups such as GALE or their related resource lists are not approved for use or redistribution in the Surrey School District.

[49]During the April 10, 1997 meeting, the Superintendent of Schools advised the School Board that the request for approval of the three books as educational resource materials would be on the agenda of the April 24, 1997 meeting.

[50]On April 24, 1997 the School Board considered the request for approval of the three books. The meeting was broadly attended. Submissions on the issue were received from Mr. Warren and another person from GALE, from the B.C. Civil Liberties Association and from one parent from the elementary school at which Mr. Chamberlain teaches. Some of those in attendance supported approval, some did not.

[51]The discussion of the school trustees on April 24, [1997] centered on concern that the books raised sensitive issues in which parents should be involved and their concerns given weight.

[52]By a four to two vote, the School Board declined to approve the books, saying in its resolution (the "Books resolution"):

THAT the Board under Policy #8800 – Recommended Learning Resources and Library Resources, not approve the use of the following three (3) learning resources:

> Grade Level K-1 Personal Planning
> Elwin, R. & Paules, M. (1990). *Asha's Mums.*
> Newman, L. (1991). *Belinda's Bouquet.*
> Valentine, J. (1994). *One Dad, Two Dads, Brown Dad, Blue Dads.*

IV. THE SCHOOL ACT ISSUES

[53]I turn now to the legal issues that arise in the field of administrative law.

[54]The petitioners and the intervenor contend that the two resolutions are *ultra vires* the Board of School Trustees because they are outside its authority delegated by the *School Act*. The petitioners also say the resolutions are void because they were based on irrelevant considerations, failed to take into account relevant considerations and were discriminatory and thus an abuse of power. Further, they say that the conduct of some of the School Trustees who comprise the School Board demonstrated actual malice.

[55]In answer to this administrative law argument, the School Board says its decision was made in consideration of strong parental concern about introducing the subject of same-sex parents into the early education classroom. The School Board says that the School Act incorporates parent participation into education decisions and permits the School Board to integrate parent participation into curriculum issues, that consideration of parental views on sensitive issues is wise, and that some trustees campaigned for office on the platform of facilitating parental participation. The School Board further says that the resolutions were consistent with the *School Act* and were motivated by consideration of the well-being of children and their families. The School Board relies upon evidence that many in the community hold strong religious and moral views against homosexuality, and says that introduction of the three books would both infringe the parents' rights to give moral guidance to their children and abridge the parents' freedom of religion. The School Board says its corporate decision was made in the best interests of the children, and that introduction of the books into the classroom would raise a subject inappropriate for young children.

[...]

The Books Resolution

[61]The Books resolution was passed by the School Board under its authority to approve educational resource material. All parties agree that the books required approval of the School Board before a teacher could use them as educational resource material to teach the curriculum. The issue is whether the School Board, in reaching its decision, acted in excess of its jurisdiction or in a fashion which renders the decision invalid.

[62]The School Board, as a delegated level of government, derives its authority from the *School Act*. It may act only in accordance with the Act, the principles of natural justice and in accordance with laws of general application, most significantly the *Charter of Rights and Freedoms*.

[63]The history of public education in British Columbia is of a non-denominational school system supported by the public. Unlike school systems in other jurisdictions which were denominational and in which some religious training or teaching was incorporated, the public schools in British Columbia have been based upon an independence of school from church.

[64]The first statutory provision relating to religion in public schools was passed in 1865, *The Common School Act, 1865,* No. 6, 28 & 29 Victoria (1865), an Act governing the colony of British Columbia. It provided in s. XIII:

All Schools established under the Provisions of this Act shall be conducted strictly upon Non Sectarian Principles. Books inculcating the highest Morality shall be selected for the Use of such Schools and all Books of a

Religious Character, teaching Denominational Dogmas shall be strictly excluded therefrom.

[65] For a short time, from 1869 to 1872 the requirement that a school be non-sectarian disappeared, but was revived after Confederation in the *Public School Act, 1872* S.B.C. No. 16, 35 Vict. (1872). Section 35 of that Act provided:

> All Public Schools established under the provisions of this Act, shall be conducted upon strictly non-sectarian principles. The highest morality shall be inculcated, but no religious dogmas or creed shall be taught. All Judges, Clergymen, Members of the Legislature, and others interested in education, shall be school visitors.

[66] The section went on to preclude clergy, public political and judicial figures from taking significant involvement in the schools.

[67] In 1876 the word "secular" was added:

> All Public Schools established under the provisions of this Act, shall be conducted upon strictly secular and non-sectarian principles ...

> Public Schools Act, 1876, S.B.C.
> No. 2, 39 Vict. (1876), s. 41

[68] In 1891 the section was amended to permit usage of the Lord's Prayer (*Public School Act, 1891*, S.B.C. 1891, c. 40). The next substantial change in the Act concerning matters religious came in 1948, when reference to the Lord's Prayer was amended from a discretionary "may" to a mandatory "shall," and reading of a passage of scripture became mandatory (*Public Schools Act*, R.S.B.C. 1948, c. 297, s. 155).

[69] In 1989, in *Russow v. B.C. (A.G.)*, 35 B.C.L.R. 29 (S.C.), Mr. Justice Hollinrake struck down the portion of the statute requiring a reading of a passage of the scripture and recitation of the Lord's Prayer, severing and leaving in force the portion of the section requiring schools to be conducted on a strictly secular and non-sectarian basis. He did so on the basis that the provision infringed s. 2(a) of the *Canadian Charter of Rights and Freedoms* for the reasons given in *Zylerberg v. Sudbury (Bd. of Educ.)* (1988), 65 O.R. (2d) 641, 52 D.L.R. (4th) 577 (C.A.).

[70] Consistent with *Russow v. A.G. (B.C.)*, the Act, now the *School Act*, was amended in 1989 to exclude mention of the Lord's Prayer and readings from scripture. The section became reminiscent of those Act's prior to 1891 Act, providing in s. 95:

> (1) All schools and Provincial schools shall be conducted on strictly secular and non-sectarian principles.

(2) The highest morality shall be inculcated, but no religious dogma or creed shall be taught in a school or Provincial school.

[71] Today, s. 76 of the *School Act* continues this section with minor modifications. It follows the long-standing habit of public school statutes in British Columbia, consistent with the broad diversity of the peoples of British Columbia, of emphasizing a non-religious school system but one bound to inculcate high moral values. Section 76 provides:

(1) All schools and Provincial schools must be conducted on strictly secular and non-sectarian principles.

(2) The highest morality must be inculcated, but no religious dogma or creed is to be taught in a school or Provincial school.

[72] Teachers have the primary task of implementing the statutory requirements set out in s. 76. They assume a parental role, one commented on by Mr. Justice La Forest in *R. v. Audet,* [1996] 2 S.C.R. 171 at p. 196:

> In my view, no evidence is required to prove that teachers play a key role in our society that places them in a direct position of trust and authority towards their students. Parents delegate their parental authority to teachers and entrust them with the responsibility of instilling in their children a large part of the store of learning they will acquire during their development.

[73] At p. 198 of *R. v. Audet,* Mr. Justice La Forest approved the following passage from *R. v. Forde,* [1992] O.J. No. 1698 (Gen. Div.):

> ... In our society the role of the teacher is second in importance only to the parent. I dare say that the parent views the teacher as being in his or her place while the child is away from the control of the parent. The parent entrusts the teacher with the parent's responsibilities, preparing the youths to compete and to contribute and to develop their individual talents in this very difficult world, both in our own community, in our national community and in the international community, an extremely difficult time for young people and their parents....

[74] The school's role as a communicator of values was described in *Ross v. School District No. 15,* [1996] 1 S.C.R. 825 at 856–57:

> A school is a communication centre for a whole range of values and aspirations of a society. In large part, it defines the values that transcend society through the educational medium. The school is an arena for the exchange of ideas and must, therefore, be premised upon principles of tolerance and impartiality so that all persons within the school environment feel equally

free to participate. As the Board of Inquiry stated, a school board has a duty to maintain a positive school environment for all persons served by it.

[75]I turn then to the question of whether the School Board, by its Books resolution, acted contrary to s. 76. This is really a question of whether it acted contrary to s. 76(1), whether by its decision it failed to conduct the schools on strictly secular and non-sectarian principles. This is both a question of interpretation of s. 76(1) and a question of fact.

[76]There is no question that the resolution is non-sectarian. The issue is whether it infringes the requirement that the schools "be conducted on strictly secular ... principles."

[77]The petitioners contend that the School Board made its decision on a religious basis, running afoul of s. 76(1). The School Board contends that it acted in the best interests of the children, with consideration for the parents' rights to teach their children their religious and moral values and beliefs regarding homosexual conduct.

[78]The words "conducted on strictly secular ... principles" have been part of the requirements of public schools for a very long time, but, to the court's knowledge, have not been judicially considered prior to this case. In the education setting, the term secular excludes religion or religious belief. Combining the word "secular" with the words "strictly" and "principles," and considering the history of schools in British Columbia as being beyond overt church or religious intervention or influence, I conclude that the words "conducted on strictly secular ... principles" precludes a decision significantly influenced by religious considerations. This interpretation is consistent with the increasingly pluralistic nature of modern British Columbia and accords with the obligation to give statutory provisions a fair, large and liberal interpretation: *Interpretation Act*, R.S.B.C. 1996, c. 238, s. 8.

[79]The School Board submits that the section does not require it to place into the classroom books which are morally contentious. It says that the books in issue here, presenting families with same-sex parents as normal and same-sex parents as not "bad," are morally contentious, may tend to confuse children and may interfere with parental education on religious and moral matters.

[80]These submissions must be viewed in light of all the language in s. 76. Section 76(1) directs a School Board, administrators and teachers to refrain from religious based education or management motivated by religious considerations. At the same time s. 76(2) directs the moral education of children to a high plain by language requiring inculcation of the highest morality. Section 76 has the effect of distinguishing religious influence from issues of morality, precluding the first while requiring the second.

[81]The issue underlying this case illustrates this difference. Affidavits placed before the court by the School Board depose that some religions or churches with adherents in the community hold that homosexual activity is wrong. Yet in

considering the highest morality as those words are used in the *School Act,* it is appropriate to consider the values embodied in the *Charter of Rights and Freedoms* and import them into the moral standard that must be applied: *Hills v. A.G. (Canada),* [1988] 1 S.C.R. 512, at 518. Recent cases under s. 15 of the *Charter of Rights and Freedoms* state that s. 15 protects equality rights for those of a homosexual orientation: *Egan v. Canada,* [1995] 2 S.C.R. 513; *Vriend v. Alberta,* [1998], 1 S.C.R. 493.

[82] The School Board says that s. 15 of the Charter protects persons, not conduct, and thus that it protects homosexual persons, not homosexual conduct. On this reasoning, the School Board says that it sought to balance tolerance for homosexual persons with the views of some parents that homosexual conduct is not acceptable. This position is not consistent with the observations at p. 595 in *Egan v. Canada* by Mr. Justice Cory that:

> ... individuals, because of their uniqueness, are bound to vary in these personal characteristics which may be manifested by their sexual preferences whether heterosexual or homosexual. So long as those preferences do not infringe any laws, they should be tolerated.

The protection of the *Charter* is not intended to be hollow. Where a defining characteristic of a person is his or her conduct and the conduct is not unlawful, s. 15 of the *Charter* protects equality rights for that person complete with his or her conduct. I conclude that s. 76 does not protect a decision based on religious views as to homosexual conduct.

[83] I conclude, therefore, that s. 76(2) requires a school board to adhere to a high moral line which is consistent with the *Charter of Rights and Freedoms,* at the same time that s. 76(1) of the *School Act* precludes a school board from making a decision based in a significant way on religious considerations.

[84] On this reading of s. 76 of the *School Act,* the question is whether the Books resolution was based in a significant way on religious considerations. This is a question of fact.

[85] The primary evidence on the basis of the School Board's decision is from the lone trustee who provided evidence and from the Superintendent of Schools.

[86] The deponent trustee, one of the four trustees who voted in favour of the motion, deposed that prior to the April 24, 1997 School Board meeting she had received hundreds of calls from members of the Surrey community, the vast majority of whom supported the April 10, 1997 GALE resolution. She deposed that in reaching her decision on April 24, 1997 she considered as relevant to the motion the questions of age appropriateness of the books' subject matter, their necessity to teach the curriculum and whether they dealt with the subject matter in a way that reflects the needs and values of the Surrey community including parents. She deposed that another trustee who voted in favour of the motion expressed concern that the books would initiate discussion on a sensitive issue.

A third trustee in support of the motion expressed concern that if the Board approved the books kindergarten and grade one students in the School District would be exposed to the issues (same-sex parents) raised by them, and stated that he considered the books to be age inappropriate because they would create confusion and conflict.

[87] In cross-examination on her affidavit, the trustee testified that she did not consider that the books by themselves would have an adverse effect on children. She spoke of the lack of community consensus on introducing the books into the classroom, and said that the lack of consensus was a factor in not approving the books. She agreed that the focus of discussion centered on the fact that the books raised issues of a sensitive nature, and weight was given to the concerns of parents. She confirmed her view that teaching on the subject of same-sex relationships should allow a child to validate beliefs that the relationship would be morally wrong from their religious viewpoint.

[88] In his affidavit, the Superintendent of Schools acknowledged his anticipation that approval of the three books as educational resource material would be a very controversial decision among parents. On cross-examination he testified that he felt parents would feel the decision was "values sensitive" for them. He stated that he had questions concerning the age appropriateness of the concepts in the books, but it is clear from the record that he did not recommend that the books not be approved.

[89] In its submissions the School Board referred to affidavits from parents and members of the community in support of its argument on s. (2) of the *Charter* that it had protected the parents' and children's freedom of religion by passing the Books resolution. This affidavit evidence from parents included the following statements:

(i) "If the Three Books were used in either of our sons' classes, our children would be confused at the challenge to their own faith and family values";

(ii) "... I am opposed to the introduction of the Three Books into Kindergarten and Grade One classrooms for the following reasons:

(a) the Three Books portray same-sex couples ... in a manner contrary to my personal religious beliefs";

(iii) "The Three Books would introduce to children in Kindergarten and Grade One a particular worldview or brand of morality. The morality or worldview is directly in conflict with deeply held family and religious values";

(iv) "We believe, and would like to teach our children that according to our religious views, the homosexual lifestyle is wrong";

(v) "This is a matter of significant religious importance to me and the views expressed by the Three Books conflict with my religious views and those of my family";

(vi) "My concern is that I and my wife be able to teach our children according to our religious beliefs without having the school teach them something, at an early age, which runs counter to what we believe";

(vii) "I am opposed in accordance with my religious beliefs to my children being taught a redefinition of the traditional family";

(viii) "We are opposed to the introduction of the Three Books ... for the following reasons:

(a) Surrey Schools should not negate our right as parents to teach our children ... in accordance with our family and religious views;

(b) it is our strongly held religious belief that homosexual behaviour, including same-sex couples, is contrary to the teaching of the Bible;"

(ix) "I wish to teach my children according to my own religious beliefs and oppose lessons at school which contradict what I am attempting to teach my children";

(x) "The Three Books raise issues with respect to homosexuality and same-sex couples that are morally contentious. If used in Kindergarten and Grade One classrooms in Surrey they would create conflict between many families in the District who have religious or moral beliefs opposed to the views presented in the Three Books, and the teacher or school";

[90] Affidavit evidence filed by the School Board includes numerous other similar assertions of concern on religious and moral bases. Some of these affidavits also express the views that the books raise issues of sexual behaviour, advocate a "homosexual lifestyle," and introduce confusing issues to children not yet of an age to learn about sexuality.

[91] The respondent also filed affidavits from persons who deposed they do not hold religious convictions but are opposed on moral grounds to approval of the books as educational resource material, or simply do not wish the subject approached in school.

[92] In addition, the School Board filed affidavits from several religious leaders. These affidavits were countered by the petitioners with affidavits from other persons formally associated with churches. The affidavits from religious leaders filed by the School Board in support of its position include the following statements:

(i) from the Steering Committee of the Surrey Evangelical Churches: "Our Churches are extremely concerned that the Three Books present same-sex couples and introduce the issue of homosexuality in a positive light, contrary to the Biblical teachings and doctrine which form the basis of our beliefs";

(ii) from a pastor of a church: "The Three Books would introduce to children at the Kindergarten and Grade One levels a unique board of morality or worldview. This morality or worldview is directly in conflict with the morality and worldview of most members of the Evangelical Free Church";

(iii)   from a priest of a Roman Catholic Church: "I am of the view that the Three Books create an irreconcilable conflict between the views stated in the Three Books regarding the topic of homosexuality, and the doctrine of the Church.

"... I am opposed to the introduction of issues relating to homosexuality and same-sex couples, which issues necessarily bring into conflict religious and moral views on the subject";

(iv)   from a Muslim who is on the Surrey/Delta Management Committee of the B.C. Muslim Association: "The Three Books present homosexuality and homosexual conduct as acceptable and morally equal to heterosexuality. This contradicts the teachings of the Qur'an and the beliefs of Muslims";

(v)   from a leader of the Guru Nanak Sikh Gurdwara Society: "In the Sikh faith, homosexuality is considered a moral and social sin which we are instructed to resist.

"I have read the books. ... This message directly conflicts with the religious teachings of the Sikh faith";

(vi)   from a leader of the Verdic Hindhu Society: "... This message [from the books] directly conflicts with the teachings of the Hindhu faith. The Three Books display a lifestyle which we, as Hindhus, believe is immoral...."

[93] On review of all the evidence in this case on the basis of the School Board's decision, I conclude that when the School Board passed the Books resolution, some of the trustees who voted in favour of the resolution were motivated to a significant degree by concern that parents and others in the School District would consider the books incompatible or inconsistent with their religious views on the subject of same-sex relationships.

[94] In addition to the respondent's affidavit evidence and its submissions in court to the effect that it did consider, and was entitled to consider, the views of parents that use of the books in the classroom would be contrary to their sincerely held religious and moral views, there is evidence that at least one trustee who voted for the motion (who did not provide an affidavit), has campaigned for several years to promote a greater role for religion in governance of the community, including on the issue of homosexuality. The evidence on the views and activities of this trustee, in the absence of an affidavit in explanation, reasonably supports the conclusion that this trustee's decision was significantly influenced by personal religious considerations on the issue of homosexuality.

[95] I conclude that by giving significant weight to personal or parental concern that the books would conflict with religious views, the Board made a decision significantly influenced by religious considerations, contrary to the requirement in s. 76(1) that schools be "conducted on strictly secular ... principles."

[96] In concluding that the Board's decision on the Books resolution is contrary to s. 76(1) of the *School Act*, I have not addressed several issues raised by the School Board. The first is that some of the deponents whose affidavits were filed by the School Board expressed concerns that the books raise issues of sexuality and sexual practices. All parties concede such issues are inappropriate for kindergarten and grade one classes. In this case, however, the books simply do not raise these issues.

[97] Further, I note that there is direct evidence that *One Dad, Two Dads* and *Asha's Mums* have been used in the classroom elsewhere in British Columbia, and *One Dad, Two Dads* in the State of Washington, without ill effect.

[98] An accurate description of the books was given by the Superintendent of Schools in Surrey who said they give the message:

> that there are alternative family models, that these family models include models [with] same-sex parents, that these ought to be valued in the same way as other family models, that they are peopled by caring, thoughtful, intelligent, loving people who do give the same warmth and love and respect that other families do.

[99] Second, the School Board emphasized the responsibility of trustees to consider the views of parents when making decisions, and it referred in particular to the election platform of some trustees who pledged to listen to and work with parents. The court acknowledges the unique bond between school trustees, entrusted with educating the young, and the parents whose children are being educated. However, that obligation, pledge or bond exists within the framework of the *School Act*. A school board is not permitted to implement a decision made upon religious views; s. 76(1) of the *School Act* enjoins such religious consideration.

[100] Third, the School Board contends that it was protecting parental freedom of religion in the decision it made.

[101] Freedom of religion includes freedom from religion. *R. v. Big M Drug Mart Ltd.*, [1985] 1 S.C.R. 295, Chief Justice Dickson discussed freedom of religion as protected by s. 2(a) of the Charter at pp. 346–47:

> Religious belief and practice are historically prototypical and, in many ways, paradigmatic of conscientiously held beliefs and manifestations and are therefore protected by the *Charter*. Equally protected, are expressions of non-belief and refusals to participate in religious practice.

[102] Section 76 is an example of legislated protection for freedom of religion, presuming the public school is a place independent of religious considerations.

[103] Lastly, opinion evidence was filed by the respondent from educators and persons expert in child psychology to the effect that the books were age inappropriate, would create harmful confusion and would be harmful to children's cognitive development. Contrary opinion evidence was filed by the petitioners in response.

[104] This evidence in support of the Books resolution centered largely on "dissonance" between the information in the books and home teaching, the issue which was critical to the School Board's decision and consideration of which, I find, is inconsistent with s. 76(1).

[105] While there is an academic debate on this topic, I accept the perspective of Dr. Kagan, Professor of Psychology at Harvard University, that the issue is not one of harm to children but is a "legal and ethical question that lies outside of science." This accords with the evidence of the trustee that she did not consider that the books, by themselves, would have an adverse effect upon children.

V. CONCLUSION

[106] This decision is based upon a very old provision of the *School Act* enjoining religion or overt religious influence in the conduct of the schools. Many other issues were raised by the petitioners under the principles of administrative law. The petitioners also relied upon the *Charter of Rights and Freedoms,* s. 2(a) freedom of religion, s. 2(b) freedom of expression and s. 15 equality rights. In doing so the petitioners and the respondent cited many cases expressing great principles of law, including *Roncarelli v. Duplessis* (1959), 16 D.L.R. 689, [1959] S.C.R. 121 and those cases dealing with race and science in the schools. Given my conclusion on s. 76 of the *School Act,* and for the reasons of Mr. Justice Hollinrake in *Russow v. B.C. (A.G.), supra,* I do not address those issues.

[107] I conclude that the Books resolution is contrary to s. 76(1) of the *School Act,* and is therefore *ultra vires.*

[108] The Books resolution is hereby quashed. [...]

✗ **NO**

Opinion in *Chamberlain v. Surrey School District #36*
JUSTICE KENNETH MACKENZIE

INTRODUCTION

[1] This appeal involves the correct interpretation of ss. 76(1) and (2) of the *School Act*, R.S.B.C. 1996, c. 412. Those subsections read as follows:

76 (1) All schools must be conducted on strictly secular and non-sectarian principles.

(2) The highest morality must be inculcated, but no religious dogma or creed is to be taught in a school or Provincial school.

[2] These statutory directions raise three formidable questions of interpretation. What is the relationship of religion to morality in the public schools? What is the meaning of "strictly secular" in its context? What is the "highest morality" that must be inculcated?

[3] These issues arise in the context of a resolution, referred to as the "Three Books resolution," passed by the Board of Trustees of the Surrey School District on 24 April 1997 as follows:

THAT the Board under Policy #8800 – *Recommended Learning Resources and Library Resources,* not approve the use of the following three (3) learning resources:

Grade Level K-1 Personal Planning
Elwin, R. & Paules, M. (1990), *Asha's Mums.*
Newman, L. (1991), *Belinda's Bouquet.*
Valentine, J. (1994), *One Dad, Two Dads, Brown Dad, Blue Dads.*

The three books each depict children with same-sex parents. The books were proposed for use in kindergarten and grade one classes—children of five and six years of age.

[4] Mr. Chamberlain and the other petitioners commenced proceedings under the *Judicial Review Procedure Act*, R.S.B.C. 1996, c. 241, to quash this resolution and another resolution passed by the Board two weeks earlier referred to as the "GALE" resolution. A Supreme Court judge in chambers quashed both resolutions. The Board has appealed the decision to quash the Three Books resolution. The decision to quash the GALE resolution has not been appealed.

BACKGROUND

[5] Mr. Chamberlain is a primary school teacher teaching kindergarten classes at schools within the Surrey School District. He is a member of the British Columbia Teachers Federation ("BCTF") and the Gay and Lesbian Educators of B.C. ("GALE"). Mr. Chamberlain took the initiative that has led to these proceedings.

[6] The Three Books resolution and the GALE resolution were both challenged as contrary to ss. 76(1) and (2) of the *School Act* and to the *Canadian Charter of Rights and Freedoms*. The Chambers judge quashed both resolutions as being contrary to the *School Act*. She did not find it necessary to address the Charter issues.

THE DECISION UNDER APPEAL

[7] There were several evidentiary issues raised on the hearing of the petition before the Chambers judge and a significant portion of her reasons for judgment address those issues. There is no appeal on evidentiary issues and the record on this appeal is therefore the record determined by the Chambers judge on the basis of her evidentiary rulings.

[8] The Chambers judge concluded that the Three Books resolution offended s. 76 because the members of the Board who voted in favour of the resolution were significantly influenced by religious considerations, specifically opposition to homosexual conduct, contrary to the requirement that the schools be "conducted on strictly secular ... principles." She summarized her conclusion in these terms:

> A school board is not permitted to implement a decision made upon religious views; s. 76(1) of the *School Act* enjoins such considerations. [at para 99]

[9] She rejected the submission of the Board that this interpretation was in conflict with the guarantee of religious freedom expressed in the *Charter*. She relied on the opinion of Dickson J. (later C.J.C.) in *R. v. Big M Drug Mart Ltd.*, [1985] 1 S.C.R. 295. In that case the Supreme Court of Canada declared the federal *Lord's Day Act* to be unconstitutional as contrary to the freedom of conscience and religion guaranteed by s. 2 of the *Charter*.

RELIGION AND MORALITY

[10] I agree with the Chambers judge that *Big M* must be the point of departure for the analysis of the issues. The narrow issue in *Big M* was whether the prohibition in the *Lord's Day Act* against the sale of goods on Sunday could be supported on non-religious grounds as mandating a day of rest. Such a rationale was consistent with American authorities upholding Sunday observance legislation. The Supreme Court rejected that view and concluded that the *Lord's Day Act* historically was so infused with Christianity that justification for a secular purpose

was not possible. The legislation inescapably enacted long held Christian doctrine. It bound all to a sectarian Christian ideal "inimical to the spirit of the *Charter* and the dignity of all non-Christians ... Non-Christians are prohibited for religious reasons from carrying out activities which are otherwise lawful, moral and normal." [p. 337]

[11] The wide-ranging implications of the case prompted Dickson J. to reflect on fundamental principles underlying the *Charter*. He concluded that the idea of a truly free society infuses all elements of democratic rights and freedoms. He described the truly free society in strong and evocative terms at p. 336:

> A truly free society is one which can accommodate a wide variety of beliefs, diversity of tastes and pursuits, customs and codes of conduct. A free society is one which aims at equality with respect to the enjoyment of fundamental freedoms and I say this without any reliance upon s. 15 of the *Charter. Freedom must surely be founded in respect for the inherent dignity and the inviolable rights of the human person.* The essence of the concept of freedom of religion is the right to entertain such religious beliefs as a person chooses, the right to declare religious beliefs openly and without fear of hindrance or reprisal, and the right to manifest religious beliefs by worship and practice or by teaching and dissemination. [Emphasis added]

[12] This passage highlights "respect for the inherent dignity and the inviolable rights of the human person" as the first principle of freedom. Dickson J. cited no authority for this proposition and he obviously regarded it as a proposition too well established to require authority. It is properly regarded as so generally accepted by Canadians as to be beyond controversy.

[13] Nonetheless, in the context of the issues before us it may be useful to reflect briefly on the historical origins of the proposition. There is little doubt that the idea of the inherent worth and dignity of each individual human person originated in our political history as an insight of Christianity and the democracy of Periclean Athens. It gained ascendancy with the spread of Christianity and the Christian belief that every person is unique and irreplaceable as a child of God.[1] While the association with Christianity deserves acknowledgement, it is not an insight that is exclusive to Christianity. It is shared with other religious traditions and is in that sense religiously inclusive or "pluralist." It is also embraced by those who do not adhere to any religious faith or tradition. For that reason it is properly characterized today as a cultural rather than religious norm. That clearly is the context in which it is formulated by Dickson J. in *Big M.* But it remains a normative or moral proposition.

[14] The extension of this cultural or moral norm beyond its religious origins highlights the distinction between religion and morality. A moral proposition may originate from a religious insight but religion is more than morality and moral positions are not necessarily derived from religion. Section 76(2) emphasizes this

distinction by mandating teaching of "the highest morality" while prohibiting teaching of any "religious dogma or creed."

[15]The relationship between religion and morals was a subject that intrigued the American philosopher, William James. In his famous Gifford Lectures published as *The Varieties of Religious Experience*,[2] James examined the experiential dimension of religion and its connection to morals. James characterized the essence of the religious life as the belief that there is an unseen order and that our supreme good lies in harmoniously adjusting to that order.[3] At the heart of all religions is the experience of a dimension of reality which is "wholly other." The great western religions—Judaism, Christianity and Islam—identify the essence of this transcendent or immanent greater reality as God. Eastern religions share the experience but describe the source in different terms.

[16]James emphasized that the religious experience of the wholly other is not in itself normative or moral. The moral implications usually flow from reflection on the experience, in answer to the questions "What does the experience mean?" and "How should life be lived, individually and socially, in the light of the experience?" Sacred texts and traditions record and elaborate these reflections in doctrines and moral precepts.

[17]The experiential dimension of religion is powerful. It may change lives. But law is concerned with the mundane world and its normative rules. Experiential religion is beyond its terms of reference.

[18]The distinction between religion as experience and morals is a useful one for analytical purposes in the context of this litigation. It emphasizes that religion and morality are not synonymous terms. A religious person acknowledges the reality of the wholly other dimension, either on the basis of personal experience or by accepting as authentic the religious experience of others, as maintained through a religious tradition or otherwise. For a religious person, moral precepts are related to that experience, usually filtered through the sacred texts and tradition of a faith shared in common with others. As the ecclesiastical authority of religious institutions has waned, the conscience of a religious person has become more a matter of choice than ecclesiastical fiat. Increasingly individuals are said to form their convictions *à la carte,* and other non-religious factors influence the conscience. It is a commonplace observation that religious adherents can be found across a wide spectrum of views on contentious moral issues. Positions are likely to reflect a variety of factors, some pragmatic or otherwise unrelated to religious insight. Causal linkage between religion and a particular moral position cannot be assumed.

[19]Of course many people do not recognize the authenticity of any religious experience. Their moral precepts and convictions will be derived from other sources but their moral positions taken as positions of conscience are entitled to full participation in the dialogue in the public square where moral questions are answered as a matter of law and social policy.

[20] There is a broad social consensus on many moral subjects. For example most of the conduct sanctioned by the *Criminal Code* is within that consensus as morally unacceptable. Some aspects of human sexuality remain morally controversial including homosexual or "same sex" relationships. The division of moral conviction on this subject cuts across society and divides religious communities as well as people of no religious persuasion. The moral position of some on all sides of particular issues will be influenced by their religion, others not. There is no bright line between a religious and a non-religious conscience. Law may be concerned with morality but the sources of morality in conscience are outside the law's range and should be acknowledged from a respectful distance.

The Interpretation of "Strictly Secular" in s. 76(1)

[21] Section 76 originated in an early enactment of the colony of Vancouver Island, *The Common School Act, 1865,* No. 6, 28 & 29 Vict. (1865) [Tab 122], which contained the following provisions:

> XIII. All schools established under the Provisions of this Act shall be conducted strictly upon Non Sectarian Principles. Books inculcating the highest Morality shall be selected for the Use of such Schools, and all Books of a Religious Character, teaching Denominational Dogmas shall be strictly excluded therefrom.

> XIV. It shall be lawful for the Clergy of every Denomination at stated Intervals to be fixed by the General Board of Education to visit such Schools and impart in a separate Room Religious Instruction to the Children of their respective Persuasions.

The tenor of these provisions is aimed toward a non-denominational system of public education and prohibition of control by any denominational establishment. Doctrinal instruction, by clergy, was restricted.

[22] Section 13 of the statute of 1865 was repealed by *The Common School Ordinance* of the combined colony of Vancouver Island and mainland British Columbia in 1869, S.B.C. No. 21, 32 Vict. (1869). Section 14 was reenacted as follows:

> XII. It shall be lawful for every Clergyman and Minister of any denomination, at such times, before and after the regular school hours, as shall be approved by the Governor in Council, to visit the Public School of the District in which such Clergyman or Minister is resident or officiates, and impart such religious instruction as he may think proper to the children of his denomination.

[23] Section 12 of the ordinance disappeared and s. 13 of the 1865 enactment reappeared in modified form in one of the first statutes of the Province of British Columbia, *Public Schools Act, 1872,* S.B.C. No. 16 (1872), thus:

> 35. All Public Schools established under the provisions of this Act, shall be conducted upon strictly non-sectarian principles. The highest morality shall be inculcated, but no religious dogmas or creed shall be taught. All Judges, Clergymen, Members of the Legislature, and others interested in education, shall be school visitors.

[24] The word "secular" first appears in the reenactment of s. 35 as s. 41 of the *Public Schools Act, 1876,* S.B.C. No. 2 (1876). The wording has then remained essentially unchanged in the several revisions to the statute over the intervening years.

[25] In 1891 an amendment permitted recitation of the Lord's Prayer. A further amendment in 1948 made recitation of the Lord's Prayer and reading of a passage of scripture mandatory. These provisions were struck down as contrary to the *Charter* by *Russow v. B.C. (A.G.)* (1989), B.C.L.R.(2d) 29 (S.C.).

[26] There was no verbatim record of debates in the B.C. legislature in 1876 and the rationale for adding "secular" to "strictly non-sectarian" is obscure. I think it can be inferred, however, that the addition was intended to reinforce the non-denominational character of the public schools. The fact that the Lord's Prayer was introduced in 1891 without any perceived inconsistency with "strictly secular" implies that the prohibition was aimed at denominational indoctrination and ecclesiastical control rather than morality associated with non-denominational Christianity. In the social and political culture of the times, I have little doubt that the architects of the 1876 amendment would have been startled and dismayed at the suggestion that secular required religious unbelief.

[27] No doubt the political culture in British Columbia in 1876 was predominantly Christian and non-Christian religions would have been barely visible on the political landscape, although the number of adherents of non-Christian religions in the population likely was larger than their relative political invisibility would indicate. The frequency with which the public schools legislation was reviewed and the tinkering with the religion sections in the early years of British Columbia suggests that the subject was politically sensitive and the legislature was at pains to avoid denominational control and indoctrination in the public schools. At the same time it would be assumed that the "highest morality" flowed from a non-doctrinaire and non-sectarian Christianity.

[28] Can "strictly secular" in s. 76(1) of the *School Act* be interpreted as limited to moral positions devoid of religious influence? Are only those with a non-religiously informed conscience to be permitted to participate in decisions involving moral instruction of children in the public schools? Must those whose moral positions arise from a conscience influenced by religion be required to

leave those convictions behind or otherwise be excluded from participation while those who espouse similar positions emanating from a conscience not informed by religious considerations are free to participate without restriction? Simply to pose the questions in such terms can lead to only one answer in a truly free society. Moral positions must be accorded equal access to the public square without regard to religious influence. A religiously informed conscience should not be accorded any privilege, but neither should it be placed under a disability. In a truly free society moral positions advance or retreat in their influence on law and public policy through decisions of public officials who are not required to pass a religious litmus test.

[29] A contrary interpretation is not only insupportable in principle, it would raise immense practical difficulties. How would it be determined that a moral position is advanced from a conscience influenced by religion or not? If the restriction were applied only where the religious conviction was publicly declared it would privilege convictions based on a conscience whose influences were concealed over one openly proclaimed. The alternative would be to require inquiry as to the source of a moral conviction, whether religious or otherwise. Both alternatives are offensive and indefensible.

[30] In a recent article entitled *Two Concepts of Secularism* a respected scholar[4] acutely summarizes the issue lurking in the term "secularism" as follows:

> ... First, the secular can be understood as an opponent of established belief—including a *nonreligious* establishment—and a protector of the rights of free exercise and free association. Second, it can be understood as a proponent of established *unbelief* and a protector of strictly individual expressive rights.
>
> The former view, on the one hand, is a minimal, even "negative" understanding of secularism, as a freedom "from" establishmentarian imposition. For it, the secular idiom is merely a provisional lingua franca that serves to facilitate commerce among different kinds of belief, rather than establish some new "absolute" language, an Esperanto of postreligious truth. The latter view, on the other hand, is the more robust, more assertive, more "positive" understanding of secularism ... —the one that affirms secularism as an ultimate faith that rightfully supersedes the tragic blindness and destructive irrationalities of the historical religions, at least so far as activity in public is concerned. By understanding religious liberty as a subcategory of individual expressive liberty, it confines religion to a strictly private sphere, where it can do little public harm—and little public good. [Emphasis in original]

To interpret secular as mandating "established unbelief" rather than simply opposing "established belief" would effectively banish religion from the public square.

[31] Today, adherents of non-Christian religions and persons of no religious conviction are much more visible in the public square than a century ago and any truly free society must recognize and respect this diversity in its public schools. "Strictly secular and non-sectarian" must be interpreted in a manner that respects this reality. That respect precludes any religious establishment or indoctrination associated with any particular religion in the public schools but it cannot make religious unbelief a condition of participation in the setting of the moral agenda. Such a disqualification would be contrary to the fundamental freedom of conscience and religion set forth in s. 2 of the *Charter*, and the right to equality in s. 15. It would negate the right of all citizens to participate democratically in the education of their children in a truly free society.

[32] "Non-sectarian," while originally it may have been limited to a Christian context of various denominations and sects, must now be extended to include other religious traditions as well as those who do not adhere to any religious faith or tradition. The section precludes the teaching of religious doctrine associated with any particular faith or tradition (except in a context which is intended to educate students generally about the various religious traditions for the purpose of advancing religious tolerance and understanding and does not advance any particular doctrinal position over others).

[33] In my opinion, "strictly secular" in the *School Act* can only mean pluralist in the sense that moral positions are to be accorded standing in the public square irrespective of whether the position flows out of a conscience that is religiously informed or not. The meaning of strictly secular is thus pluralist or inclusive in its widest sense. This interpretation accords with *Big M*, where the fatal flaw in the *Lord's Day Act* was its link to exclusively Christian doctrine rather than morality. It also accords with the distinction between morality and dogma or creed in s. 76(2).

[34] No society can be said to be truly free where only those whose morals are uninfluenced by religion are entitled to participate in deliberations related to moral issues of education in public schools. In my respectful view "strictly secular" so interpreted could not survive scrutiny in the light of the freedom of conscience and religion guaranteed by s. 2 of the *Charter* and the equality rights guaranteed by s. 15.

The "Highest Morality" in s. 76(2)

[35] Section 76(2) of the *School Act* clearly distinguishes between "the highest morality" and religious dogmas or creeds. Subsection (2) reinforces the non-doctrinal emphasis of s-s. 1 but it also mandates that the highest morality be taught. That morality, while it may originate in religious reflection, must stand independently of its origins to maintain the allegiance of the whole of society including the plurality of religious adherents and those who are not religious. In this context, the highest morality is public virtue in a truly free society. Public virtue upholds

the dignity of the individual, the first principle which underlies the *Charter* and informs all of public life in a truly free society. The cultural norm and Christian morality coincide on this point and an inclusive Christianity reinforces the truly free society and the *Charter* foundation.

[36]It is clear on the authorities that human dignity and *Charter* principles prohibit discrimination on grounds of sexual orientation. Any doubts on that question have been laid to rest by the decisions of the Supreme Court of Canada in *Egan v. Canada,* [1995] 2 S.C.R. 513 and *Vriend v. Alberta,* [1998] 1 S.C.R. 493. Cory J. stated the position eloquently in *Egan,* at p. 595:

> In our democratic society, every individual is recognized as important and deserving of respect. Each individual is unique and distinct. Because of the uniqueness of individuals, their tastes will vary infinitely from matters as prosaic as food and clothing to matters as fundamental as religious belief. Religious belief and the form of worship are personal characteristics. These characteristics may seem extremely peculiar and vastly perplexing to the majority. Yet, so long as the form of worship is not unlawful, it must be not only tolerated but also protected by the *Charter*. Similarly, individuals, because of their uniqueness, are bound to vary in those personal characteristics which may be manifested by their sexual preferences whether heterosexual or homosexual. So long as those preferences do not infringe any laws, they should be tolerated. In its attempt to prohibit discrimination, the *Charter* seeks to reinforce the concept that *all* human beings, however different they may appear to be to the majority, are *all* equally deserving of concern, respect and consideration. [Emphasis in original]

Discrimination against children because of the sexual orientation of their parents would be even more invidious.

[37]The *Charter* protects against legal discrimination and in that sense can be said to be reactive rather than proactive. However, in my view, that principle of non-discrimination is sufficiently compelling as a public value in a truly free society that it must be included within any definition of the highest morality for the purposes of s. 76(2) of the *School Act*. In that context, non-discrimination on the basis of sexual orientation is a moral principle which the legislation directs as mandatory for education in the public schools. The members of the school board are elected public officials who by virtue of their office are required to carry out that mandate within the limits of their jurisdiction. A public official must discharge his or her public responsibilities in accordance with the law.

[38]The Surrey Superintendent of Schools, with the concurrence of the Board, sent a directive to the Surrey schools on 9 May 1997 under the heading TOLERANCE FOR SEXUAL ORIENTATION. The directive stated in part:

There has been extensive media coverage regarding recent Board motions on learning resources and sexual orientation. Let there be no confusion with regard to the District's expectation in terms of how we treat the matter of sexual orientation. The District will not accept any action of intolerance or discriminatory treatment of students, staff, or parents on the basis of their sexual orientation. Administrative officers must be vigilant in their responsibility and must confront instances of intolerance to ensure that they cease and that appropriate action results.

Board Regulation 10900.1, Multicultural, Anti-Racist and Human Rights, states, in part:

> "... any form of discrimination that results in disparagement towards others based on identifiable group features is unacceptable."

Our Board is committed to providing a working and learning environment that is safe, supportive, and free of discrimination based on a person's sexual orientation. *The promotion of intolerance is unacceptable.* [Emphasis in original]

This directive was a clear, emphatic and unambiguous statement of District policy.

[39] It cannot be ignored, as the Supreme Court stressed in *Vriend*, that discrimination against gays and lesbians can range from insults and ostracism to vicious and violent acts. Schools are not immune and all those involved in teaching and administration must be vigilant in prevention of all forms of discrimination and abuse. However, I do not think that there is any reason not to take this directive at its word or to conclude that the Board did not stand behind its admonition.

Summary of s. 76 Interpretation

[40] The answers to the questions posed at the outset of these Reasons can be briefly summarized as follows. Section 76 of the *School Act* is directed to moral education and not to religious education. The public schools must eschew religious indoctrination. Positions on moral issues should not be differentiated on the basis of their source in a religious or non-religious conscience. The public schools must teach in accordance with the highest morality and the fundamental principles of a truly free society are attributes of the highest morality. That highest morality includes non-discrimination on grounds of sexual orientation. The public schools must positively espouse that moral position and they cannot teach a morality that is inconsistent with it. Members of school boards as well as teachers and school officials must carry out their duties mindful of these legal obligations arising from the combination of the *School Act* and the *Charter*.

[41] In my respectful view, the reason given by the Chambers judge for quashing the Three Books resolution, namely that the Board majority was significantly influenced by religion, cannot be sustained. The question then is whether the Three Books resolution is fatally flawed on other grounds. It is first necessary to examine the jurisdiction of the Board.

THE JURISDICTION OF THE BOARD

[42] The Board's jurisdiction flows from s. 85(2) of the *School Act* as follows:

85 ...

(2) Without limiting subsection (1), a board may, subject to this Act and the regulations, do all or any of the following:

   (a) determine local policy for the effective and efficient operation of schools in the school district;

   (b) subject to the orders of the minister, approve educational resource materials and other supplies and services for use by students;

   (c) make rules

   (i) establishing a code of conduct for students attending educational programs operated by or on behalf of the board,

   (ii) respecting suspension of students and the provision of educational programs for suspended students,

   (iii) respecting attendance of students in educational programs provided by the board,

   (iv) respecting the establishment, operation, administration and management of

   (A) schools operated by the board and educational programs provided by the board, and

   (B) transportation equipment used for the purposes of the board,

   (v) respecting the provision of volunteer services,

   (vi) respecting the management of student housing facilities and the supervision of students accommodated in them, and

   (vii) respecting any other matter under the jurisdiction of the board;

   (d) suspend students, in accordance with the rules under paragraph (c)(ii), so long as the board continue to make available to those students an educational program;

   (e) if approved by the council of the municipality in which the school is located, provide a system of traffic patrols to assist in the control of motor vehicle traffic on highways or elsewhere in that municipality so far as the traffic may affect students going to or from school;

   (f) provide housing accommodation for students;

(g) subject to the orders of the minister, permit persons other than students to utilize board facilities, equipment and personnel;

(h) subject to the orders of the minister, evaluate and recognize educational activities of an educational program undertaken by a student outside of the school;

(i) develop and offer local programs for use in schools in the school district;

(j) subject to the orders of the minister, cause an educational assessment to be made of students or groups of students;

(k) establish loan funds or bursaries for students resident in the school district and spend money received by donation. ...

[43] The Board's jurisdiction is subject to ministerial order specifically to Ministerial Orders 143/89 and 165/93. The portion of the orders pertinent to this litigation is the following:

1. (1) In addition to the educational program guides referred to Ministerial Order 165/93, the Educational Program Guide Order, a board may only use the following educational resource materials:

(a) the educational resource materials referred to as authorized or recommended in the most recent "Catalogue of Learning Resources, Primary to Graduation," published from time to time by the Ministry of Education;

(b) other educational resource materials that, subsequent to the publication of the Catalogue referred to in paragraph (a), are designated by the minister as authorized or recommended; and

(c) educational resource materials that the board considers are appropriate for individual students or groups of students.

(2) Where a board uses educational resource materials referred to in subsection 1(c), the board shall establish evaluation and selection criteria and procedures to approve those educational resource materials.

[44] Mr. Arvay submitted that the Ministry has largely deferred to local school boards in the selection of educational resource materials. The text of the order quoted above does not support that conclusion. The Ministry has assumed the responsibility for a catalogue of learning resources, primary to graduation, and the Board's jurisdiction is limited to subsection (c) "educational resource materials that the board considers are appropriate for *individual students* or *groups of students*." [Emphasis added]

[45] The terms of the ministerial orders in my opinion clearly place the primary responsibility for the selection of educational resource materials in the hands of the Ministry and assign an ancillary jurisdiction to local boards in relation to individual students or groups of students.

[46] It is common ground that the three books are not included in the catalogue of learning resources published by the Ministry. Efforts by Mr. Chamberlain to have the three books approved by the Ministry were unsuccessful. Mr. Chamberlain's correspondence with the Ministry covered a wider list of resources than the three books at issue but Mr. Chamberlain was candid in stating that the reason for adding the recommended books to the list of approved resources was for the purpose of "discussing the realities of same-sex family structures." Mr. Chamberlain received a polite but non-committal response from the Ministry. He then took up the matter with the District.

"Recommended Learning Resources" and "Library Resources"

[47] The ministerial order required the Board to "establish evaluation and selection criteria and procedures to approve those educational resource materials" considered appropriate under s. 1(i)(c) of the Ministerial Order. The Board did so by passing Regulation 8800.1 entitled *Recommended Learning Resources and Library Resources*.

[48] Regulation 8800.1 distinguishes between "Recommended Learning Resources" and "Library Resources." Before us, the Board's position was that it has no objection to the three books as library resources and the Three Books resolution was directed only to the question of the approval of the books as recommended learning resources. Consequently, there is nothing to prevent the three books being placed in school libraries within the District and made accessible to teachers and students in the same manner as other resources within a school library. In the context of K-1 classes where the students are just learning to read, use would presumably mean being read to the class by the teacher in story time or some similar circumstances with perhaps a discussion period about the story afterward.

[49] The distinction between recommended learning resources and library resources and the Board's acquiescence to the three books as library resources apparently was not drawn to the attention of the Chambers judge. The Chambers judge was also under the apprehension that:

> In 1996 the School Board by resolution, prohibited the use of resource material for the family life component of the Personal Planning curriculum that was not on an existing list of approved materials issued by the Ministry or School Board.

The parties are agreed this is in error and there is no resolution of the Board containing such a blanket prohibition. Apart perhaps from the quashed GALE resolution which has not been appealed by the Board, there is no resolution of the Board or Ministry order that would prevent the books becoming library resources.

[50] The criteria for a library resource is set out in the Board's regulation:

Library Resources

1. The library resource shall support and be consistent with the general educational goals of the province, district, and the aims and objectives of individual schools and specific courses.

2. The library resource shall meet high standards of quality in factual content and presentation.

3. The library resource shall be appropriate for the curriculum and for the age, emotional development, ability level, learning style, and social development of the students for whom the materials are selected.

4. The library resource shall have aesthetic, literary, historical, and/or social value.

5. The physical format and appearance of a library resource shall be suitable for its intended use.

6. The library resource may be chosen to motivate students and staff to read for the purpose of recreation.

7. The library resource shall be chosen to help students gain an awareness of our pluralistic society as well as an understanding of the many important contributions made to our civilization.

8. The library resource shall be chosen to motivate students and staff to examine their own attitudes and behaviors, and to comprehend their own duties, responsibilities, rights, and privileges as participating citizens in our society.

9. The library resource is fair, objective, free from gratuitous violence, propaganda and discrimination, except where a teaching/learning situation requires illustrative material to develop critical thinking about such issues.

[51] The Board's position by necessary implication means that the Board does not dispute that the three books meet this criteria for library resources. It should be noted that there is a procedure for challenging materials by parents which ends with a decision of the Board in the event that the challenge is not resolved by agreement through the extensive process set out for dealing with a challenge. The three books have not been challenged and the likely outcome of any challenge is not within the purview of this appeal. I think that we must assume based on the Board's position that for the purposes of this appeal the Board accepts that the three books meet the library resource criteria.

[52] The criteria set out for a recommended learning resource by Regulation 8800.1 is similar to that for a library resource and specifically repeats library

resource item 9 *mutatis mutandis*. The difference between a recommended learning resource and a library resource appears to be that a recommended learning resource "is relevant to the learning outcomes and content of the course or courses" whereas a library resource is intended to be merely "appropriate for the curriculum."

[53] Mr. Dives, on behalf of the Board, attempted to draw a distinction between a recommended learning resource and a library resource in terms of classroom use and submitted that a library resource could only be used in the library and not in a classroom. With respect I do not think that limitation can be sustained. It would lead to the absurd result that a K-1 teacher could not take any story book out of the library and read it to the class. I think the only sensible distinction that can be made between a recommended learning resource and a library resource, having regard to the criteria set out in Regulation 8800.1, is that a recommended learning resource is recommended for instructional purposes generally in classes throughout the district whereas a library resource is made available for use as appropriate in the discretion of the particular teacher. A prudent teacher should consult with colleagues, parents and the principal before using sensitive materials. But if the books are in the library and otherwise age appropriate stories, incidental classroom use by a teacher is primarily a matter for the professional judgment of the teacher rather than one of general policy for the Board.

THE ISSUE BEFORE THE BOARD

[54] The three books in issue are short story books. Each could be read to a class of K-1 students at a story time or like occasion. At least two of the three books depict parents and children who are ethnically diverse and *Belinda's Bouquet* rebuts adult criticism of a little girl that she is too fat by emphasizing that children, like flowers, are each beautiful and valued in their own way. The common message that the books are intended to convey is that there are family models other than families with one father and one mother. Parents in alternative families love and care for their children equally as much as other parents.

[55] The contentious feature of these three books is that they each depict two "same-sex" parents. Mr. Arvay submitted that the books were not intended to convey any message with respect to the sexual orientation of the parents. The stated object is simply to convey the message that parents of children in alternative family models generally love and care for their children equally as much as parents in stereotypically "traditional" families.

[56] The difficulty with this submission is that each of these three books depicts a family model distinguishable from other alternative family models only by reason of the sexual orientation of the parents. A wide variety of alternative family models undoubtedly are present in the Surrey school district. Indeed, it may be well be that over half of school age children grow up in "non-traditional" families. That is certainly true if one were to limit the traditional family model to one in which the mother does not work outside the home. Some of the "alternative"

families obviously will involve more than one father or more than one mother in heterosexual contexts. For example it is not uncommon for a grandmother or aunt to take on a surrogate mother role for a birth mother. The children may well regard both women as mothers in such circumstances. In many families a mother may have separated from the birth father and formed a new relationship taking the children with her but allowing access to the birth father. In that situation the children might easily consider themselves to have two fathers. One need not multiply examples. The point is that the three books in issue appear to have been selected by Mr. Chamberlain through criteria which emphasizes one form of alternative family, that involving same-sex parents, over others equally capable of conveying the same general message to the students. The same-sex factor is the only element that distinguishes these three books from other books available to make the same point in a variety of alternative family contexts.

[57] Sexual orientation issues raise strong emotions and Mr. Chamberlain must have known that by advancing these three books for status as recommended learning resources for the Surrey School District he was inviting a confrontation before the Board. The views of Board members and some parents on issues of sexual orientation were well-known. Passions were raised to the point where gross and vituperative epithets were shouted at Board members by spectators during the Board meeting when the resolution was being considered. No doubt some supporters of the Board were also insulting to their opponents.

[58] The irony of all this was that the battle was ostensibly over the means of conveying the value of loving and caring family relationships, whatever their form. It is hard to resist the thought that K-1 children may have a better appreciation of that value than any of the contending adults. Alternative family arrangements must now be a fact of life for virtually every child in public schools in Surrey either as a result of personal circumstances or the circumstances of friends and classmates well-known to them. K-1 children for the most part are too young to form critical normative judgments. They simply accept the variety around them as fact and welcome all the love and care they receive.

[59] I cannot accept that the initiative of Mr. Chamberlain and the other petitioners was aimed only at demonstrating the presence of nurturing values in alternative families generally. The three books in issue were selected for their sexual orientation dimension. While Mr. Chamberlain could reasonably expect five and six year olds in the classroom to be oblivious to that dimension of the stories he could also expect that by promoting the books as recommended learning resources the books would come to the attention of parents who would object to the sexual orientation dimension as morally offensive. The anticipated confrontation would be an adult confrontation, but as it would involve parents, teachers and the Board, children would inevitably be drawn in.

[60] Discrimination aside, parental views on matters of sexual orientation are entitled to be respected even if in the words of Cory J. in *Egan* quoted earlier they

"may seem extremely peculiar and vastly perplexing to the majority." Canada is a signatory to the *International Covenant on Civil and Political Rights* which confirms parental rights in these terms—:

4. The States Parties to the present Covenant undertake to have respect for the liberty of parents and, when applicable, legal guardians to ensure the religious and moral education of their children in conformity with their own convictions. [Article 18, para. 4]

[61] Under the *Covenant* the liberty of parents to ensure the religious and moral education of their children is "subject only to such limitations as are prescribed by law and are necessary to protect public safety, order, health, or morals or the fundamental rights and freedoms of others." That caveat provides ample authority to take reasonable measures to protect against discrimination, but not to otherwise override parental views.

[62] According to a parents' petition filed in the proceedings, Mr. Chamberlain appears to have the support of a large majority of the parents of his students to use the three books in his classes. As discussed above I do not think that the Three Books resolution or the position prevailing before the Three Books resolution came forward precluded reading the books in class or using them as illustrations to generate discussion on a general topic of nurturing families in his classroom. The petitioners, however, were pursuing a broader agenda that was bound to be confrontational at the adult level and it is hard to see how children at the K-1 level could be well-served by that confrontation having regard to the ultimate objective of the curriculum of celebrating the nurturing value of families.

[63] Ultimately this litigation has a certain *Alice in Wonderland* quality. Like the Cheshire Cat, the issues slowly vanish on close examination. The parties appear to agree that issues of sexual orientation do not belong in K-1 classrooms. In my opinion, the Three Books resolution is consistent with that objective and within the jurisdiction of the Board.

[64] I would allow the appeal. It follows that the cross appeal by the petitioners for a mandatory injunction directing the Board to approve the three books as recommended learning resources should be dismissed. The parties may make written submissions on costs.

NOTES

1. See Jean Bethke Elshtain, *Democracy on Trial*, The Massey Lectures 1993, Anansi Press 1993, pp. 128–9.

2. First published in 1902, Penguin Classics Edition 1985.

3. Ibid., at p. 53.

4. Wilfred M. McClay, *The Wilson Quarterly*, vol. XXIV, no. 3, 2000, p. 54 at pp. 63–4.

POSTSCRIPT

These court rulings deal directly with the question of the legitimacy of using religiously based arguments in debating and deciding matters of public policy. Contemporary liberal political theorists have often been critical of the use of religiously based arguments in political debates. They frequently argue that the modern liberal democratic polity has to be protected from the potentially divisive and destabilizing impact of public religious conflict. To do this a two-fold strategy must be used: politics must be secularized, and religious beliefs must be kept to the private realm, not the public.

Some contemporary liberal theorists take these assumptions to mean that all religiously based lines of reasoning should be excluded from the public square. Instead, citizens should employ only "secular" or "rational" positions that are accessible to all. Richard Rorty, for example, in an article entitled "Religion as Conversation Stopper" argues that in contemporary society it should "seem bad taste to bring religion into discussions of public policy." (*Philosophy and Social Hope,* London: Penguin, 2000, p. 169). In her judgment, Justice Saunders seems to have gone even beyond this position, contending that even if religious arguments are not employed, any proof that public policy decisions could be rooted in religious beliefs could be a basis for excluding such decisions.

Other contemporary liberal theorists take a less exclusionary point of view. Robert Audi and John Rawls both maintain that such a limiting approach is discriminatory and serves only to silence religiously motivated advocates. They assert instead that citizens may use religiously motivated arguments as long as they also advance other arguments in support of their position that do not depend in any way on religious belief. Governments and courts should rely on these broader arguments, which are open to everyone, as the ultimate basis for making their decisions.

Jonathan Chaplin gives a detailed examination and critique of these issues in "Beyond Liberal Restraint: Defending Religiously Based Arguments in Law and Public Policy," *UBC Law Review* 33, Special Issue (2000): 617–46. Chaplin puts forward that there is little real evidence that religiously based arguments will contribute to greater divisiveness in society, and he sets out his own views on the appropriate role for religiously based argumentation in the public sphere. In addition to Chaplin's article, this special issue of the *UBC Law Review* on "Religion, Morality, and Law" contains a useful collection of articles dealing with the relationship between religion and public policy. And John von Heyking's "Harmonization of Heaven and Earth? Religion, Politics, and Law in Canada" (in this same issue) provides helpful background to this debate.

Students will also find instructive the following materials on the interaction between religion and law in Canada: Paul Horwitz, "The Sources and Limits of Freedom of Religion in a Liberal Democracy: Section 2(a) and Beyond," *University of Toronto Faculty Law Review* 54, no. 1 (Winter 1990): 1–64; Timothy Macklem, "Faith as a Secular Value," *McGill Law Journal* 45, no. 1 (2000): 3–63; and Albert Menendez, *Church and State in Canada* (Amherst, N.Y.: Prometheus Books, 1996). John von Heyking, who is a professor of political science at the University of Lethbridge, also maintains a useful list of resources covering the relationship between religion and politics; the list can be accessed via his homepage at the university's website. Students may also wish to examine the following articles on the two court decisions presented in this Issue: Shaheen Shariff, Roland Case, and Michael Manley-Casimir, *Education and Law*, vol. 10 (2000); and Shaheen Shariff, Roland Case, and Linda LaRoque, "Begging the Question: The Court of Appeal Decision to the Surrey School Board Book Controversy," in *Education and Law*, vol. 11 (2001).

The plaintiffs in the Surrey school board suit appealed the decision of Justice Mackenzie to the Supreme Court of Canada. The Supreme Court agreed to hear the case and issued a ruling in December 21, 2002. In a 7–2 vote, the court ruled, in the words of Chief Justice Beverley McLachlin, that "parental views, however important, cannot override the imperative placed upon the British Columbia public schools to mirror diversity of the community and teach tolerance and understanding of difference." Nevertheless, the court returned the decision of whether to approve the books back to the school board. In June 2003, the school board voted again, by a 5–2 margin, to ban the books, citing issues relating to poor grammar and inappropriate content, scope, and depth for the age group as the reasons for the decision. Following this decision, James Chamberlain, the teacher who initially launched the case, announced that he would not be party to any further legal action since it had become too expensive to continue. Later in the same month, it was announced that the District Standing Advisory Committee for Learning Resources had recommended that the two of the titles in question be included in the list of recommended resources for Surrey classrooms.

Contributor Acknowledgments

The editors wish to thank the publishers and copyright holders for permission to reprint the selections in this book, which are listed below in order of appearance.

Issue 1

Paul Nesbitt-Larking, "Canadian Political Culture: The Problem of Americanization," © Nelson, a division of Thomson Canada Limited, 1994.

Anthony A. Peacock, "Socialism as Nationalism: Why the Alleged Americanization of Canadian Political Culture Is a Fraud," © Nelson, a division of Thomson Canada Limited, 1994.

Issue 2

John A. Olthuis and Roger Townshend, "The Case for Native Sovereignty," © Nelson, a division of Thomson Canada Limited, 1994.

Thomas Flanagan, "Native Sovereignty: Does Anyone Really Want an Aboriginal Archipelago?" © Nelson, a division of Thomson Canada Limited, 1994.

Issue 3

Nelson Wiseman, "Going Nowhere: Conservatism and the Conservative Party," © Nelson, a division of Thomson Canada Limited, 2005.

Faron Ellis, "Twenty-First Century Conservatives Can Succeed," © Nelson, a division of Thomson Canada Limited, 2005.

Issue 4

Robert Martin, "The Canadian Charter of Rights and Freedoms Is Antidemocratic and Un-Canadian," © Nelson, a division of Thomson Canada Limited, 1994.

Philip L. Bryden, "The Canadian Charter of Rights and Freedoms Is Antidemocratic and Un-Canadian: An Opposing Point of View," © Nelson, a division of Thomson Canada Limited, 1994.

Issue 5

Andrew Heard and Daniel Cohn, "The Federal Government Should Stay Involved: The Case for a Strong Federal Role in Health Care," © Nelson, a division of Thomson Canada Limited, 2005.

Paul Barker, "The Case Against a Strong Federal Role in Health Care," © Nelson, a division of Thomson Canada Limited, 2005.

Issue 6

Justice Duncan Shaw, "Opinion in *R. v. Sharpe*," reproduced from Dominion Law Reports: 169-*Regina v. Sharpe*, pp. 540–54, with permission of Canada Law Book.

Chief Justice Beverley McLachlin, "Opinion in *R. v. Sharpe*," reproduced from Dominion Law Reports: 194-*Regina v. Sharpe*, pp. 16–50, with permission of Canada Law Book.

Issue 7

Patrick J. Monahan, "Doing the Rules: An Assessment of the Federal *Clarity Act* in Light of the *Quebec Secession Reference*," reprinted with permission of the C.D. Howe Institute.

Claude Ryan, "Consequences of the Quebec *Secession Reference:* The Clarity Bill and Beyond," reprinted with permission of the C.D. Howe Institute.

Issue 8

Donald J. Savoie, "*Primus:* There Is No Longer Any *Inter* or *Pares*," from *Governing From the Centre* (University of Toronto Press © 1999) pp. 71–108. Reprinted with permission of the publisher.

Paul Barker, "Limits on the Power of the Prime Minister," © Nelson, a division of Thomson Canada Limited, 2002.

Issue 9

F.L. Morton, "Why the Judicial Appointment Process Must Be Reformed," © Nelson, a division of Thomson Canada Limited, 2005.

H. Patrick Glenn, "Parliamentary Hearings for Supreme Court of Canada Appointments?" © Nelson, a division of Thomson Canada Limited, 2005.

Issue 10

David Kilgour, John Kirsner, and Kenneth McConnell, "Discipline versus Democracy: Party Discipline in Canadian Politics," © Nelson, a division of Thomson Canada Limited, 1994.

Robert J. Jackson and Paul Conlin, "The Imperative of Party Discipline in the Canadian Political System," © Nelson, a division of Thomson Canada Limited, 1994.

Issue 11

Tim Schouls, "Why Group Representation in Parliament Is Important," © Nelson, a division of Thomson Canada Limited, 1998.

John H. Redekop, "Group Representation in Parliament Would Be Dysfunctional for Canada," © Nelson, a division of Thomson Canada Limited, 1998.

Issue 12

Andrew Coyne, "The Right to Vote, and the Obligation," *National Post,* December 20, 2000, A19. Material reprinted with the express permission of "National Post Company," a CanWest Partnership.

Clifford Orwin, "You Can Lock Me Up, But You Can't Make Me Vote," from the *National Post,* December 20, 2000. Reprinted by permission of the author.

Issue 13

John L. Hiemstra and Harold J. Jansen, "Getting What You Vote For," © Nelson, a division of Thomson Canada Limited, 2005.

Christopher Kam, "The Limits of Electoral Systems and Electoral Reform—or How I Came to Love SMP," © Nelson, a division of Thomson Canada Limited, 2005.

Issue 14

Michael Walzer, "Political Action, the Problem of Dirty Hands," *Philosophy and Public Affairs* v32, i, 1975, pp. 160–168. Reprinted with permission of Blackwell Publishing.

David P. Shugarman, "Chapter Fourteen: Democratic Dirty Hands?" copyright © 2000 by David P. Shugarman, reprinted from *Cruelty & Deception: The Controversy Over Dirty Hands in Politics,* edited by Paul Rynard and David P. Shugarman, Ontario: Broadview Press, 2000, pp. 234–236, 238–244. Reprinted by permission of Broadview Press.

Issue 15

Margaret Somerville, "Getting Past the Myth of Medicare (and response)," *National Post,* June 21, 2004. Reprinted by permission of the author.

Colleen Flood, "Two-Tier Medicine Isn't the Answer (and response)," *National Post,* August 3, 2004. Reprinted by permission of the author.

Issue 16

Jonathan Rauch, "For Better or Worse?" © Jonathan Rauch 1996. First published in *The New Republic,* May 6, 1996. Reprinted with permission.

Daniel Cere and Douglas Farrow, "War of the Ring," from *Divorcing Marriage,* McGill-Queen's University Press, 2004. Reprinted with permission.

Issue 17

Michael Krashinsky, "Canada Needs an Early Childhood Education and Care Program," © Nelson, a division of Thomson Canada Limited, 2005.

Beverly Smith, "Equal Benefit to Children: What It Really Means," © Nelson, a division of Thomson Canada Limited, 2005.

Issue 18

Justice Mary Saunders, "Opinion in *Chamberlain v. Surrey School District #36*," B.C.S.C. Doc. No. Vancouver A972046, retrieved September 19, 2001, from http://www.courts.gov.bc.ca.

Justice Kenneth Mackenzie, "Opinion in *Chamberlain v. Surrey School District #36*," C.A.B.C. Doc. No. Vancouver CA25465, retrieved September 19, 2001, from http://www.courts.gov.bc.ca.